The Rating Agencies
and their Credit Ratings

For other titles in the Wiley Finance series
please see www.wiley.com/finance

The Rating Agencies and their Credit Ratings

What They Are, How They Work and Why They Are Relevant

Herwig M. Langohr

and

Patricia T. Langohr

A John Wiley and Sons, Ltd., Publication

Other Wiley Editorial Offices

John Wiley & Sons Inc., 111 River Street, Hoboken, NJ 07030, USA

Jossey-Bass, 989 Market Street, San Francisco, CA 94103-1741, USA

Wiley-VCH Verlag GmbH, Boschstr. 12, D-69469 Weinheim, Germany

John Wiley & Sons Australia Ltd, 42 McDougall Street, Milton, Queensland 4064, Australia

John Wiley & Sons (Asia) Pte Ltd, 2 Clementi Loop #02-01, Jin Xing Distripark, Singapore 129809

John Wiley & Sons Canada Ltd, 6045 Freemont Blvd, Mississauga, Ontario, L5R 4J3, Canada

Wiley also publishes its books in a variety of electronic formats. Some content that appears
in print may not be available in electronic books.

Library of Congress Cataloging-in-Publication Data

Langohr, Herwig M.
  The rating agencies and their credit ratings : what they are, how they work and why they are relevant /
Herwig M. Langohr, Patricia T. Langohr.
  p. cm.–(Wiley finance series)
  Includes bibliographical references and index.
  ISBN 978-0-470-01800-2 (cloth)
  1. Credit ratings. 2. Credit bureaus. I. Langohr, Patricia T. II.
Title.
  HG3751.5.L364 2008
  332.7–dc22

                                                                                          2008026792

British Library Cataloguing in Publication Data

A catalogue record for this book is available from the British Library

ISBN 978-0-470-01800-2 (HB)

Typeset in 10/12pt Times by Laserwords Private Limited, Chennai, India
Printed and bound in Great Britain by Antony Rowe Ltd, Chippenham, Wiltshire

Contents

Foreword   ix

Preface   xiii

1 Introduction   **1**
- 1.1 Context and Premises   1
  - 1.1.1 The Benchmarking of Default Prospects Remains Deeply Rooted in Business Analysis   1
  - 1.1.2 Credit Ratings Play a Unique Role in Overcoming Information Asymmetries on the Information Exchanges   9
  - 1.1.3 Under the Spotlight as Unique Infomediaries, the CRAs became Strictly Regulated   13
- 1.2 Book Chapters   17
- 1.3 Supporting Materials   18

PART A CREDIT RATING FOUNDATIONS   **21**

2 Credit Ratings   **23**
- 2.1 The World of Corporate Defaults   24
  - 2.1.1 What are Corporate Defaults?   27
  - 2.1.2 The Drivers of Corporate Defaults   35
  - 2.1.3 Recovery Rates from Defaults   39
- 2.2 Credit Rating Scales   40
  - 2.2.1 Fundamental Ordinal Credit Rating Scales   43
  - 2.2.2 Rating Scales and Observed Bond Market Credit Spreads   64
  - 2.2.3 Market-Implied Cardinal Rating Scales and Default Probabilities   72
- 2.3 The Interpretation of Credit Ratings   74
  - 2.3.1 Interpreting from the Scale   75
  - 2.3.2 Correctly Interpreting versus Misinterpreting Ratings   78
  - 2.3.3 Special Issues   85
- 2.4 Credit Ratings: Summary and Conclusions   88

3 The _Raison d'Être_ of Credit Ratings and their Market   **89**
- 3.1 Needs for Credit Ratings – or the Demand Side of Ratings   89

3.1.1   Principals: Issuers/Borrowers   91
3.1.2   Principals: Fixed Income Investors   99
3.1.3   Prescribers   104
3.2   Credit Ratings as a Solution to Information Asymmetry: Economic
Analysis   111
3.2.1   Economics of Ratings: Intuition   111
3.2.2   Economics of Ratings: Analysis   113
3.2.3   The Economic Analysis of Ratings: Summary and Implications   124
3.3   Credit Rating Segments – or Scale and Scope of the Rated Universe   126
3.3.1   Industry Segments or Type of Rated Issuers   126
3.3.2   Product Segments or Types of Rated Issues   138
3.3.3   Geographical Segments or Location of the Obligor   149
3.4   Summary   158
3.5   Technical Appendix   158

4   **How to Obtain and Maintain a Credit Rating**   **161**
4.1   The Rating Preparation   161
4.1.1   The Issuer Client   163
4.1.2   The Rating Adviser-Intermediary   165
4.1.3   The Credit Rating Agency Supplier   168
4.2   The Rating   170
4.2.1   The Rating Action   170
4.2.2   Rating Follow-Up   174
4.2.3   The Rating Agreement   179
4.3   Quality of the Rating Process   187
4.3.1   Objectivity   188
4.3.2   Diligence   189
4.3.3   Transparency   191

PART B   CREDIT RATING ANALYSIS   **195**

5   **The France Telecom Credit Rating Cycle: 1995–2004**   **197**
5.1   From Sovereign Status to Near Speculative Grade (1995–2002)   198
5.1.1   How Sovereign Aaa Status of June 1995 Adjusts to Corporate Aa1
in July 1996   198
5.1.2   A Company that went Public on Aa1 Status in October 1997 is
Downgraded to Aa2 in December 1999   200
5.1.3   Rapid Extension of FT's Reach and Two Notches Downgrade to
A1 in September 2000   202
5.1.4   A Wake-up Call: the Orange IPO and Surprise Two Notches Downgrade to A3 in February 2001   211
5.1.5   The Slide Downward to Baa1 in September 2001   219
5.1.6   Looming Crisis and Two Notches Downgrade to Baa3 in June 2002   222
5.2   Turning Point and Rating Recovery (Fall 2002–Winter 2004)   229
5.2.1   Improvement in Outlook in September 2002   229
5.2.2   A New Start in October 2002 and Recovery Actions   238

	5.2.3	Recovery Implementation and the Sequence of Rating Upgrades through February 2005	244
5.3	Analysis and Evaluation		247
	5.3.1	Risk Shifting at France Telecom and its Fundamental and Market-Implied Ratings	248
	5.3.2	The Restraint of the CRAs during the 2002 Crisis	253
	5.3.3	The Value of Ratings to Issuers	254

6 Credit Rating Analysis   **257**
6.1	Fundamental Corporate Credit Ratings		257
	6.1.1	Corporate Credit Risk[2]	257
	6.1.2	Credit Risk of Corporate Debt Instruments	260
	6.1.3	Putting it All Together: the Rating[8]	265
6.2	Corporate Ratings Implied by Market Data		274
	6.2.1	The Concept	274
	6.2.2	Mechanics of Extracting Default Probabilities from Market Prices[21]	276
	6.2.3	Market-Implied Ratings	284
6.3	Special Sector Ratings		286
	6.3.1	Sovereign Ratings	286
	6.3.2	Financial Strength Ratings	291
	6.3.3	Structured Finance Instruments Ratings	296
6.4	Technical Appendix		304
	6.4.1	Step 1: Computing the Implied Market Value of Assets and Asset Volatility	305
	6.4.2	Step 2: Computing the Distance to Default	305
	6.4.3	Step 3: Calculating the Default Probability Corresponding to the Distance to Default	306

7 Credit Rating Performance   **307**
7.1	Relevance: Ratings and Value		307
	7.1.1	Structural Relevance: Rating and Credit Spreads	310
	7.1.2	Impact Relevance: Rating Actions and Security Price Changes	325
	7.1.3	Evaluation: How Relevant are Fundamental Credit Ratings?	331
7.2	Preventing Surprise in Defaults: Rating Accuracy and Stability		332
	7.2.1	Metrics of Accuracy and Stability	334
	7.2.2	Analysis of the Prevention of Surprise in Defaults	353
	7.2.3	Summary, Evaluation and Conclusion	356
7.3	Efficiency Enhancement: Stabilization in Times of Crisis?		356
	7.3.1	The Asian Macroeconomic Financial Crisis	356
	7.3.2	The Western Microeconomic Equity Crisis	363
	7.3.3	The Subprime Mortgage Related Crisis	364
	7.3.4	Criticisms: the Ratings in Crisis?	369

PART C   THE CREDIT RATING BUSINESS   **371**

8 The Credit Rating Industry   **375**
| 8.1 | The Rise of the Credit Rating Agencies | | 375 |

		8.1.1 Origins	375
		8.1.2 Macroeconomic Forces Shaping the Current Industry	378
		8.1.3 The Current Structure of the Industry	384
	8.2	Industry Specifics and How They Affect Competition	407
		8.2.1 Agencies Compete for the Market rather than in the Market	407
		8.2.2 The Business Model and Profit Drivers	411

8.1.1   Origins   375
8.1.2   Macroeconomic Forces Shaping the Current Industry   378
8.1.3   The Current Structure of the Industry   384
8.2   Industry Specifics and How They Affect Competition   407
8.2.1   Agencies Compete for the Market rather than in the Market   407
8.2.2   The Business Model and Profit Drivers   411
8.2.3   Some Dynamic Aspects of Competition among CRAs: A Small
        Number of Players can be Consistent with Intense Rivalry   418
8.3   Industry Performance   419
8.3.1   Performance for CRA Shareholders   419
8.3.2   Performance of Ratings as a Public Good   420
8.3.3   Performance for Issuers   427
8.3.4   Performance for Investors   427
8.4   Conclusion   428

9   Regulatory Oversight of the Credit Rating Industry   **429**
9.1   The Regulatory Uses of Ratings   430
9.1.1   Prudence   435
9.1.2   Market Access   436
9.1.3   Investor Protection   439
9.2   The Regulation of the Industry   440
9.2.1   The Regulatory Options   440
9.2.2   Worldwide Regulatory Initiative: the 2004 IOSCO Code of
        Conduct   443
9.2.3   The 2005 European Union Policy on Credit Rating Agencies   444
9.2.4   The US 'Credit Rating Agency Reform Act of 2006'   448
9.3   Analysis and Evaluation   455
9.3.1   The EU and the US Approaches Compared   455
9.3.2   The Positions of the Main Stakeholders   461
9.3.3   Comments and Evaluation on Regulatory Options   466

10 Summary and Conclusions   **469**
10.1 The Challenges Facing Rating Agencies Today   469
10.1.1 From Regulatory Legitimacy to Market Legitimacy   469
10.1.2 Financial Innovation   472
10.1.3 Growth and Globalization   473
10.2 Conclusion   473

References   **475**

Index   **495**

Foreword

Credit ratings have become ubiquitous these days. Virtually everywhere in the capital market, investors, issuers, and regulators have come to depend upon these alphanumeric report cards. Issuers know that their rating affects their financing costs in a very fundamental way. Investors depend heavily on these scores to determine their buying (and selling) decisions. And today, regulators have woven these ratings into everything from allowable investment alternatives for many institutional investors to required capital for most global banking firms.

For a long time, most people felt comfortable with the situation. Someone was issuing report cards; someone was watching the store – to mix my metaphors. They were comfortable, at least until the spring of 2007, when the stress of a deflating boom in the US housing market and the implication of this stress on residential mortgages spread to structured debt instruments of various kinds. Concern over the associated weakness in the real economy led investors and regulators alike to look more closely at the credit risk imbedded in various financial instruments and to question how well they understood the financial instruments in circulation.

Surely there was nothing to worry about. Most of the relevant investments were rated investment grade, and the rating agencies were watching out for them. But as the news of the potential losses imbedded in various structured products became evident, and as rating agencies began to review their evaluation of these instruments, it became clear that the world was a far riskier place than some had imagined.

Recriminations followed. In the case of subprime mortgages, how could borrowers have agreed to unsustainable financial conditions? In the case of private equity deals, how risky were many of these transactions? In the case of the banks that created these instruments, how could they have issued so much risky debt? Where were the underwriting standards that many investors had come to expect? And where were the rating agencies? Who was watching the store? How could they have issued such positive ratings, and how could they have changed their minds so quickly, leaving many investors with substantial losses?

It soon became clear that blindly following a credit rating agency grade was an ill-conceived investment strategy, an ill-conceived way to issue debt, and an ill-conceived way to regulate institutions and their capital market investments. It also became clear that most of the participants in the financial markets had little idea of what these credit agencies really do, why they do it, and what to expect from them.

The answers to these questions are contained in this book. The title says it all: The Rating Agencies and Their Credit Ratings, *What they are, how they work and why they are relevant.*

In the many pages that follow, the authors, Herwig M. Langohr from INSEAD and Patricia T. Langohr from ESSEC, inform, enlighten, and educate the reader. In 10 chapters, the world of credit ratings is laid out before us. It is a masterful work – a blend of history, context, and process. It touches on a wide range of issues, from the history of both the credit rating process and the leading firms, to their methodological approach. The book extensively discusses what these rating do and do not do, how they should and should not be used, as well as their value to various participants in the financial markets.

> Credit rating agencies and their output play a unique, indeed important, role in overcoming the information asymmetries that are endemic to the capital market. The fruits of their labor have value to issuers, investors, and regulators alike; but that value is often misunderstood. To the authors, the recent controversy over the role of the rating agencies in the current liquidity crisis is as much evidence of that misunderstanding as it is a failure of these organizations.

The authors' view is quite clear: the value of credit ratings is the objective feedback they provide to all concerned about the long-term implications of the firm's current credit risk posture. By offering this view, they help issuers to integrate the long-term consequences of their actions into their current decision making. Hopefully, therefore, they make better decisions. In addition, they help issuers to gain access to the capital markets by offering buyers the place of various issuers on the long-term default risk spectrum, and by doing so they reduce information asymmetries between issuers and investors. To these investors, credit rating agencies offer a product that is an opinion about credit risk that respects a set of minimum standards, including objectivity, consistency, comparability, stability, and transparency. By so doing, the agencies provide the market with an independent evaluation of borrower creditworthiness, based on company fundamentals, making it easy for investors to compare different potential investments. As such, they support bond portfolio managers in the implementation of strategic asset allocations to default risk classes. They allow them to tactically select bonds that belong to a class, relying on the large sample statistical anchors of the long-term default probability of a particular issuer or issue for which a rating is a proxy.

Crucial to performing their role, the rating agencies must adhere to four principles: their actions must be independent and objective, keep all non-public information confidential, enhance transparency and disclosure, and reduce informational asymmetry. This is a tall order.

Yet, this is their mandate, and governments and regulators everywhere are demanding more accountability. The litany of the recent spate of rules and regulations under which these firms operate is a particularly useful part of this book, which those unfamiliar with the array of regulators and oversight bodies will find quite informative. These organizations are not, as some suggest, unregulated entities.

And in light of the recent financial market crisis, they are feeling the heat, not only from these regulators, but from their clients – both buyers and sellers. The authors have some valuable advice for the agencies in the current environment. They remind the firms that issue these ratings that their usefulness is dependent upon two self-reinforcing elements: reputation and general acceptability. The value of a rating to the markets depends on its statistical ability to gauge the likelihood of default. That ability and the reputation for accuracy are the result of continuous improvement and constant updating of the techniques employed. Recent failures, if they are proven to be failures, beg for more investment and improved techniques. As instruments become more complex, ratings need to be more sophisticated. It also should be remembered that market participants use the ratings of leading credit rating agencies because the market trusts their ratings and participants know that other players will also accept their evaluation. Issuers seek such general acceptance. Bond portfolio managers too look for a generally accepted rating that springs from both accurate and complete coverage of their full range of investment opportunities. Ratings thus require general trust and acceptance that can only come from statistical evidence of relevance and a general level of acceptance of the validity of credit ratings emanating from the industry leaders. This suggests that the most effective response to the current crisis of confidence is a greater attention to detail – what went wrong and what in the rating process that needs to be improved, rather than emphasis on public discourse and the inevitable blame game.

And so, there is much in this volume to recommend it to the reader. Whether you are a financial executive who depends upon these ratings to gain access to the capital market, or an investor who looks to these ratings for their informational content, or a regulator overseeing the entire process, you will be smarter after reading this book. You also will be much better informed. I was, and recommend it to you

Anthony M. Santomero

McKinsey & Company.

Preface

This monograph offers a 360-degree introduction to credit ratings. It is written for the professional with some background in economics, finance, and political economy. Our purpose is to develop the reader's understanding of the fascinating, fog-piercing world of credit ratings and the credit ratings agencies (CRAs) that produce them. The reader should not therefore expect to become an expert in any particular rating technique after reading this book. Some types of ratings are highly technical, others are based on a number of inputs, including quantitative analysis. In all cases, a rating action is a complex business judgment decision that integrates the past, the present, and the likely future of the issuer, its competitive environment and the political economy within which it operates.

Credit rating agencies do not have a crystal ball, they cannot see if or when a specific default will occur. But market participants and legislators sometimes behave as if they consider CRAs to be psychic. When catastrophic default disasters struck South-East Asia in 1997, the US in 2001–2002, and Europe in 2002–2003, the CRAs only spotted them at the last minute, and the world berated the agencies for failing to give investors sufficient lead time to protect themselves from credit losses. Regulators around the world seized the opportunity to rein in the CRAs with new rules in a seeming attempt to exorcise the supposed evil influence of CRAs as the masters of capital. This led to CRAs around the world adopting a voluntary code of conduct. In Europe, it gave rise to the December 2005 Communication from the Commission on Credit Rating Agencies; and in the US, to the Credit Rating Agency Reform Act of 2006.

Against that background, this book offers an understanding of what ratings and CRAs are by explaining how they work. The reader should not expect another round of sensation. There has been plenty of that: 'The new masters of capital: American bond rating agencies and the world economy'[1]; 'The credit rating agencies caught with their pants down?'[2]; 'The credit rating agencies let the American public down;' 'CRAs are superpowers in the world today. They can destroy you by downgrading your bonds',[3] etc., etc. We want to develop the reader's understanding in the following context. First, as an application of business economics, credit analysis remains deeply rooted in the fundamentals of business analysis. Next, as information products, credit ratings compete for attention in the information or

---

[1] Sinclair, T.J., 2005, *The New Masters of Capital*, Cornell University Press, Ithaca and London, 1–186.

[2] Irvine, S., 1998, Caught with their pants down?, *Euromoney*, January, 51–53.

[3] Public Broadcasting Service, 1996, Paraphrased from Friedman, T., The News Hour with Jim Lehrer: Interview with Thomas L. Friedman, February 13.

security markets. Lastly, as highly visible infomediaries in these markets, CRAs have been forced to live under the spotlight.

The explanations are based on one basic insight at the firm, industry, and economy levels. First, the core activity of a CRA is the benchmarking of default prospects. Next, given the nature of a ratings product, the CRA industry is naturally going to be concentrated. Lastly, the role of CRAs in the economy is bound to expand. We will explain how modern-day rating agencies work, how they achieve their ratings, and how they play a unique role in global financial markets, without trying to sharpen anyone's technical expertise in solving any specific ratings problem.

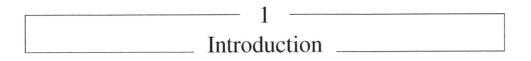

1
Introduction

> *Not all that glitters is gold. Often have you heard that told.*
>
> Shakespeare: *The Merchant of Venice.*

1.1 CONTEXT AND PREMISES

1.1.1 The Benchmarking of Default Prospects Remains Deeply Rooted in Business Analysis

> There is not in this country ... a central point at which all companies are required to present annual statements of their affairs. It is not uncommon for leading companies to publish no reports whatsoever. Some make them unwillingly, with no design to convey information upon the subjects to which they relate. Results that are full and explicit are accessible only to a small number of parties interested. Fewer still have the means of comparing results for consecutive years, without which it is impossible to form a correct opinion as to the manner in which the work has been conducted or of its present or prospective value.[1]

Henry Varnum Poor rendered the description above in 1860. He was editor of *The American Railroad Journal.* The country was the United States. The audience was a group of London-based investors being asked to fund infrastructure growth in the United States without a hint of the risks involved.

Poor's purpose was to alert investors to the need to be informed about default risks involved in lending money. Many of the London-based investors lost vast amounts of money when railroad and canal companies that they financed went bankrupt – as any investor today loses on average 65% of the face value of a bond when it defaults.[2] Henry Poor went on to say that:

> what is wanted is a work which shall embody ... a statement of the organization and condition of all our companies, and at the same time present a history of their operations from year to year which would necessarily reflect the character of their management, the extent and value of their business, and supply abundant illustrations with which to compare similar enterprises that might be made the subject of investigation and inquiry.[3]

---

[1] O'Neill, L.C., President and Chief Rating Officer - Standard & Poor's, 1999. Building the new global framework for risk analysis, Remarks to Professional bankers association at World Bank Headquarters in Washington, D.C., March 26, 1–5, page 2.

[2] Cantor, R., Hamilton, D.T., Ou, S., and Varma, P., 2004. Default and recovery rates of corporate bond issuers: A statistical review of Moody's ratings performance, 1920–2003, *Special Comment*: Moody's Investors Service, January, Report 80989, 1–40.

[3] O'Neill, L.C., President and Chief Rating Officer – Standard & Poor's, 1999. Building the new global framework for risk analysis, Remarks to Professional bankers association at World Bank Headquarters in Washington, D.C., March 26, 1–5, page 2.

Three types of businesses emerged in the 19th century to publish reports that enabled investors to make better-educated investment decisions and to, directly or indirectly, pressure obligors to respect their obligations – the specialized financial press, credit reporting agencies, and investment bankers. One of the first specialized business publications on record was *The American Railroad Journal*, which was started in 1832. Henry Poor transformed it into a publication for investors in railroads when he became its editor in 1849.[4] To fill the gap he had identified, Poor eventually created his own firm. It embarked upon collecting operating and financial statistics on US railroad companies. The company started publishing the results annually in 1868 as the *Manual of the Railroads of the United States*.[5] One of the first credit reporting agencies, founded in 1841, was The Mercantile Agency. Through a network of agents, it gathered information on the business standing and creditworthiness of businesses all over the US, and sold its service to subscribers.[6] The merchant banker was of course the consummate insider, insisting that securities issuers provide all relevant information related to company operations on an ongoing basis, sometimes insisting on being on the board for that purpose.[7] One of their hallmarks was also that they 'vouched for the securities they sponsored', as had already happened in 1835–1845 when the debts of several American States had been restructured.[8]

The foundations of these businesses lay in their grasp of the issuer's business in its competitive environment, so credit analysis originated as business analysis.[9] It focused strongly on the quality of the portfolio of opportunities that companies were actually pursuing, on the success with which management was pursuing them, on the ability to respect the debt obligations that the companies had incurred to finance their development, and on the character of the management to be willing to honor them. These businesses formed the information infrastructure in which the bond markets expanded in the 19th century. The fact that business reporting and financial statements are vastly better today in many parts of the world than they were in 1860 is in no small part due to the activities of these 19th-century businesses, which predated the CRAs.

In 1909, John Moody initiated agency bond ratings in the US, marking the expansion of business analysis to include credit risk analysis for rating purposes. Originally, this only covered the bonded debt of the US railroad companies.[10] The purpose of the analysis became more targeted toward rating an issuer's relative credit quality, but the foundations of the ratings continued to focus on the issuer's business fundamentals.

---

[4] Sylla, R., 2002. An historical primer on the business of credit ratings, in Ratings, Rating Agencies and the Global Financial System, edited by Levich, R., Majnoni, G., and Reinhart, C. Boston: Kluwer, 19–40, page 25.

[5] This was the ancestor of the rating agency Standard & Poor's formed in 1941: Sylla, R., 2002. An historical primer on the business of credit ratings, in Ratings, Rating Agencies and the Global Financial System, edited by Levich, R., Majnoni, G., and Reinhart, C. Boston: Kluwer, 19–40, page 26.

[6] Sylla, R., 2002. An historical primer on the business of credit ratings, in Ratings, Rating Agencies and the Global Financial System, edited by Levich, R., Majnoni, G., and Reinhart, C. Boston: Kluwer, 19–40, page 24: the Agency became R.G. Dun & Bradstreet in 1859 and its paying subscribers grew to 40 000 in the 1880s, its reports covering more than a million businesses.

[7] Sylla, R., 2002. An historical primer on the business of credit ratings, in Ratings, Rating Agencies and the Global Financial System, edited by Levich, R., Majnoni, G., and Reinhart, C. Boston: Kluwer, 19–40, page 26.

[8] See, Chernow, R., 1990. *The House of Morgan: An American Banking Dynasty and the Rise of Modern Finance*, Touchstone, New York, 1–812, pages 3–5.

[9] Some defend a credit analysis approach that does not get distracted from soft issues such as the borrower's corporate strategy, the forces that drive competition in its industry, the capability of management to run the business, etc. Several of our colleagues and friends, board members and successful entrepreneurs – support that view because they don't want a CRA to tell them how to run their business.

[10] Sylla, R., 2002. An historical primer on the business of credit ratings, in Ratings, Rating Agencies and the Global Financial System, edited by Levich, R., Majnoni, G., and Reinhart, C. Boston: Kluwer, 19–40, page 23.

   Rating actions in the automobile industry highlight the extent to which ratings continue to focus on business fundamentals. As an example, consider S&P's December 12, 2005, downgrade of General Motors (GM) corporate credit to B, affecting $285 billion. Exhibit 1.1 reproduces the action announcement *in extenso*. Summing it up, note how S&P refers at length to GM's business position as the key driver of the downgrade. S&P emphasizes the point by going out of its way to remind investors that GM's liquidity position and borrowing capacity give it substantial staying power. But that power is limited by GM's ability to generate positive free cash flow (FCF), and that ability is currently impaired due to the difficulties in turning around the performance of GM's North American automotive operations. S&P explains that GM suffers from meaningful market share erosion related to a marked deterioration of its product mix, despite concerted efforts to improve the appeal of its product offerings. S&P also refers to the aging of GM's SUV models. Credit rating is, and remains, thus deeply rooted in business analysis. No spreadsheet ratings can replace this.

Exhibit 1.1   S&P Research Update: General Motors Corp. Corporate Credit Rating cut to 'B'; Off Credit Watch; Outlook Negative (December 12, 2005)

Credit Rating: B/Negative/B-3

Rationale

On December 12, 2005, Standard & Poor's Ratings Services lowered its corporate credit rating on General Motors Corp. (GM) to 'B' from 'BB-' and its short-term rating to 'B-3' from 'B-2' and removed them from Credit Watch, where they were placed on October 3, 2005, with negative implications. The outlook is negative. (The 'BB/B-1' ratings on General Motors Acceptance Corp. [GMAC] and the 'BBB-/A-3' ratings on Residential Capital Corp. [ResCap] remain on Credit Watch with developing implications, reflecting the potential that GM could sell a controlling interest in GMAC to a highly rated financial institution.) Consolidated debt outstanding totaled $285 billion at September 30, 2005.
   The downgrade reflects our increased skepticism about GM's ability to turn around the performance of its North American automotive operations. If recent trends persist, GM could ultimately need to restructure its obligations (including its debt and contractual obligations), despite its currently substantial liquidity and management's statements that it has no intention of filing for bankruptcy.
   GM has suffered meaningful market share erosion in the US this year, despite prior concerted efforts to improve the appeal of its product offerings. At the same time, the company has experienced marked deterioration of its product mix, given precipitous weakening of sales of its midsize and large SUVs, products that had been highly disproportionate contributors to GM's earnings. This product mix deterioration has partly reflected the aging of GM's SUV models, but with SUV demand having plummeted industry wide, particularly during the second half of 2005, it is now dubious whether GM's new models, set to be introduced over the next year, can be counted on to help to restore the company's North American operations to profitability.
   In addition, GM is paring the product scope of its brands. The company has also announced recently that it will be undertaking yet another significant round of production capacity cuts and workforce rationalization. But the benefits of such measures could be undermined unless its market share stabilizes without the company's resorting again to ruinous price discounting.
   One recent positive development for GM has been the negotiation of an agreement with the United Auto Workers providing for reduced health care costs. Yet, this agreement (which is pending court

approval) will only partly address the competitive disadvantage posed by GM's health care burden. Moreover, cash savings would only be realized beginning in 2008 because GM has agreed to make $2 billion of contributions to a newly formed VEBA trust during 2006 and 2007. It remains to be seen whether GM will be able to garner further meaningful concessions in its 2007 labor negotiations.

This year has witnessed a stunning collapse of GM's financial performance compared with 2004 and initial expectations for 2005. In light of results through the first nine months of 2005, we believe that the full-year net loss of GM's North American operations could approach a massive $5 billion (before substantial impairment and restructuring charges) and that the company's consolidated net loss could total about $3 billion (before special items). With nine-month 2005 cash outflow from automotive operations a negative $6.6 billion (after capital expenditures, but excluding GMAC), we expect full-year 2005 negative cash flow from automotive operations to be substantial. GMAC's cash generation has only partly mitigated the effect of these losses on GM's liquidity.

Deterioration of GM's credit quality has limited GMAC's funding capabilities. On October 17, 2005, GM announced that it was considering selling a controlling interest in GMAC to restore the latter's investment-grade rating. GM recently indicated that it is holding talks with potential investors. As we have stated previously, we view an investment-grade rating for GMAC as feasible if GM sells a majority stake in GMAC to a highly rated financial institution that has a long-range strategic commitment to the automotive finance sector. Even then, GMAC still would be exposed to risks stemming from its role as a provider of funding support to GM's dealers and retail customers. However, we believe a strategic majority owner would cause GMAC to adopt a defensive underwriting posture by curtailing its funding support of GM's business if that business were perceived to pose heightened risks to GMAC.

One key factor in achieving an investment-grade rating would be our conclusions about the extent to which financial support should be attributed to the strategic partner. We will continue to monitor GM's progress in this process and the potential for rating separation; however, if the timeframe for a transaction gets pushed out, or if there is further deterioration at GM, GMAC's rating could be lowered, perhaps to the same level as GM's. Ultimately, in the absence of a transaction that will significantly limit GM's ownership control over GMAC, the latter's ratings would be equalized again with GM's.

The ratings on ResCap are two notches above GMAC's, its direct parent, reflecting ResCap's ability to operate its mortgage businesses separately from GMAC's auto finance business, from which ResCap is partially insulated by financial covenants and governance provisions. However, we continue to link the ratings on ResCap with those on GMAC because of the latter's full ownership of ResCap. Consequently, should the ratings on GMAC be lowered, the ratings on ResCap would likewise be lowered by the same amount. Or, if the ratings on GMAC are raised, as explained above, ResCap's ratings also could be raised.

Short-Term Credit Factors

GM's short-term rating is 'B-3'; GMAC's rating is 'B-1.' GM's fundamental challenges are short- and long-term in nature. The rapid erosion in GM's near-term performance prospects points up its high operating leverage and the relative lack of predictability of near-term earnings and cash flow. Still, GM should not have any difficulty accommodating near-term cash requirements for the following reasons:

- GM has a large liquidity position; cash, marketable securities, and $4.1 billion of readily available assets in its VEBA trust (which it could use to meet certain near-term benefit costs, thereby freeing up other cash) totaled $19.2 billion at September 30, 2005 (excluding GMAC), compared with loans payable in the 12 months starting September 30 of $1.5 billion.
- As of September 30, 2005, GM had unrestricted access to a $5.6 billion committed bank credit facility expiring in June 2008, $700 million in committed credit facilities with various maturities,

and uncommitted lines of credit of $1.2 billion. We are not aware of any financial covenants that appear problematic.

- GM could save some cash by cutting the common dividend.
- Under current regulations, GM faces neither ERISA-mandated pension fund contributions through this decade nor the need to make contributions to avoid Pension Benefit Guaranty Corp. variable-rate premiums. Its principal US pension plans are overfunded for financial reporting purposes. However, under certain pending legislative proposals, the size of GM's pension liability could increase for ERISA purposes.
- Given the intense competitive pressures the company faces, GM has little leeway to curtail capital expenditures, which are budgeted at $8 billion for 2005.
- GM has virtually no material individual, non-strategic, parent-level assets left that it could divest, excluding GMAC and its assets.

GM's liquidity could be bolstered by the sale of a portion of its ownership stake in GMAC, and we would expect sale proceeds to represent adequate compensation for the related loss of GMAC earnings and dividends. We assume that GM would retain such proceeds as cash or equivalents, or use them to reduce debt or debt-like liabilities. On the other hand, owing to GMAC's enhanced independence, we believe there is increased risk that, in certain circumstances, GMAC could curtail its funding support of GM's marketing operations, precipitating potential problems for GM.

For GMAC, the key element of its financial flexibility is its ability to use securitization and whole-loan sales as funding channels, and we believe the ABS and nascent whole-loan markets are now accommodating issuance by GMAC in the near term without materially affecting market pricing, but this remains a risk factor.

Consistent with the practices of its finance company peers, GMAC relies heavily on short-term debt, albeit less so than historically. As of September 30, 2005, GMAC's short-term debt totaled $85 billion (including current maturities of long-term debt and on-balance-sheet securitizations, but not including maturing off-balance-sheet securitizations). GMAC's unsecured bond spreads have been extraordinarily volatile and wide. Given current capital market conditions, GMAC is highly unlikely to issue any significant public term debt in the near term. Between likely persisting market jitters and the size limitations of the high-yield market, it is uncertain whether and to what extent GMAC will be able to access the public unsecured debt market economically.

GMAC's managed automotive loan and lease asset composition is highly liquid, given that about half of its total gross receivables is due within one year and that a substantial portion of receivables is typically repaid before contractual maturity dates. However, we take only limited comfort from this because GMAC is constrained in its ability to reduce the size of its automotive portfolio, given its need to support GM's marketing efforts.

Several factors support GMAC's liquidity:

- As a first line of defence, GMAC has a large cash position – $24.3 billion at September 30, 2005 (including certain marketable securities with maturities greater than 90 days).
- GMAC also has substantial bank credit facilities. As of September 30, 2005, it had about $49 billion of bank lines in addition to auto whole-loan capacity and conduit capacity, not all of which were committed lines. Of the $7.4 billion facility, $3.0 billion expires in June 2006 and $4.4 billion in June 2008. We are not aware of any rating-related triggers that will impede GMAC from accessing the committed facilities in the wake of the recent downgrades. There is a maximum leverage covenant of consolidated unsecured debt to total stockholders' equity of 11.0 to 1.0. At September 30, GMAC's actual leverage under the covenant was 7.3 to 1.0. The $7.4 billion facility was established largely for backup purposes, and we believe GMAC would be loathe to borrow under it except as a last resort.
- Most of GMAC's unsecured automotive debt issues and borrowing arrangements include an identical, fairly strict negative pledge covenant. Subject to certain exceptions, the granting of any

material security interest (other than through securitizations) would cause all unsecured automotive debt to become secured.

GMAC uses the ABS market extensively. The company can securitize almost all of its major asset types. GMAC securitizes automotive retail and wholesale loans and retail leases through various markets and in different countries. In its mortgage business, it also securitizes retail and commercial mortgage loans, commercial mortgage securities, and real estate investment trust debt. Retail automotive loans in general are highly regarded in the ABS market because they are secured, carry low prepayment risk, and are of relatively short duration. GMAC's retail automotive loans are particularly high quality, given the company's relatively conservative and consistent underwriting standards. GMAC securitizes its automotive finance assets through public and private term debt issuances and through committed, multiseller bank conduit programs and asset-backed commercial paper programs. Even amid the turmoil surrounding GMAC in recent months, credit spreads on GMAC public term securitizations have barely changed.

Apart from ABS financing, GMAC also uses the whole-loan market, selling portfolios of automotive retail receivables and mortgage loans to third-party purchasers, with GMAC remaining the servicer but not retaining any ownership interest in the loans otherwise. The mortgage whole-loan market is large and liquid and has existed for many years. The automotive whole-loan market has grown only in the past several years – fortuitous timing for GMAC. Through September 30, 2005, GMAC had completed automotive whole-loan transactions totaling $9 billion. The company has agreements under which certain third parties have committed to purchase up to $11 billion of auto loans from GMAC within a stipulated period. In addition, GMAC has established a $55 billion, five-year arrangement to sell auto finance loans (with GMAC remaining the servicer) of up to $10 billion annually. And in December 2005, GMAC announced a similar five-year purchase agreement for up to $20 billion with another financial institution.

ResCap is a non-captive finance company. We assume GMAC would divest its stake in ResCap in a distress scenario. In fact, GM has publicly expressed its intention to explore alternatives with respect to ResCap. ResCap has completed a $4 billion private offering and a $1.25 billion public deal and used some of the proceeds to repay intracompany debt owed to GMAC. In July, ResCap closed on $3.55 billion of bank facilities, further relieving GMAC of the burden of funding ResCap.

In conjunction with the pending sale of 60% of the commercial mortgage unit, this unit is expected to raise third-party financing to repay all intercompany loans to GMAC. This will slightly enhance GMAC's liquidity and, as with ResCap, relieve GMAC of the burden of funding the commercial mortgage unit. If GMAC experienced heightened financial pressures, we believe it could sell the remaining 40% of its mortgage operations outright. Likewise, it could also divest at least some of the business lines in its insurance operations. We do not wish to give an estimate of the potential proceeds, but they could be substantial.

Outlook

The rating outlook on GM is negative. Prospects for GM's automotive operations are clouded. The ratings could be lowered further if we came to expect that GM's substantial cash outflow would continue beyond the next few quarters due to further setbacks, whether GM-specific or stemming from market conditions. Even though the concern over the situation at GM's bankrupt lead supplier, Delphi Corp., was the primary factor behind the rating downgrade of October 10, 2005, events at Delphi could precipitate a further review if GM were to experience severe Delphi-related operational disruptions or if GM agreed to fund a substantial portion of Delphi's restructuring costs. GM's rating could also be jeopardized if the company were to distribute to shareholders a meaningful portion of proceeds generated from the sale of a controlling interest in GMAC.

GM would need to reverse its current financial and operational trends, and sustain such a reversal, before we would revise its outlook to stable.

Ratings List

General Motors Corp.

To From
  Ratings Lowered and Removed from Credit Watch Corporate credit rating B/Negative/B-3 BB-/
Watch Neg/B-2
Short-term rating B-3 Watch Neg/B-2

Ratings Remaining on Credit Watch

General Motors Acceptance Corp.

Corporate credit rating BB/Watch Dev/B-1

Residential Capital Corp.

Corporate credit rating BBB-/Watch Dev/A-3
  Complete ratings information is available to subscribers of RatingsDirect, Standard & Poor's web-based credit analysis system, at www.ratingsdirect.com. All ratings affected by this rating action can be found on Standard & Poor's public website at www.standardandpoors.com; under Credit Ratings in the left navigation bar, select Find a Rating, then Credit Ratings Search.
  Analytic services provided by Standard & Poor's Ratings Services (Ratings Services) are the result of separate activities designed to preserve the independence and objectivity of ratings opinions. The credit ratings and observations contained herein are solely statements of opinion and not statements of fact or recommendations to purchase, hold, or sell any securities or make any other investment decisions. Accordingly, any user of the information contained herein should not rely on any credit rating or other opinion contained herein in making any investment decision. Ratings are based on information received by Ratings Services. Other divisions of Standard & Poor's may have information that is not available to Ratings Services. Standard & Poor's has established policies and procedures to maintain the confidentiality of non-public information received during the ratings process.
  Ratings Services receives compensation for its ratings. Such compensation is normally paid either by the issuers of such securities or third parties participating in marketing the securities. While Standard & Poor's reserves the right to disseminate the rating, it receives no payment for doing so, except for subscriptions to its publications. Additional information about our ratings fees is available at www.standardandpoors.com/usratingsfees.

  The point of a rating is to benchmark default likelihoods. This is the core activity of a CRA, to scale the default prospects of issues and the likely losses of issuers and, to varying degrees, investors in the event of a default. These benchmarking and scaling actions can only be properly understood in the context of an industry and the life of a company. Since both of these continuously undergo or initiate changes, ratings aim at moving targets.
  To be of use to investors, the performance of the ratings is of paramount importance. What is this performance of ratings? Ratings are like quality grades about an obligor's prospects in carrying out its financial obligations. Significant changes in these prospects rarely move like a random walk time series, going up, staying put, or falling down from one moment to

the other in arbitrary sequences. Thus ratings must show sufficient stability to be pertinent. But these prospects do change and some obligors are more prone than others to fail on their obligations. Ratings must reflect this. To be useful, ratings must thus demonstrate a sufficient degree of accuracy in predicting the likelihood of such failures. Between the two desired rating qualities of stability and accuracy, there exists unfortunately an unavoidable trade-off. A fast real-time on-line nano information processing engine could possibly very well follow on its heels the real day-to-day micro changes in default prospects of an issuer. It could trace them like a cardiogram. It may even produce precise accuracy about small day-to-day changes in default prospects. But it would probably be a schizophrenic graph. Periods of an emotional and unstable random walk of successive minute changes would be separated by moments of sudden discontinuities – small or large – or cliffs reflecting actual changes in insights and thinking about the default prospect. Of course, what the investors really expect from ratings is to catch these discontinuities. Even better, they would like ratings to reflect so much thinking and insights that they anticipate these shifts sufficiently ahead of actual occurrence to become alerted of likely material upcoming risk shifting by the issuer. Investors want rating changes to reflect the cliffs; they do not expect ratings to reflect minute-to-minute changes in prospects. They can get these in any case from all sorts of market prices for issuer securities that are continuously traded. From ratings, investors expect more stability, disregarding the more or less random, albeit accurate, minor day-to-day changes.

To gauge the performance of a rating one needs to determine if it offers the best trade-off between accuracy and stability. This is the trade-off that reflects, for a given degree of stability, the maximum achievable accuracy or, conversely, that reflects, for a given degree of accuracy, maximum stability. Of course, depending on the reference point for one or the other, there may be many such points. Economists call the connection between these many points an efficient frontier and they recognize that different users of ratings may want to be on different points of the frontier. That is, different users of ratings may value accuracy more than stability, and vice versa. In conclusion, to be a performing rating, it has to lie on that efficient frontier. A performing rating system should offer sufficient points on the frontier to suit the needs of a diverse group of investors with different accuracy/stability trade-offs.[11]

An early analysis described corporate bond quality and investor experience by shedding light on the following questions that this book also addresses.[12] What does performance mean? How do ratings size up future bond risks and returns, relative to the grades that they assign ex ante and relative to the grades that other participants, such as bond buyers and sellers, assign as shown in credit spreads? How well do they perform in the short term as opposed to the lifetime of a bond? Do rating changes reveal a lot to the market or are they market followers? What in fact do agency ratings intend vis-à-vis market ratings? What are the particular ways in which CRAs reach their ratings and what sets them apart from market ratings? Dealing with these questions also, this book highlights that CRAs conduct their work in a world of varying degrees of information asymmetry between bond investors and issuers.

---

[11] For an excellent more technical discussion of these insights, see Cantor, R., and Mann, C., 2006. Analyzing the tradeoff between ratings accuracy and stability, *Special Comment*: Moody's Investors Service, September, Report 99100, 1–8.

[12] Hickman, W.B., 1958. *Corporate Bond Quality and Investors Experience*, Princeton University Press, New Jersey, 1–536.

1.1.2 Credit Ratings Play a Unique Role in Overcoming Information Asymmetries on the Information Exchanges

Securities markets, for which ratings are produced, are really information exchanges. About 20 years ago, shortly after the Boesky affair, M. Phellan, then chairman of the NYSE, argued to the MBA Corporate Finance class at Insead that the name of the stock exchange ought to be changed to information exchange. Today, it is a truism that securities markets are actually information markets. The paradigm of the informational efficiency of these markets has been one of the more powerful and useful inventions of modern finance. Yet the degree, extent, conditions, and consequences of that efficiency remain controversial. Credit ratings compete for attention in one of the most efficient information markets, and few would question that.

The niche that ratings occupy is called 'information asymmetry.' One of the most critical impediments to investor rights is their ignorance of what goes on in a company, i.e. the information asymmetry between outside investors and insiders who control company operations. This is the context in which CRAs operate and where they add economic value. With ratings, CRAs aim to remedy the information shortage for fixed income investors.

Why, with all the regulations in place, do investors suffer from information asymmetry and lack valuable knowledge about the company? Would legislated full transparency not be sufficient to close the gap? Full transparency could mean:

- imposing prompt disclosure of material price-sensitive facts;
- making the full managerial line responsible for the completeness and accuracy of financial statements;
- increasing the level of detail of financial statements (including, among other critical information, the compensation paid to individual board members);
- eliminating conflicts of interest between the auditing and advisory businesses of audit firms;
- putting the audit committee in charge of the external auditors, etc.

The truth is that insiders always know more than outsiders, however transparent the management of the company. Companies are not cubic feet of lumber, barrels of oil, or pork bellies whose substance and quality one can readily inspect and measure. They are extremely complex, continuously adapting organisms whose competitive advantages are based on unique knowledge and proprietary information that cannot, and should not, be communicated to outsiders. The information gap can never be fully bridged.

So can outside investors ever know enough if insiders always know more? Consider the case of large shareholders. Through the board, they have better access than creditors to company-specific data in normal times. As the residual claimant, they have stronger incentives than creditors to mine the data to acquire valuable information. Hence, one can reasonably expect that shareholders know more than bondholders.

Evidence shows that general shareholders know less than insiders.[13] Consider the graph in Figure 1.1. It shows the cumulative daily abnormal returns of shares that are legitimately traded by insiders at date 0. The graph covers data of about three million legitimate inside trades over a thirty year period. The dotted line shows returns when insiders purchase at date 0, whereas the solid line shows returns when insiders sell at date 0.

---

[13] See the seminal contribution of Seyhun, H.N., 1986. Insiders' profits, costs of trading, and market efficiency, *Journal of Financial Economics*, Vol. 16, 189–212.

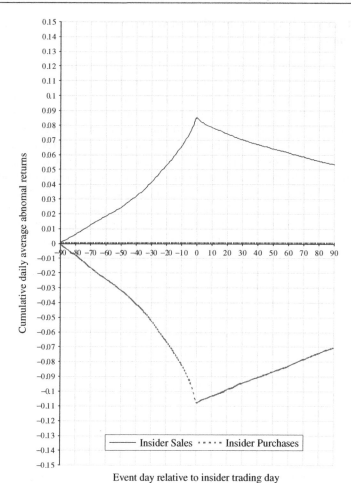

Figure 1.1 Abnormal stock returns to legitimate insider trades around 3 015 624 stock trades by insiders during 1/1975–12/2005, relative to equally weighted index.
Source: Seyhun, H.N., 1986, Insiders' profits, costs of trading, and market efficiency, *Journal of Financial Economics*, June, Vol. 16, No. 2, 189–212, page 197, Fig. 1 (updated).

Insiders act upon their superior information. They buy upon irrational bad market news and vice versa on irrational exuberance. Interpret the dotted line as one depicting companies that pursue unusually profitable complex proprietary strategies that outsiders only gradually come to understand. There is, suddenly, bad news: the company doesn't hit quarterly consensus EPS estimates, or an analyst writes a bad story, or there is a business accident. Collapse. But insiders believe that the bad news is merely transient or, if lasting, that its impact is immaterial. They cannot communicate this, since either the market would not believe them after the bad news, or they would have to give away significant proprietary information to demonstrate their credibility, thus putting the interest of their shareholders at stake (it is hard indeed to share valuable secrets with shareholders without competitors getting hold of them as well). But insiders have the right to legitimately trade on their beliefs that the market is negatively overreacting. They buy. After a while, the market recognizes that they were right. It positively adjusts and rewards the insiders with 4.3% abnormal returns. The solid line depicts the converse story. For this competitive company, nothing special happens, investors get normal returns for the risk taken. Then, suddenly, the company gets on the radar, and extensive purchases take place . . . for no real good reason. The insiders know this and, consequently, sell. After a while, the market comes back to its senses. It rewards the insider for having sold: they can buy back their original stake at a 2.2% discount.

In conclusion, outsiders and, in particular, creditors ride on the insiders. There is always going to be an information gap that only insiders can bridge. Outsiders have no means of ever knowing what goes on within the company. Insiders believe that they detect market mispricing and act upon it, usually correctly, as shown by their average profits. Along the way, they help long-term outside shareholders to reap fair risk–reward returns. What does that mean in terms of our concerns regarding the information position of outsiders? It means that insiders always outsmart outsiders. This being the case for inside shareholders *vis-à-vis* outside shareholders, it is *a fortiori* the case *vis-à-vis* bondholders and creditors generally.

Moral hazard puts creditors especially at the mercy of information asymmetry about what insiders are up to. Think about it in the following way. Making a risky loan is like lending at the risk-free rate and getting a price discount for the poor-quality grade of the loan due to its default risk. Fischer Black and others have demonstrated that the value of that discount is equal to the value of a put option on the firm assets with the face value of the debt as the exercise price; i.e. if the value of the assets is below the amount due at the due date, the lender has to accept only the value of this asset in payment. So, making a risky loan is like buying a riskless government bond and shorting that put option.[14] The upside of this deal is limited.

For equity, however, it is the other way around – the upside of equity is unlimited. In fact, holding equity is like holding a call option on the firm's assets with the face value of the debt of the firm as the exercise price. The shareholder gets all the upside, provided the debt is paid when it is due. Now, to see where the devil of moral hazard is hidden, consider a firm that starts increasing the idiosyncratic risk of its business and the total riskiness of its business increases over and above the riskiness that was expected at the time of its latest bond issue. There is no change in the systematic component of the risk, which is the only one that is priced to determine the enterprise value. But asset total volatility has increased. As a result, the value of the put and of the call on the assets both increase. Of course, there is a little difference in detail. For the bondholder who is short the put, the value of his stake declines. For the shareholder who is long the call, the value of his stake increases. With the increase in volatility, the likelihood that the bond will default increases without a corresponding increase in the upside, whereas for the shareholder, the likelihood of hitting a real upside increases, without a corresponding increase in the downside. The essential moral hazard in debt is thus the perverse incentive of the shareholder to surreptitiously increase business risk once the debt has been issued, thereby shifting value from the bondholders to himself.

From a fixed income investor standpoint, moral hazard is one type of exposure to event risk. Event risk is 'a deliberate change of the risk parameters of an issuer, a change that results in an immediate benefit to equity investors at the expense of fixed income investors.'[15] Examples of event risk include leveraged buyouts, leveraged breakup bids, or a borrower itself substantially changing its risk characteristics through a balance sheet restructuring. The last is the moral hazard type of event risk in corporate debt.

---

[14] Nowadays, holders of many of these risky bonds can buy that put option 'back' from credit risk insurers in the credit derivatives swap (CDS) market.
[15] Working group of investment institutions ('Gang of 26'), 2003. Improving market standards in the Sterling and Euro Fixed Income Credit markets, Proposals Paper, October, 1–8, page 2.

Exhibit 1.2   Worldwide storage of original information

Storage medium	2002 terabytes: upper estimate	1999–2000 terabytes: upper estimate	% Change: upper estimates
Paper	1 634	1 200	36%
Film	420 254	431 690	−3%
Magnetic	4 999 230	2 779 760	80%
Optical	103	81	28%
Total	**5 421 221**	**3 212 731**	**69%**

Sources: Lyman, P. and Varian, H.R., How Much Information? 2003. Reproduced with permission; and Mauboussin, M.J., 2006, *More Than You Know: Finding Financial Wisdom in Unconventional Places*, Columbia University Press, New York, 1–268.

Moral hazard is also very pervasive in the structured finance segment, although it is a couple of layers further away from the rating agency. In structured finance the moral hazard would be the perverse incentive of the borrower, such as a mortgage holder, to make risky bets to increase its potential upside as equity holder, while having only limited liability. Moreover, there is also moral hazard when originators and/or arrangers exert low effort on the due diligence on the assets being structured, or fail to disclose relevant information. It is useful to highlight that in the structured finance segment there is no auditing of the underlying assets and that no party has clearly its reputation at stake for disclosing the due diligence on these assets. Both the rating of a corporate bond and that of a structured finance transaction, even if a large part of the latter consists in rating-to-a-model, essentially should bridge the asymmetric information between the ultimate insiders and outsiders.

In this world of information asymmetries, how serious is the danger that excess information about issuers will create scarcity of attention to ratings? Bond investors nowadays appear to be confronted with an information glut rather than with a shortage. As a measure of the glut, consider the worldwide storage of original information in Exhibit 1.2.[16] What original information, if any, can credit ratings add to a world like that and in which in which hedge funds use high-tech filters to harvest market gossip with automated systems that 'trawl' through more than 40 million internet sources – from blogs to regulatory filings.[17] Or in a hypothetical brave new world in which issuers will have switched from quarterly standard accounts to on-line real-time customized reporting of upstream information about income and assets?[18] How original and proprietary is the bit of information that casts a forward-looking opinion about a binary event: default or non-default? Such a forward-looking opinion is something quite abstract, non-committing, even when cast in numbers. It is intangible, transient, maybe even fungible.

So what value do ratings add to whatever information is already embedded in security prices? Just bear in mind that rated issues are often securities traded on some of the more competitive securities markets that exist. The rating may very well stick to an asset, but this asset is continuously ground through one of the most powerful information mills of the world: the security markets. What is there left of the rating once the markets have

---

[16] A terabyte is one trillion bytes.

[17] Scholtes, S., 2006. Hedge funds to use high-tech filter to harvest market gossip, *Financial Times*, September 21, page 1.

[18] BDO International, Deloitte, Ernst&Young, Grant Thornton International, KPMG International, and PricewaterhouseCoopers International Limited, 2006. Global capital markets and the global economy: a vision from the CEOs of the International Audit Networks, November, 1–24, pages 15–18.

processed all available information to set the price of a bond? This question is particularly relevant now that theoretical models, numerical methods, databases, inferential techniques, and computing power are all at work to extract an issuer's default probability from freely available observables. These probabilities are called market-implied ratings (MIRs). Even some legislators have called these more 'reliable' than fundamental credit ratings.

Of course, while such endorsement makes these MIRs more legitimate, it doesn't make them more reliable.

Information asymmetries will persist because one can never fully move from the outside to the inside. Insiders will always be ahead of the crowd, and will always know more than outsiders. And forceful analysis and arguments exist for the case that new and growing gaps will emerge in increasingly diverse and unconventional places.[19] The space for traditional ratings to occupy may in fact expand, rather than contract. It will be up to the CRAs to keep focusing their work and their output on bridging the information gaps between insiders and outsiders, and so avoid disappearing into oblivion. But market participants will only pay attention to traditional fundamental ratings if they offer something unique. And if corporate bond issuers are expected to continue to pay a fee for a rating that will be ground away a few seconds after trading starts, that uniqueness has to be valuable. Where is that value in a world of excess information that is freely embedded in market prices? It is in the space where there is information about default prospects that is not embedded in market prices.[20]

Credit ratings will thus specialize in resolving information asymmetries between issuer and creditor. As long as fundamental ratings are anchored in information asymmetries, they are in a unique spot. Secondary markets will continue to pay attention to them in a different way to how they view MIRs, because fundamental ratings add to markets, whereas MIRs express the markets. In fact, in turbulent times MIRs may very well express market excesses, whereas fundamental ratings are in a strong position to dampen them. How will the relationship between CRA ratings and MIR ratings of the same securities evolve? It is sufficient to spend a few hours browsing the websites of on-line real-time market price providers, the CRAs, risk management solution providers, investment banks, asset management firms, bond market information aggregators, news agencies, and other information distributors to observe that both of these ratings are part of the same world. Will they fuse or further split apart? One cannot isolate CRAs from the market, MIRs, and competing fixed income information providers. Increasingly, CRAs are integrating MIRs into their analysis in order to sharpen their focus and deepen their insight at the margin of information uniqueness that is their *raison d'être*.

1.1.3 Under the Spotlight as Unique Infomediaries, the CRAs became Strictly Regulated

Poor's words are as relevant today as they were 140 years ago. They are a good description of the state of financial affairs in Thailand prior to the Asian economic crisis of 1997, Russia prior to the 1998 crisis, and several US and European large public companies, as became clear after the Internet bubble burst in 2000. They even relate well to the information vacuum

---

[19] See Mauboussin, M.J., 2006. *More Than You Know: Finding Financial Wisdom in Unconventional Places*, Columbia University Press, New York, 1–268.

[20] See Halov, N., and Heider F., 2006. Capital structure, risk and asymmetric information, NYU Stern School of Business and European Central Bank Working Paper, April 15, 1–58, page 27: 'the adverse selection cost of debt is irrelevant for firms that have any rating, and vice versa, suggesting that ratings appear to bridge the information gap between firms and outside investors about risk.'

concerning the quality of many mortgages and mortgage backed securities, as appeared in the subprime mortgage crisis. Many of these companies and assets suffered from similar deficiencies that Poor saw in his day and that legislative changes across OECD countries are attempting to remedy since then.

But now, the role of the CRAs has expanded significantly. When the bond markets started displacing commercial banks and official lending agencies as primary sources of credit to industry and to institutional borrowers, both domestically and internationally, there was a vacuum. Who was going to do the credit risk due diligence on all these bonds that were increasingly offered to the capital markets in lieu of credits granted by commercial banks? Not the credit analysts at the commercial banks, because the bond market was substituting for the credit-granting activities of commercial banks. These banks were not the primary lenders through these bond instruments. They would purchase some corporate bonds in the primary and secondary markets, but were not granting the credit and incurring the cost of the credit analysis as they had previously when deciding on a long-term investment credit for a corporation. Who filled the vacuum? It was the credit analysts at the CRAs. They became real infomediaries between issuers (originators of information), and investors (users of information). The major CRAs thus came to play an increasingly important and influential role in capital markets. Today, they are the credit risk compass for the asset allocation of institutional investors as private capital moves freely around the world in search of the best trade-off between risk and return.

However, as the activities of CRAs expanded, so did their exposure, on both sides of the investment equation. Since 1997, the CRAs have been caught in the middle, or worse, between the hammer and the anvil, in several highly visible instances. Issuers sometimes claim that it is the rating action that affects their creditworthiness and reputation, rather than the underlying conditions that led to the action. Bond investors sometimes believe that somehow CRAs possess a crystal ball about an issuer's future or that issuers are unable to hide anything from them. So different stakeholders in the level, timeliness and predictive accuracy of a rating and its changes tend to become very angry at CRAs when they are perceived to be making mistakes. And since 1998 the CRAs have been going through a difficult period of significant controversy.

The major CRAs have been strongly criticized for failing to raise the alarm ahead of credit crises. They were accused of failing to spot the Asian crisis that broke out on July 2, 1997. S&P rated Korea investment grade until December 21, 1997, and Indonesia until December 30. Were the CRAs 'caught with their pants down,' as a *Euromoney* article title suggested?[21] More recently, investors and opinion leaders have criticized CRAs for failing to spot the Enron, WorldCom, and Parmalat collapses. Moody's and S&P rated Enron investment grade until November 27, 2001 – six days before it declared bankruptcy. Similarly for Worldcom, which Moody's rated investment grade until May 8, 2002 and S&P until May 9, about two months before it declared bankruptcy. And S&P rated Parmalat SpA investment grade until 18 days before it declared bankruptcy on December 27, 2003. Finally, in July 2007, the rating agencies massively downgraded residential mortgage backed securities that had been issued just a year earlier, because of origination issues such as aggressive residential mortgage loan underwriting. But, of course, ratings require the full and honest participation of the debt issuer. And the CRAs have pointed out that these collapsed issuers repeatedly misled them.[22]

---

[21] See Irvine, S., 1998. Caught with their pants down?, *Euromoney*, 345, January, 51–53.

[22] See, for example, the Standard & Poor's press release of December 19, 2003. Parmalat Finanziaria, Parmalat cut to D on missed payment of put option, ratings withdrawn, stating 'Continued lack of access to reliable information

Alternatively, issuers complained that CRAs were too harsh on them. Obligors accused them of creating the bad weather, rather than being just the weathermen. According to the *Wall Street Journal Europe*, Alcatel SA Chief Serge Tchuruk likened the agencies to 'pyromaniac firemen,' while Vivendi Universal SA CEO Jean-René Fourtou called them 'the executioner.' And France Telecom SA's former CEO, Michel Bon, said an 'unjustified' downgrade by Moody's helped to initiate a debt crisis that cost him his job.[23]

As a result, most interest groups with stakes in rating actions mobilized. They scrutinized the CRAs or had regulators and legislators scrutinize them, and possibly muzzle them, asking questions such as: 'Are issuers faced with too many agencies keen to charge them fees or with not enough of them to have bargaining power?' The Committee of European Securities Regulators (CESR), International Monetary Fund (IMF), the International Organization of Securities Commissions (IOSCO), the Securities and Exchange Commission (SEC), and the US Senate, to name the major ones, conducted investigations, hearings, and made proposals for reform from 2003 through today, leading so far to the Credit Rating Agency Reform Act of 2006 in the US. The CRAs individually engaged alongside industry associations of major users such as the Bond Market Association (BMA) and the International Group of Treasury Associations (IGTA).[24]

Regulators have demonstrated a particular eagerness to have a say in agency credit ratings. It should be no surprise. They feel responsible for the quality of the information that is available to investors and are for the soundness of the financial sector. They worry occasionally about possible biases in ratings, because typically agencies earn their revenues from the fees that rated issuers pay to be rated. Alternatively, the speed of adjustment of ratings to changing issuer conditions causes concern. Sometimes they are afraid that downgrades that are too prompt make things worse for the debtor, and therefore also for the investor. Sometimes the regulators complain that agencies are too slow in downgrading, particularly so when hindsight makes it easy to predict a default that has already occurred.

However, whatever the regulators' complaints about rating agencies, they use them. A major international regulatory lobby, the Basel Committee on Banking Supervision, under the auspices of the Bank for International Settlements (BIS), assigned credit ratings a central role in its revised framework for bank capital measurement and capital standards, announced in June 2004. Accordingly, the equity capital that banks must have will be based upon the credit risk of their assets as measured, among others, by CRA credit ratings of these assets.[25] In addition, many critics of CRAs rely on them to provide objective information to facilitate investment decisions – for instance, pension funds, which base their investment criteria on bond ratings.

---

on the group's exact financial position,...left Standard & Poor's with no other option than to withdraw all of the ratings on Parmalat and related entities.'

[23] Delaney, K.J., 2002. France Inc. is fuming at top rating agencies – Anger over downgrades is sign of new accountability; 'Search for a Scapegoat,' *The Wall Street Journal Europe*, November 20.

[24] CRAs themselves don't have an industry association out of respect to antitrust legislation in the US.

[25] This will become the case as national bank prudential regulatory authorities enact in their own jurisdictions the revised framework on the international convergence of capital measurement and capital standards of the Basel Committee on Banking Supervision at the Bank for International Settlements. Central bank governors and the heads of bank supervisory authorities in the Group of Ten (G10) countries endorsed this new capital adequacy framework commonly known as Basel II on June 26, 2004. See Basel Committee on Banking Supervision, 2004. *International Convergence of Capital Measurement and Capital Standards: A Revised Framework*, Bank for International Settlements, Basel, June, 1–251.

Publicly available data suggests that the CRA business is generally extraordinarily profitable, growing fast and highly concentrated, which prompts another host of questions. Is this the competitive result of significant and sustainable competitive advantages? Are the reputational and network barriers that a new entrant has to overcome so high that an oligopoly is not only unavoidable but also more efficient than any other industry organization? Or are there many artificial barriers to entry in this industry that ought to be abolished? Do agencies possess unreasonable pricing power? Are the recent profit results of major CRAs just transient, the consequence of the demand for ratings expanding at a speed far in excess of supply? Or is there a structural misalignment between the public interest role that agencies play through the many regulatory uses of the CRAs' product – and in consequence the demand for it – and the private shareholders' interest in the conduct of their business? These are complicated questions that deserve careful analysis before answering, and hence meticulous observation and realistic explanation of how the CRAs actually work. The CRA industry is in fact naturally concentrated. Incumbents compete with intensive rivalry against each other. Contesting new entrants make gallant attempts to break in. The US Credit Agency Reform Act of 2006 strictly regulated the agencies' conduct while simultaneously removing some artificial regulatory hurdles for entering the industry.

Ill-prepared for the spotlight, the CRAs are now living in it. There is little doubt that the rating process has played a major role in inducing companies and countries to become more transparent in their dealings with investors, and that the credit rating industry review process since 2003 is inciting the CRAs themselves to become ever more transparent, diligent, and deontological in their own work. But the technological and industrial environment of this work has become ever more challenging.

To sum up, we discuss CRAs and their credit ratings in the context of traditional business analysis, the moral hazard incentives of shareholders, sovereigns or originators, and the re-invigorated modus operandi of the CRAs following the 2003–2006 industry review. We have decided not to treat the structured finance segment as a wholly separate part in the book, but we rather insist on its main specificities relative to the more traditional rating segments. Structured finance ratings have been in many headlines the last year but we found that the fundamental issues were really recurring ones such as conflicts of interest, due diligence, disclosure, transparency, investor communication, timeliness and accuracy. Three basic insights guide us. The CRAs' core activity is benchmarking default prospects in a world of ever-lasting, and expanding, information asymmetries. The bizarre CRA industry is extremely interesting because it combines intensive rivalry with high concentration, and public service with the private pursuit of profit. Finally, not withstanding the current financial crisis, the trend of capital markets penetrating more deeply and broadly into all economies worldwide continues, the role of CRAs is bound to expand and evolve and, correspondingly, to be challenged.

The book hopes to stimulate the reader's own thinking about CRAs and credit ratings. We try to combine breadth of perspective, substantiation of arguments, and depth in reflection – without mathematics. We cover the role of credit ratings in the economy, the industry organization of the ratings agency business and how to get to a rating. We guide the reader through what credit ratings really are, how credit rating agencies actually work, and why this whole activity is in fact relevant through the following chapter steps.

1.2   BOOK CHAPTERS

The book is organized in three parts: Credit Rating Foundations (A), Credit Rating Analysis (B), and The Credit Rating Business (C). Credit Rating Foundations explains in three chapters what credit ratings are, reviews how broad and diverse their applications are, and describes how an issuer obtains and maintains a credit rating.

Chapter 2 reviews what value credit ratings add in a world of corporate defaults, what scales they use, and how to interpret them. It explores the notion that ratings are opinions, not statements of fact, and reviews how CRAs ensure honesty and diligence in their own processes. We also discuss the things that a CRA is not – an auditor or a fraud detective.

Chapter 3, on the application of credit ratings, explains how important it is for borrowers and investors that ratings reduce information asymmetries between them. It notes the success of CRAs through the wide use of ratings by prescribers such as private contractors, trustees, boards of directors, corporate finance advisers, underwriters, brokers, and regulators, none of whom is a principal in any rating action.

Chapter 4 describes how to obtain and maintain a credit rating. We discuss the rating process and the players involved, and how the eventual rating decision is made. The actions following a rating decision are described, and the increasing importance of monitoring and communication is explored. Legal liability, confidentiality, and the cost of obtaining a rating are also discussed.

Part (B), Credit Rating Analysis, begins in **Chapter 5** with a study of France Telecom and the company's credit ratings between 1995 and 2004, when it went from sovereign status to near speculative grade and then back up to investment grade. The case study covers the rating actions, the business climate in which France Telecom was operating and impact on management. The case study is used to illustrate how rating actions and inactions interact with the market, offer a forward-looking perspective, and provide a degree of anticipation akin to the traditional perspective of bank credit committees. The France Telecom story shows the importance of analyzing fundamental default risk and the prospects of recovery in case of default.

Chapter 6, on Credit Analysis, deals mostly with corporate issuer analysis. It starts with reviewing the principles, methodologies, and approaches underlying fundamental credit analysis. It also explains how to extract default probabilities from market prices, explains both approaches, and clarifies how they are different and complementary. The chapter concludes with a brief review of the essentials of special sector ratings, including sovereigns, financial strength, and structured finance instruments.

Chapter 7, on Credit Rating Performance, addresses the questions of their accuracy, and how rating actions and inactions interact with the market. How accurate are ratings in predicting actual defaults and in avoiding false predictions of defaults that never occur? What do ratings and ratings changes add to the pricing of securities? How rationally and diligently did the CRAs act during periods of crisis?

Part (C), the Credit Rating Business, analyses in **Chapter 8** the credit rating industry – where it comes from, its main characteristics, how the main players compete, and the results it produces for issuers, investors, and shareholders.

Chapter 9, the regulatory oversight of the industry, covers first the regulatory uses of ratings and next the regulation of the industry. This entails both industry structure issues and conduct of business issues. We first discuss the self-regulatory approach – 'comply with the consensual code of conduct or explain why you don't' – of the EU, so far, and next the administrative oversight approach of the SECs rule to implement the Credit Rating Agency Reform Act of 2006 in the US.

We conclude in **Chapter 10** by giving our perspective on the value that rating agencies add for issuers, investors, and CRA shareholders. We also offer our view of the challenges they face, before sharing some final thoughts.

The structured finance vignettes throughout this book provide descriptions of various aspects of structured finance to the reader. SPVs (Vignette 1), the supply of and the demand for SFI (Vignettes 2 and 3), Taganka Car loan (Vignette 4), synthetic CDOs (Vignette 5), the rating process for SFI (Vignette 6), structured finance ratings and spreads (Vignette 7), and the stability of SFI credit ratings (Vignette 8).

1.3 SUPPORTING MATERIALS

We complement the text in many chapters by providing Exhibits, Tables, and Figures. As often as possible we try to refer to the original dataset, when it is difficult to access or compute we refer to data from intermediary sources.

We used a multiplicity of sources as references.

Credit Rating Agency Documents

There are two broad types of CRA documents: rating actions and others. We refer to rating actions as the agency public documents referencing and describing any new rating, rating or rating outlook change or affirmation after a review. The rating actions that are quoted or commented on in the main text, are referred to only in the footnotes and by the agency name, document title and date. For parsimony, we omit them from the list of references at the end of the book.

Among others, CRAs produce abundant periodic reports. These cover how they produce ratings and the various methods used in doing so; how well these ratings perform; and how they run their organizations. In addition, they publish occasional concept papers and policy statements. When deciding how to reference all of these, we bore in mind the interest of the reader and the differential treatments across CRAs of the identification of the authors of the periodic reports. We choose as the most logical and useful solution for the reader to always mention just the company name for the periodic reports and also the authors name for occasional concept papers and policy statements.

Interest Group Documents and Interviews

We benefitted from the extensive CRA industry review that took place in 2003–2006 and 2007–2008. We learned a lot about CRAs from hours and hours of field interviews and discussion with the different stakeholders: issuers, investors, CRAs themselves, bankers, risk managers, and regulators.

Economic Research

Great minds in economics have devoted at one point of their academic or professional career some of their talent to solve some important problems dealing with credit rating agencies and their ratings. Our purpose in this book is not to compete with these, but to pay them tribute. Their vast contributions, for which we are grateful, enabled us to write the synthesis expressed in this book. We recognize this by making extensive use of selective referencing. Our references are illustrative, but in no way exhaustive. We apologize beforehand to the many contributors to the issues that we discuss. If their work has not been cited, it is for reasons of parsimony or simply our ignorance. We cite many quotes and research findings in the book, but it is always done to support or illustrate the points that we make in our narrative, not to demonstrate anything. We focus on rigor in explaining intuition, not in deriving proofs that mathematics allows. We make one important exception concerning the kernel of our book that accurate ratings resolve adverse selection and moral hazard problems between bond issuers and investors. This point is so central that we provide illustrative proofs of it in a special annex to **Chapter 3**. By necessity, our narrative becomes occasionally quite verbose without supporting analytical derivations. It is mostly in this circumstance that we appeal to the authority of notorious contributors to our subject. All errors in doing so are ours. We did our best at never misconstruing someone else's point. If we failed occasionally, we express our regrets and ask our apologies to be accepted. To alleviate the text in order to be reader friendly, we omit to cite their names in the narrative and do so only in footnotes and the list of references.

Part A
Credit Rating Foundations

Part A reviews in three chapters what credit ratings are, how broad and diverse their applications are, and how an issuer obtains and maintains a credit rating.

Chapter 2 defines credit ratings and shows how they emerged from the world of corporate defaults which it reviews. In the event of default, investors do not typically lose their full investment, thus the chapter goes on to discuss recovery rates from defaults. In communicating, credit ratings use a variety of scales that the chapter discusses in some detail. Fundamental ratings rank default prospects on an ordinal scale, and market credit spreads, being driven by the same underlying risk of default as the ratings, reflect to some extent that ordinal scale. Market implied ratings estimate actual default probabilities on a cardinal scale. They are born out of the 'revolutionary idea of finance' that has shown the world how to extract from observing an issuer's security prices and financial commitments, its actual probability of default.* **Chapter 2** then goes on to interpret the notches on the rating scales and the generics of ratings generally. Ratings are fine opinions, not statements of fact. CRAs ensure honesty and diligence in their own processes of reaching their views; they do not vouch, like auditors, for the accuracy and fairness of the financial statements of rated issuers. Nor are CRAs detectives to expose company fraud.

Chapter 3 reviews the variety of rating applications. It explains how important it is for borrowers and investors that ratings reduce information asymmetries between them. It notices the success of CRAs in doing so by the wide use that prescribers – such as private contractors, trustees, boards of directors, corporate finance advisers, underwriters, brokers, and regulators – have made of credit ratings without being a principal in their actions. It reminds the reader that, in the beginning, there were the ratings of US railroad bonds and that, nowadays, ratings span a vast array of products, industries and regions, cross-border and in multiple currencies.

Chapter 4 describes how to obtain and maintain a credit rating. During the rating process, the analyst of the credit rating agency supplier interacts with the issuer client and his rating adviser-intermediary in preparation of the rating case that she will have to propose to the rating committee. This committee is discretionary in its sovereign decision made by a majority of votes. Once taken, informing the issuer in time for the rating action, communicating it properly to the market, and following it up diligently are becoming increasingly relevant parts of the rating agreement between the issuer and the CRA. The legal liability that the CRA engages with this agreement tends to be rather limited, the confidentiality of the information that the issuer shares with the CRA is paramount and the pricing of the service tends to be negotiated on the basis of a standard public commission-based schedule at least in segments other than structured finance.

---

* Mehrling, P., 2005. *Fischer Black and the Revolutionary Idea of Finance*, John Wiley & Sons, Inc., Hoboken, New Jersey, 1–374.

2
Credit Ratings

The credit ratings world is an extremely busy place. More than 745 000 securities from over 42 000 issuers, and representing at least $30 trillion, are rated from AAA or P-1 through C by about 150 different CRAs spanning over 100 countries.[1,2] But what exactly are credit ratings?

There is no industry definition or standard to describe credit ratings, and no trade association of CRAs.[3] During the 2003–2006 worldwide review of the credit rating industry, various regulatory bodies from around the globe offered their definition of a credit rating. For the US Securities and Exchange Commission (SEC), 'a credit rating reflects a rating agency's opinion, as of a specific date, of the creditworthiness of a particular company, security, or obligation.'[4] For the International Organization of Securities Commissions (IOSCO) and the Committee of European Securities Regulators (CESR), 'a "credit rating" is an opinion regarding the creditworthiness of an entity, a credit commitment, a debt or debt-like security or an issuer of such obligations, expressed using an established and defined ranking system ... They are not recommendations to purchase, sell, or hold any security.'[5] According to the European Commission, 'Credit rating agencies issue opinions on the creditworthiness of a particular issuer or financial instrument. In other words, they assess the likelihood that an issuer will default either on its financial obligations generally (issuer rating) or on a particular debt or fixed income security (instrument rating),'[6] and according to the US Credit Rating Agency Reform Act of 2006, 'The term "credit rating" means an assessment of the creditworthiness of an obligor as an entity or with respect to specific securities or money market instruments.'[7]

---

[1] Bolger, R.M., Managing Director, Global Regulatory Affairs & Associate General Counsel – Standard & Poor's, 2005, The credit rating agency duopoly relief act of 2005, Testimony before the House Subcommittee on Capital Markets, Insurance and Government Sponsored Enterprises, June 29, 1–17, Exhibit A.

[2] Estrella, A., 2000, Credit ratings and complementary sources of credit quality information, *Basel Committee on Banking Supervision Working Papers* No. 3: Bank for International Settlements, Basel, August, 1–186, page 14.

[3] Senior managers at CRAs point out that *vis-à-vis* US antitrust enforcers a trade association could create presumptions of collusion on competitive behavior and on pricing.

[4] US Securities and Exchange Commission, 2003, Report on the role and function of credit rating agencies in the operation of the securities markets, January, 1–45, page 5.

[5] Technical Committee of International Organization of Securities Commissions, 2004, Code of conduct fundamentals for credit rating agencies, December, OICV-IOSCO PD 180, 1–12, page 3, and The Committee of European Securities Regulators, 2005, The use of ratings in private contracts, Technical Advice to the European Commission on possible measures concerning credit rating agencies, March, CESR/05-139b, 1–93, page 12.

[6] Commission of the European Communities, 2005, Communication from the Commission on credit rating agencies, December 23, 2005/11990, 1–9, page 2.

[7] United States House of Representatives, 2006, H.R. 2990, Short Title: Credit Rating Duopoly Relief Act of 2006 (Version H.R. 2990 RFS – Referred to Senate Committee after being received from House of Representatives), July 13, 1–26, page 4 and United States Senate, 2006, Credit Rating Agency Reform Act of 2006 (S.3850), 109th Congress, 2D Session, September 22.

While these definitions give a comprehensive picture of the essential ingredients of a credit rating, the best place to find the answer to our question is the CRA industry itself.[8] Each CRA has its own definition of a credit rating.

The largest three CRAs (in alphabetical order) are Fitch, Moody's and Standard & Poor's (S&P), and their definitions of credit ratings are given below. Other definitions, from agencies in geographical or functional niches, will be drawn on where appropriate.[9]

> Fitch's credit ratings provide an opinion on the relative ability of an entity to meet financial commitments... They are used by investors as indications of the likelihood of receiving their money back in accordance with the terms on which they invested... Depending on their application, credit ratings address benchmark measures of probability of default as well as relative expectations of loss given default.[10]

> A Moody's credit rating is an independent opinion about credit risk. It is an assessment of the ability and willingness of an issuer of fixed-income securities to make full and timely payment of amounts due on the security over its life.[11]

> A credit rating is Standard & Poor's opinion of the general creditworthiness of an obligor, or the creditworthiness of an obligor with respect to a particular debt security or other financial obligation, based on relevant risk factors.[12]

The differences between these three definitions illustrate the divergence among CRAs. Fitch emphasizes that ratings are all *relative* and concerned with *default.* Their definition highlights the distinction between the *probability* that default occurs and the potential *loss* to the investor. Moody's stresses the *independence* of its opinion, which deals with *credit risk* and the *willingness* of the obligor to perform. For S&P, ratings deal with *creditworthiness,* either that of the *issuer* itself, or that of a particular *issue*, and its opinion is based on *relevant risk factors*. Whatever the differences, the big three CRAs all agree that a credit rating is an *opinion* about whether the issuer of a fixed income security will pay amounts due on time and in full. The common thread is that ratings deal with defaults and place an issuer or an instrument on a scale from least likely to default to most likely to default, so in order to understand credit ratings, we must first understand defaults.

2.1 THE WORLD OF CORPORATE DEFAULTS

Default is one of the more ambiguous notions in law. Yet, prospective default analysis is the core of the CRA business. As one of the most influential intellectual shapers of default analysis put it: 'the appropriate measure of default risk and the accuracy of its measurement

---

[8] BIS and CEBS have conducted extensive studies on the use of external credit assessments by financial institutions for determining the risk weights of their exposures, no definition of the 'credit ratings' or 'credit assessments' has been stated.

[9] Australian Rapid Ratings Pty Ltd; Canadian Dominion bond rating service limited (DBRS), Japan, credit rating agency Ltd and US Egan-Jones Rating Co.

[10] See Fitch Ratings, 2007. Fitch ratings definitions: Introductions to rating, *Resource Library*, March 26, 1–4, page 1.

[11] Moody's Investors Service, 2004, Guide to Moody's ratings, rating process, and rating practices, June, Report 87615, 1–48, page 9. An older definition was somewhat more elaborate: 'A credit rating is an opinion of the future ability, legal obligation, and willingness of a bond issuer or other obligor to make full and timely payments on principal and interest due to investors, over the life of the security.' See Moody's Investor Service, 1999, How to use Moody's ratings, *Ratings*.

[12] Standard & Poor's, 2005, *Corporate Ratings Criteria* 1–119, page 8.

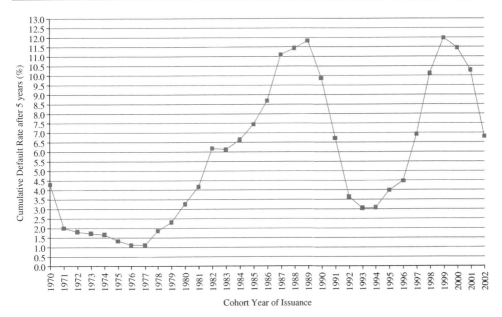

Figure 2.1 Moody's cumulative 5-year issuer weighted default rates, all corporate bonds, issue cohorts (1970–2002).
Source: Cantor, R., Hamilton, D.T., Ou, S., and Kim, F., 2007. Corporate default and recovery rates, 1920–2006, *Special Comment:* Moody's Investors Service, June, Report 102071, 1–48, page 28.

are critical in the pricing of debt instruments, in the measurement of their performance, and in the assessment of market efficiency.' We had better be clear about what default is.

Default is 'failure to pay money due.'[13] This dictionary definition allows us at least to start looking at the world of corporate defaults. Whoever the issuer and however infrequent defaults are, history has taught that all bonds are at risk of default.[14] This risk can be large or small, but no bond can be guaranteed absolutely. Since we cannot predict the future, all risk assessments are necessarily subjective estimates, and, since they can be arrived at in different ways, they represent different degrees of accuracy.

Defaults are a market-wide phenomenon. Figure 2.1 gives default rates for corporate bonds between 1970 and 2002, a period during which 4627 issuers defaulted overall. Of all corporate issuers exposed to the risk of default in a given year, 5.5% have typically defaulted by the end of five years. This default rate varies greatly over time, reaching a high of 12.0% for issuers exposed to the risk of default in 1999, the middle of the Internet bubble. The average default rate also cycles over time and is currently on an upwards trend, as the lows and highs are getting higher.

The stakes of specific issuers in defaults can be impressively high, as Exhibit 2.1 suggests. The 10 largest defaults on internationally traded debt since 1998 have involved bonds with

---

[13] *Webster's New World Dictionary of the American Language*, 1970, Second college edition, The World Publishing Company, New York and Cleveland, 1–1692.
[14] Corporate bonds, the traditional rated instruments, are debt securities that companies issue to raise money for a variety of purposes, such as building a new plant, purchasing equipment, growing the business, buying back equity, etc. The bond gives the investor an IOU on the company, but no ownership interest, unless the bond defaults.

Exhibit 2.1 Ten largest losses to bond and note investor (1998–2002).

Issuer	Defaulted Year	Defaulted bonds (US$ billion)	Wtd-avg-recovery (%)	Loss (US$ billion)	Moody's ratings prior to default[a] (mos)			
					3	6	12	24
Argentina	2001	82.27	28.60	58.74	Caa1	B2	B1	B1
WorldCom, Inc	2002	29.01	12.75	25.31	A3	A3	A3	A3
Russian Federation[b]	1998	32.32	52.75	15.27	Ba2	Ba2	Ba2	n/a
Enron Corp.	2001	10.14	15.86	8.53	Baa1	Baa1	Baa1	Baa2
NTL Incorporated	2002	11.23	34.35	7.37	Caa2	B3	B2	B3
Asia Pulp & Paper Company Ltd	2001	7.27	14.05	6.25	B1	B1	B1	B2
United Pan-Europe Communications NV	2002	6.51	19.05	5.27	Caa3	Caa1	B2	B2
Conseco Inc	2002	5.09	10.94	4.54	B2	B2	B1	B1
Global Crossing Holdings Ltd	2002	4.81	5.67	4.54	B2	Ba2	Ba2	Ba2
Adelphia Communications Corporation	2002	10.52	57.12	4.51	B2	B2	B2	B1

[a] Estimated sr. unsecured rating of primary family member (defined by debt size).
[b] Foreign currency rating.

a face value of $199.2 billion and caused expected losses to investors of $140.3 billion, or 70.4% of principal plus accrued interest. These included both sovereign risk (such as Argentina and the Russian Federation) and corporations world wide.

Given that on average 5.5% of the total value of corporate bonds default within five years, investors naturally want to know which issues are least likely to default. For instance, on June 30, 2005, S&P had rated 7028 corporate issuers around the world. The 5.5% average default rate suggests that between 300 and 400 of these will have defaulted by June 30, 2010. The job of the CRAs is therefore to try to identify the corporations that belong in this group.

Were it not for defaults, there would be no need for credit ratings. Put bluntly, defaults are the bread and butter of the credit ratings business.

2.1.1   What are Corporate Defaults?

As with credit ratings, there is no unique, global definition of what constitutes a default. Some call default the 'failure to pay money due' at the first occurrence of non-payment after a contractual grace period has lapsed; some see it as occurring 90 days after that period has lapsed, assuming that it has not been remedied during that period; yet others place it after bankruptcy. True default always entails one or another form of non-payment. Following rating industry practice, we use the first and most restrictive of the previous three interpretations.[15]

Technical default occurs if a borrower breaches a financial obligation other than debt service payment. For example, debt covenants may stipulate several balance sheet restrictions, such as minimum liquidity or solvency ratios, which the borrower has to respect in order to be allowed to reimburse a loan at maturity. Were the borrower to violate these restrictions, the bank would have the right to call the loan immediately. While such covenant violations constitute technical defaults, they typically do not trigger what is more normally called default, and they do not appear in the usual default statistics. Nevertheless, such financial obligations will be of great interest to credit rating analysts. A borrower's ability to honor any restrictions, and the likelihood that he will do so, clearly affects his subsequent ability to pay amounts due on time and in full. Hence an essential part of the CRAs' analysis is to scrutinize the covenants of all an obligor's loan contracts, including those that are private or unlisted.

But what is non-payment? According to Moody's, it is an 'event that changes the relationship between the bondholder and the bond issuer from the relationship that was originally contracted, and subjects the bondholder to an economic loss.'[16] It includes three types of credit events:

1. A missed or delayed disbursement of interest and/or principal, including delayed payments made within a grace period.

S&P Cuts Damovo Rating after Default on Debt

That was the headline in the *Financial Times* on October 31, 2006, the day after S&P said 'that it lowered to "D" from "CCC+" its long-term corporate credit rating on UK-based telecommunications services provider Damovo Group S.A.' The downgrade followed Damovo's announcement

---

[15] Ganguin, B., and Bilardello, J., 2005, *Fundamentals of Corporate Credit Analysis*, McGraw-Hill, New York, 1–437, page 195.

[16] See Cantor, R., Hamilton, D.T, Ou, S., and Varma, P., 2005, Default and recovery rates of corporate bond issuers, 1920–2004, *Special Comment*: Moody's Investors Service, January, Report 91233, 1–40, page 39.

the same day that it would defer a €18.9 million semi-annual coupon payment due that day. S&P's credit analyst went on to say that 'Although the bond indenture includes a 30-day grace period to complete the payment, we do not have enough assurances that Damovo will be able to make the payment or that a restructure would not entail significant capital losses for note holders.'[17]

Telecom Argentina in Record Default

So said the BBC news website in April 2002 when it emerged that Telecom Argentina had suspended all principal payments on debts of $3.2 billion, and the event was reported as the largest corporate default ever in Argentina. The second biggest telecom company in the country, Telecom Argentina was jointly controlled by France Telecom and Telecom Italia at the time. The Argentine peso had been devalued in January 2002 and had subsequently fallen by around 65%, and this was blamed for the company's debt problems. Telecom Argentina's announcement was only one of many as Argentine firms struggled to repay dollar loans in the face of currency instability. Fitch Ratings downgraded the company to 'DD' from 'C'. This 'indicates that the company is in default and that the recovery rate is expected to be in the range of 50%–90%.'[18]. Analyst Rafael Ber of Argentine Research told the BBC, 'The company has no money to make payments and it has already suggested that what it will do is exchange debt for equity.' A delegation from the International Monetary Fund was dispatched to Argentina to explore options to aid the country's economy.

2. Bankruptcy, administration, legal receivership, or other legal blocks (perhaps by regulation) to the timely payment of interest and/or principal.

Entergy Corporation's New Orleans Subsidiary Files Chapter 11 Petition

Entergy Board Approves Debtor-in-Possession Financial Package to Facilitate Business Continuity

September 23, 2005

New Orleans, La. – To protect its customers and ensure continued progress in restoring power and gas service to New Orleans after Hurricane Katrina, Entergy Corporation (NYSE: ETR) announced today that its New Orleans subsidiary – Entergy New Orleans, Inc. (Entergy New Orleans) – has filed a voluntary petition for reorganization under Chapter 11 of the US Bankruptcy Code.

Simultaneous with this filing, Entergy New Orleans filed a motion with the Court for 'debtor-in-possession' financing that contemplates Entergy Corporation making loans up to $200 million to Entergy New Orleans to address Entergy New Orleans' current liquidity crisis. The petition also requests that up to $150 million of these loans be approved on an interim basis. These funds will enable Entergy New Orleans to meet its near-term obligations, including employee wages and benefits, payments under power purchase and gas supply agreements, and its current efforts to repair and restore the facilities needed to serve its electric and gas customers.[19]

Moody's had placed the ratings of Entergy New Orleans under review for possible downgrade on September 8, due to the extraordinary damage that Hurricane Katrina had caused to the utility's infrastructure and service territory. It downgraded it twice in a few days, on September

---

[17] Standard & Poor's, 2006, Damovo Group Cut to 'D' On Coupon Payment Deferral, Rating Action, October 30, 1-1.

[18] Fitch Ratings, 2002, Fitch Ratings downgrades Telecom Argentina S.A. to 'DD', April 9, 1-1.

[19] Entergy Corporation, 2005, Entergy Corporation's New Orleans subsidiary files Chapter 11 petition. Press Release, September 23.

20 and 22 and withdrew its rating on December 29 in accordance with Moody's practice of withdrawing the debt rating of issuers in bankruptcy.[20]

3. A distressed exchange where: (i) the issuer offers bondholders a new security or package of securities that amounts to a diminished financial obligation (such as preferred or common stock, or debt with a lower coupon or par amount, lower seniority, or longer maturity); or (ii) the exchange had the apparent purpose of helping the borrower avoid default.'[21]

Embassy of Ukraine to the United States of America

29 September 1998

For immediate release

Standard & Poor's qualifies Ukraine's bond conversion as default; Government officials disagree

The Standard & Poor's international credit rating agency issued a statement defining as default the recent rescheduling of Ukraine's domestic debts into longer-term bonds.[22] Standard & Poor's qualifies debt rescheduling terms as default if the terms are less favorable than the original terms, the statement said. According to Standard & Poor's, investors were forced to agree to the conversion because they practically had no choice. However, Ukrainian government officials have rejected the Standard and Poor's opinion. Valeriy Lytvytskiy, an adviser to President Leonid Kuchma on economic issues, told journalists that there were no grounds to define the bond conversion as default. According to him, the relevant agreements with investors were reviewed on a voluntary basis before they expired, adding that not a single investor could claim that he was refused repayment. Vyacheslav Kozak, an adviser to Deputy Prime Minister Serhiy Tyhypko, stressed that default is the fact of non-payment. Nothing of the sort occurred in Ukraine, he added. According to him, Ukraine is fulfilling its current obligations.

---

[20] Moody's Investors Service, 2005, Successive rating actions on Entergy of September 8, 20 and 22 and December 29.

[21] See Cantor, R., Hamilton, D.T, Ou, S., and Varma, P., 2005, Default and recovery rates of corporate bond issuers, 1920–2004. *Special Comment:* Moody's Investors Service, January, Report 91233, 1–40, page 39.

[22] Standard & Poor's, 1998, Ukraine debt exchanges constitute a default, *Rating Action*, September 24, 1–2. S&P comments were remarkable inasmuch that it did not rate at that time Ukraine. Consider also the fuller picture that S&P provided after it started rating Ukraine on December 21, 2001 at the B level: 'Ukraine stopped paying debts to official creditors and began restructuring commercial debt in 2000. In April 2000, the restructuring agreement on commercial debt was concluded. It comprised an exchange offer for US$2.1 billion of four Eurobonds due March 2000–February 2001 and one so-called "Gazprom" bond due in 2001 (bonds issued in exchange for gas debts owed Russia in 1995 and subsequently traded on secondary market). They were exchanged at par for an equal amount of euro- and dollar-denominated new bonds In addition, US$0.6 billion of "Gazprom" bonds due 2002–2007 were exchanged at a discount for US$0.4 billion (holders of US$0.2 billion in these bonds did not agree to an exchange, but these bonds had been serviced). Altogether, US$2.6 billion of commercial debt was restructured into new eurobonds to be repaid by 2007. Yields on new eurobonds are still relatively high, 11% on dollar-denominated issues and 10% on euro-denominated issues. Principal payments were rescheduled to start in 2001 (US$120 million) with repayment less than US$0.5 million a year in 2003–2004. The schedule looks smooth, without any peaks, so that Ukraine should not face repayment difficulties on commercial debt over the next few years under the reasonable scenario. Debt to the Paris Club, which has not been serviced since 2000, was recently rescheduled following the agreement with IMF. The agreement comprises US$580 million out of the total US$1 billion debt outstanding. The debt is restructured into 18 equal semiannual payments to be repaid over 12 years, with repayment starting in 2004. The deal excludes US$280 million due to Turkmenistan, which should be rescheduled in early 2002. Bilateral gas debt owed to Russia has also been recently rescheduled. Taken together, the current account surplus, reduced debt servicing costs, and growing exports and international reserves notably reduced Ukraine's external debt burden. Net public external debt in terms of exports declined to an estimated 34% of exports, down from 44% in 2000 and a peak of 63% in 1999. Net quoted from Standard & Poor's, 2001, Ukraine (Republic of), Analysis, December 26, 1–14, page 12.

The government began converting its domestic debts into longer-term bonds in late August. Ukrainian banks were asked to convert bonds maturing in 1998-1999 into bonds maturing in 2001–2004; foreign investors were asked to covert their bonds into new bonds maturing in 2000. According to bankers, investors agreed to convert either under government pressure or for fear that lack of funds will force the Finance Ministry to default. However, investors have not protested officially against the government's action.[23]

A default is the first occurrence of any one of these three events. It typically (but not always) occurs when a firm's operating cash flow is insufficient to make a contractually required payment (such as trade credits or interest expenses). Inasmuch as an all-equity firm is free from such leverage requirements, poor performance does not lead to any of these events. But a leveraged firm that does poorly may become insolvent on a cash flow basis and encounter such an event, putting itself in financial distress and forcing it to take corrective action to improve its cash flows and balance sheet.[24] Corrective action involves steps such as selling major assets, merging with another firm, and/or reducing capital spending and research and development. Financial restructuring could involve issuing new securities, negotiating with banks and creditors, exchanging debt for equity, or, eventually, filing for bankruptcy.

Bankruptcy is the 'court-supervised process for breaking and rewriting contracts.'[25] It is a binary prospect: the company either files for it or it doesn't. As one of my economics teachers used to say, it is like being pregnant: you are or you are not, you cannot be just a bit pregnant. Many attempts have been made to determine company characteristics that make it drop on either side of the fence of the binary event. Seminal work initiated an industry about this, both academic and commercial using multivariate discriminant analysis to define types on the basis of observable financial ratios ahead of the event by hitting a success rate of 95%.[26] Under this approach, the value of each ratio is weighted by its factor to produce its term in the discriminant function. The sum of these terms producing the value of the function is called the overall index Z.[27] The initial sample used to estimate the value of the factors finds that 2.675 is the critical Z-score that discriminates best between bankrupt (score smaller) and non-bankrupt (score higher) firms. This result holds of course... provided that firms don't take corrective action once they know their score. A Board of Directors' weighting between filing for Chapter 11 bankruptcy protection in light of continuing financial difficulties or carrying on with sufficient grounds to expect to be able to overcome the difficulties must consider, in its decision, the preservation of enterprise and, hence, also of debt value. CRAs in their mission of preventing surprise in defaults and benchmarking expected losses in the event of default must thus also be experts in covering bankruptcy. Not only are they

[23] Part of a press release issued by Embassy of Ukraine to the United States of America, 1998. President Kuchma Receives Co-Chairperson of Ukrainian–German Interbank Group. Press release, September 29.

[24] A firm in financial distress is *insolvent on a flow basis*, it is unable to meet current cash obligations. Flow-based insolvency gives unpaid creditors the rights to demand restructuring because their contract with the firm has been breached. A firm could be *insolvent on a stock basis*: has a negative economic worth in that the present value of its cash flows is less that its total obligations, and yet not be in financial distress because its claims are paid to date. See Wruck, K., 1990, Financial distress: reorganization and organization efficiency, *Journal of Financial Economics*, October, Vol. 27, No. 2, 419–444, page 421.

[25] Bankruptcy and liquidation are sometimes incorrectly used as synonyms for financial distress. Following Wruck, *liquidation* is 'a sale of the firm's assets and distribution of proceeds to claimants' and *bankruptcy* as just defined, page 422.

[26] Altman, E.I., 1968, Financial ratios, discriminant analysis and the prediction of corporate banktruptcy, *Journal of Finance*, September, Vol. 23, Issue 4, 589–609 explains that in the case of general manufacturing the best ratios for this are X_1: working capital/total assets, X_2: retained earnings/total assets, X_3: EBIT/total assets and X_4: stock market capitalization/book value of debt, and X_5: Sales/Total assets.

[27] $Z = 0.012X_1 + 0.014X_2 + 0.033X_3 + 0.006X_4 + 0.999X_5$.

users of such bankruptcy prediction models (among many other tools and approaches) but also announcers of ratings that are information, analysis, and judgment synthesizers. And preparation for that starts upstream of bankruptcy, for example, by monitoring management's propensity to take corrective action when confronted with worsening scores.

New Century Financial Corporation Files for Chapter 11; Announces Agreement To Sell Servicing Operations

After diligently exploring a variety of other potential solutions that would have enabled New Century to continue its operations, the Chapter 11 process provides the best means for selling our servicing and loan origination operations to financially sound parties.[28]

Credit ratings gauge the exposure of an obligor to financial distress. They identify the options available if distress were to occur. And there are many such options, as a representative historical sample in Figure 2.2 shows.[29]

Financial distress typically follows poor shareholder returns. Among the firms in the bottom 5% for three years in succession, 49% experience no actual financial distress.[30] Almost half (47%) of those that do experience financial distress manage to resolve their problems through shareholders, creditors, and management renegotiating their contracts privately. The remaining 53% of distressed firms, which resort to the bankruptcy courts, almost always survive (67% to 95% of the known cases), either independently after reorganization or after a merger. Only 2.7% of financially distressed poor performers die under liquidation.

Credit rating agencies must evaluate the extent to which poor performance might lead to financial distress. They evaluate the likelihood that a well-performing firm may try to walk away from its dues, and they must assess correctly the ability and willingness of a distressed firm to resolve its problems privately with creditors or file for bankruptcy. The CRA has to figure out the consequences for creditors and calculate unbiased odds on each of these possibilities occurring. The agency must pay careful attention to the company's resources, the resiliency of its structures, and the competences and character of its management. In short, the CRA must grade the firm, or one of its securities, in the form of a rating that is, usually, announced publicly.

It is interesting to observe that Moody's definition of a rating explicitly includes an assessment of an issuer's 'willingness' to perform when cash flows are sufficient to honor dues. Ratings include a highly qualitative judgment about the character of the issuer, in the same way that traditional bank credit decisions did.[31] In an era in which executives behave as resourceful, evaluative, maximizing men (REMM) and where shareholders and creditors try to maximize self-interest, assessing willingness to perform is certainly not a redundant task for a credit analyst.[32]

---

[28] Morrice B.A., President and Chief Executive Officer–New Century Financial Corporation, 2007, quoted in the company's news release, April 2, 1–2, page 1.

[29] See Wruck, K., 1990, Financial distress: reorganization and organization efficiency, *Journal of Financial Economics*, October, Vol. 27, No. 2, 419–444, Figure 2.

[30] The 381 poorly performing firms is the population of all New York (NYSE) and American Stock Exchange (AMEX) firms whose three-year cumulative stock price performance is in the bottom 5% of all firms listed on the two exchanges between 1978 and 1987. See Gilson, S.C., 1989, Management turnover and financial distress, *Journal of Financial Economics*, December, Vol. 25, Issue 2, 241–262, page 242.

[31] See Brouw, R., 1968, De techniek van de kredietonderhandeling, Standaard Wetenschappelijk Uitgeverij Antwerpen Universitaire Pers Rotterdam, Antwerpen, 1–376, pages 43–48.

[32] See Brunner, K., 1987, The perception of man and the conception of society: two approaches to understanding society, *Economic Inquiry*, July, Vol. XXV, 367–388, pages 370–371.

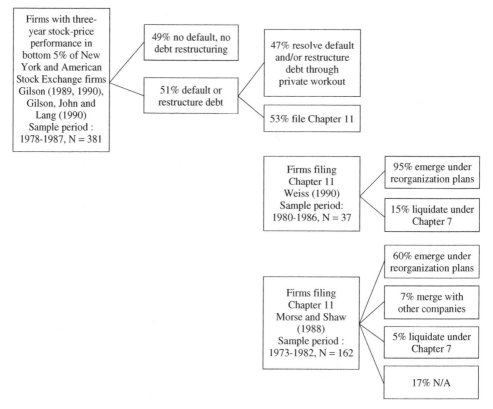

Figure 2.2 What happens in financial distress? Evidence on the outcomes of financial distress based on the data from five empirical studies on US samples of corporates (1973–1987).

The trees trace the frequency distribution of outcomes for firms in financial distress. The first box in each tree presents the authors of the studies and summarizes their sample period, size, and selection criteria.

The original sources are: Gilson, S., 1989, Management turnover and financial distress, *Journal of Financial Economics*, Vol. 25, 241–262; Gilson, S., 1990, Bankruptcy, boards, banks and blockholders, *Journal of Financial Economics*, Vol. 27; Gilson, S., John, K., and Lang, L., 1990, Troubled debt restructurings, *Journal of Financial Economics*, Vol. 27; Morse, D. and Shaw, W., 1988, Investing in bankrupt firms, *Journal of Finance*, Vol. 43, 1193–1206; Weiss, L., 1990. Priority of claims and ex-post re-contracting in bankruptcy, *Journal of Financial Economics*, Vol. 27.

Source: Wruck, K., 1990, Financial distress: reorganization and organization efficiency, *Journal of Financial Economics*, October, Vol. 27, No. 2, 419–444, Figure 2, page 426.

SF Vignette 1

SPVs: Corporations Structured to be Bankruptcy-Remote

What are Special Purpose Vehicles (SPV)?[33] SPVs are legal entities such as a limited liability company, a trust, or corporation. They can be public or private and appear

---

[33] They are also called Special Purpose Entities (SPE) and other similar designations.

in many varieties.[34] Of interest for credit ratings are financial SPVs that are set up to transform existing financial assets that generate cash flows, into new securities to be reimbursed by these cash flows.[35] These SPVs are designed so that they cannot go bankrupt and to live a predetermined lifetime, setting them thereby apart from regular business corporations as ongoing concerns that can go bankrupt. Financial SPVs tend to have the following common characteristics.

They are created by a sponsor to carry out a specific purpose or a series of specific transactions, such as managing a determined pool of financial assets purchased with money raised in the securities markets.[36] SPVs have assets purchased from the asset originator, liabilities issued to pay for these assets, and a portion of economic, if not legal, equity.[37] The structure of a standard securitized transaction and different market participants are described in Figures 2.3A and 2.3B. The originator sells a pool of assets to the SPV. The SPV issues several classes or 'tranches' of securities with different priorities of claims on the cash flows of the SPV and the pool of assets that backs them. Having different risk profiles, different tranches of securities tend to deserve and also get different credit ratings. The assets in the pool can range from cash instruments such as mortgages, credit card receivables, loans, corporate bonds, notes, or previously structured instruments such as CDOs, to synthetic instruments, such as credit default swaps (CDSs). The tranching is realized through the prioritization of payments. For instance the most senior tranches (class 'A' claims) will receive the cash flows from the underlying asset pool first, the class 'B' and 'C' claims (or mezzanine tranches) after, and the class 'D' claims (or equity tranche) last. Hence the most junior tranches are the ones that absorb first credit losses and thereby insulate the most senior claims from default risk.

The original purpose of the SPV is to protect its creditors from the default and potential bankruptcy (and all related bankruptcy costs) of the originator – or previous owner of its assets. Hence, the SPV is segregated from other entities and acquires the assets from the originator, via a true sale.[38] It is in this sense that an SPV is said to be bankruptcy-remote from the originator. This allows originating firms to finance themselves off-balance sheet via such SPV at a lower cost of capital than otherwise.

Moreover, the legal arrangements of the SPV itself are such that it *de facto* forsakes its own rights to seek court protection from its own creditors.[39] This aspect of bankruptcy

---

[34] In asset securitization SPVs take the legal form of a trust and most often a charitable trust (they are mostly off-shore entities, often based in countries such as the Cayman Islands, or Jersey).

[35] For clarity, in this vignette we focus on cash-based SPV transactions as opposed to synthetic. The principle behind synthetic transactions is the same except that instead of assets being physically transferred to the SPV and the transfer funded by notes issued by it, the SPV is exposed to the credit risk of the underlying portfolio by entering into credit derivative contracts such as credit default swaps (CDS), total return swaps or equity default swaps. Vignette 6 discusses the specificities of synthetic transactions.

[36] The sponsor of an SPV can be the originator of the assets, or the arranger (also called structurer) of the transaction, or even the investment manager in the case of actively managed transactions (as opposed to just static). In the case where the assets are not provided directly by the originator's balance sheet, an investment manager builds the pool by buying the assets on the capital markets, a process called ramping up.

[37] Typically in cash transactions the equity would represent from 5 to 10% of the face value of the liabilities.

[38] In case of synthetic transaction there is no true sale, as there is no physical transfer of assets.

[39] Although, in the US, it is not possible to waive the right to have access to the government's bankruptcy procedure, an SPV is structured so that there cannot be an 'event of default' that would throw the SPV into bankruptcy. A voluntary bankruptcy is technically possible if voted unanimously by the directors of the SPV, but highly unlikely especially if there are independent directors, something rating agencies will check for. The bankruptcy remoteness of the SPV imposes many restrictions on the activities of the SPV. This discussion is based on field interviews, original indenture documentation and on Gorton, G., and Souleles, N.S., 2006, Special purpose vehicles and securitization, in Carey, M. and Stulz, R.M. (Eds), *The Risks of Financial Institutions*, 549–597, University of Chicago Press, Chicago and London.

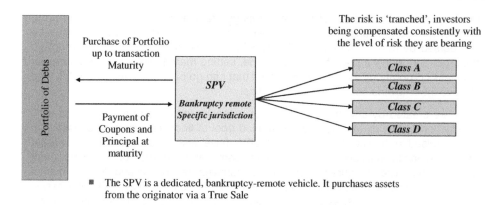

Figure 2.3A   Standard securitization structure.
Source: Marjolin, B., 2007, *Securitization – ESSEC Presentation*, Moody's Investors Service, March 16, page 4.

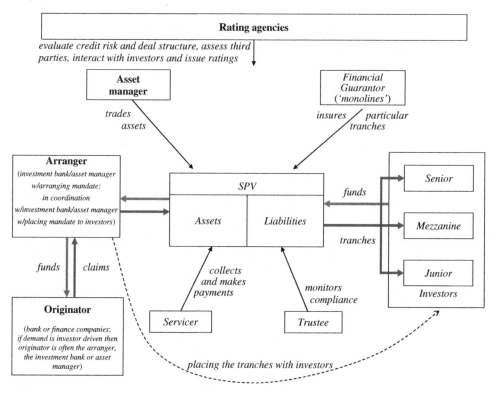

Figure 2.3B   Standard securitization structure.
Source: Committee on the Global Financial System, 2005, The Role of Ratings in Structured Finance: Issues and Implications, Bank for International Settlements, January, 1–63, page 6.

remoteness reinforces the incontestability of the priority rights of these creditors. The risk of shortfall of the SPV's cash inflow below its obligations is minimized through credit enhancements such as the diversification of cash flows, the presence of equity, the tranching of liabilities, over-collateralization, or guarantee by monoline insurers.[40]

What an SPV can do is very narrowly and carefully circumscribed. Its activities are 'preprogrammed' in a very detailed legal document called an indenture. SPVs are in principle, relatively to regular corporations, more like automata. The key aspect of the SPV-related program is that all the necessary functions are disaggregated and outsourced to separate profit centers and legal entities in order to minimize potential conflicts of interests and opportunities for risk shifting. Much of the contractual structure of the finite-lived SPV is devoted to specifying the rights and responsibilities of the note holders and these third parties involved in the transaction. These provisions replace the discretionary control rights granted to equity holders in long-lived ongoing concerns. An SPV, per se, has no management or employees, other than independent directors that serve on a board and audit committee. It has a trustee who acts on behalf of the note-holders, for instance, to monitor compliance with the indenture. An administrator performs the administrative functions and the assets of the SPV are serviced by a servicer according to a servicing contract.

In many SPVs the asset pool does not change over time. It is static. The pool gradually liquidates as the assets pay their dues and reach maturity. In such case there is very little decision-making discretion by any party to the SPV. But other pools are set up for active management to enhance their performance and/or to replace maturing assets during a re-investment period. In that case, an investment manager will have been appointed with a management mandate according to strict management prescriptions. The manager has a reasonable amount of control when there are changes to the SPV and the indenture.

The value-added of the SPV-based asset securitization relies on three key attributes: the pooling of assets, the de-linking of the credit risk of the pool from that of the originator, and the tranching of the SPV's liabilities. The careful circumscription of the rights and responsibilities of all the parties involved with an SPV, as opposed to attributing discretionary control right to one of them, is crucial. It makes the credit risk of the tranches issued against the pool relatively lower than if they were 'tainted' by the credit risk or potential actions of the originator. The tranching transforms the risk characteristics of the collateral pool into classes of securities with distinct, transaction-specific risk features. This allows distributing the cash flows from the underlying pool to investors with different degrees of risk tolerance. The issuing and selling to investors of tranches backed with the pool of assets requires ratings. This market has been a rated market from the beginning and we will view the rating process of these particular instruments in Chapter 4.

2.1.2 The Drivers of Corporate Defaults

Bad times for an economy or a sector do not necessarily mean bad times for all companies involved. There are always excellent companies that perform well under adverse conditions, but conversely, some companies will do badly even in good sectors or during economic expansion.

---

[40] The analog to corporate default occurs at the security level of the SPV, and is often referred to as impairment. Impairment is said to occur when structured finance securities sustain a payment shortfall. More on this in Chapter 6.

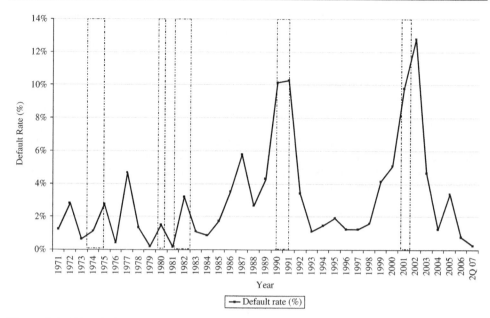

Figure 2.4 Historical default rates and recession periods in the US High Yield Bond Market (1971–2007Q2).
Source: Altman, E. and Karlin, B.J., 2007, Defaults and returns on high yield bonds and distressed debt: first half 2007 Review, *Special Report*, NYU Salomon Center, 1–25, page 5.

Periods of Recession: 11/73–3/75, 1/80–7/80, 7/81–11/82, 7/90–3/91, 4/01–12/01.

Macroeconomic Activity and Overall Default Rates

Corporate default rates increase during recessions and decline during expansions, reflecting the fact that credit risk is cyclical. Figure 2.4 shows historical annual default rates for the US corporate bond market and the five periods of recession from 1971 through 2004. It illustrates clearly the cyclic nature of credit risk. In all cases, the default rate peaked at or soon after the recession ended, and in most instances began to rise ahead of the recession.[41]

Economic Sectors and Variations in Default Rates

As business risk varies across industrial sectors, default rates tend to be sector driven. Revenues in the leisure time, media, and toys sectors are highly sensitive to the business cycle because discretionary spending is the first hit when consumers feel the pinch. So these tend to be high business risk sectors. Health care, insurance, financial institutions, and utilities represent low business risk sectors. With that in mind, it should be no surprise to see the distribution of default rates by industry shown in Figure 2.5. The left-hand scale measures the default rate and the sectors are listed in descending order of risk. In the leisure time and media sector, 2.66% of issues defaulted on average during any given year,

---

[41] Aguiar, J.M., and Altman, E.I., 2005, Defaults and returns in the high yield bond market: the year 2004 in review and market outlook, *Special Report:* New York University Salomon Center, and Leonard N. Stern School of Business, January, 1–49.

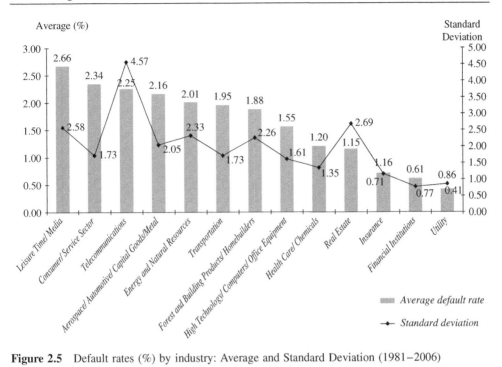

Figure 2.5 Default rates (%) by industry: Average and Standard Deviation (1981–2006)
Includes investment-grade and speculative-grade rated entities.
Source: Vazza, D., Aurora, D., and Erturk, E., 2007, Annual 2006 global corporate default study and rating transitions, *Research:* Standard & Poor's, February 5, 1–39, pages 11–12.

whereas for utilities it was 0.41%. The right-hand scale measures the standard deviation or unpredictability of the annual default rate. While it is very tricky to draw inferences from patterns, it is interesting to note that the sectors most prone to bond defaults tend to be sectors where it is more difficult to predict when defaults are going to occur and, when they occur, how hard the sector will be hit. Leisure time and media, for example, is not only a sector with a chronic positive default rate (23 out of the 26 years), but also fairly unpredictable, with a standard deviation of 2.58%. Default rates in this sector occasionally jump to several times the typical annual rate, as they did to around 9.85% and 6.90% in the recession years 1990 and 1991, and to 4.91% during the 2001 recession, as shown in Table 2.1. The table documents how the sensitivity of sectoral revenues to the business cycle shows up in the cycle of sectoral default rates.

In addition, sectors go through technological and regulatory revolutions. These affect companies both in terms of the number of competitors and the nature of competition creating thereby distress conditions for companies in the sector. Some will default. For example, telecommunications is not only a high default sector, but also has the highest standard deviation at 4.57%. This sector has the most unpredictable default rate, even though the number of phone calls made by subscribers is not particularly sensitive to the business cycle. The range and the time distribution of defaults in this sector are quite revealing and help us to appreciate the difficulties faced by credit rating analysts. For 12 of the 26 years shown in Table 2.1, there were no defaults whatsoever in the telecommunications sector.

Table 2.1 Annual default rate by industry (1981–2006).

Year	Aerospace/ Automotive/ Capital Goods/ Metal	Consumer/ Service Sector	Energy and Natural Resources	Financial Institutions	Forest and Building Products/ Homebuilders	Health Care/ Chemicals	High Technology/ Computers/ Office Equipment	Insurance	Leisure time/ Media	Real estate	Telecommunications	Transportation	Utility
1981	0	0	0	0	0	0	0	0	0	0	0	2.06	0
1982	1.28	1.64	0.8	1.03	2.7	0	1.45	3.23	2.08	0	0	2.04	0.4
1983	0.91	1.24	2.5	0	0	0	0	5.13	0	0	0	1	0
1984	0	0.41	5.43	0	1.41	0	2.9	0	0	0	0	2.94	0
1985	1.25	1.55	4.8	0	0	2.11	0	1.64	2.47	0	0	0	0
1986	4.23	0.34	10	0	1.27	1.87	3.45	0	0.94	0	0	0.88	0
1987	1.81	1.31	4.46	0	1.1	0.82	0	0	0.72	0	1.39	0	0.37
1988	1.13	1.9	1.94	1.99	1.02	3.13	0	0	3.23	0	1.28	0	0.72
1989	2.33	1.25	0	2.45	0	0	1	0.66	7.33	9.38	0	1.69	0
1990	1.99	4.81	0	1.42	8.08	0	4.55	0	9.85	8	2.6	3.6	0
1991	3.06	6.34	2.97	1.88	8.14	1.74	2.7	1.58	6.9	5.56	0	6	1.03
1992	1.73	2.81	0.93	1.81	1.33	0	4.23	0.78	1.85	5.56	0	0	0.98
1993	1.68	1.01	1.65	0.24	0	0	2.53	0.33	0.82	0	0	0	0
1994	0.4	1.23	0.76	0	0.97	0.6	1.14	0.3	2.84	0	0	1.6	0
1995	0	3.72	0.68	0.51	2.54	1.09	1.03	0.27	1.72	0	0	2.36	0
1996	0.99	1.87	0.61	0	0	0	0	0	1.95	0	0.95	0	0
1997	0.89	2.43	0	0.28	0	0.47	0.9	0.22	0.44	0	1.65	0.71	0
1998	1.03	3.3	1.41	1.22	1.16	2.07	0	0	2.83	0.78	1.18	1.85	0.2
1999	3.85	3.13	5	0.25	1.56	3.09	1.2	0.68	5.11	0	1.88	4.86	0.38
2000	3.86	5.29	0.88	0.12	3.61	4.3	4.14	1.48	4.03	0	3	4.47	0.52
2001	9.56	6	1.73	1.43	4.32	4.18	4.71	0.34	4.91	0	12.4	3.37	4.16
2002	5.43	2.94	3.32	0.74	4.92	1.8	1.75	0.5	5.81	0.58	18.72	4.86	1.51
2003	3.55	3.06	1.18	0.3	1.12	2.47	2.21	0.5	0.99	0	10.88	2.34	0.17
2004	2.28	1.59	0.78	0.09	1.6	0.32	0	0.49	0.94	0	1.63	0.97	0.32
2005	1.53	1.02	0.36	0.09	0.49	0.86	0	0	0.62	0	0.49	2.25	0
2006	1.31	0.68	0		1.41	0.28	0.5	0.28	0.89	0	0.45	0.89	0

Includes investment-grade and speculative-grade rated entities.

Source: Standard & Poor's Global Fixed Income, *Research*: Standard & Poor's CreditPro®; and Vazza, D., Aurora, D., and Erturk, E., 2007, Annual 2006 global corporate default study and rating transitions, *Research*: Standard & Poor's, February 5, 1–39, pages 11–12.

Then a shock wave hit, starting in 1995 and building to an all-time, cross-sector high of near 18.72% in 2002, finally shrinking back to 1.63% by 2004. This pattern illustrates that industry transformation can be a material source of default risk, so rating analysts must be constantly on the look-out for storms ahead.

To sum up, issuers belong to industries. Each industry tends to have its own, typical business risk and structure, both of which affect how much a particular company within the industry is exposed to the probability of default.

Company Specifics that Lead to Corporate Default and Influence its Consequences

From these, we can draw a number of insights about the drivers of company-specific default. It occurs in the context of a country and industrial sector. It is rarely the result of a single factor, but rather of a multiple interaction of several factors. The primary source of all value and risk is the business itself. The financial risk factor alone is an interacting network of seemingly unrelated variables such as liquidity and corporate governance. The end result of these drivers, whether or not a company will default, can never be captured in a simple, quantitative, linear formula.

Whereas a corporate bond rating depends on the generation of cash flows (for debt payment) from an ongoing business, structured finance ratings depend on the cash flows from the portfolio of finite duration. This makes these ratings more akin to leveraged finance or project finance ratings. The concept of company-specific drivers to corporate default do not apply to SPVs as they do not have a business activity, cannot take substantive decisions, and cannot themselves default. The performance of an SPV depends directly on the performance of the underlying asset-pool. The concept similar to default that is relevant to structured finance securities or tranches is that of impairment. Some drivers of impairment will be reviewed in Chapter 6 on credit rating analysis applied to structured finance instruments.

2.1.3 Recovery Rates from Defaults

Default automatically provides investors with a number of remedies to limit their losses. These can include a call for immediate repayment of the entire issue amount, or the right to force the issuer into bankruptcy. Losses in the event of default of a security or of an issuer will not necessarily be the defaulted amount, but only that fraction of it that investors are unable to recover:

Expected loss-given-default (ELGD) = Amount defaulted

$$\times \ (1 - \text{expected recovery-given-default}).$$

Instrument ratings include the expected loss-given-default or, as shown in the equation above, its complement, the expected recovery-given-default. The expected recovery is indicated by notching the instrument rating up or down from the issuer rating relative to how much the expected recovery differs from a baseline recovery rate determined from historical observations. The expected recovery of a specific instrument depends on the seniority and collateral structure of the security. The default rates in Figure 2.1 thus overestimate the losses to bond investors in the event of default because bondholders recover part of their investment, as Figure 2.2 suggests and Exhibit 2.1 documents.

Estimating mean recovery rates for different types of defaulted paper on the basis of realized recoveries presents a number of difficulties. One must determine not only values of securities used to pay creditor claims – often illiquid equity and derivative instruments – but also the timing and net amounts of payments received during the recovery process and the proper discount rate to apply to these cash flows. To circumvent these difficulties, a frequently used measure for the recovery rate is based on the market price of the defaulted instrument, observed roughly 30 days after the date of default. The recovery rate is then defined by the ratio of the price relative to its face value (par). For many investors who liquidate their positions after default, post-default trading prices represent, in fact, realized recovery rates. For investors who hold defaulted securities until final resolution, prices observed shortly after default are widely accepted measures of the risk-adjusted, present value of long-term expected recovery amounts.

Using market prices after default, the mean (median) percent recovery rate for 2443 defaulted bonds during 1982–2004 was 42.2% (43.1%).[42] According to Exhibit 2.1, the recovery rate on Adelphia bonds and notes was 57.12%, and on Global Crossing 5.67%. Obviously, junior subordinated debt holders recover less than senior secured ones, and so on along the spectrum of protection – or lack of it. We thus find that recovery rates are strongly correlated with the defaulted instrument's seniority in the capital structure. While the relationship may not always hold exactly in samples drawn from a single year of defaults (as was the case in 2002), the expected relationship holds true over longer periods, such as presented in the 1982–2006 column of Table 2.2.

Using actual recoveries after default has led to a new ratings product called recovery ratings.

Recovery rates are procyclical. It would be very dangerous to assume that recovery rates stay constant over the business cycle. Security on loans and bonds is there to protect the investor and to 'secure' repayment when the borrower hits bad times. Unfortunately, the recovery rates decline as the economy contracts and overall defaults increase. Recovery rates and default rates tend to be negatively correlated. Figure 2.6 illustrates the association between annual default and recovery rates. It shows the unpleasant paradox that as security becomes more necessary, it becomes less available! To illustrate this embarrassing fact of life, Table 2.3 documents that the recovery rate drops significantly below the average during periods of recession.

The decline in recovery rates as defaults increase – as shown in Figure 2.6, measured using bond prices shortly after default – is better explained by the supply and demand for defaulted securities than by the common dependence of default and recovery on the state of the economic cycle. The supply of defaulted bonds (the default rate) tends to exceed demand that comes mostly from niche 'vulture' investors who intentionally purchase bonds in default in high default years.[43]

2.2 CREDIT RATING SCALES

Credit rating agencies summarize their opinions about obligors in ratings that are graded symbols, such as AA−, BBB+, or Caa1. Each symbol represents a group within which the

---

[42] Cantor, R., Hamilton, D.T, Ou, S., and Varma, P., 2005, Default and recovery rates of corporate bond issuers, 1920–2004, *Special Comment:* Moody's Investors Service, January, Report 91233, 1–40, Exhibit 27, page 34.

[43] Altman, E.I., Default recovery rates and LGD in credit risk modelling and practice : an updated review of the literature and empirical evidence, Working Paper, November, 1–36, page 13.

Table 2.2 Mean recovery rates on defaulted instruments by priority in capital (1982–2006[a]).

Defaulted instrument	Value weighted						Issuer weighted					
	2006	2005	2004	2003	2002	1982–2006	2006	2005	2004	2003	2002	1982–2006
Bank Loans												
Sr Secured	68.4	91.8	84.7	76.0	63.1	64.7	76.0	82.1	86.1	64.6	65.9	70.4
Sr Unsecured	–	36.7	–	80.0	99.1	46.0	–	36.7	–	80.0	99.0	54.0
Bonds												
Sr Secured	75.3	78.4	70.7	54.1	56.8	58.7	74.6	69.2	59.9	60.3	49.8	54.4
Sr Unsecured	71.2	48.2	85.7	44.4	30.9	37.0	58.3	55.5	78.7	41.2	31.9	38.4
Sr Subordinated	39.8	33.6	67.8	29.2	20.7	29.3	43.6	31.0	53.2	36.6	25.3	32.9
Subordinated	61.1	11.9	43.8	12.0	29.0	29.5	56.1	51.3	47.5	12.3	27.9	31.6
Jr Subordinated	–	–	78.4[b]	39.7	NA	17.4	–	–	82.9[b]	40.4	NA	24.5

[a]Based on 30-day post-default market prices.
[b]Based on three observations.

Sources: Cantor, R., Hamilton, D.T., Ou, S., and Varma, P., 2004, Default and recovery rates of corporate bond issuers: a statistical review of Moody's ratings performance, 1920–2003, *Special Comment*: Moody's Investors Service, January, Report 80989, 1–40, page 13; Cantor, R., Hamilton, D.T., Ou, S., and Varma, P., 2006, Default and recovery rates of corporate bond issuers, 1920–2005, *Special comment*: Moody's Investors Service, March, Report 96546, 1–51, page 12; Cantor, R., Hamilton, D.T., Kim, F., and Ou, S., 2007, Corporate default and recovery rates, 1920–2006, *Special Comment*: Moody's Investors Service, June, Report 102071, 1–48, page 8.

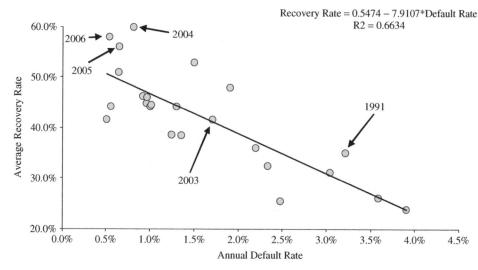

Figure 2.6   The association between recovery and default rates (1983–2006).
Sources: Cantor, R., Hamilton, D.T., Ou, S., and Varma, P., 2006, Default and recovery rates of
corporate bond issuers, 1920–2005, *Special Comment:* Moody's Investors Service, March, Report
96546, 1–51, page 13; Cantor, R., Hamilton, D.T., Kim, F., and Ou, S., 2007, Corporate default
and recovery rates, 1920–2006, *Special Comment:* Moody's Investors Service, June, Report 102071,
1–48, pages 18, 20.

credit risk characteristics are broadly the same. The first such symbolic heuristic was used
by Moody's in 1909.[44] There are many ways to classify ratings and each CRA maintains its
own set of rating systems.[45] Within their systems, most CRAs distinguish between issuer
ratings and instrument ratings.

An issuer rating rates the issuer as a whole, regardless of the particular debt instrument.
For example, an Issuer Credit Rating from Standard & Poor's is 'not specific to any particular
financial obligation, because it does not take into account any particular obligation,' rather
it 'provides an overall assessment of a company's creditworthiness.'[46] In the special world
of money, securities, derivatives, foreign exchange, interest rate, and commodities trading,
an issuer rating is known as a counterparty risk rating. Counterparty risk is the risk that the
counterparty to a financial contract will not meet the terms of the contract.

In contrast, an instrument rating deals with the performance of one particular instrument.
Its primary purpose is to evaluate the ability of the issuer to deliver on the terms of the
specific security it has issued. Instrument ratings combine the risk of default and the expected
loss-given-default. For example, a fully secured bond issue will probably carry a higher
credit rating than a subordinated debenture from the same issuer, since the investor holding
the secured bond is more likely to receive all of the scheduled interest and principal payments
in the event of bankruptcy. The subordinated debenture holder would normally receive such
payments only after all secured bondholders are paid.

---

[44] Moody's Investors Service's website: http://www.moodys.com.
[45] Moody's reports to 'maintain 32 global systems, with the number growing every year', Moody's Investors
Service, 2007, *Moody's Rating Symbols and Definitions*, March, 1–52, page 1.
[46] Standard & Poor's, 2006, *Corporate Ratings Criteria*, 1–128, page 9.

Table 2.3 Overall issuer weighted recovery rates and global default rates (1983–2006).

Year	Global corporate default rate	Issuer-weighted recovery rates
1983	0.96%	44.81%
1984	0.92%	46.25%
1985	1.00%	44.19%
1986	1.89%	47.87%
1987	1.50%	52.94%
1988	1.36%	38.48%
1989	2.34%	32.33%
1990	3.58%	26.06%
1991	3.23%	35.06%
1992	1.31%	44.19%
1993	0.94%	46.03%
1994	0.56%	44.13%
1995	1.03%	44.54%
1996	0.51%	41.53%
1997	0.65%	51.07%
1998	1.23%	38.67%
1999	2.16%	35.89%
2000	2.36%	25.50%
2001	3.80%	23.81%
2002	2.97%	31.22%
2003	1.73%	41.55%
2004	0.79%	59.85%
2005	0.60%	55.92%
2006	0.54%	57.97%

Sources: Cantor, R., Hamilton, D.T., Ou, S., and Varma, P., 2006, Default and recovery rates of corporate bond issuers, 1920–2005, *Special Comment:* Moody's Investors Service, March, Report 96546, 1–51, page 13; Cantor, R., Hamilton, D.T., Kim, F., and Ou, S., 2007, Corporate default and recovery rates, 1920–2006, *Special Comment:* Moody's Investors Service, June, Report 102071, 1–48, pages 18, 20.

Instrument and issuer ratings are never fully independent of each other, even though they are quite distinct in meaning. To understand how the analysis that precedes a rating works, what is being rated, and what is made of ratings, one must distinguish between them. However, for the purpose of explaining credit rating scales and analyzing and evaluating what credit ratings are – and what they are not – this is not necessary. We will come back to this distinction in later chapters.

There are essentially three types of credit rating 'scales': the fundamental ordinal scale, which is used by CRAs to position the creditworthiness of an issuer or instrument; financial market credit spreads, which result from the investment decisions of bond investors; and market-implied credit ratings, which are derived from a combination of mathematical modeling of the arbitrage equilibrium prices of an issuer's equity and assets, probability theory, and empirical observations of past defaults.

2.2.1 Fundamental Ordinal Credit Rating Scales

A rating expresses an opinion on the relative credit strength of an issuer or an instrument over its lifetime. The distinctive characteristic of this credit rating scale is its ordinality. The ordinality implies that all ratings along this scale are comparable. Rating agencies, especially the global ones, work purposefully hard to reach consistency across all classes of issuers, industries, instruments, and regions.[47] Hence, the same scale is used for sovereigns, corporate bonds, notes, financial institutions, and structured finance instruments. Since the beginning of the subprime mortgage related crisis there are wide discussions as to whether structured finance instruments should be rated on a different scale. This very wide consistency of the rating scale is essential for the utility of ratings to global investors, and we further discuss the drivers of the economic value-added of credit ratings in Chapter 3.

These credit strength opinions are actually more complex than the rating on the scales that we are about to discuss now. For instance, many of the more subtle nuances will come into play during rating follow-ups, to be discussed in Section 4.2.2. Long-term ratings provide an opinion of the credit-worthiness of an issuer or an instrument over a time horizon that extends three to five years in the future. Short-term ratings which are provided for the short-term financial instruments market, are primarily concerned with the coming year. Short-term ratings use a smaller rating scale than long-term ratings, although both types of rating assess the likelihood of default over the full period to maturity[48]

Long-term Credit Rating Scales

Exhibit 2.2 describes the long-term issuer credit rating scale currently used at S&P.[49] This scale measures credit risk on a risk index, with AAA rated securities having the lowest risk and C the highest. It is an index, not an absolute measure. Therefore, while the scale says that BB rated instruments are more likely to default than A rated ones, or that a B is less likely to default than a CC, it does not say how much more or how much less likely. Nor does it define the absolute default probability of an AA or CCC rated instrument. It is in this sense that rating scales are ordinal scales.[50]

There are two important separating lines on the rating scale: between BBB and BB and below CC. Instruments rated BBB or above are known as 'investment grade'. The average annual global issuer-weighted default rate on such bonds issued by corporates during the period 1980–2004 was a mere 0.07%, with a maximum of 0.49% in 1985. The bulk of

---

[47] The global rating agencies all have chief credit officers whose responsibility is to guarantee consistency of the ratings across all segments. They have to monitor for instance, that a BBB+ on a security of an Asian airline company means the same credit risk as a BBB+ tranche of a US synthetic CDO.

[48] Default for issuers (except Moody's whose Corporate Family Rating includes both), default and recovery for instruments.

[49] Moody's produced the first such scale in 1906. We use in Exhibit 2.6 Standard & Poor's scale because in 2006 it had more bond ratings outstanding than any other CRA. The following are mentioned on CRA websites as of September 2006:

- *Fitch Ratings* currently maintains coverage of 3100 financial institutions, rates over 1200 corporate issuers and 89 sovereigns, and maintains surveillance on over 45 000 municipal transactions.
- *Moody's* ratings and analysis track debt covering more than 100 sovereign nations, 11 000 company issuers, 25 000 public finance issuers, 70 000 structured finance obligations.
- *S&P*

  — The total amount of debt S&P rated in 2005 was approximately US$4.7 trillion. The total amount of out-standing debt rated by S&P globally is approximately US$34 trillion.
  — In 2005, S&P Ratings Services published more than 500 000 ratings, including 294 000 new ratings and 260 000 revised ratings. We have issued ratings on debt securities in more than 100 countries.

[50] Ordinal: 'expressing order or succession, specifically of a number in a series'. Ordinal number: 'any number used to indicate order (e.g., second, ninth, 25th, etc.) in a particular series': distinguishes from cardinal number. See *Webster's New World Dictionary of the American Language*, 1970, The World Publishing Company, New York and Cleveland, 1–1692.

Exhibit 2.2 Long-term issue credit rating major scale: Standard & Poor's description (2004).

Major rating category	Standard & Poor's description
	Investment-grade rating
AAA	**Extremely Strong capacity** to meet financial commitments – Highest rating.
AA	**Very Strong capacity** to meet financial commitments.
A	**Strong capacity** to meet financial commitments, but somewhat more susceptible to adverse economic conditions and changes in circumstances.
BBB	**Adequate capacity** to meet financial commitments, but more subject to adverse economic conditions.
	Sub-investment grade bond status
BB	**Less vulnerable** in the near-term but faces major ongoing uncertainties and exposures to adverse business, financial and economic conditions.
B	**More vulnerable** to adverse business, financial and economic conditions but currently has the capacity to meet financial commitments.
CCC	**Currently vulnerable** and dependent on favourable business, financial and economic conditions to meet financial commitments.
CC	**Currently highly vulnerable.**
	A marked shortcoming has materialized
C	A bankruptcy petition has been filed or similar action taken but payments or **financial commitments** are **continued**.
D	Payment **default** on **financial commitments**.

Source: Standard & Poor's, 2007, *Standard & Poor's Ratings Definitions*, September 21, 1–93.
Notes: Ratings in the BB, B, CCC, CC, and C categories are 'below investment grade' and regarded as having significant speculative characteristics. The ratings from AA to CCC may be modified by the addition of a plus or minus sign to show relative standing within the major rating categories.

rated issues are investment grade. According to bond index provider Iboxx, for example, \$4096 billion or 86.48% of the nominal value of all traded US\$ bonds outstanding were investment grade.[51] Such bonds are predominantly held by institutional investors who are averse to any credit loss, or are prohibited, by either internal or external regulations, from investing in instruments that are below investment grade. The decision to rate an issue above or below investment grade thus has material repercussions for the issuers.

Instruments rated BB or less are below investment grade, and are also known as specu-lative grade or junk bonds. Their average default rate for 1980–2004 was 3.85%, reaching 10.59% in 1984. The high-yield, speculative bond market first flourished in the 1920s, dried up during the Great Depression, and re-emerged in the 1980s in the US.[52] Since the introduction of the euro, this market developed rapidly in Europe. More recently, Chinese

---

[51] Iboxx as of March 23, 2006.

[52] This segment of the US bond market happened to be so successful in the 1980s because it was both demand and supply driven. In the context of the Volcker measures to eradicate inflationary expectations, yields were skyrocketing and the prices of the existing bonds were collapsing. The more sophisticated bond investors were looking for very high coupon instruments to drastically shorten the duration of their portfolios in order to immunize portfolios against interest rate risk while diversifying credit risk across their portfolios. The demand for junk bonds emerged. On the supply side, fast growing high tech companies that were already profitable but that were still high risk so that they could not access the senior bond market and so that their equity suffered from chronic under valuation due to information asymmetries, had poor access to capital because the offering was incomplete. The supply of high yield debt had emerged. Financial entrepreneurs saw the opportunity and helped create the market, with some excesses. As investors became increasingly comfortable with the idea of buying high risk, the supply of high yielding bonds from fast growing companies in search of large amounts of growth capital exploded. A number of investment banks (most notably the now defunct Drexel Burnham Lambert) played an important role

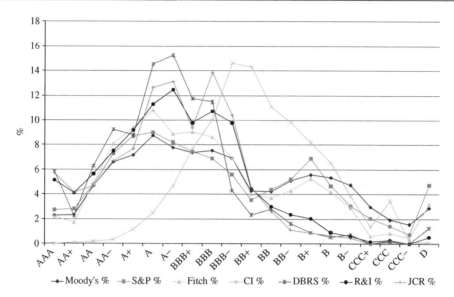

Figure 2.7   Quality distribution of issuer ratings for seven major rating agencies (1999–2004).
Source: Barton, A., 2006, Split credit ratings and the prediction of bank ratings in the Basel II environment. Thesis submitted for the degree of Doctor of Philosophy, University of Southampton, Faculty of Law, Arts and Social Sciences, School of Management, 1–205, page 119.

toll-road operator Fuxi Investment Holdings saw its one billion yuan (US$127 million) bond issue downgraded to below investment grade. This was the first Chinese debt issue to be assigned a junk credit rating.[53] Speculative bonds appeal to investors seeking a high return, often specialized funds and high net-wealth investors. The probability of default is material for speculative grade bonds, and so CRAs provide an explicit evaluation of the severity of loss-given-default used in their analysis.[54]

Below CC, a marked shortcoming has been found in the debtor. If you are holding a security rated C or below, it is probably too late to call your broker and sell. All major CRAs use an issuer credit rating scale and important separating lines that look broadly similar with that of S&P, but are in fact dissimilar. The cumulative effect of many small differences between them makes each CRA's scale quite idiosyncratic. This can be seen for example in Figure 2.7 by comparing the quality distribution of over 15 000 issuer credit ratings assigned by major agencies around the world across industries and countries.[55] It suggests that the rating distributions of Fitch, Moody's, and S&P have a lower density

in developing the market by introducing issuer to their clients and structuring high yield (or junk) deals that had previously been financed in the syndicated loan market or the equity markets. The US high yield market became less active in the early part of the 1990s when many high yield issuers were not able to service their debt and had to declare bankruptcy. The Euroland high yield market started taking off in 1999.

[53] Areddy, J.T., 2006, Chinese firms disclose more – Transparency shows ties to government as scandals unfold, *The Wall Street Journal Europe*, November 13.

[54] Marshella, T., Rowan, M., and Subhas, M., 1999, Moody's analytical framework for speculative grade ratings, *Global Credit Research:* Moody's Investors Service, May, Report 40026, 1–8, page 2.

[55] We take issuer credit ratings as shorthand for long-term senior unsecured or senior subordinated debt issue ratings. Data are drawn from the base produced by Dale, R.S., and Thomas, S.H., 1999–2004 (eds) *Financial Times Credit Rating International* (FTI), London as processed and discussed in Barton, A., 2006, Split credit ratings and the prediction of bank ratings in the Basel II environment, Thesis submitted for the degree of Doctor

of high ratings than the other agencies. One explanation of this could be selection bias, meaning that each group of CRAs specializes or rates samples of issuers that come from universes with intrinsically different characteristics. In this case one can expect significant differences in densities even if the scales and the applied standards at each CRA were identical. Another explanation is that the three major global incumbents use different scales and/or follow stricter rating standards. At this point, it is important to be aware of these differences in densities across rating agencies and to bear that in mind during our discussion of credit rating scales. The rating scales and their describers that are shown in Exhibit 2.3 below is just one example among many.

Exhibit 2.3 Fine rating rankings of competing credit risk indexes (2004).

Ranks						Default Probabilities %
Alphanumeric ratings			Numeric ratings			
S&P (1)	Fitch (2)	Moody's (3)	Constant increments (4)	Random increments (5)	Altman equivalents (6)	KMV (7)
AAA	AAA	Aaa	1	1	16	0.02
AA+	AA+	Aa1	2	6	16	0.05
AA	AA	Aa2	3	100	15	0.08
AA−	AA−	Aa3	4	112	14	0.13
A+	A+	A1	5	113	13	0.21
A	A	A2	6	216	12	0.32
A−	A−	A3	7	240	11	0.42
BBB+	BBB+	Baa1	8	242	10	0.54
BBB	BBB	Baa2	9	325	9	0.70
BBB−	BBB−	Baa3	10	340	8	0.90
BB+	BB+	Ba1	11	345	7	1.15
BB	BB	Ba2	12	350	6	1.48
BB−	BB−	Ba3	13	352	5	2.09
B+	B+	B1	14	400	4	2.95
B	B	B2	15	401	3	4.14
B−	B−	B3	16	460	2	6.66
CCC+	CCC+	Caa1	17	500	1	10.64
CCC	CCC	Caa2	18	727	1	17.00
CCC−	CCC−	Caa3	19	753	1	17.95
CC	CC	Ca	20	811	1	20.00
C	C	C	21	819		20.00
D	DDD		22	945		
	DD		23	947		
	D		24	999		

Sources: (1) Standard & Poor's, 2004, Rating definitions and terminology, March 18, 1–12; (2) Fitch Ratings, 2005, Fitch Ratings definitions – international long-term credit ratings, 1–2; (3) Moody's Investors Service, 2004, Guide to Moody's ratings, rating process, and rating practices, June, Report 87615, 1–48; (4) and (5) the authors; (6) Altman, E.I. and Rijken, H.A., 2003, How rating agencies achieve rating stability, Working paper, December, 1–48; (7) Authors' computation of average EDF at that rating rank in June 2004 according to Moody-KMV's EDF data.

---

of Philosophy, University of Southampton, Faculty of Law, Arts and Social Sciences, School of Management, 1–205, pages 92 and 119.

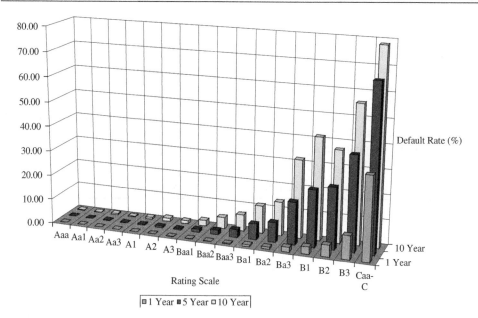

Figure 2.8 One-, five- and 10-year average issuer-weighted cumulative default rates by rating category (1983–2006).
Sources: Cantor, R., Hamilton, D.T., Kim, F., and Ou, S., 2007, Corporate default and recovery rates, 1920–2006, *Special Comment:* Moody's Investors Service, June, Report 102071, 1–48, page 24.

Historical evidence suggests that the grades on these symbolic scales provide a fairly predictable system for default rates. As Figure 2.8 shows, higher grades yield consistently lower default rates over 1-, 5-, and 10-year horizons. Note from the figure that the inverse relationship between ratings and default rates holds for any given time horizon from the year of issuance. For instance, for the 5-year time horizon, the Aaa cumulative default rate was 0.18%, the Aa2 0.28%, rising to 2.11% for Baa2, 8.82% for Ba2 and 31.24% for B2. The order is by and large, but not exactly, preserved over longer time horizons. Figure 2.8 also shows that defaults increase exponentially as one goes down the grading scale, particularly below investment grade, from Ba1 downwards.[56]

For all grades, default rates increase rapidly with bond age, particularly by the fifth year for bonds rated Baa1 and below. Five years after issuance, 50.8% of the amounts of speculative grade bonds that are going to default over a 20-year period have already defaulted. Only 18.6% of investment grade bonds default within five years, and so the frequency of unpleasant surprises later on is clearly higher. Recovery rates following default decline as ratings go down, as shown in Figure 2.9

Different rating agencies use different indices or scales, and Exhibit 2.3 ranks the competing default risk indexes for long-term debt currently in use.

---

[56] Consistent with the importance of the investment grade/non-investment grade distinction, the probability of default rises most dramatically once the investment grade barrier is reached. Cantor, R., and Packer, F., 1994, The credit rating industry, *Quarterly Review:* Federal Reserve Bank of New York, Summer-Fall, 1–26 note a Moody's study that shows a default probability that is six times higher for bonds rated BB than for those rated BBB. The same study notes that the one year default rate is zero for all bonds rated A and higher. This rises to two-tenths of one percentage point for BBB issuers and 1.8% and 8.3% for BB and B rated issuers respectively.

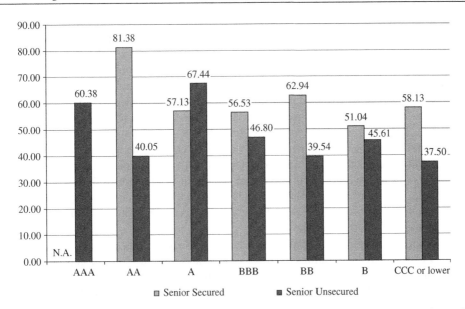

Figure 2.9 Standard & Poor's recovery rates as a function of original rating category for senior secured and senior unsecured issues (1981–2000). The study was based on 762 US dollar-denominated bonds that defaulted between 1981 and 2000.
Source: Griep, C.M., 2002, Higher ratings linked to stronger recoveries, *Research:* Standard & Poor's, March 11, 1–6.

There are two fully equivalent ways of presenting the indices: either using alphanumeric symbols, such as S&P (1), Fitch (2) and Moody's (3), or using numerical equivalents, starting at 1 for the best rating and going up in constant increments to 21 (4).[57] One could also juxtapose a column of random increments (5) or one going down from 16 to 1 (6). S&P introduced its plus or minus fine rating modifiers on its major scale in 1979. Moody's followed this with its numerical 1 or 2 or 3 modifiers in 1981.

The alphanumeric symbols on each row represent the same rank order in rating quality for each CRA, with an S&P AAA, a Fitch AAA or a Moody's Aaa all representing their best rating. Similarly, S&P and Fitch BB+ and Moody's Ba1 are their highest speculative grade rankings.

The metrics behind the letters are different from one CRA to the other. Identical symbols have different meanings for different CRAs. One cannot infer that a Moody's C is the same as an S&P C. Moody's, for instance, integrates loss in the event of default into its Corporate Family Ratings for speculative grade issuers, whereas S&P ranks only the probability of default.[58] A B2 security according to Moody's, therefore, does not have the same default probability as a B security according to S&P. At first sight, different agencies may assign the same rating to a security because they label the value that a security has in their index

---

[57] Alphanumeric symbols AAA/Aaa through C have their numeric equivalents from 1 through 21 for the three CRAs. The numeric equivalent 22 applies for S&P and Fitch, 23 and 24 being only relevant for Fitch.

[58] Note that loss given default or recovery rate per se does not make sense for issuer rating but just for instrument rating. Fitch now only uses probability of default in issuer rating. Moody's still includes both PD and LGD in their Corporate Family Rating (used only for speculative grade) but now splits out the probability of default in a separate rating. The CFR provides a global expected loss, which breaks down into varying levels for each instrument.

similarly, but every agency uses its own metrics to position securities and the index values are unrelated. Therefore comparing different rating agencies at arbitrary index values is, strictly speaking, like comparing apples and pears.

Even if the metrics were identical, ratings would still represent relative rankings. To illustrate this, we added the two numerical columns (4) and (5) to the rankings. Both start with 1 as the index for the lowest default risk and show increasing numbers to rank increasing default risk. Index (4) increases with the arbitrary constant 1 to reach 24 for the highest default risk. Index (5) increases randomly through 999 for the highest default risk. Both indexes order increases in default risk in 23 steps, but none of the numerical values per se tells us anything about the probability of default at that step, nor do the distances between the numbers tell us anything about the actual change in default probability between steps. For example, the $+1$ in each step of series (4) has exactly the same meaning as any of the random numbers $+5$, $+94$, $+12$, $+1$, $+103$, etc., of series (5), and the value 24 in series (4) means the same as 999 in (5).

Ratings are thus very much *relative,* as Fitch makes clear in its definition, they are not measures of absolute risk. Ratings exist for a large and diverse group of entities and debt instruments, which allows investors to assign an individual issuer or debt instrument a credit risk class *vis-à-vis* the overall universe of debt issuers and instruments. As Fitch puts it, 'Entities or issues carrying the same rating are of similar but not necessarily identical quality since the ratings are relative measures of risk and ratings categories may not fully reflect small differences in the degrees of risk.'[59] Since only a limited number of rating classes are used in grading a continuum of thousands of different bonds, the symbols cannot reflect the shadings of risk that actually exist.

Short-term Credit Rating Scales

Exhibit 2.4 describes the short-term credit rating scales of the three largest CRAs, particularly relevant in the commercial paper market.[60] Short-term credit ratings provide an opinion of the ability of an issuer to make timely payments on short-term financial commitments. The focus of short-term ratings is on the liquidity of the issuer. Short-term instruments have a maximum 390-day period, although the average maturity of US commercial paper is about 30 days. For speculative grade issuers, the rating focuses on the expected liquidity over the upcoming 13 months, whereas for investment grade issuers the expected liquidity over the 3- to 5-year horizon of the long-term rating is considered.

Short-term ratings are assigned to the issuer, but they can also be applied to a specific program to sell instruments when requested. Requests are generally made for issuance programs for instruments that will benefit from an improved rating (i.e. above that of the issuer rating) due to enhancement or support, such as commercial paper backed by a letter of credit. Unlike long-term instrument ratings, short-term instrument ratings do not include the severity of loss-given-default in their analysis, as most short-term instruments are investment grade where default risk is the primary concern of investors. The short-term rating scale measures credit risk on a risk index, as with long-term ratings. It says that an A-2 rated

---

[59] Fitch Ratings, 2007, Fitch ratings definitions: Introduction to Ratings. *Resource Library*, March 26, 1–4, page 1.
[60] Commercial paper is a short-term debt obligation of a corporation. Creditworthy companies are able to use the commercial paper market to fund their short-term financial needs, as opposed to setting up short-term credit lines with commercial banks. Investors in the capital markets buy commercial paper as a short-term liquid investment from only the most creditworthy companies.

Exhibit 2.4   Short-term obligation ratings scales of major CRAs (2004).

Rating Categories of CRAs			Description
S&P	Fitch	Moody's	
			Investment-grade rating
A-1+	F1+		Extremely strong *capacity* for timely payment of short-term financial commitments.
A-1	F1	P-1	Strong/superior *capacity* for timely payment of short-term financial commitments.
A-2	F2	P-2	Satisfactory/strong *capacity* for timely payment of short-term financial commitments.
A-3	F3	P-3	Adequate/acceptable *capacity* for timely payment of short-term financial commitments.
			Speculative-grade rating
B (B-1, B-2, B-3)	B	SGL-1, SGL-2, SGL-3	Speculative/Not Prime. Minimal capacity for timely payment of short-term financial commitments. Faces major ongoing uncertainties, *vulnerable* to near term changes in financial and economic conditions
C	C	SGL-4	High Default Risk. Default is a real possibility. Capacity for meeting financial commitments is reliant upon a sustained, favorable business and economic environment
SD/D	RD/D		Payment default on financial commitments

Sources: (1) Moody's Investors Service, 2007, website – rating definitions, short-term ratings; (2) S&P Ratings-Direct, 2004, Rating definitions and terminology, March 18, 1–12; (3) Fitch Ratings, 2007, Fitch ratings definitions: International short term ratings, *Resource Library*, March 26, 1–3.

issuer is more likely to default than an A-1 rated one, but it does not say how much more or how much less likely. Neither does it define the absolute default probability of an A-1+ or B rated issuer.

The short-term rating scale is much shorter than the long-term rating scale because credit risk for a given issuer is generally lower in the short term. The relationship between the long-term scales and the short-term scales, as demonstrated in Exhibit 2.5, results from the fact that liquidity concerns, which are dominant for short-term ratings, also play an important role in long-term ratings.

Short-term ratings were introduced as a solution to a market problem that was exposed by the collapse in 1970 of Penn Central, a major railroad that was an important issuer of commercial paper. In the 1960s, commercial paper sold on the capital markets developed as a new source of short-term funds for large companies, increasingly replacing bank loans. The market grew much more quickly than the understanding of the risk of these new instruments – a situation glaringly revealed by the unexpected collapse of Penn Central, leading investors to pull back from the commercial paper market and precipitating the default of other companies. The introduction of short-term credit ratings provided essential information to allow investors to manage their risk. In 1997, the much larger commercial paper default of Mercury Financing caused virtually no disruption to the markets.

Exhibit 2.5   Correspondence of Fitch's short-term ratings with long-term ratings.

Long-term Issuer Rating	Short-term rating
Investment Grade	
AAA	F1+
AA+	F1+
AA	F1+
AA−	F1+
A+	F1+ or F1
A	F1
A−	F1 or F2
BBB+	F2
BBB	F2 or F3
BBB−	F2 or F3
Speculative Grade	
BB+	B
BB	B
BB−	B
B+	B
B	B
B−	B
CCC	C
CC	C
C	C
RD/D	D

Source: Fitch Ratings, 2007, Short-term ratings criteria for corporate finance, *Criteria Report*, June 12, 1–16, page 2.

The global short-term debt market is very large indeed. At the end of November 2007, the amount of outstanding commercial paper was $1.86 trillion (including financial, non-financial, and asset-backed categories) in the US market, €228 billion ($336 billion) in the euro market, and £55 billion ($115 billion) in the sterling-denominated market.[61]

Figure 2.10 gives default rates for short-term instruments between 1981 and 2006, a period during which only 77 defaults were recorded. Short-term defaults are thus extremely rare. Of all issuers, on average only 0.2% had defaulted by the end of a given year.

As Figure 2.11 shows, the relationship between default frequency and short-term credit rating has the same characteristics as with long-term ratings. Higher grades of short-term ratings yield consistently lower default rates over the time horizons from one month to one

---

[61] US Federal Reserve and Euroclear websites, December 11, 2007.

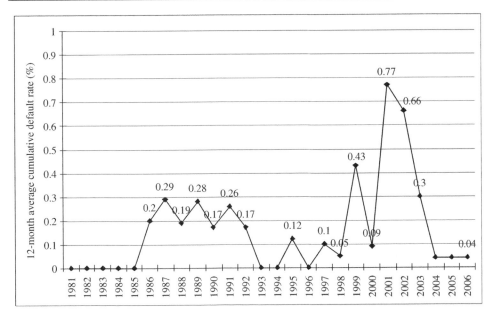

Figure 2.10 S&P's global short-term annual default rates for each calendar year (1981–2006).
Source: S&P RatingsDirect, 2007, Default, transition and recovery, *Global Short-Term Default Study and Rating Transitions*, June 21, 1–28, page 5.

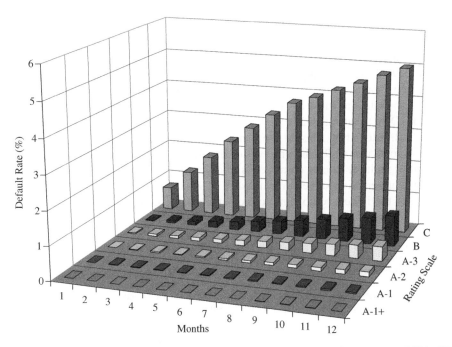

Figure 2.11 One- to 12-month short-term cumulative default rates by rating category (1981–2006).
Source: S&P RatingsDirect, 2007. Default, transition and recovery, *Global Short-Term Default Study and Rating Transitions*, June 21, 1–28, page 28.

year. Also, the inverse relationship between ratings and default rates holds for any given time horizon, with defaults increasing exponentially as one goes down the scale, particularly below investment grade.

The extremely low level of defaults seen in the short-term credit markets stems from the nature of the short-term securities market which typically only accepts issues from companies with the best creditworthiness. The risk aversion of the short-term market means that access to the markets is rationed. As the credit rating of an issuer declines, investors are likely to refuse to roll over maturing short-term debt, such that issuers with short-term ratings of '3' or lower often exit the CP market, drawing on bank loan and alternative funding sources instead.[62] This rationing behavior of the short-term markets is in contrast to what occurs in the long-term debt markets, where the debt markets adjust to issues of lower credit quality by demanding a larger interest rate spread. In the US market, for example, Tier-2 ratings constituted only $68 billion in outstanding commercial paper at the end of November 2007, representing only 4% of the $1616 billion of Tier-1 commercial paper outstanding.[63] Furthermore, during periods of stress, the Tier-1 commercial paper market has proven to be substantially more liquid than the Tier-2 market. The development of the asset-backed commercial paper market has partially mitigated these constraints, allowing companies that are not rated investment grade to receive funding by using asset-backing to create commercial paper that is highly rated.

Multiple Ratings, Inter-rater Agreement and Split Ratings

Most issues are rated by more than one CRA, leading to multiple ratings for the same issue or issuer. For example, 62 496 new US Domestic Public Offerings of Non-convertible debt from 1976 through 2006 were credit rated. Of these, only 1.8%, were rated by just one of the three main agencies, the remainder 98.2%, had multiple ratings: 67.3% by two of the three CRAs and 30.8% by all three.[64] Moody's had rated 99.0% of all these, S&P 98.3% and Fitch 28.9%.[65] Considering corporate bonds outstanding at the end of March 1997, on a representative sample of 2514, Moody's had ratings on 92.5% and S&P 90.7%. Only 7.2% of the sample was rated by just one CRA; 4.1% was unrated. Duff & Phelps Credit Rating Co. (DCR) had rated 23.6% of these bonds and Fitch IBCA 9.9%. Considering these four CRAs together, 5.3% of the bonds were rated by all four CRAs, 21.4% by any three of the four, and 61.9% by any two of the four – virtually all Moody's and S&P.[66] This extent of multiple ratings corresponds in order of magnitudes to the one found as the result of a representative survey conducted in 1999 among US industrial issuers. It finds that 97.4% of the issuers responding to the survey buy credit ratings from more than one

---

[62] A short-term rating of '3' refers to an A-3 rating at S&P or its equivalent at other rating agencies. Similarly, a rating of '1' refers to an A-1 or A-1+ rating at S&P or its equivalent, while a rating of '2' refers to an A-2 rating at S&P or its equivalent.

[63] Federal Reserve website. In the US, short term securities purchased by money market mutual funds must be rated within the two highest short-term rating categories (referred to as Tier-1 and Tier-2) by at least two NRSRO rating agencies. Furthermore Tier-2 holdings may not constitute more than 5% of the assets of all funds, except those that are tax-exempt.

[64] Security Data Corporation, 2007, *US Domestic Public Offerings* Data Base, Non-convertible, non-short term debt, All issuer and issue types.

[65] For the years prior to Fitch acquisition of Duff & Phelps, the ratings of these two were aggregated.

[66] Jewell, J., and Livingston, M., 2000, The impact of a third credit rating on the pricing of bonds, *Journal of Fixed Income*, December, Vol. 10, 69–85, page 72.

credit rating agency. About three-quarters hire two rating agencies and one-fifth hire three or more.[67]

Among multiple ratings, split ratings of outstanding and of new issues are widespread. Observationally split ratings (in short, split ratings as they are conventionally called) occur when at least two CRAs give different ratings to the same issuer or issue. At the level of outstanding issuer ratings, a sample of 22 752 globally representative observations of these from 1999 through 2004, shows that even though S&P and Moody's ratings are highly correlated at 0.940, 40.0% of their ratings were split at the main category level. For S&P and Fitch, it is 48.2% out of 5630 matched pairs and a correlation of 0.936 and for Moody's and Fitch, it is 49.7% out of 5837, correlation 0.921.[68] The differences between these top three agencies with respect to nine other agencies world wide are often much larger. They increase also moving down the credit scale toward non-investment grade issuers, as Figure 2.12 illustrates.[69] The level of consensus shown for each fine rating grade is the average of the agreements for matched pairs of ratings among the seven agencies in Figure 2.7. Companies that receive split ratings from Moody's and S&P are much more

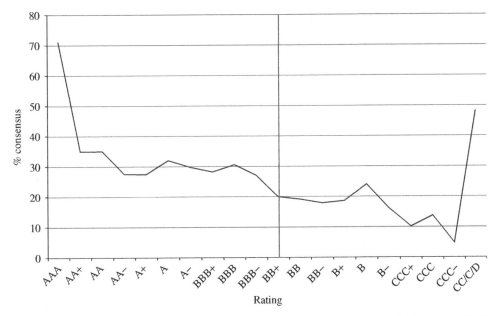

Figure 2.12 Average observational consensus by fine rating notch among seven CRAs (1999–2004). *Source:* Barton, A., 2006, Split credit ratings and the prediction of bank ratings in the Basel II environment. Thesis submitted for the degree of Doctor of Philosophy, University of Southampton, Faculty of Law, Arts and Social Sciences, School of Management, 1–205, page 122.

---

[67] Baker, H.K., and Mansi, S.A., 2002, Assessing credit rating agencies by bond issuers and institutional investors, *Journal of Business Finance and Accounting*, November/December, Vol. 29 (9) and (10), 1367–1398, page 1377.
[68] Barton, A., 2006, Split credit ratings and the prediction of bank ratings in the Basel II environment, Thesis submitted for the degree of Doctor of Philosophy, University of Southampton, Faculty of Law, Arts and Social Sciences, School of Management, 1–205, page 115.
[69] Barton, A., 2006, Split credit ratings and the prediction of bank ratings in the Basel II environment, Thesis submitted for the degree of Doctor of Philosophy, University of Southampton, Faculty of Law, Arts and Social Sciences, School of Management, 1–205, pages 121–122.

likely to go after a third rating.[70] Consider now the previously discussed sample of new issues that has 61 349 multiple ratings. Of these, Moody's and S&P had 60 987 joint ratings and 50.9% of them were split; Moody's and Fitch had 19 508 joint ratings and 59.7% of them were split; and Fitch and S&P had 19 398 joint ratings, of which 63.3% were split. Of these splits, less than one-third are two fine notches or more. Exhibit 2.6 shows the distributions of these splits across the rating scales. For example, the largest fraction of splits of Fitch from S&P occurs at S&P's AA+ level, 84.3%, Fitch assigning AAA 249 times where S&P assigns AA+. Similarly, at Fitch AA+ level, S&P disagrees 91.0% of the time, rating 63.3% of the issues below the Fitch level. Or comparing the 676 new issues that Moody's rated Ba1, 588 were also rated by S&P, of which 442 received a rating that was different from Moody's or 75.2%. Of these differences, there were 328 cases of below investment grade according to Moody's, to which S&P had assigned an investment grade. Split ratings thus represent an interesting and sometimes surprising variety of ratings.

The interpretation of multiple ratings, split or not, deserves close scrutiny. Before being able to interpret them, there has to be a way to compare them. And this is not obvious, in the light of our previous analysis that reached the conclusion that comparing ratings from different CRAs at given index values is strictly speaking meaningless. The following contrasting situations could occur. On the one hand, identical alphanumeric symbols could benchmark varying degrees of creditworthiness. In such a case, one could erroneously infer that the multiple CRAs concur with each other, whereas in fact they do not. On the other hand, different alphanumeric symbols could in fact benchmark identical degrees of creditworthiness. One could then erroneously infer that these split ratings, as they are commonly called, benchmark split degrees of creditworthiness. It is often said that splits occur in case of disagreement among CRAs about creditworthiness, whereas in truth an alphanumeric split is neither a sufficient nor a necessary condition to reflect substantive disagreement. Each CRA follows its own approach to preventing surprise in default. It should thus be no surprise to find that CRAs can disagree about the creditworthiness of an issuer/issue at a particular point in time. Each CRA also defines its own rating index scale. It could thus very well happen that even in agreement about creditworthiness, the position of an issuer on the scales of different CRAs could be different – or vice versa. In addition, random errors by the CRAs form part of the explanation of split ratings.

Observationally split ratings occur due to systematic differences across CRAs. The initial evidence about this was ambiguous, not to say contradictory. Yet the overall findings that are now available point to cross CRA idiosyncrasies in rating. Early research on 493 US industrial bond new issues between 1975 and 1980 that were rated B or above by Moody's and S&P found that

> split ratings represent random differences of opinion on issues whose creditworthiness is close to the borderline between ratings... In only a decided minority of cases do splits appear to represent a more fundamental difference of opinion, and in those cases the differences appear to be with respect to aspects of the issue other than the public accounting information.[71]

---

[70] Beattie V., and Searle S., 1992, Bond ratings and inter-rate agreement, *Journal of International Securities Markets*, Summer, Vol. 6, 167–172.
[71] Ederington, L.H., 1986, Why split ratings occur, *Financial Management*, Spring, Vol. 15, Issue 1, 37–47, page 46.

Exhibit 2.6 Distribution of new issues multiple and split ratings Fitch, Moody's and S&P (1976–2006).

A: Distribution of new issues multiple and split ratings between Fitch and Moody's

Moody's	1 AAA	2 AA+	3 AA	4 AA−	5 A+	6 A	7 A−	8 BBB+	9 BBB	10 BBB−
1 Aaa	**749**	34	9	15	3	8	3		2	
2 Aa1	292	**473**	203	148	7		1	1		
3 Aa2	34	100	**697**	730	155	8	1	2		
4 Aa3	23	18	1639	**2340**	724	43	44	5	2	1
5 A1	27	16	87	1098	**1090**	317	49	7	1	
6 A2	6	1	49	111	1794	**1188**	403	32		
7 A3		1	12	126	236	717	**422**	115	11	13
8 Baa1	6		1	1	14	115	418	**346**	161	13
9 Baa2	2		1	6	3	41	71	347	**238**	50
10 Baa3	1		1	2	1	16	117	82	151	**204**
11 Ba1					1		67	17	17	63
12 Ba2	3						2	1	10	21
13 Ba3		3						1		6
14 B1							1	4		6
15 B2										1
16 B3										
17 Caa1										
18 Caa2										
Multiple	1143	646	2699	4577	4028	2453	1599	960	593	378
Split	394	173	2002	2237	2938	1265	1177	614	355	174
Split %	34.5	26.8	74.2	48.9	72.9	51.6	73.6	64.0	59.9	46.0

Exhibit 2.6 (continued)

A: Distribution of new issues multiple and split ratings between Fitch and Moody's

Fitch (cons.)

Moody's	11 BB+	12 BB	13 BB−	14 B+	15 B	16 B−	18 CCC	Multiple	Split	Split%
1 Aaa			1					824	75	9.1
2 Aa1								1125	652	58.0
3 Aa2					1			1728	1031	59.7
4 Aa3	1	5				2		4847	2507	51.7
5 A1								2692	1602	59.5
6 A2	2							3586	2398	66.9
7 A3			1					1654	1232	74.5
8 Baa1	10	2						1087	741	68.2
9 Baa2	6	5	2					772	534	69.2
10 Baa3	16	7	2					600	396	66.0
11 Ba1	47	33						245	198	80.8
12 Ba2	18	35	8	1				99	64	64.6
13 Ba3	63	26	17	2				118	101	85.6
14 B1	3	19	18	16	13	2		81	65	80.2
15 B2	2	2	7	10	4			27	23	85.2
16 B3				11	5	2		18	16	88.9
17 Caa1				1	1	2		5	4	80.0
18 Caa2							1	0	0	
Multiple	168	134	56	41	24	8	1	19508	11639	
Split	121	99	39	25	20	6	0	11639		
Split %	72.0	73.9	69.6	61.0	83.3	75.0	0.0	59.7		59.7

B: Distribution of new issues multiple and split ratings between Fitch and S&P

Fitch (cons.)

S&P	1 AAA	2 AA+	3 AA	4 AA−	5 A+	6 A	7 A−	8 BBB+	9 BBB	10 BBB−
1 AAA	789	246	20	11	6	6	1	1	2	
2 AA+	249	58	18	37	5			1		
3 AA	29	232	554	114	6	5	4	1		1
4 AA−	28	88	1713	1345	196	21	4	6	1	
5 A+	8	16	280	2436	1247	134	50	9	1	
6 A	4	4	54	574	2265	1625	177	92	6	
7 A−	3	1	41	31	203	595	572	288	38	
8 BBB+	6		1	5	16	78	336	324	264	18
9 BBB			9	7	39	7	340	224	241	52
10 BBB−	3			1	6	25	100	8	23	224
11 BB+										59
12 BB						24	1		1	6
13 BB−							1		1	4
14 B+										1
15 B										
16 B−										
17 CCC+										
18 CCC										
19 CCC−										
20 CC										
Multiple	1119	645	2690	4561	3989	2520	1586	954	578	365
Split	330	587	2136	3216	2742	895	1014	666	314	141
Split %	29.5	91.0	79.4	70.5	68.7	35.5	63.9	69.8	54.3	38.6

Exhibit 2.6 (continued)

B: Distribution of new issues multiple and split ratings between Fitch and S&P

Fitch (cons.)

S&P	11 BB+	12 BB	13 BB−	14 B+	15 B	16 B−	18 CCC	Multiple	Split	Split%
1 AAA								1083	294	27.1
2 AA+		3	1					370	312	84.3
3 AA	1							947	393	41.5
4 AA−		2			1			3400	2055	60.4
5 A+	5							4178	2931	70.2
6 A	1							4719	3094	65.6
7 A−	2					2		1545	973	63.0
8 BBB+	10	1	1					790	502	63.5
9 BBB	8	7	2					1061	797	75.1
10 BBB−	76	7	1					840	616	73.3
11 BB+	41	6	2	1				139	98	70.5
12 BB	7	57	12	1				154	97	63.0
13 BB−	1	18	27	4				85	58	68.2
14 B+	3	6	7	19	5			40	21	52.5
15 B			3	13	6			25	19	76.0
16 B−				1	12	7		20	13	65.0
17 CCC+				1				2	1	50.0
18 CCC							1			
19 CCC−										
20 CC										
Multiple	155	107	56	39	24	9	1	19398		
Split	114	50	29	20	18	2	0	12274	12274	
Split %	73.5	46.7	51.8	51.3	75.0	22.2	0.0	63.3		63.3

C: Distribution of new issues multiple and split ratings between Moody's and S&P

Moody's / S&P	1 AAA	2 AA+	3 AA	4 AA-	5 A+	6 A	7 A-	8 BBB+	9 BBB	10 BBB-	11 BB+
1 Aaa	4178	134	84	35	5	9	16	4			
2 Aa1	686	699	782	459	91	8				1	
3 Aa2	121	370	1845	2124	920	69	62	9	1	1	
4 Aa3	44	117	885	4875	4106	707	163	5	4	3	
5 A1	13	56	262	1038	3678	3373	330	20	8	1	
6 A2	26	13	68	284	1831	6602	1456	190	6	7	
7 A3	1	21	24	110	414	1579	2261	645	121	21	1
8 Baa1	1			1	10	369	712	1339	452	341	37
9 Baa2		4	4	8	16	67	132	554	705	503	14
10 Baa3			2	1	1	20	22	105	1475	1756	87
11 Ba1					1	1		22	599	156	146
12 Ba2	1			1					148	79	95
13 Ba3			3	1	5	10		1	23	40	36
14 B1	1					1			6	2	13
15 B2					1			1	1		1
16 B3							1		1		
17 Caa1									1		
18 Caa2							1				
Multiple	5072	1414	3959	8937	11079	12815	5156	2896	3551	2911	430
Split	894	715	2114	4062	7401	6213	2895	1557	2076	1155	284
Split %	17.6	50.6	53.4	45.5	66.8	48.5	56.1	53.8	58.5	39.7	66.0

Exhibit 2.6 (*continued*)

C: Distribution of new issues multiple and split ratings between Moody's and S&P

Moody's	S&P 12 BB	13 BB−	14 B+	15 B	16 B−	17 CCC+	18 CCC	19 CCC−	20 CC	Multiple	Split	Split%
1 Aaa										4466	288	6.4
2 Aa1										2726	2027	74.4
3 Aa2										5525	3680	66.6
4 Aa3			3							10913	6038	55.3
5 A1										8780	5102	58.1
6 A2										10598	3996	37.7
7 A3		1								5530	3269	59.1
8 Baa1	3	2								3520	2181	62.0
9 Baa2	4	138								2915	1440	49.4
10 Baa3	20	10								2627	871	33.2
11 Ba1	78	24	5	7						588	442	75.2
12 Ba2	212	56	24	9	3					509	297	58.3
13 Ba3	125	149	87	21	6					485	336	69.3
14 B1	39	100	172	141	52	1				524	352	67.2
15 B2	6	27	121	321	215	30	11			734	413	56.3
16 B3	4	3	29	106	238	65	32	4		483	245	50.7
17 Caa1			1	1	15	14	5	1	2	39	25	64.1
18 Caa2			1		9	7	7			25	18	72.0
Multiple	491	510	443	606	538	117	55	5	2	60987	31020	50.9
Split	279	361	271	285	300	103	48	5	2	31020		
Split %	56.8	70.8	61.2	47.0	55.8	88.0	87.3	100.0	100.0	50.9		

Notes: (1) Covering 65 992 investment grade, high-yield and emerging market investment grade corporate, and agency, supranational and sovereign new issues of which about 13% bonds, 30% CDS, and 56% notes. Of these, 62 496 were rated by Fitch, Moody's or S&P and 1150 by only one of these three.
(2) Fitch and Duff rating are consolidated for the period that they co-existed.
Source: Authors' calculations based on Security Data Corporation, 2007, *US Domestic Public Offerings Database,* Non-convertible, non-short term corporate debt. All issuer and issue types, 1976–2006.

But the findings on a global representative sample of 1853 issuer ratings assigned by the world's 12 most important CRAs tell a different story. In fact, they say the opposite: that many CRAs have division points in their scales that are consistently different between them. For example, on a 11-point numeric fine scale from 1 (Aaa) to 10 (Baa3) plus 1 (all below investment grade collapsed), of the 65 jointly rated bonds The Japan Bond Research Institute (JBRI) rated on average 1.75 notches below Moody's; of the 1398 joint ratings, S&P rated on average 0.06 notches above Moody's, both pairwise differences being statistically significant. Interestingly – they eventually merged – IBCA, Fitch, and Duff&Phelps rated the same, on average.[72] In a similar vein, the analysis of a sample of 1137 issuer ratings as of December 31, 1993, of US corporations out of the same database as the previous case concludes that 'observed differences in average ratings reflect differences in rating scales.'[73] All firms in the sample were rated by Moody's and S&P, whose ratings the study compared with those of Fitch and of Duff&Phelps Credit Rating Agency (DCR). The sample revealed 'that DCR and Fitch give systematically higher ratings on jointly rated issues than Moody's and S&P.'[74] Another potential explanation for this would have been a selection bias – that is, the firms that seek and publish a third rating from Fitch do so because they expect to get a higher rating than the prevailing ones. However, in this study, no strong evidence of selection bias is found. In addition to individual raters' rating scales that differ, raters may rely or focus on different factors or give different weights to the same factors in reaching a rating. Several more recent findings all suggest that each CRA follows its own approach, leading to its own results in preventing surprise in defaults.[75] One result among these is of particular interest here. 'Firms with large information asymmetry problems are more likely to have split bond ratings.'[76] This suggests that the heterogeneity among CRAs is most valuable when most needed. As creditworthiness becomes more opaque, the different ways that CRAs use to extract relevant signals about expected loss and the uncertainty surrounding it lead to increasingly different appreciations across agencies. As long as each one provides its own judgment about it – independent and in different ways from its competitors – the combined information to the market in the split ratings should be valuable extra information to investors. In fact, as we will review later, that extra information is priced indeed.

Summing up and concluding, ratings rank default benchmarks according to the idiosyncrasies of the agency doing the rankings. They do this on ordinal scales. The most refined of these deal with the long-term prospects of the issuer, but there are also short-term scales. Each CRA has its own proprietary approach to benchmarking and summarizing this in a rating. The symbols and verbal qualifiers attached to them look quite similar across CRAs, but this does not prevent their ability to show variety. Across agencies, all scales have some key breaking points. Their ratings show all monotonic increases in defaults and declines

---

[72] Beattie, V., and Searle, S., 1992, Bond ratings and inter-rate agreement, *Journal of International Securities Markets 3*, Summer, Vol. 6, 167–172, page 170.

[73] Cantor, R., and Packer, F., 1997, Differences of opinion and selection bias in the credit rating industry, *Journal of Banking and Finance*, Vol. 21, 1395–1417, page 1416.

[74] Cantor, R., and Packer, F., 1997, Differences of opinion and selection bias in the credit rating industry, *Journal of Banking and Finance*, Vol. 21, 1395–1417, page 1400.

[75] See, for example, Morgan, D., 2002, Rating banks: risk and uncertainty in an opaque industry, *American Economic Review*, Vol. 92, No. 4, 874–888; Barton, A., 2006, Split credit ratings and the prediction of bank ratings in the Basel II environment, Thesis submitted for the degree of Doctor of Philosophy, University of Southampton, Faculty of Law, Arts and Social Sciences, School of Management, 1–205.

[76] Livingston, M., Naranjo, A., and Zhou, L., 2005, Information asymmetry, bond split ratings, and rating migration, Working Paper, January, 1–35, page 22.

in recovery rates as their level goes down. So the structure of the outputs of the rating systems of the different CRAs shows similar contours, but each CRA has in the end its own language for qualifying risk. This is one of the reasons why different CRAs produce rating quality distributions with their own densities, why issuers often seek multiple ratings, and why these multiple ratings have a high propensity to be 'split' or observationally different.

2.2.2 Rating Scales and Observed Bond Market Credit Spreads

It is often suggested that credit ratings determine the cost of borrowing. For example, on October 19, 2006, Fitch and S&P downgraded Italy's debt by one notch to AA−. In its lead article the next day, *The Wall Street Journal* commented, 'the downgrades ... raise [Italy's] cost of borrowing' and 'yield spreads between Italian 10-year government bonds and German government bonds widened by 0.015 percentage points, the sharpest rise in seven months.'[77] Both statements suggest that, since spread increases followed rating downgrades, somehow credit ratings create the spread or cause the cost of borrowing. But is this really the case? Was it the increase in Italy's credit risk that the CRAs revealed with their rating action that widened the spread, or was it the rating action per se?

It is not obvious to what extent the agencies either cause the bad weather in the credit spreads or announce, just like the weatherman, that bad credit weather lies ahead, the market immediately reflecting that forecast by repricing the credit spread. These spreads tend to wander around rating levels and changes in these levels in a way that seems quite unpredictable. Consider for this the case of Germany's Deutsche Post World Net.

It obtained its initial issuer credit ratings of Aa3/AA− of Fitch and S&P and of A1/A+ of S&P on May 8, 2002. Then, it issued a €1.0 billion maturity 2012 senior unsecured Eurobond, newly issued and rated in June 2002. Figure 2.13 graphs the Deutsche Post AG Fitch, Moody's and S&P ratings along with the mid asset swap spread on the bond.[78] It is not clear on February 7, 2003 and the following few days, when the mid asset swap rate shoots up, how much is caused by the announcement that DPWN is going to buy Airborne or by S&P setting the credit watch to negative. Similarly on March 26 when Moody's sets DPWN on credit watch negative and again when S&P actually downgrades DPWN to A+ on May 12.

Do people thus seek shelter upon the weatherman's announcement or do they simply ignore him? Is it because they had figured out already on their own the upcoming bad weather, or because they learned from experience that the weatherman is unreliable? These are questions of life and death for credit rating agencies that we will answer when discussing credit rating performance in Chapter 7. Prior to that, we need to define what credit spreads are and what the distinctions are between promised, expected, and required returns of a bond. We will then have an introductory discussion of the association between credit ratings and credit spreads. The section concludes that changes in a rating and in the spread of the rated bond share the change in the default risk of the bond as a common cause, rather than the rating change really causing the spread change, or vice versa.

---

[77] Di Leo, L., and Perry, J., 2006, Italy credit downgrade may undermine euro zone, *Wall Street Journal*, October 20, pages 1 and 2.

[78] The mid asset swap spread generally, when there are no arbitrage opportunities, reflects the price a buyer would be willing to pay to protect itself from credit default risk. Hence, the larger the default risk of the underlying bond, the greater the spread.

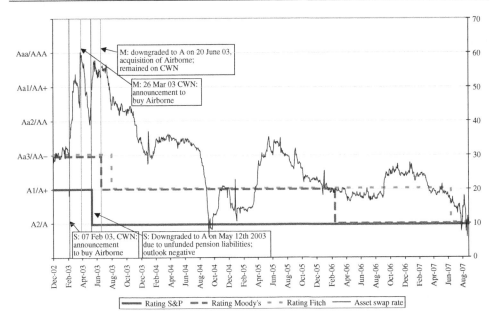

Figure 2.13   DPWN ratings and asset swap spread (2002–2007).
Source: Atkinson, R., Managing Director, Global Capital Markets, Morgan Stanley, 2006, DPWN: The initial credit rating of a major corporation, January 13, 1–20, page 19.

What are Credit Spreads?

Bond market credit spreads are the difference between the yield to maturity and the default risk-free rate of equal maturity. This holds for all debt instruments: bonds, notes, CDs, commercial paper, bills, etc. Investors price the pure time value of money in the instrument by discounting the cash flows in the first place at the prevailing market risk-free rate. But the yield to maturity on a defaultable instrument, say a corporate bond, will typically be higher than that risk-free rate. That difference is called the credit spread. For example, the credit spread between below investment grade rated high-yield 10-year corporate bonds and US Treasury bonds, was 4.90% on average from 1987 through 2004.[79] Ratings and spreads are inversely related, also at the level of gross ratings. Table 2.4 tabulates this on an annual basis, showing spreads in yields between each gross rating and US Treasuries from 1980 to 2005. It documents the existence of a systematic relationship between rating and spread, but albeit a variable one.

These spreads are neither constant over time nor identical for all bonds. Figure 2.14 illustrates that during the period 1978–2004 the spread went through two macro cycles, going from 2.81% to 10.50% and back down to 3.16% through 1978–1996, and then swinging to 9.44% in 2000 and back down to 3.14% by year end 2004.

Several ups and downs interspersed these cycles. High spreads were observed during times of both high overall interest rates, as in 1990, and low overall rates, as in 2002 – and vice versa. At the peak year of overall rates in 1982, the spread was a mere 3.98%. It was at an

---

[79] Altman, E.I., and Hotchkiss, E., 2006, *Corporate Financial Distress and Bankruptcy*, John Wiley & Sons, Inc., Hoboken, New Jersey, 1–354, Table 7.14.

Table 2.4 Average spreads in yields between Corporate bonds and US Treasuries (1980–1997).

Year	AAA	AA	A	BBB	BB	B	CCC
1980	0.60	1.00	1.30	1.90	3.00	3.80	
1981	0.60	1.10	1.30	2.20	3.40	4.10	
1982	0.60	1.00	1.40	2.60	3.60	4.90	9.20
1983	0.70	0.75	0.90	1.57	2.70	3.60	7.60
1984	0.55	0.73	1.04	1.75	2.80	3.10	5.60
1985	0.20	0.58	0.65	1.46	3.10	4.00	6.20
1986	0.95	1.59	1.70	2.33	3.70	4.70	7.90
1987	0.58	1.02	1.18	1.82	2.43	4.03	7.23
1988	0.42	0.79	1.29	1.75	2.07	3.12	7.22
1989	1.28	1.61	2.08	2.49	3.76	4.95	11.91
1990	1.02	1.34	1.77	2.52	4.78	8.57	23.65
1991	0.82	1.13	1.61	2.71	3.92	8.93	12.95
1992	0.90	1.08	1.54	1.77	3.29	4.34	6.46
1993	0.70	0.76	1.74	1.96	2.82	4.15	6.15
1994	0.29	0.62	1.01	1.37	2.23	3.12	6.38
1995	0.43	0.60	1.17	1.49	2.45	4.25	8.75
1996	0.25	0.35	0.54	0.88	2.00	4.08	8.43
1997[a]	0.28	0.39	0.57	0.83	1.53	3.30	7.29

[a] 1997 data is of 3rd quarter

Note: Based on equally weighted averages of monthly spreads (basis points over treasuries) per rating category.
Source: Caouette, J.B., Altman, E.I., and Narayanan, P., 1998, *Managing Credit Risk: The Next Great Financial Challenge*, John Wiley & Sons, Inc., New York, 1–452, page 75.

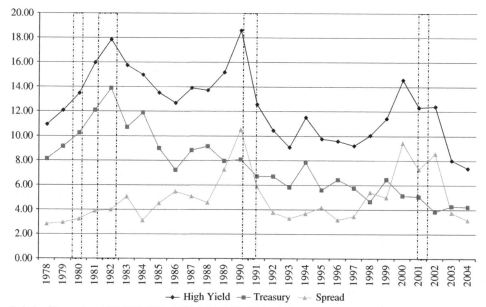

Periods of Recession: 1/80–7/80, 7/81–11/82, 7/90–3/91, 4/01–12/01

Figure 2.14 Yield to maturity on 10-year Treasury and high-yield bonds and the credit spreads between them (1978–2004).
Source: Altman, E.I. and Hotchkiss, E., 2006, *Corporate Financial Distress and Bankruptcy*, John Wiley & Sons, Inc., Hoboken, New Jersey, 1–354, Table 7.14.

almost all-time low of 3.14% when Treasury yields were also at one of their lowest troughs, at 4.21%. The level and variation of spreads thus cannot be associated with the level and changes in overall nominal interest rates in a simple way, but they do follow a pattern that reminds us of Figure 2.4, showing peaks around periods of recession, sometimes leading (1990–1991), sometimes surrounding a recession (2001), and sometimes closely lagging (1981–1982).

The Components of Credit Spreads that Relate to Creditworthiness

These spreads reflect several quite distinct 'spread' components. Some of these are more or less intertwined and their relative influences are difficult to disentangle – even though some claim that they are independent of each other. There are exogenous influences unrelated to the characteristics of the issuer or the instrument (and *a fortiori* to any rating), such as differential tax, liquidity, and transaction cost on defaultable corporate versus default-free government bonds. And there are two endogenous ones that relate to the issuer and the instrument. One is closely linked to the credit rating, the other to the market pricing of risk. Bearing these three categories in mind will help the reader to understand the drivers of credit spreads.

The component that is most closely related to the rating is the expected loss on the bond. Investors do not discount the promised cash flows of the bond, but the expected cash flows. A bond may default and the losses on it in the event of default could vary significantly, as we saw during our discussion of recovery rates from defaults in Section 2.1.3. Investors integrate that in their pricing of the bond. The expected cash flows that investors discount are the promised cash flows minus the expected shortfalls in coupon and principal on them due to the likelihood of default and to the lack of recovery in the event of default. If, for example, the expected cumulative default probability on a 10-year bond that currently rates B were 43% and the average recovery rate on such a bond were 51%, the expected loss on that bond for that holding period would be 22%. The expected cash flows would thus be only 79% of the promised ones, roughly speaking.[80]

The component that is somewhat more related to the possible unexpected changes in expected losses, and which investors worry about, is the risk premium. This is a pure return premium over and above the risk-free rate that investors require to buy and hold the bond. It is less related to the current rating and probably more to the likelihood of rate changes, and the reasons for these changes.[81]

Spreads and Expected or Required Return

The integration of expected losses in pricing means that the promised yield on a bond is an unreasonable approximation to its expected return.[82] The observed yield spread is also an unreasonable approximation of the expected return spread. 'The promised yield, figured by calculating the return earned if the promised payments on the bond are made, is in fact the

---

[80] This holds strictly only for a zero coupon bond.
[81] See for an analysis of this: Amato, J.D., and Remolona, E.M., 2004, The pricing of unexpected credit losses, *Working Paper*: Bank for International Settlements, October, 1–49.
[82] This is calculated by taking its yield to maturity: the internal rate of return of the promised cash flows with respect to the prevailing market price.

maximum that the bond can earn.'[83] It is only for AAA bonds that this yield comes close to the expected return. As John Moody's put it in 1909 in his 'Key to the Bond Ratings' found at the beginning of his first 'Moody's Analyses of Railroad Investments'[84]:

Aaa   The bonds...given this rating are regarded of the highest class...Practically all
      such issues are dependent for their prices on the current rates of money, rather
      than the fluctuations in earning power. In other words, their position is such that
      their value is not affected, or likely to be affected, by any normal changes in the
      earning capacity of the railroad itelf, either for better or for worse.

Fortunately, in equilibrium bond prices adjust to make the expected return at that price equal to the return required to hold the bond at that price. However hard it is to observe expected return directly, trading rallies it closely to investors' required return on the bond. And this can be approximated in a similar way as is done for stocks.

In practice, spreads are often used as a proxy for the risk premium on the bond because it is easily observable. But this proxy overestimates the true fair risk premium because, as we have just discussed, it is made up of both the fair risk premium plus the expected loss. As a consequence, the higher the expected loss, the higher the upward bias in the credit spread as a proxy for the risk premium or for the return expected and required above the risk-free rate. So, speculative grade bonds compensate investors for expected losses by promising much higher returns than investment grade bonds. Their credit spread, i.e. the promised yield to maturity minus the benchmark risk-free rate, is higher. But caveat: that is only an expected premium to the extent that none of these high yield corporate bonds would ever default, which is a highly unlikely condition to hold. In all other cases of bond defaults, the expected and likely realized return premium will be less than the 4.90%, the average spread between high yield 10-year corporate bonds and US Treasury bonds from 1987 to 2004 (see Figure 2.14). To conclude, 'corporate bonds do earn an expected excess return over default-free bonds, even after correcting for the likelihood of default.'[85] But bear in mind that this excess return is less than the observed credit spread!

Patterns of Credit Spreads

Changes over time in observed spreads occur because expected losses and the risk premium fluctuate. From the association of historical default rates, for instance, with recessions displayed in Figure 2.4, it should be no surprise that the average spread varies considerably over time. What do these observations tell us? For sure, that credit risk, and investors' taste for it, has an important, yet complex macro-context. Credit spreads also change from bond to bond. We saw that credit ratings are negatively correlated with default frequencies and that credit spreads increase with credit risk. We also find that credit spreads go up as credit ratings go down – that they are statistically negatively correlated with credit spreads. For an arbitrary day on the euro investment grade corporate bond market in 2005, Figure 2.15

---

[83] Merton, R.C., 1990, The financial system and economic performance, *Journal of Financial Services Research*, December, Vol. 4, Issue 4, 263–300, page 277.

[84] Quoted from Moody's Investors Service, 2007, *Moody's Rating Symbols & Definitions*, March, page 6.

[85] Driessen, J., 2005, Is default event risk priced in corporate bonds?, *Review of Financial Studies*, Vol. 18, No. 1, 165–195, page 165.

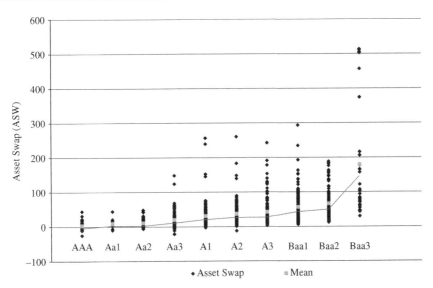

Figure 2.15 Average spread and spread dispersion of Euro investment grade corporate bonds by fine rating category as of November 30, 2005.
Source: Merrill Lynch, 2005. EMU Corporate Index, November 30.

documents the monotonic increase in average spreads from 2 bps for an AAA rating to 102 bps as the rating declines to Baa3.[86]

The increases in average spreads as the rating declines are not linear, but exponential, as Figure 2.15 also shows. The market correctly anticipates that, as the fine ratings go down one notch at a time, the default risk increases with more than a constant increment. Figure 2.15 showed that changes in rating at the high quality end are relatively granular differentiators of default risk, whereas differences at the lower quality end are less closely defined. This is a historical consequence of the traditionally strong interest of institutional investors such as pension funds and life insurance companies in high-quality bonds, which led Moody's to pay a lot of attention to high-quality bonds and the subtle differentiation of quality among them.

Individual spreads within a particular rating category vary substantially around their mean. The relationship between *average* bond spreads and ratings is fairly consistent, but the dispersion can be particularly large at any point in time, increasing as the rating goes down, as Figure 2.15 also illustrates and Table 2.5 documents. For example, the issues of FSA Global Fund for the maturity date of June 29, 2015, which are rated AAA, have their asset swap at 44, 40.95 points away from the mean, 3.05. The asset swap of Barclays Bank PLC's issue, which is rated Aa3, for the maturity date of March 15, 2020, is 148, 128.17 points away from its mean, 19.83. For Baa3 rated issues of Ford Motor Credit for the maturity date of January 14, 2008, their asset swap at 513 is 333.97 points higher than the mean, 179.03. Or take the example in October 2006 of Countrywide Financial, the largest mortgage lender in the US. Spreads on bonds of rivals with identical credit rating had risen 2 bps since May, but its spread widened by 24 bps at the same rating level.[87]

---

[86] The spread in this figure is measured by the asset swap (ASW) rate in bps.
[87] Bloomberg News, 2006, Doubt on lender's debt (folo) Citigroup sees advance in global equity market, October 17, as reported in the *International Herald Tribune*, page 21.

Table 2.5 Spread dispersion summary of Euro investment grade corporate bonds by fine rating category as of November 30, 2005.

Rating	Number of observations	Asset swap				Standard deviation
		Minimum	Maximum	Median	Mean	
AAA	99	−25	44	2.00	3.05	8.83
Aa1	28	−10	44	7.50	9.32	10.03
Aa2	114	−6	48	8.00	10.70	10.63
Aa3	109	−21	148	14.00	19.83	23.32
A1	183	−3	256	22.00	30.78	34.75
A2	146	−12	260	30.50	37.07	32.95
A3	176	3	242	31.50	41.94	35.91
Baa1	122	6	293	47.00	55.78	45.03
Baa2	82	12	188	47.50	65.83	46.77
Baa3	33	30	513	102.00	179.03	167.13

Source: Merrill Lynch, 2005. EMU Corporate Index, November 30.

Between individual rating distributions, spreads overlap significantly. Notice, for instance, that in Table 2.5 there are 28 issues rated Aa1 whose asset swaps overlap with Aa2, and 176 issues rated A3 whose asset swaps are in the same range as Baa1's.

To sum up, the relation between the fundamental credit rating of a bond and its credit spread at any point in time and over time is a very noisy one. The easily observable patterns in the relationship correspond on average to what one would expect, but there are a number of non-rating factors that affect the spread such as the maturity of the instrument: income tax treatment of the coupon and capital gains, the liquidity in trading of the instrument, and the dynamics of the mutual adjustment over time of spreads and ratings.

Bond Maturity

The maturity of the bond explains part of the variability in the relationship. Table 2.6 illustrates this by tabulating across the maturity buckets for 1–3 years, 3–5 years, and 5–7 years and across six gross rating categories, the average spreads of US corporate debt over

Table 2.6 Average US corporate bond spreads across gross rating categories per maturity bucket (1997–2003).

Rating	1–3 years	3–5 years	5–7 years
AAA	49.50	63.86	70.47
AA	58.97	71.22	82.36
A	88.82	102.91	110.71
BBB	168.99	170.89	185.34
BB	421.20	364.55	345.37
B	760.84	691.81	571.94

Spreads are averages over the period January 1997–August 2003 of Merrill Lynch option-adjusted spread indices for US corporate bonds.
Sources: Bank for International Settlements, 2003, International Banking and Financial Market Developments, *Quarterly Review*, December, 1–103, page 52; and Amato, J. and Remolona, E., 2003, The credit spread puzzle, *BIS Quarterly Review*, December, pages 51–63.

equivalent US government debt for the period 1997–2003.[88] It first confirms that spreads are inversely related to the rating for all maturities. For short-term debt, the spread on AAA debt averaged 49.5 bps, going up to 58.97 bps for the AA category, to 88.82 on the A, and to 168.99 on the lowest investment grade category, BBB. Below investment grade, the BBs commanded 421.20 bps in spread and the Bs 760.84. Note that spreads increase significantly at lower ratings down to BBB, and even more so across sub-par investment grade debt. The relationship is exponential, rather than linear.

The spread itself is related to maturity at each rating level. In fact, the spread curve is never flat over maturity; it increases with maturity bucket up to the BBB category. For AAA bonds, spreads increase from 49.5 bps in the 1–3 years bucket to 70.5 bps in the 5–7 years bucket. But the the spread curve inverts for the below investment grade categories. The spreads decline for BBs from 421.2 bps at the short end to 345.4 bps at the long end, and for Bs from 760.8 to 571.9. Economists are still trying to explain this paradox. The market considers long-term very-risky bonds to be less risky than short-term very-risky bonds. Maybe the intuition is that, if an issuer in a relatively bad financial shape but proves to harness the staying power to survive the short term (however unlikely that may be), he will have purchased time to sort things out. Put differently, there may be many occurrences in which financial distress and short-term risk of default are due to liquidity and debt structure problems, rather than to solvency and capital structure problems.

Spreads change with the rating at different speeds in different maturity buckets. This is a corollary to the slope of the spread curve. This occurs at all maturities, but particularly so for the short-term ones were spread to increase by 711.34 bps when the rating goes down from AAA to B, whereas at the long-term end bps increase by only 501.47 across the same range.

Transitory Market Conditions

During several periods the relation between credit ratings and spreads weakened. Similar to stock markets, credit markets go occasionally through cycles of irrational credit exuberance or pessimism. For example, during the 1980s, there were the so-called 'story bonds.' These were bonds issued at below investment grade for which pricing was not just a function of credit risk but also of the special interest that underwriters created in them. Drexel Burnham Lambert, the high-yield bond house that went bankrupt in 1990, would talk about the intangibles of management vision and drive to offset risky balance sheets when marketing a high-yield offering. And there was often a noticeable increase in price between the time when the underwriter is engaged in preliminary price talk and when the bond is issued. While a portion of this will be due to improvement in the credit condition of the borrower, it is plausible that the 'story' told by underwriters to investors and analysts about the credit plays a role. These bonds (especially those of high-yield first time issuers) were often heavily marketed and oversubscribed.[89]

Research measuring the relative influence on spreads of transitory market conditions and of ratings settled largely in favor of the latter. Subjecting to close scrutiny the extent to which one can establish objective valuation criteria for these bonds, one finds that 'nevertheless, 56% of the variance in risk premiums is explained by quantifiable factors, such as rating,

---

[88] This section draws from BIS, 2003, *Quarterly Review*, page 52.
[89] 'Bonds are sold, they are not bought,' it is often said.

term, and secondary-market spreads. At the same time, the underwriter's effectiveness in presenting the issuer to investors appears to materially influence pricing.'[90]

Of course, one can think of several transitory market conditions that, at times, could weaken the relationship. In conjunction with their 'story' attractiveness that reduced the expected loss premium in the yield, and thus the observed credit spread, there was an interest cycle effect in the demand for these bonds. Bond coupons were generally at historically high levels due to the policy of the Federal Reserve to eradicate inflationary expectations. The higher the coupon on a bond, the larger the proportion of the value of the bond that comes from its near term coupon flows. As a result, the more apt the bond in satisfying bond portfolio investors' demand for stable value in their portfolios.[91] After the tremendous shocks in portfolio values following Volcker's change in monetary policy regime, bond portfolio managers were keen to find instruments that would immunize portfolio values from changes in market interest rates.

Conclusion: The Consistency of Ratings and Observed Bond Market Credit Spreads

The non-ratings factors that influence spreads do not make these inconsistent with ratings. 'Adjusting for economic determinants of spreads and allowing for the dynamic adjustment of ratings and spreads largely eliminates inconsistencies.'[92] This conclusion was based on the rigorous analysis of the 1991–1998 price data of a very clean sample of 1430 US dollar-denominated bonds, 90% of which were Eurobonds. It found that, on average, between one-fifth and one-quarter of AA bonds are priced in a way that is inconsistent with their ratings, with smaller fractions of AAA and A rated bonds. Thus, the credit quality ordering that CRAs attribute to obligors is distinct from the one that the bond market assigns. However, about a third of the inconsistencies are eliminated by adjusting for tax, liquidity, and term premiums. After these adjustments, around a half of the remaining inconsistencies disappear after six months, during which time spreads and ratings adjust dynamically. Either the spreads adjust to the rating, or rating actions occur bringing the rating in line with the spread. That this takes time 'is intuitive given the deliberative process used by rating agencies to implement rating changes.'[93] Hence, ratings and spreads suitably adjust in a reasonably consistent way after some time, yet significant variability in the relationship remains.

2.2.3 Market-Implied Cardinal Rating Scales and Default Probabilities

From the previous sections, it is clear that ratings order issuers and instruments according to their future default expectations and that credit spreads in the markets by and large reflect that ordering. Yet the order remains approximate in several respects. One is that default prospects increase in discrete steps from 1 to 22, but the actual probability of default has a much greater granularity. It can be any real number on a continuum between 0 and 1. The

---

[90] Fridson, M.S., and Garman, M.C., 1998, Determinants of spreads on new high-yield bonds, *Financial Analysts Journal*, March/April, 28–39.

[91] See Blume, M.E., and Keim, D.B., 1987, Lower grade bonds: their risks and returns, *Financial Analysts Journal*, July–August, Vol. 43, 26–33 who find that lower grade bonds have lower volatility from interest changes than risk-free, lower coupon Treasuries.

[92] Perraudin, W., and Taylor, A., 2004, On the consistency of rating and bond market yields, *Journal of Banking and Finance*, Vol. 28, September, 2769–2788.

[93] Cantor, R., 2004, An introduction to recent research on credit ratings, *Journal of Banking and Finance*, Vol. 28, September, page 2569.

other is that ratings are strictly only comparable for constant maturities. Take, for example, two instruments, S and L, that are identical in all respects, except maturity. S has a 3-year maturity, L a 10-year one. Let both be rated A2 (rank 6). The default prospect embedded in the A2 has not quite the same meaning for S as for L, since on S it is a statement for three years whereas it is one for 10 years on L. Ratings are not strictly comparable in the time horizons of the default prospects that they express. Again, the probability of default is defined for a constant horizon across the prospects. Investors want a method that assesses the default prospects in such a way that they obtain a cardinal measure of this probability of default at identical horizons. This is called the expected default frequency (EDF), typically taken with a one-year horizon.[94] How do we determine EDF?

Until the early 1980s, credit analysts lacked a way of adequately quantifying default risk, and corporate credit analysis was viewed as an art rather than a science. Changes began in 1984, when Oldrich Vasicek published his now famous research results on credit valuation.[95] He asserted that 'credit risk should be measured in terms of probabilities and mathematical expectations, rather than assessed by qualitative ratings. When performed in this manner, we can refer to a credit valuation model.'[96] Vasicek's method of quantifying EDF was based on the stock price of an issuer and gave rise to equity-implied ratings, 'the credit category assigned to a firm based on the performance of its equity.'[97] This approach follows the insight that the equity of an issuer is like a call option on the company's assets, with an exercise price equal to the face value of the debt, and its time to expiration equal to the maturity of the debt. The observed stock market capitalization of the firm's equity thus corresponds to the market value of a call option on the firm's assets. The trick – the technicalities of which we shall explain in Section 6.2.2 – is to use that correspondence to estimate the market value of the firm's assets and the volatility of these assets. With these, and the face value and maturity of the debt, one can then estimate the probability that the value of the firm will be insufficient to pay the debt when due.

Moody's KMV maps EDF values to equity-implied ratings through the following steps. Take the median EDF value of the firms in each major rating class Aaa to B on a monthly basis and determine fine rating EDF values by geometric interpolation between the major class EDF values.[98] While interpolating, impose monotony, i.e. EDF always increases when the rating goes down, and convexity, i.e. for each incremental notch down, EDF increases more than with the previous notch down.[99] Every month, therefore, ordinal fine rating grades are mapped with cardinal EDF values, as Figure 2.16 illustrates for six points in time during the period 1994–2004. Hence we can rank Moody's KMV EDFs alongside the competing credit risk indexes, as column (7) in Figure 2.16 does.[100] This column therefore shows the cardinal scale mean equivalents, at a particular point in time, of ordinal ratings.

Using EDFs helps us to appreciate the differences in meaning of the alphanumeric ratings at the same level between CRAs. For example, an S&P B+ (level 14) does not have the

[94] The one-year horizon reflects industry practice, not analytical necessity.

[95] Vasicek, O.A., 1984, Credit Valuation, *White Paper*: KMV Corporation, March 22, 1–16.

[96] Vasicek, O.A., 1984. Credit valuation, *White Paper*: KMV Corporation, March 22, 1–16, page 1.

[97] Cantor, R., Fons, J., Mann, C., Munves, D., and Viswanathan, J., 2005. An explanation of market implied ratings, Moody's Investors Service, November, SP1325, 1–19, page 11.

[98] Below B, Moody's KMV applies an EDF constant of 17% for the Caa grade and 20% for Ca and C.

[99] Cantor, R., Fons, J., Mann, C., Munves, D., and Viswanathan, J., 2005. An explanation of market implied ratings, Moody's Investors Service, November, SP1325, 1–19, pages 11–13.

[100] LLC (KMV) was an independent San Francisco based corporation until Moody's acquired it in April 2002. Since then, it became Moody's KMV.

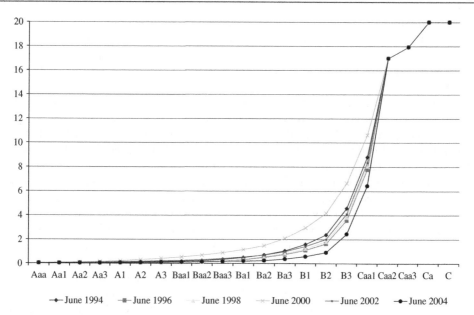

Figure 2.16 Mapping of Moody's fine ordinal rating scale and Moody's KMV cardinal ratings (Bi-annually on June 30 1994–2004).
Source: Moody's Investors Service.

same probability of default as a Moody's B1 (level 14), even though they ordinally rank the same (see Exhibit 2.4). At one point, EDFs from 4 through 10 bps correspond to ratings from AA through A (levels 3 through 6) at S&P and from Aa2 to A1 (levels 3 through 5) at Moody's.[101] Accordingly, a Moody's A2 has the same rank of 6 as an S&P A, but it signals a higher probability of default than its S&P counterpart. Practitioners suggest that S&P is tougher than Moody's because it tends to rank at a lower grade. The truth is slightly more subtle, with Moody's signaling a higher EDF than S&P at the steps A1/A2 (A+/A) and Ba1/Ba2 (BB+/BB). When one reads in the newspapers that an issue has been downgraded more by S&P than by Moody's, this does not necessarily mean that S&P believes that the EDF of the downgraded issue is higher than Moody's. It simply means that S&P has to descend its symbolic ladder more than Moody's to reach the same EDF.

2.3   THE INTERPRETATION OF CREDIT RATINGS

How should we interpret all the information about creditworthiness drawn from these three different sources: fundamental ratings, credit spreads, and market implied ratings? Let's first take a look at the differences in meaning along the gradations on the fundamental scale. We will then deepen and refine our understanding of what fundamental credit ratings really convey and conclude this section with a discussion of three special topics: a fundamental credit rating as an opinion, credit ratings and fraud, and CRAs and auditors.

---

[101] See Crouhy, M., Galai, D., and Mark, R., 2000, *Risk Management*, McGraw-Hill, New York, 1–717, Table 9.3, page 379.

2.3.1 Interpreting from the Scale

By rating an issuer or instrument, the CRA positions it in the world of possible defaults. In doing so, the agency considers capacity to meet financial commitments, exposure to business, financial and economic conditions, and actual payment default and its consequences. The CRA reduces the rating in steps as the level of adversity accumulates. Initially it does so as the capacity to meet financial conditions weakens. Next, it reduces the rating when vulnerability to adverse business, financial and economic conditions increases. Lastly, the rating gets stepped down as the obligor's options are reduced due to the urgency of its situation. In the end, payment default is highlighted if and when it occurs. Below are examples of company, organization, or country situations and their corresponding credit ratings rationale going down the scale (in this case, S&P as per Exhibit 2.3).

Investment Grade Ratings

AAA – *Extremely strong capacity to meet financial commitments*

The Wellcome Trust is the second largest charitable foundation funding biomedical research in the world, having over £12 billion in investment assets and spending over £450 million per year on research and other activities aimed at improving human health. In July 2006, the Wellcome Trust announced that it had been graded AAA by S&P and also top-rated by Moody's, and planned to use its new status to issue sterling-denominated bonds to help to fund a wider range of research programs in the long term. S&P believed 'that the Trust has the size, flexibility, and financial sophistication to withstand even significant downturns in the equity markets.'[102]

AA – *Very strong capacity to meet financial commitments*

The long-term corporate credit rating of Genentech Inc. was raised from A+ to AA by S&P in September 2006. The rating increase reflected the 56% ownership of Genentech by Roche Holdings AG (recently initiated at the AA+ level), and S&P pointed out that the increasing contribution of Genentech's novel products to the results of its parent company strengthened its position. S&P believed, among others, that 'the company has significant financial stamina to cushion potential unforeseen hits to its operating performance.'[103]

A – *Strong capacity to meet financial commitments, but somewhat more susceptible to adverse economic conditions and changes in circumstances*

Norinchukin Finance (Cayman) Ltd, the overseas subsidiary of Japanese Norinchukin Bank, received a rating of A for a series of subordinated bonds in September 2006. Commenting, S&P stated that the ratings were 'one notch lower than the long-term counterparty credit rating on the parent bank, reflecting their subordinate status.' This

---

[102] Standard & Poor's, 2006, UK based Wellcome Trust and its debut LT bond issue assigned AAA rating; outlook stable, *Rating Action*, July 3, 1–3 stated: 'The rating on the Trust is supported by its independent financial position based on its sizable and well-diversified investment portfolio, its high level of financial flexibility, and its minimal debt position. Furthermore, the Trust has mitigated much of the risk posed by its dependence on the performance of equities, and on the judgment of fund managers.' The announcement also quoted the above-mentioned belief.

[103] Standard & Poor's, 2006, Genentech Inc. corporate credit raised to AA/Stable/A-1+, *Rating action*, September 19, 1–4, quoted 'The conservative financial policies and internally generated growth sustain the rating ... The product diversity sufficient for the company to receive a rating upgrade is not an early prospect. On the other hand, the company has significant financial stamina to cushion potential unforeseen hits to its operating performance. The absence of any formal financial support from Roche precludes consideration of an equalization of the ratings.'

parent is the central cooperative bank for agriculture, forestry, and fisheries and the largest among Japanese banks. Since 1991, it had enjoyed first AAA and then for six years AA status. But in 1998 the crisis environment affected Japan. In September S&P lowered Norinchukin Bank to 'A+', reflecting the bank's deterioration 'stemming from the worsening economic conditions in Japan in September 1998' and the 'challenging operating conditions surrounding the Norinchukin's group.' S&P's announcement then goes on to point out the strong capacities of the bank itself in terms of size, liquidity, profitability, and capitalization.[104]

BBB – *Adequate capacity to meet financial commitments, but more subject to adverse conditions*

In October 2005, Bulgaria saw its long-term foreign currency sovereign credit rating reach BBB 'On Sustained Fiscal Prudence.'[105] Impending EU accession was one factor in the improved rating. S&P's credit analyst Remy Salters said, 'The upgrade reflects the ongoing reduction in the general government debt burden, underpinned by the maintenance of prudent fiscal policies through the recent government change.'

Below-Investment, Speculative, or Junk Bond Status

BB – *Less vulnerable in the near term, but faces major ongoing uncertainties and exposures to adverse business, financial and economic conditions*

General Motors was downgraded to non-investment grade BB by S&P on May 5, 2005, reflecting S&P's 'conclusion that management's strategies may be ineffective in addressing GM's competitive disadvantages. Still, GM should not have any difficulty accommodating near-cash requirements.'[106] The downgrading was due to a number of factors, including GM's falling share of the US car market, and the impending health care and retirement costs of its numerous and aging workforce. Ford saw its debt ratings downgraded to BB+, a shade better than GM but still junk, or speculative, status. The BBC news website reported that 'The downgrades, affecting debt worth about $290 billion, are the largest cuts to junk in a single day.'[107]

B – *More vulnerable to adverse business, financial and economic conditions, but currently has the capacity to meet financial commitments*

Having had its debt downgraded to junk status, BB+, in May 2005, to BB− in January 2006, and to B+ on June 28, 2006, September 2006 saw Ford's debt status drop again, this time to B. The downgrade followed Ford's announcement that it was revising its turnaround plan and would now shed 10 000 employees and close an additional two plants. This followed a month of suspended production as Ford tried to shift excessive inventories. Shares in Ford fell 2% on the day of the announcement. The latest S&P 'downgrade reflects the seemingly relentless deterioration in Ford's North American automotive operations, which are now expected to remain unprofitable until at least 2009.' Ford's challenges accelerated in 2006, 'leading to a higher than anticipated use of cash since we last lowered Ford's rating in June.'[108]

---

[104] Standard & Poor's, 1998, S&P lowers Norinchukin Bank to 'A+'; off creditwatch. *Rating Action*, September 4, 1–2.

[105] Standard & Poor's, 2005, Bulgaria L-T FC rating raised to 'BBB' on sustained fiscal prudence. *Research Update*, October 27, 1–4, page 1.

[106] Standard & Poor's, 2006, General Motors Corp. downgraded to 'BB' on concerns about business prospects, *Research Update*, May 5, 1–5.

[107] BBC News, 2005, GM and Ford downgraded to junk, May 5.

[108] Standard & Poor's, 2006, Ford Motor and Ford Credit ratings lowered one notch to 'B' *Research Update*, September 19, 1–5, page 1.

CCC – *Currently vulnerable and dependent on favorable business, financial and economic conditions to meet financial commitments*

Energis, a UK telecoms group, saw its shares fall 70% on one day in February 2002 and drop further to just 3p the following day (from an all-time high of around 850p) as investors became convinced the company would collapse. Energis had been valued at almost £14 billion just 14 months previously. But S&P now downgraded the company's creditworthiness to CCC, following 'a strategic review statement ... and the announcement that the group is considering the restructuring of its £562 million outstanding bond obligations.'[109] Deutsche Bank was quoted as saying, 'The story for equity holders is over; if you can, exit,' and S&P pointed out that, 'a restructuring operation that would worsen the bondholders' original position would be treated as a selective default.'

CC – *Currently highly vulnerable*

Fedders Corporation, a US manufacturer of a wide variety of air-treatment products, was rated CC by S&P in July 2005. The company was facing stiff competition from imports as American consumers began to seek out more energy-efficient appliances. The company had a turnover of $399.4 million in 2004, but this fell to $297.72 million by the end of 2005, and losses over the same period more than doubled, from $26.11 million in 2004 to $62.08 million in 2005. The downgrade followed 'Fedders announcement that an event of default (under its senior note indenture) has occurred as a result of the company's failure to file its annual report on Form 10K with the SEC within the specified 30-day grace period'...As a result, representatives of at least 25% 'of the senior notes outstanding can declare all senior notes to be due and payable immediately.'[110]

Unrespected Financial Commitments

C – *A bankruptcy petition has been filed or similar action taken, but payments or financial commitments are continued*

America West's unsecured debt was downgraded from CC to C in November 2001 as the implications of the September 11 attacks for airlines became apparent. Airlines were obliged to back their borrowings with aircraft as security. America West had 69% of its assets pledged this way. Speaking about a raft of downgrading for nine airlines, S&P said, 'The ratings actions do not indicate a changed estimate of default risk, but rather poorer prospects for recovery on senior unsecured obligations if the affected airlines were to become insolvent.'[111]

D – *Payment default on financial commitments*

Adelphia Communications, a cable television operator that had recently celebrated its 50th birthday, hit S&P's lowest corporate credit rating of D when it missed a $45 million interest payment on its senior unsecured note in May 2002.[112] The founding family was forced to give up control of the company and options to rescue Adelphia, the fifth largest issuer of junk bonds in the US at the time, were actively pursued. Investigations

---

[109] Standard & Poor's, 2002, Long-Term CCR on Energis PLC cut to 'CCC–' after possible bond restructure, *Research Update*, February 21, 1–2, page 1.

[110] Standard & Poor's, 2005, Fedders ratings lowered on concerns of meeting future obligations under its note indenture, *Research Update*, July 1, 1–3, page 1.

[111] Standard & Poor's, 2001, Airline unsecured debt ratings lowered; other ratings unaffected, *Rating Action*, November 29, 1–4, pages 1 and 2.

[112] Standard & Poor's, 2002, Adelphia Comm corporate credit rating lowered to 'D,' after missed interest payment, *Rating Action*, May 20, 1–1.

by the SEC, two state grand juries, and federal officials into questionable transactions, along with the threat of being de-listed from NASDAQ and, not surprisingly, a record low share price, all added to Adelphia's woes.[113]

Rating levels are like different steps on a pyramid of facts and considerations relevant to benchmark default prospects. On top stands AAA/Aaa. With foundations shaky as a D, it is impossible to climb. The short visits just made to each one of the randomly selected rating actions tell a story about what it takes for an issuer to enduringly climb the pyramid. The stairs have to stay level on all sides, the four vectors rising together to the common top. The macroeconomic, industrial sector, business quality, and financing vectors need to keep in pace with each other so that the whole structure remains stable as you move up. Every single story above tells something about each vector of the issuer, albeit with different emphasis – depending on where the issuer stands on the pyramid. Yet the financing vector is more readily measurable than the other three. The benchmarks on that vector can thus be more easily compared across ratings. Financial leverage is one of the most widely used proxies for financial risk.

Interpreting the rating scale, leverage tends to monotonically increase as the issuers ratings go down. Table 2.7 documents this for ratings from AAA/Aaa to CCC+/Caa1 or below.[114] For example, the top four credit ratings have median debt to total capital ratios ranging from 31% to 44%, whereas the bottom four credit ratings have these ratios ranging from 66% to 72%. It is equally interesting, if not more, that the standard deviations around the mean of each rating class are relatively high and increase with the rating. This means that other drivers than sheer leverage play an increasing role to further improve the rating, consistent with our pyramidal four vectors story.

2.3.2   Correctly Interpreting versus Misinterpreting Ratings

By emphasizing here some important correct interpretations of ratings we want to overcome many remaining misunderstandings about them. Ratings have been in use for more than 100 years, and yet the business community, regulators, legislators, academics, and journalists occasionally have unrealistic expectations of what the ratings actually mean.[115] The following, correct interpretations of ratings deserve particular explanation:

- Ratings address benchmark measures of probabilities of default; they are not probabilities.
- Ratings maintain a time perspective on credit risk for at least as long a period as the maturity of the instrument.
- Ratings are descriptive, not prescriptive, of a debt situation.
- Ratings measure credit risk, they don't price it.
- Credit ratings are . . . credit ratings, not equity ratings.

---

[113] Schepp, D., 2002, Family cedes control at Adelphia, BBC News, May 23.

[114] Kisgen, D.J., 2006, Credit ratings and capital structure, *The Journal of Finance*, June, Vol. 61, No. 3, 1035–1072, Table 1, page 1049.

[115] Consider for example the misinterpretation of what ratings are in the statement of US Rep. M.G. Fitzpatrick (PA): 'In light of the mistakes S&P and Moody's made by telling investors that Enron and WorldCom were safe investments just days before they filed for bankruptcy, the current state of regulation in the credit rating industry could not stand anymore' (House Committee on Financial Services, 2006, President signs credit rating agency reform act of 2006, S.3850, into law, Press Release, September 29).

Table 2.7 Ratings and leverage.

Means, medians, and standard deviations of debt/(debt + equity) by credit rating within the sample, and the number of firm-years (out of the total sample of 12 336 firm-years) that had the indicated rating at the beginning of the firm-year. The sample is Compustat firms from 1986 to 2001, excluding firms with missing values for regularly used variables in the empirical tests of the paper (these include credit ratings, total assets, debt, and equity). Debt/(debt + equity) is book long-term and short-term debt divided by book long-term and short-term debt plus book shareholders' equity (leverage statistics exclude firms with D/(D + E) greater than 1 or less than 0).

	AAA	AA+	AA	AA−	A+	A
Number of Firm-Years	342	199	622	703	1135	1380
Debt/(Debt + Equity)						
Mean	39.3%	30.7%	39.0%	43.2%	46.7%	45.2%
Median	30.5%	37.4%	41.1%	44.1%	46.6%	46.1%
Std Dev.	28.2%	16.7%	18.2%	19.5%	20.5%	18.7%

	A−	BBB+	BBB	BBB−	BB+	BB
Number of Firm-Years	1067	1083	1149	847	521	636
Debt/(Debt + Equity)						
Mean	46.4%	46.9%	48.9%	50.2%	55.4%	55.3%
Median	40.3%	42.1%	45.7%	48.6%	53.1%	53.6%
Std dev.	16.6%	15.9%	16.4%	17.4%	17.9%	17.7%

	BB−	B+	B	BB−	CCC+ or Below	
Number of Firm-Years	785	1067	419	172	209	
Debt/(Debt + Equity)						
Mean	59.5%	63.3%	68.0%	68.0%	62.5%	
Median	57.9%	66.2%	72.1%	70.6%	71.4%	
Std dev.	19.0%	21.0%	18.9%	23.0%	28.6%	

Source: Kisgen, D.J., 2006, Credit ratings and capital structure, *The Journal of Finance*, June, Vol. 61, No. 3, 1035–1072, Table 1, page 1049.

Ratings Address Benchmark Measures of Probabilities of Default; They are Not Probabilities

A probability of default, or *default risk*, is the measurement on a continuous scale from 0 to 1 of the likelihood that the counterparty will default. For an instrument with a given rating at a particular point in time, a subjective assessment of its default probability within, say, the next five years could be taken statistically from past observations. One could observe the historical default frequencies of an instrument with a similar rating over several 5-year time periods and obtain several estimates of the 5-year default frequency. The average of these observations would give a statistical measure of the EDF. If this EDF is believed to be representative, unbiased, and efficient, it could be accepted as the default probability over the next five years for an instrument in the same rating category. For example, the 5-year EDF of all investment grade corporate long-term public debt for the period 1920–2004 was 1.84% on average.

Estimating the likelihood of default by its EDF over 1920–2004, one can estimate the default probability over the next five years of any randomly selected current investment grade corporate long-term bond to be 1.84%. However, if the period 1970–2004, which yields a 5-year EDF of 0.92%, is believed to be more representative for what the next five years may bring, the 5-year default probability looking forward might be taken as 0.92%. And similarly, it would be set at 0.96% based on 1983–2004 5-year EDFs. For 1-year horizons, these EDFs would be 0.15%, 0.07%, and 0.08% respectively. For 10 years, they would be 4.47%, 2.31%, and 2.03%.[116]

But the assigned probabilities of default to different ratings in this way need to be interpreted carefully. As the previous example illustrates, the apparently objective and statistical way becomes easily extremely subjective, not to say indeterminate or arbitrary. Hence Fitch, for instance, says clearly that these ratings are benchmark measures of the probability of default. Which is not quite the same as a probability itself.

Ratings Maintain a Time Perspective on Credit Risk at Least as Long as the Maturity of the Instrument, through the Business Cycle

Ratings measure credit risk until the maturity of the instrument. CRAs thus evaluate the fundamental drivers of creditworthiness over the long term. These drivers cover the financial condition of the issuer that raters analyze over several years to avoid transitory anomalies.[117] But they include also a broad spectrum such as management, strategy, technology, R&D, regulatory trends, and the company's legal status. For example, a draft bill was released in France in May 1996 proposing to change France Telecom's legal status to a regular corporation subject to common law. Moody's immediately placed France Telecom's sovereign top Aaa rating under review for possible downgrade, even though nothing in the company's current condition had actually changed.

Ratings thus look at structural company characteristics, which typically do not change with the business cycle. Ratings aim to be cycle neutral, and are not systematically adjusted up during booms or down during recessions. For instance,

> In rating cyclical companies, Fitch analyzes credit-protection measures and profitability through the cycle to identify a company's equilibrium or mid-cycle rating. The primary challenge in rating a cyclical issuer is deciding when a fundamental shift in financial policy or a structural change in the operating environment has occurred that would necessitate a rating change.[118]

To sum up, ratings want to be cycle-neutral. They do not swing up and down with transient business or supply–demand conditions, or to reflect the last quarter's earnings report. This prevents, for instance, a security from being rated conservatively because of poor short-term performance if the issuer is expected to recover and prosper in the long term. This intended cycle-neutrality of ratings is one of the contributors to the stability of ratings.

---

[116] See Cantor, R., Hamilton, D.T., Ou, S., and Varma, P., 2005, Default and recovery rates of corporate bond issuers, 1920–2004, *Special Comment:* Moody's Investors Service, January, Report 91233, 1–40, Exhibits 17, 18 and 19.

[117] For example, Kaplan, R.S., and Urwitz, G., 1979, Statistical models of bond ratings: a methodological inquiry, *Journal of Business*, Vol. 52, No. 2, 231–261, use systematically a 5-year arithmetic average of all financial ratios they use to estimate the determinants of bond ratings because they 'believe that bond raters look beyond a single year's data to avoid temporary anomalies,' page 245.

[118] Fitch, 2006, Corporate rating methodology: corporate finance, *Criteria Report*, June 13, 1–7, page 2.

Ratings are Descriptive, not Prescriptive, of a Debt Situation

The optimal amount of debt for a company is adjustable from the perspective of the share-holder. The shareholder optimizes the amount that the firm should borrow in order to maximize shareholder value. In this quest, the shareholder may have a legitimate interest in pushing a company's ability to pay the amounts due to the limits. In so doing, the company would intentionally opt for a lower credit rating. For example, S&P reports that in 2006

> investment grade companies in Europe adopted more aggressive financial policies to satisfy shareholders and ward off potential acquirers. The largest 30 European nonfinancial issuers spent a staggering €149 billion on shareholder-driven activities. Consequently, debt levels at these firms are on the rise again as cash flows are no longer sufficient to finance these activities on top of regular capital expenditures. And cash flow as a percentage of total debt for these issuers declined to 29% from 33%. Overall, M&A contributed to about 40% of all downgrades involving European industrials, while a further 25% arose from changes to financial policies that increased value for shareholders.[119]

The shareholder trades off the cost of a lower credit rating against the benefits of more debt. This works as follows. Keeping business risk constant, corporate income taxes and the agency costs of equity favor increasing debt. But the corresponding increases in interest cost of debt, expected costs of financial distress, and agency costs of debt, push in the other direction. So somewhere there is an optimal debt-to-assets ratio that maximizes enterprise value to the benefit of the shareholders and minimizes a company's overall cost of capital.

To minimize the overall cost of capital, a firm does not need to minimize its cost of debt and maximize its credit rating. An issuer could probably achieve a lower cost of debt and a higher credit rating by moving away from its lowest cost of capital; it would just have to issue equity to retire debt. The ratings of the residual debt would probably increase, but so would the overall cost of capital to the firm because the cost of equity, or the required rate of return on equity, is always higher than that on debt. So the firm would have changed the mixture by replacing a cheap source of funds with an expensive one.

The optimal credit rating for a company's debt at a given point in time may be any-where from speculative to the safest investment grade.[120] Take, for example, the case of a corporate event (merger, acquisition, spin-off, financial restructuring, LBO, etc.). To enable the event, the company may very well have to go through a financing scheme that moves it opportunistically and temporarily away from its long-term sustainable financial struc-ture. For example, high debt financing of an acquisition leading to the issuance of below investment grade debt. The issuer rating may decline. This is not necessarily 'bad' in any normative sense for the company at that point in time, as long as after transitory financing reactions to a corporate event the company resumes to grow and develop along the path of its optimal debt-to-assets ratio. Thus, depending on a company's circumstances, a weak credit rating may be better than a strong one, or even none at all.

But, of course, that doesn't obliterate that ratings are relevant to financing choices. As a matter of fact, survey results find that for CFOs credit ratings are their second highest

---

[119] Quoted freely from Ganguin, B., and De Toytot, A., 2006, Private equity activity and uncertainty threaten the outlook for European credit quality in 2007, *Research:* Standard & Poor's, December 13, 1–7. The reference period is the 12 months ending June 30, 2006.
[120] Standard and Poor's, 1998, *Corporate Credit Ratings: A Guide*, page 2.

concern when determining their capital structure.[121] Ratings are not only a proxy for default risk and the concomitant cost of debt, they can also generate discrete costs and benefits to firms. CFOs do integrate ratings and possible rating changes in their financing choices. For example, some regulations reduce the liquidity of bonds when they move from investment to below investment grade. Demand drops in a discrete way, more than related to the changing risk characteristics of the bond. The cost of capital of the bonds makes a once and for all shift off the equilibrium risk–return security market line. This is a real once and for all sunk cost to the firm. CFOs will integrate the likelihood and extent of this occurrence when they weight the trade-offs between alternative sources of financing.

Thus ratings are relevant. And so are possible rating changes relevant for financial choices. For example, suppose it is known that a firm's rating is under review for a possible change. In other words, the fact of the review reveals to investors uncertainty surrounding the creditworthiness of the firm – to the better or the worse. This uncertainty makes not only fair public pricing harder than it would otherwise have been, but it can also give the issuer an edge over the market by having a better knowledge of the reasons and likely outcome of the review. In these circumstance, the CFO may very well wait to issue debt until the situation is clarified. Evidence finds that this is indeed the case. 'Firms near a credit rating upgrade or downgrade issue less debt relative to equity than firms not near a change in rating.'[122]

Nor does a rating say anything about the optimality of a sovereign debt. Speaking about an optimal sovereign rating could equally lead to errors in judgment. The level of successive public deficits is one instrument in an overall economic policy mix. What counts for the country is the optimality of the mix, not so much the rating of its public debt at a particular point in time or in relation to its neighbors. Not that this rating is irrelevant, but the policy objectives are at a higher level. The statement in S&P's rationale 'The downgrade [of Italy from AA− to A+ on October 19, 2006] reflects the new government's inadequate response to Italy's structural economic and fiscal challenges' leads in the wrong direction. By using the term 'inadequate,' it passes a value judgment about the optimality of Italy's public policies.[123] Focusing on the risk-shifting implications of that policy would have corresponded more closely to what a rating does. But the media tend to push CRAs into opinions of value judgment. On the Italian downgrade, to continue on the same example, two journalists wrote, 'The ratings agencies' move is a vote of no confidence in Prime Minister Romano Prodi's ability to tackle Italy's twin ills of slow growth and rising public spending.'[124] No opinion is formulated in the rating actions rationale about the Prime Minister's abilities in conducting the macroeconomic policy, so one should be extremely careful in shedding the right light on what a rating says.

Ratings Measure Credit Risk, they Don't Price It

Credit ratings *grade* credit risk. That Moody's puts this in its definition reminds us that ratings don't value the instrument. They couldn't, because default risk is only one factor of

---

[121] Graham, J.R., and Harvey, C.R., 2001, The theory and practice of corporate finance: evidence from the field, *Journal of Financial Economics*, May, Vol. 60, Issue 2–3, 187–243.

[122] Kisgen, D.J., 2006, Credit ratings and capital structure, *Journal of Finance*, June, Vol. 61, No. 3, 1035–1072.

[123] Standard & Poor's, 2006, Republic of Italy L-T rating cut to 'A+' from 'AA−' on poor fiscal prospects. *Research Update*, October 19, 1–3, page 1.

[124] Di Leo, L., and Perry, J., 2006. Italy credit downgrade may undermine euro zone, *Wall Street Journal*, October 20, page A4.

security risk. The other factor that drives the market value of the obligation is *market risk*, also known as *credit exposure*.[125]

Credit rating agencies and their ratings have little to say about market risk. As a result, bond prices live their own life, distinct from the life of bond ratings. Initial ratings and the yield at issuance tend to interact closely with each other, but thereafter, in the secondary market, yields and ratings are only occasionally synchronized.

Ratings change discretely, bond yields move continuously. They move sometimes with the market, and sometimes against the market. Figure 2.17 illustrates this by showing the yield to maturity, spread, and Moody's ratings of the France Telecom 6.25% Eurobond maturing on November 3, 2006.

Note that from January 1999 through April 2000, the yield to maturity on the France Telecom bond very closely followed that on an equal maturity benchmark French government bond. The yield on the France Telecom bond followed the cyclical increases in rates from May 1999 through March 2000 and reflected almost one-for-one the very short-term, small spikes or drops in the general level of interest rates during that period. The vertical

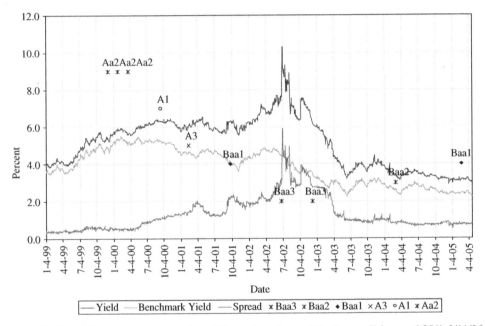

Figure 2.17   Yield to maturity, spread and Moody's ratings of the France Telecom 6.25% 3/11/06 bond (1999–2005).
Note: The Spread (over Benchmark). To calculate 'Spread,' the maturity and yield of a bond is compared with the equivalent government benchmark bond for the bond's currency of denomination. The spread is expressed as yield difference (bond minus benchmark) in basis points. Because the maturities for most of the bonds for which the spread is calculated will not exactly match the maturity of the available government benchmark bonds, linear interpolation is used to estimate the yield of a government benchmark with the same maturity as the bond that is analyzed.
Source: Thomson Datastream, author analysis.

---

[125] Jorion, P., 2001, *Value at Risk*, second edition, McGraw-Hill, New York, 1–544, page 314.

distance between the two series remained more or less constant, as one can see in the spread series.

But then, things changed. It seems that in May 2000, the France Telecom yield started living a life of its own, disconnecting from the general interest rate movement. In fact, while the general level of interest rates started declining, the France Telecom rate increased. It stayed high at around 6% while the general rates dropped to below 4% in November 2001. By then the France Telecom spread had more than quintupled to slightly over 200 bps. The divergence continued to increase, reaching a spread peak of almost 600 bps, with France Telecom bonds yielding about 10%, whereas the general rates stayed at 4%. After a period of hesitation and ups and downs, the stable, pre-May 2000 relationship re-established itself, albeit at a higher spread.

The ratings of this bond invite two quite typical observations describing the relationship between ratings and credit spreads. Firstly, through the cycle of credit spreads – stable, then deteriorating, followed by recovery and then again stabilizing – the ratings show a similar overall pattern. Secondly, the ratings do not reflect the very short-term changes in credit spread at all, unless exceptionally, as in October 2000 or July 2002. In other words, ratings reflect changes in creditworthiness discontinuously and in discrete steps, while the bond market reflects these changes continuously, with marginal steps.

Credit Ratings are . . . Credit Ratings, not Equity Ratings

Many of the analytical tools that credit rating analysts use are also used by equity analysts, yet credit ratings are quite different from equity ratings. Ratings deal with an obligor's ability to make full and timely payments of amounts due from the perspective of a creditor's interests, with a particular eye on possible delays and payment shortfalls.

Credit ratings focus on the downside risk. Bondholders require regular revenues and their money back. Equity analysis looks more at the upside potential of a company. For example, a highly leveraged transaction may boost the share price of a company (good for the equity holders) but the extra debt taken on may decrease cash flow and could even lead to insolvency or bankruptcy.

Credit ratings look more deeply into the future than financial analyst equity ratings (2-year window before and after). At the very least, they are expected to give an opinion of the creditworthiness of the company during the lifetime of the security being rated. Equity reports often focus on current earnings announcements, or on the expected performance of a stock over the next 6 to 12 months (the so-called target price).

With some forms of debt, credit analysis is a combination of macroeconomic, equity and credit research. Consider, for example, high-yield debt, which is considered to be a hybrid source of financing between equity and debt. As a European high-yield telecom analyst at Morgan Stanley puts it, 'the high-yield investor focuses on the upside as does the equity holder, but a high-yield investor is still much more concerned about asset protection on the downside.'[126] Or take variable coupon and/or inflation-linked and/or income bonds, for which the dues are fixed according to a formula rather than in amounts: the ratings analysts will pay great attention to the drivers and their impact on the dues, e.g. fluctuations in short-term interest rates, inflation, and relevant income.

---

[126] Ramakrishnan, B., 1999, quoted in Telling the wheat from the chaff by Bream, R., *Euromoney*, April, Issue 360, 128–134, page 42.

2.3.3 Special Issues

A Credit Rating as Opinion: Accountability and Contestability

Credit ratings are fundamentally forward-looking. They are not statements of historical fact but rather the rating agent's judgment about the degree of credit risk. Ratings are not performance guarantees. They are beliefs about the downside risks surrounding promised future outcomes. Because the future cannot be known, credit ratings are, by nature, opinions, and necessarily come with various degrees of uncertainty.

Credit ratings are neither market ratings nor investment advice. Unlike sell side analyst research reports, they are not buy, sell, or hold recommendations, and do not take into account yield, price, other market factors, or specific investor risk preferences. They are intended only to measure the risk of credit loss, not the appetite for risk nor the liquidity with which the risk can be traded.

However non-controversial these characterizations are, they have a deep implication about immunity. How accountable is a CRA for its rating? Are there any legal means to contest a rating? There is a firm position of the CRAs about that: they naturally point out that their role in rating is not that of a consultant giving private investment advice but rather one of expressing openly to the public at large an opinion about the creditworthiness of a borrower. 'They, therefore, conclude that they act in a journalistic capacity, consequently they should be protected by the principles of the freedom of the Press' (in the US specifically by the First Amendment of the US Constitution, a claim that has been tested and upheld in American courts).[127]

This raises a thorny issue due to the regulatory uses of ratings.[128] This use leads to the following equally natural argument made by a European legislator: 'Freedom of the press implies the right, on the part of the public, to ignore the opinions expressed in the press without suffering legal consequences. This is not the case with the opinions expressed by rating agencies, since an investment grade rating is a prerequisite for being able to place one's bonds with institutional investors.'[129] Some institutional investors impose voluntary internal portfolio governance rules that refer to ratings, other have such rules imposed by law and regulations, as we will review in Chapter 9.

The resolution of the ensuing tension between producers and users of ratings is not seen at the horizon. The tension exists and can be material. The rating of a bond affects its regulatory eligibility for certain institutional portfolios. Hence, a rating change may impose sunk portfolio adjustment costs on regulated portfolios. Negligently maintaining too high a rating could cause losses for the portfolio beneficiaries that the ratings-based regulations were supposed to protect. The stakeholders in these portfolios thus argue reasonably that they have a product quality right over the ratings. How can we reconcile CRAs' rights under freedom of the Press and rating users rights of rating quality as a consequence of the regulatory uses of ratings? Many reactions in the aftermath of the reverses that the CRAs suffered with the Asian ratings crisis of 1997, the spectacular unpredicted corporate bankruptcies in 2001–2002, and the ongoing subprime mortgage related crisis are an expression of these tensions. But they have not yet been addressed head on, probably

---

[127] Katiforis, G., 2004, Report on role and methods of rating agencies, European Parliament, January 29, Session document A5-0040/2004, 1–11, page 10.

[128] To be discussed in detail in Chapter 9.

[129] Katiforis, G., 2004, Report on role and methods of rating agencies, European Parliament, January 29, Session document A5-0040/2004, 1–11, page 11.

Exhibit 2.7 Differences between rating agencies and auditors (2005).

Very different roles, processes and uses

Auditors:
- 'Pass–fail' grade on reporting of *historical periods*
- Externally prescribed content and processes
- Passing grade needed for many regulatory purposes
- Commoditization of services can *require* access to information

Rating agencies:
- Multiple levels of opinion about *future* creditworthiness with indicative information (outlooks and watchlists)
- Prescribe own content and process methodologies
- Limited use in regulation (except in United States)
- Need to avoid CRA or ECAI legislation or regulation prescribing static or commoditizing methodologies
- Receive information that is voluntarily provided by issuers

---

Source: Rutherfurd Jr, J., Senior Adviser – Moody's Corporation, 2005. Rating agencies and auditors, IOSCO Technical Committee meeting Panel 5: *Securities Regulation and Financial Stability – Learning the Lessons of Recent Corporate Failures*, Frankfurt, Germany, October 6, 1–18, page 17.

because they are too complex to easily resolve. It may have to start with a rethinking of the regulatory uses of ratings, a subject that is just starting to be considered for the agenda very recently.

Rating Agencies and Auditors: Insurance

Rating agencies and auditors play highly distinguishable roles, use different processes, and produce different outcomes. Exhibit 2.7 summarizes these differences.

Auditors grade the reporting of historical periods and assign a pass–fail grade to a current situation. In contrast, rating agencies express a forward-looking opinion about future periods. In practice, auditors work with the audited firm until it earns a pass grade, because companies tend to be reluctant to report a financial condition that fails the auditors' tests. Auditing is labor-intensive and therefore time consuming, so the markets often become aware of near-fail grades through delays in the publication of financial statements.

Rating agencies give multiple levels of forward-looking opinions, nuanced with indicative ancillary information. Ratings are normally made public, and once a company has been rated, it will be constantly monitored and any adjustments in rating announced. There are two exceptions. The first concerns an already rated company, where a CRA might produce private and confidential rating assessments for specific clients who wish to understand particular issues. The second concerns unrated companies, where a CRA client can request a rating and keep that rating private if so desired, i.e. the CRA has no right to disclose it and the company has no duty to do so.

Auditors can require access to information that CRAs cannot. They have a legal right to request certain data and to establish certain facts. Rating agencies rely on information provided voluntarily by issuers. The CRA does not walk around the business as an auditor does. Many areas are off-limits to the CRA, few are off-limits for the auditor.

Rating Agencies and Detectives: Company Fraud

Parmalat was an Italian success story. Having inherited the business from his father in 1960, Calizo Tanzi brought the Tetra Pak to Italy and revolutionized the milk distribution business. By the end of the 1960s, Parmalat was a nationwide brand, and during the next 20 years expanded enormously overseas, eventually going public in 1990. But business analysts began to suspect Parmalat's figures in 2003, particularly the levels of debt. When Parmalat's accountants were forced to admit that they could not certify the accounts, top management ordered all evidence of financial activities to be destroyed. On December 19, 2003, a Parmalat press release indicated that Bank of America has denied the authenticity of a document used to certify the existence of about €3.95 billion of securities and bank deposits. These represented almost all of the firm's liquidity. Immediately, S&P withdrew its rating on Parmalat 'as the reliability of all key information supporting a credit opinion is now questioned.' Default on a bond payment followed on December 27, 2003, and Tanzi was soon imprisoned. Investigations revealed that Parmalat's accounts had been falsified for 13 years, and that Tanzi had probably siphoned almost €1 billion out of his once-proud company.[130,131]

Rating agencies rely on financial transparency from the rated obligors, but 'fraud is an extreme form of lack of transparency or false transparency.'[132] Some of the largest expected losses from recent defaults, WorldCom, Inc. $25.3 billion in 2002, Enron Corporation $8.5 billion in 2001, and Adelphia Communications Corporation $4.5 billion in 2002, included fraud.[133] And until six days prior to its default on December 3, 2001, Enron was still rated investment grade B2/B−. So was WorldCom (Ba2/BB) until almost three months before its July 17, 2002 default. WorldCom was rated as having strong capacity to meet financial commitments and Enron as having adequate capacity−both investment grade ratings. Three months prior to its May 20, 2002 default on interest payments, Adelphia had the weaker B2/B below investment grade status, rated as being more vulnerable to adverse conditions, but with a current capacity to meet financial obligations. None of the three was considered to be currently highly vulnerable, or even vulnerable, but they later declared bankruptcy. Is, then, the probability of fraud not a relevant risk factor that CRAs should have integrated in their ratings?

Credit ratings analysis is not a means for auditing for fraud. Were the CRAs not at fault for not having detected fraud? Definitively not, is the answer of the CRA industry.[134]

---

[130] Standard & Poor's, 2003, Parmalat Finanziaria SpA *Research Update*, December 19, page 1.

[131] It is worth recalling that Parmalat bond spreads did not sharply widen in the months leading up to its default.

[132] Rutherfurd Jr, J., Senior Adviser – Moody's Corporation, 2005, Rating agencies and auditors, IOSCO Technical committee meeting Panel 5: Securities regulation and financial stability – learning the lessons of recent corporate failures, Frankfurt, Germany, October 6, 1–18, page 4.

[133] Expected losses are measured as Amount defaulted × (1 − the recovery rate), the recovery rate being defined as bond price/par one month after default, not eventual recovery. Eventual recoveries may be larger or smaller than recoveries given. See Rutherfurd Jr, J., Senior Adviser – Moody's Corporation, 2005, Rating agencies and auditors, IOSCO Technical committee meeting Panel 5: Securities regulation and financial stability – learning the lessons of recent corporate failures, Frankfurt, Germany, October 6, 1–18, pages 5–6.

[134] McDaniel, R., President of Moody's Investor Services, 2005, Examining the role of credit rating agencies in the capital markets, Testimony before the US senate committee on banking, housing and urban affairs, February 8, 1–14, page 9.

Ratings are based on publicly available information and on private information willingly provided by the issuer. The CRA's financial analysis is based largely on the audited financial statements, with the exception of the most recent quarterly reports. Credit rating agencies thus rely on the auditors to assure the veracity of the public information with which they work. To avoid duplication of professional effort, rating agencies do not perform detailed verification of information obtained about the issuer, and the CRAs do not repeat the work of the auditors. Nevertheless, in the aftermath of the 2001–2003 reverses, the major CRAs recruited specially trained accountants to conduct forensic accounts analysis on issuers. The credit analysts can call upon these in-house forensic experts to support them with the interpretation of the financial statements on which they do their credit analysis.

Individual cases of ratings failure, particularly when occasioned by fraud, are not in themselves evidence of the failure of a rating agency. Ratings reflect the chance or probability of default; they do not predict if and when a default will happen in any individual case. In appropriate support of that, the European legislator argues that a system can only be said to have failed 'if the number of occasions of default diverges markedly from the benchmark for that rating or if grounds of suspicion of fraud in specific egregious cases were too obvious to be neglected.'[135]

The CRAs do of course have the option to refuse to rate. They can withdraw existing ratings when the information on which to base the rating is deemed inadequate and/or unreliable, as S&P did in the case of Parmalat.

2.4 CREDIT RATINGS: SUMMARY AND CONCLUSIONS

A Credit Rating is a Holistic, Relative, Highly Specialized Opinion

Credit rating agencies offer a product that is an opinion about credit risk, and which respects a set of minimum standards of objectivity, consistency, comparability, stability, and transparency. The agencies provide the market with an independent heuristic of creditworthiness, based on company fundamentals, that indicates gradations of creditworthiness, making it easy for credit investors to compare different potential investments without undertaking their own credit analysis.

True Ratings Measure Credit Risk and Should Not Price It

There is no paradigm shift from fundamental ordinal ratings to market-implied cardinal ratings. These two are complementary. Cardinal estimated default probabilities are mapped in fundamental ordinal ratings and add additional insight when interpreting ratings, but the ratings themselves retain the characteristics of fundamental ratings.

---

[135] Katiforis, G., 2004, Report on role and methods of rating agencies, European Parliament, January 29, Session document A5-0040/2004, 1–11, page 6.

3

The *Raison d'Être* of Credit Ratings and their Market

Why do credit ratings exist? Who needs them? What is the scale and scope of their applications? Credit ratings are an information good at the intersection between borrowers and investors, respectively the demand and supply for capital. Providers and users of ratings all agree that they are an opinion on the relative ability of an entity to meet a financial commitment. This chapter explains in sequence the different needs that credit ratings satisfy – each actually corresponding to a somewhat distinct function of credit ratings, the original economic function of credit ratings, and the current rated universe in terms of issuers, products, and regions. More specifically, we distinguish in Section 3.1 the three different functions of ratings and follow through on how issuers, investors, and prescribers use them. After this description, we provide in Section 3.2.3 a more formal economic analysis of a credit rating as a solution to information asymmetry, what we refer to as the original and fundamental function of credit ratings. In Section 3.3, we describe along three segment categories – issuers, products, and geography – the current scale and scope of the rating universe that follows from the demand for ratings.

3.1 NEEDS FOR CREDIT RATINGS – OR THE DEMAND SIDE OF RATINGS

Many economic agents need credit ratings in a variety of ways. This section provides an overview of the various ways by which credit ratings bring value to market participants, to capital markets, and the economy in general. Credit ratings shorten the distance between lenders and borrowers because they satisfy needs on both sides. Investors need information on the quality of their investments and issuers need access to funds. Satisfying these needs facilitates optimal investment decisions on the part of investors and optimal issuing decisions on the part of borrowers. For the former, a credit rating reduces the cost of information; for the latter, it reduces the cost of market access.

Investors and issuers have a direct stake in ratings as principals. They are the market participants that rating agencies consider fundamentally as their clients. To these users, ratings aim to achieve the somewhat conflicting objectives of accuracy, comparability of rating information, timeliness, and stability of the rating actions. Prescribers have a stake in ratings as they use ratings as contractual references in, for instance, investment guidelines or regulatory activities. Although prescribers are not clients of the rating agencies, they use ratings extensively and hence are an important driver of the demand for ratings. This section outlines the various functions of ratings for the main categories of users that demand them.

A rating's first function is to objectively *measure the credit risk* of the issuer's business and its debt financing and to resolve information asymmetry about it. This is the *raison d'être* of credit ratings, or what we referred to as the original economic function of credit ratings. In the development of the credit rating industry, this function was initially performed by credit reporting, which essentially consists in describing an issuer's ability to meet its financial obligations, but not necessarily in the form of a rating. Information asymmetry describes the fact that the two parties in an economic transaction do not have access to the same information. The concept has special power when the two parties do not have incentives to reveal all the information relevant to the other party. This is a fundamental issue in finance and many other fields in economics as it plagues many transactions. At a macroeconomic level, credit ratings enhance capital market efficiency and transparency by reducing the information asymmetry between borrowers and lenders. In this function, the demand for ratings is driven by the fact that ratings are a measure of an underlying default probability, and the more accurate the rating in terms of predictive power of default, the better it will lift information asymmetry and the more value-added it will bring to its users. This is the function that issuers are most willing to pay for, as we explain in Section 3.1.1.

The second function of ratings is to provide a *means of comparison* between all issues of the credit risks embedded in them. Indeed, a large part of the production process of rating agencies, especially global ones, is the consistency of the rating scale across all possible types of issues. This is the function investors are most willing to pay for as they rely on ratings to constitute portfolios. The demand for ratings driven by investors is reviewed in Section 3.1.2.

Lastly, the third function is that ratings from a given credit rating agency provides market participants a *common standard* or language to refer to credit risk. A rating is an independent credit opinion expressed in a single contractible measure. By contractible we mean that a rating from a given rating agency is both *observable* and *verifiable*.[1] Observable means that it is public and all parties in a contract can observe it at a given point in time, in the same unambiguous way. Verifiable means that a court can acknowledge the level of a given credit rating at any given point in time. Hence a contract clause based on an observable and verifiable measure can be enforced in court. In a statistical sense, a credit rating aggregates the likelihood of all the future contingencies where an issuer is unable or unwilling to meet its financial commitments. However, future states of nature cannot all be foreseen, cannot all be described, at least in a contractible way, and are uncountable.[2] This makes the nature of a credit rating unique. It is not just a credit report that bridges the information asymmetry and rank orders issues by increasing risk. It does so, but in a particular way: by concentrating a mass of private and public information that is payoff relevant to the investor into one single contractible measure. It is because of this contractibility feature that credit ratings are used by so many agents other than issuers and investors directly. We review this application of ratings by prescribers in Section 3.1.3.

---

[1] Here we refer to ratings from agencies that have an issuer-pays subscription model. Indeed, subscription based ratings are not publicly observable; they are only observable to parties who pay the rating agency.

[2] Unforeseen contingencies and undescribable states of nature are often invoked bases for the incomplete contracting literature in economics pioneered among others, by, Coase, R.H., 1937, The nature of the firm, *Economica*, 4, 1–44; Williamson, O., 1975, *Markets and Hierarchies: Analysis of Antitrust Implications*, New York, Free Press; and Grossman, S., and Hart, O., 1986, The costs and benefits of ownership: a theory of lateral and vertical integration, *Journal of Political Economy*, Vol. 94, 691–719. Interestingly, Maskin, E., and Tirole, J., 1999, Unforeseen contingencies and incomplete contracts, *Review of Economic Studies*, Vol. 66, 83–114, argue that '[the incomplete contract literature] usually assumes that contractual incompleteness is due to transactions costs of describing – or even foreseeing – the possible states of nature in advance. We argue, however, that such transaction costs need not interfere with optimal contracting (i.e. transactions costs need not be *relevant*) provided that agents can probabilistically forecast their possible future *payoffs* (even if other aspects of the state of nature cannot be forecast). In other words, all that is required for optimality is that agents be able to perform dynamic programming (...).' The nature of credit ratings is to forecast the event of default which is the critical event to determine possible future payoffs. This research justifies the use of credit ratings in writing complete contracts, and hence the efficiency enhancing aspects of using ratings in contracts and guidelines.

The three distinct functions of ratings as *a measure of credit risk*, as *a means of comparison* between issues, and as *a common standard to refer* to credit risk are complementary.[3] These functions are often difficult to disentangle and are complementary in the sense that the demand for one of the functions of ratings is enhanced by the fact that ratings fulfill the three functions. For instance, the function of measuring credit risk could be provided by just a credit report or a grade, but if this grade is not comparable across all issues it will be of small use to investors. Similarly, if the grade or rating is comparable across issues but is not observable publicly, as is the case for subscriber-paid credit ratings (an investor pays an agency to privately get a rating on a given issue), the total economic value-added of the rating is smaller than if the rating had all three functions embedded. Fundamental, issuer-pays credit ratings, from global rating agencies have all three functions.

3.1.1 Principals: Issuers/Borrowers

Issuers' demand for ratings is essentially driven by the fundamental function of credit rating that provides a measure of credit risk. Issuers need to inform investors that they are creditworthy.

Credit ratings deal with all sorts of obligors. These have different capacities as issuers of fixed income securities, those that entail predetermined commitments by their issuer to disburse predefined amounts at preset dates to their holders. For some issues – such as variable coupons, inflation protected, or income debt – the exact amount of the dues are not rigidly prefixed, but formula-fixed. They are thus fixed income for our purposes because the exact functions that determine the future disbursements are prefixed.

These issuers include four main categories: corporates, incorporated asset pools, financial institutions, and governmental bodies. For corporates, 'the most important factors affecting debt policy are maintaining financial flexibility and having a good credit rating.'[4] This is particularly the case for large firms that are in the Fortune 500.

Why should any of these issuers seek a costly credit rating? A rating is expensive in direct and indirect costs. Directly, the agency charges a fee for rating a company. Indirectly it is intrusive and time-consuming. An agency scrutinizes the company in depth and accesses significant confidential information, and management at several levels, from the top down, are involved.

Some rating requests or minimum rating objectives are simply *business driven,* regardless of costs. A reinsurance company needs to keep a rating of A or higher to be able to underwrite new reinsurance treaties ... and to maintain it to avoid seeing its contracts being cancelled.[5] SCOR, for instance, the ninth largest global reinsurance group, had several reverses

---

[3] As an analogy, one can think of the three functions of money: as a store of value (comparable to a measure of credit risk), medium of exchange (means of comparison) and unit of account (common standard to refer to credit risk). One could then think of the three main agencies' ratings being comparable to three competing currencies, where in some countries or issue segments one currency dominates the others depending on whether it is widely accepted (has investors' confidence). An issuer's demand for a given agency's rating will depend on the value it will get from the rating, or the market spread that will correspond to the rating on the given instrument. The spread will be driven by how well the agency's rating performs its three functions.

[4] Graham, J.R., and Harvey, C., 1993. The theory and practice of corporate finance: evidence from the field, *Journal of Financial Economics*, May, Vol. 60, Issue 2–3, 187–243; Version: July 29, 1999, page 2. Table 5 reports that in 1999, out of a large cross-section of approximately 4440 US firms, for 57.10% of a representative sample of 392 Chief Financial Officers the credit rating is important to very important in choosing the appropriate amount of debt for their firm. This is second most important out of 14 possible factors, the No. 1 factor being financial flexibility (important to very important to 59.38% of the respondents).

[5] Chart 1, Global reinsurance companies rating distribution, 2005 and 2006, documents that more than 70% of reinsurers have an A rating or more, according to S&P, 2006, Industry Report Card: global reinsurance companies bounce back from a catastrophe riddled 2005, *Research*, April 5, page 3/12.

in 2001–2002 leading to a cumulative loss of about 71% of its total equity in two years and ratings downgrade to BBB− in November 2003. This restricted SCOR's access to primary rating sensitive insurance markets outside of its core areas, from which it eventually withdrew. To be able to participate in money market trading banks will typically need an AA counter-party rating. Local authorities that invite banks to tender for the opportunity to give credit may request that the tendering bank has a rating above a certain threshold. Or distribution contracts between a distributor and a product manufacturer may be conditional on the supplier maintaining a minimum credit rating. In addition to these business-driven requests for a rating, any issuer may seek a rating for one or more of the following reasons.

Some businesses or deals would not even exist without ratings. Take incorporated pools of cash flow generating financial assets. Because the structured finance market is rated by definition, the demand drivers of ratings in this segment are directly related to the demand for structured finance instruments.

SF VIGNETTE 2

Originators' Supply of Structured Finance Instruments (*and Demand for Capital and Credit Ratings*)

We refer here to an originator, in its general economic sense, as an issuer of a specific type of security: structured finance instruments.[6] We are interested here in understanding the value drivers of structured finance instruments to its issuers, that is, the party who captures the value from the selling of the tranches. As we have discussed previously, the originator does not directly issue structured finance instruments such as ABSs or CDOs, it only does so through an SPV. Also, it is the fundamental characteristics of structured finance that we have mentioned previously: the *pooling of the assets*, the *delinking of the assets from the credit risk of the originator* and *the tranching of the notes* issued against the pool of assets, that are at the heart of the originator's specific demand for capital in the form of a supply of structured finance instruments. How do the pooling, delinking and tranching create value, partially captured by the issuer-originator?

Firstly, pooling enables the transformation of illiquid assets into liquid shares in them. Suppose a single type tradeable security with pro-rata title to all the value in the segregated pool is issued against the pool. Clearly, in that case, the individual illiquid assets – the individual loans in the pool – are transformed into shares of a liquid asset: the securities issued by the pool. These securities are easier, cheaper, and less risky to trade than the illiquid assets in the pool, which increases their total value above the sum of the illiquid values of the assets in the pool. As a consequence, the market re-rates the value of the pool and the illiquidity discount is removed. For example, where the price of a highly liquid bond is 100, the market price of its otherwise fully identical illiquid counterpart could very well be as low as 90, depending on characteristics and circumstances. Conversely, transforming an illiquid pool of credit card receivables into a liquid pool of ABSs re-rates the value of the pool, easily by more than 5%. This potential profit margin offers originators a sufficient incentive to securitize these pools. In principle, the improved risk evaluation of a whole pool of assets and the increased liquidity of the securities issued by the pool, explain

---

[6] More strictly speaking, in finance, an originator is a party that in its regular course of business originates financial assets by either granting loans or underwriting newly issued securities to sell to investors.

the benefits of pooling, common to the traditional pass-through securitization without structuring.

Moreover, the pooling of assets and the portion of the pool retained by the originator serves as a signal that allows for the resolution of adverse selection between the originator and investors.[7] The adverse selection issue in question is that the originator has private information regarding the quality of the assets it would like to sell, and the investors are less informed. In this setting it is known that the portion of an asset that an issuer sells serves as a signal of its quality and is a decreasing function of its quality.[8] Hence, an informed originator could prefer to sell each asset individually rather than selling them in a pool, as it can then maximize the benefit of having private information by optimally choosing the portion it sells of each individual asset – assuming that the originator does not sell portions of assets in a pool, or that the signaling effect of the retained portion of an asset is lost, it is an ('information destruction' effect). However, depending on the originator's type of private information, the positive diversification effect may be greater than the information destruction effect of pooling. This would be the case, for instance, if the private information on the asset values in a pool is general, in the sense that it is correlated across assets, then pooling is preferred to selling the assets individually. The portion of the whole pool of assets that the originator sells then serves as a signal regarding the quality of the pool as an entity. In particular, originators' investment in the equity tranche of an SPV serves as an important signal regarding the quality of the asset pool. Mortgage-backed securities (MBS) are such a case, where the originator's or arranger's private information is rather general (or correlated across the assets in the pool). MBS are then, accordingly, natural candidates to pooling, as the early wave of pass-through securitization of mortgages in the 1970s suggests.

Secondly, the de-linking of the assets from its originator allows a transaction to be very carefully circumscribed through an SPV. As a result, the scope for misaligned governance incentives is reduced to its minimum. Hence, the delinked assets and the notes issued by the SPV are isolated as much as possible from the credit risk management – and potential moral hazard involved in it – of the parties involved in the transaction. In particular, the overall credit risk of the pool of assets in such a structured transaction is better defined than that of the originator.

Thirdly, the tranching of the notes based on the pool of assets allows for the subtle resolution of adverse selection between informed investors and uninformed investors.[9] This occurs when investors have different degrees of information regarding the quality of the assets sold. This adverse selection is specifically alleviated by selling assets together

---

[7] The concept of adverse selection in the lending relationship is reviewed in Section 3.2.2.

[8] This is the classical result of Leland, H. and Pyle, H., 1977, Informational asymmetries, financial structure, and financial intermediation, *Journal of Finance*, Vol. 32, No. 2, pages 371–387. In a more general corporate setting, it is shown that when the owners of a firm or project have private information about a project, the portion of their own funds invested in the project will be interpreted as a signal of its quality. In equilibrium, the higher the quality of the project, the greater the portion of equity that will be retained by the owner, and the higher the market valuation of the firm.

[9] This discussion on adverse selection issues in pooling and tranching of securities is essentially based on DeMarzo, P., 2005, The pooling and tranching of securities: a model of informed intermediation, *Review of Financial Studies*, Vol. 18, No. 1, 1–35. Further fundamental references on the topic are: Boot, A. and Thakor, A. 1993. Security design, *Journal of Finance*, Vol. 48, 1349–1378; DeMarzo, P. and Duffie, D., 1999, A liquidity-based model of security design, *Econometrica*, Vol. 67, No. 1, 65–99. A useful literature review is: Mitchell, J., 2004, Financial intermediation theory and the sources of value in structured finance markets, Working Paper, National Bank of Belgium, pages 1–13.

as a pool. When uninformed investors know that they are competing with informed investors who can identify and buy the highest quality assets, they are willing to pay less for the assets that are available to them. Uninformed investors require a premium when investing alongside informed investors to compensate for the fact that informed investors can identify the high-quality assets available on the market, leaving the uninformed investors with a lower average quality of assets to invest in. The pooling of assets before their placement mitigates this problem as informed investors are then less able to adversely select the individual assets for which they have positive information. The tranching of the pool of assets improves upon the mere pooling as it allows for investors with different amounts of information and risk preferences to invest in the same pool of assets while the adverse selection problem amongst them is substantially reduced.[10]

More generally, a rating gives the issuer *access* to the public bond markets. It thereby opens up a wider range of funding alternatives in terms of size, length of maturity, geographic market, diversity of instruments and investor base, range of currencies and covenant packages.[11] This is so true that firms with ratings have 35% more debt, ceteris paribus.[12] This reduces an issuer's capital rationing, making it less reliant on one particular set of creditors, giving it more flexibility in times when credit becomes tight. Ratings can also be helpful for a firm that is negotiating leases or other long-term contracts. It is quicker and easier to establish the credibility and financial standing of a firm when an independent opinion is available from one of the rating agencies. A strong rating can be an important asset that a bidder brings to the party in discussions with a would-be target.

Consider now the Russian MDM Bank that, in the fall of 2006, had an Issuer Credit rating and Senior Unsecured instrument ratings of BB− or below investment grade.[13] In 2006 it used an SPV to issue $430 million asset-backed Irish loan notes to refinance a loan book consisting of 34 623 Russian auto loans with an average outstanding Auto Loan value of $13 357. Of the loan notes, 6.3% were a non-rated subordinated loan of MDM Bank; and 12.7% were C Notes rated BB, still below investment grade but already one notch above MDM Bank. Then, the B Notes, 18% of the total, were rated BBB and the A Notes, 63.0% of the total, were rated A−, both above investment grade and several notches above MDM Bank. The overall weighted average rating (WAR) for all the Notes was about BBB, investment grade. In other words, by pooling the loans, de-linking them from MDM Bank's own credit risk and tranching the Notes, MDM improved the overall credit rating of the funding of its car loan book by approximately four notches. In October 2006, that corresponded to a ceteris paribus reduction in credit spread of about 150 bps or about $6 million per year gross. The subordinated loan represented a 6.3% equity buffer that MDM Bank retained in the transaction, significantly less than the different

---

[10] As described more extensively in Section 2.3.2, a potential driver for the supply of structured finance instruments is that the bulk of the tranched pool, that is rated AAA because the credit risk is very low, is actually overpriced given that, conditional on defaulting they will systematically default in bad economic states. The overpricing would occur because investors in fixed-income tend to be myopic and focus excessively on expected returns and ratings. This creates an arbitrage opportunity for originators who will then have the incentive to supply a large volume of structured instruments and senior tranches more specifically. Coval, J., Jurek, J., and Stafford, E., 2007, Economic catastrophe bonds, Working Paper, July, pages 1−42 estimate that investors in senior CDO tranches are grossly undercompensated for the highly systematic nature of the risks they bear.

[11] As noted above, the US capital markets provide borrowers with longer-term funds and a vast pool of institutional investors. In addition, bond covenants for issuers tend to be less onerous than covenants which commercial banks demand of borrowers.

[12] Faulkender, M., and Peterson, M., 2006, Does the source of capital affect capital structure?, *Review of Financial Studies*, Vol. 19, No. 14, 45−79, page 45.

[13] Both these ratings were Global Scale S&P ratings: Foreign Currency.

levels of its own equity capitalization.[14] The rated Notes, sold to global investors, allowed MDM Bank, through the Taganka Loan Finance Plc, to reach into the global capital markets much more broadly, and at a cheaper cost, than it would otherwise have been able to. This illustrates both the originators' supply of structured finance instruments, and concomitantly their demand for credit ratings, to improve the terms of access to capital markets. The following vignette shows the transaction structure as a typical classical, static asset-backed vehicle to buy cash by selling structured finance instruments.

SF VIGNETTE 3

New Issue – Taganka Car Loan Finance Plc $403.025 million Asset-Backed Floating-rate Notes

Figure 3.1 presents the whole structure of the Taganka SPV transaction, providing an opportunity to emphasize each party's economic function, legal function and relationship to the structure and to illustrate the different financial flows.

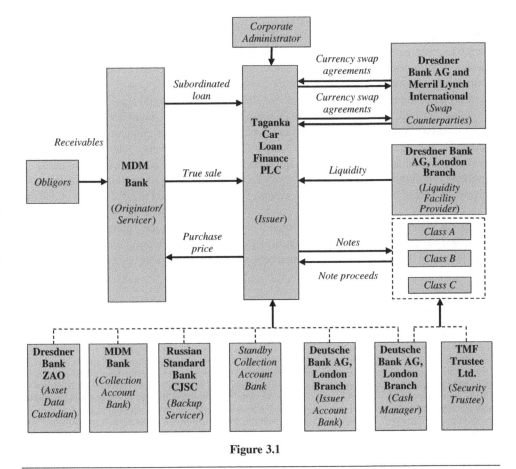

Figure 3.1

---

[14] Depending on the exact ratio used, that capitalization was 15.2 to 22.9%.

Ratings can help companies to *compete*. For this reason alone they take them very seriously. Credit ratings and credit spreads tend to be negatively correlated. Issuers will thus tend to want a higher rating rather than a lower one in order to pay a lower yield at issue and economize on interest expenses. For example, in the fall of 2006 Toyota Motor Corporation's LT Issuer Rating was Aaa, compared with Caa1 for General Motors Corporation. Depending on the specific characteristics of the instruments, GM's cost of debt would at least be 300 bps more than Toyota's, already otherwise a lower cost competitor to GM. Other things being equal, as higher ratings are associated with a lower cost of capital, they can become a real advantage when competing in the product market . . . and vice versa. In fact, for some borrowers success of an issue may mean 'a tighter spread relative to a competior.'[15] In the Toyota case, the AAA rating is both the product of its business and financial success as a purposeful strategy of an efficient just-in-time manufacturer. Just-in-time manufacturing requires close coordination between the assembler or manufacturer and parts supplier. Toyota's supplier should be willing to make major relationship-specific investments only if it is confident enough that Toyota will be around long enough to sustain its business. Having a high credit rating is then part of the Toyota business model and contributes toward sustaining it. On the other hand, there is also a strategic effect that can accompany a higher leverage than a pure direct cost reduction effect would suggest. Indeed a higher leverage, and hence a lower rating, can serve as a commitment device for a firm to be more aggressive in the product market. In this case the rating, in its contractibility function, strengthens the commitment in that it makes the commitment publicly and unambiguously observable.[16]

A rating gives the company *name recognition*. This by itself is also invaluable for a company. A large, established, locally well-known company may be able to issue debt in its domestic public market without a rating. In the Eurobond market, for example, companies raising capital traditionally did not need a credit rating,[17] and well-known borrowers could easily raise large amounts of capital from the proverbial Belgian dentist based on name recognition alone.[18] The dentist is still there, but industry has globalized and bond issues have become too large to be absorbed locally by retail investors. Nowadays, local names need to raise capital in distant markets where they are unknown. A company well known in Benelux will not be able to raise capital in the US public market without a credit rating. Investors, particularly large US institutional ones, demand credit ratings for international issuers entering the US market.[19] If they want to tap the international bond markets, such companies will have difficulty raising

---

[15] John Winter, head of European investment banking at Barclays Capital, as quoted in Oakley, D., 2007, Ford bond a matter of timing, February 14, *Financial Times*, page 41.

[16] See for instance the classic reference: Brander, J., and Lewis, T., 1986, Oligopoly and financial structure: the limited liability effect, *American Economic Review*, December, Vol. 76, No. 5, 956–970.

[17] A Eurobond is an international bond denominated in a currency other than that of the country where the bond is issued. The country of issue is determined by reference to the location of the investment bank that is structuring the issue. If the London office of Morgan Stanley Dean Witter (a US investment bank) structures a US$ bond issue for a French company this is considered to be a Eurobond. If the same French company issues a US$ bond that is structured by the New York office of Morgan Stanley, the bond is known as a 'Yankee bond' and will be subject to different SEC enforced rules and regulations. The Eurobond market is generally considered to be centred in London, however, Eurobonds can be issued in any country as long as the above definition is complied with. The Eurobond market is a much less regulated market than the US capital market and is a major source of finance for large companies.

[18] An important part of the Eurobond investor base has always been the rich retail investor (individual investors who buy Eurobonds to minimize domestic personal income taxes on coupon revenue). The Belgian dentist phrase was coined by Euromarket participants to represent the typical European retail buyer of Eurobonds.

[19] Large institutional investors (such as pension funds, insurance companies and mutual funds) are the most important purchasers of bonds in the US capital markets.

funds if they are not well known by the investor base. A rating gives them the name recognition they need. By providing a standard of comparison to investors about their investments in debt obligations, ratings increase the marketability of debt issues. They enable issuers to access investors in different geographical regions, and different investor categories. In short, ratings are almost always a prerequisite for international issues, given the higher level of information asymmetries between investors and issuers.

The Royal Borough of Kensington and Chelsea in London was given an AAA rating by Standard & Poor's in March 2001. The BBC explained, 'This means that [the Borough] is thought more likely to repay its debts than, for example, Spain.' At the time, the Borough's AAA credit rating also put it ahead of countries such as Argentina (BB), Japan (AA) and Morocco (BBB). It was unusual for a UK local government institution to seek a credit rating, as the UK did not have an active local government bond market at the time. Kensington and Chelsea decided that an AAA rating would raise their profile in Europe, encourage investment from outside the UK, and enable them to issue bonds if they needed to. They also cited the reduced funding costs associated with a top rating.[20]

Ratings also allow issuers to sell securities to *regulated investors*. Some regulations create a specific need for ratings. For example, every registered security sold in the US market must have a credit rating from a NRSRO in order to be sold to US institutional investors. In 2005 alone, these investors' net purchases of corporate and foreign bonds amounted to $463.2 billion, and all had to be rated by a NRSRO.[21] This requirement creates a regulatory benefit, because having a rating increases the marketability and liquidity of an issue, which is particularly important for enhanced access to funds for issues of $50 million or more.

Companies also use credit rating agencies to *assess major strategic moves*. By engaging the rating assessment service of a CRA, companies simulate the likely rating impact for hypothetical 'what if' scenarios. This can have several benefits. One, if the Board disapproves of the likely rating impact of a move, it may ask company management to redesign, postpone, alter or cancel an intended transaction. Two, if the hypothetical 'what if' scenario becomes reality, the CRA will understand it sooner and better than it otherwise would have, permitting it to integrate major corporate actions promptly in its ratings. Both issuers and investors benefit from this promptness in uncertainty resolution, which is unavailable for non-rated issues.

For some institutions there is also a competitive *prestige factor*. Just a few years ago there were a number of international banks with a triple-A credit rating. Among this select group were JP Morgan, Deutsche Bank, and UBS, all of whom have lost their AAA rating in recent years. Initially, this was seen as a loss of reputation and generally received negative publicity; however, because of the substantial number of downgrades recently, much of the negative stigma associated with the loss of AAA status has been removed.[22] An AA+ rating enables

---

[20] *Financial Times*, May 29, 2006 and BBC news dated March 5, 2001, Kensington wins top credit rating.

[21] *Federal Reserve Bulletin*, 2006, Table F.212, September 19, page 44.

[22] The World Bank is able to fund itself at sub-LIBOR levels. This allows the institution to offer very low cost loans to highly indebted countries. It has kept its AAA rating despite its business in risky and volatile emerging markets. This allows it to raise money on international capital markets at extremely low rates. In order to keep its AAA rating however, the World Bank will not transact certain types of business with banks, which have ratings below the AA level. In addition, over half of the World Bank's assets are invested in risk-free US Treasuries that provide the institution with liquid assets in case of problems elsewhere in the portfolio.

Exhibit 3.1   Pros and cons of obtaining a credit rating

Advantages
- Diversification of funding sources
  - Ability to access a broader and deeper investor base
- Opportunity to extend maturity profile
- Greater financial and strategic flexibility
  - Market timing
  - Terms/covenants
  - Amortization
- Reduced duration-adjusted cost of borrowing
- Enhanced transparency, recognition and credit standing in the international capital markets
- Improved bargaining power with relationship banks, suppliers, and other non-financial counter-parties

Issues to Consider and Related Mitigating Factors
- Economic costs: initial and surveillance fees
  - Fairly modest and generally associated with the amount of rated debt; best treated as part of all-in financing cost
- Initial management time
  - Minimized to the most optimal level by Morgan Stanley's active involvement and effective advice
- Unfavorable outcome
  - In Europe, by and large, rating agencies give issuers the option to keep ratings confidential for as long as desired
- Ongoing time commitment and relationship with a new external constituency
  - To be treated as part of the overall investor relations effort, with minimal additional interaction
- Ongoing scrutiny
  - Transparency and open dialogue advised to build mutual trust; agencies can be relied upon for confidentiality
- Possible repercussions of future negative rating actions
  - Initial and ongoing management of rating agencies' expectation is crucial

---

Source: Morgan Stanley Credit Advisory Group, 2006, Pros and cons of obtaining credit ratings, Overview of the rating process, Overview of the credit rating process – Morgan Stanley's integrated rating advisory approach, December 12, 1–3.

banks to access the capital markets at extremely attractive conditions and therefore to provide credit to their customers at highly competitive rates.

To sum up, Exhibit 3.1 lists the pros and cons of obtaining a credit rating as seen by a major investment bank that offers credit rating advisory services.

Almost all *issuers use the ratings services of two or more CRAs*. And, interestingly, most of the ensuing multiple ratings are observationally split ratings, which is evidence of 'the complexity and subjectivity of bond credit-worthiness evaluations.'[23] Why do issuers engage the extra expense of a second rating? What is the benefit to an issuer to see its ratings split? One answer is that an issuer unhappy with its first rating might go rate shopping and pay for a second rating. If the second is higher than the first, the issuer decides to release it. If not, it remains confidential. Then all new issues with a multiple rating ... would have a split rating. So opportunism cannot be the full story. In anticipation of later discussion, one needs

---

[23] Ederington, L.H., 1986, Why split ratings occur, *Financial Management*, Spring, Vol. 15, Issue 1, 37–47, page 46.

already have in mind that once an issuer has agreed to release an initial rating, it has no longer any control whatsoever on the release or not of follow-up ratings and change in these. For an issuer to go for a dual or triple rating regime, there is more to it than a possible advantage from instant short-term rating shopping. What is it? Why is it of benefit to the issuer to incur the extra cost? The more so that, in fact, below investment grade, a split rating significantly increases the underwriter spread![24]

Investors value a second rating. That is what has been found since the early 1990s by exploring certification value of ratings.[25] This shows that 'bond issues with two identical ratings have yields significantly less than issues receiving that rating from only one rating agency.' Now, why would investors value a second and identical rating, if it were to be a replica of the first? Somehow, to add value over and above the first rating, whether split or not, the second rating ought to be independent of the first, not a copy of it. Both CRAs normally use the same information and analyze it in the same manner, as will be discussed in Chapter 6. Yet, the two resulting evaluations of creditworthiness are not identical. Albeit equivalent summaries of the available information, each rating represents in the final analysis a subjective interpretation of that information as outcome of a deliberative process. 'It is this subjectivity that leads most users to demand a second rating ... Since any one rating is subject to error, a second is normally sought. The value of the second rating, or opinion, arises primarily from the fact that it is independent of the first.'[26]

3.1.2 Principals: Fixed Income Investors

Institutional investors often view credit risk as their most important investment holding risk. This was again reported in a recent international survey. Of these investors, 80% indeed claimed that credit risk was from very to extremely important, compared to 78% for management, 75% for market, 67% for operational, and 29% for geopolitical risk. 'Credit risk was a major factor for all of the institutional investors surveyed. All agree that overextending debt and credit rating downgrades and defaults are the most important credit risk factors.'[27] It goes beyond doubt that credit risk comparison is of great interest to investors.

The means of comparison that ratings provide is of foremost use to long-term fixed income investors. We saw in Chapter 2 that ratings temporarily anchor the default risk of an issuer or issue in an ordinal space. By benchmarking long-term default risk, ratings, in the first place, address the needs of long-term bondholders and portfolio investors, which are different to those of short-term bond investors and event, name, or spread traders.

Credit ratings enable investors to *understand better* the risks and uncertainties they face while investing. This is particularly important for investments overseas, and became increasingly relevant in the 1990s, when the flow of private capital to emerging markets increased rapidly. As the pie charts in Figure 3.2 show, in 1989, $16.1 billion or 19% of $84.5 billion

---

[24] Jewell, J., and Livingston, M., 1998, Split ratings, bond yields, and underwriter spreads, *Journal of Financial Research*, Summer, Vol. XXI, No. 2, 185–204.

[25] Tompson, G.R., and Vaz, P., 1990, Dual bond ratings: a test of the certification function of rating agencies, *Financial Review*, Vol. 25, No. 3, August, 457–471.

[26] Ederington, L.H., 1986, Why split ratings occur, *Financial Management*, Spring, Vol. 15, Issue 1, 37–47, page 46.

[27] See: Russell Reynolds Associates, 2005, International survey of institutional investors: a world of risk, *Business Evolves, Leadership Endures*, Series No. 8, 1–21, page 5. These finding are based on 101 globally stratified respondents of a survey conducted by Harris Associates. Sample sizes were as follows: Asia 14, Europe 46, and North America 41.

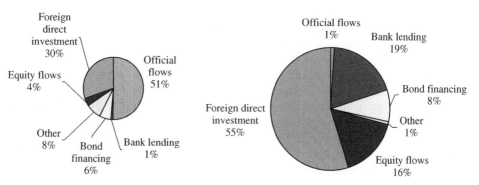

Total net long term resource flow = $84.50 billion   Total net long term resource flow = $569.60 billion

Figure 3.2   Net long-term resource flows to developing countries: 1989 versus 2006
Sources: The World Bank, 1994, *World Debt Table: External Finance for Developing Countries 1994–1995*, A World Bank book, December, 1–30, page 4. The World Bank, 2007, *Global Development Finance 2007*, 1–162, Table 2.1, page 37.

of net resource flow to developing countries went through the capital markets in the form of bank lending, bond financing, equity financing, and others (trade financings). In 2006, the proportion that flowed through capital markets rose to 44%, representing $250.6 billion out of a total flow of $569.6 billion. As investment opportunities become generally more global and diverse, it becomes more difficult to decide not only which companies, but also which countries, are good fixed-income investment opportunities. There are advantages to investing in foreign markets, but the risks associated with sending money abroad are considerably higher than those associated with investing in the domestic market. It is important to gain insight into different investment environments and to understand the risks and advantages these environments pose. Ratings help to satisfy investors' need to understand by being based on information from a wide variety of sources, and encompassing the country in which the issuer operates, the nature of the economy and the issue.

Ratings *save* investors the costs of doing their own analysis to evaluate risk prospects. These costs have been increasing with international diversification and the rising complexity of securities. In addition to helping to understand the risks and uncertainties of investments, the independent benchmark of default risk that credit ratings provide makes it easier for investors to compare different potential investments. This need for comparability grew significantly with the international diversification of financial portfolio investment. Table 3.1 and Figure 3.3 document the rise in the overseas securities portfolio of residents of major countries relative to their home security holdings over the period 1970–2005. In 1970, UK residents held a foreign portfolio (stocks plus bonds) that was worth 9.5% of their domestic portfolio. This increased to 48.1% by 2005. Foreign bondholdings alone represented 42.1% of domestic bondholdings in the UK in 2005, 25.7% in Germany, 3.6% in Canada, and 2.3% in the US. This trend was underpinned by the development of cross-border securities markets and the ensuing demand for globally comparable information about securities. Credit ratings filled the information gap for investors needing to compare globally the relative credit standing of different bond issues and other fixed income securities.

Table 3.1 Overseas securities investments as percentage of home ones (1970–2005)[a] (% of domestic market capitalization)

	1970	1975	1980	1985	1990	1995	2000	2005
Canada								
Total portfolio investment	2.0	1.9	2.1	2.4	6.0	12.9	18.7	14.3
Equity	3.1	3.2	3.6	3.5	9.6	25.4	29.3	21.2
Bonds	0.7	0.6	0.4	1.3	1.9	2.2	3.2	3.6
Germany								
Total portfolio investment	4.9	2.4	2.7	5.8	10.2	14.5	30.0	31.1
Equity	–	–	–	–	–	16.9	37.8	42.1
Bonds	–	–	–	–	–	13.0	23.0	25.7
Japan								
Total portfolio investment		1.3	2.0	6.9	10.7	12.1	13.6	16.7
Equity	–	–	–	–	2.2	4.0	8.3	9.9
Bonds	–	–	–	–	–	–	–	–
United Kingdom								
Total portfolio investment	9.5	8.6	11.4	27.5	34.0	37.1	42.6	48.1
Equity	–	–	–	–	33.1	33.5	40.9	52.4
Bonds	–	–	–	–	35.6	43.4	46.4	42.1
United States								
Total portfolio investment	1.5	2.1	2.3	2.2	3.5	6.4	7.8	7.4
Equity	0.8	1.1	1.3	2.0	5.6	9.3	10.5	12.7
Bonds	2.7	3.1	3.3	2.4	2.1	3.5	3.8	2.3

[a]The investment position in stocks is the domestic investment position in foreign equities as a fraction of the end-of-year domestic stock market capitalization. The investment position in foreign bonds is the investment position in foreign bonds as a fraction of the end-of-year domestic bond market capitalization. Portfolio investment is the sum of investment in foreign stocks and bonds. Overseas portfolio investment has increased since 1970.

Source: International Monetary Fund, 2005, *Globalization and External Imbalances*, Staff Survey, April, 109–156, page 114.

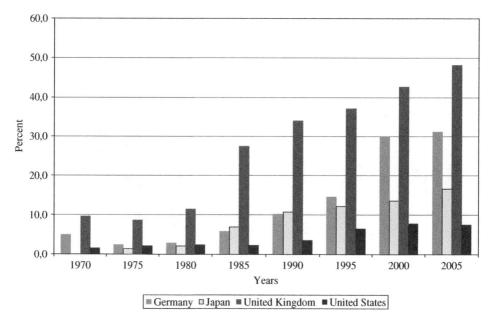

Figure 3.3 Overseas securities investments as percentage of home ones (1970–2005)
Source: International Monetary Fund, 2005, *Globalization and External Imbalances*, Staff Survey, April, 109–156, page 114.

The default frequencies produced by CRAs are an invaluable input for those *constructing a bond portfolio* for a buy and hold strategy. Figure 2.8 showed 1-, 5-, and 10-year average issuer-weighted cumulative default rates for 17 fine rating categories for the period 1983–2006. This figure mimics the typical default experience for a systematic investor over an extended period of time in any one of the 17 rated corporate bond categories on offer in the market. Inasmuch as the forecasting ability of the historical frequency distributions associated with the rating categories is reasonably powerful, this data provides invaluable inputs for long-term bond portfolio management.

SF VIGNETTE 4

Investors' Demand for Structured Finance Instruments (*and Supply of Capital*)

Investors' demand for structured finance instruments is based on two drivers of value-added to them. The first is that the creation of structured finance instruments improves the allocation efficiency of financial markets, in theory it is said that it makes financial markets more complete.[28] The issuance of structured finance instruments tailored to specific investor groups facilitates the insurance in contingencies yet uncovered by the financial markets. Related to this driver is that structured finance instruments provide arbitrage opportunities in a segmented market, improving thereby market pricing efficiency. Note that the creation of these instruments, although ultimately driven by investors' demand, is often materialized by the intermediary of an investment bank's

---

[28] Arrow, K., 1964, The role of securities in the optimal allocation of risk-bearing, *Review of Economic Studies*, Vol. 31, 91–96.

structurer (also called arranger) or asset manager, or even an independent investment manager.

The idea of market completeness is that structured finance instruments create assets with payoff characteristics that are not replicable by simply combining existing ones. The large range of structured products offerings such as Asset Backed Securities (ABS), Mortgage Backed Securities (MBS), Collaterized Debt Obligations (CDO) or Collateralized Loan Obligations (CLO), allows investors to take direct exposures and diversify into consumer risk, real estate risk, and leveraged or managed exposure to all types of corporates risks. CDOs allow investors to choose underlying assets, leverage, rating, and maturity and disconnect their choice of credit risk (given by the rating of the tranche) from their choice of asset class (given by the asset class in the pool). For instance with a CDO, a given investor can access noninvestment-grade collateral while securing a high grade rating for his investment. Moreover, products such as synthetic CDOs and single-tranche CDOs have enabled structurers to offer payoffs that are entirely tailored to address specific investor demands or concerns.[29] Life insurance companies, for example, are known to invest in such instruments that are tailored to close particular gaps in the cash inflows they need in order to match cash outflows.

Structured finance instruments have allowed many investors to make the best of portfolio restrictions. In particular, many fixed-income investors have strict rating constraints for their investments while also facing yield targets. The tightness of spreads the last few years has encouraged these investors to find new products that would allow them to get higher spreads while maintaining the credit exposure of their portfolio within their rating restrictions and guidelines. The initial success of cash CDOs pertains to these investors. CDOs are typically higher yielding than non-structured assets for a given rating. 'For example, in December 2005, AAA corporate bonds were trading at a spread of 5 basis points over Libor, whereas CDOs with comparable maturities were offering spreads between 25 basis points (AAA CLOs) and 50 basis points (AAA synthetic investment-grade CDOs).'[30]

An additional function is to aid *identification of parties to deal with*. These could be investment targets for investors and could also help to determine acceptable counterparties and collateral levels for outstanding credit exposures as per regulatory or self-imposed rules for several groups of institutional market participants, such as commercial banks and insurance companies.

Short-term investors and traders focus on rating changes and *bet* on singular events that unwind over a relatively short time span. They very willingly take diversifiable risks on the basis of their beliefs. The bond trader tends to focus on the arrival of new information. Anticipating this correctly is critical for dealing purposes, regardless of how transient the information will be once it arrives. While forward-looking in his pricing decisions in the bond

---

[29] For a very useful description of investment motives in cash and synthetic CDOs refer to: Renault, O., 2007, Cash and synthetic collateral debt obligations: Motivations and investment strategies, pages 373–396 from *Handbook of Structured Finance*, de Servigny, A. and Jobst, N., ed. Standard and Poor's, McGraw-Hill.

[30] Renault, O., 2007, Cash and synthetic collateral debt obligations: Motivations and investment strategies, page 377 from *Handbook of Structured Finance*, de Servigny, A. and Jobst, N., edited by Standard and Poor's, McGraw-Hill. Known reasons for the higher yield in any rating category rating are the presence of a liquidity premium because the secondary market liquidity on tranches of CDOs is lower than that of corporate bonds, the fact that CDOs are more leveraged and have higher mark to market volatility, CDOs are likely to have lower recovery rates and there is a perception among investors that CDOs are simply more risky than cash assets despite having the same rating, in the sense of all other risks but credit risk.

market, the trader's perspective is essentially short-term. For these market participants, the level of fundamental credit ratings are not all that important because they say relatively little about near-term singular events. As we will see in more detail when discussing credit rating performance in Chapter 7, large sample statistical inference techniques are needed to evaluate the accuracy of ratings, and the power of ratings to discriminate between defaults and non-defaults increases with sample size and with time. For instance, claims such as, 'Rapid Ratings have far outperformed Moody's and S&P in assessing credit risks. It predicted financial distress at Enron and Parmalat well before [these agencies] downgraded their debt,' miss these essential rules of inference.[31] Of course, short-term traders will be interested in betting on correctly anticipating, before others, if and when rating changes will occur. Rating changes serve as a warning system for investors in the case where a particular issuer's creditworthiness changes over time.

3.1.3 Prescribers

Prescribers are stakeholders in a rating without being party to a rating action in the same way as a CRA or an issuer. Nor do they use credit ratings to make investment decisions in debt instruments in the same way as a fixed income investor – they have their own business interest in a rating. Prescribers use the contractibility function of credit ratings to increase the efficiency and completeness of the contracts they write. Private contractors refer to the rating of one of the contracting parties to impose obligations on it and give rights to the other party. Other users include equity investors, investment banks, and boards of directors. Regulators refer to credit ratings in a number of prudential, capital requirement, market access, and investor protection regulations that we shall discuss in Chapter 9. The role of regulators in the use of credit ratings has become tremendous if one judges it by the volume of debt exchanged that is subject to one or another regulatory reference to a rating. We reserve a whole chapter to the role of regulators in the credit rating market and refer to that chapter for an extensive discussion of the regulatory uses of ratings.

Rating Constraints and Guidelines in Asset Manager Contracts

Trustees of asset managers use ratings as an instrument of *governance*. They impose ratings-based portfolio constraints on the managers they supervise. For example, investors are some-times constrained to only invest or retain issues that are investment grade, according to the ratings given by some specific agencies. The institutionalization of investments requires spon-sors or trustees of institutional portfolios to monitor their agents' portfolio holdings.[32] These include collective investment schemes like mutual funds, pension funds, and insurance com-panies.[33] The total value of mutual funds has increased at the fastest rate, by 25-fold since the early 1990s. Figure 3.4 shows the growth of institutional assets in terms of percentage

---

[31] Partnoy, F., 2006, Take away the credit rating agencies' licenses, *Financial Times*, March 13.

[32] Institutionalization refers to the increased purchase of securities via collective investment vehicles, such as mutual funds, pension funds and life insurance. Rather than providing funds directly via the financial market, households invest in collective vehicles to obtain diversification benefits and thus higher expected returns, while keeping their risk levels acceptable. The increased size and sophistication of financial markets has made investing in collective vehicles relatively cheaper than entering into securities markets directly. Also this process has been very rapid in Europe. In most continental European countries, all types of collective investment have increased much faster than direct holdings of securities.

[33] In some jurisdictions these are the only investors in fixed income securities.

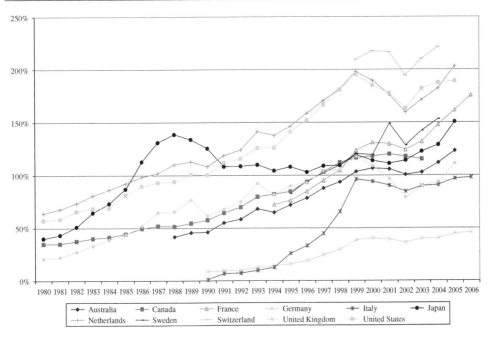

Figure 3.4   Financial assets of institutional investors as % of GDP
Source: OECD, 1980–2006, in framework of System of National Accounts.

of GDP for selected countries over the period 1980–2006. As is apparent from the figure, institutional assets have grown several times since the 1980s. These investors use ratings in their internal rules for restrictions on investments. CalPERS, for instance, uses composite ratings of Fitch, Moody's, and S&P to monitor its bond portfolios.[34] Such rating-based portfolio governance is one of the reasons why rating changes can produce real consequences that are costly to reverse.[35] This leads investors to value a proper degree of ratings stability.[36] A survey of 200 plan sponsors and investment managers in the US and Europe regarding the use of credit rating guidelines in the conduct of their investment activities finds that ratings-based guidelines are widespread and seem to be more driven by the private sector than by regulation. This survey also finds that market participants express a slight preference of accuracy over stability, but effectively they do not include credit outlooks in their guidelines, although these could increase accuracy. Interestingly, this survey finds that although guidelines commonly include asset retention, forced selling upon downgrade remains infrequent, limiting the potential destabilizing effect of downgrades.[37] Finally, buy-side fixed-income financial analysts use credit ratings as endorsement, check or input for their own research.

---

[34] Fitch was added in 2005 and celebrated this event in its annual report. Fimalac S.A., 2006, *Annual Report* 2005, 1–211, page 9.

[35] For an empirical estimation of feedback losses and changes in asset volatilities around downgrades refer to: Fulop, A., 2006, Feedback effects of rating downgrades, September, *ESSEC Working Paper series*, 1–38.

[36] Cantor, R., and Mann, C., 2006, Analyzing the trade off between ratings accuracy and stability, *Special Comment*: Moody's Investors Services, September, Report 99100, 1-8, page 1.

[37] Cantor, R., Gwilym, O.A., and Thomas, S., 2007, The use of credit ratings in investment management in the US and Europe, *Journal of Fixed Income*, Fall.

CalPERS is the California Public Employees Retirement System. It is the largest public pension fund in the US and manages a $210 billion portfolio for its 1.4 million members. The stated aim of CalPERS is to 'maximize returns at a prudent level of risk' and it does this through careful consideration of how its funds are allocated across a diverse range of bonds, securities, and other investments. Of the total funds under management, 26% is allocated to Global Fixed Income. Investment policy regarding international fixed-income investments limits exposure to emerging markets and single countries, and stipulates investment grade ratings for local currency debts of national governments and all debts of corporates and sub-national governments, i.e. Baa3 from Moody's or BBB— from Fitch and S&P. Investment managers are required to 'Consider macro- and microeconomic factors including, but not limited to, economic growth, monetary and fiscal policy of eligible countries, the credit risk of market and issuer, and risk-adjusted yields,' all of which are taken into account when defining an issuer or instrument credit rating.[38]

Private Contractors

Private contractors use ratings triggers extensively in loan and bond covenants.[39] These triggers are 'contractual provisions that give counterparties and lenders the right to terminate the credit availability, accelerate credit obligations, or have the borrower post collateral, in the event of specified rating actions, such as if the rating of the borrower's fixed-income securities falls below a certain level.'[40] Moody's reported that in 2001, 'out of 771 US corporate issuers rated Ba1 or higher, only 12.5% reported no triggers, while the remaining 87.5% reported a total of 2819 rating triggers.[41] Exhibit 3.2 tabulates the common features and the frequency of these triggers. It shows a wide variety in what is being triggered, some with possibly wide-ranging consequences.

Rating triggers are not a new practice and involve both demand- and supply-side factors. For example, they were a part of the 'super poison put provisions' popular in the late 1980s, which allowed bondholders to sell their bonds to the issuing company at par value or at a premium after the occurrence of a "designated event" combined with a 'qualifying downgrade.'[42] More recently, institutional corporate bond market participants in Europe, in their efforts to improve standards in the sterling and euro fixed-income credit markets, proposed a minimum covenant for corporate investment grade issuers that include such a put. It would link a change of control provision to a rating downgrade (normally below investment grade). The basic principle would be that 'if the borrower is acquired, the deal has to be financed so that it is consistent

---

[38] www.calpers.com

[39] For an excellent survey, see Committee of European Securities Regulators (CESR), 2005, The use of ratings in private contracts, Technical advice to the European Commission on possible measures concerning credit rating agencies, March, CESR/05-139b, 1-93, pages 87–93.

[40] Committee of European Securities Regulators (CESR), 2005, The use of ratings in private contracts, Technical advice to the European Commission on possible measures concerning credit rating agencies, March, CESR/05-139b, 1-93, page 38.

[41] Committee of European Securities Regulators (CESR), 2005, The use of ratings in private contracts, Technical advice to the European Commission on possible measures concerning credit rating agencies, March, CESR/05-139b, 1–93, page 89.

[42] Gonzalez, F., Hass, F., Johannes, R., Persson, M., Toledo, L., Violi, R., Wieland, M., and Zins, C., 2004, Market dynamics associated with credit ratings, *Occasional Paper* No. 16: European Central Bank, June, 1–40, page 13.

Exhibit 3.2 Rating triggers: common features and frequencies (2001)

Trigger	Frequency
Collateral, letter of credit, bonding provisions	21.6%
Pricing grid	21.1%
Acceleration	29.1%
of which – Termination	8.5%
– Material adverse change	5.4%
– Default	5.3%
– Acceleration	4.0%
– Put	3.0%
– Early amortization	2.9%
Other	28.2%

Source: Coppola, M., and Stumpp, P., 2002, Moody's analysis of US corporate rating triggers heightens need for increased disclosure. *Special Comment*: Moody's Investors Service, July, Report 75412, 1–16, page 6.

with the predetermined ratings level, otherwise existing bonds will have to be refinanced as well.'[43]

On the demand side, counterparties often require triggers as a kind of security. Lenders may require rating triggers as protection against credit deterioration, asymmetric information problems, and prospective losses, especially in cases where a borrower faces a serious likelihood of bankruptcy or default. The rights given to the creditors usually vary from an increase in the nominal coupon to a put option.[44]

There is, however, also a supply-side reason for rating triggers to reduce the cost of debt. Borrowers are willing to include such triggers because, without them, lenders, out of fear of event risk, would demand a higher initial spread on debt contracts, or they would see the markets shut down for them.[45] As an example, a rating change may trigger coupon adjustments on corporate bonds, according to the bond covenant. France Telecom, in relative hardship circumstances, was nevertheless able to sell a mammoth €17.6 billion bond package in March 2001 rated A– (S&P)/A3 (Moody's) thanks to its step-up clauses. It granted investors an additional 0.25% in interest payments for each notch below the A category by which either Moody's or S&P lowered its rating.

Rating triggers vary in degree of impact from severe to benign. On the high end of the risk spectrum are triggers that cause a loss of availability under credit lines, events of default, acceleration or puts. The liquidity implications of these rating triggers can be severe, since such triggers exacerbate liquidity strains at the precise moment when an issuer is least able to deal with such problems.[46]

Somewhat less damaging are collateral clauses. These do not result in a change in the initial financing conditions but require the borrower to pledge additional collateral.[47] These clauses

---

[43] Working group of investment institutions ('Gang of 26'), 2003, Improving market standards in the Sterling and Euro fixed income credit markets, *Proposals Paper*, October, 1–8, page 2.

[44] Gonzalez, F., Hass, F., Johannes, R., Persson, M., Toledo, L., Violi, R., Wieland, M., and Zins, C., 2004, Market dynamics associated with credit ratings, *Occasional Paper* No. 16: European Central Bank, June, 1–40, pages 12, 13.

[45] Gonzalez, F., Hass, F., Johannes, R., Persson, M., Toledo, L., Violi, R., Wieland, M., and Zins, C., 2004, Market dynamics associated with credit ratings, *Occasional Paper* No. 16: European Central Bank, June, 1–40, page 12.

[46] Coppola, M., and Stumpp, P., 2002, Moody's analysis of US corporate rating heightens need for increased disclosure, *Special Comment*: Moody's Investors Service, July, Report 75412, 1–16.

[47] Gonzalez, F., Hass, F., Johannes, R., Persson, M., Toledo, L., Violi, R., Wieland, M., and Zins, C., 2004, Market dynamics associated with credit ratings, *Occasional Paper* No. 16: European Central Bank, June, 1–40, page 13.

are not entirely harmless. For example, in the case of Enron, rating triggers gave counterparties the right to demand cash collateral, which increased the company's financial difficulties.[48] At the lowest end of the risk spectrum are the relatively benign pricing grids, which consist of a requirement to reset pricing according to rating downgrades.[49]

A 2001 survey found that a large proportion of rating triggers consist of pricing grids.[50] This finding was consistent with a 2002 S&P survey which revealed that around 50% of surveyed issuers were exposed to some sort of ratings-linked contingent liability, but less than 3% were seriously vulnerable to rating triggers that could turn a moderate decline in credit quality into a liquidity crisis.[51,52]

Until recently, disclosure of ratings-based triggers by issuers was rather neglected. It remained largely ignored by analysts and investors. Under US (GAAP/FAS), UK (FRS), and international accounting standards (IAS), there is an obligation to disclose material triggers, but the interpretation of 'material' by different issuers may result in important information not being reported.[53] As the 2001 survey found, nearly 87.5% of companies whose debt is rated Ba1 or higher reported that they had rating triggers but only 22.5% of the triggers were disclosed in their SEC filings. Moreover, as more than half of the disclosed triggers related to pricing grids, a much higher proportion of the most problematic triggers may not have been disclosed.

CRAs themselves are championing the cause of better disclosure of rating triggers. As stated in the above-mentioned Moody's study, 'in view of the importance of rating triggers, Moody's will highlight, where possible, the existence of these in each issuer's financial structure. Although Moody's will not disclose the particulars of any undisclosed triggers due to confidentially constraints, it intends to factor the effects of each rating trigger (whether or not publicly disclosed by the issuer) into the rating. In addition the issuer's refusal to provide information about its rating triggers to Moody's will be considered a negative factor in the rating process.'

ABB provides an example of a bank loan transaction that uses rating downgrades as a trigger for the right to recall a loan or ask for additional collateral. The Swiss–Swedish electrical engineering group went through a financial crisis starting in 2001.[54]

---

[48] US Securities and Exchange Commission, 2003, Report on the role and function of credit rating agencies in the operation of the securities market, January, 1–45.

[49] Coppola, M., and Stumpp, P., 2002, Moody's analysis of US corporate rating triggers heightens need for increased disclosure, *Special Comment*: Moody's Investors Service, July, Report 75412, 1–16, page 1.

[50] Coppola, M., and Stumpp, P., 2002, Moody's analysis of US corporate rating triggers heightens need for increased disclosure, *Special Comment*: Moody's Investors Service, July, Report 75412, 1–16, page 1.

[51] Samson, S.B., 2002, S&P releases survey on rating triggers, contingent calls on liquidity, *Research*: Standard and Poor's, May 15, 1–2.

[52] Another use is in derivative transactions. Take for example the ISDA clause for derivative transactions in the event of a rating downgrade, with the number of notches specified for each transaction.

[53] Gonzalez, F., Hass, F., Johannes, R., Persson, M., Toledo, L., Violi, R., Wieland, M., and Zins, C., 2004, Market dynamics associated with credit ratings, Occasional Paper No. 16: European Central Bank, June, 1–40, page 14.

[54] ABB incurred significant net losses in 2001, 2002, and 2003, with a smaller loss in 2004, and positive net income in 2005. The company reached near bankruptcy in 2002. The losses were partly as a result of a greater-than-anticipated increase in the number of and amounts demanded to settle certain asbestos-related claims against its subsidiary, Combustion Engineering ... as well as the weak performance of some of the businesses that were later classified as non-core activities, discontinued operations, and an overall weakening of global markets that started in 2001. (*Source*: ABB Ltd, 2006, Form 20-F for fiscal year ended December 31, 2005 filed with United States Securities and Exchange Commission, April 19, File No: 001-16429, 1–224, page 5 and ABB Ltd, 2003, Form 20-F for fiscal year ended December 31, 2002 filed with United States Securities and Exchange Commission, June 30, File No: 001–16429, 1–224, page 57, press reports.)

In March 2002, a rating downgrade to Baa2 by Moody's triggered a minimum rating clause in the company's $3 billion revolving credit facility provided by a group of 24 banks. According to this clause, if the company's long-term debt rating fell below either A3 or A− from Moody's and S&P, respectively, the terms of the facility were to be renegotiated. Given the financial position of the company, withdrawal of the facility, resulting in a serious liquidity crisis, seemed imminent. The immediate crisis was averted when, in April 2002, the company was able to negotiate with its banks to replace the rating trigger with certain financial covenants. The negotiated terms also included repayment of the entire outstanding by December 2002, followed by replacement of the old facility with a new facility of $1.5 billion, to be reduced to $1 billion by December 2003, with further reductions at future dates from specified proceeds.

Of course, the banks did not wish to stand by passively if the situation deteriorated during this period, rather than stabilized and began gradual recovery. In fact, unless the situation did stabilize and gradually improve, the banks wanted to be able to call the loans immediately under certain conditions. In this particular case, the continued availability of the new facility to ABB depended on it being able to comply with a number of stringent market-related financial covenants with respect to minimum interest coverage (EBITDA to gross interest expense), total gross debt, a maximum level of debt in subsidiaries other than those specified as borrowers under the facility, a minimum level of consolidated net worth during 2003, as well as specific negative pledges. An additional covenant was that the company should obtain minimum levels of proceeds from the disposal of specified assets and businesses and/or equity issuances during 2003. In addition, the facility prohibited the voluntary prepayment of any other banking facility, the prepayment or early redemption of any bonds or capital market instruments, the repurchase of any shares of ABB and the declaration or payment of dividends by ABB Ltd as long as the facility was outstanding.[55]

The use of credit ratings as ratings triggers cause rating changes to have real consequences that are costly to reverse. One will appreciate that this use of ratings explains 'that many market participants have a strong preference for credit ratings that are not only accurate but also stable.'[56] This is also the case of rating-based portfolio management.

Other Prescribers

USERS OF COLLATERAL   Lenders impose minimum rating standards on securities to be accepted as collateral for a loan. This can be the result of voluntary lending policy guidelines, or a (possibly indirect) result of the regulatory uses of ratings, to be discussed in Chapter 9. But it is said that the practice is rather widespread. Central banks, for instance do not accept securities below investment grade as collateral for commercial bank borrowing. Bank of France Governor Christian Noyer reminded market participants of that:

> ... the Euro offers little cover to countries that struggle to meet financial obligations. The market seems to believe that there will be a bailing out of euro-zone countries that get into financial

---

[55] ABB Ltd, 2003, Form 20-F for fiscal year ended December 31, 2002 filed with United States Securities and Exchange Commission, June 30, File No: 001-16429, 1–224, pages 98, 99.
[56] See Cantor, R., and Mann, C., 2006, Analyzing the tradeoff between ratings accuracy and stability, *Special Comment*: Moody's Investors Service, September, Report 99100, 1-8, page 1.

difficulties after living above their means. That simply cannot happen and will not happen. Nor will the ECB accept as collateral the bonds of any government whose debt is rated below investment grade.[57]

EQUITY INVESTORS   Equity financial analysts use credit ratings as an indicator of corporate quality and equity risk. Although credit ratings are not investment advice, they function as one of the indicators of equity valuations.

INVESTMENT BANKS   Initial ratings help price and place new issues at the time of the offering. They compare the lifetime credit risk at a particular point in time for a very broad universe of different securities and position a specific new issue in that universe. Thereby, they attest to the relative quality of an issue and to the accuracy of the accompanying information about the issuer.[58] Investors will almost always demand a greater return from securities that carry a higher risk and hence have a lower rating. Initial ratings thus serve to price new securities on that basis and are an important data point for investment banks.

Rating advisory groups assist clients with initial ratings in a similar way that equity advisers assist private companies with initial public offerings (IPOs). Getting the rating right is not too dissimilar from getting the IPO price right. For debt underwriters, the rating helps to pitch new issues to the proper investor segments and, therefore, to reduce underwriting risk. For sell-side, fixed-income financial analysts, ratings are used as a check on their own independent research – an input in the overall opinion to buy, hold, or sell.

BOARDS OF DIRECTORS   Boards of Directors sometimes use credit ratings to monitor management. Boards direct corporate strategy and authorize broad asset and liability structures. If the Board decides a rating benchmark for the firm, it constrains strategy and balance sheet structure. By seeking and maintaining a credit rating, the Board obtains an independent, external review of management and its performance. Credit quality correlates in many respects with the concerns of a Board of Directors and some firms have found the rating review meetings and assessment a valuable management tool.

The Lafarge Group is one of the top building materials companies in the world. Launched in 1833, its first major international contract was to provide lime for the construction of the Suez Canal. The company is listed in Paris and New York, and 2005 sales amounted to €16 billion. The Board of Directors stipulates the conditions under which certain financial arrangements can be made, as described in the Corporate Governance chapter in the 2005 Company Report. For bond issues of less than €300 million, the Board only needs to be informed after the fact, for issues between €300 million and €1 billion, the Board must be informed before the issue is launched, but for amounts above €1 billion, full Board approval of the issue and its terms must be obtained. Prior approval from the Board must also be sought for an 'issue and its terms in case of bond issues convertible or exchangeable into shares.'[59]

---

[57] Di Leo, L., and Perry, J., 2006, Italy credit downgrade may undermine euro zone, *Wall Street Journal*, October 20, pages 1 and 2.
[58] See also Beattie, V., and Searle, S., 1992, Bond ratings and inter-rate agreement, *Journal of International Securities Markets*, Summer, Vol. 6, 167–172.
[59] www.Lafarge.com

3.2 CREDIT RATINGS AS A SOLUTION TO INFORMATION ASYMMETRY: ECONOMIC ANALYSIS

3.2.1 Economics of Ratings: Intuition

The different demand drivers of market participants for ratings, as documented in Section 3.1, are expressions of a common need to resolve information asymmetries about the credit quality of an issue. At the time of an initial rating or at the time of a new issue, it is the adverse selection problem that is most salient. Adverse selection describes the fact that investors have less information than issuers on the quality of an issuer and its debt claim before they invest. Therefore, they may invest (i.e. select) a 'bad' debt claim with returns that are inferior to a 'good' one. Adverse selection occurs when there is hidden information on the quality of a good that is traded. Later, once an instrument or an issuer obtains its initial rating, the problems of moral hazard can begin to emerge. Moral hazard describes the fact that once an issuer has sold its debt claim, it may have an incentive to take actions, unobservable to the investor, that are in its own interest but against those of the debtholder. Moral hazard occurs when an agent (here the issuer) can take hidden actions that negatively affect the principal's (the investor's) payoff.

Consider adverse selection in the lending relationship.[60] Investors demand higher credit spreads to compensate for a higher default risk on the part of the issuer, but they know much less about this risk than the issuer.[61] This makes it hard for investors to discriminate between risky and safe issues. As a result, the market will just price issues according to the average risk they face across all issues in the market, without discrimination. Given that safe issues decrease the average riskiness of issues, whereas the risky issues increase it, safe issues may thus find themselves charged with spreads that are too high for their true riskiness – and truly very risky ones with spreads that are too low. It is what we call cross-subsidization (good issues subsidize the spread of the bad issues). The existence of risky issues that cannot be distinguished from safe issues not only increases the spread for safe issues, but if there are too many very risky issues, the credit market could be rationed or even break down. Relatively safe issuers will prefer to get funding elsewhere or will invest in signaling their quality and the public credit market could be left only with the riskiest issues.

The market frictions that adverse selection brings about create value-adding opportunities for certifiers of risk quality. These could, for instance, be credit ratings that reduce information asymmetries between issuers and investors, or commercial banks that provide funds to borrowers and monitor them.[62,63] One can analyze this mechanism in the situation where all types of issuers are pooled together and their qualities cannot be distinguished by outsiders.[64] So, in this case, to outsiders truly good bonds look like truly bad ones. If then the two types of issuers – safe types and risky types – gather funds on the debt market, the risky type will issue the same type of debt claim as the safe type. Investors cannot distinguish them and risky issuers will benefit from cross-subsidization. Alternatively, in some circumstances, the safe type can issue a type of debt claim that would be too costly for the risky type to

---

[60] The pioneering article on adverse selection in market transactions is: Akerlof, G., 1970, The market for lemons, qualitative uncertainty and the market mechanism, *Quarterly Journal of Economics*, Vol. 88, 488–500.

[61] We refer here to default risk in its generic sense that includes the probability of default, the expected loss in the event of default and the standard deviation surrounding that expected loss.

[62] Leland, H., and Pyle, D., 1977, Information asymmetries, financial structure and financial intermediaries, *Journal of Finance*, Vol. 32, 371–387.

[63] Diamond, D., 1984, Financial intermediation and delegated monitoring, *Review of Economic Studies*, Vol. 51, 393–414.

[64] This situation leads to what is called a pooling equilibrium with adverse selection.

mimic.[65] Hence, this costly signal for the safe type can help to differentiate the safe issuer from the risky issuer and get a better cost of capital.

Our formal analysis shows how much a safe issuer would be willing to pay for that certification. It emphasizes that there exists a rational, value-maximizing, willingness to pay for an accurate rating. The good entrepreneur's willingness to pay for the rating increases with the proportion of bad borrowers on the market willing to mimic the good borrower, with a measure of the intensity of the adverse selection problem and the amount of capital borrowed from the capital markets. The reduction in information asymmetry helps rated companies to access funds at a cost that corresponds better to their true risk than if they were unrated. For truly safe companies, a correct rating lowers the cost of debt from what it would have been without a rating, and vice-versa for truly risky ones.

The CRAs also reduce the moral hazard costs of debt financing associated with risk shifting. The hazard exists in the sense that an issuer, once the terms of the issue have been set corresponding to the risk level at the time of the issue, may start increasing business or financial risk, thereby shifting value from unprotected creditors to shareholders. Inasmuch as CRAs continuously monitor the risks of issuers and change the ratings if warranted, they guard investors against the moral hazards that firm managers would cause when, in the absence of being monitored, they would be tempted to indulge in risk shifting on the behalf of their shareholders, whose agents they are.

The Marriott Corporation Announced a Major Spin-off Plan on October 5, 1992

This plan would entail significant asset and liability restructurings shifting risks from shareholders to creditors. This would benefit shareholders at the expense of creditors. Upon the announcement, Marriott's bond ratings were notched down from Baa3 to Ba2, long-term bonds dropped by 30%, its 13 senior Notes by 16.51%, but its Hotel sector adjusted stock price shot up by 13.1%. The transaction eventually did not materialize as initially announced. But the case illustrates extremely well the moral hazard risks to which bondholders are exposed and thus the potential concomitant costs to debt financing.[66]

Shirking is another form of moral hazard cost of debt that CRAs can reduce. Once the terms of the issue have been set, an issuer may be tempted to simply mismanage the investment project for which he borrowed funds and divert resources to get a private benefit. The private benefit is inefficient in that its value to the borrower is smaller than the forgone profit; however, given that the borrower receives only part of the profit but the entire private benefit, it is in his interest to do so, at the expense of the lenders. The borrower must then keep a sufficient stake in the outcome of the investment project in order to have an incentive not to waste money. With moral hazard, the issuer should then be credit rationed to maintain a large enough stake in a project's payoff. One of the main consequences of moral hazard in debt is credit rationing.[67,68]

---

[65] This is what is called a separating equilibrium, the situation where truly good quality issuers are able to separate themselves from truly bad ones. So, in this case, outsiders can distinguish between truly good bonds and truly bad ones. It is often costly for the good issuer to separate from the bad issuer.

[66] Parrino, R., 1997, Spinoffs and wealth transfers: The Marriott Case, *Journal of Financial Economics*, February, Vol. 43, Issue 2, 241–274.

[67] Stiglitz, J., and Weiss, A., 1981, Credit rationing in markets with imperfect information, *American Economic Review*, Vol. 71, 393–410.

[68] Jensen, M., and Meckling, W.R., 1976, 'Theory of the firm: managerial behavior, agency costs and ownership structure,' *Journal of Financial Economics*, No. 3, 305–360.

A would-be borrower is said to be *rationed* if he cannot obtain the loan he wants even though he is willing to pay the interest that the lenders are asking, perhaps even a higher interest. In practice such credit rationing seems to be commonplace: some borrowers are constrained by fixed lines of credit which they must not exceed in any circumstances; others are refused loans altogether.[69]

Empirically, there is evidence that firms that have a debt rating have significantly more leverage than firms that do not, even after controlling for firm characteristics.[70]

3.2.2 Economics of Ratings: Analysis

We now turn to formally analyze the core problems of information asymmetry between issuers of debt claims and investors, and their solutions. As explained, they relate essentially to adverse selection and moral hazard. The following short models are based on the advances in the last 30 years of information economics and theoretical corporate finance. They are intended here just as a more detailed analytical transcription of the intuitions described earlier.[71]

Initial Ratings as a Solution to the Adverse Selection Problem in Debt

In this section we review the adverse selection problem embedded in debt claims, its consequences, and how a credit rating can solve them. From there we will be able to derive a good borrower's willingness to pay for ratings.

To illustrate the adverse selection problem in debt, we consider a very simple one-period model. Initially, at time $t = 0$, an entrepreneur (also called the issuer or borrower) invests in a risky project. He invests part of his own cash and borrows the rest from the public debt market. Investors (also called debt or bondholders or the lender) buy the bond issued by the entrepreneur at this time. At the end of the period, at time $t = 1$, the risky project returns a payoff, of which investors get a promised amount according to the terms of the debt claim. The entrepreneur keeps the residual.

$t = 0$ $t = 1$

The entrepreneur invests in a risky
project. He borrows on the public
debt market. Investors buy the
debt claim after having observed the
entrepreneur's quality
(case of symmetric information).

The project is realized and returns a payoff.
Investors get compensated according to
the realized payoff and the face value of the bond.
The entrepreneur gets the residual claim.

Timeline of the basic model with symmetric information.

Notation and assumptions

1. The entrepreneur and all investors are risk neutral hence there is no risk-premium associated to any investment. ρ is the one period (risk-free) interest rate.

---

[69] Bester, H., and Hellwig, M., 1987, Moral Hazard and Credit Rationing: an Overview of the Issues, in *Agency Theory, Information, and Incentives* (ed. G. Bamberg and K. Spremann), Heidelberg, Springer.

[70] Faulkender, M., and Petersen, M., 2006, Does the source of capital affect capital structure?, *Review of Financial Studies*, Vol. 19, 45–79.

[71] The notation and presentation of this section are based on Tirole, J., 2006, *The Theory of Corporate Finance*, Princeton University Press, Princeton and Oxford, 1-644, an excellent classic reference.

2. Capital markets are competitive, so that in expectation, investors get a rate of return of ρ, wherever they invest.
3. The entrepreneur invests in a risky project that costs I. He has an amount A of cash on hand, and borrows $I - A$ from the public debt market by issuing a standard bond with face value D.
4. There are two types of entrepreneurs: good types (in proportion α) or bad types (in proportion $1 - \alpha$). Both entrepreneurs have the same characteristics except for the project's distribution of payoffs. The good entrepreneur's project will have a return of $R \in [0, +\infty)$ with (pdf) $p(R)$, the bad entrepreneur's project return will also have a return R but with a probability density function (pdf) $\tilde{p}(R).p$ first order stochastically dominates (f.o.s.d.) $\tilde{p}$.[72]

Symmetric Information

Case 1: The Bad entrepreneur is not Creditworthy

His project has a negative expected net present value (NPV): $E(\tilde{R}) = \int_0^{+\infty} R\tilde{p}(R) \, dR < (1 + \rho)I$.[73,74] Given that investors observe the entrepreneur's quality, they only invest in projects by the good entrepreneur and only the good entrepreneur borrows from the public debt markets. The good entrepreneur issues a standard debt contract. At time $t = 0$ he borrows an amount $I - A$ with face value D. Define $w(R, D)$ as the entrepreneur's payoff at $t = 1$ from the project after having paid the investors:

$$w(R, D) = \begin{cases} 0 & \text{if } R < D \\ R - D & \text{if } R \geqslant D \end{cases}$$

Investors who buy the good entrepreneur's debt claim get:

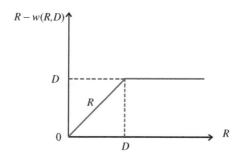

$$R - w(R, D) = \begin{cases} R & \text{if } R < D \\ D & \text{if } R \geqslant D \end{cases}$$

---

[72] p first-order stochastically dominates (f.o.s.d.) $\tilde{p}$ if and only if, for any non-decreasing function $u : \mathbb{R} \to \mathbb{R}$, $\int u(x)p(x) \, dx \geqslant \int u(x)\tilde{p}(x) \, dx$, this implies that the mean of p is greater than the mean of $\tilde{p}$.

[73] Note that we abuse notation by setting: $E(R) = \int_0^{+\infty} Rp(R) \, dR$ and $E(\tilde{R}) = \int_0^{+\infty} R\tilde{p}(R) \, dR$.

[74] Investors buy the bad entrepreneur's bond only if they expect the return to be greater or equal to $(I - A)(1 + \rho)$. The entrepreneur invests in the project only if he expects a payoff greater or equal to $A(1 + \rho)$, his opportunity cost of capital. Hence if $E(R) < I(1 + \rho)$, there exists no claim based on this project that can satisfy both parties' participation constraints.

The good entrepreneur issues a standard debt contract with face value D to maximize its payoff subject to the constraint that investors get their market return p:

$$\max_{D \geqslant 0} \int_{D}^{+\infty} (R - D)p(R)\,dR$$

$$\text{s.t.} : (1 + \rho)(I - A) - E(R) + \int_{D}^{+\infty} (R - D)p(R)\,dR \leqslant 0$$

The solution to this problem yields a debt contract with face value D^* and is defined by the following relationship:

$$C(D^*) = D^*[1 - P(D^*)] + \int_{0}^{D} Rp(R)\,dR = (1 + \rho)(I - A)$$

where P is the cumulative distribution function (cdf) of p.

The good entrepreneur borrows an amount: $I - A$ at $t = 0$, an expected cost of $C(D^*)$ at $t = 1$.

Investors invest an amount $I - A$ at $t = 0$ and expect to get in return $(1 + p)(1 - A)$ at $t = 1$.

We refer to D^* later in the text. D^* as the reference face value of the debt claim when the good entrepreneur borrows $I - A$ under symmetric information, and provides the market return ρ to investors.

Case 2: The Bad Entrepreneur is Creditworthy

The good entrepreneur will still issue the same debt claim as above with face value $D = D^*$, because the good entrepreneur can still be identified as such by investors. This time the bad entrepreneur is creditworthy, his project has a positive expected NPV, hence there exists a debt claim that allows him to borrow $I - A$ with face value $\tilde{D}$ to finance his project. The bad entrepreneur's reward is:

$$w(R, \tilde{D}) = \begin{cases} 0 & \text{if } R < \tilde{D} \\ R - \tilde{D} & \text{if } R \geqslant \tilde{D}. \end{cases}$$

Given that information is symmetric and that the bad entrepreneur will have to provide investors with the market's competitive expected return $(1 + \rho)(I - A)$, the bad entrepreneur's bond will be uniquely defined by its face value $\tilde{D}$ such that:

$$C(\tilde{D}) = \tilde{D}(1 - \tilde{P}(\tilde{D})) + \int_{0}^{\tilde{D}} R\tilde{p}(R)\,dR = (1 + \rho)(I - A)$$

We can thus compare both contracts using the equality:

$$D^*(1 - P(D^*)) + \int_{0}^{D^*} R\rho(R)\,dR = \tilde{D}(1 - \tilde{P}(\tilde{D})) + \int_{0}^{\tilde{D}} R\tilde{p}(R)\,dR$$

$$D^* - \tilde{D} = \int_{0}^{D^*} P(R)\,dR - \int_{0}^{\tilde{D}} \tilde{P}(R)\,dR$$

which implies that $D^* < \widetilde{D}$ (see Proof 1 in the technical appendix on page 162). Although, in expectation, investors get the same return, the face value of debt of the bad entrepreneur is higher. That is, when the project return is normal or high, investors will get a higher return, but it will default more often.

The bad entrepreneur borrows an amount: $I - A$ at an expected cost of:

$$\int_{\widetilde{D}}^{+\infty} (R - \widetilde{D})\widetilde{p}(R)\,dR = (1 + \rho)(I - A)$$

Investors invest an amount, $I - A$ and get in return $(1 + \rho)(I - A)$. The bad entrepreneur then has an expected cost of capital ρ that is identical to the good entrepreneur's (remember that all agents are risk neutral).

ASYMMETRIC INFORMATION

This is the real interesting case that we will compare to the symmetric information case. When investors cannot distinguish ex-ante whether the entrepreneur is good or bad, there exists two types of equilibria that need to be distinguished according to the value of the parameters. One where the good entrepreneur is able to separate himself from the bad entrepreneur by offering investors conditions that the bad entrepreneur has no incentive to imitate, we call this the separating equilibrium. The other equilibrium is where the good entrepreneur is not able to separate himself from the bad entrepreneur, whether the bad entrepreneur is creditworthy or not. We call this case the pooling equilibrium. The timing of information and actions is slightly different from the symmetric information case.

$t = 0$ $t = 1$

Both the good and the bad entrepreneur have the possibility of investing in a risky project. If so, they borrow from the public debt market by issuing a debt claim with the same (*pooling equilibrium*) or different (*separating equilibrium*) observable characteristics. Investors decide whether to buy the debt claim **without** observing the entrepreneur's quality per se beforehand.

The project is realized and returns a payoff. Investors get compensated according to the realized payoff, which varies with the entrepreneur's type, and the face value of the bond.
The entrepreneur gets the residual claim after having paid investors.

Case 1: Separating Equilibrium: the Good Borrower can Separate
(A Sufficiently Big)

The good borrower's payoff is then:

$$w(R, D^s) = \begin{cases} 0 & \text{if } R < D^s \\ R - D^s & \text{if } R \geqslant D^s. \end{cases}$$

The good entrepreneur will set D^s so as to maximize its payoff subject to the constraint of investors getting a market return, in expectation (IR constraint), and the bad entrepreneur preferring not to invest in a project (keep the cash and get market return on the cash A) rather than investing on the same terms than the good entrepreneur (IC constraint). Such that:

$$\max_{D^s \geqslant 0} \int_{D^s}^{+\infty} (R - D^s) p(R) \, dR$$

$$\text{s.t.} : (1 + \rho)(I - A) \leqslant D^s[1 - P(D^s)] + \int_0^{D^s} Rp(R) \, dR \qquad \text{(IR)}$$

and
$$\int_{D^s}^{+\infty} (R - D^s) \tilde{p}(R) \, dR \leqslant (1 + \rho)A \qquad \text{(IC)}$$

Consider the case where the bad entrepreneur's incentive compatibility (IC) constraint is binding:

The good entrepreneur has to set $D^s > \tilde{D}$ to make the *IC* constraint just binding. Hence the bad borrower becomes indifferent between investing in the risky project and borrowing $(1 + \rho)(I - A)$ from the public debt market or just keeping its cash and collecting $(1 + \rho)A$. The bad borrower does not borrow from the public debt market and hence, although there is asymmetric information initially, in equilibrium, investors will know that only the good borrowers issue debt. However, because $D^s > \tilde{D}$, in expectation investors earn more than the competitive rate of return, indeed:

$$C(D^s) = [D^s(1 - P(D^s)] + \int_0^{D^s} Rp(R) \, dR > (1 + \rho)(I - A)$$

Define s^s as the spread that investors earn above the competitive rate of return, it is:

$$C(D^s) = (1 + \rho + s^s)(I - A)$$

Because of asymmetric information and the presence of bad entrepreneurs, **the good entrepreneur has to leave an informational rent on the table to separate himself from the bad entrepreneur.** To summarize this case:

- The good entrepreneur borrows an amount $I - A$ at an expected cost of:

$$(1 + \rho + s^s)(I - A).$$

  Its expected cost of capital is $\rho + s^s$.
- Investors invest an amount $I - A$ at $t = 0$ and expect to get in return

$$C(D^s) = (1 + \rho + s^s)(I - A) \text{ at } t = 1.$$

- The bad entrepreneur does not invest in a risky project, he just keeps his cash the whole period and gets $(1 + \rho)A$.[75]

---

[75] This case only makes sense if the bad entrepreneur is not creditworthy. If he were creditworthy, but not able to imitate the good entrepreneurs by issuing the same debt claim, he would still have an interest in issuing a debt claim on its own specific terms rather than not investing in a positive NPV project at all.

Case 2: Pooling Equilibrium: the Good Borrower cannot Separate (A Relatively Small)

The setting is the same as previously, except that not only can investors *not* distinguish ex-ante (before investing) among good borrowers or bad borrowers, but in equilibrium both types of borrowers offer bonds with the same characteristics. Bad entrepreneurs take advantage of the fact that investors cannot distinguish among them before investing by imitating the good entrepreneur and offering the same type of debt claim. Bad entrepreneurs can then have better borrowing conditions than in the case of symmetric information. However, the good entrepreneur is worse off. In the pooling equilibrium of the model, both types offer bonds with face value D^p.[76]

Recall that a proportion α of the entrepreneurs are 'good' types, the remainder $(1 - \alpha)$ of the entrepreneurs are 'bad' types: the stochastic return R on their investment has a pdf of $\tilde{p}$, as before p f.o.s.d $\tilde{p}$.

First consider the case where the good entrepreneur can still get financing in the pooling equilibrium (α large or bad borrower is creditworthy).

$$w(R, D^p) = \begin{cases} 0 & \text{if } R < D^p \\ R - D^p & \text{if } R \geqslant D^p. \end{cases}$$

The good entrepreneur will issue a debt claim with face value D^p such that:

$$\max_{D^p \geqslant 0} \int_{D^p}^{+\infty} (R - D^p)p(R)\, dR$$

$$\text{s.t}: \quad (1 + \rho)(I - A) - \alpha \left[\int_0^{D^p} R\tilde{p}(R)\, dR + D^p[1 - \tilde{P}(D^p)] \right]$$

$$- (1 - \alpha) \left[\int_0^{D^p} R\tilde{p}(R)\, dR + D^p[1 - \tilde{P}(D^p)] \right] \leqslant 0.$$

which we write as:

$$(1 + \rho)(I - A) - \alpha C(D^p) - (1 - \alpha)\tilde{C}(D^p) \leqslant 0$$

Solving this we find that:

$$\alpha C(D^p) + (1 - \alpha)\tilde{C}(D^p) = (1 + \rho)(I - A)$$

Overall in expectation investors will still make $(1 + \rho)(I - A)$, but they expect to make more from the good entrepreneurs and less from the bad ones: $C(D^p) \geqslant \tilde{C}(D^p)$ (see Proof 2 in the technical appendix on page 162). **There is cross-subsidization: investors get in expectation an above market competitive return from good entrepreneurs and a below market competitive return from the bad entrepreneurs.** Therefore, good entrepreneurs have a greater cost of capital whereas bad entrepreneurs have a lower cost of capital than in the symmetric information case.

---

[76] The necessary condition for a pooling equilibrium to exist is that:

$$(1 + \rho)A < \int_{D^p}^{+\infty} (R - D^p)\tilde{p}(R)\, dR$$

which holds if A is relatively small.

To summarize:

- The good entrepreneur borrows an amount $I - A$ at $t = 0$ at an expected cost of:

$$C(D^p) > C(D^*) = (1 + \rho)(I - A) \text{ at } t = 1.$$

Hence there exists a spread s^g such that: $C(D^p) = (1 + \rho + s^g)(I - A)$.

The good entrepreneur's cost of capital is $\rho + s^g$, higher than in the symmetric case.

- Investors invest an amount $I - A$ and get in return $(1 + \rho + s^g)(I - A)$ at $t = 1$ if they invested in a good entrepreneur's bond, or $(1 + \rho - s^b)(I - A)$ if they invested in a bad entrepreneur's bond. Because they do not observe ex-ante, what type the entrepreneur is, in expectation they get:

$$\alpha(1 + \rho + s^g)(I - A) + (1 + \alpha)(1 + \rho - s^b)(I - A) = (1 + \rho)(I - A)$$

- The bad entrepreneur borrows an amount $I - A$ at $t = 0$ at an expected cost of $\tilde{C}(D^p) < C(D^*)$ at $t = 1$. Hence there exists a spread s^b such that:

$$\tilde{C}(D^p) = (1 + \rho - s^b)(I - A).$$

The bad entrepreneur's cost of capital is $\rho - s^b$ which is lower than in the symmetric case.

Now the case where the good entrepreneur cannot get financing (α small and bad borrower not creditworthy) is when no investor is willing to lend any capital because in expectation they cannot get the market competitive rate of return.

The presence of too many bad borrowers that are not creditworthy leads to a market breakdown for public debt. The adverse selection problem leads to an infinite cost of capital.

Ratings and Adverse Selection (no Moral Hazard) The good entrepreneur is creditworthy and would like to raise funds on the public debt markets to realize a risky project but is worried about the cross-subsidization problem due to the presence of bad entrepreneurs.[77] Suppose that, at a cost c, the good entrepreneur can have access to a reputable rating agency that will accurately disclose the quality of the project (in the sense that it perfectly reveals whether it is a good or bad project). The entrepreneur borrows this cost in addition to other necessary funds to undertake the risky project. Hence with the certification, the good entrepreneur will issue debt with face value D^c to maximize its return, subject to the constraint:

$$\max_{D^c \geqslant 0} \int_{D^c}^{+\infty} (R - D^c) p(R) \, dR$$

$$\text{s.t.: } C(D^c) = D^c[1 - P(D^c)] + \int_0^{D^c} Rp(R) \, dR \geqslant (1 - \rho)(I + c - A)$$

Given that $(1 + \rho)(I + c - A) \geqslant (1 + \rho)(I - A)$ and that the investors' constraint is binding, we get $D^c > D^*$, and $C(D^c) = (1 + \rho)(I + c - A)$ defines D^c.

---

[77] Here we compare the rated bond case with the information asymmetry pooling equilibrium case, however for some parameter values, one should really compare it to the separating equilibrium case. The drivers behind the willingness to pay for a rating though are similar.

The good entrepreneur is willing to pay a cost c to the rating agency to lift the information asymmetry as long as its net payoff with the certification is higher than in the pooling equilibrium, or as long as:

$$E(R) - C(D^P) < E(R) - C(D^c)$$

$$(1+\rho)(I + c - A) < C(D^P)$$

$$(1+\rho)c + \alpha C(D^P) + (1 - \alpha)\tilde{C}(D^P) < C(D^P)$$

$$(1+\rho)c < (1 - \alpha)\lfloor C(D^P) - \tilde{C}(D^P)\rfloor$$

$$c < \frac{1-\alpha}{1+\rho} \int_0^{D^P} (\tilde{P}(R) - P(R)) \, dR$$

Finally, we get:

$$c < \underbrace{\frac{1-\alpha}{1+\rho} \int_0^{D^P} [\tilde{P}(R) - P(R)] \, dR}_{\tau} = \frac{1-\alpha}{1+\rho}\tau$$

The good entrepreneur's willingness to pay for the rating is an increasing function of $(1 - \alpha)$ the proportion of bad borrowers willing to mimic the good borrower, and τ a measure of the intensity of the adverse selection problem. Indeed, as the cumulative distribution of the bad entrepreneur's payoffs $\tilde{P}$ converges to the good one P, the adverse selection problem disappears and the good entrepreneur's willingness to pay for the rating converges to 0. Finally, the cost c is also directly increasing with the bond's pooling equilibrium face value D^P. The higher D^P the more the good entrepreneur subsidizes the bad entrepreneur by borrowing a large amount of capital. Moreover, D^P is directly increasing with $I - A$, the amount of capital borrowed from the capital markets. Hence it makes sense that large issues have a higher willingness to pay for ratings than smaller ones.

Here we compare the issuer's willingness to pay for an accurate rating to a situation where good and bad issuers cannot be distinguished. However, there are other ways an issuer can signal its quality in order to separate himself from bad borrowers. One effective way of doing so is issuing putable bonds:

Marks & Spencer included its First Poison Puts in £400M of Notes Issued in March 2007

Marks & Spencer, the biggest British clothing retailer, is providing a refuge for bond-holders ravaged by the wave of leveraged buyouts sweeping Europe. Bondholders at European consumer companies have lost $92 million during 2007-Q1 amid speculation that buyouts would push up debt, eroding the value of existing bonds.

Poison puts, or change-of-control covenants that guarantee the value of bonds in the case of leveraged buyout, were included in at least $8.9 billion of securities sold by European companies in the past five weeks, more than half the total. By protecting bondholders, companies save almost 50 bps in annual interest, according to analysts at Bank of America.

Marks & Spencer issued its first putable debt after more than 100 bond offerings totalling over $10 billion in the past two decades without the clauses. It used the put feature to entice buyers to its first bond sale since an approach three years ago by billionaire Philip Green wiped \$136 million off the value of the retailer's debt securities.[78] Fitch called the M&S issue 'Bondholders armour from potential takeovers.'[79]

Ratings Follow-up as a Solution to the Moral Hazard Problem in Debt

In this section we describe the moral hazard problem more formally and highlight how the monitoring by a rating agency can solve the moral hazard problem.

To illustrate the moral hazard problem in debt, we again consider a simple two-period model. Initially, at time, $t = 0$ an entrepreneur (also called the issuer or borrower) invests in a risky project. He invests part of his own cash and borrows the rest from the public debt market. Investors (also called debt-holders or lenders) buy the bond issued by the entrepreneur at this time. At the end of the period, at time $t = 1$, the risky project returns a payoff, of which investors get a promised amount according to the terms of the debt claim. The entrepreneur is the residual claimant.

We keep the same notation as previously. Assumptions 1, 2, and 3 of the previous section are maintained, but use assumption 4b instead of assumption 4.

> 4b. After he has invested, the entrepreneur now has the opportunity to put more or less effort, respectively e_h and e_l, in the execution of the project. The entrepreneur gets a private benefit B from lowering his effort. The project's return is $R \in [0, +\infty)$ with a pdf $p(R/e_h)$ when the entrepreneur puts in a high level of effort, or $p(R/e_l)$ if the entrepreneur puts in a low amount of effort. $p(./e_h)$ f.o.s.d. $p(./e_l)$.

Finally, we just consider the case where the project has a negative expected NPV if the entrepreneur misbehaves.

Symmetric Information

In the case of symmetric information, we assume that the investor perfectly observes the entrepreneur's effort. We assume that the effort is either verifiable by a court or/and that the entrepreneur's effort is sufficiently observable by outside parties that instances of shirking are revealed publicly so that reputation mechanisms ensure that the entrepreneur exerts a high effort to comply with the terms of the contract and not divert resources from the project to obtain private benefits. In a two-period model the reputation mechanism cannot be modeled explicitly, but assume that there are no opportunities for the entrepreneur to take hidden actions.

That is: conditional on exerting the high level of effort, the entrepreneur's project has a positive expected NPV: $E(R/e_h) = \int_0^{+\infty} R p(R/e_h) \, dR \geqslant (1 + \rho)I$. The entrepreneur issues a standard debt contract. At time $t = 0$ he borrows an amount $I - A$ with face value D. Define $w(R, D)$ as the entrepreneur's payoff at $t = 1$ after having paid the investors:

$$w(R, D) = \begin{cases} 0 & \text{if } R \in [0, D) \\ R - D & \text{if } R \in [D, +\infty). \end{cases}$$

---

[78] Adapted from: Bloomberg News, 2007, Some take refuge in poison puts, *International Herald Tribune*, April 4, page 14.
[79] Fitch Ratings, 2007, Bondholders' armour from potential takeovers, *Press Release*, March 26, 1 page.

Investors who buy the good entrepreneur's debt claim will get:

$$R - w(R, D) = \begin{cases} R & \text{if } R \in [0, D) \\ D & \text{if } R \in [D, +\infty). \end{cases}$$

The good entrepreneur will set D in order to maximize his payoff subject to the constraint that investors should be rewarded at the competitive market rate ρ.

$$\max_{D \geqslant 0} \int_0^{+\infty} (R - D) p(R/e_h) \, dR$$
$$\text{s.t.:} \quad (1 + \rho)(I - A) - E(R/e_h) + \int_D^{+\infty} (R - D) p(R/e_h) \, dR \leqslant 0$$

Given the entrepreneur's maximization problem, he will just issue the bond with the lowest possible face value D^* such that investors get in expectation their competitive market return given their investment of $(I - A)$. The maximization problem is relatively simple in the sense that the entrepreneur is just the residual claimant of the project. Define the solution D^* by:

$$C(D^*) = D^*[1 - P(D^*)] + \int^{D^*} R p(R/e_h) \, dR = (1 + \rho)(I - A)$$

The entrepreneur borrows an amount $I - A$ at an expected cost of $(1 + \rho)(I - A)$. Investors invest an amount $I - A$ at $t = 0$ and expect to get in return

$$C(D^*) = (1 + \rho)(I - A) \quad \text{at} \quad t = 1$$

The entrepreneur then has a competitive expected cost of capital ρ.

Asymmetric Information: Moral Hazard Without Monitoring

In this case investors do not observe the entrepreneur's effort; they only observe the realization R of the outcome of the project. We assume that the project is viable (positive expected NPV) only if the entrepreneur exerts a high level of effort, i.e. $E(R/e_h) \geqslant I(1 + \rho)$. The project has a negative NPV, even taking into account the private benefit if the entrepreneur 'shirks':

$$E(R/e_l) + B < I(1 + \rho)$$

Hence, no loan that gives an incentive to misbehave will be provided.

That is, given that the net value created is negative, there is no way of splitting the project's return that can satisy both the investors and the entrepreneur. Hence, for the entrepreneur and investors to invest in the project, the entrepreneur needs to have the incentives to exert the high level of effort. Without incentives, monitoring, or effort observability, after the loan agreement, the entrepreneur will always be better off shirking, at the expense of the investor. Hence, in this case the entrepreneur will issue a debt claim provided that the claim's face value D is sufficiently high for investors to get in expectation a competitive return on their investment, but as low as possible for the entrepreneur to have a sufficient stake in the project that he will not want to divert resources for his private benefit. His optimization program then becomes:

$$\max_{D \geq 0} \int_{D}^{+\infty} (R - D)p(R/e_h)\, dR$$

$$\text{s.t:} \quad \int_{D}^{+\infty} (R - D)p(R/e_h)\, dR \geq \int_{D}^{+\infty} (R - D)p(R/e_l)\, dR + B \tag{IC}$$

$$(1 - \rho)(I - A) - E(R/e_h) + \int_{D}^{+\infty} (R - D)p(R/e_h)\, dR \leq 0. \tag{IR}$$

As before, the investor's IR constraint defines:

$$C(D^h) = E(R/e_h) - \int_{D^h}^{+\infty} (R - D^h)p(R/e_h)\, dR = (1 + \rho)(I - A)$$

However D^h must be sufficiently small for the entrepreneur to have a large enough residual claim or stake in the return of the project, that is:

$$\int_{D^h}^{+\infty} (R - D^h)[p(R/e_h) - p(R/e_l)]dR \geq B.$$

Because $C(D^h)$ is increasing in D^h and $C(D^h) = (1 + \rho)(I - A)$, a debt claim satisfying both the investor's individual rationality constraint and the entrepreneur's incentive compatibility constraint will exist if $A \geq \overline{A}$, that is if the entrepreneur has a large enough stake.[80]

Hence, for any $A < \overline{A}$, even though the project is positive NPV, it will not be funded. The entrepreneur's net payoff or utility will then be:

$$U = \begin{cases} 0 & \text{if } A \geq \overline{A} \\ \int_{D^h}^{+\infty} (R - D^h)p(R/e_h)\, dR - A(1 - \rho) & \\ \quad = E(R/e_h) - (1 + \rho)I & \text{if } A \geq \overline{A} \end{cases}$$

---

[80] $\overline{A}$ is defined by:

$$C^{-1}[(1 + \rho)(I - A)] = D^h$$

$$\int_{D^h}^{+\infty} (R - D^h)[p(R/e_h) - p(R/e_l)]\, dR \leq B$$

equivalent to

$$\int_{D^h}^{+\infty} [P(R/e_l) - P(R/e_h)]\, dR \geq B$$

which implies

$$\int_{C^{-1}[(1+\rho)(I-\overline{A})]}^{+\infty} [P(R/e_l) - P(R/e_h)]\, dR = B$$

The implication of moral hazard is the existence of **credit rationing**. That is, there are positive expected NPV projects that do not get funding because the entrepreneur does not have a large enough stake in the project to provide sufficient incentives against hidden actions such as diverting resources from the project for personal benefits (B) or not putting enough effort in the realization of the project $E(R/e_l) \leqslant E(R/e_h)$ or preferring riskier projects that favor him relative to the lender: $p(./e_h)$ f.o.s.d. $p(./e_l)$.

Ratings and Moral Hazard (no Adverse Selection)   The entrepreneur is creditworthy and would like to raise funds on the public debt markets to realize a risky project but cannot because he does not have enough cash ($A < \overline{A}$) to invest in the project to gain investors' trust that he will not be subject to moral hazard. Suppose that at a cost c the entrepreneur can have access to a reputable rating agency that will accurately monitor the entrepreneur's effort in the execution and follow-up of the project. Thanks to the monitoring of a rating agency, investors will be willing to lend to the entrepreneur even if his personal stake in the project is low ($A < \overline{A}$), knowing that the agency's monitoring aligns the entrepreneur's incentives with the lenders. The entrepreneur borrows this cost in addition to the other necessary funds for his risky project. Hence with the certification, the entrepreneur will issue debt with face value D^c such that:

$$\max_{D^c \geqslant 0} \int_{D^c}^{+\infty} (R - D^c) p(R/e_h) \, \mathrm{d}R$$

$$\text{s.t}: \; C(D^c) = D^c[1 - P(D^c/e_h)] + \int_0^{D^c} Rp(r/e_h) \, \mathrm{d}R$$

$$\leqslant (1 + \rho)(I + c - A)$$

Given that $(1 + \rho)(I + c - A) \geqslant (1 + \rho)(I - A)$ and that the investors' constraint is binding, we get $D^c > D^*$, and $C(D^c) = (1 + \rho)(I + c - A)$ defines D^c. The entrepreneur is willing to pay a cost c to the rating agency to lift the information asymmetry as long as its net payoff with the certification is positive:

$$E(R/e_h) - (1 + \rho)(I + c) \geqslant 0$$

or
$$c \leqslant \frac{E(R/e_h)}{1 + \rho} - I$$

The entrepreneur's willingness to pay for a rating is relatively high, because in this case ($A < \overline{A}$), without it he would not have access to funds that would allow him to undertake the project.

3.2.3   The Economic Analysis of Ratings: Summary and Implications

None of the above suggests that it is in a borrower's economic interest to have access to as cheap credit as possible, or, as a result, thus 'to have a high credit rating. In fact, a foundation paper of modern corporate finance elucidates the merits of capital being costly.[81]

---

[81] Jensen, M.C., 1996, Agency costs of free cash flow, corporate finance and takeovers, *American Economic Review*, Vol. 76, No. 2, May.

And evidence suggests that costly credit leads to better investment decisions.[82] A high credit rating would be in the economic interest of the borrower's shareholders, conditional on the issuer having an optimal capital structure, as we hinted when we discussed the misinterpretation of ratings in Section 2.3.2. In fact, obtaining a high credit rating per se is very easy. Just maximize equity financing, at whatever cost. Would this make any sense? No. It is in the firm's economic interest to have an optimal capital structure. At a particular point in time, the search for optimality trades-off the expected agency and bankruptcy costs of debt against the benefits of debt in generating a tax shield and in reducing the agency cost of equity. Dynamically, the search for optimality trades off the access to debt and the flexibility that equity provides against the upside potential to equity that debt provides.

It is in the lasting borrowers' interest to have an accurate credit rating. Accuracy is the key, not the level. Think about it in the following way. With any optimal amount of debt there is associated a true, but unknown, likelihood of default and loss in the event of default. The optimal rating is the one that embeds an unbiased and efficient estimate of the likelihood and that loss. This is the kernel of the quest of credit rating agencies: to get it right. That is what investors expect from a credit rating in order to use it in their supply of capital decisions, and what issuers desire in order to be able to access the capital markets at the best price for the optimal capital structure they wish to maintain. For some companies in such circumstances this could be well below investment grade rating and, for others, a high investment grade one.

It would be against the issuers' economic interest if ratings failed the accuracy test. Public investors might cease trying to discriminate between bad and good credit. In that case suppliers will protect themselves by assuming that all credit is more or less bad, thereby overcharging good credit and undercharging bad. Myopically, this may be in the economic interest of the bad ones, but that cannot last. Being cross-subsidized by good credit, bad credit will overinvest, thereby eventually guaranteeing self-destruction. This is hardly in its long run economic interest.

The entrepreneur has alternatives to protect the investment from moral hazard other than monitoring from a rating agency. The formal analysis assumed that this was not the case. Actually, there are alternatives such as offering investors the option to convert the regular debt claim into a share, if the project's prospects become favorable. In this case, investors may still suffer from the diversion of resources to private benefits and from the lower expected return, but they would then also benefit from the increased riskiness of the project.[83] Alternatively, lenders may require to protect themselves against the entrepreneur's misbehavior by writing loan covenants that force the firm to exert care. These covenants are in place to help lenders to monitor the entrepreneur by setting goals for certain financial ratios, or requiring certain actions or forbidding others.[84] (Rating triggers used in bond covenants are discussed in Section 3.1.3.) Moreover, credit rating agencies are not the only players in the financial markets monitoring managers of firms, but they certainly are the main monitors for debtholders. Other parties, such as underwriters, financial analysts, large

---

[82] See for instance: Rehman, Z., 2007, Does costly credit lead to better investment decisions? Evidence from Bank- and Bond-Financed acquisitions, March 27, Working Paper, 1–73.

[83] Brennan M., and Schwartz, E., 1988, The case for convertibles, *Journal of Applied Corporate Finance*, Vol. XX, 55–64.

[84] A reference on the economic analysis of bond covenants is Smith, C., and Warner, J., 1979. On financial contracting: an analysis of bond covenants, *Journal of Financial Economics*, Vol. 7, 117–161.

shareholders or bondholders, and venture capital firms also monitor crucial aspects of moral hazard in managerial behavior, but none monitor the possibility of firms' risk-shifting at the expense of bondholders as explicitly as rating agencies.

This section thus explained the critical role ratings play in reducing information asymmetry problems between investors and borrowers. If not resolved, adverse selection and moral hazard greatly increase the cost of external financing, may exclude the better issuers from the market, and lead to credit rationing. The wide range of organizations that use credit ratings – not only the principals in a loan arrangement, but also prescribers such as private contractors, regulators, trustees, boards of directors, corporate finance advisers, underwriters, and brokers – suggest that credit rating agencies perform this task very successfully.

3.3 CREDIT RATING SEGMENTS – OR SCALE AND SCOPE OF THE RATED UNIVERSE

We now turn to the scale and scope of the credit rating market. We describe where credit ratings have developed, by segment, and the equilibrium where credit ratings meet the supply of rating opportunities. The original ratings in 1909 were for US railroad bonds, but today credit ratings span a vast array of products, industries, countries, regions, and currencies, as we will see now during our discussion of the broad spectrum of rated parties across issuer, product and geographical sectors.

When John Moody published the first credit rating in 1909, it was for a US railroad bond although the railroad bond market dated back to the 1850s. Until that time, the investment bankers who underwrote, purchased, and distributed the bonds from railroad companies placed their reputation behind the bonds they sold through their networks of wealthy American and European investors. However, the new investors that emerged with the growth of the US economy increasingly wanted to benefit from the access to detailed information enjoyed by investment bankers. The introduction of credit ratings by John Moody was a response to this demand, combining elements of the functions previously performed by the investment bankers, financial journals, and credit reporting firms.

The number of different rated instruments has expanded greatly, from bonds to other financing instruments such as commercial paper, bank deposits, structured finance instruments, and loans. And among those, agencies differentiate between short-term and long-term credit ratings. In summary, the various types of ratings are a combination of the issuer (e.g. corporate (large and SME) vs sovereign vs municipal vs structured finance), the instrument (e.g. bonds, commercial paper, loans), the country of the issuer, and the target market of the issue (domestic or international). The following sections discuss the most important recent developments in each of these segments.

3.3.1 Industry Segments or Type of Rated Issuers

As per S&P's definition,

> an issuer credit rating is an opinion of the obligor's overall capacity to meet its financial obligations. This opinion focuses on the obligor's capacity and willingness to meet its financial commitments as they come due. The opinion is not specific to any particular financial obligation,

because it does not take into account the specific nature or provisions of any particular obligation. Issuer credit ratings do not take into account statutory or regulatory preferences, nor do they take into account the creditworthiness of guarantors, insurers, or other forms of credit enhancement that may pertain to a specific obligation. Counterparty ratings, corporate credit ratings, and sovereign ratings are all forms of issuer credit ratings.[85]

The landscape of issuers is made up of about six groups. Figure 3.5 shows the distribution of issuer ratings by issuer class and by geographic region. Industrials and corporates form the largest group, followed by the financial sector, where rated insurance companies are more numerous than rated commercial banks and insurance companies. Special purpose vehicles (SPV) for securitized asset pools represent a significant group that has grown in importance since the publication of this data.. Unsurprisingly, there are more rated sub-sovereigns than sovereigns.[86]

These issuer groups are real business segments. CRAs tend to separate the work of credit analysts and organize divisions of activities along the lines of these issuer groups. This

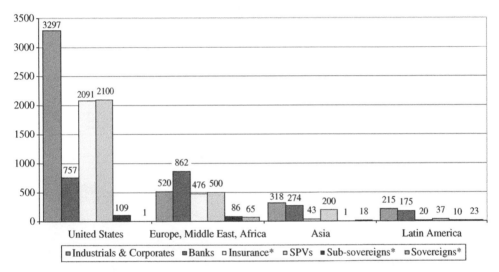

Figure 3.5   Issuer rating by issuer class and geographic region (2000)
Notes:

1. Due to lack of data, the highest number of rated issuers by one of 4 credit rating agencies (DCR, Fitch, Moody's, and S&P).
2. For insurance firms, ratings are FSR (Financial Strength Rating), a measure of a company's ability to pay out their insurance claims rather than the likelihood of them defaulting on the repayment of issued debt.

Source: Estrella, A., 2000. Credit ratings and complementary sources of credit quality information, Basel Committee on Banking Supervision, Working Papers No. 3: Bank for International Settlements, Basel, August, 1-180, pages 33–34.

---

[85] S&P, 2005, *Corporate Ratings Criteria*, page 9.
[86] Although the data is relatively old, it is one of the few available by issuer (not issue), segment and geographic region.

suggests that these groups have sufficient common default risk characteristics to make them distinct from other groups.

Industrials and Corporates

The last 35 years have witnessed radical changes in the global industrial segment. As Figure 3.6 illustrates, the number of global rated issuers grew at a compounded annual rate of 4.7%, quintupling in 35 years from 1045 in 1970 to 5767 in 2006.[87] Periods of uninterrupted high economic growth saw above-average spurts of new issuers entering the debt-financing market through rated securities: 791 or 54% new issuers during 1985–1988 and 2702 or 214% during 1993–2000, but it was not just economic growth that drove the changes.

Corporations significantly increased their use of capital markets to obtain credit, although this occurred at the expense of commercial banks, thereby expanding the supply of opportunities to 'credit rate.'[88] For example, of the $207.7 billion financial debt that corporate business had outstanding in the US in 1965, $93.7 billion or 45.1% was in the form of loans and $114.0 billion or 54.9% in the form of bonds. Out of a total of $10 979.3 billion in 2006, the share of loans had declined to 21% and the share of bonds had increased to

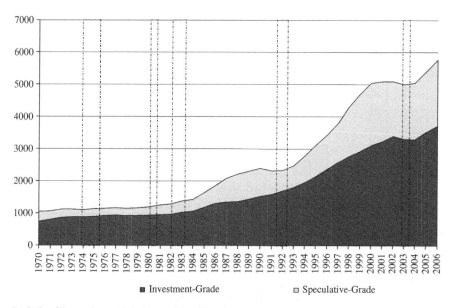

Periods of Recession: 11/73–3/75, 1/80–7/80, 7/81–11/82, 7/90–3/91, 4/01–12/01.

Figure 3.6   The number of different corporate issuers (1970–2006)
Source: Moody's Investors Service, 2007, *Corporate Default and Recovery Rates, 1920–2006,* Exhibit 33.

---

[87] Moody's rated corporate issuers from Exhibit 42, Moody's special comment (revised version), 2006, Default and recovery rates of corporate bond issuers, 1920–2005, March, Moody's Investors Service, 52 pages.

[88] Broadly speaking, debt capital can be supplied either in the form of bank loans from commercial banks or in the form of bonds which are issued to investors in the capital markets. While commercial banks still supply the majority of debt financing in Europe, companies in the United States have access to cheaper, longer term money in the capital markets and therefore the importance of bank loans has declined over time.

79%. Over the same period, the ratio of loans to bonds in the financial debt of non-financial corporations declined from 77.6% to 46.5%.[89]

This intensified use of capital markets in lieu of bank credit had several reasons that reinforced each other and we will discuss the most important ones. Interest rates went up almost continually during the late 1960s and the 1970s, the US prime rate reaching an all-time high of 20.5% in August 1981. Borrowers became ever more price sensitive to the cost of borrowing which, other things being equal, is lower for liquid investment vehicles such as bonds, than for illiquids such as loans. Market interest rates exceeded regulatory interest rate ceilings on commercial bank time deposits, and commercial banks were prevented from paying competitive interest rates on time deposits, driving them to the securities market for funding. Thus, the rising interest rates drove both banks and corporations to the capital markets for funding. Concurrently, the institutionalization of investable asset pools, which were gathering/welcoming/embracing the funds withdrawn from the commercial bank time deposits, increased the demand for the rated paper that banks and corporations were offering.

Of the corporate issuers, the fastest growing rated segment was speculative grade firms. These tend to be firms that pay particular attention not only to the costs of distress in choosing their ideal amount of debt, but also to their credit ratings.[90] The speculative grade segment grew at a rate of 6.2% per year, reaching 2048 issuers by 2006, or over one-third of all issuers and more than all issuers together in 1970. It is also a volatile segment, as Figure 3.7 shows. It experienced a real boom during the four go-go years 1985–1988,

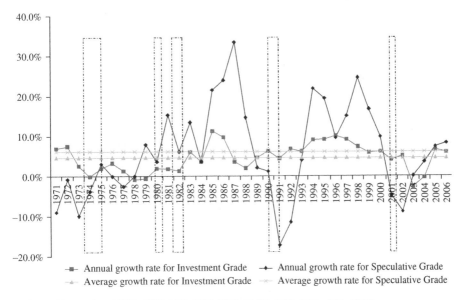

Periods of Recession: 11/73–3/75, 1/80–7/80, 7/81–11/82, 7/90–3/91, 4/01–12/01.

Figure 3.7   Growth rate and volatility of new participation of corporate issuers (1970–2006)
Source: Moody's Investors Service, 2007, *Corporate Default and Recovery Rates, 1920–2006,* Exhibit 33.

---

[89] Federal Reserve, Flow of funds accounts of the United States historical data, L.212, L.215, L.216.
[90] Graham, J.R., and Harvey, C.R., 2001, The theory and practice of corporate finance: evidence from the field, *Journal of Financial Economics*, May, Vol. 60, Issue 2-3, 187-243, page 17.

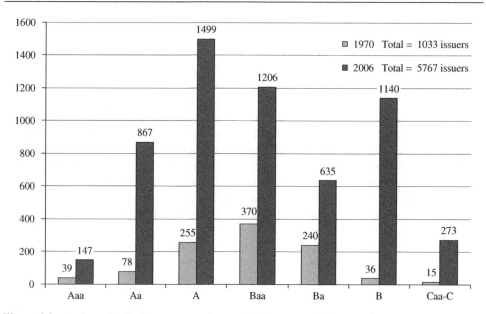

Figure 3.8 Ratings distribution corporate issuers (1970 versus 2006)
Source: Moody's Investors Service, 2007, *Corporate Default and Recovery Rates, 1920–2006*,
Exhibit 33.

when the number of issuers more than doubled from 368 to 847. It then went through
the 1991–1992 bust, losing 231 issuers through defaults or otherwise. In the process, the
overall rating distribution became bi-modal and shifted to the right, as Figure 3.8 illustrates.
In 1970, the distribution had one mode at the Baa level. By 2006, it had a mode at the
A level and another at the B level.

The change in the distribution of ratings of corporate issuers over the last 35 years is
related to the industry composition of corporate issuers, shown in Figure 3.9. The largest
sector is the financial sector, consisting of financial institutions and insurance companies
followed by the Consumer/Service and the Aerospace/Automotive/Capital goods/Metals sectors. Looking at the fine rating distribution of the individual sectors, as shown in Figure 3.10,
we see that the bi-modal rating distribution of the corporate segment, as shown in Figure 3.8,
is really made up of two rating class sub-segments with their own distribution and industrial
fiber underneath them. The financial and utilities sectors constitute the bulk of investment
grade distribution, with single modes at A+ and BBB respectively. The consumer and capital
goods sectors constitute the bulk of speculative grade distribution, with single-modes at B+.

Special Purpose Vehicles (SPVs) for Securitized Asset Pools

Almost non-existent about 30 years ago, SPVs for asset pools have seen the fastest growth
rate of all issuer segments since then. The expansion of this segment has been due to four
main drivers.

The first driver of growth started with banks selling assets to raise cash that was hardly
available otherwise. When market interest rates in the US increased in the mid-1970s,
such that they exceeded the maximum rates that commercial banks and similar financial

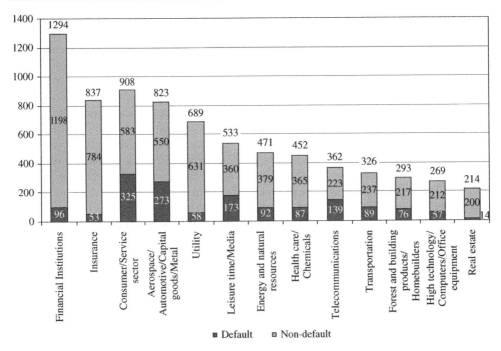

Figure 3.9 Global rated corporate issuers by industry as of June 30, 2007
Note: 'D' rating (or Default) is accumulated since 1981.

Source: Standard & Poor's, 2007, *Data from CreditPro 7.71*, August 1.

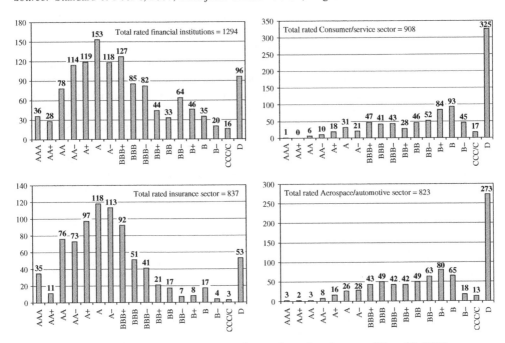

Figure 3.10 Top 4 industries' rated corporate issuers by rating class as of June 30, 2007
Source: Standard & Poor's, 2007, *Data from CreditPro 7.71*, August 1.

intermediaries were allowed to pay on their time deposits, the banks became subject to severe liquidity drains as consumers withdrew substantial amounts of funds for placement in instruments with higher rates of return, such as money market funds. To replenish their liquidity, the banks started raising cash by pooling some of their loans and selling them to new corporations, called SPVs, created for that purpose. Soon this technique for raising cash became relatively standardized and was also used in other circumstances.

The second driver was newly imposed stringent equity capital requirements for some financial intermediaries such as commercial banks, but not for others. This increased the amount of equity that banks needed to hold to back up their earning assets. This made capital more expensive for those financial intermediaries subject to capital requirements for the holding of earning assets than for those to whom these capital requirements did not apply. As the cost of funding became uncompetitive, banks downsized their loan portfolios. They slowed down their own funding of some of the earning assets that they generated by selling existing loans to SPVs, making new loans with the cash raised in this way, pooling sets of assets to sell to SPVs, raising cash again, etc.

The next driver, subtly different from the previous one, was balance-sheet driven transactions for 'capital requirement regulatory arbitrage.' Specifically, these are cases of originators supplying asset-backed securities in order to optimize their return on capital. For example, SPVs enabled banks to sell particular sets of assets to reduce regulatory capital while maintaining some of the return. A bank selling some of its assets to a SPV clears its balance sheet from these assets and invests instead in a portion of the equity tranche issued by the SPV. Under capital requirements that prevailed until recently, that equity tranche required no more capital (often less) for the bank than the loans sold.[91] But as the equity tranche is the first-loss (or most subordinated) tranche, it is also the one with the highest expected return. This operation allows the bank to extend new loans and to have access to cheaper capital than if it just securitized pools of assets without structuring, or if it borrowed from the market using the assets as collateral. For many commercial banks, the issue of asset-backed securities is seen as a cheap source of funding.

Lastly, SPV techniques became standard instruments for risk management. Market participants adopted several documentation standards. With advances in theoretical knowledge and experience, originating asset holders improved their mastering of the risk–return characteristics of these asset pools, They became better at segregating them from their balance sheets and at designing securities that could be issued to finance them through SPVs at a better credit rating than otherwise would have been the case. For example, a segregated mortgage portfolio would back exclusively the securities of the SPV, whereas as part of the commingled assets of a lender, that same portfolio could have to support many different types of claims in case of an emergency. Therefore, the securities issued against that portfolio as the sole asset of an SPV would command a lower default probability and a higher credit rating than the securities implicitly issued against that portfolio as part of a larger

---

[91] This has changed under the new Basel II capital requirement regulations that countries, and banks in these countries have started applying. Indeed, under Basel II, the amount of the equity that a bank has in an SPV obtains a 100% risk weight and a 100% capital charge. Indeed, one of the objectives of Basel II is to reduce the volume of transactions motivated by capital arbitrage. The new system of capital charges preserves on and off balance sheet neutrality, i.e. the capital that banks must hold is the same whether they hold a pool of loans on balance sheet or if they securitize it and retain all the tranches. It has become attractive for banks to unwind their SPVs to save equity capital, a process that has already started in Europe. For a clear reference see: Perraudin, William, 2007, Securitization in Basel II, Chapter 15, the *Handbook of Structured Finance*, Standard and Poor's, McGraw-Hill, 675–696.

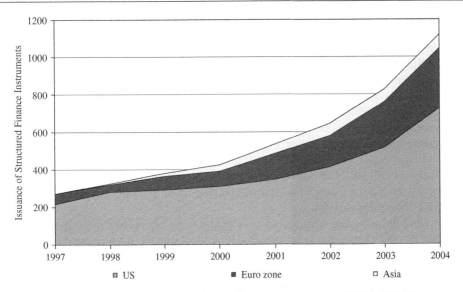

Figure 3.11 SPV Issuance of Structured Finance Instruments by region (1997–2004)*
*Billions of US dollars, includes cash issuance and funded portion of synthetics.
Source: JP Morgan Structured Finance Research from the *BIS Quarterly Review*, June 2005.

commingled asset pool with other liabilities outstanding against it. With continued competitive and regulatory pressure on financial intermediaries to optimize their values at risk,
the SPV techniques were further transformed to legitimate instruments of risk segregation,
allocation, and risk–return management in their own right.[92]

As a result of the above drivers and trends, the use of SPVs has seen continuously strong
growth over the last decade. Figure 3.11 illustrates this by showing the growth in the value
of the structured finance instruments issued by SPVs to fund themselves. Over that period
of time, issuance in the US has more than tripled and become well established in Europe.
In Asia, however, structured finance is still in a relative fledgling state.

Sovereigns

Governments seek a rating in order to ease their access – and the access of companies
domiciled within their borders – to the international capital markets.[93] Institutional investors
in particular are not likely to purchase the bonds of risky emerging market borrowers unless
the securities have an adequate rating from a reliable credit rating agency. While foreign
governments generally cooperate with the agencies, there have been bitter disputes over
ratings that governments have felt to be unjustified. When Japan lost its AAA rating in
2001, it openly criticized the reliability of ratings.[94] On the other hand, numerous emerging
market governments could not have tapped the world capital markets without the credit

---

[92] There have, very unfortunately, also been many illegitimate uses of SPVs by unscrupulous highly indebted
corporations in attempts to hide some of their liabilities. Enron is probably the most well known case of this.
[93] This section draws on S&P, 2006, The future of sovereign ratings, *Research*, September 5 for data and examples.
[94] For example, in 2002, Haruhiko Kuroda, Ministry of Finance Vice Minister for International Affairs, was bluntly
public about his opinion regarding the rating agencies. 'Considering the strong fundamentals of the Japanese
economy, the current ratings of Japanese Government Bonds are already too low and any further downgrading

rating agencies' reputation in resolving information asymmetries between them and would-be investors.

The history of sovereign ratings started in 1927 in the US and moved slowly until 1988. Standard Statistics and Poor's Ratings were the first to assign ratings to sovereigns issuing debt. These ratings assessed the default risk of the debt obligations of sovereign countries.[95] The governments of these countries were not necessarily comfortable with an outside opinion about their creditworthiness, particularly if it was less than AAA. For a long time, foreign government interest in obtaining a credit rating remained limited, particularly as they didn't need a rating when government debt was easily sold domestically and when foreign markets for government paper were relatively small and fragmented, and thus not attractive for an issuer. Before 1975, S&P had just two foreign currency sovereign issuer ratings outstanding (Canada and the US), a number that started creeping up in 1975 to become 18 in 1984, to stay at that level through 1988.

From 1989 onwards, the coverage of sovereign ratings expanded rapidly as Figure 3.12 illustrates. In 1983 Denmark was downgraded to AA+, losing the AAA rating it had received just two years earlier. In 1986, Australia was similarly downgraded, losing the AAA status it obtained in 1981. This helped governments to overcome the stigma of seeing their debt rated less than AAA, and facilitated a more realistic access to the international bond markets.

In 1989 emerging market debt ... emerged as a new asset class needing ratings. A severe crisis in Latin America in the 1980s had led to massive debt defaults. Private and government short- to medium-term illiquid debt in the form of bank or public loans were in default or quasi-default. In March 1989, the international financial community followed

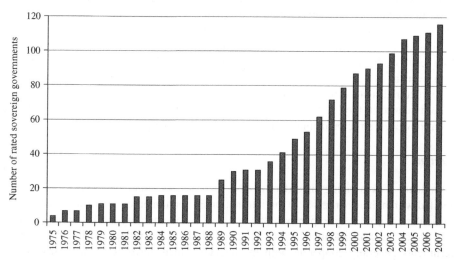

Figure 3.12   The number of S&P foreign currency sovereign credit ratings (1975 – September 28, 2007)
Source: Beers, D.T., 2007, Credit FAQ: The future of sovereign credit ratings, *Research*: Standard & Poor's, October 16, 1–12, Chart 1.

---

is unwarranted. Your explanations regarding rating decisions are mostly qualitative in nature and lack objective criteria, which invite questions about the larger issue of the reliability of ratings itself.'
[95] There exist several types of sovereign ratings to capture divergent risks. For example, for each nation, Fitch sovereign ratings include Long- and Short-term Foreign Currency and Local Currency Debt Ratings. See Fitch website. This section refers essentially to long-term foreign currency sovereign debt ratings.

the leadership of US Treasury Secretary Nicholas Brady in agreeing to exchange these for more liquid and long-term bonds. These 'Brady bonds' introduced emerging markets as an asset class to international investors and launched the issuer segment of foreign currency sovereign credit ratings.

In addition, the supply of countries, mostly in the emerging markets class, increased. In 1990–1991, the Soviet Union broke up, creating 15 new sovereigns. Yugoslavia followed suit and its break-up added a few more. More recently, in June 2006, Montenegro expanded the ratable universe to more than 200, according to S&P. With the globalization of capital markets, many emerging market borrowers tapped the international capital markets for the first time during the 1990s. Mexico and Hungary issued their first speculative-grade sovereign Yankee bonds in 1992. In 1995, Jordan became the first rated Arab state, and Trinidad and Tobago became the first rated Caribbean sovereign in 1996.

Typically, a government will go to the capital markets first, setting a country benchmark. This then allows the country's top corporations and financial institutions to follow it to market. Governments often seek a rating just to ease access to the international capital markets for companies domiciled within their borders. For instance, this was the case for Chile in 1992 and Georgia in 1995. US investors in particular are not likely to purchase the bonds of risky emerging market borrowers unless the securities have an adequate rating from a US-based rating agency.

One of the reasons that such sovereign ratings are so important to the private sector is that a rating agency will rarely assign a higher rating on the foreign currency debt of a company than the 'country ceiling,' which is directly linked to the sovereign rating and is either equal to or notched upward from the sovereign rating. The 'country ceiling' makes it very hard for a company – no matter how creditworthy – to obtain low-cost funding if the political environment in which it operates is deemed to be volatile and high risk by the rating agencies. Exhibit 3.3 suggests how hard it would have been for companies in some countries to obtain a high rating on January 10, 2000. Note the unforgiving low Caa1 rating for Pakistan (spread of 1800 bps) and Ukraine and the high dispersion of sovereign ratings and credit spreads across countries.

The lower the sovereign rating the more likely it will act as a ceiling for private sector ratings. However, a country downgrade does not need to imply a downgrade of issuers in the country, nor does a country ceiling really exist at all times, everywhere, and with all CRAs. For example, on October 19, 2006, Fitch and S&P downgraded the Republic of Italy's issuer credit rating one notch to AA− and A+, respectively.[96] A few months later, S&P reported that the downgrade 'had no effect on the ratings on major Italian banks, which continue to show steady progress.'[97] In fact, Banca Nazionale del Lavoro SpA maintained S&P's AA− rating, now higher than Italy's sovereign rating.

A last driver for traditionally unrated countries to seek a rating has been public corporate governance reform. The IMF and the World Bank, in cooperation with the international financial community, started this movement in the aftermath of the 1997–1998 Asian and Russian financial and the African credibility crisis. Eventually, many governments began to appreciate how sovereign ratings could contribute to transparency in the economic situation of the country and in their own public finances. This has been a significant factor in the

---

[96] On the same day, Moody's affirmed Italy's Government bond rating at Aa2: Moody's, 2006, Global credit research announcement, Government of Italy, October 19.

[97] Ganguin, B., and De Toytot, A., 2006, Private equity activity and uncertainty threaten the outlook for European credit quality in 2007, *Research*: Standard & Poor's, December 13, page 4.

Exhibit 3.3 Illustrative Sovereign credit ratings (2000)

Country	Moody's	Standard & Poor's	Pricing[a]
Argentina	B1	BB	572
Australia	Aa2	AA+	90
Brazil	B2	B+	503
Belgium	Aa1	AA+	73
Canada	Aa2	AA+	74
China	A3	BBB	228
Greece	A2	A−	124
Hungary	Baa1	BBB	97
Indonesia	B3	CCC+	609
Japan	Aa1	AAA	8
Pakistan	Caa1	B−	1800
Russia	B3	SD	N/A
South Africa	Baa3	BB+	331
South Korea	Baa2	BBB	274
Ukraine	Caa1	N/R	N/A
United Kingdom	Aaa	AAA	44
United States	Aaa	AAA	0

[a]Basis points over 10 year US Treasuries
Note: The pricing in column 3 is taken from Bloomberg and should be used for
illustrative purposes only to show general pricing relationships. Where available,
the pricing is based on the outstanding 10-year international sovereign issue. In
some cases, a bond of a shorter maturity had to be utilized given the lack of a
10-year benchmark outstanding bond.
Source: Bloomberg as of January 10, 2000

rapid expansion of sovereign rating participation for sub-Saharan Africa: Senegal (B+) in
2000, Botswana (A) 2001, Ghana (B+), Cameroon (B-), and Benin (B+) in 2003, Burkina
Faso (B), Madagascar (B), Mali (B), and Mozambique (B) in 2004. Many of these 'rating
entrants' benefited from the New Partnership for Africa's Development (NEPAD) program
of the United Nations Development Programme (UNDP) in having the private and public
sectors joining forces to develop the financial market infrastructure of emerging countries.
As the UNDP stated, one initiative of this program

'consists in helping countries obtain a credit rating from world-renowned rating agencies such
as Standard & Poor's, Fitch, or Moody's. These ratings are critical for international private
investors to decide on coming to a given country. UNDP has established a trust fund to
support selected countries with positive macroeconomic indicators obtain these ratings. This
program, which is to last several years, will also provide financial and technical assistance to
countries to negotiate with the credit rating agencies and monitor their performance indicators
successfully.'[98]

The above forces have vastly expanded the opportunities in favor of an increasing number
of countries being rated. To see the enrichment in the diversity of the sovereign rating
universe from the late 1980s until 2006, consider Figure 3.13. Layer upon layer of sovereign
rating participation has been added with lower and lower credit ratings. Comparing the
2007 end point of this movement and its 1975 starting point with a histogram of sovereign
ratings, Figure 3.14 shows a quasi tri-modal distribution centered around AAA, A and B

---

[98] Diabré, Z., UNDP Associate Administrator, Partnership with the private sector for financing Africa's growth
through NEPAD, Statement on April 15, 2002 in Dakar, Senegal, page 3.

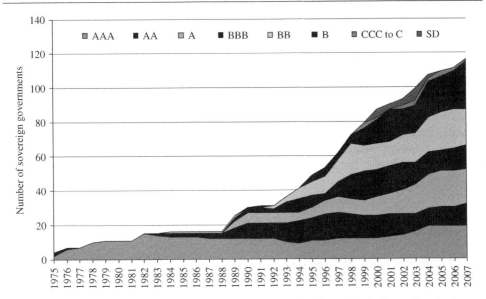

Figure 3.13 Distribution of foreign currency sovereign credit ratings (1975 – September 28, 2007)
Source: Beers, D.T., 2007, Credit FAQ: The future of sovereign credit ratings, *Research*: Standard & Poor's, October 16, 1–12, Chart 2.

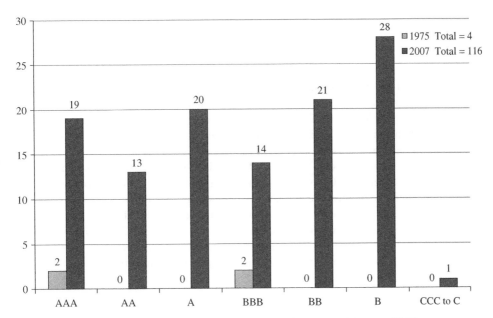

Figure 3.14 Histogram of rating dispersion of sovereign issuers (1975 versus 2007)
Note: 2007 ratings as of September 28, 2007.

Source: Beers, D.T., 2006, Credit FAQ: The future of sovereign credit ratings, *Research*: Standard & Poor's, September 5, pages 1–8, and October 16, pages 1–12.

respectively. A probably represents countries in transition from emerging B to mature AAA, and vice versa.

3.3.2 Product Segments or Types of Rated Issues

As the name suggests, issue ratings are specific to a particular instrument. Instrument ratings are issued for obligations of issuers across the whole spectrum of issuers and obligations. Hence, different obligations of the same obligor can have different ratings depending on seniority, security, covenants structure, tenor, etc. And as Fitch points out, these 'can be above, below or equal to the Issuer Default Rating IDR, depending on the security's priority among claims, the amount of collateral and other aspects of the capital structure.'[99]

Amazon.com, Inc: Moody's Current Ratings on 11 December 2006.

- LT Corporate Family Ratings – domestic: Ba2;
- Subordinate – domestic and foreign: Ba3;
- Senior Unsecured Shelf – domestic: (p) Ba1;
- Preferred Shelf – domestic: (p) B1.[100]

Of the many rated products, we will briefly review bonds and structured finance instruments because their markets and ratings have seen the most interesting developments.

Bonds

The Dutch started the bond markets some 300 years ago, in the early 17th century. The English emulated them about a century later, the US another hundred years after that. The US stood apart in that it had relatively minor national debt, which was entirely paid off in 1836.[101] Most bond investing until 1850 was in sovereign debt, universally considered to be a safe investment, and thus not needing a rating.[102]

In the US, the corporate bond market took the place of the government bond market from the late 18th century. Corporations, including banking and insurance, as well as transportation, actively entered the market. Manufacturing and public utilities companies that needed to access large pools of funds also started issuing bonds. The US corporate bond market continued to grow without credit ratings until the early 20th century. Finally, demand for greater disclosure of information about the huge US corporate bond market, hitherto the private domain of investment bankers, prompted the production of the first credit ratings.

---

[99] Fitch, 2006, Corporate rating methodology, *Corporate Finance Criteria Report*, June 13, page 1.

[100] Moody's Investors Service, 2004, Rating History on Amazon.com, Inc., April 24.

[101] Most states had withdrawn from the bond markets by the early 1840s, following a string of defaults.

[102] Sylla, R., 2001. An historical primer on the business of credit ratings, NY University Salomon Center, Conference on Rating Agencies and the Global Financial System, June 1, 1–29.

Nowadays, bond ratings have become very much a global activity, spanning multiple currencies, sectors, and borders.[103] Figure 3.15 illustrates the growth in the global bond markets. The gross issuance of international bonds and notes, virtually all rated, reached $3.8 trillion in 2005, 6.6 times higher than a decade previously. Interestingly, this growth was highly unequally distributed. The annual issuance – and correspondingly bond rating activity – in euros expanded by a factor of 8.7 over a decade, not least due to the adoption of the euro. Issuance in yen shrunk by 26%, an expression of the Japanese deflation. By 2005, yen gross issuance – and hence yen bond rating activity – was reduced to a mere 3% of gross issuance, with euro issuance taking the lions share of 48%, and exceeding gross dollar issuance since 2003.

In relation to sectors, annual issuance by financial institutions expanded by a factor of 7.0, representing 83% of all gross issuance in the international bond and note markets in 2005 and thereby creating the bulk of market growth – and the ratings business related to it. This was driven by three main forces, as discussed more fully in Section 8.1 Firstly, financial institutions entered international markets on the coat-tails of new sovereigns entering these markets. Secondly, within the broad financial institutions sector, non-commercial banks (investment banks, other financial institutions, etc.) expanded their activities much faster than commercial banks and the traditional reliance on funding through demand and time deposits was superseded by funding through securities markets. Finally, corporate tax rates prompted financial institutions that were subject to minimum capital requirements to fully use the long-term debt component of the requirements.

Sovereigns and international organizations increased their international issuance steadily (with the exception of 2001) over the period. This is very much in line with the increased sovereign participation in the markets discussed earlier. International corporate bond and note gross issuance expanded least overall. It was highly volatile: nearly doubling during the 'irrational exuberance' year of 1999 to $477 billion, but then contracting severely post-bubble by about 30% per year in 2001 and 2002. In addition to the withdrawal of commercial banks from direct international corporate lending – discussed earlier – the trend growth of international corporate bond issuance was due to the globalization in the organization of business and privatizations.

When industrial sectors consolidate and companies reorganize, redeploying globally, foreign investment grows along with the size of the surviving companies. The balance sheets and funding needs of an obligor tend to expand along with it. The expansion of foreign direct investment from $25.7 billion in 1989 to $165.5 billion in 2004, growing at the compounded annual growth rate of 12.3%, is an expression of that.[104] The universe of international companies seeking, naturally, international funding, has thus expanded correspondingly. And each time a government privatizes a company, a new supplier of corporate bonds also comes to the market. Both globalization and privatization became widespread around the turn of the century, and so the supply of corporate bonds has expanded.

---

[103] As a result, CRAs differentiate between instruments raised for the domestic market versus those targeted at the international markets, and between those in the currency of the target market or otherwise.

[104] World bank global development finance 2005, page 138.

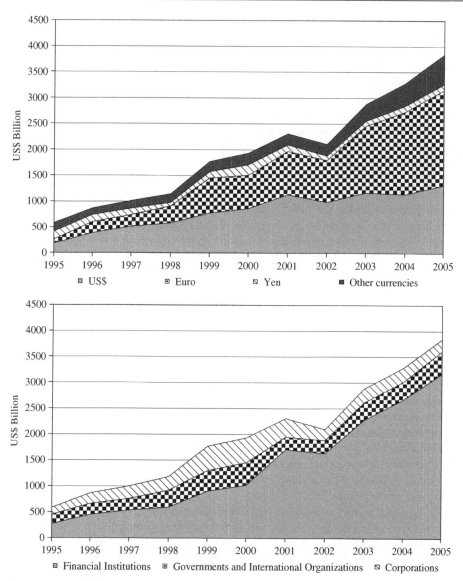

Figure 3.15 Gross issuance in the international bond and notes markets by currency and by institution type (1995–2005)

Note: The $81 billion of 1995 for gross issuance in euro are in fact issues in Deutschmark.

Sources:

1. Bank for International Settlements, 1997, International Banking and Financial Market Developments, *Quarterly Review*, November, 1–34, page 17. (1995 data)
2. Bank for International Settlements, 1998, International Banking and Financial Market Developments, *Quarterly Review*, November, 1–40, page 19. (1996 data)
3. Bank for International Settlements, 1999, International Banking and Financial Market Developments, *Quarterly Review*, November, 1–45, page 15. (1997 data)
4. Bank for International Settlements, 2000, International Banking and Financial Market Developments, *Quarterly Review*, August, 1–45, page 23. (1998 data)

Structured Finance Instruments

Structured finance instruments (SFIs) are claims on the future cash flow stream of the assets of an SPV. Unlike the early untranched, pass-through asset-backed securities, the claims that SPVs issue against their asset pools are bundled into different categories of seniority called tranches or classes. Indeed, 'structured' finance instruments are so called precisely due to the active process that goes into defining the properties of each class of security.

Exhibit 3.4 provides an overview of the various types of structured finance instruments and how they fit into the broader universe of all asset-backed securities. Each tranche has a different risk and return profile. In some sense, the SPV transforms the asset pool into a set of securities with different risk profiles, with the equity, preferred stock, and junior tranches absorbing the initial credit losses. The diagram in Exhibit 3.5 describes how the overall risk on a portfolio is tranched into classes of different risk and remuneration.

This tranching of claims makes the rating of structured finance instruments inherently different to rate than bonds. It has specific complexity because the mapping of pool cash flows to different tranches requires, as a prerequisite, an estimate of a loss distribution on the portfolio of ultimate obligors. But each of these obligors has its own unknown, but estimated, loss distribution, and losses that are correlated with that of other obligors are correlated with each – other. One therefore needs thus to appreciate that the smooth histogram of expected portfolio loss that Exhibit 3.5 shows is the result of a complex mathematical, statistical, and judgmental inference process that is unique to each CRA and specific to the ultimate obligors of the assets in the portfolios and the correlations among their performances. Detailed transaction and tranche-specific documentation, and the involvement of multiple parties, also increase the complexity of these instruments. In addition, the credit risk of the tranches can be affected by risks that are unrelated to the default risk embodied in the underlying asset pool, such as the quality of the work of the servicer (who tracks and collects payments on the asset pool against a fee).

CRAs are involved with SFIs in multiple ways that are distinct from traditional issuer or instrument ratings. They rate the different tranches, assess third parties involved in the transaction, and ensure the legal soundness of the structure, including the proper de-linking of the default risk of the asset pool from the default risk of the originator. Moreover, due to the greater complexity of structured finance instruments, credit ratings play a more significant role in removing information asymmetries concerning credit risk than in the case of bonds. The rating of structured instruments is considered inherent to the instrument. Indeed, the

---

Figure 3.15 *continued*

5. Bank for International Settlements, 2001, The International Debt Securities Market, *Quarterly Review*, September, 23–28, page 25. (1999 and 2000 data)
6. Bank for International Settlements, 2003, International Banking and Financial Market Developments, *Quarterly Review*, December, 1–103, page 28. (2001 and 2002 data)
7. Bank for International Settlements, 2005, The International Debt Securities Market, *Quarterly Review*, Part 3, June, 31–40, page 32. (2003 data)
8. Bank for International Settlements, 2006, International Banking and Financial Market Developments, *Quarterly Review*, June, 1–83, page 28. (2004 and 2005 data)

Exhibit 3.4   Structured finance products: an overview of the ABS universe

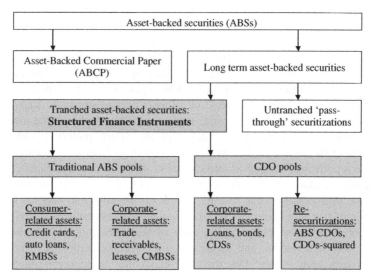

Source: Committee on the Global Financial System, 2005, The role of ratings in structured finance: issues and implications, Bank for International Settlements, Basel, January, 1–59, page 5.

Exhibit 3.5   The tranching of a risky portfolio into different classes of securities

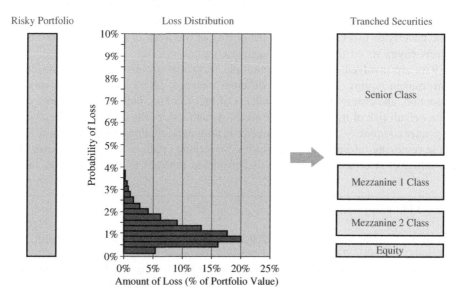

The overall risk on the portfolio is 'tranched' into classes of different risk and different remuneration

Source: Marjolin, B., 2007, *Securitization* – ESSEC presentation, Moody's Investors Service, March 16, page 8.

rating process occurs at the same stage as the instrument is structured by the structurer. Structurers design the instruments to meet agencies' rating requirements, because investors rely heavily on the rating to make their investment decision. The reliance on ratings, and hence merely credit risk, has been excessive in the light of the current market turmoil and the materialization of other risks such as model risk, liquidity risk and systemic risk. On the one hand this has the major advantage to allow all market participants to be better informed and have a better understanding of where a given rating comes from, but on the other hand it has also allowed structurers to game the rating, that is, to structure instruments to optimize the ratings. This in itself could very well be economically efficient if credit risk were the only risk that mattered or if investors also sufficiently considered the other risks involved. The value-added of ratings to this class of instruments is tremendous as there is almost no other public information available on the structured instruments and the collateral pool, which is probably one of the reasons why investors have focused so much on the ratings.

The first untranched pass-through securities were issued in 1970 when the US Government National Mortgage Association (commonly known as Ginnie Mae) developed and guaranteed the first mortgage-backed securities (MBS).[105] This was a significant development, creating a liquid secondary mortgage market that allowed loan originators to renew their capital and thereby extend additional loans. However, these pass-through mortgage securities had several limitations. They only appealed to investors with a certain investment horizon and they were exposed to prepayment risk. Homeowners are motivated to refinance their mortgage and prepay the loan when interest rates go down, precisely at the moment that fixed-income reinvestment opportunities are worsening. The advent of structured finance provided a solution to these limitations. In 1983, the US government sponsored Federal Home Loan Mortgage Corporation (commonly known as Freddie Mac) issued the first collateralized mortgage obligations (CMOs).[106] By structuring the asset pool into different tranches, CMOs were able to meet investor demand for a wider range of investment time frames and greater cash flow certainty.

MBSs and CMOs backed by US government agencies (such as Ginnie Mae) or US government sponsored enterprises (such as Freddie Mac and Fannie Mae) are collectively known as agency securities and marketed without a credit rating. They benefit from their association with the US government and the fact that the guarantees provided to the securities are senior to the AAA rated debt issued by these 'agencies.' Agency securities represent a large majority of the US residential mortgage securities market. Private label issuers, on the other hand, need to have their securities rated. Standard & Poor's started rating mortgage-backed securities in 1976.

Structured finance instruments soon expanded to other types of collateral and became collectively known as asset-backed securities. The type of collateral in a given asset pool remained homogeneous, containing only credit card receivables or only corporate equipment leases, for example. Exhibit 3.6 depicts a brief historical overview of the expansion in the types of assets used as the collateral for SFI. These types have expanded into exoticism such as the risk that the World Cup would be canceled or the risk of fluctuations in the value of a large stock of Champagne.

---

[105] www.ginniemae.gov

[106] www.freddiemac.com

Exhibit 3.6   Historical overview of the expansion of assets used to back structured finance instruments

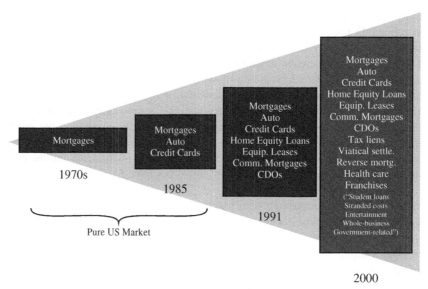

Source: Marjolin, B., 2007, Securitization – ESSEC presentation, Moody's Investors Service, March 16, page 10.

In 1987, the techniques of structured finance were extended by Drexel Burnham Lambert to corporate credit, in the form of bonds and loans, resulting in the first collateralized debt obligation (CDO).[107] Whereas an ABS pool generally contains many homogeneous assets, for example 100 000 commercial mortgages, a CDO will usually contain a smaller number of much higher value loans or bonds, for example 50 to 150 corporate bonds but also very heterogeneous assets.

The first CDOs were driven by the desire of banks to transfer credit risk away from their balance sheets and thereby to release economic and regulatory capital. Such CDOs are known as *balance sheet CDOs*. As shown in Figure 3.18, the majority of CDOs now issued are *arbitrage CDOs*. Arbitrage CDOs are typically initiated by the arranger who buys assets in the secondary market and structures them into new securities with interest and principal payments lower than the expected cash flows provided by the underlying securities. The arranger captures part of the value created by the pooling and tranching by retaining the equity portion of the issuance. Investors were attracted to CDOs, whose senior tranches are invariably rated AAA as demonstrated in Exhibit 3.7, as they are able to broaden their exposure to asset classes while staying within typical rating restrictions imposed on investment portfolios.

The type of collateral used as the underlying asset for the CDO gradually expanded to include other structured finance instruments such as ABSs and even other CDO tranches, giving rise to so-called CDO^2 (CDOs-squared). With the development of the credit derivatives

---

[107] Salas, C., and Hassler, D., 2007, CDOs may bring subprime-like bust for LBOs and Junk Debt, Bloomberg.com, March 13.

Exhibit 3.7   CDO ratings distribution by amount outstanding, as of July 20th 2008

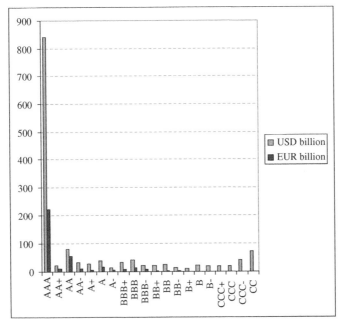

Source: Standard & Poor's

market came the possibility to avoid the complications of ensuring the true sale of the underlying assets to the SPV by writing a credit derivative contract instead. SF Vignette 5 (page 150) discusses synthetic CDOs, as they are known, in more detail.

The issuance of structured finance instruments experienced very strong growth until recently, as shown in Figure 3.11 and Figures 3.16 to 3.18. Structured ABSs related to the housing market (RMBS and home equity loans) expanded along with the residential property markets. The volume of issued CDOs has become a significant portion of the structured finance universe, with spread 'arbitrage' representing the dominant motivation for the issuance of CDOs.

The theoretical value drivers behind the strong growth in structured finance are discussed in detail in the SF Vignettes 2 and 3.

For the banks who originate the assets, selling loans to investors via SPVs allows them to reduce their capital reserve requirements and release capital to make new loans and expand business. For the investment banks and other financial intermediaries who arrange structured finance transactions, keeping the equity tranche allows them to profit from the difference that exists between the cash flows from the underlying assets (loans, CDSs, etc.) and the payments that must be made to the securities issued by the SPV. Since spreads on both sides are partly driven by ratings, it is often possible to structure the tranches of a portfolio such that the weighted average spread on the rated securities results in payments going out that are significantly lower than the incoming payment streams from the assets.

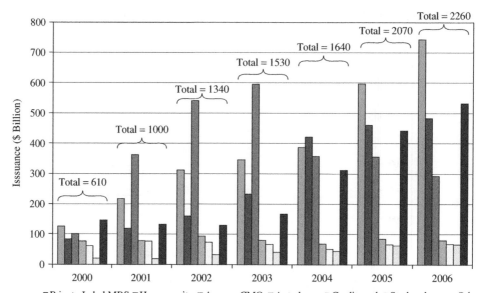

Figure 3.16 US asset-backed security issuance (2000–2006)
Note: Agency collateralized mortgage obligations (CMOs) are marketed without the need for credit ratings. They thus do not drive demand for credit ratings.
Sources: Bond Market Association, 2001–2007, *Research Quarterly*, February.

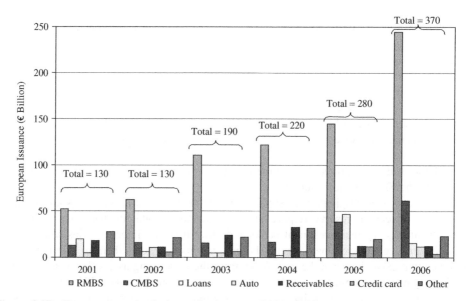

Figure 3.17 European asset-backed security issuance (2001–2006)
Note: European issues consist of ABS and MBS issues placed in the Euromarket or in European domestic markets having underlying collateral from Europe.

   1. European Securitization Forum, 2002–2007, *ESF Securitization Data Report*, Spring (2002), Winter (2003–2007).

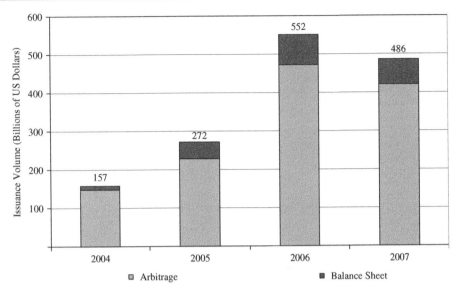

Figure 3.18 Global CDO Issuance (2004–2007)
Source: Securities Industry and Financial Markets Association, 2008, *Global CDO Market Issuance Data*, January, 1–3.

For investors, a common objective is to improve returns under rating constraints, since some investors, such as life insurance companies, can only invest in securities with ratings above a certain level. Another motivation is to achieve portfolio diversification. By investing in structured finance instruments, investors can incorporate different asset classes with various exposures into their portfolios. Lastly, investors can obtain customized assets with tailored risk and return profile and while investing in a very similar process to that of investing in bonds.

SF VIGNETTE 5
Synthetic vs Cash CDO Transactions

Cash CDOs and synthetic CDOs mainly differ in their underlying assets, thus resulting in further difference in contractual and payment arrangements. Cash CDOs use cash instruments as underlying assets while synthetic CDOs use non-cash instruments, which take the form of credit default swaps (CDS) as underlying assets.

Unlike cash CDOs, synthetic CDOs do not necessarily involve SPVs. Everything can be handled on a bank's balance sheet without true sale of assets to third parties, which is known as unfunded synthetic CDOs. The bank will "sell protection" on a pool of single-name bonds (take on only credit exposure instead of buying the physical assets), and "buy protection" on defined senior/subordinated/junior portfolio swaps (pass on the credit exposure to investors). Since CDSs are contingent claims and have zero value when entered, no exchange of cash will occur when the transaction is closed. An illustration of the transaction is presented in Figure 3.19.

Nevertheless, most synthetic CDOs introduce an SPV feature to allow for credit-linked notes (CLN) to be issued to investors, which case is known as "funded synthetic CDOs".

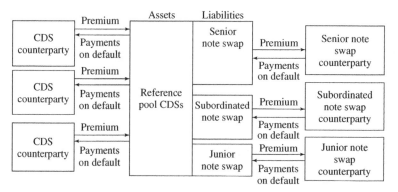

Figure 3.19   Structure of an unfunded synthetic CDO

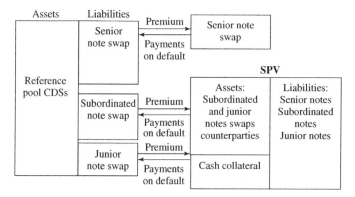

Figure 3.20   Structure of a funded synthetic CDO

The structure is shown in Figure 3.20. Note that the SPV invests in the cash collateral the proceeds from issuance of notes to generate interest return. This return plus the credit premium from the reference pool CDSs pays the preset coupon on these notes. As defaults on the underlying reference pool occur to a certain level, it will affect certain swaps in the liability side of the bank balance sheet, for example, the surbordinated note swap, which will have to make the contingent payment to the corresponding swap counterparties who suffer from defaults on their reference bonds. The credit losses are then paid by SPV to these swap counterparties. At swap maturity, the remainder of the original sale of notes is then returned to the note holders.[108]

In recent years, growth in synthetic CDOs has dramatically outpaced the growth of cash CDOs. The reasons for this dramatic growth include:

1. Relative value: compared with similarly-rated cash CDOs and corporate debts, synthetic CDOs usually have wider spreads.
2. Shorter maturities: synthetic CDOs often have shorter maturity profiles (3–7 years) than cash CDOs (12–35 years).

---

[108] For a detailed illustration on CLN and funded synthetic CDOs, see S&P's *Global Cash Flow and Synthetic CDO Criteria*, March 2002, pages 9–12.

3. Credit risk focused: synthetic CDOs allow for return for credit risk solely, since the structure separates the credit component from other risks associated with a cash asset (interest rate risk, currency risk, market risk).
4. Smooth execution: synthetic CDOs have less complicated legal and administrative procedures than cash CDOs. This has spurred the creation of taylor-made synthetic CDOs for each investor in the form of a single-tranche with subordination and thickness to be agreed upon with them.
5. Lack of availability of some cash-settled debt instruments and extending arbitrage to the traded spread products in the derivatives markets.

3.3.3 Geographical Segments or Location of the Obligor

Geography affects the likelihood of defaults and recovery prospects in the event of default in many different ways. This makes it a quite meaningful way of segmenting the ratings universe. Sovereign governments set the ground rules for the regulatory framework, tariffs, fiscal, and monetary policy, foreign currency control, and political and legal risks. Of particular interest are the disincentives against defaulting, and creditor rights and prospects in the event of default. The infrastructure of a country and the quality of private and public corporate governance all affect the creditworthiness of issuers and the repayment prospects of issues.

Financial intermediation systems may function by relying very heavily on securities markets or, alternatively, on institutions. This distinction is in fact an important starting point for appreciating the differences in rating scenarios between Euroland, the US, and Japan, as Table 3.2 documents. Notice that the ratio of debt securities to bank loans outstanding in 2002 was 3.0 in the US versus just 0.98 in Euroland. Over the last few years the ratio has expanded in Euroland and Japan, while in the US it has contracted slightly.

Figure 3.21 sums up the relative importance of the different regions in corporate ratings. The US still dominates, but the three other major regions have become quite significant, particularly the emerging markets.

The differences in the distributions of the fine ratings across the three continents is also typical. The fine rating profiles, shown in Figure 3.22, indicate their maturity, reliance on security markets, industrial infrastructure, and sovereign country ceilings. Overall, the US has a bi-modal distribution, centered around BBB and B. The first mode consists of the most established and mature corporations that, for instance, make up the S&P 100 index.

Table 3.2 Euro, US, and Japan financial structure (1999 and 2002) (amounts outstanding of debt securities, and bank loans as % of GDP)

	1999			2002		
	Debt securities	Bank loan	Ratio of securities/loans	Debt securities	Bank loans	Ratio of securities/loans
Euro Area	89%	100%	0.88	105%	108%	0.98
United States	165%	48%	3.40	154%	51%	3.00
Japan	127%	107%	1.18	160%	101%	1.59

Sources: 1. European Central Bank, 2004, *The Monetary Policy of the ECB*, 1–128, pages 34, 39.
2. European Central Bank, 2000, *Monthly Bulletin*, January, 1–120, page 39.

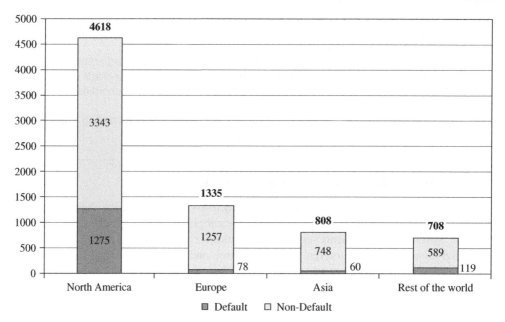

Figure 3.21   Global rated corporate issuers by region as of June 30, 2007
Note: 'D' rating (or Default) is accumulated since 1981. Europe comprises Western and Eastern Europe in Credit Pro classification.
Source: Standard & Poor's, 2007, *Data from CreditPro 7.71*, August 1.

The rating distribution of all the firms in this index as of February 2006 was as follows: 5% (AAA), 16% (AA), 42% (A), 25% (BBB), 5% (BB), and 7% (B). The median and mode of this rating distribution are the A. The second mode B+ reflects the early development in the US of the high-yield bond market. A similar market is developing in Europe, but the A to BBB+ classes clearly dominate the others, reflecting the fact that the high-yield market only really developed around 2000. Asia is still very much uni-modal in the A− to BBB+ classes, having relatively high country ceilings and low degrees of penetration for the high-yield segment of the bond markets. Emerging markets are equally uni-modal, but due to the relatively low country creditworthiness, the mode is BB−.

A last interesting point of contrast between the US and Euroland segments is the degree of penetration achieved in securitization issuance by 2006. While significant at about €370 billion, the European flow of asset-backed securities is still less than 17% of that in America, at $260 billion. Mortgage-backed securities are the most important sectors in both markets, but otherwise what stands out is the absence of home equity in Europe and its high degree of activity in receivables securitization.

The United States

Turning to the US, the size, breadth, and depth of the market for bonds issued in that country – amounting to $27 trillion by the end of 2006 taken across all issuer, currency, and nationality categories, almost all rated – dominates the picture, as shown in Figure 3.23.

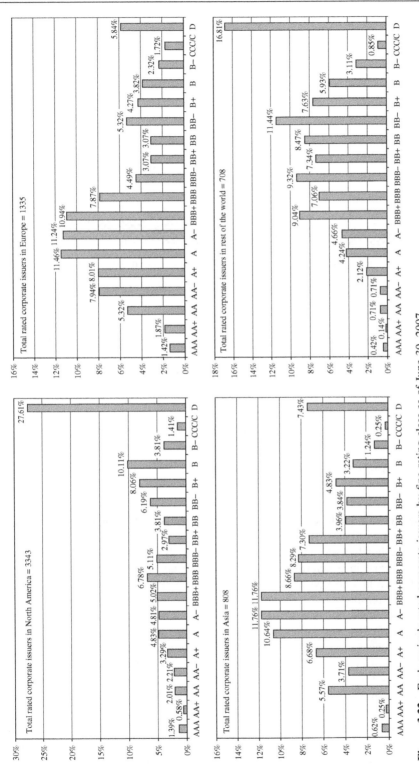

Figure 3.22 Each region's rated corporate issuers by fine rating class as of June 30, 2007

Note: 'D' rating (or Default) is accumulated since 1981. Europe comprises Western and Eastern Europe in Credit Pro classification.

Source: Standard & Poor's, 2007, *Data from CreditPro 7.71*, August 1

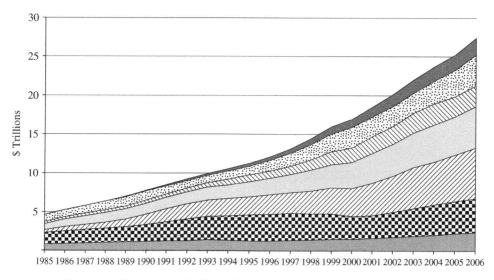

◨ Municipal ◧ Treasury ▨ Related ▫ Debt ◩ Securities ◰ Money Markets ▪ Asset-Backed

Figure 3.23 US bond market debt outstanding (1985–2006)
Notes:

1. Includes bonds issued in the US market only by any corporation, US or Non-US, in US dollars or any other currency.
2. Debt and asset-backed: The Securities Industry and Financial Markets Association estimates.
3. Treasury: Interest bearing marketable public debt.
4. Related: Includes GNMA, FNMA, and FHLMC mortgage-backed securities and CMOs and private-label MBS/CMOs.
5. Money markets: Includes commercial paper, bankers acceptances, and large time deposits. Beginning in 2006, bankers' acceptance are excluded.

Source: The Bond Market Association, 2007, *Outstanding US Bond Market Debt*, Statistical data.

This enormous stock of bonds leads naturally to a bond market that is large and liquid, with daily trading volume estimated at $23 billion.

Most corporate bonds trade anonymously in the over-the-counter (OTC) market. This market does not exist in a central location; it is made up of bond dealers and brokers from around the world who trade debt securities over the phone or electronically. Market participants are increasingly utilizing electronic transaction systems to assist in the trade execution process. Some bonds trade in the centralized environments of the New York Stock Exchange (NYSE) and American Stock Exchange (AMEX), but the bond trading volume on the exchanges is small. The OTC market is much larger than the exchange markets, and the vast majority of bond transactions, even those involving exchange-listed issues, take place in this market. This huge secondary market for corporate bonds makes it thus very economic to de-link the original lender from the issuer who purchased the bonds at the time of the issue from the current investor in the same bond.

The tremendous influence that disintermediation has had on corporate funding and on the growth of the need for credit ratings is shown in Figure 3.24, which graphs corporate non-financial loans versus bonds outstanding. It clearly highlights how disintermediation

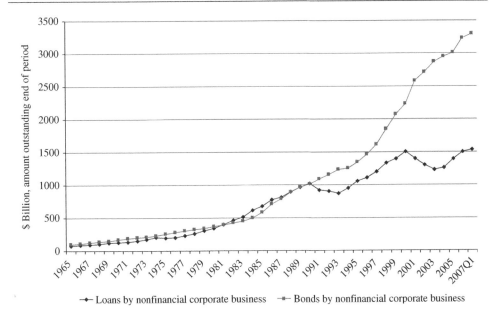

Figure 3.24 US non-financial corporate funding: loans versus bonds (1965-2007Q1)
Sources:

1. Board of Governors of the Federal Reserve System, 2005, *Flow of Funds Accounts of the United States Historical Data: 1965–1994*, December 8, L.212, L.215, L.216.
2. Board of Governors of the Federal Reserve System, 2006, *Flow of Funds Accounts of the United States Historical Data: 1995–2005*, September 19, L.212, L.215, L.216.
3. Board of Governors of the Federal Reserve System, 2006, *Flow of Funds Accounts of the United States. Flows and Outstandings, First Quarter 2007*, June, L.212, L.215, L.216.

has caused the growth trajectories of loans and bonds to decouple since 1991, and thereby increase the relevance of ratings for corporates in the US.

The fastest growing ratable sub-segment in corporate debt issuance, and also the most volatile, was high yield, as shown in Figure 3.25. This segment grew by 17.1% since 1990, compared with 10.5% for investment grade corporate bonds.[109]

It has also been shown that the bonds of this very fast growing high-yield segment are traded in an informationally highly efficient way. Since 1994 this trading has been supported by an electronic quotation and surveillance system known as the fixed income pricing system (FIPS). Through this system, investors can track bond price, volume, and transactions on a continuous basis. Analyzing these intraday data, it turns out that the informational efficiency of that segment 'is similar to that of the underlying stocks [...] stocks do not lead bonds in reflecting firm-specific information [...] Information is quickly incorporated in both bond and stock prices, even at short return horizons. [...] Measures of market liquidity are no poorer for the bonds in our sample than for the underlying stocks.'[110]

---

[109] www.bondmarkets.com.

[110] Hotchkiss, E.S., and Ronen, T., 2002, The informational efficiency of the corporate bond market: an intraday analysis, *Review of Financial Studies*, Winter, Vol. 15, 1325–1354, page 1325. The sample consisted of daily and hourly transactions for 55 high-yield bonds included on the NASDFIPS system between January 3, 1995, and October 1, 1995 (page 1326).

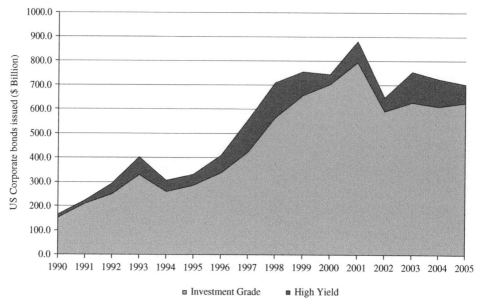

Figure 3.25 Rated US corporate bonds issuance (1990–2005)
Notes:

1. Includes all non-convertible corporate debt, MTNs and Yankee bonds, but excludes all issues
   with maturities of one year or less, CDs and federal and agency debt.
2. Includes bonds issued in the US market only by any corporation, US or Non-US, in US dollars
   or any other currency.

Source: The Bond Market Association, 2006, *Corporate Bond Issuance – Yearly*, Statistical data, June
30, 1–1.

Europe

Both the contrast and similarity of Europe with the US show clearly in Figure 3.26. Historically, the European debt capital markets were quite small due to the predominance of bank
financing. The European capital market has been growing in recent years. As Figure 3.26
shows, loans remain by far the dominant source of corporate funding over debt securities
but, as in the US, debt securities have seen a faster growth rate since 1997.

To appreciate the context of this, consider Figure 3.27. This shows, on the one hand, how
the non-financial corporate sector is dwarfed by the government and financial sectors, while
on the other hand, this same sector experienced significant expansion since the Euro was
introduced in 1999.

Figure 3.28 confirms the latter picture in terms of the corporate penetration of rated issuers
and also shows the increased presence of non-investment grade corporate issuers in Europe.
European companies that did approach the rating agencies usually did so only because they
were interested in tapping the US capital markets. The number of rated companies in the
EU is dwarfed by the number of rated companies in the US. The last remarkable evolution
in the European segment has been the rapid expansion of securitization issuance and the
corresponding expansion in ratings activity.

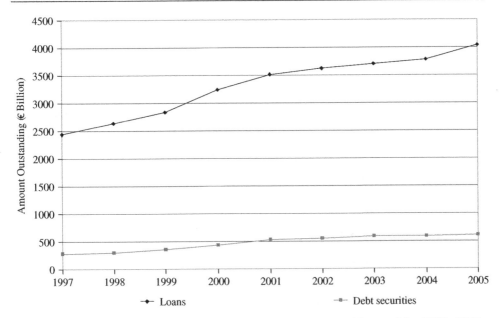

Figure 3.26 Euro area non-financial corporate funding: loans versus debt securities (1989–2006)
Notes:
1. Euro area: the area formed by those EU Member States in which the euro has been adopted as the single currency in accordance with the Treaty.
2. Loans: Loans taken from euro area MFIs and other financial corporations.
3. MFIs (including Eurosystem) comprises the ECB and the national central banks of the euro area and other monetary financial institutions.
4. Debt security: a promise on the part of the issuer (i.e. the borrower) to make one or more payment(s) to the holder (the lender) at a specified future date or dates. Such securities usually carry a specific rate of interest (the coupon) and/or are sold at a discount to the amount that will be repaid at maturity. Debt securities issued with an original maturity of more than one year are classified as long-term.

Sources:
1. European Central Bank, 2006, Euro area statistics: section 3.2 – Main liabilities of non-financial sectors, June.
2. European Central Bank, 2006, Debt securities issued by euro area residents by original maturity; currency and sector of the issuer – outstanding amount, July.

The first trend that underlies the tendency toward disintermediation in Europe has been the declining profitability in lending. Banks suffered from declining spreads on bank loans – a result of heightened competition. In early 2004, A and BBB rated corporates in Europe were being funded at around 40–50 bps. In June 2005, this was down to around 20–30 bps in the UK and 10–20 bps on the continent – a substantial reduction in pricing across the corporate spectrum.[111] When combined with a substantial drop in fees, this decline in margins has driven out banks unable to compete in the investment grade market.

---

[111] Fitzgerald, I., 2005. Uncertainty in the European Loan Market, Lloyd's TSB, June 13, pages 1–3.

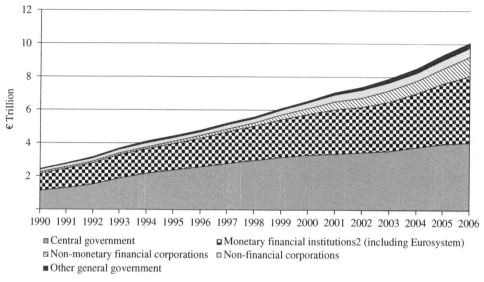

□ Central government   ▣ Monetary financial institutions2 (including Eurosystem)
▨ Non-monetary financial corporations   □ Non-financial corporations
■ Other general government

Figure 3.27   Euro-Area long term debt securities outstanding (1990–2006)[1]
Notes:
1. Debt securities issued by euro area residents (fixed composition) by original maturity; currency
   and sector of the issuer.
   (Euro includes items expressed in the national denominations of the euro.) Amounts outstanding (EUR billions; end of period; nominal values)
2. MFIs (monetary financial institutions): financial institutions which together form the money-
   issuing sector of the euro area. These include the Eurosystem, resident credit institutions (as
   defined in Community law) and all other resident financial institutions whose business is to
   receive deposits and/or close substitutes for deposits from entities other than MFIs and, for
   their own account (at least in economic terms), to grant credit and/or invest in securities. The
   latter group consists predominantly of money market funds

Source: European Central Bank, 2007, Debt securities issued by euro area residents (fixed composition) by original maturity; currency and sector of the issuer, June.

Another is the development of the European capital markets. For over 40 years, the US
dollar has been the currency of choice for international debt contracts. In January 2002,
the euro was introduced for both retail and capital market transactions in the European
Union. The Economic and Monetary Union (EMU) in Europe has reduced the issue costs of
euro-denominated bonds (compared with bonds denominated in the legacy currencies) and
increased liquidity due to the elimination of currency risk, reduction of home bias among
investors, and reliance on local syndication expertise, consolidation and economies of scale
in new issuance, and greater attractiveness (for all of the above reasons) to non-European
investors wishing to diversify their portfolios.[112] CRAs believe that the EMU will continue
to facilitate disintermediation, with borrowers increasingly obtaining more financing through
the public debt markets rather than through banks.

---

[112] Melnik, A., and Nissim, D., 2004, Issue costs in the Eurobond market: the effects of market integration, *Journal
of Banking and Finance*, February, pages 8–10.

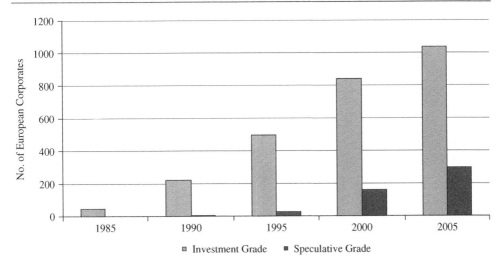

Figure 3.28   European Issuers 1985–2006
Source: Zazzarelli, A., De Bodard, E., Cantor, R., Hamilton, D., and Emery, K., 2006, European Corporate Default and Recovery Rates, 1985–2006, *Special Comment*: Moody's Investors Service, March, Report 102492, 1–28, page 5.

Corporate bond investors are now substituting for commercial banks investing in the loans they originate. These include institutional investors such as pension funds, endowments, mutual funds, insurance companies, and banks. Individuals, from the very wealthy to people of modest means, also invest in corporates because of the many attractions these securities offer.[113]

Emerging Markets

Emerging markets became an increasingly important segment for credit ratings with the rise of cross-border securities markets through the globalization of capital markets. Figure 3.29a compares the evolution of official and private flows to the developing world, with private flows broken up into foreign direct investments and capital market investments (both debt and equity). Private flows sharply increased since 1992, when they first overtook official flows. The share of the international capital markets reached a high of 48.5% in net long-term flows in 1996, but after the onset of the 1997 financial crisis the flow of international private capital to emerging markets slowed significantly in 1998 and dried up completely in 2001. Once the crisis was resolved, private capital started flowing again, rapidly surpassing official flows from mid-2002. The flows of foreign direct investment were less volatile, contracting by 13% from 1999 to 2002 before picking up again in 2004.

   The composition of the capital market flows themselves has undergone a dramatic transformation. Figure 3.29b shows that since the 1990s, bond issuance has surpassed bank lending as the dominant source of international private capital for developing countries, expanding the need for credit ratings. Of course, domestic capital is still more important than international capital. It represents about 90% of a typical country's investable capital.

---

[113] www.bondmarkets.com.

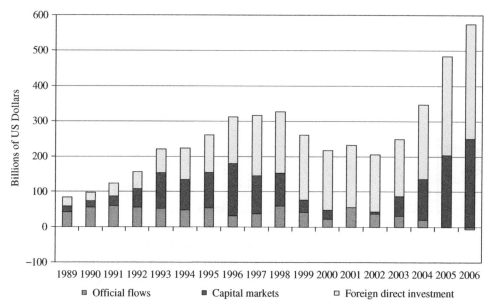

Figure 3.29a   Net total long term resource flows to developing countries (1989–2006)
Sources: World Bank, 1994, *World Debt Table: External Finance for Developing Countries 1994–1995*, A *World Bank Book*, December, 1–30, page 4. (1989 data); World Bank, *Global Development Finance 2000*, 35–54, Table 2.1, page 36. (1970, 1980, & 1990 data); World Bank, *Global Development Finance 2001*, 33–57, page 36. (1991–1996 data); World Bank, *Global Development Finance 2004*, 1–248, Table 1, page 4. (1997 data); World Bank, *Global Development Finance 2006*, 1–221, Table A.1, page 173. (1998–2004 data); World Bank, *Global Development Finance 2007*, 1–162, Table 2.1, page 37. (2005–2006 data).

3.4   SUMMARY

To sum up and conclude this chapter, credit ratings have become a real pillar of the economic infrastructure of capital markets. From our formal analysis of the effectively documented needs of investors and issuers, and the broad spectrum of uses across issuer, product, and geographical sectors, it is clear that CRAs strengthen this infrastructure when they reduce information asymmetries between issuers and investors in an independent and objective way. When these qualities are lacking, or when confidence in these qualities are lacking, they damage it. Beyond doubt, credit ratings generate public interest externalities and CRAs play a public interest role.

3.5   TECHNICAL APPENDIX

Proof 1:   Note that $\int_0^{\tilde{D}}(P(R) - \tilde{P}(R))\,dR < 0$ by f.o.s.d. Hence:

$$D^* - \tilde{D} < \int_{\tilde{D}}^{D^*} P(R)\,dR,$$

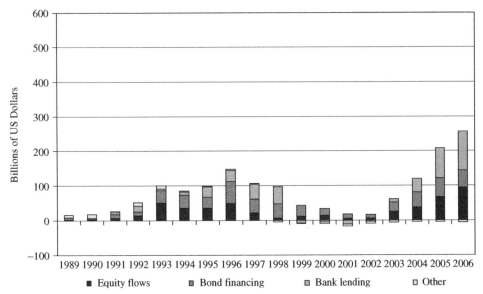

Figure 3.29b   Net capital market resource flows to developing countries (1989–2006)
Sources: World Bank, 1994, *World Debt Table: External Finance for Developing Countries 1994–1995*, A *World Bank Book*, December, 1–30, page 4. (1989 data); World Bank, *Global Development Finance 2000*, 35–54, Table 2.1, page 36. (1970, 1980, & 1990 data); World Bank, *Global Development Finance 2001*, 33–57, page 36. (1991–1996 data); World Bank, *Global Development Finance 2004*, 1–248, Table 1, page 4. (1997 data); World Bank, *Global Development Finance 2006*, 1–221, Table A.1, page 173. (1998–2004 data); World Bank, *Global Development Finance 2007*, 1–162, Table 2.1, page 37. (2005–2006 data).

If $D^* \geqslant \widetilde{D}$, then

$$(D^* - \widetilde{D})P(\widetilde{D}) \leqslant \int_{\widetilde{D}}^{D^*} P(R) \, dR \leqslant (D^* - \widetilde{D})P(D^*),$$

which implies:

$$D^* - \widetilde{D} \leqslant (D - \widetilde{D})P(D^*),$$

but because $0 \leqslant P(D^*) < 1$, this is only true if $D^* - \widetilde{D} < 0$, which contradicts the case. Hence: $D^* < \widetilde{D}$. $\square$

Proof 2:   Note that

$$C(D^p) - \widetilde{C}(D^p) = \int_0^{D^p} Rp(R) \, dR + D\left[1 - P(D^P)\right]$$

$$- \int_0^{D^p} R\widetilde{p}(R) \, dR + D^p\left[1 - \widetilde{P}(D^p)\right]$$

Integrating by parts yields:

$$C(D^p) - \tilde{C}(D^p) = \int_0^{D^p} [\tilde{P}(R) - P(R)] \, dR \geqslant 0 \text{ by f.o.s.d.}$$

Hence: $C(D^p) \geqslant \tilde{C}(D^p)$. Moreover, given that

$$\alpha C(D^p) + (1 - \alpha)\tilde{C}(D^p) = (1 - \rho)(I - A)[= C(D^*)],$$

it must be that $C(D^p) > C(D^*)$.

With $C'(D^p) < 0$, we get $D^* < D^p$, so that investors who have invested in a good entrepreneur's debt, will get a higher return than would be obtained not only on the bad entrepreneur's debt, but also on the good entrepreneur's debt in the case of symmetric information. □

4

How to Obtain and Maintain a
Credit Rating

Despite the various approaches that CRAs may take in rating issuers, the largest international CRAs tend to follow similar procedures for similar types of instruments. The rating process itself is designed to facilitate analytical consistency and capitalize on area expertise. At the core of it is a rating committee.[1]

This chapter describes how to obtain and maintain a credit rating according to the current rating process. The architecture of this process, if not all the details, the technology, and the analytical methods used, has been followed since the 1970s after the introduction of issuer fees. A rating assessment is prepared by an analyst from the credit rating agency, working in conjunction with the issuer client and his rating adviser-intermediary. A rating committee then decides whether or not to approve the suggested rating. This committee is discretionary and its decision is made by a majority vote. Once the rating is confirmed, informing the issuer, communicating with the market, and following up diligently are increasingly relevant parts of the rating agreement between the issuer and the CRA. The legal liability that the CRA engages with this agreement tends to be rather limited, the confidentiality of the information that the issuer shares with the CRA is paramount and the pricing of the service, for all issues but structured finance, tends to be negotiated on the basis of a standard public, commission-based schedule.

By default we describe the corporate and sovereign rating process and in each section describe specificities of the rating process in structured finance when appropriate. We believe that the role and function of the rating agency is fundamentally the same as in the corporate/sovereign market and hence highlight the differences rather than treating structured finance in an entirely separate section.

4.1 THE RATING PREPARATION

Prior to a debt issue, the issuer typically contacts a CRA. The process normally begins with an informal telephone call or a meeting requesting information on the rating process, prior to sale or registration of a debt issue. The usual concerns of a company are what the ratings process entails, the likely time frame, how confidential information is dealt with, and the cost of the rating.

An initiating rating is like a debt IPO and the company will learn up front that its approach is quite fundamental. The process entails much more than computing and sorting financial ratios based on its published accounts, or deriving quantitative default probabilities from market prices or credit spreads. As S&P puts it, 'proper assessment of debt protection levels

---

[1] Technical Committee of the International Organization of Securities Commissions, 2003. Report on the activities of credit rating agencies, September, OICV-IOSCO PD 153, 1–20, page 5.

requires a broader framework, involving a thorough review of business fundamentals, including judgments about the company's competitive position and evaluation of management and its strategies.'[2] A rating decision will be influenced by business risk issues, the inherent risk of the company regardless of its financing, and the firm's financial condition. The latter can make a company more risky, or less risky, than its inherent business risk would warrant. In sum, 'ratings should be understood as professional credit opinions that look beyond each day's news in order to provide a much more stable signal than a market-based mechanism.'[3]

Obtaining a rating is thus a laborious, time-consuming and intrusive process. The client must be prepared to submit an impressive number of files and documents, to have its management contribute to extensive meetings with the CRA, to share confidential information, to organize facility tours for the CRA, and to have staff available to respond to the CRA's follow-up questions. The process is thus highly confidential and expensive, particularly so for a first rating. The length of time between the initial request and the company being advised of the decision of the agency is usually 6 to 12 weeks, but varies considerably.

The Initial Credit Rating of a Major Corporation

While it is typically expected to take around three months to secure an initial credit rating, for Deutsche Post World Net (DPWN), the initial rating process in 2002 took eight months. This was intentional. Morgan Stanley, DPWN's advisers, made sure that the rating process was carefully designed and structured from the start, and that it was synchronized with DPWN's five-year internal planning process. The standard route of preliminary organization, preparation for meeting with the CRAs, meetings and finally decisions was augmented by a period of education and internal preparation within DPWN to ensure that all the relevant employees had the knowledge they needed to help the rating exercise to succeed.

Preliminary organization in this case comprised four months collecting and preparing the data needed to support the rating application, and identifying areas of potential concern to the CRAs. Morgan Stanley's widespread experience from previous ratings of German DAX companies, recently privatized incumbents and other European logistics companies meant that it was well placed to anticipate the issues that would be most important for the CRA analysts. A list of potential areas of concern was drawn up, including such things as changes in off-balance-sheet liabilities, German labor regulations, and competition. Methods and communication tools for approaching each issue were developed. The education and internal preparation phase then followed, taking another month.

Thus DPWN and Morgan Stanley had already invested five months of effort by the time they began detailed preparations for their meetings with the CRAs. The credit story that DPWN would present to the CRAs tackled all the potential concerns identified in the data mining and preparation phase, pointing out how each issue would be tackled and highlighting DPWN's strengths across a range of financial parameters. Preparations for CRA meetings took six weeks, and the meetings themselves took place over a three-week period.

Three weeks after the CRA meetings ended, DPWN received the rating decisions from the agencies. S&P rated DPWN A+, Moody's rated the company Aa3, and Fitch gave

---

[2] Standard & Poor's, 1998. *Corporate Credit Ratings: a Guide*, page 4.
[3] Mahoney, C., 2002. The bond rating process in a changing environment, *Special Comment*: Moody's Investors Service, January, Report: 73741, 1–4, page 3.

the company a rating of AA−, all within the rating target range originally defined by DPWN. Of the potential concerns, several were not mentioned in the CRAs reports and others were taken as having various degrees of negative impact. The strengths that had been highlighted in documentation were noted and deemed to have a positive impact on the ratings achieved. Fitch pointed to the 'significant contribution of the stable, regulated, monopoly-status, sizeable and profitable Mail division,' Moody's expected DPWN to 'remain the leading postal service provider in Germany,' and S&P also highlighted the company's 'leading positions in the European and global express and logistics industries.'

The result of this exercise played a significant part in the success of DPWN's first Eurobond issue. A well-attended pan-European roadshow introduced the transaction to over one hundred institutional investors across eight financial centers. Originally proposed at €1 billion, the issue was six times oversubscribed and subsequently upsized by 50% to €1.5 billion, and split into tranches of 5 and 10 years. Both tranches priced aggressively against the spread talk, and the order books closed 24 hours after the price guidance was published. The orders were spread across Europe, and included hundreds of institutional accounts.

With thanks to Rupert Atkinson, Managing Director, Morgan Stanley Global Capital Markets, and Dirk Northeis, Managing Director, Morgan Stanley Investment Banking.

However frustrating at times, the process outcome tends to be enlightening to the issuer and beneficial to the issue. Companies that wish to know precisely how their quantitative and qualitative situation maps into the rating obtained – perhaps to enable them to 'improve' it – tend to be frustrated because this exactness is typically not achieved. However diligent a CRA is in giving the rationale behind its credit rating decision, an issuer will never find out exactly how the credit analysis transforms into a specific rating grade. This will, to some extent, always remain somewhat of a 'black box.' Knowing exactly what is in this box would, without doubt, strengthen the hand of the issuer client *vis-à-vis* the CRA rater-supplier, and, not surprisingly, the CRAs would prefer this not to happen in order to preserve their independence and reputation for objectivity. But the company will learn a lot, as we will see, about what is important and how the CRA looks at its business, as well as identifying some of the critical red flags or benchmarks. Would-be investors in the instrument will worry less about being stuck with a 'lemon' and, therefore, are more likely to pay a just price rather than have no rating.

To conclude and introduce the next sections, Figure 4.1 shows a summary of the rating process as a major rating adviser would typically present it to a client of its advisory service. Note how the company and the rating agency interact with each other during what is roughly an eight-step process. The issuer's rating adviser plays a valuable role in bringing all his or her experience to bear so that both CRA and issuer understand and respect each other's perspectives and accept the outcome of the process. We consider now each one of these roles in more detail throughout the process.

4.1.1 The Issuer Client

In most commercial transactions, the client sits in the driver's seat and steers the process of dealing with the service supplier, so one might think that the rated corporation, as the client, would drive the CRA, its supplier. But for credit ratings, it is the other way around. The CRA

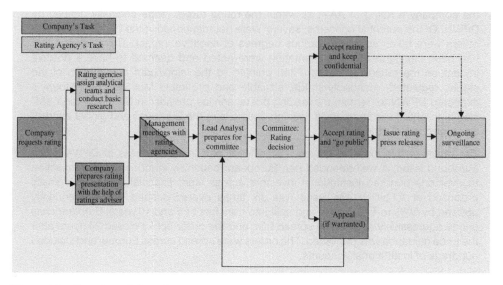

Figure 4.1   Overview of the rating process.
Source: Morgan Stanley Credit Advisory Group, 2006, Pros and cons of obtaining credit ratings, Overview of the credit rating process – Morgan Stanley's integrated rating advisory approach, December 12, 1–3.

drives the process in the same way that the corporate finance department of an investment bank drives a client through the process of issuing securities or preparing, deciding and executing a major transaction. The finance department of the issuer needs to understand this in order to guide the general management team through the initial rating process.

The *written information* that the issuer usually supplies to the rating agency at the beginning of the process would include:

- relevant industry and company positioning information;
- up-to-date descriptions of operations, products, and risk management;
- a business plan;
- audited annual financial statements for five years;
- interim financial statements for several recent sub-periods; and
- draft registration statement or offering memorandum or equivalent covering the to-be-rated issue, if available.

CRAs must accept of course that the issuer limits what it provides. Data that is very confidential, such as budgets, or that is immaterial in relation to their disponibility are often withheld.

The Meetings

In-depth interviews with company management are an integral part of the rating process. S&P considers these 'critical in helping to reach a balanced assessment of a company's circumstances and prospects. The purpose of these is to review in detail the company's key operating and financial plans, management policies, and other credit factors that have an impact on the rating.'[4] Or, as Moody's puts it, 'Meetings also frequently help the analyst to become familiar with local officials, as management capability is a key rating factor.'[5]

The issuer will be responsible for conducting these meetings: planning, scheduling, preparing, and participating. Subsequent meetings, with both senior and more junior employees at the company, will cover the business and financial elements of the issuers' operations. While senior management is often subject to intense scrutiny at these meetings, management teams that are perceived as already successful are probably subject to much less intense questioning. When the latest in a long line of bond issues for General Electric is being rated it is probably safe to say that the CFO has a great deal of credibility, given the historical success of the firm. However, the CFO of Amazon.com probably faced a more skeptical credit analyst when it entered the US high-yield market on a Caa2 rating on May 5, 1998, given by Moody's.[6]

Facility Tours

A significant and increasing proportion of meetings take place on company premises, and CRAs actively encourage this. To S&P, these serve

> 'to facilitate increased exposure to management personnel – particularly at the operating level; obtain a first-hand view of critical facilities; and achieve a better understanding of the company by spending more time reviewing the business units in depth ... touring major facilities can be very helpful in gaining an understanding of a company's business. However, this is generally not critical. Given the time constraints that typically arise in the initial rating exercise, arranging facility tours may not be feasible. Such tours may well be a useful part of the subsequent surveillance process.'[7]

To Moody's, analysts are most interested in a balanced and accurate view of the issuer. A tour itinerary should, therefore, highlight both the issuer's strong points and problem areas.[8]

4.1.2   The Rating Adviser-Intermediary[9]

Issuers seeking an initiating rating may appoint a rating adviser.[10] This is typically an investment bank. His role is to assist the issuer in obtaining the most appropriate rating

---

[4] Standard & Poor's, 2005. *Corporate Ratings Criteria*, 1–119, pages 15–18.

[5] Moody's Investor Services, 2004. Guide to Moody's ratings, rating process and rating practices, June, Report 87615, 1–48, page 19.

[6] The rated instrument was approximately $325 million gross proceeds ($275 million net proceeds) or $530 million (face value) 10% senior discount note due 2008 and not to pay cash interest until 2003. In the year ended December 1997, Amazon.com, Inc. had revenues of about $148 million. The proceeds from the bond issue were to be used to repay a $75 million term loan closed in December 1997, and to fund future operating losses and business development. Moody's rating action states that the company "will have extremely high leverage after the note issue, which will require significant growth in revenues and profitability to eventually service the debt. The company's ability to achieve these goals is tied to significant uncertainties." S&P initiated Amazon's rating three months later, on August 20, 1998, and three notches higher at B.

[7] Standard & Poor's, 2005. *Corporate Ratings Criteria*, 1–119, pages 15–18.

[8] Moody's Investor Services, 2004. Guide to Moody's ratings, rating process and rating practices, June, Report 87615, 1–48, page 19.

[9] The authors thank Rupert Atkinson, Managing Director at Morgan Stanley Global Capital Markets who heads Morgan Stanley's rating advisory team in Europe, for several insightful conversations on this topic.

[10] Investment banking industry sources suggest that this occurs in most initiating rating cases, but we did not see representative evidence of this.

and, therefore, the best access to the fixed income public capital market. Permanent access to this market is not predicated upon being rated as highly as possible initially, in the same vein as permanent access to the public equity market may not be served by conducting an IPO at the highest possible share price. The investment bank will thus advise the issuer regarding the credit rating process and the default risk positioning of the issue. The bankers will act as an intermediary between the issuer and the rating agency throughout much of the process, with access to the same confidential information about the client as the CRA.

As Figure 4.2 conveys, the adviser has an important process management role and participates in meetings between the CRA and the issuer. Issuers who are new to the capital markets are most likely to need the services of an independent adviser. This happens frequently in cases of privatizations, after IPOs generally, in emerging markets, and after an issuer comes out of distress.

The adviser smoothes the sometimes contentious relationship between CRA and issuer. Issuers have a natural tendency to believe that they deserve a higher rating than that which the CRA is prepared to give them. This is not completely unlike CEOs, who tend to claim that their company is worth more than the market thinks, or like students who are deeply convinced that they deserve a better grade.

The adviser mimics the actual rating process with the client. For the client, this is often its first experience, and not unlike preparing for an IPO. But the corporate finance fixed income team of the investment bank is practiced in acting as an intermediary between an issuer and a rating agency. It is thus well positioned to conduct a 'mock' rating for the client, making the client familiar with the types of analysis that agencies carry out and the basis by which they reach a rating. The accounts are thus carefully verified and consolidated

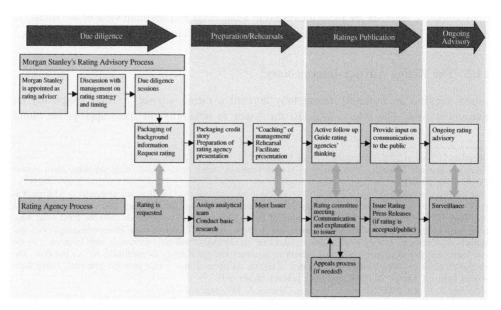

Figure 4.2   Overview of integrated advisory approach.
Source: Morgan Stanley Credit Advisory Group, 2006. Pros and cons of obtaining credit ratings, Overview of the credit rating process – Morgan Stanley's integrated rating advisory approach, December 12, 1–3.

in cooperation with the client's external auditors so that they are presented in ways that facilitate comparability with similar companies and shows consistency over time.

An investment bank with credit rating exposure has a strong incentive to give a correct mock rating. An underwriter has market price – including credit rating – exposure during the short period of time between the pricing-signing and the CRA's rating announcement. Getting the rating right is thus of paramount importance to the investment bank. The investment bank does not say what it thinks the right rating should be, but should forecast, preferably accurately, the rating the agency will give the issuer or the issue.

The rating advisory business is laborious for the adviser. A significant amount of scarce and expensive resources is often mobilized, yet investment bankers usually only charge a nominal fee that only covers out-of-pocket expenses for a rating advisory assignment. This is not due to the generous spirit of the bankers. Ratings advisory is normally considered to be a loss leader – it positions the firm to win lucrative underwriting business at a later date when the issuer goes to the bond markets. The service thus tends to be offered primarily to would-be or actual clients that are on the bank's radar screen for important corporate finance business such as restructuring, privatization, IPO, M&A, LBO, etc. One can fairly say that the demand, supply, revenues, costs, and profits of the service are bundled into more generic corporate finance services and products. The rating advisory business has no business model of its own. It is ancillary to, or a component of, the overall relationship engagement of the bank with a client.

The bank adds value to the client by putting the client in the driver's seat in front of the CRA. Sometimes, CRAs have a tendency to behave as somewhat intrusive 'regulators' who feel that they are in a position to request all sorts of information and data from an issuer or to expect that the issuer volunteers and discloses everything imaginable that would facilitate the CRA's work. The bank can certainly help to remind the CRA that the issuer is the client and that the CRA is the provider of a paid service, so the value it adds should be worth the cost to the issuer. The bank can thus protect the client against an overintrusive CRA by reminding it that the issuer is responsible for the conduct of its business and is fully entitled to exercise due business judgment in deciding what it is ready to disclose to the CRA and what it is not.

This being argued, it is in the issuer's interest to be open, transparent, and cooperative with the CRA, particularly when bad news is on the way. No market participant loves bad news, certainly not when it comes as a surprise (except maybe the hedge funds that are short in the hit security). In a sense, the surprise of bad news is almost worse than the bad news itself. The bank as rating adviser plays an important smoothing role in managing the flow of confidential information between the issuer and the CRA, and CRAs generally look on the rating adviser as a facilitator in their interactions with issuers.[11]

The rating advisory assignment provides a unique window of opportunity for the investment bank to deepen its advisory relationship with the client. The task requires analysis and evaluation of a significant amount of confidential information about the company. Of course all this information must stay within the corporate finance department. None of it should cross the Chinese wall between the corporate finance and trading activities of the adviser. There are at least four reasons for that: (1) it would violate a private contract:

---

[11] The CRAs are rather sparse in their views on the role of advisers, beyond acknowledging the fact that they exist. Example: 'Outside advisors may be helpful in preparing an effective presentation. We neither encourage nor discourage their use: it is entirely up to management whether advisors assist in the preparation for meetings, and whether they attend meetings,' Standard & Poor's, 2005. *Corporate Ratings Criteria*, 1–119, page 15.

the confidentiality agreement of the corporate finance division with the issuer; (2) it would violate a public regulation: regulation fair disclosure that says that no public issuer may disclose confidential information to one market party without disclosing it to the market as a whole; (3) it would lead to criminal conduct: a trader could only inflate its bottom line by trading on the information surreptitiously, i.e. criminally violating insider trading laws and regulations; and (4) it would violate the internal employment conditions at an investment bank: a trespasser would be fired on the spot for professional misconduct.

4.1.3   The Credit Rating Agency Supplier

The Team

Internally, the agency rating process is not unlike that in asset management firms. An analyst who is responsible for an industry or a region, will be assigned coverage of a particular company or country. This lead analyst will follow a given issuer and handle day-to-day contact, with the support of a team of experienced analysts assigned to the rating relationship with each issuer. S&P divides the work of analysts by industry, rather than by instrument. Their analysts generally concentrate on a limited number of industries, covering the entire spectrum of credits within these industries.[12] To build the foundations of a rating proposal, the lead analyst directs extensive research.

The Research

This focuses primarily on finding a conditional, unbiased, and efficient estimate of the obligor's default probability. Several other 'gems' are being mined, for example recovery in the event of default, but without default probability they are less meaningful. The research is very result oriented, and is conducted to find things out. Whatever the analyst team digs up, its contribution toward estimating the default probability is conditional on the relevant data, the capability to understand and interpret it and the methods available to make inferences from it at the time of the research. After the event, many enlightened souls can explain perfectly why a particular company went into default and blame CRAs for not forecasting it properly. A statement such as 'the mistakes S&P and Moody's made by telling investors that Enron and Worldcom were safe investments just days before they filed for bankruptcy' is such an example of enlightened hindsight.[13] The default probability that is benchmarked by the rating is an estimate, and everyone knows this. CRAs do not have a crystal ball, and the quality of ratings cannot be judged on the basis of a few singular events, as the US Congress erroneously did to justify its Credit Rating Agency Reform Act.[14] Quality can only be assessed on the basis of large samples – as we will discuss in Chapter 7. Research thus tries to establish estimates that are unbiased (i.e. accurate on average) and efficient (i.e. with smaller individual errors on both sides of the average than any other type of estimate). The research methods reflect that.

---

[12] 'Such specialization allows accumulation of expertise and competitive information better than if junk-bond issuers were followed separately from high-grade issuers,' Standard & Poor's, 2005. *Corporate Ratings Criteria*, 1–119, page 15.

[13] House Committee on Financial Services, 2006. President signs Credit Rating Agency Reform Act of 2006, S.3850, into law, Press release, September 29.

[14] United States Senate, 2006. Credit Rating Agency Reform Act of 2006, S. 3850, 109th Congress, 2nd Session, September 22.

To get it right, the lead analyst brings together understanding, data, methods, and a strong personal drive in conducting the research. Deep country, sector, issuer and product technical understanding is brought to bear through the composition of the team that works with the lead analyst. The enormous proprietary databases contain massive amounts of cross-section and time series issuer and issue data. Pooling this data and applying proper, often proprietary, statistical methods allows the CRA to track the record of obligors and the antecedents and conditions of defaulters. And the compelling driver that steers this powerful engine is the credit analyst's ambition to get it right, i.e. to properly map the conditions of the issuer in that space. Getting it right means that the frequency of defaults among the analyst's sample of rating recommendations corresponds to the default frequency of that rating in the corresponding universe. Imagine that she has been in the trade for three years and has made 150 issuer recommendations at B−/B3. Suppose that the five-year historical cumulative default frequency of the B−/B3 universe is 6.0%. Then, she will have got it right if, over a five-year period, nine issuers in her set have defaulted. Not more, because that would mean that she has a bias toward not detecting problems and declaring 'safe' that which is 'unsafe' (Type I error); nor less, because that would mean that she has a bias toward seeing problems where there aren't any and falsely declaring 'unsafe' what is 'safe' (Type II error).

The outcome of the research positions the obligor in the default and recovery spectrum. A rating is in no sense an absolute statement nor is it a value judgment. The issuer, and market participants in general, should understand that it is a positioning in a spectrum. Understanding the spectrum and the issuers and issues within it is as important as understanding the case at hand. This, of course, requires that a lot of accumulated knowledge and experience is brought to bear on a rating decision. One of our friends in the trade sums this up by claiming that he 'smells' a B/B2, or the difference between an AA/Aa2 and AAA/Aaa. This sort of positioning requires a comprehensive business judgment call, which explains why rating decisions are made by a rating committee rather than by an individual. The principle is the same in structured finance but in terms of research, quantitative models carry a much larger weight in the rating. These models, or more precisely the programs running the model, are well diffused among investors to allow market participants to understand the mechanics behind an instrument's rating.

Rating Committee

At the core of the rating process is the rating committee. The lead analyst must defend her proposal – typically in the form of a draft rating action – to this committee. The proposal has to be factual in its origins and unbiased in its presentation to help the committee to reach a conclusion built on a broad base of accepted data and information. The committee is generally formed as required to initiate, withdraw, or change a rating, and is typically composed of a lead analyst, managing directors or supervisors, and junior analytical staff. At the committee meeting, the analyst will face vigorous questioning by more senior members of the firm or other analysts who come in from a different angle. For example, the lead analyst on Lafarge could be the CRA's world expert on the cement industry, but will not necessarily be the regional or issue expert, and these dimensions must be integrated in the rating proposal. The committee chairperson should thus make sure that all necessary competencies are represented at the meeting.

A rating committee does not work in a fixed way. Unlike a Board of Directors or an Audit Committee, it has no set composition, planned meeting schedule, or fixed agenda.

Rather, its chairperson composes and calls the committee when the lead analyst requests a meeting with regard to a particular rating action. Like a Board, deliberations are private and confidential to the committee, but, unlike a Board or Audit Committee, the minutes do not have to be approved by the next committee and do not form a legal record of actions and their motivations.

4.2 THE RATING

4.2.1 The Rating Action

Rating decisions are based on a simple majority vote by the committee. They represent the CRA's opinion regarding the likelihood that the issuer will repay its financial obligations. The vote is open. By voting, the committee assigns the rating for which it takes collective responsibility. This is the rating action.

Rating Disclosure to the Issuer

The issuer and adviser are immediately informed of the rating action. The analyst contacts the issuer and the underwriter before it is made public. The issuer typically has the opportunity to review the draft press release. This is normal business practice for factual verification and to ensure that confidential information is not disclosed. However, it is prone to pitfalls, incidents or misconstructions, as the following case of S&P's follow-up of its Portland General Electric ratings illustrates.

A Little Knowledge is a Dangerous Thing . . .

S&P announced that they had revised the Portland General Electric Co.'s (PGE) rating outlook to negative on February 27, 2006. The company was facing several unpredictable outcomes, including unexpected costs resulting from a power outage, litigation regarding investment in a nuclear power plant, and investigation by the City of Portland into the company's taxes and trading practices, and was in the throes of redistributing stock as it became independent of former parent company, Enron. S&P's February report highlighted that supportive regulation in Oregon was a key strength for PGE. Six months later, on September 25, an S&P research summary on PGE indicated that the 'regulatory environment may become less favorable for the company' and this was one of the factors that kept S&P's outlook for PGE negative.

PGE was about to file a request with Oregon's Public Utility Commission to increase the rates it charged to customers. In October, a lawyer for 34 of PGE's largest industrial customers subpoenaed all the previous 21 months' correspondence between S&P and PGE, and revealed that PGE had commented on and suggested amendments to S&P's rating report before publication that S&P had accepted.[15]

---

[15] *Sources:* Standard & Poor's, 2006. Portland General Electric Co.'s rating outlook revised to negative, *Rating Action*, February 27; Standard & Poor's, 2006. Portland General Electric Co., Research, March 1 and September 25; Johnston, D.C., 2006. Objectivity of a rating questioned, *New York Times*, December 12; Duin, S., 2006. Warning: PGE hasn't redlined this column, *The Oregonian*, December 14; Jaquiss, N., 2006. An Oregon senator wants regulators to look at PGE–Standard & Poor's dealings, *Willamette Week*, December 13.

Ratings agencies cannot publish rating reports without checking the facts with the issuer. They are also professionally obliged to ensure that their reports do not contain any confidential information – that which the issuer has provided in order to facilitate the ratings process, but which should not be released publicly. Hence issuer and agency work together to ensure the accuracy of their reports. However, in the above case the media instantly jumped to the quick conclusion that PGE and S&P were in cahoots, attempting to hoodwink the Public Utility Commission into granting a rate increase that PGE did not merit. But the relationship between ratings and regulated utility prices is highly complex. And among firms that have their debt rated, for utilities credit ratings are a more important determinant of debt policy than for any other category of firms.[16] Those who act in these matters clearly understand that the rating affects the regulatory outcome and the regulatory outcome affects the rating, and the objectivity of the CRA is not called into question.

This case then is a classic example of how a little learning can be a dangerous thing. It highlights how, even when market participants thoroughly understand the rating process, the issuers understand the arm's-length nature of their relationship with the CRA, and the CRA follows proper procedures of disclosure between agency and issuer, things can still be misconstrued. And inevitably, the 'Enron chorus' has raised its head yet again – it seems that any time a ratings agency gets noticed, the notion that the major ratings agencies should have predicted Enron's collapse is repeated. But the measurement of risk will never eliminate uncertainty.

The issuer normally has the chance to appeal the rating, but since the issuer is involved throughout the rating process, such appeals are rare. When the issuer does disagree strongly with the proposed rating, it may request that the rating committee reconsiders its decision. 'However, agencies may be reluctant to reconsider a decision unless the issuer presents new material information or points out the CRA's reliance on incorrect information.'[17] Occasionally, after comments are received from the issuer, the CRA makes any appropriate changes.

At an initial rating, if the issuer strongly disagrees with the proposed rating it can decide to withdraw the request for a rating and not go ahead with it by refusing its publication. The rating agency will accept this and not, instead, issue an unsolicited rating. It could do so of course once the information collected in cooperation with the issuer has become obsolete. However, for an issuer to withdraw a rating is much more difficult with subsequent ratings. In this case, it may happen that the issuer decides to stop participating in the rating process and refuses to pay the rating fee. If that happens, the rating agency usually decides to continue rating the issue and disclosing it to the market as long as it believes it has sufficient information. A public rating is the intellectual property of the CRAs and investors are also their clients even though not directly paying for the service. Rating agencies will appreciate the extent to which it is in the business interest of investors not to interrupt a rating as long as an issue is traded. They preserve the prerogative to continuously respond to needs of investors, independently from the issuer. In effect, the rating is then technically an unsolicited rating, even though it is not based on public information only.

---

[16] Graham, J.R., and Harvey, C.R., 2001. The theory and practice of corporate finance: evidence from the field, *Journal of Financial Economics*, May, Vol. 60, Issue 2–3, 187–243, page 17.
[17] Technical Committee of the International Organization of Securities Commissions, 2003. Report on the activities of credit rating agencies, September, OICV-IOSCO PD 153, 1–20, page 5.

Communicating the Rating to the Market

Usually, the CRA issues a press release with the newly decided rating. This is to communicate its decision to the market by explaining the key elements underlying the rating. For example, on May 20, 2002, S&P said 'it lowered its corporate credit rating on cable television operator Adelphia Communications Corp. to "D" from triple "C" minus following a missed interest payment on the company's $500 million 9.375% senior unsecured note issue.[18] This was a clear notch down to default that was easy to understand because a default event had occurred, and it required little further explanation. Some ratings announcements are more complex and require a lot of explanation. On August 24, 2005, Moody's lowered the rating of the Ford Motor Company (Ford) senior unsecured to Ba1 from Baa3, along with simultaneous downgrades on other Ford securities classes, moving approximately $150 billion of debt from investment grade to below the line, i.e. speculative or junk.

> The downgrades reflect further erosion in the operating results and cash flow generation of Ford in consideration of weakened market share and continued challenges in addressing its uncompetitive cost structure in North America. These factors are expected to result in a pretax loss from automotive operations in 2005. Since improvement in the company's cost structure can only be implemented over a period of time, financial performance is expected to remain weak.

Obviously, this summary was insufficient to underpin such a wide-ranging decision and too general to explain it. The announcement thus added a very detailed, quantified, and timed analysis of Ford's situation, making very explicit what was supporting the current rating level and 'what factors would contribute to downward pressure on Ford's Ba1 rating' (e.g. continuing loss of market share, escalation in price competition, erosion of liquidity).[19]

Why only *usually*? Because there are also private ratings, provided only to the issuer. Issuers and CRAs tend to keep initiating ratings confidential until the issuer has confirmed that it wishes to go public with the rating, regardless of whether or not the rating is based on material non-public information.[20] Initiating solicited ratings can thus remain private and confidential. When issuers obtain, upon their request, the assessment by a CRA of the likely rating impact of a hypothetical major transaction, these assessment are also, of course, private and confidential. A publicly listed company may decide a price sensitive transaction (major acquisition, spin-off, reorganization, etc.) that will lead to a public announcement. If also rated, the company would usually have informed its CRA beforehand. In most countries it would be a punishable infringement of securities law if the CRA were to release its transaction-related rating action ahead of the transaction announcement by the company. Unfortunately, this has happened, by accident. One reason why issuers should also be concerned about operational risk management at the CRAs, and not just only the other way around.

Follow-up ratings of a publicly rated issuer or instrument are made public. If the rating action integrates material non-public information, the CRA must disclose any rating

---

[18] Standard & Poor's, 2002. Adelphia Comm corporate credit rating lowered to 'D,' off watch, after missed interest payment, May 20.

[19] Moody's Investors Service, 2005. Moody's lowers Ford's ratings, Global credit research rating action, August 25, 1–3, pages 1–2.

[20] The Bond Market Association, 2004. Public comment on IOSCO October 2004 draft: *Code of Conduct Fundamentals for Credit Rating Agencies*, November 6, 1–12, page 9.

regarding publicly issued securities, or public issuers themselves.[21] This should be done on a non-selective basis and free of charge.

In addition to the actual rating and its justification, the CRA should also disclose whether or not the issuer participated in the rating process. In other words, each rating not initiated at the request of the issuer, i.e. unsolicited, should be identified as such.[22] Market participants insist that CRAs make this disclosure on a continuous basis and prominently, and CRAs generally do. But that doesn't mean that market data providers (e.g. Bloomberg, Reuters) disseminate such information properly to the market, and CRAs are under pressure to adopt subscript markers, or symbols, that are part of the rating itself and can be recognized by the market as unsolicited ratings.[23]

The Role of the Internet

Ratings are usually posted on the CRA's website. This makes them freely available to all market participants. For example, looking at some CRA websites on October 19, 2005, one would have read on the cover page of fitchratings.com that Fitch had placed GMAC on *rating watch*; on moodys.com that Moody's *changed* its GMAC *review to 'direction uncertain'*; and on standardandpoors.com that S&P *revised* its *outlook* on Vietnam *to positive from stable* and that it *affirmed the BB−/B foreign currency sovereign credit rating*. Without registering or logging in, any web browser could also have downloaded free of charge the 900-word summary of S&P's credit rating report coming out of Singapore. Rating actions and reports thus tend to become a 'public good' and freely available.

Arguably, what is freely available through the web are not public goods, but advertising messages. There are also time delays ensuring that the information becomes available at different times to different consumers according to their subscription – i.e. paying – levels. In fact, the free website is meant as bait, or a sneak preview of the information that actually exists on a company, in addition to its mere rating. And the free information is certainly not as user friendly as the subscription information.

Take, for example, the websites of the three major CRAs. S&P provides free rating information on its public website, but the rating analysis and rationale is available only to subscribers through its web-based real-time credit analysis system, RatingsDirect at www.ratingsdirect.com. While a few free credit reports are available on the public website, these are usually summaries and clicking on a report informs the browser that 'complete ratings information is available to subscribers of RatingsDirect.'[24] Moreover, these summaries are usually not S&P's latest analysis on the issuer and are difficult to search and access. One has to go to a separate web page, several clicks away from the Credit Ratings Lists, where search options for locating a particular company are not available. On the other hand, S&P's entire, latest research on a company, including the rating rationale, peer comparisons, industry studies, etc., are available on RatingsDirect merely by clicking on

---

[21] Technical Committee of the International Organization of Securities Commissions, 2004. *Code of Conduct Fundamentals for Credit Rating Agencies*, December, OICV-IOSCO PD 180, 1–12, measure 3.4, page 8.

[22] Technical Committee of the International Organization of Securities Commissions, 2004. *Code of Conduct Fundamentals for Credit Rating Agencies*, December, OICV-IOSCO PD 180, 1–12, measure 3.9, page 9.

[23] The Bond Market Association, 2004. Public comment on IOSCO October 2004 draft: *Code of Conduct Fundamentals for Credit Rating Agencies*, November 6, 1–12, page 10.

[24] Standard & Poor's, 2005. Vietnam outlook revised to positive from stable; ratings affirmed, bond issue rated 'BB−', *Research Update*, October 18, 1–3, page 2.

the name of the issuer, which itself can be located through a convenient search. Similarly, Moody's has research-related subscription services for different segments (Corporate Finance, Financial Institutions, Structured Products, Sovereigns, Public US Finance, and Fixed Income) offering regular updates on credit opinions, rating rationales, and other company research. Interestingly, the services offer '[A]ccess to Moody's analysts via individual consultation, and group briefings and teleconferences,' reflecting the special status of a paying subscriber.[25] Along similar lines, Fitch offers web-based subscription services like Fitch Research and Ratings Delivery Service.[26]

In conclusion, there is a lighthouse, but also a private data room. What the lighthouse on the web diffuses is public, but its light is not the most enlightening component of what CRAs produce. Credit rating opinions, their production, distribution and consumption, are less public goods than first meets the eye, but they are not easily withheld from non-subscribers and subscription revenues are not the main revenues of CRAs, as we will see later.

4.2.2 Rating Follow-Up

> *We're not feeling all that sanguine about the ratings, even at these revised levels*[27]

After-Sales Service to the Client Issuer

The issuer not only invests considerable senior management, including the Board of Directors', time and attention in obtaining an initial rating, but also has a stock of intangible capital invested in the rating and its ongoing maintenance. After the initial rating, follow-up is therefore important.

Issuers pay a considerable amount for their rating (see later) and expect to have a continuing professional relationship with their credit rating analyst. When the CFO calls the company's rating agency, he wants a knowledgable person to pick up the phone. After-sales service should include periodic feedback about the company's relative standing and how it is evolving, so the analyst needs to keep abreast of company developments.

Credit rating agencies and issuers hold divergent views about after-sales service. Issuers believe that the fee they pay gives them a claim on the time of their credit rating analyst and expect their analyst to be responsive to any requests for attention. This implies that the analyst can only follow a limited number of companies to enable her to follow the rated clients in her portfolio in real time and be responsive to each client on an ongoing basis. Agencies have a self-interest in preserving the integrity of their current ratings and proper company follow-up is thus part of their internal charter. But this is different from being available to clients at all times. In fact, it could be argued that the rating analyst should

---

[25] Moody's Investors Service website (http://www.moodys.com), 'Products and Services'.

[26] Fitch Ratings website (http://www.fitchratings.com), 'Products and Tools'.

[27] Said Scott Sprinzen, a credit analyst in Standard & Poor's Ratings Service auto group, at a conference in New York, according to Covel, S., and Hawkins Jr., L., 2005. High fuel prices, Delphi woes pressure GM's credit ratings, *The Wall Street Journal Europe*, September 29, page M4. The WSJE quoted Sprinzen as saying that S&P has grown more concerned since it last downgraded GM's rating on May 5. The double-B credit rating, which carries a negative outlook, could come under pressure.

shy away from such frequent contact to preserve her independence and objectivity. There is no ideal way to deal with this tension in the relationship between issuer client and CRA supplier, and it is mostly dealt with on an ad hoc basis. There is a growing pattern of annual review sessions combined with event-related contacts, initiated by either the issuer or the CRA.

Surveillance

Investors, issuers, and CRAs share an interest in keeping their ratings current. Once a rating action is taken, surveillance starts. Investors need to base their investment decisions on current information, therefore the grade they find on an instrument has to be up to date. Portfolio management sponsors set asset allocation boundaries using credit ratings in their governance of portfolio managers. These ratings must remain current if the governance approach is to reach its goals. Similarly, with issuers it happens that Boards of Directors use credit ratings to resolve agency problems with management by defining observable independent boundaries within which executive management must operate. As the company's environment changes and management responds accordingly, it needs up-to-date information from the rating agency to know how these responses fit within the boundaries. Surveillance is also in the interest of the CRA itself. A rating does not engage the professional liability of the agency, it is not a result contract. So, for instance, when Fitch upgraded Bulgaria to BBB in August 2005, it did not guarantee that Bulgaria will not default. But if Bulgaria had defaulted a year later without Fitch having noticed a deterioration in the country's sovereign risk during the year, Fitch would have had a problem with its reputation. All rating agencies had a bad time when outcomes went unexpectedly wrong in Thailand and at Enron, Worldcom, and Parmalat. The credit quality of a company or government can change rapidly and the rating agencies are expected to track such changes and give ample warning to investors.

CRAs differ in the timeliness with which they keep their ratings current. Sometimes, there have been significant differences in the speed of response to new information relevant to issuers. For example, during a quite recent 20-year period, rating changes in electric public utility bonds occurred in the same month in only 18% of cases. The average lead time when one agency changed first was 12 months. However, there was no significant difference over time in the propensity to change ratings earlier by either Moody's or S&P.[28] A differential rating adjustment lag among CRAs that rate the same security will then lead to splits ratings on outstanding issues. Inasmuch as investors' required return on bonds is affected – which it is – by the existence of split ratings, CRAs should avoid such transitory rating splits. Issuers are entitled to expect proper follow-up by the CRA in order to avoid disturbing transitory effects on their cost of debt due as a result.

Analysts are responsible for monitoring the credit quality of the issuers whose rating they prepared. In order to do this, they maintain close contact with the issuers they have rated. They often attend quarterly results presentations, talk to the CFO or the Treasurer regularly, and arrange annual review meetings with the issuer. CRAs organize internally for the analyst in charge of a portolio of companies to meet periodically with her or his

---

[28] See Altman, E., Avery, R., Eisenbeis, R., and Sinkey J., 1981. *Application of Classification Techniques in Business, Banking and Finance*, JAI Press, quoted in Beattie, V., and Searle, S., 1992. Bond ratings and inter-rate agreement, *Journal of International Securities Markets 3*, Summer, Vol. 6, 167–172, page 172.

superior to discuss the ratings of the portfolio. Analysts keep a closer watch on high-yield companies and usually maintain up-to-date liquidity scorecards. There are often important developments with regard to a particular company or the economy in general that will have a significant impact on a rating. In cases such as this, the agency will notify the market, and the monitoring may lead to a rating review. Moody's started to rate bonds in 1909 but only began announcing reviews in 1985 (and did not consider reviews to be formal rating actions until 1991). Standard & Poor's introduced reviews in 1981 and outlooks in 1986.[29] S&P will place the issuer on its *Credit Watch* for possible upgrade or downgrade. Moody's will use Rating Outlooks and Watchlists to achieve a different mix of accuracy and stability than the actual ratings, making its full rating system more informative than would be obtained by the juxtaposition of its silos.[30]

Rating Outlooks

Rating outlooks indicate the potential direction of a rating over the intermediate term (typically six months to two years). In determining a rating outlook, consideration is given to any changes in the economic and/or fundamental business conditions. An outlook is not necessarily a precursor of a rating change, and is often used to maintain the stability of long-term ratings, while enhancing its precision. A *positive* outlook means that a rating may be raised; *negative* means that a rating may be lowered; *stable* means that a rating is not likely to change; and *developing* means that a rating may be raised or lowered.

For example, S&P recently lowered Italy's credit outlook from stable to negative. It cited increased risks to public finances from low growth and the failure of politicians to address economic problems ahead of the 2006 general elections. Moritz Kraemer, S&P's analyst, said, 'The negative outlook could revert to stable if structural measures were implemented that would ensure the resumption of an unambiguous, significant, and sustainable downward trend of the government debt ratio. Conversely, the rating would be lowered within 18 months if no signs of a coherent debt reduction strategy emerge after the 2006 elections.' Italy currently has a rating of AA− from S&P, and a lever higher at Aa2 with a stable outlook from Moody's.[31]

At Moody's, for example, issuers that experience above or below normal earnings growth are often assigned positive or negative outlooks during the period in which a rating committee awaits additional evidence that demonstrates whether the change in the firm's credit posture is temporary or enduring. During these periods of uncertainty, Moody's typically maintains the issuer's rating but signals the nature of the risk through the Outlook assignment.[32] If and when a rating changes according to the outlook, at Moody's it reflects typically a change in benchmark default probability that corresponds to one rating notch.

---

[29] Micu, M., Remolona, E., and Wooldridge, P., 2006. The price impact of rating announcements: which announcements matter?, Working Paper No. 207: Bank for International Settlements, June, 1–31, page 2.
[30] Cantor, R., and Mann, C., 2006. Analyzing the tradeoff between rating accuracy and stability, *Special Comment*: Moody's Investors Services, September, Report 99100, 1–8, pages 6–7.
[31] Associated Press Newswires, 2005. Standard & Poor's lowers Italy's credit outlook from stable to negative, August 8.
[32] Cantor, R., and Mann, C., 2006. Analyzing the tradeoff between rating accuracy and stability, *Special Comment*: Moody's Investors Services, September, Report 99100, 1–8, pages 6–7.

Rating Reviews: Rating Alerts, Watchlists or CreditWatches[33]

Reviews give a stronger indication of future rate changes than outlooks. They indicate that there is a very high probability that the issuer rating will change, even though the direction of change may be uncertain. Names published for review tend to be so because of developing enduring trends or events that warrant a more extensive examination. At Moody's, for example, 'an issuer that is "in play" is usually placed on review until its merger or acquisition is completed and its rating consequences are well understood.'[34] In a random sample of 30 negative reviews over the 2001–2004 period, 60% were found to refer to a recent announcement by the company.[35] A rating review is announced solely at the discretion of the CRA, and not all issuers with ratings under review are included on a Rating Alert, Watchlist, or CreditWatch. CRAs aim to conclude listed reviews within 90 days, which gives time to clarify the impact of an announcement. Names can be removed from a published review without a change in rating.[36] If and when a rating changes according to a Moody's Watchlist, it reflects typically a change that corresponds to two rating notches (Figure 4.3).

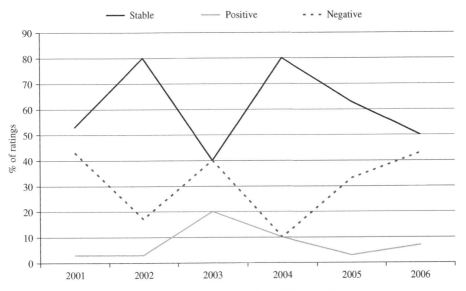

Figure 4.3   Top 30 European Industrials Rating Modifiers 2001–2006.
Note: Stable modifiers include stable and developing outlooks, and CreditWatch placements with developing implications (albeit there are none of the latter in this case). Negative modifiers include negative outlooks and CreditWatch placements with negative implications. Positive modifiers include positive outlooks and CreditWatch placements with positive implications.
Source: Ganguin, B., Jones, R., and Six, J.M., 2006, It's all a game of snakes and ladders for the top 50 European corporate entities, *Industry report card*: Standard & Poor's, November 2, 1–22, page 6, Chart 2.

---

[33] Fitch says that it places a rating on 'Rating Alert,' Moody's on a 'Watchlist,' and S&P on 'CreditWatch.'
[34] Cantor, R., and Mann, C., 2006. Analyzing the tradeoff between rating accuracy and stability, *Special Comment*: Moody's Investors Services, September, Report 99100, 1–8, pages 6–7.
[35] Micu, M., Remolona, E., and Wooldridge, P., 2006. The price impact of rating announcements: which announcements matter?, Working Paper No. 207: Bank for International Settlements, June, 1–31, page 2.
[36] Moody's Investor Service website as of November 2, 2006. Watchlist/Fundamental Ratings.

Rating Transitions

Rating outlooks and reviews help to maintain stability in long-term ratings themselves, albeit at some expense of their accuracy.[37] The credit quality of most issuers and their obligations is not fixed and steady over time. Changes in ratings reflect variations in the intrinsic relative position of issuers and their obligations. A change in rating or rating transition may thus occur at any time in the case of an individual issue. Such change indicates that the CRA observes some alteration in creditworthiness, or that the previous rating did not fully reflect the quality of the bond as now seen. These transitions follow two distinct patterns, one that relates to the business cycle, and one that relates to the rating category.

The business cycle influences the pattern of rating transitions. Table 4.1 tabulates annual aggregate rating migration rates. It illustrates the evolution of the credit climate, or credit climate cycle, over time. It shows the annual cohort of issuer counts, increasing from 1370 in 1983 to 4810 in 2004, the percentage of these upgraded, downgraded, unchanged, or withdrawn during that year, and the ratio of downgrades divided by upgrades. The latter ratio is an indicator of the general credit climate during a given year. The highest D–U ratio was 3.85 and occurred in 1990. For 117 issuers out of 2361 that were upgraded during that year (4.96%), 450 were downgraded (19.06%). The credit climate during that year was extremely poor. At the opposite end of the spectrum is 2004, when the credit environment

Table 4.1 Annual aggregate rating migration rates (1983–2004)

Cohort year	Issuer count	% Upgraded	% Downgraded	% Unchanged	% WR	D–U Ratio
1983	1370	8.25	12.41	75.55	3.80	1.50
1984	1422	12.87	11.74	72.93	2.46	0.91
1985	1620	9.63	13.02	73.02	4.32	1.35
1986	1834	8.51	17.23	68.16	6.11	2.03
1987	2064	6.59	11.87	74.56	6.98	1.80
1988	2195	6.61	13.26	73.90	6.24	2.01
1989	2271	6.61	13.78	73.76	5.86	2.09
1990	2361	4.96	19.06	68.95	7.03	3.85
1991	2267	5.78	18.70	69.25	6.26	3.24
1992	2287	6.69	17.10	67.77	8.44	2.56
1993	2415	7.99	13.13	70.35	8.53	1.64
1994	2725	7.60	7.30	79.38	5.72	0.96
1995	3055	9.95	8.67	76.82	4.55	0.87
1996	3361	11.34	7.53	75.75	5.39	0.66
1997	3741	9.92	8.47	76.37	5.24	0.85
1998	4234	8.57	17.67	68.21	5.55	2.06
1999	4650	8.09	20.56	66.73	4.62	2.54
2000	4923	11.01	12.09	72.27	4.63	1.10
2001	4925	8.49	16.75	68.79	5.97	1.97
2002	4921	5.10	21.19	66.35	7.36	4.16
2003	4813	6.61	14.98	70.41	8.00	2.27
2004	4810	13.58	8.77	70.69	6.96	0.65

Source: Moody's Investors Service, 2005. *Annual Default and Recovery Study: 1920–2004,* June 29, Exhibit 29.

---

[37] See Exhibit 4 of Cantor, R., and Mann, C., 2006. Analyzing the tradeoff between rating accuracy and stability, *Special Comment*: Moody's Investors Services, September, Report 99100, 1–8, page 7.

Table 4.2 Average annual whole letter rating migration matrix (1970–2004)

Cohort rating	Issuer count	Terminal rating								
		Aaa	Aa	A	Baa	Ba	B	Caa–C	Default	WR
Aaa	3 179	89.48	7.05	0.75	0.00	0.03	0.00	0.00	0.00	2.69
Aa	11 310	1.07	88.41	7.35	0.25	0.07	0.01	0.00	0.00	2.83
A	22 981	0.05	2.32	88.97	4.85	0.46	0.12	0.01	0.02	3.19
Baa	18 368	0.05	0.23	5.03	84.50	4.60	0.74	0.15	0.16	4.54
Ba	12 702	0.01	0.04	0.46	5.28	78.88	6.48	0.50	1.16	7.19
B	10 794	0.01	0.03	0.12	0.40	6.18	77.45	2.93	6.03	6.85
Caa–C	2 091	0.00	0.00	0.00	0.52	1.57	4.00	62.68	23.12	8.11

Source: Moody's Investors Service, 2005. *Annual Default and Recovery Study: 1920–2004*, June 29, Exhibit 32.

was really benign. The D-U ratio stood at 0.65. For 422 downgrades out of 4810 rated issuer (8.77%) there were 653 upgrades (13.58%).

The rating category also influences the pattern of rating transitions. Table 4.2 tabulates the rating migration matrix per rating cohort. Migration increases with the age of a rating cohort. Consider, for example, the Aaa category: 11% of the ratings change after one year, 43% after five years, and 68% after 10 years. And for an Aaa, the rating can only go down. Rating changes are also more frequent among lower rated bonds than among higher rated bonds. For example, in the first year, 89% of the A rated bonds preserve their rating, down to 85% for those rated Baa; after five years it is 58% versus 47%; after 10 years it is 38% versus 27%. This partly reflects the fact that Baa rated bonds are more frequently upgraded than those rated A: 5% after one year (versus 2%); 17% after five years (versus 8%), and 20% after 10 years (versus 11%).

There is less downgrading of newly issued bonds than there is for older issues. It is interesting to note the example of the Aa cohort. After one year, 8% have been downgraded; after five years 28%, and after 10 years 40%. A company with a newly issued bond has received the face value of the issuance (in most cases) and probably has the liquidity to do many things, including service debt. In addition, in most cases, there is no significant change in credit quality in a very short period of time unless there is an external shock or the company that issued the bond has become very highly geared and is vulnerable to sudden changes in the operating environment. In addition, it is not likely that the agency would conduct a review of the issue before the first anniversary of the rating. So upgrades are also less frequent in the short term: for the Aa category, there are 1% within a year, 4% after five years, and 5% after 10 years.

To sum up, we will review the distribution of rating announcements. Table 4.3 and Figure 4.4 compare the frequencies of negative and positive announcements; they decompose each subset in rating change, review, and outlook change; they then show, for each of these rating actions per subset, the distribution per major rating agency, per prior announcement or not and, if a prior announcement occurred, what type.

4.2.3 The Rating Agreement

Once the company decides to go ahead, a rating agreement letter is usually drafted. It spells out the respective rights and responsibilities of both the rating agency and the issuer. This letter helps to avoid any misunderstandings by either side during the rating process and lays the foundation for complete confidentiality within the relationship.

Table 4.3 Distribution of rating announcements (2001–2005)

Raw sample	Negative announcements				Positive announcements			
	Downgrade	Review	Outlook change	Total	Upgrade	Review	Outlook change	Total
Total	2646	1402	994	5042	700	298	454	1452
By rating agency:								
Moody's	1561	651	324	2536	273	195	142	610
Standard & Poor's	721	590	470	1781	298	71	195	564
Fitch	364	161	200	725	129	32	117	278
Total *not* preceded by any announcement[1]	1871	880	528	3279	473	244	334	1051
Total preceded by any announcement[1,2]	775	522	466	1763	227	54	120	401
Rating change	365	270	253	888	116	20	39	175
Review	519	290	190	999	118	19	24	161
Outlook change	128	50	172	350	35	20	72	127
Same agency	143	67	97	307	63	4	14	81
Different agency[3]	632	455	369	1456	164	50	106	320

Notes:

1. Preceded by another type of rating announcement during the 60 business days prior to the rating announcement.
2. Some announcements were preceded by more than one rating announcement and so the total may differ from the sum of the preceding announcements other
3. Preceded by a rating announcement by a different rating agency

Source: Micu, M., Remolona, E., and Wooldridge, P., 2006, The price impact of rating announcements: which announcements matter?, Working Paper No. 207: Bank for International Settlements, June, 1–31.

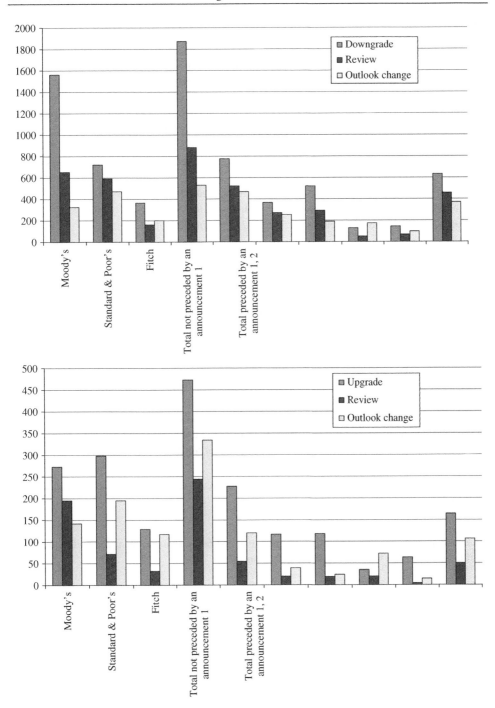

Figure 4.4   Distribution of rating announcements (2001–2005).

Notes:

1. Preceded by another rating announcement during the 60 business days prior to the rating announcement.
continued on next page

Liability

'Ratings, as forward-looking opinions on matters of public concern, should not be subject to liability standards that treat them as either statements of fact or investment recommendation.'[38] Credit opinions are expressions of freedom of speech. Their publishers, for example, are thus afforded First Amendment protections under US jurisdiction. To that extent, CRAs incur no special contractual results liability in exchange for the invoice being sent to the rated client company. Results liability exposes an agency to costly legal damages. If an agency were to be held liable for a rating that turned out to be wrong – for example, an investment grade company suddenly defaults – rating agencies would be in a very precarious financial situation.[39]

Credit rating agencies are currently exempt from legal liability. Amy Lancellotta, Senior Counsel of the Investment Company Institute, testifying to the SEC Hearings on Issues Relating to Credit Rating Agencies in April 2002, pointed out that:

'The Commission has relieved NRSROs from the accountability that would otherwise apply under the federal securities laws: it has exempted NRSROs from expert liability under Section 11 of the Securities Act if their ratings appear in a prospectus for a public offering of a security registered under that Act. As a result, issuers do not have to obtain consents from NRSROs before publishing their ratings and NRSROs are exempt from Section 11 liability if their ratings are included in a registration statement. The exemption of NRSROs from the normal liability provisions of Section 11 of the Securities Act means that NRSROs are not held to a negligence standard of care. The rating agencies also maintain that they are members of the 'media' that are providing their 'opinions,' and thus claim that they can only be liable if their conduct can be said to have been 'reckless.'[40]

The First Amendment status of publishers of credit opinions strengthens their hands *vis-à-vis* the rated client. It makes it easier for CRAs to make unbiased or unpopular observations regarding issuers and their securities. And this is certainly what the investor wishes the

---

Figure 4.4   (*Continued*)

2. Some announcements were preceded by more than one rating announcement and so the total may differ from the sum of the preceding announcements.

Source: Micu, M., Remolona, E., and Wooldridge, P., 2006, The price impact of rating announcements: which announcements matter?, Working Paper No. 207: Bank for International Settlements, June, 1–31.

---

[38] Dering, J.M., Executive Vice President for Global Regulatory Affairs and Compliance – Moody's Corporation, 2005. Remarks to the American Enterprise Institute, September 27, 1–7, page 5.

[39] If a rating agency could be held liable for a rating that turned out to be wrong, an investor who bought Korean government bonds just prior to the Asian crisis based on Korea's investment grade credit rating could hold the rating agency responsible for his losses and demand to be compensated.

[40] Lancelotta, A.B.R., Senior Counsel – Investment Company Institute, 2002. SEC Hearing on issues relating to credit rating agencies, November 21, Section III, point 4.

CRAs to do. Making the CRAs subject to litigation by issuers, investors, or others when they disagree with a rating could indeed 'have a chilling effect on the agencies' willingness to continue to publish their independent opinions.'[41]

In other words, the phrase *caveat emptor* applies to bond ratings and the buying of bonds.

Confidentiality

Credit rating agencies possess inside information about their clients. During the rating process, they acquire confidential data such as business segment analysis and three- to five-year financial projections. As the SEC has pointed out, CRAs commonly use non-public information in their analysis, such as budgets and forecasts, internal capital allocations, and contingent risks.[42] The vast majority of issuers provide such non-public information to the rating agencies.[43] As that information is probably stock price sensitive and has not been publicly disclosed, possessing it presents a dilemma for the agency. Investors demand ratings that capture all the information available to the rater. Issuers need an incentive to discuss significant events with the rater in advance of announcements. Agencies deal with this dilemma by taking the rating action that incorporates all the data but without disclosing the confidential information upon which the rating is based.[44]

To allow CRAs to access non-public information without the issuer disclosing it, the SEC exempts CRAs from its fair disclosure regulation. This regulation generally prohibits an issuer of securities from communicating non-public information to selected persons unless the information is publicly disclosed.[45] To improve the rating process, CRAs are exempted 'insiders.' This allows, for instance, Ford Motor Company to release product plans for future years that could be used by Ford's competitors if publicly available confidentially to the CRA, and helps improve the quality of the rating.[46]

By using inside information in their rating actions, CRAs reduce information asymmetry. It is a major function of the CRAs to probe inside information without disclosing it. Ratings 'attest to the relative quality of the bond issue and to the accuracy of the accompanying information about the issuing company.'[47] In most cases, the CRA makes the assigned rating public. In such rating announcements, the CRA is careful that any rationales or other information published about the company refer only to publicly available corporate information.

---

[41] Dering, J.M., Executive Vice President for Global Regulatory Affairs and Compliance – Moody's Corporation, 2005. Remarks to the American Enterprise Institute, September 27, 1–7, page 6.

[42] US Securities and Exchange Commission, 2003. Report on the role and function of credit rating agencies in the operation of capital markets, January, 1–45, pages 33–34.

[43] Standard & Poor's, 1998. *Corporate Credit Ratings: a Guide*, page 4.

[44] See also Cotton, C., and Zarin, F., 1998. Rating methodology: responses to frequently asked questions concerning confidential information, *Special Comment*: Moody's Investors Services, October, Report 38862, 1–4.

[45] August 24, 2000.

[46] Macdonald, M.S., Vice President, Finance and Treasurer – Ford Motor Company, 2002. Transcript of SEC hearings on the current role and function of the credit rating agencies in the operation of the securities markets, November 15.

[47] Wakeman, L.M., 1984. The real function of bond rating agencies, in Jensen M., and Smith C. (eds), *The Modern Theory of Corporate Finance*, McGraw-Hill, New York, 391–396, page 395.

Non-public information is provided to the CRA solely for the purpose of arriving at a rating and should be kept strictly confidential by the rating group. The confidentiality provisions of the rating agreement should always stipulate this. For example, 'it is not to be used for any other purpose, nor by any third party, including other Standard & Poor's units. Standard & Poors maintains a "Chinese Wall" between its rating activities and its equity information services.'[48]

Exhibit 4.1 Stated fee schedules (2007)

€ Thousand	Fitch	Moody's	S&P
ST or LT Issuer/Senior Unsecured Rating			
Initial Rating Fee	55–80	43.5	50–125
Annual Surveillance Fee	40–65	43.5	n.m.
Commercial Paper (CP) Program			
Initial Rating Fee	n.m.	43.5	50–125
Annual Fee –			
Initial Program	35	33.9	47.5
Second Program	35	n.m.	37.5
Subsequent Program	25	n.m.	22.5
Quarterly Usage Fee	n.m.	11.10–90.9 depending on volume o/s	n.m.
LT Debt, Preferred Stock and Private Placement			
Initial Rating Fee	n.m.	43.5	50–125
Issuance fee	4.25 bp	Up to EUR 500m = 4.5 bp (min 43.5, max 188), >EUR 500m = additional 3 bp (max 372.0)	Up to EUR 650m = 4.25 bp, >EUR 650m = additional 2.5 bp on par amount over EUR 650m
Annual Surveillance Fee	n.m.	25.3	40–90
Frequent Issuance Fee	n.m.	n.m.	260–400, additional issuance fee of 2.08–0.80 bp
Medium Term Notes			
Initial Fee	n.m.	52.5	50–125
Annual Fee	n.m.	52.5	As per CP fees
Drawdown Fee	4.25 bp	As per LT debt and preferred stock fees	>EUR 25m, as per LT Debt fees

n.m.: not mentioned.

Notes:
The initial fees in each category is only applicable if the applicant has had no definite rating in either category in the past 12 months.

Sources: Fitch Ratings, 2007. Reference fee schedule 2007 Corporate – EMEA, 1–1; Moody's Investors Service, 2007. Fee guide for per issue fees, January, 1–2; Standard & Poor's, 2007. Fee schedule for European corporates, utilities, and financial institutions, January 1, 1–4.

---

[48] Standard & Poor's, 2005. *Corporate Ratings Criteria*, 1–119, page 16.

Pricing

The pricing of different rating services is based on a public fee schedule. It varies with the type of service and from agency to agency. Is it an issuer or instrument rating; initial or follow-up; short or long term; an actual rating or a rating assessment; single or one of many for the same company?

Exhibit 4.1 compares the stated fee schedules of 2005. For each of the three major CRAs, it lists the fee structure for issuer ratings and then for three major categories of issues: long-term debt, preferred stock and private placement; medium-term notes; and commercial paper.

Fee schedules have evolved in two ways recently. Generally, they have become more standardized for the industry, converging across agencies, and they have also become more expensive.

There are no public fee schedules for the rating of structured finance instruments, only vague guidelines. The time and complexity involved in the rating of these instruments varies much more widely.

SF VIGNETTE 6

Specificities of the Credit Rating Process in SF

The general procedure of rating structured finance is briefly presented in Exhibit 4.2. It consists of an interaction between the arranger and agencies as well as some involvement of third parties such as the originator, the legal firm, and the asset manager. To reach opinions on the credit rating of a particular transaction, the rating agencies follow the specific steps below:[49]

- Review the structural basics and legal structure
- Size the default frequency of the collateral pool
- Review the collateral manager if it is a managed instrument
- Size the loss severity
- Review the transaction's collateral and structural detailed features
- Establish the required level of credit support for each rated tranche if it is a tranched instrument.

What is noticeable is that the arranger can change the structure of the transaction on receipt of preliminary ratings, while this possibility is rare in rating corporations or corporate bonds. This reflects the flexibility of structured finance instruments. Particularly in a CDO transaction, the transaction usually includes a ramp-up period during which the manager of CDO first purchases the required assets to form up to 40–60% of the value of the predetermined pool. Then with the final ratings issued by CRAs, the manager can issue notes to investors to finance for the purchase of the rest of the pool. This gives rise to an additional concern that the CRAs need to watch over the purchase of assets and estimate how likely and how much the assets the manager obtains during ramp-up comply with the assets stipulated in the transaction's contract. The reason is that the modeling of credit risk and other risks are mainly based on the analysis of the predetermined pool rather than the actual pool, resulting in affecting the soundness of the final ratings.

---

[49] Standard & Poor's, 2002. Global Cash Flow and Synthetic CDO Criteria, March, page 15.

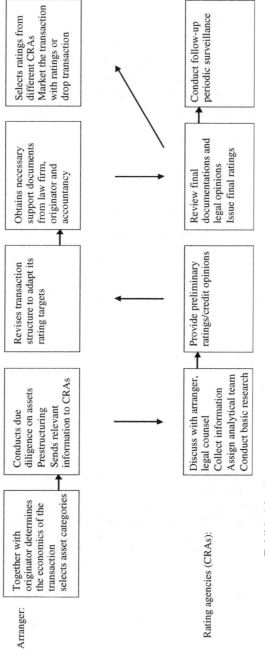

Exhibit 4.2 Securitization and rating process of a typical (cash) structured finance instrument

4.3   QUALITY OF THE RATING PROCESS

Rating outcomes stir controversy. This should be no surprise. Just bear in mind that the two main constituents of a rating are easily perceived to have conflicting stakes in a rating outcome. Concerned about their cost of capital, issuers sometimes believe that the rating grade causes the level of the credit spread. If so, they will want the rating to be higher rather than lower, ceteris paribus. Issuers would thus prefer the CRAs to set the odds of erring on the higher side of the rating, i.e. not make Type II errors (don't condemn an innocent). Investors are concerned about their return for risk. If they believe also that the rating grade causes the level of the return spread, they will want the rating to be lower rather than higher, ceteris paribus. Investors would thus prefer CRAs to set the odds of erring on the lower side of the rating, i.e. not to make Type I errors (don't acquit a murderer). The sensitivity of issuers toward cost and of investors toward return and their aversion toward different types of risk tend to set them up against each other when it comes to accepting a rating. During periods of rapid and material shifts in the credit risk of an obligor, it is easy to see how either the issuer or the investment community will find the action or inaction of a CRA controversial.

Reaching a rating action is a high-risk decision and the credit committee walks a tightrope. It must progress toward a decision, but any misstep could be disastrous for its reputation. While moving forward, it must keep contradictory forces at bay. To avoid making a Type I error, it has to focus on the issuer's downside. But to avoid a Type II error, it must focus on the issuer's upside. CRAs have a strong self-interest in wanting to avoid a reputation disaster. Either the issuer or the investment community and certainly the media will be keen to expose what appear, with hindsight, to be mistakes.

> Institutions '... relied on the ratings agencies to reassure them that the complex mortgage bonds they were buying were indeed investment-grade. But those ratings agencies did not understand how, under conditions of "stress," i.e. falling house price, those bonds would fall in value.'[50]

The CRAs take pride in standing up to controversy and are philosophical about it. As S&P's President notes,

> the fact that there is often controversy surrounding rating opinions is healthy. It speaks to the independence of the process. At S&P, our test is not whether the issuer, the underwriter or even the investor agrees with our rating. The test is whether the process was objective, whether the rating and our analysis were promptly disseminated, and whether all investors were alerted to the outcome at the same time. More importantly, is there fundamental quantitative and qualitative information to support a rating decision?[51]

The quality of the ratings process thus focuses on objectivity, diligence, and transparency.

Conflicts of Interest

In a letter to Jonathan G. Katz, Secretary of the US Securities and Exchange Commission dated November 12, 2002, Stephen W. Joynt, President and CEO of Fitch, outlined

---

[50] http://news.bbc.co.uk/2/hi/business/7086909.stm
[51] O'Neill, L., President and Chief Rating Officer of Standard & Poor's, 1999. Building the new global framework for risk analysis, Remarks to Professional bankers association at World Bank headquarters in Washington D.C, March 26, 1–5.

Fitch's views ahead of hearings relating to CRAs and the securities markets later that month. Conflicts of interest merited several pages discussing fees, why issuers request Fitch ratings, disclosure, and rating advisory services. Joynt pointed out that, 'we emphasize independence and objectivity because our independent, unbiased coverage of the companies and securities we rate is important to our research subscribers and the marketplace in general.'

Joynt went on to describe how Fitch managed potential conflict 'through our compensation policy,' whereby analysts' compensation is unrelated to fees from issuers. He also commented that fees were fixed and not influenced by any financial success or otherwise related to a particular issue or rating. Transparency is also important in avoiding conflicts of interest. Joynt stated that 'Fitch firmly believes that the disclosure of the arrangement by which an issuer pay fees to Fitch in connection with Fitch's ratings of the issuer is appropriate.'[52]

We further discuss the sensitive issue of conflicts of interest related to the issuer-pays business model in Chapters 8 and 9.

4.3.1 Objectivity

Analyst Independence

A CRA has in principle no incentive to present biased and inaccurate data as if it was unbiased and accurate. The CRA is not a claimant on the firm, except for the fee for the current rating and the value of fees for future ratings. Each individual fee is relatively so small compared to the value of the reputation for accuracy and independence – which can be measured objectively – that no CRA can afford to be biased in its opinion about the extent to which a firm in actual distress is insolvent on a stock, as well as a flow basis. This is contrary to shareholders, who have an interest in encouraging the upside mindset that a flow insolvency is not a stock one – and creditors the other way around – and management upon whom the CRAs depend for information and insights, and who will side with the party least likely to fire them.[53] Objectivity or independence of opinion is thus a cornerstone of the value that CRAs add in making predictive assessments about an obligor's future cash flows based on incomplete information, and CRAs stress that a credit rating is an independent opinion about credit risk.

Agency independence receive a lot of attention at every credit crunch, corporate scandal or financial crisis. Agencies were berated for supposedly being slow in downgrading countries such as Indonesia, South Korea, and Thailand in 1997, and companies such as Enron in 2001 and Worldcom in 2002. The CRAs were accused of delaying downgrades, because these issuers were also among their biggest customers, and paying them hefty fees. But any individual issuer represents only a small share of a CRA's revenues and the intense rivalry between agencies puts them under a lot of pressure to get it right. The fact that CRAs emphasize the independence of their opinion reflects their response to the close scrutiny that such accusations engender.

---

[52] Joynt, S.W., President and Chief Executive Officer – Fitch Ratings, 2002. Comment on the role and function of rating agencies in the operation of securities markets, November 12.

[53] See further Wruck, K., 1990. Financial distress: reorganization and organization efficiency, *Journal of Financial Economics*, October, Vol. 27, No. 2, 419–444, pages 422–424.

4.3.2 Diligence

A serious charge that has been leveled against the leading CRAs is that due diligence in the rating process is inadequate. CRAs have been blamed for taking the issuers' word at face value, undertaking improper reviews of public filings, paying inadequate attention to detail, and aggressive accounting practices in financial statements. [54]

Market participants contend that this has caused ratings to fail the 'timeliness' test, with downgrades lagging credit deterioration in the large bankruptcy cases and the subprime meltdown. For instance, Enron was rated a good credit by S&P and Moody's until four days before its collapse, Worldcom until three months before, and Parmalat until 45 days before. The CRAs' main defense against this charge is that the importance of their reputation is enough to ensure that no single issuer can affect their rating process. Also, CRAs claim that they have been misled by some issuers, who deliberately provided inaccurate and misleading information through their financial statements, which the rating agencies do not audit.[55] Another justification given by the CRAs to the delays in rating changes is that their ratings attempt to meet the dual objectiveness of both timeliness and stability, as frequent changes can affect the stability of capital markets. According to the CRAs, the objective of timeliness is met through watchlists and outlooks.

Egan-Jones Ratings Co. (EJRC) has given great publicity to its relatively greater timeliness in issuing ratings downgrades (including negative watches) prior to the bankruptcies of Enron and Worldcom. Exhibit 4.3 compares the rating downgrades of (a) Enron, (b) Worldcom, and (c) Parmalat. What emerges from the exhibit is that EJRC started to ring the alarm bells well before either S&P or Moody's. Enron was put on negative watch as much as 110 days before the bankruptcy, while Moody's issued the negative watch 48 days before, and S&P 32 days before. EJRC lowered Enron to below investment grade 38 days before the bankruptcy, while the two leading CRAs had Enron rated as investment grade as late as five days before bankruptcy. Worldcom tells a similar story. Of course, as Part B will show, one must discriminate between luck and skill, which can only be done using proper statistical inference methods based on large representative samples. And powerful performance tests should not only look at the ability to correctly forecast defaults that actually occurred, but also at avoiding forecasting defaults incorrectly. Based on that evidence, nothing substantiates the claim that the 'technical' rating scores that EJRC uses are statistically superior to the traditional 'fundamental' ones.

CRAs have thus maintained their stand against the charges of inaccuracy, ratings delays, and inadequate due diligence. They have nevertheless taken a number of measures to improve the quality of the ratings process. For example, the appointment of forensic accounting expertise by S&P to verify issuer information, appointment of analysts by Moody's to deal with off-balance-sheet exposure, and accounting disclosures, analyst training, increased liquidity, recovery analysis, etc.[56] Diligence in the structured finance segment has been the most questionable. The argument that the crisis was due to loose underwriting standards

---

[54] US Securities and Exchange Commission, 2003. Report on the role and function of credit rating agencies in the operation of the securities market, January, 1–45, page 32.

[55] Corbet, K.A., President – Standard & Poor's, 2005. Examining the role of credit rating agencies in the capital markets, Testimony before the Committee on Banking, Housing, and Urban Affairs, United States Senate, February 8, 1–12, page 7.

[56] Corbet, K.A., President – Standard & Poor's, 2005. Examining the role of credit rating agencies in the capital markets, Testimony before the Committee on Banking, Housing, and Urban Affairs, United States Senate, February 8, 1–12, page 8.

Exhibit 4.3   Enron, Parmalat, Worldcom: Timing of the CRAs Move to Non-Investment Grade Rating (2000–2003)

Senior Unsecured Ratings				
(a) Enron: Bankruptcy declared on December 3, 2001				
	Days before	Egan-Jones	Moody's	S&P
27-Jun-01	159	BBB	Baa1	BBB+
15-Aug-01	110	BBB (neg.)	"	"
16-Oct-01	48	"	Baa1 (neg.)	"
23-Oct-01	41	BBB−	"	"
24-Oct-01	40	BBB− (neg.)	"	"
26-Oct-01	38	**BB+**	"	"
29-Oct-01	35		Baa2 (neg.)	"
01-Nov-01	32		"	BBB (neg.)
09-Nov-01	24		Baa3 (neg.)	BBB− (neg.)
28-Nov-01	5		**B2**	**B−**

(b) Worldcom: Bankruptcy declared on July 17, 2002				
	Months before	Egan-Jones	Moody's	S&P
11-Jan-00	31	A− (neg.)	A3	A−
03-Nov-00	21	"	"	A− (neg)
17-Nov-00	20	BBB+ (neg)	"	"
08-Feb-01	17	BBB	"	"
27-Feb-01	17	"	"	BBB+
25-Jun-01	13	BBB−	"	"
26-Jul-01	12	**BB+ (neg)**	"	"
29-Jan-02	6	BB (neg)	"	"
07-Feb-02	5	BB− (neg)	A3 (neg)	"
19-Feb-02	5	B+	"	"
12-Apr-02	3	"	"	BBB+ (neg)
22-Apr-02	3	"	"	BBB
23-Apr-02	3	B	Baa2	"
25-Apr-02	3	B−	"	"
09-May-02	2	"	**Ba2**	"
10-May-02	2	"	"	**BB**

Source: Egan, S.J., Managing Director – Egan-Jones Ratings Company, 2005, Examining the role of credit rating agencies in the capital markets, Testimony before the Committee on Banking, Housing and Urban Affairs, United States Senate, February 8, 1–12.

Issuer Credit Rating		
(c) Parmalat SpA: Bankruptcy declared on December 27, 2003		
	Days before	S&P
15-Nov-00	3 years 1 month before	BBB−
13-Jun-02	1 years 6 months before	BBB− (pos)
15-Sep-03	103	BBB−
11-Nov-03	46	BBB− (watch neg)
09-Dec-03	18	B+ (watch dev)
10-Dec-03	17	CC (watch dev)
19-Dec-03	8	D
19-Dec-03	8	NR

Source: Standard & Poor's, 2003. *Rating history on Parmarlat SpA*, December, 1-1.

holds, but the rating agencies should have anticipated that no institution effectively had enough reputation at stake over the due diligence process; contrarily to audit firms and corporations. Moreover, it should be part of the rating process, even of structured finance instruments, to gauge under what market environments issuer and originator information becomes less reliable. The rapid pace of financial innovation has been a major issue in the loosened diligence in the structured finance segment.

4.3.3 Transparency

Transparency deals with the adequacy, fairness, and confidentiality of rating-related information. Is public disclosure of the rating basis adequate? Is the process of diffusing the rating basis fair? Do CRAs properly preserve the confidentiality of issuers' private information?

Disclosure of Rating Basis

Several market participants feel that there is inadequate disclosure of information by CRAs about rating decisions and processes, especially assumptions behind decisions, information and documents reviewed, and rating triggers in private contracts. However, the CRAs claim that rating methodologies, ratings, underlying rationale, criteria, and industry commentaries are made available on the Internet, with any change announced publicly. For structured finance ratings, the major agencies allow market participants to download the program running the rating model on which ratings are based. However, although these programs allow to anticipate some ratings and scenarios, many of the key assumptions and parameters underlying the quantitative models are not made explicit. The key issue behind transparency is to prevent surprises in a rating action and future transition, so that more than the running of a program, it should involve an explanation of the confidence around a rating and the robustness of the model to certain events. This implies that market participants also have enough incentives to make the effort to thoroughly understand a given rating and not focus excessively on the rating grade per se.

In February 2003, S&P announced that it had put 12 European companies on a watch list because of worries about pension liabilities in the face of falling European markets. ThyssenKrupp AG was the first of those companies to suffer, when S&P downgraded its credit rating to junk, lowering its long-term corporate credit rating from BBB to BB+ and its short-term rating from A-2 to B in February 2003. S&P credit analyst Olivier Beroud said that 'the rating actions reflect Standard & Poor's treatment of unfunded pensions as debt-like in character. Including unfunded pensions in the calculation of the group's indebtedness, credit protection measures are weak.' While S&P was being transparent about its processes, ThyssenKrupp reacted angrily, regarding the downgrade as 'incomprehensible.'[57]

---

[57] Standard & Poor's, 2003. ThyssenKrupp ratings lowered to 'BB+/B'; OffWatch; Otlk Stable, February 21; Benoit, B., and Bream, R., 2003, S&P downgrades ThyssenKrupp, *Financial Times*, February 22.

The requirement to disclose extends to the careful management of changes in rating methods. In fact, what did upset issuers most in the pension liabilities example that affected also US issuers was that S&P had not prepared them regarding its change in methods of accounting for these liabilities, nor about the possible repercussion of this for the ratings. The placing on the watchlist and subsequent downgrading resulted from a change in rating method, not from a change in issuer conditions. This, and other similar incidents led the major associations of corporate treasurers in the world to include in their draft Code of Standard Practices for Participants in the Credit Rating Process that:

> Each CRA should widely publicize any changes in its methodologies and allow a short period for public comment to the agency prior to the release of any rating announcement that might be the consequence of these changes.[58]

CRAs tend to respect this quite reasonable request of issuers and to take their comments into consideration. It happens that they do not implement proposed changes after a consultation process. For example, in 2006 Moody's made a detailed proposal to change their rating transitions for investment grade issuers subject to event risk.[59] This entailed a protocol-based graduating in transitions as a function of objectively measurable increases in the likelihood that the event risk would materialize. After listening to the views of their market constituents who were only lukewarm about the proposed changes, Moody's decided that they were not going ahead with their proposal. Instead they affirmed their existing approach for such situations as debt-financed acquisitions and LBOs.[60]

The Process of Diffusing the Rating

A related charge is that CRAs give subscribers preferential access to information, because subscribers have direct access to rating analysts. CRAs argue that some preferential access to subscribers, such as detailed reports and analyses, is justified, given the cost of making this information available. In addition, analysts are available to the public to answer queries.

Confidentiality of Issuers' Private Information

Another concern deals with improper leakage of material non-public information, especially since CRAs are exempt from Regulation Fair Disclosure, and that rating information might be provided before the rating is released to the public.[61] Here the CRAs respond

---

[58] Association for Financial Professionals,' Association Française Des Trésoriers D'Entreprise, and Association of Corporate Treasurers, 2004. Comments on IOSCO October 2004 draft: *Code of Conduct Fundamentals for Credit Rating Agencies*, November, 1–38, page 31.

[59] Bodard, E., Hu, C.M., Lau, C., Otsuki, E., and Stumpp, P., 2006, Rating transitions for investment-grade issuers subject to event risk: request for comment, *Rating Methodology*: Moody's Investors Service, July, Report 98024, 1–8.

[60] Bodard, E., Gates, D., Hu, C.M., Lau, C., and Otsuki, E., 2006. Event risk and investment grade non-financial companies, *Rating Practice*: Moody's Investors Service, October, Report 97134, 1–4.

[61] Regulation FD prohibits an issuer of securities from communicating non-public information to certain enumerated persons – in general, securities market professionals or others may use the information for trading – unless the information is publicly disclosed. When Regulation FD was adopted the SEC exempted CRAs on the condition that non-public information is communicated to a rating agency solely for the purpose of developing a credit rating and that the rating is publicly available.

that internal rules and regulations are in place to prevent information leakage. The main CRAs' reputation regarding confidentiality of issuers' private information is excellent so that treasurers' organizations encourage issuers to be very transparent with the CRAs: 'The Code of standard practices for participants in the credit rating process' issued by the ACT and other treasury organizations advises that 'issuers should cooperate actively with CRAs when a rating is solicited and provide adequate and timely information.'[62]

---

[62] From the The Association of Corporate Treasurers, 2006. The Treasurer's Handbook 2006, page 223. The Code of standard practices for participants in the credit rating process is issued by the ACT, the Association of Finance Professionals and L'Association Française des Trésoriers d'Entreprise on behalf of the International Group of Treasury Associations.

Part B
Credit Rating Analysis

Part B – Credit Rating Analysis – follows France Telecom's credit ratings from 1995 to 2004 and uses this fascinating case to explore fundamental and technical credit ratings before examining the technical performance of credit ratings.

Chapter 5 describes how France Telecom's credit ratings cycled from sovereign status in 1995 to near speculative grade in 2002, and back up by the winter of 2004. France is infamous as the country where issuers complain more than anywhere else that CRAs create bad weather, rather than being the weathermen who report it. However, France Telecom's story illustrates exactly the opposite.

Chapter 6 studies credit rating analysis. In preparing a rating action, CRAs use fundamental analysis of default risk and of the prospects of recovery in case of default. They complement this with the extraction of default probabilities from market prices. Both approaches are explained, and then related to France Telecom to clarify where the two factors differ and where they complement each other.

Chapter 7 answers three questions about rating performance. How accurate are ratings in predicting actual defaults and in avoiding predicting defaults that never occur? What do ratings and ratings changes add to the party of pricing securities? How rationally and diligently did the CRAs act during periods of crisis?

5
The France Telecom Credit
Rating Cycle: 1995–2004

After setting the scene with a look at the telecoms sector in the latter half of the 1990s, we explain the sequence of events that led to France Telecom (FT) experiencing a series of rating downgrades through June 2002. This leads us to explore the company's refinancing plan in November 2002 and its eventual rating recovery. We then document the timeline of the cycle, along with some financial ratios and default probabilities, in preparation for the more technical discussion of credit rating analysis in Chapter 6.

Changes in the European Union (EU) Telecommunications Industry

With technological changes ushering in a new era in telecommunications, the industrial challenges that FT faced were daunting. At the same time, regulations were being drafted that would transform the European telecommunications sector beyond recognition on January 1, 1998, going from closed markets dominated by state monopolies to one open EU market with private players. Market changes were inevitable, but would take time to materialize.

In the 1980s, changes in ICT technology galvanized the EU to introduce competition in the sector. Numerous directives focused on liberalization and harmonization, and an open and seamless telecommunications space within and between member states. A few member states acted early, privatizing telecom operators and liberalizing their markets.

Later EU directives sought to address harmonization, introducing common practices for EU countries. In 1990, the Framework Directive forced established telecom operators to open their networks to third parties. The 1997 Licensing Directive, together with earlier directives, created a common framework for authorizing companies to offer telecommunication services. The outcome was to open the European fixed and mobile telecommunications market from 1998.

In December 1998, the EU also decided that the coordinated introduction of the Universal Mobile Telecommunications System (UMTS), should be completed no later than January 2002. UMTS was created to support innovative (third generation or 3G) wireless multimedia services, while also being compatible with the old 2G network and allowing international roaming. This pushed 3G to the forefront. The consensus among telecoms analysts was that UMTS would be one of the most important value drivers in the future. No aspiring market leader could afford to miss out on this.

UMTS licenses were mostly to be auctioned by national authorities. As the operators thought that the licenses were a guarantee for future revenues, competition among bidders was fierce, encouraged by the multi-round auction system adopted in most countries. By December 2001, most major European licenses had been allocated, saddling winning bidders with multi-billion euro debts that were not forecast to be paid off for many years.[1] On top

---

[1] The UK and German governments, for example, auctioned off their 3G licenses for €37.6 bn and €48.6 bn respectively.

of this, operators' capital expenditure requirements included infrastructure investments to support UMTS.

5.1 FROM SOVEREIGN STATUS TO NEAR SPECULATIVE GRADE (1995–2002)

5.1.1 How Sovereign Aaa Status of June 1995 Adjusts to Corporate Aa1 in July 1996

Toward Liberalization on Sovereign Aaa Status

Traditionally the State provider of mainly fixed-line and data transmission services, FT became an *exploitant public* in 1991, acquiring legal existence separate from the State, ownership of its assets, and financial autonomy, although the company was still under the Government's influence. It augured well that, on November 6, 1991, Moody's assigned French sovereign Aaa status to FT's senior unsecured first domestic €304.0 mn bond issue of October 7 and first international €457.3 mn issue of November 12, 1991.[2] When FT issued €0.9 bn more bonds in the winter of 1993, Moody's rated all of them Aaa.

But the company was still subject to multi-year State agreements tackling issues such as debt reduction, service targets and tariff rebalancing across its services.[3] This rebalancing was especially important. Liberalization was expected to dramatically alter the tariffs for services, bringing them in line with costs. Historically, FT had maintained relatively low subscription charges (relevant for private users) and relatively high tariffs for daytime long-distance calls (particularly relevant for business users). In 1993, FT began rebalancing its prices to avoid wide price fluctuations once the market was liberalized, raising subscription fees and lowering tariffs to better reflect production costs, and making it more difficult for rivals to enter the market.

The State renewed FT's management contract in April 1995, set against the 1998 deadline, and a few eyebrows were raised. Moody's, in particular, commenting about the renewal of this management contract on May 30, 'As a public operator, FT cannot go bankrupt ... but ... a status change would place clear pressure on FT's rating.'[4] On June 27, 1995, Moody's assigned FT a Long Term Issuer rating of Aaa.[5]

Renewing the Business Model with Michel Bon

To prepare the company for the 1998 liberalization deadline, financial autonomy, access to the bond markets, and tariff rebalancing were not enough. The number of rivals was

---

[2] Moody's Investors Service, 2005, France Telecom rating history, Ratings Interactive, March 14, page 2. Both bonds carried a 9% coupon, with maturities of 10 and 8 years, respectively.

[3] Public sector operator or *exploitant public*; multi-year agreements or *contrats de plan* – initially for the years 1991 through 1994.

[4] Moody's Investors Service, 1995, Moody's says renewal of management contract highlights threats to France Telecom, *Rating Action*, May 30, page 2.

[5] This action was taken as a standard procedure to assign the rating level according to this new 'Issuer Rating' product to all Moody's credit rating clients. Issuer Ratings provide credit ratings as the senior unsecured level. At that time FT senior unsecured rating was Aaa. Therefore, its LT Issuer rating was automatically Aaa, without a rating committee having to take a rating action.

to grow and regulatory reductions in call tariffs and interconnection rates were going to depress existing revenues for incumbents.[6] This induced FT to make significant investments across a wide range of new products and services to diversify their sources of revenue.

Following the appointment in September 1995 of Michel Bon as Chairman and CEO, FT adopted a new strategy based on three priorities: accelerate growth by focusing on new telecom market segments, gain a position as a European global operator, and provide global services to multinational firms. This would give FT significant presence in telephony (fixed and mobile), internet and cable, but required significant investments.

On the international front, FT first turned its sights to fixed line activities, entering a strategic alliance with Sprint and Deutsche Telekom (DT) in January 1996 to launch Global One. This was to offer international data and voice services to multinational companies, transit and hubbing services for other international carriers, and calling cards for international travelers. FT initially invested €337 mn in the project. To enhance its presence in the United States, FT also purchased 10% of Sprint's outstanding voting stock for a price of €1.4 bn, as did DT.

In the new segments, FT had to be in the Internet space. French consumers had already become accustomed to accessing information on-line through Minitel, therefore they would understand Internet services more quickly once these were offered.[7] In April 1996, FT launched its Internet business under the Wanadoo brand name. The company was playing catch up with operators CompuServe and AOL as well as with a handful of French networks. It hoped that Wanadoo's wide and cheap offering would help to establish itself as the profitable market leader.

Changing French Regulations and Downgrade to Aa1 in July 1996

Continuing preparation for competition, a draft bill was released in May comprehensively reforming the French regulatory regime for telecommunications and proposing to change FT's legal status to a regular corporation subject to common law.[8] In response, Moody's immediately placed FT's Aaa LT Issuer ratings under review for possible downgrade, affecting €4.6 bn in bonds. Moody's said 'that a change in FT's legal status from public operator would remove one of the key factors supporting the rating.'[9] The downgrade to Aa1 with stable outlook came on July 10, just before the legal transformation of FT on July 26.[10]

Despite FT's investments in Global One and Wanadoo, 96% of its 1996 revenues still came from France and 90% from fixed-line, voice, and data services.

---

[6] Interconnection fee: a per minute rate that operator A has to pay to B for each call originated on network A and terminated on network B. It is subject to the approval of the National Regulatory Authority (NRA).

[7] This facility, pioneered by FT, offered some 25 000 on-line services, from travel reservations to shopping, to around 14 million users.

[8] The French government introduced an independent regulatory authority, the *Autorité de Regulations des Telecommunications* ('ART'), to encourage competition in a neutral, continuous, and efficient way and to monitor the continued provision of universal service.

[9] Moody's Investors Service, 1996, Moody's reviews Aaa senior long term debt rating of France Telecom for possible downgrade, *Rating Action*, May 7, page 3.

[10] FT was to become *Société Anonyme* as from December 31, 1996 onwards.

5.1.2 A Company that went Public on Aa1 Status in October 1997 is Downgraded to Aa2 in December 1999

The October 1997 IPO and Tapping the Debt Capital Markets

To really succeed, FT badly needed long-term capital. An IPO was the obvious route to the international capital markets and would also provide shares to use as acquisition currency.

But labor unions resisted fiercely. To overcome this, FT made a deal with them in 1996 whereby current employees would keep their civil servant status and FT would make a one-off €5.7 bn payment to the State to fund its employees' pensions. A generous early retirement plan was initiated on September 1, valued at €3.7 bn on December 31, 1996. And the state would keep at least 51% of FT's share capital.

FT also secured its financial reputation and balanced its debt structure by regularly accessing the long-term debt market in 1997, issuing €1.4 bn in bonds, assigned Aa1 by Moody's, while preparing the IPO.[11]

The IPO went ahead and trading started on October 20, 1997 with the French State selling 246 mn or 25% of FT's shares to the public at €27.0 per share, valuing FT's equity at €26.0 bn.[12]

On October 24, the IPO Global Coordinator Banque Paribas and Associate Coordinators BNP and Merrill Lynch arranged a Euro Medium Term Notes (EMTN) program for FT with nine of the world's top dealers. FT could draw on this from time to time for the issuance of debt instruments, never to exceed €3.0 bn outstanding at any time. The facility was extremely flexible. A pricing sheet would set terms for each issue of senior unsecured notes within the program framework. Moody's assigned the programme an Aa1 long-term rating, reflecting 'FT's operating strengths, Moody's expectation that it will continue to generate substantial free cash flow, and its strong association with the French government despite the recent partial privatization.' However, this rating also reflected Moody's belief that FT's capital investments 'will be funded in a way that enables the company to continue to reduce its debt over time. If the company's financing requirements increase to levels beyond those currently expected, negative rating pressure could develop.'[13]

From 1998 through 2000, telecom companies became the toast of the stock market. As a result of significant investments, debt started to pile up in the industry, but ratings kept up until mid-2000 and there was little concern. ICT stocks kept increasing, MSCI Europe ICT index peaking first at 120.2 on February 2, 1999, and holding firm to peak at 225.2 on March 28, 2000. These companies were confident enough to refinance their balance sheets when needed through debt and equity issues and assets sales.

Big Bang, Deutsche Telekom Partnership and Tapping the Equity Markets

The big bang thus occurred on January 1, 1998, opening the EU telecom market to full competition.[14] For FT, international expansion was now more important than ever, as other

---

[11] A 10 year one at 5.75% for €915 mn on February 7 and a 13-year one at 5.70% for €457 mn on July 25.

[12] Total proceeds to the French State of €6.5 bn made this transaction France's largest IPO at that time, 75 mn shares being placed in France, 150 mn internationally and 21 mn to its employees.

[13] Moody's Investors Service, 1997, Moody's assigns Aa1 long-term rating to the EMTN program of France Telecom, *Rating Action*, October 24, pages 1 and 3.

[14] In January 1998, the European Parliament and the Council approved the Directive on the application of open network provision (ONP) to voice telephony and on universal service for telecommunications in a competitive environment.

incumbents were embarking on a frenzy of acquisition activity in search of diversified sources of revenue.

Between 1998 and 2000, the entire European telecom landscape changed dramatically. The incumbents' fixed-line operations were now exposed to serious competitive threats. To protect their profitability, they had to increase revenues generated by their mobile business units. These units already had a footprint in their domestic markets and antitrust authorities monitored closely the incumbent's domestic position. Therefore, to expand their operations and conquer new sources of revenues, the main players started to acquire smaller mobile operators internationally.

The most active buyers were Deutsche Telecom (DT), Vodafone (with the ambition of becoming a pan-European mobile operator), and FT in Europe. Telefonica and Telecom Italia preferred to expand mainly in Latin America, although they also acquired stakes in other European operators. Prices, already sustained by the general optimism in the technological industry, soared to unexpected levels thanks to this acquisition rush.

Institutionalizing further the strategic partnership they had established in January 1996, FT and DT initiated a 2% cross shareholding on July 20, 1998, costing FT €1.3 bn. On November 10, the two companies signed a cooperation framework agreement (CFA) to generate operational synergies in areas such as R&D, multimedia, information systems, and telephone cards. These included the building of a European Backbone Network (EBN) by Global One, and a secure high-speed network connecting Europe's major business centers. FT invested €201 mn in Global One's March capital increase.

To finance these long-term investments, FT tapped the long-term capital markets for €3.5 bn, taking advantage of the doubling in FT's stock price. The company raised €1.5 bn with a rights issue at €59.46 per share and issued a convertible bond for the first time, raising €2.0 bn for five years.[15,16] Moody's assigned it an Aa1 rating using essentially the same considerations as the previous year's rating assessment of the EMTN program.[17]

The markets had clearly endorsed FT's new business model. For three years now, under Michel Bon, FT had achieved a significant presence in 14 European countries, mainly through joint ventures with local partners based on fixed and mobile licenses. These started to pay off when international revenues reached €2.3 bn, registering a 39% increase and accounting for 10% of total revenues. The stock closed 1998 at €58.62 or 2.17 times the IPO price.

Going after the UK, Standing Alone, and Downgrade to Aa2 in December 1999

But at the start of 1999, FT was far from where it wanted to be. It had no significant position in the UK, Europe's second largest telecommunications market with about €40 bn revenues in 1998. And the recent strategic alliance with DT had to be terminated due to DT's bid (unsuccessful) for Telecom Italia, which was opposed by FT.

---

[15] FT issued 24.614 mn new shares, the French State sold 87.5 mn of its shares in a secondary placement.

[16] On November 10, 1998, FT issued 2.538 mn bonds convertible until its maturity on January 1, 2004 in 10 FT shares per bond and carrying a coupon of 2%. The bonds are senior unsecured and unsubordinated obligations of FT, ranking pari-passu with all other unsecured and unsubordinated obligations of FT.

[17] Moody's Investors Service, 1998, Moody's assigns Aa1 long term rating to the convertible bond of France Telecom, *Rating Action*, November 9.

FT had to continue alone along the road of rapid external growth. In the following three years, FT would transform itself almost beyond recognition through an aggressive acquisition program (Exhibit 5.1).

The acquisition program was set in motion when FT announced on July 15 that it was investing €1.4 bn in NTL: €1.2 bn for a 6.4% stake in its equity, and €0.2 bn for convertible bonds.[18] NTL was a highly successful UK start-up focusing on the green-field build-out of cable TV franchises. That infrastructure provided them with a platform to offer triple-play telephone, Internet and interactive services to home and business customers.

The agreement with NTL committed FT to invest more if NTL was successful in its bid to buy Cable & Wireless Communications (CWC), the consumer cable subsidiary of Cable & Wireless Plc. NTL indeed secured the deal and FT had to top its initial investment with €5.4 bn in cash and shares.[19] This was the start of FT's efforts to establish itself as a triple-play market leader, but also drew the attention of the rating agencies. Moody's placed FT's LT Issuer rating of Aa1 on review for possible downgrade, affecting €14.4 bn of debt.

The review would

> focus on the extent to which FT's investment could constrain its future financial flexibility, despite the fact that FT has publicly stated that it will finance the transaction mostly with cash proceeds from the likely divestiture of some of FT's non-core assets. The review will also assess the risks associated with FT extending its ambitions in Europe in order to enhance its European footprint.

Recognizing that the new entity's 'combined internet access, cable telephony and telephony offerings will represent an outstanding opportunity for FT in the UK telecommunications market,' Moody's nevertheless would also 'review the extent to which this sizeable equity investment exposes FT to NTL's business and financial risks as well as to possible additional investments, in the longer term, in order to complete the consolidation process of the UK cable sector.'[20]

The review concluded in December, cutting the rating to Aa2, reflecting 'Moody's perception of increasing business risk as a result of FT accelerating its international investment strategy and anticipated further possible international investments.'[21]

5.1.3 Rapid Extension of FT's Reach and Two Notches Downgrade to A1 in September 2000

FT set up a new organization for its international activities, making business development outside of France a core focus within each of FT's units. In 2000, FT accelerated its international external growth.

---

[18] NTL stands for *National Transcommunications Limited*, but was not known as such.

[19] FT announced on July 26 that it would increase its NTL stake to 25%. NTL's deal with CWC propelled the group from number three to the top spot in Britain's fast consolidating cable TV industry, servicing 2.8 million customers and giving network access to over half of the cable TV households.

[20] Moody's Investors Service, 1999, Moody's places on review for possible downgrade France Telecom's Aa1 debt ratings, *Rating Action*, July 27, pages 4 and 5.

[21] Moody's Investors Service, 1999, Moody's downgrades France Telecom's long term debt ratings to Aa2 from Aa1, *Rating Action*, December 3, page 1 and in page 6 it further explained: '*In spite of increased risks, FT has very strong operating cash flow, one of the best networks in Europe, a very strong competitive position in France, and well respected management.*'

Exhibit 5.1 France Telecom acquisitions history (1996–2002I)

Announcement Date	Target	Industry	Country	Total Investment	Breakdown of Transaction	Interest Obtained	Financing
1996							
January	Atlas-Global One	Telecommunications		€467 mn	Atlas: €337 mn; Atlas France; €131 mn		Atlas France, €131 mn, promissory notes in the amount of €184 mn and cash of €22 mn.
	Sprint	Wireless telephony and fixed long distance services	US	€1425 mn		Acquired Class A Common Stock; representing a 10% voting interest.	
1997							
January	CI-Telecom	National Operator	Ivory Coast	€160 mn		Acquired 51% of capital	
July	Sonatel	Telecommunications	Senegal	€99 mn		Acquiring 33.33% share in the capital	
December	Casema	Dutch cable operator		€406 mn		Acquired entire share capital	
	Sema Group Plc				Receivable of €18 mn was converted into ordinary shares	Held a direct 22.56% interest	
	SGS Thomson Microelectronics					Indirect holding of 16.9%	
	Optimus	Mobile License	Portugal	€55 mn		Due to 20% share in consortium with Portuguese companies	

(continued overleaf)

Exhibit 5.1 (*continued*)

Announcement Date	Target	Industry	Country	Total Investment	Breakdown of Transaction	Interest Obtained	Financing
1998							
July	Oda	Producer of telephone directories		€366 mn			
July	Main telephony operator in El Salvador		El Salvador	€245 mn			
	Sonatel	Telecommunications	Senegal			Acquired further 9% share	
	ECMS	Mobile telephony	Egypt			Acquired 23.5% share	
	ElTele Ost	Telecommunications	Norway			Acquired 33.9% share	
August	Nortel Inversora	Holding company retaining 58.3% of Telecom Argentina's capital	Argentina	€249 mn	Purchase of shares	17.5% (increasing existing participation of 32.5% to 50%)	
April and July	Crown Castle Int'l Corporation		US	€195 mn	Purchase of shares		
	Sprint	Wireless telephony and fixed long distance services	US	€155 mn	Purchase of shares: €112 mn in Sprint PCS wireless telephony and €43 mn in Sprint FON fixed line long distance services	10.0%	

Exhibit 5.1 (continued)

Announcement Date	Target	Industry	Country	Total Investment	Breakdown of Transaction	Interest Obtained	Financing
	Remu	Cable operator	Netherlands	€106 mn	Purchase of shares	100.0%	
	Catalana	Fixed line services	Catalan	€80 mn	Purchase of shares	75.0%	
	Wind	Mobile telephony	Italy	€146 mn	Purchase of shares		
	Intelig		Brazil	€130 mn	Purchase of shares		
	Mobil Rom		Romania	€84 mn	Purchase of shares	51% (increasing existing participation of 16.8% to 67.8%)	
	Alapage.com	e-merchant site	France	€49 mn	Purchase of shares		
2000							
May	Orange	Mobile telephony	UK	€21 693 mn	Purchase of shares	100.0%	FT's isssue of a security of €2.15 bn with maturity March 2001
	NTL	Telephony, Internet access provider, cable TV	UK	€5397 mn	Purchase of shares		
March	Atlas-Global One			€4055 mn	Purchase of shares	100.0%	
March	MobilCom	Mobile telephony	Germany	€3749 mn	Purchase of shares	28.5%	Put and call agreements exercisable under certain conditions

(continued overleaf)

Exhibit 5.1 (continued)

Announcement Date	Target	Industry	Country	Total Investment	Breakdown of Transaction	Interest Obtained	Financing
October	TPSA	Network operator	Poland	€3411 mn	Purchase of shares	25.0%	
November	Orange Communications SA	Wireless operator	Switzerland	€1280 mn	€241 mn was paid in 2000, remainder to be paid in cash and Orange SA shares in 2001	42.5% (increasing existing participation of 37.5% to 85%)	Shares of Orange SA with put and call agreements exercisable under certain conditions
	BITCO (via Orange Plc)		Thailand	€388 mn	Purchase of shares	34.0%	
	Mauritius Telecom		Mauritius	€309 mn	Purchase of shares	40.0%	
July	Wind (share repurchase from Deutsche Telekom)			€2076 mn	Purchase of shares: payment recorded in other short term debts in the balance sheet at December 31, 2000	18.9%	
July	Wind (participation in capital increase)			€109 mn	Purchase of shares		
September	TPSA	Network operator	Poland	€679 mn	Purchase of shares	33.9%	
	PTK Centertel (participation in capital increase)		Poland	€124 mn	Purchase of shares		

Exhibit 5.1 (*continued*)

Announcement Date	Target	Industry	Country	Total Investment	Breakdown of Transaction	Interest Obtained	Financing
November	Orange Communications SA (through Orange SA)	Wireless operator	Switzerland	€234 mn	€175 mn for purchase of shares – €59 mn remains payable for acquisitions made during 2000	14.75% (increasing existing participation of 85% to 99.75%)	
	ECMS/Mobinil (share repurchase from Motorola)			€205 mn	Purchase of shares	25.15% (increasing existing participation of 46.1% to 71.25%)	
	BITCO (through Orange SA)		Thailand	€158 mn	Purchase of shares	15% (increasing existing participation of 34% to 49%)	
	Digita (through TDF)		Finland	€125 mn	Purchase of shares	49.0%	
	Uni2			€102 mn	Purchase of shares	31% (increasing existing participation of 69% to 100%)	
December	Indice Multimedia			€283 mn	€85 mn, was paid in cash, representing 30% stake, with the balance paid by exchange of Wanadoo SA shares	86.7%	

2002I

Source: France Telecom, Forms 20-F and Annual Report.

Global One in January 2000

FT had begun discussions in the fall of 1999 with DT and Sprint regarding their joint ownership of Global One. On January 27, they announced that FT would buy their equity interests in Global One for €3.6 bn plus €437 mn in debt repayment. On the same day, Moody's confirmed FT's LT Issuer rating at Aa2, affecting €11.7 bn in debt, with stable outlook, using reflections as last time, yet specifying 'the possibility of future additional investments' and 'Moody's believes FT's ... balance sheet is further strengthened by the possible divestiture of non-core assets, which could amount to some €17 bn' and 'the acquisition is in line with Moody's expectation that FT would significantly accelerate its international investment strategy.'[22]

Mobilcom in March 2000

FT was indeed looking for an additional foray, this time into the German market, and Mobilcom seemed to be the ideal candidate. Active in mobile, land-line, and the Internet, Mobilcom operated an advanced backbone network for combined voice/data traffic, serving over six million customers.[23] It became an FT target. In March, this resulted in a CFA between FT, Mobilcom and Mr Gerhard Schmid. Conditional upon Mobilcom winning a UMTS license, FT would invest €3.7 bn in Mobilcom to fund its purchase and further support its UMTS business. The CFA also granted FT significant approval and monitoring rights.[24]

Moody's reconfirmed the same day FT's LT Issuer rating at Aa2 with stable outlook, offering largely the same explanation as in January. But now, Moody's refers to 'the additional international investment being made' and to its belief that 'FT is most likely to divest, in the short-term, non-core assets, worth some €17.0 bn.'[25]

Orange in May 2000 and the Review for Possible Downgrade

The UK mobile market was the second largest in Europe,[26] and Vodafone was market leader in revenue per user, owning Orange Plc (Orange), a leading mobile network with comprehensive coverage and a high call success rate. Management and the markets would see FT's acquisition of this world-class asset as a real coup. In one stroke, FT would own the leading brand with a strong reputation for innovation, excellence and customer service, and the potential for rapid mobile expansion throughout Europe and globally.[27]

---

[22] Moody's Investors Service, 2000, Moody's confirms France Telecom's long term debt ratings at Aa2, *Rating Action*, January 27, page 2.

[23] Formed in 1991 and listed on the Frankfurt Neuer Market since 1997, it had a very strong founding shareowner in the face of G. Schmid, its largest shareholder and lead of the Executive Board. It generated 1999 revenues of €1.2 bn and EBITDA of €118.0 mn.

[24] FT would underwrite a capital increase to give it 28.5% of the equity and a call option from 2003 onwards to increase its stake.

[25] Moody's Investors Service, 2000, Moody's confirms France Telecom's debt ratings, *Rating Action*, March 23, page 2.

[26] It had 27.2 mn subscribers at end of Q1 2000 (equivalent to 46% penetration of the population) and still growing 84% in 1999 and 3.2 mn net adds in Q1 2000 vs 1.9 mn in Q1 1999.

[27] Orange had 22% market share and enjoyed strong customer loyalty experiencing the lowest churn rate in the market at 14.6%. The combination of FT's mobile assets, including Itineris, with Orange would be number 2 in Europe, present in 16 European and Mediterranean countries.

The opportunity arose in April 2000, when the European Commission required Vodafone AirTouch Plc (Vodafone) to divest Orange if it wanted to acquire Mannesmann AG. Very quickly FT made a deal, announcing on May 30 that it was acquiring 100% of Orange from Vodafone for €40.3 bn plus the assumption of Orange's €2.8 bn net debt.

The transaction was structured in two phases. First, FT would pay Vodafone €40.3 bn, €22.2 bn in cash and €18.1 bn in FT shares, which FT would later repurchase at €140.2 per share.[28] Next, FT would execute an IPO of 'New Orange' in 2000-Q4 or early 2001. The expected proceeds of €14.0 bn would finance FT's shares repurchase from Vodafone to honor the liquidity guarantee.

Immediately, Moody's placed FT LT Issuer Rating on review for possible downgrade, affecting €15.0 bn. It considered 'the expected financing plan which consists of the sale of non-core assets, over the next two years, with a current market value of approximately €20.0 bn and a secondary placing in the second half of 2001 of €5.0–€7.0 bn of FT shares to be repurchased from Vodafone.'[29]

By this time, the markets had become very nervous and the stock price guarantee would create a lot of debt on FT's balance sheet if the markets were to collapse. While €140.2 represented the average trading price for the short-term period preceding the announcement, there was a lot of downward pressure in the market. The European ICT sector had turned first on February 28 and the downturn had accelerated from March 7 onwards, losing 28.4% by the time FT announced it was acquiring Orange. But on the announcement, FT stock ticked upwards 5.1% to €135.5 – after it had lost a lot of ground along with the market, from its historical high of €189.7 on March 2. To get the cash to pay Vodafone, on July 31 FT signed a new credit agreement, providing it with a €20 bn facility for 364 days and a €10 bn facility for three years. Moody's rated these loans Aa2 and placed them under review for possible downgrade along with the rest.[30] FT drew upon the facility immediately to help to complete the transaction on August 22, thus giving FT full control of Orange.

More Deals and Two Notches Downgrade to A1 in September 2000

To strengthen its position as a European operator, FT had set its sights on Poland's market leader, Telekomunikacja Polska SA (TPSA), which had about 10 million fixed lines installed and 95% market share. When it was due to be privatized, FT formed a partnership with Kulczyk Holding and won the bid. FT paid €3.2 bn.[31]

Along with these efforts to occupy the space, FT also took advantage of the high stock market to execute an IPO for Wanadoo SA on July 18, listing on Euronext at €19.0 per share and raising €1.8 bn new equity from the market for its subsidiary.[32] And in August, Mobilcom, five months after its CFA with FT, successfully bid for a 3G license costing €8.4 bn. FT paid €3.7 bn. To persuade banks to lend the new entrant the remaining €4.7 bn,

---

[28] 129.2 mn new FT shares issued at €140.2, subject to a share repurchase agreement for cash by FT.

[29] Moody's Investors Service, 2000, Moody's places on review for possible downgrade France Telecom's Aa2 debt ratings and continues the review for possible upgrade of Orange at Ba3, *Rating Action*, May 30, page 2.

[30] Moody's Investors Service, 2000, Moody's rates France Telecom's bank loan Aa2 and places it on review for possible downgrade, *Rating Action*, August 1.

[31] 35% of TPSA, plus a call option for an additional 10% plus a right of first refusal for an additional 6%, were sold for €4.5 bn. FT acquired 25% of the equity.

[32] This valued Wanadoo €19.0 bn pre-money – about 15 times revenue and would create a float of 8.6%.

FT committed to guarantee residual later financing needs and promised to bankroll Mobilcom until the launch of its 3G services.[33]

All of these occurred while Moody's was reviewing FT's LT Issuer rating for possible downgrade to A1. This action was taken in September, affecting €40.0 bn in debt, with Moody's explaining that:

> Although the combination of FT and Orange will create a strong pan-European wireless operator, this transaction, together with other recent significant international investments, increases the operating and financial risk for FT, given the size and considerable short-term debt financing requirement. The rating downgrades takes into consideration management's plan to dispose of non-core assets and to use the proceeds to reduce debt.[34]

Equant in November 2000

This downgrade did not stop FT from borrowing or from further strengthening its position in the one-stop shop service to multinational business. It thus drew upon its €27.5 bn EMTN program in November to issue €5.3 bn A1 rated notes to lengthen its debt maturity profile and diversify its source of financing.[35]

FT also decided to invest €8.1 bn for a 54.3% controlling stake in Equant and to merge it with Global One. This would boost FT's position as a global provider of broadband data communications.[36] The financial deal involved related transactions consisting of FT selling 100% of Global One to Equant in exchange for 80.6 million newly issued Equant shares; purchasing 67.9 million existing Equant shares at a ratio of 2.2 Equant shares for one FT share; and subscribing 10 million Equant preferred shares for €1.0 bn.[37] In addition, to protect Equant minority outside shareholders, FT issued them with 138.4 million Cumulative Value Rights (CVRs).[38]

At once, Moody's reaffirmed the FT long-term debt ratings at A1 and the short-term one at P-1, with stable outlook, considering FT's

> intention to equity finance the acquisition . . . and our assumption that FT will execute its asset disposal plan of about €30.0 bn over the short to medium term, which, together with its strong

---

[33] Loans from suppliers such as Nokia and Ericsson swelled Mobilcom's borrowings to over €6 bn, all implicitly backed by FT.

[34] Moody's Investors Service, 2000, Moody's downgrades France Telecom's debt ratings to A1 and upgrades Orange Plc to A1, *Rating Action*, September 18, pages 2 and 5.

[35] A 20-year £450 mn issue at 7.000%; a 10-year €1.4 bn one, at 6.625%; a 5-year €1.0 bn one at 6.125%; another 5-year £500 mn one at 7.000% and finally a 3-year €1.4 bn floating rate one at 3 months EURIBOR plus 375 bps per annum. FT, pricing supplements of November 8, 2000.

[36] This Amsterdam-based company operated the world's largest commercial data communications network in terms of geographic coverage providing voice, data, Internet, integration and application services to companies around the globe with cross-border data communications needs. It served 3700 large business customers in more than 220 territories and expected 2000 revenue of about €3 bn.

[37] FT and Equant closing prices on November 14, 2000 were €99.95, respectively €34.52.

[38] The CVRs had a three-year maturity and gave its holder the right to receive a cash payment equal to the difference between the average Equant share price over a specified period and €60.0, within a limit of €15.0 per share. This would cost FT €2.1 bn if Equant's share price were to be less that €45.0. Considering Equant's share price volatility of between 52% and 55% and the interest rate 5.33%, Michel Bon estimated that the theoretical value of one CVR was €9.2 on November 14. France Telecom, 2001. Note d'Operation, May 28, section 2.4.4, page 12.

and sustainable operating cash flow, will help to substantially reduce debt. This plan includes the IPO of Orange during the first quarter of 2001, which is targeted to raise cash proceeds of some €14.0 bn.[39]

FT's approach to external growth respected the autonomy of its targets. By investing in Global One, Mobilcom, Orange, TPSA, and Equant, FT extended its strategic reach with already successful businesses headed by strong-minded, reputable management. Analysts wondered how FT was going to integrate and finance them. To FT, it was more important to ensure leading market positions in high-growth areas across Europe and in global data services to multinational firms.

All in all, FT had spent over €100 bn on acquisitions in three years, €62.1 in 2000 alone: €4.0 bn for 100% of Global One, €43.1 bn for Orange, €3.7 bn for 28.5% of Mobilcom, €3.2 bn for 25% of TPSA, and €8.1 bn for control of Equant. The law of French State majority ownership imposed an equity financing constraint on FT that most competitors did not face. As a result, over €80 bn of payments were made in cash, financed by reducing free cash flow and borrowing.

FT thus increased its financial debt from €15.1 bn at the end of 1997 to €63.3 bn at the end of 2000, with an average maturity of two years.[40] It had undertaken to reduce this debt by €25 bn in 2001 and by up to €30 bn within two to three years, mainly through the sale of non-strategic assets.[41] The company's credit rating depended critically on the €30.0 bn valuation of these assets, but the stock market downturn was upsetting plans to refinance the balance sheet.[42]

5.1.4 A Wake-up Call: the Orange IPO and Surprise Two Notches Downgrade to A3 in February 2001

One such plan was the long-promised IPO for Orange. The landmark acquisition loaded FT with more than €20 bn in short-term debt. Refinancing the deal and honoring the share repurchase agreement with Vodafone became tough. The market had been waiting for the high-profile IPO, valued at €90.0 bn at the top of the market in 2000, which was to be executed in winter 2000/2001. But by then, investors were worrying about the high costs of 3G licenses in Europe and the bursting of the dot.com bubble in the US. In this context, the Orange IPO was a real test of FT's asset sales program.

As IPO deals were becoming few and far between, competition to land the Orange IPO mandate was extremely intense, and eventually won by Dresdner Kleinwort Wasserstein, Morgan Stanley Dean Witter, and SG Investment Banking. They assembled a large syndicate of underwriters and worked hard at tough preparations. When an IPO at around €65.5 bn was proposed for the fall, Orange turned out to be insufficiently ready and FT decided to postpone, perhaps also hoping for a better price later.

---

[39] Moody's Investors Service, 2000, Moody's affirms long term debt ratings of France Telecom at A1 and short term at P-1, *Rating Action*, November 20, page 4.

[40] France Telecom, 2002, Form 20-F for the fiscal year ended December 31, 2001, June 28, 1–321, page 168.

[41] Moody's Investors Service, 2001, France Telecom analysis, Global Credit Research, June, page 3 and Fay, S., Girard, L., 2001, France Telecom carries out record bond issue (France Telecom boucle une emission obligatoire record), *Le Monde*, March 9.

[42] From €113.71 down to €79.3, December 31, 1999 to 2000, with a €189.66 high on March 2, 2000.

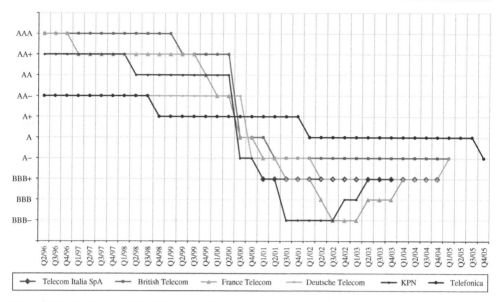

Figure 5.1 Evolution of S&P issuer credit ratings for telecom companies (1996–2005)
Source: Standard & Poor's, 2005, Issuer credit ratings history on Telecom Italia SpA, British Telecom, France Telecom, Deutsche Telecom, KPN, and Telefonica, November 30.

Yet pressure to go ahead kept mounting. After being the toast of the market, telecom companies became regarded as 'giants on glass legs,' laden with debt and suffering rating downgrades and the consequent cost of debt increases (see, for example, Exhibit 5.2, Figure 5.1, and Table 5.1).

Investors, who had been flocking to buy telecoms stocks, were suddenly critical of operators' rapid and expensive expansion into activities often outside their expertise and their apparent inability to contain ever-increasing debts. FT's share price had slid to €79.63 by the end of 2000, upsetting secondary offerings of FT shares. The Orange IPO had to happen before the IPO window was closed.

Thus the offer was launched on January 20, 2001, at an indicative price range of €11.5 to €13.5, or maximum value of €65.5 bn. By the end of the domestic offer and global placing on February 9, the IPO parties had to fix the share price at €9.5 to ensure full take up. This valued Orange at €46.1 bn, raising only €6.0 bn of the €14.0 bn expected. To partially make up for the shortfall, from February 5 through 7 the same lead managers plus CSFB had placed a two-year €3.1 bn note issue convertible in Orange shares.[43]

Immediately, the market doubted FT's ability to sell €30.0 bn in non-core assets for cash in the short term, and FT's market value dropped by €11.9 bn or 12.6%.[44] At once, the agencies downgraded FT's LT Issuer rating to A3, affecting about €60 bn of debt. The two-notch drop in the absence of prior review was rather unusual, reflecting 'Moody's expectation

---

[43] Settled on February 16 and due on February 16, 2003, it carried a 2.5% coupon plus a conversion American call option on 242.6 mn Orange shares, exercisable at €12.7. France Telecom, 2001, Note d'Operation, February 12, 1–170, pages 2 and 13, Paris.
[44] From January 20 through February 9.

Table 5.1 Evolution of S&P issuer credit ratings by quarter for telecom companies (1996–2005)

	British Telecom	Deutsche Telecom	France Telecom	KPN	Telecom Italia SpA	Telefonica
Q2/96	AAA		AAA	AA+		AA−
Q3/96	AAA		AAA	AA+		AA−
Q4/96	AAA		AAA	AA+		AA−
Q1/97	AAA		AA+	AA+		AA−
Q2/97	AAA		AA+	AA+		AA−
Q3/97	AAA	AA−	AA+	AA+		AA−
Q4/97	AAA	AA−	AA+	AA+		AA−
Q1/98	AAA	AA−	AA+	AA+		AA−
Q2/98	AAA	AA−	AA+	AA		AA−
Q3/98	AAA	AA−	AA+	AA		AA−
Q4/98	AAA	AA−	AA+	AA		A+
Q1/99	AAA	AA−	AA+	AA		A+
Q2/99	AA+	AA−	AA+	AA		A+
Q3/99	AA+	AA−	AA+	AA		A+
Q4/99	AA+	AA−	AA	AA		A+
Q1/00	AA+	AA−	AA−	AA		A+
Q2/00	AA+	AA−	AA−	AA		A+
Q3/00	A	AA−	A	A−		A+
Q4/00	A	A−	A	A−		A+
Q1/01	A	A−	A−	BBB+	BBB+	A+
Q2/01	A−	A−	A−	BBB+	BBB+	A+
Q3/01	A−	A−	BBB+	BBB−	BBB+	A+
Q4/01	A−	A−	BBB+	BBB−	BBB+	A+
Q1/02	A−	A−	BBB+	BBB−	BBB+	A
Q2/02	A−	BBB+	BBB	BBB−	BBB+	A
Q3/02	A−	BBB+	BBB−	BBB−	BBB+	A
Q4/02	A−	BBB+	BBB−	BBB	BBB+	A
Q1/03	A−	BBB+	BBB−	BBB	BBB+	A
Q2/03	A−	BBB+	BBB	BBB+	BBB+	A
Q3/03	A−	BBB+	BBB	BBB+	BBB+	A
Q4/03	A−	BBB+	BBB	BBB+	BBB+	A
Q1/04	A−	BBB+	BBB+	A−	BBB+	A
Q2/04	A−	BBB+	BBB+	A−	BBB+	A
Q3/04	A−	BBB+	BBB+	A−	BBB+	A
Q4/04	A−	BBB+	BBB+	A−	BBB+	A
Q1/05	A−	A−	A−	A−	BBB+	A
Q2/05	A−	A−	A−	A−	BBB+	A
Q3/05	A−	A−	A−	A−	BBB+	A
Q4/05	A−	A−	A−	A−	BBB+	A−

Source: Standard & Poor's, 2005, Issuer credit ratings history on Telecom Italia SpA, British Telecom, France Telecom, Deutsche Telecom, KPN, and Telefonica, November 3.

that FT's ability to reduce debt within a relatively short period, through expected asset disposals, is materially constrained by the lower non-core asset valuations ...' and that '... a significant deviation from the original [€25 bn] debt reduction plan, which was factored in the previous A1 rating, will occur.'[45]

---

[45] Moody's Investors Service, 2001, Moody's downgrades France Telecom's long-term debt ratings to A3, short-term to Prime-2 and Orange to A3, *Rating Action*, February 15, pages 2 and 3.

Exhibit 5.2 France Telecom peer group performance indicators (1996–2004)

	Y2004	Y2003	Y2002	Y2001	Y2000	Y1999	Y1998	Y1997	Y1996
France Telecom (EUR millions)[1]									
Total Assets	89 207	91 906	102 684	121 989	127 053	51 771	43 783	40 269	38 001
Total Liabilities	69 474	73 914	102 855	92 801	91 860	31 498	26 013	25 802	25 880
Book Value of Equity	19 733	17 992	−171	29 188	35 193	20 272	17 770	14 467	12 121
Market Value of Equity	60 099	54 436	17 227	44 861	91 878	116 509	60 063	28 820	
Book Value (Debt/Equity)	**3.5207**	**4.1082**	**−601.4912**	**3.1794**	**2.6102**	**1.5538**	**1.4638**	**1.7835**	**2.1351**
Book Value Debt/MV Equity	**1.1560**	**1.3578**	**5.9705**	**2.0686**	**0.9998**	**0.2704**	**0.4331**	**0.8953**	
British Telecom (USD millions)									
Total Assets	49 013	44 422	39 224	77 391	59 854	45 100	38 938	41 085	35 933
Total Liabilities	43 317	40 303	39 884	56 984	33 909	20 655	20 530	22 521	16 302
Book Value of Equity	5 696	4 118	−660	20 407	25 944	24 445	18 408	18 564	19 631
Market Value of Equity	33 242	29 125	27 222	31 931	56 016	158 666	97 359	49 953	43 558
Book Value (Debt/Equity)	**7.6054**	**9.7860**	**−60.3866**	**2.7925**	**1.3070**	**0.8449**	**1.1153**	**1.2132**	**0.8305**
Book Value Debt/MV Equity	**1.3031**	**1.3838**	**1.4652**	**1.7846**	**0.6053**	**0.1302**	**0.2109**	**0.4508**	**0.3743**
Cable and Wireless (GBP millions)									
Total Assets	4 907	7 336	16 185	23 826	21 514	17 470	13 039	9 667	9 020
Total Liabilities	2 946	4 842	6 885	7 342	10 403	9 490	7 402	4 356	4 301
Book Value of Equity	1 961	2 494	9 300	16 484	11 111	7 980	5 637	5 311	4 719
Market Value of Equity	2 821	3 186	1 066	9 154	25 265	25 529	17 780	12 152	10 865
Book Value (Debt/Equity)	**1.5023**	**1.9415**	**0.7403**	**0.4454**	**0.9363**	**1.1892**	**1.3131**	**0.8202**	**0.9114**
Book Value Debt/MV Equity	**1.0444**	**1.5200**	**6.4587**	**0.8020**	**0.4117**	**0.3717**	**0.4163**	**0.3585**	**0.3958**
Deutsche Telekom (EUR millions)									
Total Assets	107 809	116 072	125 814	164 280	123 466	93 534	77 943	81 876	89 130
Total Liabilities	69 875	82 268	90 405	97 986	80 757	57 859	52 880	57 261	65 305
Book Value of Equity	37 934	33 804	35 409	66 294	42 709	35 675	25 063	24 615	23 825
Market Value of Equity	69 851	61 035	51 296	81 436	97 250	213 842	76 875	47 486	44 029
Book Value (Debt/Equity)	**1.8420**	**2.4337**	**2.5532**	**1.4781**	**1.8909**	**1.6218**	**2.1099**	**2.3263**	**2.7411**
Book Value Debt/MV Equity	**1.0004**	**1.3479**	**1.7624**	**1.2032**	**0.8304**	**0.2706**	**0.6879**	**1.2059**	**1.4832**

Exhibit 5.2 (continued)

	Y2004	Y2003	Y2002	Y2001	Y2000	Y1999	Y1998	Y1997	Y1996
KPN (EUR millions)									
Total Assets	21 519	22 276	25 093	40 503	53 165	17 991	13 629	13 634	16 277
Total Liabilities	14 554	14 917	20 313	27 619	29 253	11 595	7 712	5 580	8 817
Book Value of Equity	6 965	7 359	4 780	12 884	23 912	6 395	5 918	8 055	7 459
Market Value of Equity	17 412	15 245	15 444	12 871	14 755	46 352	20 172	18 129	13 987
Book Value (Debt/Equity)	**2.0896**	**2.0270**	**4.2496**	**2.1437**	**1.2234**	**1.8132**	**1.3031**	**0.6927**	**1.1821**
Book Value Debt/MV Equity	**0.8359**	**0.9785**	**1.3153**	**2.1458**	**1.9825**	**0.2502**	**0.3823**	**0.3078**	**0.6304**
Portugal Telecom (EUR millions)									
Total Assets	12 471	12 974	12 849	17 136	13 216	8 518	9 277	4 990	4 355
Total Liabilities	9 144	9 336	9 219	11 151	7 594	5 493	7 082	2 970	2 313
Book Value of Equity	3 327	3 638	3 630	5 985	5 622	3 025	2 195	2 019	2 042
Market Value of Equity	11 414	10 009	8 216	10 975	9 952	11 380	7 419	8 093	4 189
Book Value (Debt/Equity)	**2.7486**	**2.5663**	**2.5400**	**1.8631**	**1.3507**	**1.8161**	**3.2261**	**1.4708**	**1.1329**
Book Value Debt/MV Equity	**0.8012**	**0.9328**	**1.1222**	**1.0160**	**0.7631**	**0.4827**	**0.9546**	**0.3670**	**0.5523**
Telefonica (EUR millions)									
Total Assets	54 209	52 912	57 735	82 034	89 118	61 780	47 711	36 852	32 248
Total Liabilities	34 782	31 663	35 500	49 059	54 063	36 298	30 286	22 087	18 351
Book Value of Equity	19 427	21 249	22 235	32 975	35 055	25 481	17 424	14 765	13 897
Market Value of Equity	68 689	57 687	41 461	70 219	76 396	80 918	39 645	24 562	17 024
Book Value (Debt/Equity)	**1.7904**	**1.4901**	**1.5966**	**1.4878**	**1.5422**	**1.4245**	**1.7382**	**1.4959**	**1.3205**
Book Value Debt/MV Equity	**0.5064**	**0.5489**	**0.8562**	**0.6987**	**0.7077**	**0.4486**	**0.7639**	**0.8992**	**1.0780**
Telecom Italia (EUR millions)									
Total Assets	74 386	76 936	80 952	93 130	94 276	74 768	7 739	4 643	5 278
Total Liabilities	54 754	56 477	60 396	66 821	62 878	47 985	5 799	3 650	4 354
Book Value of Equity	19 632	20 459	20 556	26 309	31 398	26 783	1 940	993	924
Market Value of Equity	31 049	24 210	8 598	10 494	12 505	13 574	8 377	1 248	976
Book Value (Debt/Equity)	**2.7890**	**2.7605**	**2.9381**	**2.5399**	**2.0026**	**1.7916**	**2.9886**	**3.6742**	**4.7116**
Book Value Debt/MV Equity	**1.7635**	**2.3328**	**7.0248**	**6.3678**	**5.0283**	**3.5351**	**0.6923**	**2.9253**	**4.4626**

(continued overleaf)

Exhibit 5.2 (continued)

	Y2004	Y2003	Y2002	Y2001	Y2000	Y1999	Y1998	Y1997	Y1996
Belgacom (EUR millions)									
Total Assets	4892	5362	6666	6301	5944	5778	5986	5988	5593
Total Liabilities	2262	2368	3501	3303	3197	3301	3762	4008	3814
Book Value of Equity	2630	2994	3165	2998	2748	2477	2224	1980	1779
Market Value of Equity	11504	0	0	0	0	0	0	0	0
Book Value (Debt/Equity)	**0.8601**	**0.7909**	**1.1062**	**1.1015**	**1.1634**	**1.3328**	**1.6917**	**2.0237**	**2.1435**
Book Value Debt/MV Equity	**0.1966**								
Swisscom (CHF millions)									
Total Assets	14349	16290	16548	23538	22064	20860	16844	15473	16010
Total Liabilities	7005	7870	8453	10686	13411	14144	11454	14243	16094
Book Value of Equity	7344	8420	8095	12852	8653	6716	5390	1230	−84
Market Value of Equity	29659	27011	26514	33833	31001	47366	42291	0	0
Book Value (Debt/Equity)	**0.9538**	**0.9347**	**1.0442**	**0.8315**	**1.5499**	**2.1060**	**2.1250**	**11.5797**	**−191.5952**
Book Value Debt/MV Equity	**0.2362**	**0.2914**	**0.3188**	**0.3158**	**0.4326**	**0.2986**	**0.2708**		
Hellenic (EUR millions)									
Total Assets	10218	10299	8855	8329	7682	6248	6033	5030	3984
Total Liabilities	5775	5716	5027	4546	4049	2808	2869	1974	1764
Book Value of Equity	4443	4583	3828	3784	3632	3440	3164	3056	2221
Market Value of Equity	6494	5282	5293	9224	8040	11896	11419	8029	5409
Book Value (Debt/Equity)	**1.2998**	**1.2472**	**1.3132**	**1.2014**	**1.1148**	**0.8165**	**0.9067**	**0.6457**	**0.7942**
Book Value Debt/MV Equity	**0.8892**	**1.0820**	**0.9499**	**0.4928**	**0.5037**	**0.2361**	**0.2512**	**0.2458**	**0.3261**

Exhibit 5.2 (continued)

	Y2004	Y2003	Y2002	Y2001	Y2000	Y1999	Y1998	Y1997	Y1996
Telenor (NOK millions)									
Total Assets	85 095	82 260	84 592	82 023	93 243	47 823	40 750	NA	NA
Total Liabilities	43 427	41 377	47 304	36 340	55 063	26 558	21 996	NA	NA
Book Value of Equity	41 668	40 883	37 288	45 683	38 180	21 265	18 754	NA	NA
Market Value of Equity	96 233	78 475	47 772	69 585	69 203	0	0	NA	NA
Book Value (Debt/Equity)	**1.0422**	**1.0121**	**1.2686**	**0.7955**	**1.4422**	**1.2489**	**1.1729**	NA	NA
Book Value Debt/MV Equity	**0.4513**	**0.5273**	**0.9902**	**0.5222**	**0.7957**	NA	NA	NA	NA
Teliasonera (SEK millions)									
Total Assets	180 880	175 100	190 725	126 701	119 323	74 453	65 704	64 537	NA
Total Liabilities	51 767	59 266	76 776	66 612	63 015	41 350	36 150	38 744	NA
Book Value of Equity	129 113	115 834	113 949	60 089	56 308	33 103	29 554	25 793	NA
Market Value of Equity	186 074	175 789	153 347	140 156	145 558	0	0	0	NA
Book Value (Debt/Equity)	**0.4009**	**0.5116**	**0.6738**	**1.1086**	**1.1191**	**1.2491**	**1.2232**	**1.5021**	NA
Book Value Debt/MV Equity	**0.2782**	**0.3371**	**0.5007**	**0.4753**	**0.4329**	NA	NA	NA	NA
Annual Average (Debt/MV Equity)	**0.7755**	**1.0061**	**1.0387**	**0.9598**	**0.7845**	**0.5745**	**0.7265**	**1.0286**	**0.8729**
Pooled rolling average	0.8630	0.8740	0.8551	0.8245	0.7974	0.8006	0.8760	0.9508	0.8729
Annual Average (BV Debt/BV Equity)	1.5744	1.6105	1.5774	1.4824	1.3869	1.4379	1.7428	1.2709	1.3820
Pooled rolling average	**1.4961**	**1.4863**	**1.4686**	**1.4505**	**1.4441**	**1.4584**	**1.4652**	**1.3264**	**1.3820**

Note: The difference between France Telecom's financial data in this exhibit and that of Table 5.3 is due to standardization adjustments by Worldscope.
Source: Thomson Worldscope for Financial data
Thomson Datastream for Market Value data

Operators such as BT, DT, FT, and KPN, forced to consider asset sales to reduce their combined debt of €185 bn, became worried.[46] Assets bought at the top of the market looked grossly overvalued now. The general downturn that began in mid-2000 continued, hitting them especially hard. At a time of pressing needs to reduce debt, they were suddenly denied access to equity, their most critical source of capital.

Spring 2001: Steps toward Debt Consolidation and Liquidity Enhancement. Financing with One-Step-at-a-Time Credit Protection

Under pressure to reduce its short debt as much as possible, FT accessed the international bond markets in March. Initially, between €7.0 bn and €8.0 bn were to be issued. In the end, FT sold a mammoth €17.6 bn package.[47] It extended the average maturity of FT consolidated debt from 2 to 4 years and 10 months and increased its average interest rate from 5.86% at 31 December 2000 to approximately 6.22%.[48] FT was able to do a record issue because of the attractive income it was promising investors and the protection it offered them in case its credit ratings fell. It granted investors an additional 0.25% in interest payments for each notch below the A category that either Moody's or S&P lowered its rating. It was one of the best compensations available, matching step-ups offered by BT, DT, KPN, and Olivetti, but it was not a good sign for FT. Step-ups tend to emerge in times of distress, as with Chrysler in the 1980s. Investors impose them when a company needs to de-lever and is coming to the market at an inopportune time. And they risk sending the wrong message to investors – that they are bound to fall to junk bond status.

At the March 23 press conference announcing 2000 results, Chairman Bon reiterated the company's plans to reduce debt by as much as €30 bn over the next two to three years, €20 bn with cash from selling assets.[49] One such asset was FT's 10% stake in Sprint, sold in May for €1.9 bn, realizing a pre-tax capital gain of €0.6 bn.[50]

Settling the Stock Overhang with Vodafone and Authority for More Repurchases

FT promptly used €6.6 bn of the proceeds of the bond issue to honor its liquidity agreement with Vodafone, repurchasing 64.1 million of its shares, still leaving 49.75 million of its share – or €4.97 bn – to be repurchased later.

Telecom operators had also turned to some of their value-resistant assets for liquidity, the receipts of future telephone bills. Telecom Italia had innovated with such a type of asset-backed security (ABS) to the tune of €1.0 bn, rated Aaa, in February. FT then announced that it was going to launch a similar securitization program in 2001.[51] In June, FT thus sold

---

[46] Duyn, A.V., 2001. *Financial Times*, Telecoms operators look set for long stay in debt markets: Equity markets cooling sentiment means companies must turn to debt financing to fund 3G networks, *Financial Times*, March 16.

[47] Issued on March 7 with four tranches in US Dollars (at 4.16% for 2 years, $2.0 bn at 7.20% for 5 years, $3.5 bn at 7.75% for 10 years and $2.5 bn at 8.50% for 30 years), two in € (at 7.25% for 3 years and 7.00% for 7 years) and one in Sterling (£600 mn at 7.50% for 10 years). The protective covenants are called coupon step-ups and bump up coupon payments in the event that the companies' credit rating drops beneath a certain threshold.

[48] Moody's Investors Service, 2001, France Telecom analysis, *Global Credit Research*, June, page 10.

[49] Such as a 11% stake in STMicroelectronics, valued at €4 bn and a stake in Sprint FON Group, valued €2 bn, *Wall Street Journal*, 2001, France Telecom expects revenue to grow at double-digit pace, March 23.

[50] It sold 75.9 mn shares at $19.

[51] Giddy, I., 2001, France Telecom confirms ABS, Article compiled by Giddy, I. of New York University, February 27.

trade receivables for fixed-line telephony contracts with consumers and certain businesses in France, netting €914 mn. This sale was made without recourse, as part of a securitization program with a Security Fund.[52] More cash was raised where it could be found, with €690 mn worth of future receivables from the French State being sold to a bank.[53]

Moody's Credit Analysis June 2001

In June, Moody's published an extensive credit analysis of FT (Exhibit 5.3), explaining at length that the A3 rating

> expects FT to continue executing its asset disposal plan of about €20 bn over the next three years, gradually bringing debt down. Continued strong growth in the underlying business will mean strong and stable cash flows with which to fund capital expenditure needs.

The stable outlook 'factors the execution of management's plan to dispose of non-core assets and to use the proceeds to reduce debt,' including later selling back to the market part of the FT shares to be repurchased from Vodafone.[54]

While highlighting several company strengths/opportunities, favorable company fundamentals and management strategy, Moody's also discussed the tough competitive environment and listed the following among risks/weaknesses:

- Step-up of international expansion has increased both the financial and business risk profiles, with greater operating cash flow volatility.
- FT continues to face a big challenge in its efforts to improve the deteriorated debt protection ratios over the next few years. Management has committed to achieve a net debt/EBITDA ratio of 2.5 by 2003.
- The risk of structural subordination as listed subsidiaries could raise debt on their own.[55]

Moody's expected FT's operating cash flow to strengthen on revenue growth, productivity increases and reduction in marketing and customer acquisition costs, and the real drain on cash flow, interest expense, 'to have peaked in 2000 and to gradually be reduced over time.'[56]

5.1.5 The Slide Downward to Baa1 in September 2001

Outlook Change to Negative in August 2001

But soon afterwards, the conditions that had supported the A3 rating deteriorated. Speculation mounted that FT, to refinance €5 bn of notes maturing in October, was to return to

---

[52] FT remains in charge of servicing the transferred receivables on behalf the Security Fund, *Fonds commun de créances (FCC)*. FT subscribed for €851 mn in beneficial interests in the FCC, subordinated for risk of non-recovery of the total €1765 mn receivables sold. France Telecom, 2002, Form 20-F for the fiscal year ended December 31, 2001, June 28, 1–321, page F-30.

[53] FT guaranteed to the assignee institution the existence and amount of the receivables sold and is committed to indemnify it to this regard. France Telecom, 2002, Form 20-F for the fiscal year ended December 31, 2001, June 28, 1–321, pages F-44 and F-58.

[54] Moody's Investors Service, 2001, France Telecom analysis, *Global Credit Research*, June, pages 1 and 7.

[55] Moody's Investors Service, 2001, France Telecom analysis, *Global Credit Research*, June, page 3.

[56] Moody's Investors Service, 2001, France Telecom analysis, *Global Credit Research*, June, page 10.

Exhibit 5.3   France Telecom: Moody's operating and balance sheet ratios (1997–2000)

Operating statistics	2000[a]	1999	1998	1997	5-year Avg[b]
Int. Cov. (%)	3.7	7.9	4.0	4.1	4.9
RCF/TD (%)	8.9	36.7	38.7	39.3	36.2
Op. Margin (%)	11.8	16.9	17.3	16.8	16.6
ROS (%)	10.9	10.2	8.2	9.5	8.0
ROC (pretax) (%)	10.6	14.7	16.0	15.8	12.7
Balance sheet statistics	2000	1999	1998	1997	5-year Avg[c]
TD (% Cap)	64.3	46.0	46.0	52.5	51.3
DIT & Min. Int (%)	2.1	3.6	2.4	0.6	1.9
Com. Equity (%)	33.7	50.4	51.6	46.9	46.8
Total Cap (€ bn)	98.4	37.5	32.9	30.5	22.7

[a]For the 12 months ended December 31.
[b]Five-year average 2000–1996.
[c]Five-year compound annual growth rate.

Int. Cov. (%): Interest Coverage: (Operating income + Other income – Other expense + Foreign currency translation) ÷ Interest expense.
RCF/TD (%): Retained Cash Flow/Total Debt: ((Gross cash flow – Cash dividends) ÷ Total debt) × 100.
Op. Margin (%): Operating Margin: (Operating income ÷ Net sales) × 100.
ROS (%): Return on Sales: (Net income ÷ Net sales) × 100.
ROC (pretax) (%): EBIT to Average Capitalization: ((Pretax income + Reported interest expense) ÷ Average capitalization) × 100.
TD (% Cap.): Total Debt to Capitalization: (Total debt ÷ Total capitalization) × 100.
DIT. & Min. Int. (%): Deferred taxes & Minority Interest to Capitalization: ((Deferred taxes + Minority interest) ÷ Total capitalization) × 100.
Com. Equity (%): Common Equity to Capitalization: (Reported common & surplus – (Preferred stock at liquidation value – Reported value) ÷ Total capitalization) × 100.
Total Cap. (€bn): Total Capitalization: Total debt + Minority interest + Deferred taxes + Investment tax credit + Preferred stock at liquidation value + Common and surplus – Cumulative translation adjustment.

Source: De Bodard, E., Fisher, A., Konefal, R., and Winzer, C., 2001, France Telecom, *Analysis:* Moody's Investors Service, June, Report 68 080, 1–16.

the corporate bond market with a short-dated issue of €5 bn.[57] On August 7, the Polish treasury confirmed that the FT & Kulczyk consortium had offered to increase its stake in TPSA, from 35% to 49%, costing about €1 bn.[58] And the overall equity market refused to recover. Global negativity toward telecommunications stock prevailed, with the ICT sector resuming its slide when it closed the week, down by 10% on Friday August 10, with FT down by 14.3%.[59]

Moody's noticed and changed its outlook to negative on August 13, 2001. It now expected 'that ... FT's ability to reduce debt within a relatively short period is exposed to significant execution risk and is materially constrained by the currently low non-core asset

---

[57] *Wall Street Journal Europe*, 2001, France Telecom may be near big push in Eurobond market, August 2.
[58] *Wall Street Journal*, 2001, France Telecom group may raise stake in Telekomunikacja Polska, August 22.
[59] The MSCI ICT Europe Index closed at 141.63, FT at €38.99.

valuations ...' and '... that the full de-leveraging that would comfortably position FT in the A3 rating level will take longer than originally expected.'[60]

Review for Possible Downgrade in Early September 2001

When FT presented its half-year results to financial analysts, it backed off earlier targets for debt reduction, announcing now a reduction in net debt of only €18 bn to €28 bn, excluding TPSA, and projecting net debt at €37 bn to €47 bn at the end of 2003, above the €30 bn to €40 bn it had previously forecast. This relied, among other things, on the sale of approximately 100 million FT treasury stock at the price of €70 to €100 and the conversion of FT's convertible bond and Orange exchange notes for €5 bn.[61]

Michel Bon declared the following day that 'our debt is a burden, not a risk' and that FT's mounting debt load would not affect its wireless and Internet expansion strategies.[62] But FT's shares tumbled 15.7% from €29.57 on September 4 to €24.94 on September 6, amid investor fears about the company's heavy borrowing. This revised debt reduction plan triggered Moody's to immediately review the FT Issuer rating for possible downgrade:

> in light of the current severe constraints FT faces to reduce its debt due to the negative sentiment in the equity capital markets.... In addition, Moody's will also review the extent to which FT's expected strong underlying business performance, in both fixed line and wireless, together with its strong operating cash flow will mitigate the high debt levels.[63]

Downgrade to Baa1 end September 2001

Non-core asset valuations continued to decline. On the dramatic September 11, FT's stock price and market value reached a new low of €24.34, valuing the company at €28.1 bn.[64] This forced management to shelve plans to sell the company's Treasury Stock, indefinitely. FT now, in the horrible fall of 2001, became stuck.

The rating agencies took notice on September 26. Moody's downgraded FT's and Orange's long-term debt ratings to Baa1, with stable outlook, affecting €60 bn. The main new reason was that FT's 'debt protection ratios, in the context of its increasing business risk, will be commensurate with a Baa1 long-term rating within the next two to three years.'[65] The spread on FT's uncovenanted bonds widened 10 bps early that day after S&P's rating downgrade, and another 10 bps on the news from Moody's. FT's November 2005 and 2010 bonds, which did not contain coupon step-ups, were now trading at 215 bps and 240 bps over comparable German government bonds.[66] Step-up clauses on some other bonds were expected to increase FT's interest charges, amounting to approximately €80 mn in 2002.

---

[60] Moody's Investors Service, 2001, Moody's changes to negative the ratings outlook of France Telecom and Orange Plc, *Rating Action*, August 13, pages 2 and 4.

[61] France Telecom, 2001, Financial analyst presentation – half-year results 2001, September 6, page 38.

[62] *Wall Street Journal*, 2001, France Telecom says its debt won't derail some expansion, September 7.

[63] Moody's Investors Service, 2001, Moody's places the long term debt ratings of France Telecom SA (A3) and Orange Plc (A3) on review for possible downgrade. Short term ratings is affirmed, *Rating action*, September 6, pages 2 and 3.

[64] After having peaked at €194.3 bn on March 2 and having increased it by €18.1 on August 25, 2000.

[65] Moody's Investors Service, 2001, Moody's downgrades France Telecom and Orange's long-term debt ratings to Baa1. Rating outlook is stable, *Rating Action*, September 26, page 3.

[66] *Wall Street Journal*, 2001, France Telecom bonds pressured by downgrade, September 26.

5.1.6 Looming Crisis and Two Notches Downgrade to Baa3 in June 2002

Change in Outlook to Negative in February 2002

Operating results for 2001 were strong, however. By the time the ratings were down, FT was drawing more than 60% of its revenues from new activities.[67] In just two years, Orange had overtaken competitors to become the number one mobile service provider in the UK, with a 28.2% market share, while FT's domestic long-distance traffic market share looked as if it was stabilizing around 64%. The company seemed to have achieved what it had set out to do: 'with Orange, Wanadoo, and Equant, we enjoy top-tier European status in the fastest growing segments.'

But planned capital expenditures remained impressive. FT had paid already over €11.6 bn to acquire UMTS licenses in some markets. As 2002 started, it estimated that additional UMTS licenses, investments in networks and new technology, and expenses necessary for the success of these technologies would be between €10.7 bn and €12.7 bn in 2002 and 2003.[68]

How was FT to finance them? Bank regulators had issued warnings to banks relating to telecom industry-specific risks in their lending portfolios. They had cited the large expenditures on the acquisition of UMTS licenses and related investments. As a result, banks could become unwilling to lend money to FT at acceptable rates. Furthermore, spreads on telecom debt securities had risen considerably. If FT were unable to borrow at affordable rates, it would be unable to pursue its plans.

FT also relied on the cooperation of some of its strategic partners to achieve its aims. And Mr Schmid proved difficult when it came down to respecting FT's right to approve Mobilcom's UMTS business plans. As a result, third parties could end up exercising financial claims against FT over which FT had no control. It was impossible to keep a lid on these difficulties in Germany, and in February, Moody's changed FT's ratings outlook from stable to negative, due, significantly, to 'the increasing uncertainty in respect of FT's exposure to the German market.'[69]

Review for Possible Downgrade in March 2002

When FT negotiated a €15 bn syndicated multi-currency credit line later that February to replace the one negotiated within the framework of the acquisition of Orange Plc, it was no surprise that it had to sign tough covenants, committing it to respect several coverage ratios (Exhibit 5.4).[70]

Disclosing 2001 results in a March press release, FT posted 'its best-ever operating income, but net income is negative after non-recurring provisions.'[71] Annual financial results

---

[67] The company was by now organized along four business lines: fixed line in France ('France Telecom' with 46.1% of revenues, 64.1% of EBITDA), wireless (Orange with 34.3% of revenues, 26.7% of EBITDA), fixed-line outside France (Global One with 16% of revenues, 9.5% of EBITDA) and internet (Wanadoo with 3.4% of revenues, −0.5% of EBITDA). It showed solid growth in mobile telephone traffic, accelerating take-up of Internet services with more than 8.2 mn French households connected to the Internet compared to 5.0 mn at the end of 2000 and an expanding customer base of 91 mn, up 19% from 77 mn in 2000.

[68] France Telecom, 2002, Form 20-F for the fiscal year ended December 31, 2001, June 28, 1–321, page 11.

[69] Moody's Investors Service, 2002, Moody's changes to negative the ratings outlook of France Telecom and Orange Plc, *Rating Action*, February 1.

[70] France Telecom, 2002, Form 20-F for the fiscal year ended December 31, 2001, June 28, 1–321, page F-48.

[71] France Telecom, 2002, France Telecom posts its best-ever operating income in 2001 but net income is negative after non-recurring provisions, *Press Release*, March 21.

Exhibit 5.4 Coverage ratios in covenants of February 2002 syndicated credit line

	12/31/02	6/30/03	12/31/03	6/30/04	12/31/04
EBITDA: Total Interest Costs	3	3	3.25	3.25	3.25
Total Net Debt: EBITDA	5	4.75	4.50	4.25	3.75

The ratio calculations are to be based on the consolidated financial statements prepared under French GAAP and EBITDA is calculated over the period of 12 months, by using the data corrected for acquisition and disposals that take place within the 12 preceding months.

Total Interest Costs are Net Interest Expense.
Total Net Debt is defined as Financial Debt.
EBITDA is defined as Operating Income before depreciation and amortization expense.

Sources: France Telecom, 2003, Form 20-F for the fiscal year ended December 31, 2002, March 21, 1–450; France Telecom, 2004, Form 20-F for the fiscal year ended December 31, 2003, April 16, 1–468; France Telecom, 2005, Form 20-F for the fiscal year ended December 31, 2004, May 17, 1–508.

indeed failed to reflect the operational prowess of the business. Net income was hit by valuation allowances relating to NTL, Equant, Telecom Argentina, and Mobilcom, totalling €9.4 bn. Adding to that total goodwill amortization of €5.8 bn and hefty net interest expenses of €3.8 bn resulted in the company posting a record net loss of €8.3 bn for 2001.[72] The balance sheet, burdened with €76.2 bn financial debt, could no longer support financial ratios of creditworthiness commensurate with the company's Baa1 rating. The figures revealed that FT was unable to finance investments and to service debt through cash flows from operations and had to rely instead on borrowing.

To redress the situation, FT announced another plan to reduce debt through sustained growth in EBITDA and continued asset disposals. The argument was that as the various businesses would reach maturity, they would bring about a marked decline in capital expenditures (CAPEX/revenues) and a sharp rise in EBITDA (EBITDA/revenues), releasing free cash flow estimated through 2002–2005 at €14 bn for debt reduction. Concurrently, the company had identified various non-core assets for disposal (Table 5.2), expected to produce €17 bn at current valuations.[73] Together these would generate €32 bn through 2005, enough to reduce debt by €15 bn and to cover the maximum off-balance-sheet risks, €17 bn, including €6.5 bn pertaining to Mobilcom.

The release further stated:

In a pessimistic scenario, the net debt/EBITDA ratio would be between 3.3 and 3.5 at the end of 2003 and between 2.2 and 2.6 at the end of 2005, against 4.9 at year-end 2001. In a more optimistic scenario, should the market pick up, the ratio would be between 1.5 and 1.7 around 2005.

However alarming the financial results, Michel Bon fiercely defended his approach: '... *These acquisitions were necessary. With the opening of competition in the French market, where FT generated three-quarters of its sales as a monopoly, we had to swiftly become*

---

[72] In comparison, Alcatel reported on its consolidated income statement a Net Loss for 2001 of €5.0 bn and for 2002 of €4.7 bn (see Alcatel, 2003, Consolidated income statement, Annual Report 2002, 1–176, page 37).
[73] France Telecom, 2002, France Telecom posts its best-ever operating income in 2001 but net income is negative after non-recurring provisions, *Press Release*, March 21, pages 2 and 3.

Table 5.2 France Telecom non-core assets for disposal and maximum off-balance-sheet risk (2002–2005), March 21, 2002 financial redress plan

Value of non-core listed assets (€ bn)		2002–2003	2004–2005	Total
STM stock (2.9%)	*€38*	1.0	0.0	1.0
STM Ens (soft mandatory)	*€38*	0.0	1.1	1.1
FT treasury stock	*€32*	1.6	0.0	1.6
FT Ens (soft mandatory)	*€32*	0.0	1.6	1.6
Sprint PCS stock (5.6%)	*US$11*	0.7	0.0	0.7
Total listed assets		**3.3**	**2.7**	**6.0**
Value of non-core unlisted assets (€ bn)				
Divestitures already planned: Casema, Noos, Numericable and others				3.0
New divestitures decided: Wind, TDF, satellite consortiums				8.0
Total unlisted assets				**11.0**
TOTAL LISTED AND UNLISTED ASSETS				**17.0**

Maximum additional debt from off-balance sheet commitments	2002–2003	2004–2005	Total
Vodafone put option	5.0	0.0	5.0
Eon put option (net value)	0.2	0.0	0.2
DT call option (net value)	0.0	0.0	0.0
CableCom (NTL) preferred	1.3	0.0	1.3
Kulzcyk (TPSA) put option	0.0	2.0	2.0
Equant CVRs	0.0	2.1	2.1
Total off-balance sheet commitments	**6.5**	**4.1**	**10.6**
Mobilcom risk	6.5		6.5
MAXIMUM OFF-BALANCE SHEET RISK	**13.0**	**4.1**	**17.1**

Sources: France Telecom, 2003, Annual Report 2002, March 21, 1–69; France Telecom, 2004, Annual Report 2003; France Telecom, 2005, Annual Report 2004, 1–284; France Telecom, 2006, Annual Report 2005.

bigger and more international in the most dynamic segments of our business, namely wireless and Internet' [74]

From a debt market perspective, Moody's placed FT's Issuer Rating once again under review for a possible one notch downgrade, with 'focus on the level of support of the Mobilcom debt, which FT may ultimately become responsible for.' [75]

Scrambling for Cash and Two Notches Downgrade to Baa3 in June 2002

It soon turned out that the pessimistic scenario was the realistic one. Progress in finalizing asset sales was slow. And after a week's respite following the March news, FT's stock resumed its descent, losing 21.3% or €7.6 bn in market capitalization during the month

---

[74] France Telecom, 2002, Annual Report 2001, March 20, 1–147.

[75] Moody's Investors Service, 2002. Moody's places France Telecom and Orange's long-term debt ratings on review for downgrade, *Rating Action*, March 27, page 2.

following Moody's decision, and another 18.0% during the first week into May – upon disappointing fixed telephone Q1 revenues for FT and the breaking Worldcom scandal in the US – to close at €19.81, 18.6% below the floor of the IPO price. It became extremely unlikely that FT could sell its treasury stock at €70 to yield €2 bn in the foreseeable future.

In addition, the likelihood that FT's convertible bond exchangeable in Orange shares at €12.7 would not have to be reimbursed in February 2003 became slim, as the Orange price was slipping to less than 50% of that price.

A possible liquidity crisis at FT, rather than debt reduction, started to emerge. In this climate, Moody's announced that it would expand the scope of its review. It also included the Prime-2 short-term rating on review for possible downgrade, revised its 'guidance, indicating that a downgrade of up to two notches is now possible for the long-term ratings,' and expecting 'the ratings to remain investment grade.'[76] As this expanded review went on, the problems with Mobilcom increased and FT scrambled for cash.

At the close of 2001, FT had re-examined the outlook for the mobile phone market in Germany which now had six players, two of which controlled 80% of the market. FT concluded that it would be very difficult for the four other players – including Mobilcom – to achieve a reasonable level of profitability, making consolidation inevitable within two years. FT thus thought it prudent to depreciate or amortize its full €3.9 bn direct exposure to Mobilcom for its 2001 accounts.

FT also decided that Mobilcom's best interests lay in limiting investments to meet the minimum obligations under the UMTS license, pending industry consolidation, and participating actively in the consolidation process. FT thus disapproved of Mr Schmid's business plans and refused to finance them. It already had a maximum contingent exposure of up to €7 bn corresponding to Mobilcom's current debt and to minimum investments over the next 18 months, pending consolidation of the German market.

These business disputes with Mr Schmid were extremely serious. Yet FT needed his shares if they were to take full control over Mobilcom and clean it up before disengaging from it in an orderly way. The relationship with Schmid became untenable, however, when FT discovered that he had illegally channeled €68 mn of company funds to his wife's company.[77] Clearly, Mr Schmid had to go. Early June, FT denounced its CFA agreement with Mobilcom, whose Supervisory Board relieved Mr Schmid of his functions. FT now sought to obtain an agreement with the members of the Senior Interim Facility banking syndicate for Mobilcom and to perform an in-depth overall analysis of the company before initiating further action.[78] But with only six weeks to go before Mobilcom's debts had to be refinanced, the clock was ticking.

FT's scramble for cash inspired observers to claim that it was increasingly hard to see how FT could avoid a deep discount rights issue to raise €10 bn, the bare minimum to put its finances on a firm footing. A la KPN in 2001, which issued one new share for every existing one, raising €5 bn. Or à la BT, which issued one new share at a 40% discount for every three existing ones, for FT to raise €10 bn by issuing two new shares for every three existing ones at its current market capitalization of €25 bn.[79]

---

[76] Moody's Investors Service, 2002, Moody's expands scope of France Telecom's review, placing the Prime-2 short-term rating on review for downgrade, while continuing the review of the Baa1 long-term ratings, *Rating Action*, May 13, pages 2 and 3.

[77] Raynes, P., 2002, Piece of Schmid, *Breakingviews*, May 30.

[78] France Telecom, 2003, Form 20-F for the fiscal year ended December 31, 2002, March 21, 1–450, page F-54.

[79] Monnelly, M., 2002, Bon voyage, *Breakingviews*, May 24.

Financial engineers also became creative. So it was rumoured that FT was contemplating issuing a hybrid equity in the form of a deeply subordinated perpetual convertible bond to Mobilcom's lenders (significantly the same as FT's lenders) in exchange for Mobilcom's €4.7 bn debt to these lenders. The interest payments on the bond could probably be deferred and they might even be payable in shares. In effect, Mobilcom's lenders would be swapping debt for FT equity and FT would get equity credit for the Mobilcom debt that it might have had to assume. In this case, FT would not have to rush into a discounted rights issue, which in any case the French government had ruled out.[80]

After considering probably all the options that were available to FT, Moody's eventually slashed FT's rating two notches down to Baa3 with negative outlook, affecting €70.0 bn: 'The rating actions reflect Moody's expectation that FT and Orange will not generate sufficient free cash flow in the near term to reduce its high debt levels.'[81]

Exhibit 5.5 shows Moody's Investor Services rating action on France Telecom.

Exhibit 5.5   Moody's Investors Service, rating action France Telecom, June 24, 2002

Global Credit Research
Rating Action
24-juin-02
Rating Action: Orange Plc

Moody's downgrades to Baa3 France Telecom and Orange's long-term debt ratings and France Telecom's short-term rating to Prime-3; rating outlook is negative

Approximately EUR 60 Billion of Long-Term Debt Affected

London, 24 June 2002 – Moody's Investors Service has today downgraded the long-term debt ratings of France Telecom (FT) to Baa3 from Baa1 and the short-term rating to Prime-3 from Prime-2. At the same time, the ratings of Orange Plc were also downgraded Baa3 from Baa1 due to the link between the two ratings, based on the majority ownership of Orange SA by FT as well as by the strong implicit support from FT toward Orange. The rating outlooks are negative. This concludes the review process, which was started on the 27th March 2002.

The rating actions reflect Moody's expectation that FT and Orange will not generate sufficient free cash flow in the near term to reduce its high debt levels. Despite expectations that FT's EBITDA will grow to around EUR 14 billion in 2002, FT's substantial interest and capex requirements means the company is not expected to generate material free cashflow for deleveraging in the near term. FT is dependent upon asset disposals and its treasury stock to make any significant inroads into reducing its debt.

Moody's does not expect FT to have net debt of less than EUR 70 billion at year-end 2002 (adjusted by Moody's for sale and leaseback and asset backed securitization). Furthermore, depending upon the timing of disposals and the acquisition of Mobilcom, Moody's believes that net debt could potentially be as high as EUR 75 billion at year end 2002 (adjusted by Moody's for sale and leaseback and asset-backed securitization). In regard to Mobilcom the rating agency factors either significant contingent liability arising from potential legal action or a significant increase in FT's net debt from acquiring a majority stake. This assumes that FT exchanges either FT or Orange equity for Mobilcom stock and that a mandatory, perpetual convertible bond is used to retire existing debt, which Moody's understands will not impact FT's balance sheet. Moody's further expects that Mobilcom will continue

---

[80] Monnelly, M., 2002, Bon's chance, *Breakingviews*, May 28.
[81] Moody's Investors Service, 2002, Moody's downgrades to Baa3 France Telecom and Orange's long-term debt ratings and France Telecom's short-term rating to Prime-3; rating outlook is negative, *Rating Action*, June 24.

Exhibit 5.5   (*continued*)

to be EBITDA negative in 2003, but that FT will take action to reduce the negative cashflow impact.

Moody's regard FT's ability to reduce debt within a relatively short period as having become increasingly constrained by the fall in its equity value, which reduces the potential value of the treasury stock FT holds, reducing the probability of conversion of numerous convertible bonds and potentially implying a lower realizable value for expected non-core asset disposals, although Moody's acknowledges that it is possible this may change. Additionally, the positive impact of expected asset disposals is expected to be partly offset by various contingent liabilities adversely impacting upon FT.

The negative outlook attached to the Baa3 rating reflects the execution risks associated with FT's high debt refinancing needs of this highly leveraged company. Although Moody's does not have any immediate liquidity concerns, the rating agency notes that FT faces around EUR15 billion of total long-term debt maturities in 2003.

Whilst Moody's expects that FT will make asset disposals and deepen its liquidity resources via securitisation and sale and leaseback structures, FT has a continuing and significant dependency upon access to the debt capital markets.

FT's management continues to be committed to improve the group's debt protection ratios in the medium term. Furthermore Moody's acknowledge that in times of financial stress, telecom operators such as FT have the option of curtailing capex and reducing costs in the short term without having a major detrimental impact on their future longer-term competitive position and growth objectives.

The French government holds 55.5% of the equity of FT, a company that continues to employ approximately 130,000 employees, some 80% to 90% of which are classed as civil servants. Moody's Baa3 rating of FT factors the implicit support of the French government due to its majority ownership, and the according protection afforded to bondholders, given that FT does not currently display credit metrics in line with an investment grade entity. Furthermore, the Baa3 rating factors FT's very strong domestic fixed line market position (at Q1 FT's share of local market traffic had fallen to approximately 85% and is expected to fall another 10% during the course of this year, but remain above 70% for the foreseeable future); and through Orange its leading positions in both the UK and French markets where it has approximately 28% and 49% respectively. Furthermore, Moody's expects FT to continue to grow its operational cashflow, and notes that despite the negative outlook (reflecting ongoing refinancing risk), that the reduction of the current high debt levels would remove potential liquidity concerns and place the company in a better position to exploit its strong market positions, leaving the company on a sound investment grade footing.

The France Telecom ratings downgraded to Baa3 relate to the following:

Convertible global bonds, Euro MTNs, Eurobonds, Floating Rate Euro MTNs, Floating Rate French Franc Bonds, French Bonds, Swiss Franc Bonds, its issuer rating and bank loan rating.

The short-term rating is downgraded to Prime-3

The Orange Plc ratings downgraded to Baa3 are ratings on the following bond issues:

GBP200 million 8.625% Global notes due 8/1/2008, EUR100 million 7.625% Global Notes due 8/01/2008, US$545 million 8% Global Notes due 8/01/2008,
GBP150 million 8.875% Global Notes due 6/01/2009, US$275 million 9% Global Notes due 6/01/2009, US$225 million Global Notes due 6/01/2006.

Orange SA, domiciled in London, UK, is a subsidiary of FT. Orange SA had some 40.5 million wireless subscribers as of 31 March 2002, 18.3 million of which were in France and 12.7 million

Exhibit 5.5   (*continued*)

in the UK (Orange's two most important markets). France Telecom is domiciled in Paris, France. It is the principal provider of telecommunication services in France and one of the world's leading telecommunication service providers, with activities in over 75 countries.

London
Stuart Lawton
Managing Director
European Corporate Ratings
Moody's Investors Service Ltd.
44 20 7772 5454

London
Aidan Fisher
Vice President – Senior Analyst
European Corporate Ratings
Moody's Investors Service Ltd.
44 20 7772 5454

Exhibit 5.5   (*continued*)

security and of each issuer and guarantor of, and each provider of credit support for, each security that it may consider purchasing, holding or selling.

MOODY'S hereby discloses that most issuers of debt securities (including corporate and municipal bonds, debentures, notes and commercial paper) and preferred stock rated by MOODY'S have, prior to assignment of any rating, agreed to pay to MOODY'S for appraisal and rating services rendered by it fees ranging from $1,500 to $2,300,000. Moody's Corporation (MCO) and its wholly owned credit rating agency subsidiary, Moody's Investors Service (MIS), also maintain policies and procedures to address the independence of MIS's ratings and rating processes. Information regarding certain affiliations that may exist between directors of MCO and rated entities, and between entities who hold ratings from MIS and have also publicly reported to the SEC an ownership interest in MCO of more than 5%, is posted annually on Moody's website at www.moodys.com under the heading 'Shareholder Relations – Corporate Governance – Director and Shareholder Affiliation Policy.'

FT was now only just one notch above junk status.

The downgrades increased the opportunity cost of FT's debt, made it more expensive and difficult to attract fresh cash, and made issues of existing debt with step-up clauses more onerous. The latest downgrading was expected to have an additional impact on interest charges of approximately €30 mn in 2002. The downgrades in the fall of 2001 and June 2002 were expected to have a total impact on interest charges of approximately €230 mn in 2003.[82]

The June downgrading enabled the banks to exercise their rights regarding financing the purchase of the shares in TPSA by Kulczyk Holding. FT and Kulczyk asked the banks to negotiate these provisions. In addition, the downgrading could lead to the early repayment of approximately €400 mn of this debt.[83]

5.2 TURNING POINT AND RATING RECOVERY (FALL 2002–WINTER 2004)

5.2.1 Improvement in Outlook in September 2002

Getting Close to the Default Point

One draft resolution that the FT Board of March 20 had adopted to conserve hard needed cash to repay debt was to offer shareholders the option of receiving dividends either in shares or in cash. The French State exercised the share option, thereby reducing the cash outflow associated with the €1.1 bn dividend payment in July by €662.4 mn.[85,86] FT employees also helped, subscribing to new equity for €52.5 mn in July.[87]

But the liquidity situation remained worrisome, as the following well-informed assessment suggests.

---

[82] France Telecom, 2002, Form 20-F for the fiscal year ended December 31, 2001, June 28, 1–321, page 10.
[83] France Telecom, 2002, Form 20-F for the fiscal year ended December 31, 2001, June 28, 1–321, page 11.
[85] France Telecom, 2002, Financial analysts presentation – Annual results 2001, March 21.
[86] On July 8, 2002 FT issued 33.688 mn new shares at €19.7.
[87] On July 31, 2002 FT issued 4.679 mn new shares at €11.22 to employees.

FT has a liquidity structure which is sufficient to cover its debt maturities and other cash demands during 2002. However, the rating agency does not consider the present level of facilities/expected cash inflow as ample enough to necessarily cover all of FT's demands, including some €15 bn of debt maturities in 2003.[88]

Rumours in the market that FT would follow the example of BT, KPN, and Sonera with a deeply discounted or 'rescue' rights offering abounded, as did speculation that Michel Bon, a very vocal opponent of such a tactic, might leave the company. The presence of at least three groups of minority shareholders after the partial floating of Orange and Wanadoo also made it increasingly complex to deal with all the fires.

Resignation of the CEO and Help from Big Brother Shareholder: la République Française

On September 12, 2002, Michel Bon reported to the Board of Directors that 2002-HI had produced an unprecedented €12.2 bn loss and that the company had to deal with €400 mn in negative equity. It was clear that little had been achieved to resolve the debt problem.[89] As it was increasingly difficult to service debt repayments due in 2003 from existing funding sources, FT had also an impending liquidity crisis. At that meeting, Michel Bon submitted his resignation at the helm of FT. The French government accepted this. It also announced that it will assist FT with the implementation of a financial restructuring plan; that it will participate in a future capital injection; and that it will support FT if a liquidity problem emerges. The next day, Moody's changed its outlook to stable.[90]

The turnaround challenge facing any new team was going to be tough. FT had worked hard to adapt to changes in the European telecom industry, but now it was struggling under an increasingly expensive €72.1 bn debt burden on €8.7 bn in stock market capitalization and €0.4 bn in book equity. Tables 5.3 and 5.4, show, respectively, the FT consolidated balance sheet an income statement for 1996–2001, while Exhibit 5.6 shows the FT notes to financial statements for the prime period. Just recapitulating, the rating agencies had taken ever more pessimistic rating actions[91] (see Table 5.5).

Initially, as Figure 2.17 shows, the spread on FT's long-term debt over government bonds was just a few base points. Since then, it had increased steadily to 290.7 bps by the day of the June downgrade and reached an all-time high of 591.7 bps on July 3, 2002. As Figure 5.2 shows, FT's stock price had dropped to an all time low of €6.01 on September 30, leaving a mere 22 cents to the euro to those who had subscribed to the 1997 IPO at €27.00. Shareholder value had declined €86.1 bn in five years, €743.8 bn in two and a half years since the €189.66 all time price high on March 2, 2000.

---

[88] Moody's, *Liquidity Rating Assessment 2002*, page 1.

[89] This included a €7.2 bn provision relating to Mobilcom.

[90] Ministère de l'Economie, des Finances et de l'Industrie, 2002, Situation financière de France Télécom, Communiqué, September 12; and Moody's Investors Service, 2002, Moody's changes France Telecom and Orange's outlook to stable from negative and affirms the Baa3 long-term debt ratings and Prime-3 short-term rating, *Rating Action*, September 13.

[91] These include Fitch, Moody's, Standard & Poor's. Without being identical, their rating actions and their sequence, timing, history and motivation were highly correlated during the case period. For pedagogical purposes, the case narrates in detail the actions of just one of them.

Table 5.3 FT consolidated balance sheet (1996–2002I)[92]

(€ million)	Note[a]	1996	1997	1998	1999	2000 6m	2000	2001 6m	2001	2002 6m
ASSETS										
Goodwill, net	1	228	286	872	1206	5136	36049	42551	34963	34041
Other intangible assets, net	2	355	401	646	925	2051	16289	17154	18189	19279
Property, plant and equipment, net		26028	26041	26577	28964	30081	34623	36299	31728	37128
Investments accounted for under the equity method	3	615	774	956	1066	1279	10506	10174	8912	4278
Non-consolidated investments, net		2504	2719	3738	5673	10489	10218	7700	3240	1720
Other long term assets, net		352	926	471	443	501	722	2024	1936	1517
Deferred income taxes, net	4	2353	2439	2375	2285	2204	2532	4208	5369	4040
Total long-term assets		**32434**	**33585**	**35635**	**40562**	**51741**	**110939**	**120110**	**104337**	**102003**
Inventories		397	378	420	621	987	1216	1100	900	850
Trade accounts receivable, less allowances		5604	5418	5688	6884	7879	8783	7498	7596	7730
Deferred income taxes, net (ST)	4	343	589	551	677	522	1609	819	1102	646
Prepaid expenses and other current assets		968	2126	1785	2676	3284	4782	8806	6653	5678
Receivable from divestment of real estate		0	0	0	0	0	0	0	2689	239
Marketable securities		118	198	37	211	312	216	73	1138	148
Cash and cash equivalents		489	415	2042	2424	3883	2040	3563	2943	2288
Total current assets		**7919**	**9123**	**10523**	**13493**	**16867**	**18646**	**21859**	**23021**	**17579**
TOTAL ASSETS		**40354**	**42708**	**46158**	**54055**	**68608**	**129585**	**141969**	**127358**	**119582**
LIABILITIES AND SHAREHOLDERS' EQUITY										
Share capital	5	3811	3811	3905	4098	4098	4615	4615	4615	4750
Additional paid-in capital	6	5259	5259	6629	6629	6629	24228	24228	24228	24755
Retained earnings (loss) at the beginning of the period		*3262*	*2898*	*4172*	*5255*	*6998*	*2748*	*4062*	*4682*	*-4865*
Net income (loss) for the year		*321*	*2266*	*2300*	*2768*	*3817*	*3660*	*1951*	*-8280*	*-12176*
Foreign currency translation adjustment	7	-2	52	-15	153	348	59	755	844	-2929
Own shares	8	-686	0	0	0	0	-2153	-4998	-5002	-9975
Shareholders' equity		**11966**	**14286**	**16991**	**18903**	**21890**	**33157**	**30613**	**21087**	**-440**
Minority interests	9	**155**	**181**	**779**	**1369**	**1654**	**2036**	**15586**	**8101**	**10149**

(continued overleaf)

Table 5.3 *(continued)*

(€ million)	Note[a]	1996	1997	1998	1999	2000 6m	2000	2001 6m	2001	2002 6m
Exchangeable or convertible notes		0	0	2031	2031	2654	2653	5735	10 750	7668
Other long and medium term debt, less current portion	*10*	9184	9027	10 049	10 202	15 243	27 894	37 176	43 793	41 485
Pension Plans		3712	3537	3650	3684	3915	3633	3827	3773	3346
Other long term liabilities excluding pension plans	*10*	257	244	377	498	266	1587	1368	4890	11 818
Total long-term liabilities		**13 153**	**12 808**	**16 107**	**16 415**	**22 078**	**35 767**	**48 106**	**63 206**	**64 317**
Current portion of long and medium term debt		1019	2284	1764	2551	1239	7542	7914	1596	9210
Bank overdrafts and other short term borrowings		944	4697	1302	2479	8506	25 165	17 783	11 365	13 769
Special contribution owed to the French State		5717	0	0	0	0	0	0	0	0
Trade accounts payable		3195	4103	4085	5330	5849	7618	7764	8631	7898
Accrued expenses and other payables		3020	3252	3480	4208	4159	7729	6872	7259	8255
Other current liabilities	*11*	610	422	557	1175	1380	8113	4277	2481	2638
Deferred income taxes		37	82	133	495	627	512	2789	374	456
Deferred income		538	592	960	1130	1226	1946	265	3258	3330
Total current liabilities		**15 079**	**15 433**	**12 281**	**17 368**	**22 986**	**58 625**	**47 664**	**34 964**	**45 556**
TOTAL LIABILITIES AND SHAREHOLDERS' EQUITY		**40 354**	**42 708**	**46 158**	**54 055**	**68 608**	**129 585**	**141 969**	**127 358**	**119 582**

[a]See Exhibit 5.6 for notes to this table.

Source: France Telecom, Forms 20-F, except for the year 1996 (FT Annual Report).

[92]All numbers have been converted to €1 at FF6.55957, $0.94 and £0.63, the end 2000 exchange rates.

Table 5.4 FT consolidated income statement (1996–2002I)

(€ million)	Note[a]	1996	1997	1998	1999	2000 6m	2000	2001 6m	2001	2002 6m
Sales of services and products		22 876	23 420	24 648	27 233	15 324	33 674	20 424	43 026	22 472
Cost of services and products sold		−7332	−8473	−8937	−9686	−5595	−12 733	−8405	−17 619	−9133
Selling, general and administrative expenses		−5046	−5293	−6115	−7341	−4196	−9685	−5687	−12 520	−6187
Research and development expenses		−820	−696	−658	−593	−214	−449	−266	−567	−282
EBITDA		**9679**	**8957**	**8938**	**9613**	**5319**	**10 807**	**6066**	**12 320**	**6870**
Depreciation and amortization (excluding goodwill)		−4979	−4736	−4584	−4885	−2566	−5726	−3251	−6910	−3595
Operating income before special items, net		4700	4222	4354	4728	2753	5081	2815	5410	3275
Special items, net		−2888	−217	−379	−238	−112	−225	−101	−210	−93
Operating income	12	**1811**	**4005**	**3975**	**4490**	**2641**	**4856**	**2714**	**5200**	**3182**
Net interest expense		−814	−733	−900	−662	−471	−2006	−1967	−3847	−1754
Foreign exchange gain (loss), net		60	−6	−23	−20	−49	−141	−399	−337	−87
Other non-operating income/(expense), net	13	−148	259	860	767	3336	3957	1778	−5904	−9339
Changed actuarial cost of early retirement plan		0	−218	−270	−196	−119	−237	−114	−229	−126
Income before income taxes, employee profit sharing and cumulative effect of employee profit-sharing		909	3307	3642	4379	5338	6429	2012	−5117	−8124
Equity in net income/(loss) of affiliates		98	−152	−144	−135	−107	−141	−71	−131	−51
Cumulative effect of changes in accounting principles		18	25	189	259	−105	−275	−292	−890	−163
Income taxes		−702	−915	−1438	−1797	−1158	−1313	1439	2932	−2296
Income/(loss) before goodwill amortization and minority interest		**325**	**2266**	**2249**	**2706**	**3968**	**4700**	**3088**	**−3206**	**−10 634**
Goodwill amortization		−81	−150	−82	−136	−171	−1092	−1353	−2531	−1466
Exceptional goodwill amortization	14	0	0	0	0		0		−3257	
Minority interest (net)		78	150	133	198	20	52	216	714	−76
Net income (loss)		**321**	**2266**	**2300**	**2768**	**3817**	**3660**	**1951**	**−8280**	**−12 176**
Appropriation of earnings to dividends	6	−686	−991	−1025	−1025	−1025	−1075	−1075	1056	−1056
Other movements	6				−193		−4250	−651		
Dividends paid to minority interests		−1	−4	−8	−71	−52	−213	−99	−128	−39

[a]See Exhibit 5.6 for notes to this table.
Source: France Telecom, Forms 20-F, except for the year 1996 (FT Annual Report), and casewriter adjustments to 1996 and 1997 to make them reasonably comparable with subsequent periods.

Exhibit 5.6   France Telecom notes to financial statements (1996–2002I)

		2000	2001 6m	2001	2002 6m
1	**Goodwill, net: Total**	**36 049**	**42 551**	**34 963**	**34 041**
	Orange	29 895		24 490	22 883
	Equant/Global One	3849		6290	5331
	Wanadoo	595		2908	2682
	Casema	219			
	Nortel Inversora/Telecom Argentina	173			
	TP Group				1938
	JTC	317		295	
	Mauritius			203	
	Other	1001		777	1207

The amortization period for goodwill is usually ranging from 5 to 20 years, determined after taking into consideration the specific nature of the business acquired and the strategic value of each acquisition.
Goodwill amortization is not tax deductible.

		2000
2	**Other intangible assets, net: Total**	**16 289**

- This includes licenses, patents and access rights, i.e., acquisition cost of UMTS telephony licenses in the UK and Netherlands; and GSM mobile telephony license in UK.
- This includes purchase price allocation of Orange Plc allocated to trademarks and customer relationship.
- This includes amortization expense of intangible assets, including goodwill amortization of consolidated companies

3 Investments accounted for under the equity method versus full or proportionate consolidation

The main consolidation principles are as follows:

- Companies which are wholly owned by France Telecom or which France Telecom controls, either directly or indirectly, are fully consolidated; this means that the total amount of each asset, liability, revenue and cost of the subsidiary and related to third parties is added to the corresponding item of France Telecom. That is, all third party accounts of the companies are combined.

- Investments in which France Telecom and a limited number of other shareholders exercise joint control are accounted for using the proportionate consolidation method; this means as previous, but the combinations are proportional to the FT ownership;

- Investments over which France Telecom exercises significant influence but does not control, such as joint ventures (generally a 20% to 50% controlling interest), are accounted for under the equity method; this means that these investments are initially recorded as an asset at cost to which periodically the share in the investee's net income is added against the same amount of investment revenue on the income statement.

- Material inter-company balances and transactions are in all three cases eliminated.

Exhibit 5.6 (*continued*)

	2000
Investment accounted for under the equity method: Total	**10 506**
Mobilcom	3687
TP SA	3441
Wind	2011
FT1CI	785
BITCO	370
Intelig	107
PTK	60
Pramindo Ikat	44
Television Par Satellite	−99
Other affiliates	100

	2000	
4 Long-term deferred income taxes, net asset: Total	**2532**	
Gross deferred tax assets	6106	
Valuation allowance	−1965	Allowance estimated based on the probability of deferred tax assets being realized over time.
Less: Current deferred tax assets	−1609	At December 31, 2000, this allowance related principally to tax loss carry forwards of €1859 mn.

	2000	
5 Additional Paid-in Capital: Total	**24 228**	
Balance at December 31, 1999	6629	
Increases in capital during 2000	17 599	In 2000, FT issued 129 201 742 new shares of €4.0 nominal amounting to €516.8 mn. The premium attached totaled €17 597.3 mn.

	1998	
6 Retained earnings at the beginning of the period: Total	**4173**	
Retained earnings at the beginning of the previous period	2 898	
Net income of the previous period	2 266	
Dividends accrued of the previous period	−991	Dividends are appropriated on earnings of the same period and are normally paid during the next period.

7 Foreign currency translation adjustment
The translation adjustment relates to movements in the exchange rate on goodwill, investments and reserves

Exhibit 5.6 *(continued)*

8 Own shares

During 2000:

o Acquisitions of 15.4 mn FT shares from Mannesmann at €140.2 per share.

During 2001:

o Acquisitions of 64.6 mn FT shares at an average price of €103.37, resulting mainly from two purchases in March 2001 of 64.1 mn shares from Vodafone for an amount of €6.65 bn.
o Divestiture of 31.5 mn FT shares at an average price of €56.71, including the contribution of 30.9 mn FT shares to the SITA foundation for the acquisition of Equant (see Note 3 of 20-F for year 2001). The result of these sales was offset against consolidated reserves for an amount of €1271 mn, net of tax (€778 mn).

During 2002:

o Acquisitions of 51.9 mn FT shares at an average price of €96.79, resulting mainly from purchase in March 2002 of the remaining shares from Vodafone for an amount of €4.973 bn.

	2001 6m	2001	2002 6m
9 Minority Interest: Total	**15 586**	**8101**	**10 149**
Opening balance	2036	2036	8101
Result for the year	−216	−714	76
Issuance of share capital to minority interests	57	74	11
Effect of acquisitions and divestitures	13 628	6802	2712
Appropriation of net result	−99	−128	−39
Translation adjustment	184	31	−712
Other changes	−4	0	0

10 Pension plan and other long-term liabilities

For 6m 2001, the casewriter estimated these figures by linear interpolation for pension liabilities between December 31, 2000 and 2001.

	2000	2002 6m	
Pension plan	**3881**	**3698**	
Early retirement plan for French civil servants	3633	3346	
Post retirement benefits other than pensions	134	147	
Retirement indemnities	114	205	
LT deferred tax	830	368	FT disclosed this item only for some years.
Provision for CVRs issued to Equant minority shareholders		2077	CVR intrinsic value as contingent liability relate to the commitments re the development of UMTS activities.
Provision for FT's financial risks at Mobilcom		7000	
Other long-term liabilities	509	2021	
Total	**5220**	**15 164**	

Exhibit 5.6 (*continued*)

11 Other current liabilities

The increase in €5267 mn of 'Other current liabilities' from December 31, 1999 to December 31, 2000, are vendor notes owed to: Deutsche Telekom for the acquisition of 18.9% of Wind (€2076 mn), to E.on for the acquisition of an additional 42.5% of Orange Communications SA (€1038 mn), and to Vodafone in connection with the Orange Plc acquisition for €2153 mn.

12 Special items

These are essentially the amortization for the period of adjustments in the actuarial value of the early retirement plan. A provision corresponding to an actuarial measurement of the liability under the early retirement plan in accordance with the FT law of July 26, 1996 is recorded as a liability under 'Pension plan'. Changes in actuarial assumptions are accounted for from the anniversary of the plan in the income statement in the year of change, and on a pro-rata basis over future service periods until the end of the plan on December 31, 2006 as personnel opt for early retirement.

For the year 1996: Special Items also includes:
Impairment of long-lived assets   4 979

13 Other non-operating income/(expense), net includes	2001	2002 6m	
MobilCom	−1393	−7290	At June 30, 2002: charges of €7,290 mn relating to MobilCom of which €290 mn related to the additional depreciation of loans made by FT SA to MobilCom in the course of the first 6 months of 2002 and of €1663 mn relating to provisions on NTL shares and bonds.
NTL	−5910	−1663	
Provision for losses and charges on the Equant CVR	−2077		
NTL securities representing Noos shares	−		
Wind	−		
Restructuring costs within Orange	−		
FT assets in Ivory Coast	−		
Repurchase of TP SA shares with Kulczyk Holding	−		
Other non-operating income/(expense), net*	3476	−386	*includes capital gains and losses from sales of assets, income from dilution, other provision movements, costs of the sale of receivables and dividends.
Total	*−5904*	*−9339*	

Exhibit 5.6 (*continued*)

14 Exceptional goodwill amortization	2001	
MobilCom	2509	Fully amortize the goodwill by €2509 mn, the charge being recorded as exceptional amortization.
Nortel/Telecom Argentina	185	
Ananova and Wildfire	211	Exceptional goodwill amortization in 2001 relates
Equant/Global One	349	to Ananova and Wildfire (€4211 mn) and to the restructuring and other related costs for the new Equant/Global One entity (€4349 mn) included in the acquisition cost.
Other	3	
Equant	–	
Orange Communications SA – revision of business plan	–	
JTC (Jordan)	–	
Total	*3257*	

Source: France Telecom, Forms 20-F and Annual Report.

Previous management attempts to tackle FT's financial problems with ambitious debt reduction programs had proved unattainable. As a result, credibility was badly shaken. Investors constantly speculated on management changes and bailout scenarios.

Bottoming Out

On September 30, the ICT index bottomed at 43.4. FT's share price stood at its all-time low of €6.01, 76% lower than its IPO price. The corresponding €7.2 bn market capitalization was less than FT's net loss of €12.2 bn for the first half of the year. FT was now the world's most indebted publicly listed company. It had a €70 bn net debt burden, faced an impending liquidity crisis, and 75% of the inordinate amount of debt matured within the next three years, as Figure 5.3 shows.

5.2.2   A New Start in October 2002 and Recovery Actions

The Appointment of a New CEO

When the French government appointed Thierry Breton CEO of France Telecom and reaffirmed as its main shareholder its financial commitment on October 2, 2002, there was a sigh of relief from the markets.[93] This energetic 48 year old, known for his decisive management style, had been widely credited with rescuing the French consumer-electronics maker Thomson Multimedia from near collapse in the late 1990s. Investors were hoping

---

[93] Ministère de l'Economie, des Finances et de l'Industrie, 2002, France Télécom, Communiqué, October 2.

Table 5.5 History of Fitch, Moody's, and S&P's rating actions on FT's Long-Term Issuer/Issuer Credit rating.

Date	Fitch Long-Term Issuer Default Rating				Moody's Long-Term Issuer Rating				Standard & Poor's Issuer Credit Rating			
	Alpha-numeric	Numeric	Action	Outlook	Alpha-numeric	Numeric	Action	Outlook	Alpha-numeric	Numeric	Action	Outlook
06 Nov 1991					Aaa	1	Initiating		AAA	1	Initiating	
07 Nov 1991									AAA	1		Stable
14 Nov 1991									AAA	1		Negative
24 Mar 1994												
27 Jun 1995					Aaa	1	Assigned					
07 May 1996					Aaa	1	Watch/Downgrade					
10 Jul 1996					Aa1	2	Rating lowered					
03 Mar 1997									AA+	2	Rating lowered	Stable
19 Feb 1998	AA+	2 negative	Initiating/Watch									
16 Jul 1999					Aa1	2	Watch/Downgrade		AA+	2	Watch/Downgrade	
27 Jul 1999					Aa2	3	Rating lowered					
03 Dec 1999								Stable				
21 Dec 1999	AA	3	Downgrade						AA	3	Rating lowered/Watch	Negative
22 Dec 1999												
28 Jan 2000					Aa2	3	Watch/Downgrade		AA−	4	Rating lowered	Stable
30 May 2000	AA	3	Watch negative						AA−	4	Watch/Downgrade	
23 Aug 2000									A	6	Rating lowered	Negative
11 Sep 2000	A	6	Downgrade	Stable								
18 Sep 2000					A1	5	Rating lowered	Stable				
09 Feb 2001	A	6	Affirmed	Negative								
15 Feb 2001					A3	7	Rating lowered	Stable				
16 Feb 2001									A−	7	Rating lowered	Negative
21 Jun 2001	A−	7	Downgrade	Negative								
06 Sep 2001	A−	7	Watch negative		A3	7	Watch/Downgrade		A−	7	Watch/Downgrade	
25 Sep 2001									BBB+	8	Rating lowered	Negative
26 Sep 2001					Baa1	8	Rating lowered	Stable				
28 Sep 2001	BBB+	8	Downgrade	Negative								
27 Mar 2002	BBB+	8	Watch negative									
28 Mar 2002					Baa1	8	Watch/Downgrade		BBB+	8	Watch/Downgrade	

(continued overleaf)

Table 5.5 *(continued)*

Date	Fitch Long-Term Issuer Default Rating				Moody's Long-Term Issuer Rating				Standard & Poor's Issuer Credit Rating			
	Alpha-numeric	Numeric	Action	Outlook	Alpha-numeric	Numeric	Action	Outlook	Alpha-numeric	Numeric	Action	Outlook
24 Jun 2002					Baa3	10	Rating lowered	Negative	BBB	9	Rating lowered/Watch	Negative
25 Jun 2002												
05 Jul 2002	BBB−	10	Downgrade	Negative								
12 Jul 2002									BBB−	10	Rating lowered	Stable
13 Sep 2002	BBB−	10	Affirmed	Stable								
05 Dec 2002	BBB−	10	Affirmed	Positive								
24 Mar 2003									BBB−	10	Watch/Upgrade	
14 May 2003									BBB	9	Rating raised	Positive
07 Aug 2003					Baa3	10	Watch/Upgrade					
05 Dec 2003	BBB	9	Upgrade	Positive								
18 Feb 2004	BBB+	8	Upgrade	Positive								
19 Feb 2004									BBB+	8	Rating raised	Positive
03 Mar 2004					Baa2	9	Rating raised	Stable				
14 Jun 2004	A−	7	Upgrade	Stable								
03 Sep 2004	A−	7	Affirmed	Stable								
24 Jan 2005					Baa2	9	Watch/Upgrade					
10 Feb 2005												
23 Feb 2005					Baa1	8	Rating raised	Stable	A−	7	Rating raised	Positive
24 Mar 2005	A−	7	Affirmed	Stable								
23 Jun 2005					A3	7	Rating raised	Stable				
27 Jul 2005	A−	7	Affirmed	Stable								
07 Feb 2006	A−	7	Revision IDR	Stable								
25 Apr 2006	A−	7	Affirmed	Stable								
26 May 2006												
27 Sep 2006	A−	7	Affirmed	Stable					A−	7	Affirmed	Stable
04 Jun 2007	A−	7	Affirmed	Stable								

Sources: Fitch Ratings, 2007. Long-term issuer default rating history on France Telecom, as of October 15; Moody's Investors Service, 2007. Long term issuer rating history on France Telecom, as of October 15; Standard & Poor's, 2007. Issuer credit ratings history on France Telecom, as of October 15.

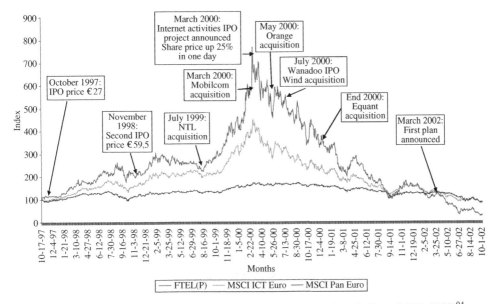

Figure 5.2   France Telecom, ICT Sector and Pan-European share indices (1997–2002)[94]

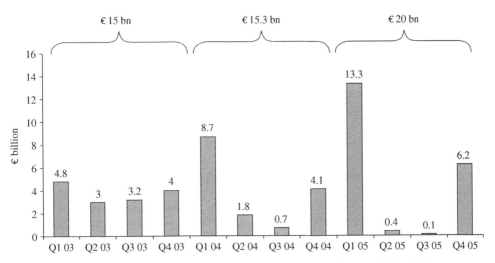

Figure 5.3   France Telecom: Quarterly debt repayment schedule (2003–2005)

he would work the same magic with FT. When he took office, wide speculation about the future of the company let up momentarily. On the morning of his appointment, he issued a statement outlining his vision for the FT group:

> ... I told (the FT employees) that my goals could not be limited to the indispensable task of reducing debt. I want to drive an ambitious policy of operational progress within the company,

---

[94] ICT stands for Information and Communication Technology.

and pursue dynamic growth based on FT's outstanding human and technological capabilities in the fixed-line, mobile and Internet businesses. But above all, I asked employees to immediately work at exceeding the company's objectives, especially in this last quarter.

In the coming weeks I will conduct an in-depth study of the company's activities. This review will enable us to rapidly define and implement solutions to loosen the financial grip in which FT is now caught and recover the necessary flexibility to pursue a great ambition. As the French government has indicated, this turnaround will be achieved with the support of the majority State shareholder, in keeping with European Union rules. . . .[95]

By the close of the same day, investors had pushed FT's stock price up 10.1% to €7.30, an increase worth about €0.8 bn.

Immediately, Thierry Breton appointed a new team, which was immediately charged with deciding what actions would get FT out of its financial distress in a timely and orderly fashion. Breton immediately ordered an in-depth independent review of FT. The markets would have to wait two months for the refinancing plan to be unveiled.

The Plan was Going to be Particularly Straightforward

On December 4, 2002, Thierry Breton presented the FT Ambition 2005 restructuring plan to the Board. The core of the plan was the '15 + 15 + 15' plan, placed in the framework of a strategy to make France Telecom a full service European telecom operator with a focus on its core brands.

The first part of the plan, named TOP (Total Operational Performance), was to generate savings within France Telecom that would release €15 bn of free cash flow over the following three years to pay down debt. Exhibit 5.7 provides a breakdown of the projected savings by type, by business area, and by year. This ambitious program was projected to achieve these savings through strict control of investments and significant cuts in operating costs primarily through streamlining of purchasing.

The most urgent measure facing France Telecom was to restructure its debt load to avoid the impending liquidity crisis in 2003. This would be achieved by a €15 bn refinancing of the debt to lengthen its average maturity. Finally, the capital structure would be stabilized by raising €15 bn from existing shareholders to pay down debt and bring shareholders equity back into positive territory. The French government announced at the meeting that it would participate in the capital increase at a level pro-rata to its shareholding, representing €9 bn. It also announced that €9 bn was being immediately made available to France Telecom in the form of a subordinated shareholder loan, provided by a holding company, as a way of circumventing EU restrictions on direct government subsidies to a corporation. The loan would be convertible into shares upon the launch of the rights issue. Indeed, the loan was only repayable in FT equity, upon maturity or sooner if FT launched an equity issue.

Wednesday, 4 December, 2002

French State Support to the Recovery Plan

In support of the recovery plan that the Board of France Telecom approved on December 4, the French government confirmed that it shall in due time participate in a €15 billion

---

[95] France Telecom SA, Paris, October 3, 2002.

Exhibit 5.7 Details of the projected €15 bn of savings to be achieved by France Telecom

By Business Unit	By Timetable	By Nature[a]

[a] Bulk of savings coming from CAPEX, purchasing and marketing
Source: Presentation to INSEAD, 2004, France Telecom, February 5.

equity increase of France Telecom in prorate of its shareholding, i.e. to the amount of €9 billion.

The French finance ministry also said the government would stand by to make, if needed, a shareholder advance of these €9 billion in anticipation of the equity increase to give France Telecom the flexibility to optimally launch the equity increase at the right time.

The finance ministry added that the French government may, if necessary, give up its majority share in the company.

State Aid

The finance ministry said the refinancing strategy was 'ambitious and realistic,' describing it as 'a cornerstone in the recovery of the company.'

The government loan, which is to be repaid at market rates, will be advanced by a state holding company, ERAP.

ERAP will take over the goverment's 55% stake in France Telecom.

The use of ERAP as an intemediary is seen as a way of getting around European Union regulations banning direct government subsidies to industry.

The plan requires the approval of EU state aid authorities before it can proceed.[96]

The aim of the plan was to bring the net debt/EDITDA ratio down below 2 by the end of 2005 from a forecast level of 4.7 at the end of 2002, with the objective of giving FT the

[96] Ministère de l'Economie, des Finances et de l'Industrie, 2002, Soutien de l'Etat au plan d'action approuvé par le conseil d'administration de France Télécom, Communiqué, December 4. BBC News, 2002, France Telecom in 9 bn euro bailout, December 4.

strategic and financial flexibility it needed to become a major player in all sectors of the European telecommunications industry.

The stock, which had doubled since Breton's appointment, opened up 11% on the morning after the announcement, and finished the day up 16%, as investors breathed a sigh of relief over the ambitious plan and its strong support by the government.

5.2.3   Recovery Implementation and the Sequence of Rating Upgrades through February 2005

Reopening of the Bond Markets

The most urgent action was refinancing of the debt to avert the looming liquidity crisis. The provision of the €9 bn shareholder loan by the French government and the ambitious plan to improve the performance of the company restored confidence that the company could rise to the challenge. The day after the announcement of the plan, Moody's confirmed its stable outlook at Baa3 for France Telecom. France Telecom wasted no time in capitalizing on the change in sentiment. A week after the Board meeting, France Telecom sold €2.5 bn in 7-year bonds carrying a 7% coupon, followed the next day by a £250 mn (€384 mn) 15-year bond carrying an 8% coupon. This marked the return of France Telecom to the bond markets after an absence of more than a year. This was followed on January 15, 2003, by a further bond offering of €5.5 bn consisting of three tranches: €1 bn 4²/₃-year bond (6% coupon), €3.5 bn maturing in 10 years (7.25%), and €1 bn maturing in 30 years (8.125%). Announced the week before at €3 bn, the amount was increased to €5.5 bn in the face of strong demand. As in December, France Telecom followed up the Euro bond with a second £250 mn bond with the same terms. In February, France Telecom added another €500 mn to the 30-year bond issued in January. It also replaced the €5 bn one-year tranche syndicated bank loan that was expiring on February 14, replacing it with a new 3-year €5 bn line of credit, taking the unusual step of self-arranging the loan to reduce banker fees.

With the replacement of the syndicated loan, France Telecom had completed the first part of the Ambition FT 2005 plan, raising €14.2 bn between December and February to refinance its debt and extend the average maturity of its debt. At the same time as it was resolving its liquidity problem, France Telecom had been putting into place the other two legs of the '15 + 15 + 15' plan aimed at reducing the €68 bn debt and strengthening the performance of the company.

In a February 2003 analysis of France Telecom, Moody's confirmed its stable outlook of Baa3, noting that it considered that the company had the ability to cover debt maturing in 2003 following the bond issuances and asset sales. Moody's based the stable rating on expectation that FT would significantly reduce debt from the planned equity increase and improvements in free cash flow generation. However, it regarded that it would be challenging for FT to achieve the planned €15 bn of cumulative cash flow, especially since only Orange was performing as expected with Wanadoo (Internet) and Equant (international fixed-line) failing to contribute in spite of large investments made on them.

Taking Control over Free Cash Flow

The second leg of the plan was formally launched in January 2003 to achieve the ambitious €15 bn in free cash flow over the next three years. The plan to reduce both operating and capital expenditures involved 100 projects grouped into programs, each of which was directly under the responsibility of a member of the Executive Committee. In the first year, France Telecom generated €6.4 bn in free cash flow (without considering cash received from asset disposals), well above expectations and went on to generate €16.6 bn over the three years of the TOP program. This performance was achieved by the strong focus on costs. Already in the first quarter of 2003, the ratio of operating expenses to revenues decreased from 68% in 2002 to 63.8%. This was brought down to 62.5% for the whole of 2003 and further improved to 61.3% in 2004, before climbing back up to 62.4% in 2005 in light of increased advertising expenses to increase client capture and retention rates.[97]

The Rights Offering

The third leg of the plan involved an increase in the capital of the firm, which was initiated by the attribution on March 24, 2003 of 1187 million warrants, entitling shareholders to subscribe to 19 shares for every 20 warrants held at a unit price of €14.50 per share. The French State immediately announced that it would exercise all of the warrants attributed to it, for a value of €9 bn, which would be paid for by the untapped shareholder loan that it had provided in December. Upon the closing of the transaction on April 15, France Telecom had raised a net amount of €14.8 bn destined for paying down debt.

Consolidating

An important part of the efforts of France Telecom to restructure included divestiture of assets to provide additional cash for paying down the debt and to redefine the perimeters of the company in light of its strategy to become an integrated European telecommunications company. In 2003, the proceeds of asset sales contributed €3 bn of the total €23.8 bn used to reduce debt, the rest of which came from the rights issue and the discretionary free cash flow.[98] Asset sales, as listed in Exhibit 5.8, allowed France Telecom to raise cash as well as divest itself of assets that were not core or not likely to perform well. Starting in December 2002, France Telecom sold off TDF, Casema, Eutalsat, and Wind. In the second half of the year however, the logic of focusing on developing itself as an integrated operator and the success of its restructuring efforts led France Telecom to announce the buyout of all minority shareholders of Orange. This was followed in February 2004 by a similar announcement to repurchase all shares of Wanadoo.

By the end of 2003, France Telecom was well on its way to achieving the ambitious turnaround goals that Thierry Breton had set for the firm. Indeed, on December 5, 2003, Moody's placed the Baa3 rating on review for upgrade, citing the continued reduction in France Telecom's very high debt burden, resulting from the increase in free cash flow through improved operational cash generation and historically low capital expenditure levels. On March 3, 2004, Moody's upgraded France Telecom to Baa2 starting a steady climb to A3 on June 23, 2005. The Baa2 rating came after the publication of the 2003 financial statements, mentioning the impressive debt reduction and generation of free cash flow of €6.3 bn, well above the 2003 objective of €4 bn set by the turnaround plan. Most significantly,

---

[97] France Telecom 20-F 2003, 20-F 2004, and 20-F 2005.
[98] Deslondes, G., 2004, France Telecom Research Report, S&P, March 22, 1–14, page 2.

Exhibit 5.8   France Telecom actions and events under the restructuring.

Date	Event

Change in Focus

2002

Date	Event
September 12	Michael Bon resigns
	French government confirms it will provide support to FT to help it reduce its debt and meet any liquidity events
September 13	Moody's changes outlook on Baa3 from negative to stable
October 3	Thierry Breton becomes CEO and Chairman of FT and announces 2-month in-depth review of the company
December 4	Main conclusions of in-depth review presented to the board of FT. Ambition FT 2005 plan is announced, including the '15 + 15 + 15' objectives.
December 12	Moody's confirms stable outlook on Baa3 rating

Rebalancing of the Capital Structure, including extension of debt maturities

2002

Date	Event
December 11	€2.5 bn 7 year bond with 7% coupon issued
December 12	£250 mn (€384 mn) 15 year bond with 8% coupon issued

2003

Date	Event
January 15	€5.5 bn bond in 3 tranches issued: a €1 bn 4$^2/_3$-year tranche with 6% coupon, a €3.5 bn 10-year tranche with 7.25% coupon, and a €1 bn 30 year tranche with 8.125% coupon
January	£250 mn (€384 mn) 15 year bond with 8% coupon issued, equivalent to the issue of December 12
February	€500 mn 30 year bond with 8.125% coupon, assimilated with the 30 year bond issued on January 15.
February 14	€5 bn 3-year syndicated bank credit line to replace the expiring €5 bn 1-year credit line.
March 24	1187 mn warrants attributed to shareholders. 19 shares at a price of €14.50/share can be purchased for every 20 warrants. French State announces it will exercise its warrants for an amount of €9 bn, thereby wrapping up its shareholder loan.
April 15	€14.9 bn (net) achieved upon closing of the rights transaction. Proceeds used to pay down debt.

Asset Divestitures and Consolidation

2002

Date	Event
December 13	€1.3 bn proceeds from closing of sale of TDF
December 26	€510 mn net proceeds from sale of Casema announced

2003

Date	Event
January 28	Sale of Casema completed
February 3	€375 mn net proceeds from sale of 23% stake in Eutelsat announced.
March 20	€1.5 bn net proceeds from sale of Wind announced
September 1	Buyout of minority shareholders of Orange announced. Offer in shares or cash of €7.1 bn for the remaining 13.9% of shares not held by France Telecom.
September 24	€4.3 mn net proceeds from sale of Menatel (Egypt) announced
December 31	French law passed to allow the French state to hold less than 50% of France Telecom.

Exhibit 5.8 (*continued*)

Date	Event
2004	
February 23	Buyout of minority shareholders of Wanadoo announced. Offer in shares or cash of €3.95 bn for the remaining shares not held by France Telecom.
June 20	€286 mn net proceeds from sale of 5.5% shareholding of Sprint PCS announced.
July 8	€600 mn net proceeds from sale of Orange Denmark announced.
July 24	€1.4 bn in proceeds from public listing of 37% of Pages Jaunes
September 7	French government sells 10.85% stake in France Telecom, bringing its holding down to 42.24%

perhaps, was the comment that Moody's Baa2 rating did not factor any implicit support from the French government. Truly, France Telecom had come a long way from September 2002.

5.3   ANALYSIS AND EVALUATION

The turmoil that was the revolution in information technology, the reorganization of the telecommunication industry, and the Internet stock market bubble took FT's credit ratings on a roller coaster ride. But interestingly, they never went below investment grade, even when theoretical default models, statistical default scores, and market credit default swap rates hinted that FT's near-term default probability was around 60%, or when the market value of its assets were estimated to fall short of its near-term debt. In fact, FT's credit ratings started sliding down from sovereign status at a time when its short-term financial health was extremely robust, and they held up above junk status when FT hit a short-term liquidity wall in June 2002.

For these reasons, FT provides an extremely interesting illustration of what credit ratings are (and what they are not); what drives them; how they accompany a company's ability and willingness to pay its dues fully and on time; and how they anticipate an issuer's resiliency and staying power, or structural weakening, from a fundamental measuring perspective, rather than from a cyclical psychological one.

One of the interests in this example is that France is infamous as the country where issuers complain more than anywhere else that CRAs create bad weather, rather than being the weathermen who report it. In *The Wall Street Journal Europe*, Alcatel SA CEO Serge Tchuruk likened the agencies to 'pyromaniac firemen,' while Vivendi Universal SA CEO Jean-René Fourtou called them 'executioners,' and France Telecom SA's former CEO, Michel Bon, said an 'unjustified' downgrade by Moody's helped to initiate a debt crisis that cost him his job.[99]

However, the fact of the matter is that the 1995–2004 rating cycle of France Telecom illustrates exactly the opposite of what Michel Bon claims. This cycle is a case of rating actions and inactions demonstrating great moderation, and of ratings setting themselves apart from credit spreads and their changes. It shows credit ratings conveying a forward-looking perspective and degree of anticipation akin to the traditional perspective of bank credit committees, which had to gauge the consequences of the lending bank being exposed

---

[99] Delaney, K.J., 2002, France Inc. is fuming at top rating agencies – anger over downgrades is sign of new accountability; 'Search for a scapegoat,' *Wall Street Journal Europe*, November 20.

to the borrower over the whole lifetime of the loan. For medium- to long-term lending, the perspective taken was unavoidably long-term.

5.3.1   Risk Shifting at France Telecom and its Fundamental and Market-Implied Ratings

Like many of its competitors, FT had over-leveraged itself to finance acquisitions, as Figure 5.4 illustrates. Figure 5.5 – the market values of FT's assets, debt, and equity for 1997–2004 – shows that FT continued to borrow heavily from June 2000, a few months after the market value of the assets in which it had invested started to decline, accelerating the downturn in its equity.

Figure 5.6 shows France Telecom's asset and equity volatility. Both moved in tandem until June 2000, when equity volatility started to diverge from asset volatility, up to about 120% in July 2002. Something else that was critical to creditors happened concurrently. The value cushion of FT's assets was deflating. The ratio of market value of assets to book value of debt – the value cushion per euro of debt, or 'cushion ratio' – became very dynamic. This ratio had reached a comfortable peak of 4.2 by March 31, 2000. But then, in just four months, it dropped dramatically to 2.1, as Figure 5.7 shows. It is worth noting that this happened two years before Moody's two-notch downgrade in June 2002, which, according to Michel Bon, supposedly triggered FT's crisis. The ratio continued its downdrift uninterruptedly from there. It hit the sensitive floor of 1.0 by March 31, 2002 and made a hard landing of 0.5 on September 30. Fortunately, it quickly bounced back to start a subsequent slow and gradual recovery.

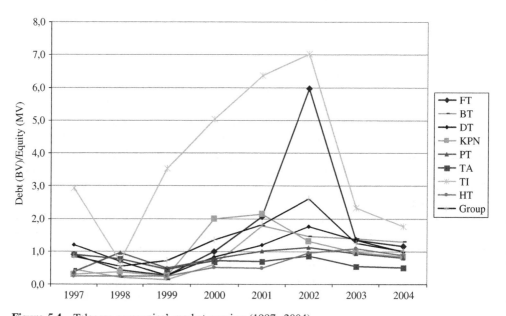

Figure 5.4   Telecom companies' market gearing (1997–2004)
Source: Thomson Datastream, FT's financial statements, the authors' analysis.

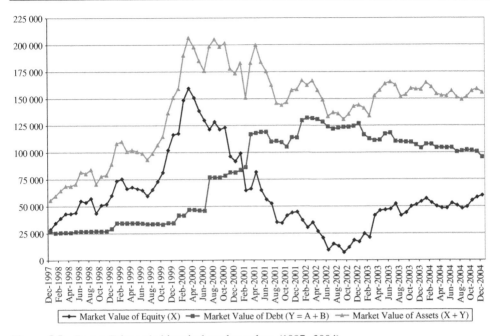

Figure 5.5   France Telecom's historical market values (1997–2004)
Source: Thomson Datastream, Euronext website, FT's financial statements, the authors' analysis.

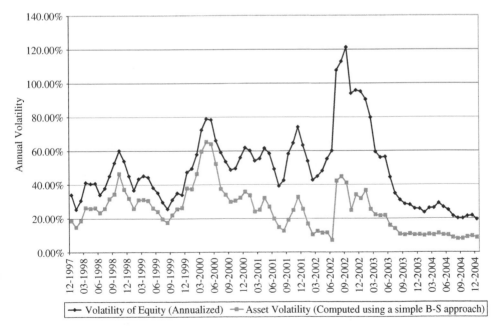

Figure 5.6   France Telecom's asset and equity return volatility (1997–2004)
Note: B-S stands for Black-Scholes.
Source: Daily returns on FT stock price.

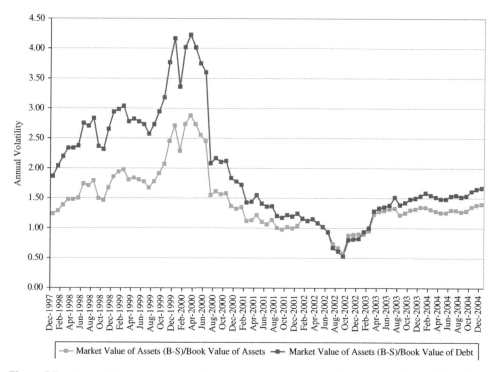

Figure 5.7   France Telecom's market value of assets to book value of assets and debts (1997–2004)
Source: Thomson Datastream, FT's financial statements, the authors' analysis.

Moody's had started following FT in 1991, leading to several initiating issue ratings in different rating classes.[100] This was followed on June 27, 1995, by an initiating Long Term Issuer Rating of Aaa, the same as the French sovereign rating, and then by regular ratings follow-up and ratings action, discussed in Sections 5.1 and 5.2 and now summarized in Figure 5.8.

These ratings stabilized once the cushion ratio had reached its trough. For 21 months, they hovered on the line between investment grade and junk, without falling below it. Until the trough, the CRAs exercised a moderating influence on management, first anticipating, then feeding back to management that it had chosen a dangerous path. But then, at a critical juncture, the CRAs' direction shifted from moderating management to moderating the markets. Interestingly, the rating never went through the investment grade floor, even though several measures, described in more detail in Chapter 6, suggested it should.

One such set of measures are default probabilities based on market prices (computed using structural Merton type models) or mechanical credit scores (statistical default probability scores, such as Altman Z-scores models – see Figures 5.9 and 5.10).

These all hinted that from June 2002 through March 2003, FT's near default probability was around 50–90% (depending on the metric used). Another market measure is France Telecom's net market worth, the implied market value of its assets minus its default point.

---

[100] It initiated its rating actions with an Aaa senior unsecured domestic currency issue rating on November 6, 1991. A similar foreign currency rating followed on July 24, 1992 and a new P-1 short-term rating on foreign currency commercial paper was initiated on June 26, 1994.

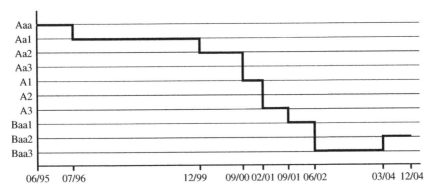

Figure 5.8   France Telecom: Moody's long term issuer ratings (1995–2004)
Source: Moody's Investors Service, 2005, Long-term issuer rating history on France Telecom, as of
December 14.

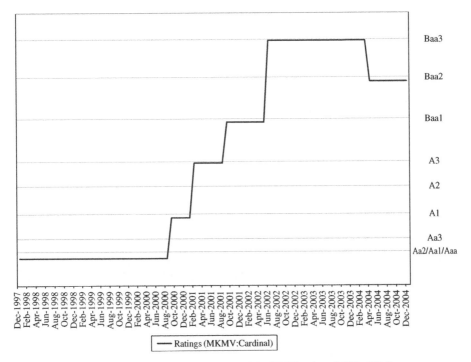

Figure 5.9   France Telecom: Moody's KMV rating (1997–2004)
Source: Moody's.

The former became negative during the third quarter of 2002, as Figure 5.11 shows. The
shaded area beneath the zero line is FT's debt due within a year, and the shortfall in net
worth is the negative dip in 2002.

Figure 5.12 shows a last indicator of the path, and the extremes of market reaction to
FT's fortunes: the market value of the put option on FT's assets that the company's creditors
implicitly shorted. This put option was almost worthless until April 2002. Then, six months

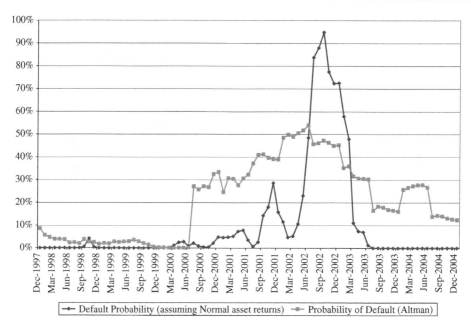

Figure 5.10   France Telecom: default probabilities and Altman Z-scores (1997–2004)
Note: Although the assumption of Normally distributed asset returns tends to exacerbate the default probability, the principle is still valid. For more detail on how the default probability is computed refer to Chapter 6, section 6.2.2.

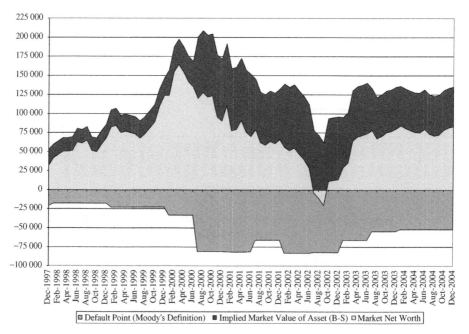

Figure 5.11   France Telecom's default point (Moody's definition) and market net worth (1997–2004)
Source: Thomson Datastream, FT's financial statements, the authors' analysis.

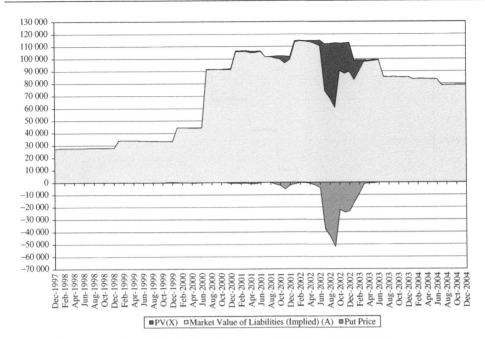

Figure 5.12   France Telecom's implied market value of liabilities (1997–2004)
Source: Thomson Datastream, FT's financial statements, the authors' analysis.

later when the time-discounted value of FT's debt was about €112 bn, it shot up to about €51 bn, reducing the overall value of FT's debt by about 54%. The debasement of the debt rapidly and almost completely disappeared within six months.

In order to make the different market measures of default probability as comparable as possible to FT's LT Issuer's rating, consider the following. Invert the traditional ordinal scale and map it on the cardinal scale of the average expected default frequency that corresponds to the ordinal ratings. Figure 5.13 plots the result from 1997 through 2004. The fundamental credit rating cycle shows similar contours to the market-implied default probabilities shown previously. But there is one distinctive difference. It is considerably attenuated, in three ways. Firstly, it starts going up sooner but climbs more gradually. Secondly, it reaches a plateau of relatively high default probability but never goes through the roof. Thirdly, it declines gradually, not abruptly. In other words, rating cycles are a moderating factor, almost like central bank interest rate movements.

The FT case thus illustrates that fundamental credit ratings aim to be weathermen, not weather makers. They tend to keep management on a leash when it risks running ahead of what is sustainable. They also tend to tame markets when they overshoot during periods of irrational depression.

5.3.2   The Restraint of the CRAs during the 2002 Crisis

During the crisis of the fall of 2002, upon the resignation of Michel Bon, the CRAs provided the company with a well needed support to face the challenge of turning the situation around. Although the financial ratios of the company were well within speculative grade range, the credit ratings stabilized their outlook just within the investment grade. They took into account

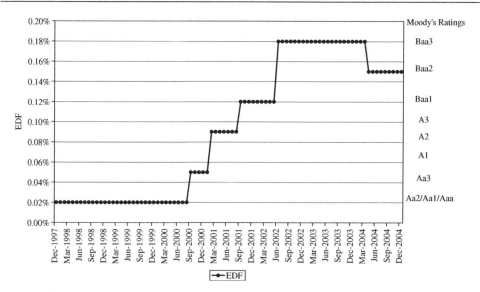

Figure 5.13 France Telecom: Moody's ordinal and cardinal rating histories (1997–2004)
Source: Authors calculations on the basis of Moody's issuer ratings history of France Telecom and its mappings of rating categories in expected default frequencies.

the repeated promises by the French Government that it would help the company with its debt load and meet any liquidity difficulties. Thus, the day after, Moody's changed its outlook from negative to stable, in spite of the fact that the company no longer had a CEO.

Upon the announcement of Thierry Breton as the CEO on October 3, the stance of the rating agencies provided an important support in his two-month review of the company and what would be necessary to turn it around. This allowed him time to develop the Ambition FT 2005 plan and the '15 + 15 + 15' objectives in December 2002 to restructure the debt and focus on cash generation by the firm.

As Figures 5.9 to 5.12 show, it can be estimated that the market gave the firm a default probability up to between 50% and 95% in the fall of 2002, which was certainly not investment grade. However, during the whole of the long autumn of 2002, the rating agencies maintained a stable outlook on the investment grade worth of the company. Given the debt covenants that increased required interest payments at every reduction in the credit rating of the company, the restraint of the CRAs gave the new management of France Telecom some welcome room to attend to the task of preparing a future with a firmer footing for the company.

5.3.3 The Value of Ratings to Issuers

To close this chapter on the 10-year FT ratings cycle, it is proper to reflect on the value added by CRAs to the issuers. What is the value of what they do to the issuers who pay the ratings bill? Corporate treasurers are sometimes quick to complain that companies only incur these costs because they are forced to, and that credit ratings are worthless to the company. Is this really so?

Let's consider what the FT case illustrates. In the face of market-implied ratings that rated FT as 'junk,' the CRAs' fundamental perspective allowed them to maintain FT's investment grade status. This moderating stance facilitated FT's new management team's work to open the bond markets again in the fall of 2002. Ratings assess the issuer from a fundamental measuring perspective, rather than from a cyclical taste-for-risk perspective. They endeavor to anticipate an issuer's relative long-term resilience and staying power, rather than express a view on the attractiveness of its bond prices.

Conversely, when the CRAs started to anticipate structural weakening in FT's credit-worthiness owing to a complex interaction of different forces, they did not hesitate to downgrade gradually, thereby acknowledging that FT was migrating from a low-risk issuer to a high-risk one. It was not the notching down of the ratings that changed FT's risk profile; it was FT's environment and expansion strategy, and the way it was financed. The rating changes were sending a series of valuable warning signals to FT's CEO and Board of Directors. These were not signals about the appropriateness of FT's business conduct, or about the pricing of its bonds. They were signals about the long-term implications of its approach to business development and financing. The reduction in the ratings did not imply that FT's business conduct somehow became 'bad'; it only meant that FT was involved in risk-shifting behavior – the reasons for which could, in fact, have been excellent. It was then up to FT management to integrate its awareness of risk-shifting activities into optimal decision-making.

Briefly, ratings provide management and Boards feedback about the long-term implications of the risk stance they maintain or alter. This long-term perspective, relative to the short-term perspective of bond spreads, shows up in the comparison between the average annual volatility of ratings versus bond yield implied ratings. Exhibit 5.9 tabulates comparative average annual volatility statistics for 1999–2002.

This long-term perspective on a borrower's downside risk is nothing new. Years ago, before disintermediation, commercial banks used it. Nowadays CRAs position an issuer on the long-term default risk spectrum as discussed in Chapter 3. By helping a company to identify its place in the distributions of its business, CRAs provide access to global capital markets. CRAs could be regarded as gatekeepers of the capital market's arena. Obtaining a credit rating for a corporation has become a normal, unavoidable necessity, although it has also been suggested that the excess of information about creditworthiness now means

Exhibit 5.9 Average annual rating volatility statistics as percentage of issuers (1992–2002).

	Moody's ratings	Bond yield implied ratings
Rating changes	25%	91%
Large rating changes (more than 2 notches)	7%	43%
Rating Reversals	1%	76%
Memo item: Average number of rating changes over 12 months for each user experiencing a rating change	1.2	4.5

Source: McDaniel, R.W., President of Moody's Investors Service, 2003, Annual meeting of the International Organization of Securities Commissions (IOSCO), Panel on the regulation of rating agencies, *Special Comment:* Moody's Investors Service, October 17, Report 79839, 1–8.

that little attention is paid to the rating itself and that, for corporates at least, the fine rating does not much matter. To borrow an analogy: a rating is like a nose; as long as you have one, nobody notices it – whatever it looks like – but beware of not having one.

In the next chapter, Credit Rating Analysis, we turn to the different techniques behind the ordinal ratings and cardinal default probability estimates presented in this chapter and the methods of their computation.

6

Credit Rating Analysis

> *Credit risk analysis is an art, not a science. It is impossible to quantify all the elements one must consider in credit analysis.*[1]

In preparing a rating action, CRAs use fundamental analysis of default risk and of the prospects of recovery in case of default. They complement this with the extraction of default probabilities from market prices. This chapter explains both approaches and clarifies their differences and complementary nature. It applies these techniques of traditional ratio analysis and Vasicek-based Merton analysis of default probabilities to FT to illustrate the practical mechanics of each one of these approaches and to discuss their strengths and weaknesses.

6.1 FUNDAMENTAL CORPORATE CREDIT RATINGS

6.1.1 Corporate Credit Risk[2]

> *As we look at the environment right now, we see no letup of the competitive environment in terms of pricing and competition. In order to recover its rating, GM will have to substantially reduce its legacy and health-care costs and see brisk sales of the new line of large sport-utility vehicles and trucks, called the GMT-900 series.*[3]

This quote nicely emphasizes the point, we believe, that ratings analysis starts with business analysis and that it then involves detailed examination of the company's operations, projection of cash flows, and assessment of the future earning power of the firm. Such analysis is necessary, because the future prospects of the firm are of primary importance to any lender.

We can best describe the perspective of CRAs on an issuer by showing in Exhibit 6.1 how a major rating adviser summarizes the focus of rating agencies.

Rating analysis has traditionally two basic components: business risk analysis and financial risk analysis.

---

[1] Emmer, E.Z., Executive Managing Director, Standard & Poor's, in Ganguin, B., and Bilardello, J. 2005, *Fundamentals of Corporate Credit Analysis*, McGraw-Hill, New York, 1–437, page x in the Foreword.

[2] This section draws heavily on the classics of the field published by the CRAs themselves, primarily: Fitch Ratings, 2006, Corporate rating methodology: corporate finance criteria report, June 13, 1–7; Moody's Investors Service, 2004, Guide to Moody's ratings, rating process, and rating practices, June, Report 87615, 1–48 and Samson, S.B., Sprinzen, S., and Dubois-Pelerin, E., 2006, *Corporate Ratings Criteria* – Standard & Poor's role in the financial markets; ratings definitions; the rating process, *Research:* Standard & Poor's, March 9, 1–13 plus some excellent publications, such as Ganguin, B., and Bilardello, J., 2005, *Fundamentals of Corporate Credit Analysis*, McGraw-Hill, 1–437.

[3] Stated by Oline, M., a credit analyst at Fitch, according to Covel, S., and Hawkins Jr., L., 2005, High fuel prices, Delphi woes pressure GM's credit ratings, *Wall Street Journal Europe*, September 29, page M4.

Exhibit 6.1   The rating agencies' focus

- Downside risk vs upside potential
- Cash flow generation vs book profitability
- Earnings quality (i.e. stability and predictability) vs EPS and growth rates
- Forward looking approach: medium- /long-term horizon
- Peer group analysis and competitive position
- Management's philosophies and policies involving financial risk
- Capital structure flexibility and liquidity cushion

Source: Atkinson, R., Managing Director, Global Capital Markets, Morgan Stanley, 2006, DPWN: The initial credit rating of a major corporation, January 13, 1–20, page 8.

Creditors lend to companies that typically compete in a particular industry and in a particular country, and so the business risk of a firm can be seen as a set of nesting spheres of risk: the company risk within the industry risk within the country risk. The business risk determines the debt capacity and how aggressive the financial policies of the company can be, and therefore conditions the evaluation of financial risk.

To determine the credit rating of a company requires a detailed analysis. The broad scope of these risk factors means that credit analysts have to conduct full company reviews that go way beyond looking at the downside of a company's situation. Rated companies perceive this type of scrutiny by credit analysts as expensive and an infringement on their privacy.

The importance of a thorough analysis in understanding and rating the credit risk of a company is expressed by S&P:

> Credit ratings often are identified with financial analysis, and especially ratios. But it is critical to realize that ratings analysis starts with the assessment of the business and competitive profile of the company. Two companies with identical financial metrics are rated very differently, to the extent that their business challenges and prospects differ.[4]

Business Risk Analysis

COUNTRY RISK   The business environment is shaped by the dynamics of the country and its government in which the company operates. These dynamics determine the framework and rules of engagement under which all companies evolve. The country risk goes beyond the elements that are considered in the determination of a sovereign rating (discussed in Section 6.3.1), to include specific country risk factors that affect the company. The country risk is used to limit the credit rating that a company can achieve, so that in high-risk countries even the best firms will not be able to achieve the highest credit ratings. To arrive at an opinion of the riskiness of a particular country, CRAs monitor the political and legal framework, the degree to which government helps or hinders business; the quality of the physical infrastructure and human capital upon which all business must rely; the development and robustness of the financial markets, especially the local banking system; and the accounting system, the macroeconomic impact of consumer spending power combined with inflation and interest rates; and finally the foreign exchange risks associated with the costs and revenues of doing business in that country.

---

[4] Standard & Poor's, 2006, *Corporate Ratings Criteria*, 1–119, page 19.

INDUSTRY RISK   The dynamics of the industry strongly influence the performance that a company can achieve. The CRAs place the company within the context of its industry in order to focus on the elements that are most pertinent to the company risk. The CRAs thus study the broad industry structure and trends and the new services and competitors appearing on the horizon. By understanding the sales and revenue prospects of an industry by classifying the industry as a growth, mature, niche, global, or cyclical sector, the CRAs are better able to understand the pricing power that companies will possess. The impact of the business cycle on the industry and the barriers to entry faced by potential new competitors allow an evaluation of the volatility in performance that individual companies will experience. As with the country risk, the industry risk evaluation is used to determine the limitations, if any, to the credit quality of the companies in an industry.

COMPANY-SPECIFIC RISK   The final layer of the business risk analysis consists of a look into the company to determine how volatile its business performance will be. The CRAs spend a great deal of effort to understand how the company compares in relation to its competitors. To do so, they identify the key competitive factors (such as price, quality, service, and ability to deliver) of an industry and their underlying drivers (such as the low-cost position if price is a key factor). These are compared with the positioning of the company being considered. The strengths of the company are evaluated in light of observed trends in market share, product and sales diversity, sales growth, and pricing power as compared to the competition. A final, but essential, consideration involves the company management. Credit analysts are expected to meet and discuss with company management, evaluate their integrity, as demonstrated by the match between announced intentions and observed actions, measure the shareholder pressures they must satisfy, and observe the financial policies they adopt to achieve their goals.

The outcome of the business risk analysis is a determination of the level of risk of the company, which can be expressed in a score that classifies the business risk from low to high risk, as discussed in Section 6.1.3. This evaluation of the qualitative level of risk of the business provides the basis for the more quantitative measurement of the financial risk.

Financial Risk Analysis

The financial risk analysis measures the ability of the company to repay its obligations and withstand shocks. It is the step that allows the credit rating agencies to validate the strength and weakness of the business. Financial ratios are used to determine trends, allow comparison with competitors, and as a basis for forecasting expected performance. The calculation of the ratios relies on an understanding of the company derived from the business risk analysis. The credit rating agencies maintain benchmark ratios for each industry, graded by credit quality to allow for comparison with other companies. The financial risk analysis also results in a score. This is combined with the business risk score to provide an overall credit score that can then be mapped to a credit rating. This process is described in more detail in Section 6.1.3.

The analysis of the financial risk can be split into four parts, consisting of:

- Balance sheet analysis
- Profitability analysis
- Cash generation analysis
- Liquidity analysis.

Exhibit 6.2   Standard & Poor's relevant business risk and financial risk factors used in the corporate rating process (2005)

Corporate credit analysis factors	
Business risk	*Financial risk*
• Country risk	• Accounting
• Industry characteristics	• Corporate governance/Risk
• Company position	tolerance/Financial policies
• Product portfolio/Marketing	• Cash-flow adequacy
• Technology	• Capital Structure/Asset Protection
• Cost efficiency	• Liquidity/Short-term factors
• Strategic and operational management competence	
• Profitability/Peer group comparisons	

Sources: Standard & Poor's, 2006, *Corporate Ratings Criteria*, 1–128, page 20; see also Standard & Poor's, 2005, *Corporate Ratings Criteria*, 1–119, pages 19–21.

Each part provides a distinct conclusion about the firm.

Evaluating the balance sheet allows a conclusion to be made about the financial risk taken by the firm. The CRAs spend a great deal of effort to fully quantify the myriad obligations on and off the balance sheet that a company may have and can lead the firm into bankruptcy if left unpaid. These obligations are compared with the assets of the firm and permit calculations of leverage ratios.

Studying the profitability of the firm allows for an evaluation of the financial performance of the assets of the firm, and is characterized by profitability ratios such as calculations of margin, return, and growth.

The cash generation ability of the firm is the most important consideration of the credit analyst as cash is what is required to repay the obligations of the firm. For this reason, the CRAs focus a great deal of attention on cash flow ratios to determine cash flow adequacy, aiming to accurately forecast future cash flows and assess their robustness to a whole variety of possible scenarios.

The liquidity, or financial flexibility, of a firm is meant to measure how and whether the firm will actually have the cash on hand when it is needed. This involves investigation of the cash needs that will potentially arise and in what ways the company will be able to meet them.

Exhibit 6.2 provides a list of factors of business and financial risk that Standard & Poor's considers when performing a corporate credit analysis.

6.1.2   Credit Risk of Corporate Debt Instruments

When analyzing debt structures, always follow the money.[5]

The vast majority of credit ratings outstanding are of debt instruments. These credit ratings include not only an evaluation of the default risk, as for issuer credit ratings, but

---

[5] Penrose, J., General Counsel and Managing Director, Standard & Poor's, in Ganguin, B., and Bilardello, J., 2005, *Fundamentals of Corporate Credit Analysis*, McGraw-Hill, New York, 1–437, page 200.

also the prospects of recovery of the specific debt instrument in the event of default. Ratings of debt instruments are notched upwards or downwards from the issuer credit rating, since timely payment of debt obligations is of primary concern and thereby trumps the expected recovery in the event of default. The credit analysis of specific debt instruments focuses on the factors that influence the expected recovery given default, as the corporate credit rating analysis already provides the default risk.

Value of the Firm in Default

The credit analysis of debt instruments must determine the value of the firm in default. The value of a firm in default depends on the reason that brought it into default, as this will determine if it can be restructured or if it will be liquidated, as demonstrated in Exhibit 6.3. A good business afflicted with an unbalanced financial structure and/or inadequate management can be restructured, whereas a company in a declining line of business or with poor fundamentals could well end up in liquidation.

For firms that are far from bankruptcy, the uncertainty surrounding the possible scenarios leading to bankruptcy are considered too remote. The CRAs use a recovery rate based on historical observations, as the base from which to notch debt issued by firms that have a low likelihood of bankruptcy.

For firms that are close to bankruptcy a distressed firm analysis is performed. An explicit expected default scenario is determined and the enterprise is valued both as a going concern and under liquidation. The going concern valuation generally involves a combination of fundamental valuation involving a discounted cash flow analysis and a market value approach using a distressed multiple of cash flow, generally proxied by EBITDA. Reorganization usually provides a higher valuation for the firm than liquidation. Whatever scenario prevails, the value of the firm is what is available for distribution to the claims, which will not only include debt but also taxes, wages, rents, leases, pensions, trade credit, guarantees, and environmental remediation.

Exhibit 6.3   Distress and insolvency outcomes.

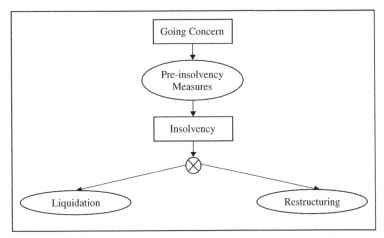

Source: Ganguin, B., and Bilardello, J., 2005, *Fundamentals of Corporate Credit Analysis*, McGraw-Hill, New York, 1–437, page 202. Reproduced with permission of The McGraw-Hill Companies.

Exhibit 6.4   Priority ranking.

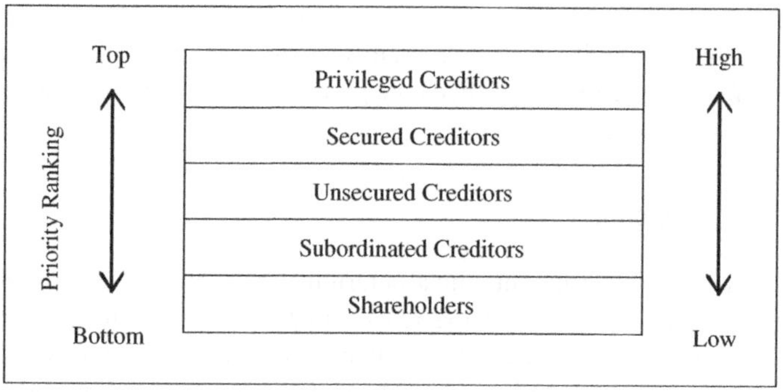

Source: Ganguin, B., and Bilardello, J., 2005, *Fundamentals of Corporate Credit Analysis*, McGraw-Hill, New York, 1–437, page 207. Reproduced with permission of The McGraw-Hill Companies.

The Influence of Priority Ranking of Debt by Classes

The most important consideration of credit risk of debt instruments is determined by the priority ranking. The priority ranking of creditors results from the sorting of creditors into classes during a bankruptcy proceeding to determine the order of payment of claims. Exhibit 6.4 demonstrates the priority ranking by classes of the claims on a firm.

The privileged creditors include the claims of the professional and court fees that are incurred inside of bankruptcy proceedings. Secured creditors benefit from collateral that they can seize to recover their money. The subordination of some creditors may be contractually agreed, in exchange for higher interest payments on their debt. The subordination may also be structural, in that debt provided to a holding company that owns operating firms will be subordinate to any debt directly incurred by those operating companies. However, this can be remedied if the operating company provides an upstream guarantee on the debt of the holding company.

The value that remains in a firm that goes into default can be seen as flowing into each class of claims, as shown in Exhibit 6.4, with any excess spilling over into the class below until no more value is left. The credit analysis therefore involves a thorough analysis of the debt documentation and the structure of the corporate family to determine the relative ranking of each instrument. The analysis must also consider the impact of violation of absolute priority rules that occur.

Debt that has better than average recovery prospects in the event of default is notched upwards. Generally, better recovery prospects are a function of the amount and quality of collateral that has been granted to the instrument. The credit analysis involves an evaluation of the quality and liquidity of collateral and whether it has been properly granted and perfected. Various post-default stress scenarios are evaluated to obtain an estimate of what value the collateral is likely to have in a distress situation.

Debt deemed to be junior to other debt issues of the company will have worse recovery prospects and is notched down.

The degree to which priority ranking levels are adhered to is subject to the insolvency regime that applies to the debt instrument. In some jurisdictions little differentiation is made between senior and junior creditors, as less importance is attached to claim priority than to a collaborative resolution of creditor claims. For example, Standard & Poor's doesn't apply notching to obligations in India, as 'distinguishing between senior and unsubordinated debt can be meaningless in India, where companies may be allowed to continue paying even common dividends at the same time they are in default on debt obligations.'[6]

Credit ratings of debt instruments are thus grounded in a thorough understanding of how creditors are treated in the applicable insolvency regime, encompassing bankruptcy law and practice. This involves understanding the influence creditors have in the process of handling firms that enter financial distress and insolvency.

The extent of notching of debt instrument credit ratings from the corporate rating is dependent on the credit grade of the corporation. For investment grade companies, the probability of default is very low and the focus of investors, and subsequently of the credit rating analysis, is on the timeliness of payment of obligations. For speculative grade companies, investors are more concerned about the recovery prospects in the event of default. This is taken into account by varying the maximum level of notching, upwards or downwards, based on the credit quality of the issuer. The notching practices of the largest three CRAs is provided in Table 6.1.

Recovery Ratings

In recent years, CRAs have started publishing recovery ratings (called loss-given-default assessments by Moody's) for debt instruments issued by low-grade issuers in response to the increased importance of recovery analysis in credit risk management. Recovery ratings are provided on instruments from industrial corporations, financial institutions, sovereigns, and structured finance.

Table 6.1 Maximum notching of debt obligations as a function of corporate credit rating for the three major CRAs

Credit rating agency	Credit rating level	Maximum upward notching	Maximum downward notching
Standard & Poor's	⩾ BBB − (Investment Grade)	+2	−1
	⩽ BB + (Speculative Grade)	+3	−2
Fitch	⩾ BBB − (Investment Grade)	+2	−2
	⩽ BB + (Speculative Grade)	+3	−3
Moody's	⩾ Caa1	+3	−3
	⩽ Caa2	+4	−4

Sources: Standard & Poor's, 2006, *Corporate Ratings Criteria*, 1–128, pages 46–50 and 54; Standard & Poor's, 2007, Recovery analytics update: Enhanced recovery scale and issue ratings framework; *Commentary Report*: May 30, 1–4, pages 2–4; FitchRatings, 2005, Recovery ratings: Exposing the components of credit risk: Special Report, July 26, 1–8, page 4; Cantor, R., Emery, K., and Stumpp, P., 2006, Probability of default ratings and loss given default assessments for non-financial speculative-grade corporate obligors in the United States and Canada, *Rating Methodology:* Moody's Investors Service, August, Report 98771, 1–16, page 12.

---

[6] Standard & Poor's, 2006, *Corporate Ratings Criteria*, 1–128, page 46.

The two primary components of credit risk – probability of default and loss-given default – are combined in instrument credit ratings. The publication of recovery ratings means that there are separate indicators for both components: the recovery rating provides the recovery indicator (for instruments of low grade issuers only) and the issuer credit rating provides the default indicator.

Recovery ratings are an opinion about the expected recovery prospects of a specific obligation in the event of default. The recovery rate compares the ultimate nominal recovery that is expected to be received at the end of the workout period to the value of the instrument (principal plus accrued but unpaid interest) at the time of default. Investors can use their own discount rate to the ultimate nominal recovery.

For sovereigns, however, given the long workout periods observed, the rating agencies generally take the additional step of determining the discounted present value of the expected recovery using an expected post-default discount factor. This is compared with the value of the instrument at the time of default to determine the recovery rate.

Recovery ratings are only made public for instruments issued by low-grade issuers, generally speculative grade, where default is close enough that fundamental issuer- and instrument-specific, scenario-based analysis can be performed. For instruments of higher grade issuers, recovery ratings are based on class-level recovery assumptions and incorporated into the instrument rating, without being made public. Whether made public or not, the recovery rating is used to determine the degree of notching of the instrument from the issuer rating, as described in Section 6.1.3.

Exhibit 6.5 describes the recovery rating/loss-given-default assessment scales of the leading CRAs.

Note that recovery ratings apply to the ultimate recovery that is expected to be achieved upon resolution of the restructuring of the firm. Credit risk models used by banks have been based on estimates of recovery rates on market prices at default, which is how recovery is determined by most published data on default recovery rates. Under the influence of Basel II guidelines, however, banks are beginning to use ultimate recoveries and not recoveries

Exhibit 6.5 Recovery rating/loss-given-default assessment scales of the major credit rating agencies

Standard & Poor's			Fitch			Moody's	
Recovery Rating	Description of recovery	Recovery range (%)	Recovery Rating	Description of recovery	Recovery range (%)	LGD Assessment	Loss range (%)
1+	Full	100					
1	Very high	90–100	RR1	Outstanding	91–100	LGD1	0–10
2	Substantial	70–90	RR2	Superior	71–90	LGD2	10–30
3	Meaningful	50–70	RR3	Good	51–70	LGD3	30–50
4	Average	30–50	RR4	Average	31–50	LGD4	50–70
5	Modest	10–30	RR5	Below average	11–30	LGD5	70–90
6	Negligible	0–10	RR6	Poor	0–10	LGD6	90–100

Sources: S&P, 2007, Recovery analytics update: Enhanced recovery scale and issue ratings framework, *Commentary Report*: May 30, 1–4, page 2; Fitch, 2007, Recovery Ratings Factsheet, 1–2, page 1; Cantor, R., Emery, K., and Stumpp, P., 2006, Probability of default ratings and loss given default assessments for non-financial speculative-grade corporate obligors in the United States and Canada, *Rating Methodology*: Moody's Investors Service, August, Report 98771, 1–16, page 5.

Exhibit 6.6   Distribution of US recovery ratings by instrument type, Fitch Ratings, September 2006.

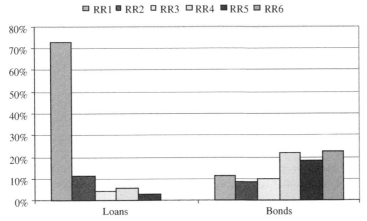

Source: May, W., Needham, C., and Verde, M., 2006, Recovery ratings reveal diverse expectations for loss in the event of default, *Credit Market Research:* Fitch Ratings, December 14, 1–11, page 4.

at the time of default. Estimates of recoveries at default are significantly higher than those at emergence from restructuring. As a conclusion to a review of the evidence on recovery rates, it is found that recovery risk is a systematic risk component that should attract risk premia and needs improved consideration in credit risk management.[7] It is clear that the realization of this will drive increasing interest in recovery ratings.

Upon the public release of recovery ratings by the CRAs have followed studies of the universe of recovery ratings, which provide some interesting observations on the expectations of recovery. Exhibit 6.6 demonstrates that loans are overwhelmingly expected to benefit from outstanding recoveries in the event of default. This is expected, given that nearly all loans require strong collateral security. In contrast, the expected recoveries on bonds cover the whole range of recovery expectations with a large proportion having distinctly poor prospects.

Looking at the distribution of recovery prospects from the perspective of the class of the instrument in Exhibit 6.7, we see that a majority of secured debt benefits from full recovery expectations, while a majority of subordinated debt has poor, if any, recovery expectations. Unsecured debt shows a full range of recovery expectations. Further analysis shows pronounced inter-industry differences, highlighting the importance of integrating industry risk in credit risk analysis.

6.1.3   Putting it All Together: the Rating[8]

The final step of the credit analysis involves expression of the credit risk of a company into a score that is mapped to the global credit risk scale, thereby ranking the firm according to

---

[7] Altman, E.I., 2006. Default recovery rates and LGD in credit risk modelling and practice: an updated review of the literature and empirical evidence, Working Paper, November, 1–36, pages 17–19.

[8] This section presents the method of scoring credit risk as presented in Chapter 10 of Ganguin, B., and Bilardello, J., 2005, *Fundamentals of Corporate Credit Analysis*, McGraw-Hill, 1–437.

Exhibit 6.7 Distribution of US recovery ratings by broad seniority types, Fitch Ratings (September 2006)

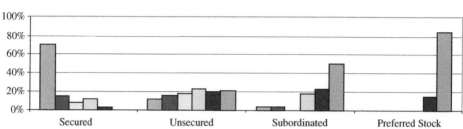

□ RR1 ■ RR2 □ RR3 □ RR4 ■ RR5 □ RR6

Source: May, W., Needham, C., and Verde, M., 2006, Recovery ratings reveal diverse expectations for loss in the event of default, *Credit Market Research:* Fitch Ratings, December 14, 1–11, page 1.

its credit quality and allowing the evolution of the credit quality to be tracked over time. The two primary components of credit risk – the risk of default and the risk of loss-given-default recovery expectation – each has its own rating scale. The rating for the probability of default is applied to the whole corporation, whereas the recovery expectation is applied to the individual instruments. These are then combined to provide an overall rating of credit quality of the instruments.

The following section describes how credit analysis can be transformed into a rating which allows for global comparison. The ability to make comparisons across the range of credit quality and across time allows for the pricing of debt instruments with a risk premium and benchmarking relative to all other instruments.

A. Determining the Overall Credit Rating

Figure 6.1 provides an overview of the process of obtaining a rating that expresses the likelihood of default based on the analysis of the corporation.

CREDIT SCORE AND MAPPING TO THE RATING   The first element of determining a credit score is the use of a default score mapping table which provides a numerical graduation of default risk that ranges from very low risk to very high risk and permits mapping the score to a default rating, as described in Table 6.2. Of course, the rating agencies will use a scale with at least 22 increments, corresponding to the number of rating steps in the scale they use.

BUSINESS AND FINANCIAL RISK SCORE   The second element of determining a credit score is the use of a business and financial risk table that splits the default risk into the component parts of the credit risk analysis. Table 6.3 provides a possible scoring of the business and financial risk components of default risk.

SCORING THE BUSINESS RISK   With the above two elements, it is possible to score the business risk based on the business risk analysis that has been performed. The first two layers of the business risk analysis, country risk and industry risk, limit the credit quality

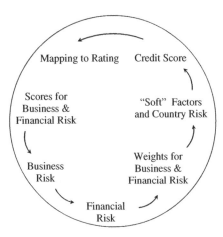

Figure 6.1 Obtaining a credit rating from a credit analysis

of the majority of companies. The industry risk directly limits the score for business risk, whereas the limit imposed by country risk is taken into consideration when determining the overall credit score.

With the company placed in the context of its industry risk, the key competitive factors that define the success of the firm in its industry, as determined in the business risk analysis, are weighted relative to their importance in the performance of a given firm in that industry. Each key competitive factor is scored, taking into account the limit imposed by the overall industry risk, and the overall business risk score is computed by taking the weighted average of the competitive factor scores.

As an example, let us consider France Telecom at the end of the crisis year of 2002. In the telecommunications industry the foremost competitive factor is the scale of operations, which provides a good cost position. This is followed by the expanse of service territory (international, domestic, regional) and revenue mix (wireless and wireline, voice, data and

Table 6.2 Default risk score and mapping to a rating

Default risk	Score	Mapping to rating
Very low risk	1	AA
	2	
Low risk	3	A
	4	
Moderate risk	5	BBB
	6	
High risk	7	BB
	8	
Very high risk	9	B
	10	

Table 6.3 Default risk scoring: scoring the business and
financial risk components

Business risk	Score	Financial risk	Score
Very low risk	1	Very conservative	1
	2		2
Low risk	3	Conservative	3
	4		4
Moderate risk	5	Moderate	5
	6		6
High risk	7	Aggressive	7
	8		8
Very high risk	9	Very aggressive	9
	10		10

video, business, and residential).[9] As shown in Table 6.4, France Telecom has a strong cost
position. Given the medium industry risk, this warrants a score of 3 for the cost position.
Thanks to its role as France's historical phone company and its recent acquisitions it has
a very good service territory, warranting a score of 4. It has a well-diversified revenue
mix, with strong positions in all sectors of the telecommunications business although the
acquisitions still need to be integrated, resulting in a score of 5. Since telecommunications
is a medium risk business, a score of 3 is the best that a telecommunications company can
receive. The weighted average business risk score is thus 3.7.

SCORING THE FINANCIAL RISK   The financial risk also needs to be scored, based on the
results of the analysis of the firm's profitability, balance sheet, cash flow adequacy, and
financial flexibility. As with the business risk scoring, each of these factors receives a score
that is weighted to determine an overall financial risk score.

The scores of the profitability, balance sheet, and cash flow adequacy factors are based on
a combination of historical ratios that show the track record and prospective ratios resulting
from a cash flow model. The benchmark ratios for each level of risk are dependent on the
industry and the economic conditions that prevail. The rating agencies regularly publish these
benchmarks. For example, consider Table 6.5 indicating the benchmarks used by Moody's.

Table 6.4 Scoring the business risk of France Telecom

Industry risk: Medium				
Competitive factors	Weighting		Competitive factor scores	Weighted score
Cost position	50%	×	3	= 1.5
Expanse	30%	×	4	= 1.2
Revenue mix	20%	×	5	= 1.0
Total	**100%**			**3.7**

---

[9] Moody's, 2007, Global telecommunications industry: *Rating Methodology*, December, 1–36, pages 11–12.
Although this report is focused on 2007, most key factors have not changed since 2002 except for the need
to provide new services such as video on demand.

Table 6.5 Benchmark free cash flow/debt ratios used by
Moody's in two different industries and for two different years

	Free cash flow/debt ratio		
Telecommunications Industry			
	Aaa	**Baa**	**B**
2007	$\geqslant 25\%$	10–15%	2–6%
2005	$\geqslant 25\%$	10–15%	0–5%
Tobacco Industry			
	Aaa	**Baa**	**B**
2007	$\geqslant 40\%$	10–15%	0–5%
2004	$\geqslant 40\%$	15–15%	0–10%

Source: Moody's, 2007, Global telecommunications industry, *Rating Methodology*: December, 1–36, page 27; Moody's, 2005, Global telecommunications industry, *Rating Methodology*: February, 1–24, page 10; Moody's, 2007, Global tobacco industry, *Rating Methodology*: November, 1–33, page 21; Moody's, 2004, Global cigarette and smokeless tobacco industry, *Rating Methodology*: December, 1–28, page 20.

The lowest risk companies in the tobacco sector have a much higher FCF/Debt ratio than those in the telecommunications industry. However, at the high-risk end of the scale, the telecommunications companies have better ratios. For tobacco companies, the ratios that indicate a given level of risk have become looser from 2004 to 2007, while the opposite has occurred in the telecommunications industry. This shows that the benchmark ratios vary from industry to industry and from year to year.

The score for the financial flexibility ratio is based on more qualitative measures, such as liquidity concerns that develop either from events, predictable or unexpected, possible liquidity sources, and the management of liquidity risks.

The first column of Table 6.8 provides a suggested range of weightings to be given to each of the four main elements of the financial risk score. The cash flow adequacy is weighted the most, unless debt service is very tight, in which case financial flexibility becomes paramount.

Continuing the example of scoring France Telecom we need to strongly weight financial flexibility since France Telecom had an extremely large debt load with a short average maturity. Table 6.6 provides some of France Telecom's key financial ratios in 2002 and the two prior years.

The exceptionally high leverage ratio shows us that France Telecom has taken a very high level of financial risk; however, the strong EBITDA margin shows that assets are performing well although the low return seems to indicate that efficiency improvements can be made.

Comparing the France Telecom ratios to the median 2002 credit statistics from Standards & Poor's, shown in Table 6.7, we see that profitability is equivalent to a moderate financial risk, meriting a score of 5 whereas cash flow adequacy is somewhere between aggressive and very aggressive, meriting a score of 9. Given the exceptional leverage, we assign a score of 10 to the balance sheet. For the qualitative judgment of the financial flexibility of France Telecom, the strong statement of backing and the €9bn shareholder loan from the French government indicate a moderate risk, so we assign a score of 6 for financial flexibility.

We can now go on to determine the weighted financial risk score, shown in Table 6.8, which works out to a score of 6.9.

Table 6.6 Key Financial Ratios of France Telecom

	2002	2001	2000
The balance sheet			
Total debt/total capita	74%	53.1%	48.6%
Profitability			
EBITDA/sales	32.6%	29.2%	32.7%
Free cash flow/sales	6.0%	−3.2%	−23.9%
Return on avg net adjusted permanent capital	5.9%	4.1%	5.9%
Cash flow adequacy			
Debt payback ratios			
Fund from operations/total debt	11.8%	11.1%	11.2%
Operating cash flow/total debt	15.1%	9.7%	9.8%
Free cash flow/total debt	3.6%	−1.9%	−12.0%
Total debt/EBITDA ($\times$)	5.2	5.8	6.1
Payment ratios			
EBITDAR interest and rent coverage ($\times$)	3.1	2.8	n/a
EBITDA gross fixed charge coverage ($\times$)	3.5	3.1	5.0
EBIT gross fixed charge coverage ($\times$)	1.7	1.4	2.4

Source: Ganguin, B., 2006, Standard & Poor's credit ratings and France Telecom, presentation at INSEAD, Fontainebleau – January 12, 2007, 1–37, page 26.

Table 6.7 Standard & Poor's median credit statistics by degree of risk for 2002

	Conservative	Moderate	Aggressive	Very aggressive
Free cash flow/sales	7.7%	5.4%	3.2%	1.9%
Funds from operations/total debt	38%	28.6%	17.9%	10.4%
Free cash flow/total debt	19.9%	11.8%	5.8%	2.2%

Source: Ganguin, B., 2006, Standard & Poor's credit ratings and France Telecom, presentation at INSEAD, Fontainebleau – January 12, 2007, 1–37, page 37.

DETERMINING THE BUSINESS AND FINANCIAL RISK WEIGHTING   With the business and financial risks having been scored, we now pass to the question of the appropriate weighting of these two scores. It is apparent that greater emphasis is put on the financial score as the credit quality worsens. The focus on repaying the interest and principal increases as the risk of default increases. A low business risk allows for more aggressive financial risks to be taken. Table 6.9 provides a gradient of weightings depending on the credit risk of the firm.

LIMITS ON THE CREDIT SCORE FROM COUNTRY RISK AND 'SOFT' FACTORS   The final element before determining the overall credit default score is to consider whether any limits to the final credit score should be applied due to country risk or any overriding 'soft' factors.

The credit score of companies operating in high-risk countries is limited to lower scores, even though a company may deserve a high score on its own merits. This limit does not apply for corporations in low-risk countries or those with a global presence that diversifies their country risk.

Table 6.8 Scoring the financial risk of France Telecom

	Range of weighting	Example weightings		Scores		Weighted score
Profitability	10%–25%	10%	×	5	=	0.5
Balance Sheet	10%–25%	10%	×	10	=	1.0
Cash flow adequacy	10%–50%	20%	×	9	=	1.8
Financial flexibility	30%–70%	60%	×	6	=	3.6
Total	**100%**					**6.9**

Table 6.9 Weighting business risk and financial risk as a function of business risk

Business risk		Business risk weighting		Financial risk weighting
Very low risk	→	50–70%	→	30–50%
Low risk	→	50–60%	→	40–50%
Moderate risk	→	40–50%	→	50–60%
High risk	→	20–40%	→	60–80%
Very high risk	→	10–20%	→	80–90%

Most of the 'soft' factors, such as the quality of management and the aggressiveness of financial policies, are already incorporated into the business and financial risk scores. However, overriding issues, such as poor accounting policy or weak corporate governance, can require a limit to be placed on the overall credit score. In our example, France is a low-risk country and France Telecom under Thierry Breton moved to significantly strengthen its corporate governance with the replacement of Board members from the government with capable French business leaders.

DETERMINING THE FINAL CREDIT SCORE AND MAPPING TO THE RATING SCALE   It is now possible to combine the business and financial risk scores to determine the overall credit default score, taking into account any capping of the credit score based on country risk or other 'soft' factors. Table 6.10 presents the calculation of the overall credit score for France Telecom.

Table 6.10 Determining the final score of France Telecom and mapping to a rating

	Scores		Weighting		Weighted Scores
Business risk	3.7	×	30%	=	1.1
Financial risk	6.9	×	70%	=	4.8
Total			**100%**		**5.9**
'Soft' factor discount	None				
Country risk cap	None				
Final credit score	5.9 → 6	**Mapping to credit rating**			**BBB**

For France Telecom, we have thus determined an overall credit score and mapped it to a corresponding credit rating of BBB. Given the high financial risk of the firm, we have weighted it more than the business risk. However, the support of the French government has mitigated some of the very poor financial ratios and kept the rating within investment grade level.

Having completed the business risk analysis, the financial risk analysis, and determined a globally comparable rating, the following step in a credit rating agency is to convene a credit rating committee and make a final decision of the rating to assign to the company.

B. Determining an Instrument Rating

Having determined the issuer credit rating, which is an expression of the default risk, it is now possible to consider the risk of the individual instruments that have been issued by the firm. The rating of the instruments includes both a consideration of the default risk and of the risk of loss-given-default. As the default risk is of greater importance, the instrument rating is notched from the issuer credit rating based on the recovery expectations. The risk of default has been expressed in the issuer credit rating. The use of a recovery scale along with notching guidelines allows the instrument rating to be based on the issuer credit rating.

THE RECOVERY SCALE AND NOTCHING The first element of determining an instrument rating is the use of a table to score the range of risk of loss-given-default and the associated recovery expectations. Since the primary weight of instrument ratings are on the default risk, the recovery expectations are combined with notching relative to the recovery expectations. Table 6.11 provides a numerical graduation of recovery expectations and corresponding notching.

DETERMINING THE RECOVERY RATING The main element of determining the instrument rating is to score the recovery prospects. The determination of the recovery prospects is discussed in Section 6.1.2. It involves determining the value of the post-default firm for speculative grade firms where the possible paths to default can be envisaged, or using historical observations for instruments issued by investment grade firms that have a low

Table 6.11 Scoring and notching of recovery expectations

			Instrument rating notches	
Risk of loss-given default	Recovery expectations	Recovery score	Investment grade issuer	Speculative grade issuer
Very low risk	90–100%	1	+2	+3
Low risk	70–90%	2	+1	+2
Moderately low risk	50–70%	3	+1	+1
Average risk	30–50%	4	0	0
High risk	10–30%	5	−1	−1
Very high risk	0–10%	6	−2	−2

Table 6.12 Scoring the Recovery Expectations of Debt Obligations

Current issuer credit rating: **B**
Estimated enterprise value in scenario of default: $100 mn

Priority ranking	Type of claim	Claims amount (million)	Expected time to recovery	Expected recovery	Recovery score
Privileged	Post-bankruptcy fees, wages and taxes	$10mn	<6 months	100%	1
Secured	Secured loan	$30mn	<30 months	100%	1
Unsecured	Unsecured debt, suppliers	$90mn	>30 months	67%	3
Subordinated	Subordinated debt	$30mn	>30 months	0%	6

probability of default. The expected recovery of a given instrument will depend on its priority ranking and the value of the firm available for recovery for instruments of its class. To illustrate with an example, let's consider the case of a company with a speculative grade credit ranking of B which has $150 mn worth of debt spread over the three standard classes of debt and whose enterprise value in the case of default has been determined to be only $100 mn. Table 6.12 provides an example of the recovery score and the mapping to an instrument rating.

In Table 6.12, the enterprise value in a default situation of $100 mn is enough to pay off the privileged and the secured creditors entirely, which gives them a recovery score of 1. The 67% expected recovery of the unsecured debt gives it a recovery score of 3.

NOTCHING TO THE INSTRUMENT RATINGS The final step is to determine the instrument ratings, based on the recovery scores. This is done by notching up or down from the issuer credit rating. Table 6.13 provides an example of mapping instruments with recovery scores to an instrument rating.

THE 'CURRENCY' OF CREDIT RATINGS The transformation of the credit analysis into credit ratings for the issuer and the instruments issued provides a common standard by which to measure and compare the relative credit risks of different investments. A scoring system, such as the one described above, is used by the credit rating agencies to achieve this. The risk of default is rated using the issuer credit rating, and the instrument credit rating consists of a combination of the risk of default and the recovery rating.

Table 6.13 Notching the debt obligations

Current issuer credit rating: **B** (speculative grade)

Debt instrument	Recovery score	Degree of notching	Instrument rating
Secured loan	1	+3	**BB**
Unsecured debt	3	+1	**B+**
Subordinated debt	6	−2	**CCC+**

6.2   CORPORATE RATINGS IMPLIED BY MARKET DATA

> *Traditional credit analysis is not necessary. This is not because future prospects of the firm are not of primary importance – they most definitely are. It is because an assessment, based on all currently available information of the company's future, has already been made by the aggregate of market participants, and reflected in the firm's current market value.*[10]

6.2.1   The Concept

Assessing default risk deals with predicting the default probability of an issuer. And the business of doing this exploded after Oldrich Vasicek published at KMV in 1984 his philosophy and model of credit valuation.[11] His idea was that 'credit risk should be measured in terms of probabilities and mathematical expectations, rather than assessed by qualitative ratings. When performed in this manner, we can refer to a credit valuation model.'[12] This was a real notice to the credit rating agencies who until then had been reluctant to link their scales to mathematical probabilities. In fact, it is fair to say that in the 1980s corporate credit analysis was viewed as an art and not a science. Credit analysts lacked a way to adequately quantify default risk. They were ranking instruments and issuers in terms of relative default likelihood, but they were not assigning absolute default probabilities to either. This was going to change.

Vasicek continued with his summons that 'a credit valuation model requires a theory that describes the causality between the attributes of the borrowing entity (a corporation) and its potential bankruptcy ... This model should be consistent with modern financial theory, particularly with option pricing theory.[13] Now, this could be revolutionary. Traditionally, credit analysis has been the job of accountants, lawyers, CFAs, and credit officers. Bringing in financial theory sounds very academic, a way to open the field of credit analysis to financial economists. Even worse, throwing in option pricing theory could open the gates to the credit rating agencies to engineers, mathematicians, and physicists. This is exactly what has happened to the gates of efficient frontier securities dealing rooms and equity portfolio management firms in the wake of Black and Scholes, 1973 publication of their option pricing model based on the economic concept of equilibrium and on the cross market forces of profit-seeking arbitrage that impose it on prices. Could a similar invasion threaten the desks of credit analysts and the bottom line of incumbent credit rating agencies?

It sounded like it, if we further follow Vasicek. 'The various liabilities of a firm are claims on the firm's value, which often take the form of options.'[14] The 'theory provides means to determine the value of each of the claims, and consequently allows one to price the firm's debt.' Throwing the uses of option pricing theory in the toolkit for evaluating bankruptcy risk was really encroaching on the turf of the credit rating agencies. This was threatening. Just as Markowitz's mean variance theory of optimal portfolio

---

[10] Vasicek, O.A., 1984, Credit valuation, White Paper: KMV Corporation, March 22, 1–16, page 1.

[11] Vasicek, O.A., 1984, Credit valuation, White Paper: KMV Corporation, March 22, 1–16.

[12] Vasicek, O.A., 1984, Credit valuation, White Paper: KMV Corporation, March 22, 1–16, page 1.

[13] See Black, F., and Scholes, M., 1973, The pricing of options and corporate liabilities, *Journal of Political Economy*, May-June, Vol. 81, Issue 3, 637–654.

[14] See Merton, R., 1974, On the pricing of corporate debt: the risk structure of interest rates, *Journal of Finance*, May, Vol. 29, Issue 2, 449–470.

construction and Linter's capital asset pricing models were to the relevance of traditional portfolio advisers. Or as Fama's theory of market efficiency and Sharpe's theory of betas to indexes and measures of portfolio performance were to active portfolio management. Or as Modigliani and Miller to traditional corporate finance. Or Black and Scholes to traditional option trading. Or as Merton to the traditional corporate finance departments at investment banks.[15]

But the extension for what these tools could be used became an actual warning shot to the credit rating agencies.

> If the credit model provides a realistic description of the relationship between the state of the firm and the probability of default on its obligations, it will also reflect the development in the borrower's credit standing through time. This means that the model can be used to monitor changes and give an early warning of potential deterioration of credit. Obviously this is only possible if the model is based on current, rather than historical, measurements. It also implies that the relevant variables are the actual market values rather than accounting values.[16]

Vasicek's direct hit at the credit rating agencies came in his next paragraph. This

> means parting ways with some of the traditional credit analysis, involving detailed examination of the company's operations, projection of cash flows, and assessment of the future earning power of the firm. Such analysis is not necessary. This is not because future prospects of the firm are not of primary importance – they most definitely are. It is because an assessment, based on all currently available information of the company's future, has already been made by the aggregate of market participants, and reflected in the firm's current market value . . . We do not assume that this assessment is accurate in the sense that its implicit forecasts of future prospects will be realized. We only assume that any one person or institution is unlikely to arrive at superior valuation.[17]

This was a bomb with impact similar to the claims that traditional equity financial analysts were redundant in most cases because they failed to lead to investment strategies that outperformed the market. Indexers started to take market share from active managers.

Then follows the core of his approach.

> The most junior claim on the firm's assets is equity. If the future earnings of the corporation start looking better or worse than before, the stock price will be the first to reflect the changing prospects. Our challenge is to properly interpret the changing share prices.[18]

Interesting technological innovations often break into existing industries because entrepreneurial new entrants successfully create new business that incumbents notice too

---

[15] Some investment banks had such deeply ingrained liberal arts, lawyers and accountants culture in their corporate finance departments still in the beginning of the 1990s that they rapidly lost commercial relevance and were taken over by state of the art rivals. When one of us was called in with a team of other academics from INSEAD to mentally recycle the prevailing such mindsets at one of the more prominent investment banks and held a couple of sessions explaining that corporate finance was all about options, he was almost thrown out of the classroom. Eventually, many of the participants were thrown out of their job after the bank was taken over.

[16] Vasicek, O.A., 1984, Credit valuation, White Paper: KMV Corporation, March 22, 1–16, page 1.

[17] Vasicek, O.A., 1984, Credit valuation, White Paper: KMV Corporation, March 22, 1–16, page 1.

[18] Vasicek, O.A., 1984, Credit valuation, White Paper: KMV Corporation, March 22, 1–16, page 2.

late because they are busy fighting their existing rivals. And so it happened in the credit agency business with the start-up KMV. Eventually, Moody's Investors Services decided to use a Merton approach to predict default which became the *de facto* standard for default-risk measurement in the world of credit risk.[19, 20]

6.2.2   Mechanics of Extracting Default Probabilities from Market Prices[21]

The most widely used model to extract default probabilities from market prices, in this case equity prices, is Moody's KMV model and the Expected Default Frequency it generates. It has become a useful tool applied by many financial institutions as it provides a fairly rapid feedback about the quality of a firm's credit. The commonly referred to KMV model is based on Merton's (1974) credit valuation model, itself based on the Black and Scholes (1973) option pricing model. The theoretical model generating the cardinal measure of probability of default, or commercially available EDF[TM] measure is the Vasicek–Kealhofer (V-K) model (Vasicek 1984; Kealhofer 2003a, 2003b). The KMV model is, strictly speaking, the (proprietary) model used by Moody's KMV, previously KMV Corporation. There are many adjustments in the implementation of the KMV model compared to the purely theoretical Vasicek-Kealhofer model.

There are now several extensions and academic research improving on the basic V–K model. Early V–K models where found to underestimate observed spreads, but the inclusion of jumps in asset values and liquidity premia seem to improve the ability of these types of models to explain both observed credit spreads and default probabilities.[22] There has been a debate as to the relevance of each type of model. It should really depend on the quality of the data available and the application of the credit risk model.[23]

In this section we focus on the basic V–K model in its publicly available version. We first pursue an explanation of the main intuition behind the model; we then review the theoretical analytics, using the simple Black–Scholes approach to get asset volatility and value; and finally we apply the model to our France Telecom case.

---

[19] See Kealhofer, S., 2003. Quantifying credit risk I: default prediction, *Financial Analysts Journal*, January–February, 30–44, page 30.

[20] See Cass, D., 2000, Moody's launches risk model, *Risk*, June, Vol. 13, No. 6, 14–15.

[21] This section draws on Crosbie, P., and Bohn, J., 2003, *Modeling Default Risk*, Moody's KMV, December 18, 1–31

[22] This literature is known as that of 'structural models', as it seeks to extract default probabilities from the market's assessments of firm asset value. In structural models the time to default is predictable, whereas in the models known as 'reduced form', it is inaccessible. There has been a debate as to the relevance and performance of each type of model. The relevance of either type really depends on the quality of the data available and the application of the credit risk model. The structural model is mostly useful for practitioners in the credit portfolio and credit risk management fields. The economic interpretation of the key variables (asset volatility as a proxy for business risk, market's assessment of enterprise value and leverage) of the models allows for corporate transaction analysis. In the credit trading arena, many practitioners have tended to use reduced form models for the greater mathematical tractability.

[23] For further references on structural and reduced form models, for empirical performance see Arora, N., Bohn, J.R., and Zhu, F., 2005, Reduced form vs. structural models of credit risk: a case study of three models, Moody's K.M.V., February 17, 1–39, and for a theoretical comparison refer to: Jarrow, R.A., and Protter, P., 2004, Structural versus reduced form models: a new information based perspective, *Journal of Investment Management*, second quarter, Vol. 2, No. 2, 1–10.

Principles underlying the KMV model

- Equity is a call option on the firm's assets with strike price equal to book value of liabilities. This link can be inverted to obtain the asset value and the asset volatility using only a time series of equity observations. It is important that the procedure only necessitates the book value of liabilities but not the market values, because the latter is hardly ever available in practice.
- The book value of liabilities defines the *default point* – the actual cash liabilities that the company has promised to repay. If the value of the underlying security (assets) exceeds the strike price (company debts) at maturity, then the option will be exercised and the value to the option holder (stockholders) will be equal to the excess amount of assets over debt. Otherwise the company is in default.
- The *distance to default* (DD) is calculated as the number of standard deviations between expected asset value and the default point (a cardinal measure).
- Finally, based on extensive historical data (compiled by KMV), and not a theoretical distribution, DD is matched to an actual default frequency.

The resulting cardinal measure is called EDF™ – Expected Default Frequency. EDF measures are actual probabilities of default; they lend themselves to decision making and can be incorporated into valuation and portfolio models.

There are essentially three steps to determine the default probability of a firm: (1) estimate asset value and volatily, (2) calculate the distance-to-default, and (3) calculate the default probability corresponding to the distance to default.

1. *Estimating asset value and volatility:* When the market price of equity is available, the market value and volatility of assets can be determined directly using an options, pricing based approach, which recognizes equity as a call option on the firm's net worth, with a strike price equal to the book value of the firm's liabilities and with same maturity. Hence, in practice, the solution to the following system of simultaneous equations

$$
\begin{bmatrix} \text{Equity value} \\ \text{Equity volatility} \end{bmatrix} = \text{OptionFunction} \left(\begin{bmatrix} \text{Asset} \\ \text{value} \end{bmatrix}, \begin{bmatrix} \text{Asset} \\ \text{volatility} \end{bmatrix}, \begin{bmatrix} \text{Capital} \\ \text{structure} \end{bmatrix}, \begin{bmatrix} \text{Interest} \\ \text{rate} \end{bmatrix} \right)
$$

yields our values for asset value and volatility.

2. *Calculating distance-to-default DD.* There are six variables that determine the default probability of a firm over some horizon, from now until time H: (1) the current asset value, (2) the distribution of the asset value at time H, (3) the volatility of the future assets value at time H, (4) the level of the default point, the book value of the liabilities, (5) the expected rate of growth in the asset value over the horizon, (6) the length of the horizon, H.

   The asset value and asset volatility are estimated in the first step and the time horizon is defined by the analyst. The expected growth rate of assets has little discriminating power in terms of predicting default. The future asset distribution and the level of the default point are the critical variables in this step.

   If the value of the assets falls below the default point, then the firm defaults. Therefore, the probability of default is the probability that the asset value will fall below the default point. This is the shaded area EDF on Figure 6.2, below the default point on the

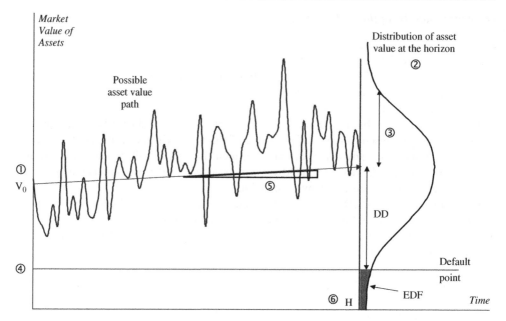

Figure 6.2   Asset value path and distance to default.
Source: Crosbie, Page, and Bohn, J., 2003, Modeling default risk, Moody's KMV, December 18, page 13.

distribution of assets at time H. If the distribution of the distance to default were known, then the probability of default would simply be the likelihood that the distance to default is zero or negative. The usual normal or lognormal distributions be used, as changes in asset value and changes in leverage (hence change in default point) are correlated.[24]

Distance to default is measured as the number of standard deviations the asset value is away from default:

$$[\text{Distance to default}] = \frac{[\text{Market value of assets}] - [\text{Default point}]}{[\text{Market value of assets}][\text{Asset volatility}]}$$

3. *Calculating the default probability corresponding to the distance to default.* Moody's KMV estimate the relationship between distance to default and default probability from their data on historical default and bankruptcy. For instance, to determine the default probability over the next year of a firm that is 7 standard deviations away from default, take the proportion of the firms that defaulted in the following year that were 7 standard deviations from default. This is about 0.05%.[25]

---

[24] This is one of the reasons why the distribution of distance to default really has fat tails.

[25] MKMV database covers firms with sales exceeding $300 million in order for the database to be uniform. This is due to the problem of information availability, as well as higher flexibility of smaller firms in 'concealing' default. Debt repayment with stock or cash injections by owners is not uncommon For more information on this see Dwyer, D., and Qu, Shisheng, 2007, EDF™ 8.0 Model Enhancements, Moody's KMV, January, 1–36, page 23.

The Basic Theoretical Model using the Simple Black–Scholes (BS) Model

The probability of default is the probability that the market value of the firm's assets will be less than the book value of the firm's liabilities by the time the debt matures:

$$p_t = \Pr\lfloor V_A^t \leqslant X_t | V_A^0 = V_A \rfloor = \Pr\lfloor \ln V_A^t \leqslant \ln X_t | V_A^0 = V_A \rfloor \tag{6.1}$$

where p_t = the probability of default by time t,
V_A^t = the market value of the firm's assets at time t, and
X_t = the book value of the firm's liabilities due at time t.

It can be assumed that the change in the value of the firm's assets is described by the following stochastic process: $dV_A = \mu V_A \, dt + \sigma_A V_A \, dz$, where dz is a Wiener process. Thus the value at time t, V_A^t given that the value at time 0 is V_A, is given by the equation:

$$\ln V_A^t = \ln V_A + \left(\mu - \frac{\sigma_A^2}{2}\right) t + \sigma_A \sqrt{t} \varepsilon \tag{6.2}$$

where μ = the expected return on the firm's asset,
σ_A = the standard deviation of asset returns,
ε = the random component of the firm's return.

The relationship given by the above equation describes the evolution in the asset value path that is shown in Figure 6.2. Combining (6.1) and (6.2) we can write the probability of default as:

$$p_t = \Pr\left[\ln V_A + \left(\mu - \frac{\sigma_A^2}{2}\right) t + \sigma_A \sqrt{t} \varepsilon \leqslant \ln X_t\right] \tag{6.3}$$

After rearranging,

$$p_t = \Pr\left[-\frac{\ln \dfrac{V_A}{X_t} + \left(\mu - \dfrac{\sigma_A^2}{2}\right) t}{\sigma_A \sqrt{t}} \geqslant \varepsilon\right] \tag{6.4}$$

The BS model assumes that the random component of the firm's asset returns is normally distributed, $\varepsilon \sim N(0, 1)$ and as a result we can define the default probability in terms of the cumulative Normal distribution, Φ

$$p_t = \Phi\left[-\frac{\ln \dfrac{V_A}{X_t} + \left(\mu - \dfrac{\sigma_A^2}{2}\right) t}{\sigma_A \sqrt{t}}\right] \tag{6.5}$$

Recall that the distance to default is simply the number of standard deviations that the firm is away from default and thus in the BS world it is given by:

$$DD = \frac{\ln \dfrac{V_A}{X_t} + \left(\mu - \dfrac{\sigma_A^2}{2} \right) t}{\sigma_A \sqrt{t}} \tag{6.6}$$

At this stage the key question is how to get the value of V_A, μ and σ_A.

The option nature of equity is used to derive the market value and volatility of the firm's underlying assets implied by the equity's market value. The BS model allows only two types of liabilities, a single class of debt and a single class of equity. If X is the book value of the debt which is due at time T then the market value of equity and the market value of assets are related by the following expression:

$$V_E = V_A \Phi(d_1) - e^{-rT} X \Phi(d_2) \tag{6.7}$$

where, V_E is the market value of the firm's equity,

$$d_1 = \frac{\ln \left(\dfrac{V_A}{X} \right) + \left(r + \dfrac{\sigma_A^2}{2} \right) T}{\sigma_A \sqrt{T}} \tag{6.8}$$

$$d_2 = d_1 - \sigma_A \sqrt{T} \tag{6.9}$$

and r is the risk-free interest rate.

Also, deriving (6.7) and taking the expectation yields the following relationship between equity and asset volatility:

$$\sigma_E = \frac{V_A}{V_E} \Phi(d_1) \sigma_A \tag{6.10}$$

Equations (6.7) and (6.10) can be solved simultaneously to obtain the implied asset volatility and the asset value which can then be used to compute the distance to default DD. Note that equations (6.7) and (6.10) are the specific BS equivalent of the general simultaneous equations from in the previous section.

Remarks on Essential Enhancements in the KMV Model over the Black–Scholes–Merton Model

A word of caution about practical implementations of (6.10). It represents a snapshot of the equity and asset values, and hence of the leverage. In rapidly changing circumstances (new debt issues, debt repurchases, etc.) the relationship can over- or underestimate the actual asset volatility. Moody's KMV uses an iterative procedure which starts with a reasonable guess of asset volatility and uses this volatility to back out the asset values. Then it computes a new iterate for the volatility by computing the volatility of the implied asset values. After a couple of iterations this procedure usually converges. Further, there is an unspecified Bayesian correction toward size, industry, and country averages.[26]

While the basic Black-Scholes–Merton model assumes a single liability and no dividends or other cash payouts, the KMV model is much less constrained in that it allows for different types of equity (e.g. preferred stock on top of common stock), as well as warrants and convertible debt. Dividends and other payouts are allowed. Note that default is considered as a companywide event, i.e. when in default, the company defaults on all its obligations.

In the original BS–Merton model default occurs only at the defined horizon and equity is a call option on assets, expiring at the maturity of debt. In the V–K model default can also occur before the defined horizon and equity is a perpetual call option on the assets.

In the V–K model the default point is empirically determined whereas in the basic framework the default point is defined as total liabilities. Based upon empirical analysis, KMV has found that the most frequent default point is at a value equal appoximately to current liabilities plus 50% of long-term liabilities. We call this default point the Moody's default point.

Finally, the essential advantage and commercial value-added from the KMV model is that the distribution of the distance to default is empirically determined from calibration to historical data.

Extracting France Telecom's EDFs

We now present the EDF on France Telecom's bonds. Following its IPO in 1997 and the opening of European telecommunications market, France Telecom embarked on an acquisition program. To finance acquisitions the company turned to capital markets. The task was somewhat facilitated by rising stock prices. Following the end of the internet bubble, however, the market changed its view of France Telecom.

Exhibit 6.8 shows the historical redemption yield and credit spread over time for the France Telecom Long-Term Bond 1993–2006 6.25%. The Equivalent Benchmark Bond Yield (EBBY) is also shown on the same graph for comparison and to show the credit spread over the same time period. As seen on Exhibit 6.8, spreads are stable from January 1999 to May 2000, after which they start to widen. The spreads narrow down to a stable range in June 2003. The interval between January 1999 and June 2003 marks a period of high uncertainty for FT due to growing leverage and a stock market crash in 2002.

The leverage was increased due to the debt increase by FT to finance its growth plan through acquisitions: July 1999, NTL acquisition; March 2000, Mobilcom acquisition; March 2000, Orange acquisition; July 2000, Wind acquisition; and end 2000, Equant acquisition.

Exhibit 6.9 shows the historical rating actions of Moody's on FT since December 1997. From a rating of Aa1, FT is downgraded all the way to Baa3 between December 1999 and June 2002. The increase in leverage along with the erosion of FT equity market value contributes to this. One can also observe the MKMV Translation EDF on the left Y-Axis. This is a translation of the Moody's equivalent rating to the KMV Expected Default Frequency (probability of default).

---

[26] Crosbie, P., and Bohn, J., 2003, *Modeling Default Risk*, Moody's KMV, December 18, 1–31, page 17. Barath, S., and Shumway, T., 2008. Forecasting Default with the KMV-Merton Model, Review of Financial Studies, Vol.21, No.3, May, 1333–1369, Working Paper, December 17, page 17 describes the iterative procedure and the SAS code that they use to compute both asset volatility and value.

Exhibit 6.8   FT 1993–2006 6.25% and credit spread

Source: Thomson Datastream.

Exhibit 6.10 shows the relationship between Moody's ratings and the EDF that we computed, as explained in the appendix at the end of this chapter. This figure is based on Moody's definition of default point, and on the assumption of normal asset returns, as in Equation (6.5). The latter assumption explains the extended periods of zero default probability. A calculation based on the historical default frequencies would have provided more realistic values. Nevertheless, the example demonstrates the power of the method to highlight in a timely manner the increasing risk of default.

Our estimated EDF peaks at 78.14% probability of default while the rating during the same time, although the worst in the history of FT, shows significantly lower default probability (0.18%). Between June 2002 and March 2003 the EDF indicates a very high probability of default while the ratings do not change. Moody's changed its outlook to stable following the publication of a communiqué by the French government, stating that it will assist with the implementation of a financial restructuring plan of FT, and that it will participate in a future capital injection. Furthermore the government has stated that it will support FT if a liquidity problem emerges.

Conclusion

EDFs are cardinal measures that provide an estimate of a probability of default based on the equity value of the firms. Hence, the EDF of a given firm changes with its equity price.

Exhibit 6.9 FT ratings history

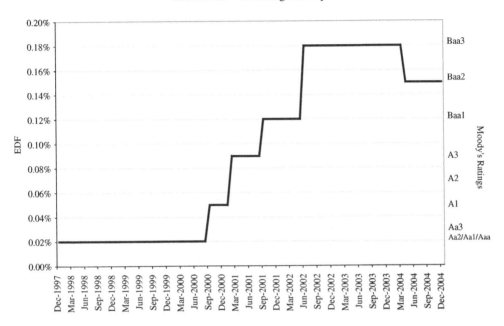

Exhibit 6.10 FT estimated EDF, assuming Normal asset returns

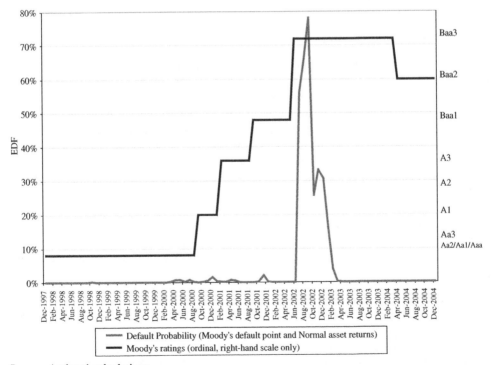

Source: Authors' calculations

This makes EDFs very volatile, but also very timely. The key characteristics that drive the demand for EDFs are its cardinality and its timeliness. EDFs being estimates of default probabilities, they are easily incorporated into different valuation models. Moreover, the timeliness of EDFs is especially useful to manage the dynamics of risk and to measure credit risk correlations. As a direct consequence of the timeliness of the EDF measure, at a given point in time, EDFs are better predictors of default than other measures. Moody's KMV is now at least in the fifth generation of the V–K model and as it has learned over time from empirical data and performance results, it has been able to improve and calibrate the model even better. According to Korablev–Dwyer (2007) MKMV EDF credit measures consistently perform better in terms of timeliness, default predictive power and level than agency ratings (S&P and Moody's), Merton's structural model and Altman's Z-score.[27]

However, it is important to bear in mind that EDF measures are totally dependent on stock prices (and book value of liabilities) for its information content. They assume a direct link between market values and default probabilities. The EDF model does not try to explicitly predict or forecast future events as agency ratings do, its predictive power relies on the fact that the current value of the firm is a good predictor of future value. Asset volatility is a measure of business risk; it reflects the uncertainty around market value of the business and the degree of difficulty in forecasting future cash flows. Three drivers are behind a public firm's probability of default: the market value of its assets, its volatility, and its current capital structure. Distance to default is an ordinal measure and, according to the KMV model, contains all the relevant information to determine relative default risk across companies. Any industry, geography, and firm size effects are incorporated via the asset value and volatility. The mapping of distances to default to EDF credit measures is essentially built on listed defaults in the United States.[28]

6.2.3 Market-Implied Ratings

Market-implied ratings (or MIRs) are all ratings derived from market data. These are essentially ratings implied by equity prices, as described extensively above, ratings implied by bond spreads, and ratings implied by credit default swap (CDS) spreads.[29]

The idea underlying these measures is to extract a market-based measure of creditworthiness from the signal given by bond and CDS spreads and equity prices. The relation between ratings and bond spreads is examined in more detail in Section 7.1. A CDS is, by definition, an insurance contract against a default by a given company or sovereign entity. The CDS spread is the cost per year for protection against a default by the company. Hence CDS prices are a fairly direct indicator of credit risk.

In practice, there are four main types of methodologies using bond price data, CDS data or equity data. First there is a simple mapping of spreads of instruments with a given rating to identify a range of spreads, which then determines a market-implied rating, based on the observed spread. Another methodology is regression analysis which captures, among others,

---

[27] Korablev, I., and Dwyer, D., 2007, Power and level validation of Moody's KMV EDF credit measures in North America, Europe and Asia, September 10, 1–56.

[28] Crosbie, P., and Bohn, J., 2003, *Modeling Default Risk*, Moody's KMV, December 18, 1–321, 3, 1339–1369 page 21.

[29] In practice the main global rating agencies now offer explicitly market implied ratings: Fitch Ratings, 2007, Fitch CDS Implied Ratings Model, June 13, *Research Special Report*; Fitch Ratings, 2007, Fitch Equity Implied Rating and Probability of Default Model, June 13, *Research Special Report*; Moody's Investors Service, 2005, An Explanation of Market Implied Ratings, November, 1–19.

observed relations between spread, recovery, industry, and rating. And finally, reduced-form or structural models, as discussed previously.

Uses

Market-implied ratings essentially are used as an early warning or surveillance tool; they have been compared to the canary in the coalmine. There are essentially three types of uses: identification of default candidates, prediction of rating changes, and relative value analysis. A lot of the information is given by differences between an issuer's implied rating and actual rating. Indeed the implied rating brings all market information relevant to creditworthiness on a rating scale that compares with fundamental ratings. Market-implied ratings can help to identify default candidates earlier as default rates are known to be significantly higher for issuers whose securities trade with negative gaps compared to their fundamental rating. A relative value analysis is most useful for fund managers and traders as it can be used as a signal that a bond may rise or fall against a broader market index. In essence, MIRs help market participants to pick out the important information in the market concerning creditworthiness.[30]

An interesting question is whether it is important that the creditworthiness information in market prices be expressed on the same scale as a fundamental rating or whether it would be better expressed as a probability of default. Obviously, the leading fundamental rating firms have an economic interest in expressing them on the same scale as their traditional ratings, but an argument in favor of expressing them on the same scale is that MIR rather than probability of defaults are less volatile and fundamental ratings even less so. For instance: 'around 90% of Moody's market implied ratings change in the course of one year, and some 76% reverse that move during the next 12 months. By comparison around 20% of Moody's ratings change throughout a year, with a reversal rate of just 1%.'[31] If one admits that fundamental ratings are accurate and represent the deeper and stable trends of creditworthiness, expressing default probabilities on the same scale helps to identify transient variations from more fundamental ones.

Clarifying the Differences

With mathematical creativity and rigor, Vasicek made many highly valuable contributions to our understanding of credit valuation and of the probabilities of loss of an issuer or a whole portfolio of them. Nevertheless, his recommendations to part with traditional credit analysis and fundamental ratings are based on three regrettable flaws in thinking.

Firstly, Vasicek confounds the measurement of risk with the appetite for risk. Stock prices do not only reflect expectations of free cash flow, but also the market price for risk at which they are being discounted. Prices are different beasts from risk analysis. They play as much in the field of appetite for risk as in the field of risk measurement. Credit analysis plays only in the field of risk measurement.

Secondly, the purpose of credit analysis is not to achieve superior valuation; it is to produce relevant insight in the lasting downside characteristics of free cash flow distributions.

---

[30] *Credit*, 2006, Upgrading the rating process, October, 1–6.
[31] *Credit*, 2006, Upgrading the rating process, October, page 5.

Thirdly, changes in information do indeed tend to lead to changes in prices. But there is another side to the coin, which is that prices occasionally change independently of changes in information.

Conclusion

We find that fundamental ratings and MIR really are complements and not substitutes. They have different purposes and so their respective performance should be measured in the light of their purposes. As we have explained in Chapter 3: fundamental ratings provide consistent, across all issues, contractible measures of creditworthiness and hence require a certain stability. Market-based measures also aim to measure default probability, but they have no stability constraints and as they are based just on publicly available information and market prices, they are much more volatile. They do not have the same contractibility (in the economic sense) feature as they are not publicly observable. Interestingly, Löffler (2007) finds that when it comes to default prediction the optimal combination of agency credit ratings and quantitative estimates of default risk is to put equal weight on both measures. His results show that each measure provides information not contained in the other. The value of ratings increases with the forecast horizon, as agencies employ a long-term horizon, but it decreases with decreasing credit quality. Indeed, the higher a company's default risk, the more important short-term developments are for its survival. Notwithstanding this, combining EDFs with ratings still increases the accuracy ratios.[32]

6.3 SPECIAL SECTOR RATINGS

6.3.1 Sovereign Ratings

As previously seen, the demand for sovereign credit ratings – the risk assessments assigned by the rating agencies to the debt obligations of governments – has increased dramatically in recent years as ever more governments seek a rating in order to ease their access, and the access of companies domiciled within their borders, to the international capital markets.

Credit rating agencies rate the risk that sovereign governments may default on their debt obligations to private creditors, in particular those issued in the capital markets. As with corporate ratings, sovereign ratings measure the ability and willingness to repay in full and on time. However, the sovereign credit ratings do not relate to public creditors such as other governments, the IMF, or the World Bank; nor do they apply to payments to suppliers of the sovereign government.

A sovereign entity has, by definition, freedom from a higher authority, which gives it characteristics that make it unique from other entities that borrow from the capital markets. Sovereign governments can change the rules that apply to entities within their jurisdiction (risk of interference) and cannot be forced to respect 'outside' rules (risk of indifference).[33] Thus, CRAs consider qualitative factors to evaluate the willingness to repay debt.

---

[32] Löffler, G., 2007, The complementary nature of ratings and market-based measures of default risk, *Journal of Fixed Income*, summer, 38–47.
[33] Truglia, V., and Cailleteau, Page, 2006, A guide to Moody's sovereign ratings, *Special Comment*: Moody's Investors Service August, 1–10, page 1.

LOCAL CURRENCY AND FOREIGN CURRENCY RATINGS   Sovereign credit ratings exist in both foreign currency and local currency ratings. The servicing of local currency debt obligations of a sovereign are met through its powers of taxation and its control of the monetary and financial systems. Foreign currency debt, in contrast, must be serviced by obtaining foreign exchange, usually through exchanging local currency on the currency markets, although some governments can obtain foreign currency directly through their control of the country's commodity resources. Since governments have more means at their disposal for repaying local currency debt, the ratings on local currency debt are at least at the same level as the ratings on foreign currency debt.

Sovereign Rating Analysis

Sovereign credit rating decisions are made by a rating committee, just as for corporate credit ratings. Sovereign ratings are even less of an exact science than a corporate bond rating.

The Philippines saw borrowing costs rise in July 2005 when Moody's became the third major credit rating agency to downgrade the country's sovereign debt outlook. Moody's downgraded its B1 long-term foreign and local currency ratings from stable to negative. The downgrade was blamed on the uncertain political climate and the fact that the Philippines had suspended changes to its Value Added Tax that would have helped the government to curb its budget deficit. Legislators had attempted to raise VAT rates from 10% to 12% and expand the number of items covered by VAT, but a legal challenge had postponed the introduction of the new rates. Eventually, the Philippine High Court approved the VAT increases in October 2005 and the new rates came into effect in November that year. An analyst speaking to the BBC pointed out that, 'the higher VAT will raise the chances of the Philippines getting an upgrade from credit rating agencies.' In February 2006, Fitch revised long-term issuer default and local currency long-term issuer default ratings back to stable, and upgraded the country ceiling to BB+ in August 2006.[34]

The nature of sovereign ratings involves the use of a whole range of qualitative factors added to a variety of quantitative indicators. Exhibit 6.11 shows the variables listed by S&P as being key determinants of a sovereign rating.

Sovereign credit ratings are broadly consistent with macroeconomic fundamentals. Of the large number of criteria used, it has been determined that 90% of the variation in sovereign credit ratings could be explained by six factors.[35] These factors are:

- GDP per capita on a purchasing power basis
- Real GDP growth
- Inflation rate
- External debt relative to export earnings
- Level of economic development (i.e. whether classified as industrialized by the IMF or not)
- Default history (whether has defaulted since 1970 or not on international bank debt).

---

[34] BBC News, 2005, Philippines' credit woes escalate, July 13.

[35] Cantor, R., and Packer F., 1996, Determinants and impact of sovereign credit ratings, FRBNY *Economic Policy Review*, October, 37–53.

Exhibit 6.11   Summary determinants of sovereign ratings at S&P (2004)

1. *Political risk*
   - Stability and legitimacy of political institutions
   - Popular participation in political processes
   - Orderliness of leadership succession
   - Transparency in economic policy decisions and objectives
   - Public security
   - Geopolitical risk

2. *Income and economic structure*
   - Prosperity, diversity, and degree to which economy is market-oriented
   - Income disparities
   - Effectiveness of financial sector in intermediating funds; availability of credit
   - Competitiveness and profitability of non-financial private sector
   - Efficiency of public sector
   - Protectionism and other non-market influences
   - Labor flexibility

3. *Economic growth prospects*
   - Size and composition of savings and investment
   - Rate and pattern of economic growth

4. *Fiscal flexibility*
   - General government revenue, expenditure, and surplus/deficit trends
   - Revenue-raising flexibility and efficiency
   - Expenditure effectiveness and pressures
   - Timeliness, coverage, and transparency in reporting
   - Pension obligations

5. *General government debt burden*
   - General government gross and net (of assets) debt as a percent of GDP
   - Share of revenue devoted to interest
   - Currency composition and maturity profile
   - Depth and breadth of local capital markets

6. *Offshore and contingent liabilities*
   - Size and health of nonfinancial public-sector enterprises
   - Robustness of financial sector

7. *Monetary flexibility*
   - Price behavior in economic cycles
   - Money and credit expansion
   - Compatibility of exchange-rate regime and monetary goals
   - Institutional factors such as central bank independence
   - Range and efficiency of monetary policy tools

8. *External liquidity*
   - Impact of fiscal and monetary policies on external accounts
   - Structure of the current account
   - Composition of capital flows
   - Reserve adequacy

Exhibit 6.11 (*continued*)

---

9. *Public-sector external debt burden*
- Gross and net public-sector external debt, including structured debt, as a percent of current account receipts
- Maturity profile, currency composition, and sensitivity to interest rate changes
- Access to concessional funding
- Debt service burden

10. *Private-sector external debt burden*
- Gross and net financial sector or external debt, including deposits and structured debt, as a percent of current account receipts
- Gross and net non-financial private sector external debt, including structured debt, as a percent of current account receipts
- Maturity profile, currency composition, and sensitivity to interest rate changes
- Access to concessional funding

Source: Beers, D.T., and Cavanaugh, M., 2005, Sovereign credit ratings: A primer, *Research*: Standard & Poor's, September 27, 1–17, Table 1, page 3.

The remaining variance corresponds to the qualitative judgment exercised by the CRAs. Indeed, a study of the rating actions of the two major CRAs around the East Asian financial crisis of 1997–1998 compared the ratings predicted by macroeconomic factors with the actual ratings to test the claim that CRAs had exaggerated the cycle by being originally too enthusiastic and then too pessimistic during the crisis.[36] In fact, foreign currency sovereign credit ratings proved to be sticky, correctly rating the crisis but remaining over-conservative after the crisis. The CRAs thus acted with inertia but did not overreact.

Cantor and Packer found that the opinions of the rating agencies independently affect market spreads, particularly for speculative grade sovereigns. Although the ratings have a largely predictable component, they also appear to provide the market with information that goes beyond that available in public data. Sovereign credit ratings thus appear to be valued by the market in pricing issues.

The credit rating agencies have only recently begun to rate sovereigns and only since the 1990s for many developing countries. Ratings are meant to provide an estimate of the likelihood that borrowers will fulfill the obligations in their debt issues. Whether sovereign ratings are properly and reliably scored remains yet to be demonstrated. Table 6.14 shows that sovereign default rates are lower than corporate default rates at most rating levels.

If sovereign ratings have indeed been properly performed, then sovereign default probabilities should in time match those of corporate ratings. It is still early to make a judgment, because of the combination of the low number and short history of sovereign ratings and the low number of sovereign default due to the availability of international emergency credit (most problems being liquidity rather than solvency related) and the high cost of future credit if a government does default. Exhibit 6.12 shows the defaults on foreign currency bond debt as compiled by Standard & Poor's. It shows the minimum rating assigned in the year prior to default and the ensuing rating during default. The exhibit provides some interesting data. Only 15 countries have defaulted on foreign currency bond debt since 1975 (although many more have defaulted on bank debt), some defaulting countries were often not even rated, and some of the countries were not downgraded to default status.

---

[36] Mora, N., 2006, Sovereign credit ratings: guilty beyond reasonable doubt?, *Journal of Banking and Finance*, Vol. 30, 2041–2062.

Table 6.14   Sovereign and corporate default rate comparison

(% of rated issuers)	One-year		Three-year		Five-year	
	Sov.	Corp.	Sov.	Corp.	Sov.	Corp.
AAA	0	0	0	0	0	0.1
AA	0	0	0	0.1	0	0.3
A	0	0	0	0.2	0	0.6
BBB	0	0.3	2.1	1.3	5.6	2.8
BB	1.1	1.1	5.6	6	8.8	10.7
B	3	5.4	8.8	17.1	17.6	24.2
CCC/CC	40	27	58.9	40.9	58.9	47.6

Note: Implied senior ratings through 1995; issuer credit ratings thereafter. Sovereign foreign currency ratings for 1975–2005; corporate local currency ratings for 1981–2005.
Source: Beers, T., and Cavanaugh, M., 2006, Sovereign credit ratings: A primer, *Criteria*: Standard & Poor's, October, 1–17, Table 1, page 2

Exhibit 6.12   Sovereign defaults on foreign currency bond debt 1975–2002

	Years	Rating in previous year		Rating during period of default	
		Moody's	S&P	Moody's	S&P
Argentina	1989; 2001–2002	Ba3; B1	N.A; BB−	B3; Ca	N.A; SD
Bolivia	1989–1997				
Costa Rica	1984–1985				
Ecuador	1999–2000	B3		Caa2	SD
Former Yugoslavia	1992–2002				
Guatemala	1989				
Ivory Coast	2000–2002				
Moldova	1998–2002	Ba2; Caa1		B2; Caa1	
Nigeria	1986–1988; 1992				
Pakistan	1999	Caa1	CC	Caa1	SD
Panama	1987–1994				
Russia	1998–2000	Ba2	BB−	B3	SD
Ukraine	1998–2000	B2		Caa1	
Venezuela	1995–1997	Ba2	B+	Ba2	B
Zimbabwe	1975–1980				

Note: Ratings refer to the minimum ratings given during the period, and for Ukraine the previous year is the new rating issued on 2/6/1998.
Source: Mora, N., 2006, Sovereign credit ratings: Guilty beyond reasonable doubt? *Journal of Banking and Finance*, Vol. 30, 2041–2062, Table 1, page 2043.

Special Issues

SOVEREIGN NOTCH DIFFERENTIATIONS   A great deal of controversy is often created by very small rating differentials between countries, making the sovereign rating business dangerous ground for the agencies. Trying to differentiate between a BBB and a BB country in terms of overall credit risk can often be difficult, and even the rating agencies have very different views regarding the risk of particular countries. Within a country, there are a greater number of qualitative factors such as the robustness of political and legal institutions, relations with other nations and other factors that are not relevant for corporate ratings.

THE COUNTRY CEILING   Sovereign ratings are also important to the private sector because the 'country ceiling,' which caps the foreign currency corporate credit rating, is directly notched upward from the sovereign foreign currency rating, thereby impacting the cost of foreign funding that a company can obtain. The 'country ceiling' measures the 'transfer and convertibility risk,' the risk that a sovereign government facing an external payments crisis will block outflows of foreign exchange to meet its own foreign currency obligations. Furthermore, the sovereign rating is correlated to (but not the same as) the country risk that limits the local currency credit rating of any company based in that country. The local currency rating of a company, limited by the country risk, will thus generally be higher than the foreign currency rating of the same company, capped by the 'country ceiling' that measures the transfer and convertibility risk.

The rating agencies will also indicate whether a sovereign has a positive, negative, or stable outlook, and will occasionally place a country on its watchlist for possible upgrade or downgrade. Ratings announcements have been shown to have a significant impact on bond yields, particularly for emerging market sovereigns.

6.3.2   Financial Strength Ratings

When one looks at the balance sheet and income statement of a bank or an insurance company, one notices immediately how different they are from any other business. Their equity is minuscule relative to their assets (in the order of 4% to 8%), their liabilities to their commercial customers make up the bulk of the right-hand side of their balance sheet (between 85% and 95%), and what is usually called debt is small relative to their equity (in the order of 10% to 20%). Similarly, sales revenue on the income statement is only a small fraction of certain type of gross inflows and outflows such as interest revenue minus interest costs and there are no costs of goods sold.

But there are significant stocks of raw materials, on both sides of the balance sheets. Banks purchase cash raw materials from depositors in exchange for a certain capital guarantee plus regular income. This is a liability of the bank, also called a bank deposit. Insurance companies similarly purchase cash raw materials in exchange for a contingent capital guarantee plus, sometimes, an amount of accumulated investments. This is a liability of the insurance company typically called policyholder provisions. In contrast to industrial companies, both banks and insurance companies perform very little transformation of that raw material and re-sell it rapidly, mostly and largely in exchange for all sorts of credit, to some extent in exchange of equity.

In addition, banks and insurance companies need government licenses to conduct their businesses. To keep the license, they have to satisfy a whole battery of regulatory requirements and financial ratios.

The financial strength ratings of either a bank or an insurance company grade the point-in-time quality of the 'raw materials' of the business, the ability to generate sufficient margin after operating expenses to be sustainable, and the economic adequacy of the equity buffer to absorb occasional raw material quality impairments. In addition, the financial strength ratings integrate compliance with regulatory constraints and any safety margins maintained over and above these constraints. While a financial strength rating sounds and looks very 'financially' oriented, it is in fact fundamentally business oriented. But the business happens to be a financial business.

Banks

As a financial business, banks play an essential part in the economy through their role in the supply and demand, and hence price, of money. The stock of money – cash plus deposits – is higher the greater the fraction of money the public is willing to hold as deposits. This is due to a money multiplier effect that follows from the lending on of deposits. This multiplier effect, if it is run in reverse and on a large scale, can cause a severe contraction in the stock of money. Since banks are illiquid as a result of having resold their raw material, a widespread movement by depositors to demand a cash-out of their deposits at a given bank will cause that bank to put pressure on other banks by calling loans, selling investments, or withdrawing its deposits. This can generate a similar process at additional banks if this weakens depositor confidence in other banks and result in a full-blown bank run and a dramatic decline in money supply and circulation. Given the dire effects monetary contraction has on the real economy, the government will do whatever is necessary to maintain confidence in the banking system.

Banks and insurance companies are inherently more opaque than other firms, meaning that it is harder to know the true riskiness of a given bank or insurance company than that of a company in any other industry. A study of US bonds issued between 1983 and 1993 found that Moody's and S&P have substantially more often split ratings on issues by banks and insurance firms than on other issues.[37] The split became larger as the rating declined, indicating that uncertainty is related to the risk of the bank. The asset profile of the bank is what affects the degree of uncertainty. The lower the capital level and the greater the level of loans and trading assets at a bank, the larger the rating split. The quality of a bank loan portfolio is difficult to observe. Trading assets are easy to change and positions are easy to conceal, as demonstrated by the bankruptcy of the Barings bank by trader Nick Leeson. This is amplified by the highly leveraged nature of banks. Banks are thus inherently more opaque and risky than other businesses.

Bank regulators certainly do not want to exacerbate this by providing a sense of impunity to bankers that will encourage risky behavior and generate moral hazard.

In other words, banks occupy such an important place in the financial system that only the smaller ones are likely to default. Instead of defaulting, most banks in trouble will experience failure, defined by Fitch as follows:

- A bank has failed if it is kept going only by state support or support from a (deposit) insurance fund.
- A bank has failed if it is kept going only by being acquired by some other corporate entity.
- A bank has failed if it is kept going only by an injection of new funds from its shareholders or equivalent.

---

[37] Morgan, D., 2002, Rating banks: risk and uncertainty in an opaque industry, *American Economic Review*, September, 874–888.

- A bank has failed if it has defaulted (defined as failure of an obligor to make timely payment of principal and/or interest on its financial obligations).[38]

Thus, a bank default is considered a failure, but failure is a broader definition that includes any situation in which a bank is rescued. The failure rate of banks is substantially higher than their default rate, and this difference is support, typically provided by governments. The intrinsic risk of a bank getting into stress therefore is more accurately measured by its failure rate than its default rate. The default rate is dominated by support, so much so that bank default rate is substantially below that of all corporates, even though bank failure rate is higher than the overall corporate default rate.[39]

Given a low occurrence of bank default but a high occurrence of failures, the rating agencies proceed to determine the probability of default by first determining a financial strength rating, which is independent of any possible support and looks at the bank as if it were any other independent business. This is useful to know, because even if a given bank is expected to be bailed out, investors and counterparties to the bank, such as corporate treasurers, will prefer to avoid the uncertainty of being involved with a bank that goes through failure and rescue. The rating agency then forms an opinion on the likelihood of support a failing bank will receive. The financial strength rating and the likelihood of support are considered together to arrive at the likelihood of default, expressed as a standard rating as used for all other issuers.

DEFINITION   The CRAs provide *financial strength ratings* on the banks, which are an opinion on the stand-alone strength of the bank to assess how it would fare if it could not rely on external support. The financial strength rating can be understood as a measure of the likelihood that a bank will require support.

The rating analysis of a bank is like that of any other company and consists of two components: the business profile and the financial profile.

Business Profile   The analysis of the business profile of a bank begins with a consideration of the country risks. Of particular importance is the strength and prospective performance of the economy, the structure and relative fragility of the financial system, accounting and disclosure policies, and the quality of banking regulation and supervision. Consideration of the business itself focuses on the market position and brand name of the bank, and the diversification and stability of its business lines.

Financial Profile   Bank credit analysts have traditionally used the CAMEL framework consisting of analysis of the Capital, Asset quality, Management, Earnings, and Liquidity to evaluate the financial profile of a bank.

- *Capital* –The equity capital of the bank available to absorb potential losses allows the bank to offset its portfolio and business risks. Better capitalized banks have greater flexibility to ride out a downturn and thus avoid insolvency.

---

[38] Fitch Ratings, 2007, Global bank individual ratings transition and failure study – 1990–2006: Special Report, June 12, 1–20, page 2.
[39] Fitch Ratings, 2007, Global Bank Individual Ratings Transition and Failure Study – 1990–2006: Special Report, June 12, 1–20, page 6.

- *Asset quality* – This is the most important part of bank analysis as it is the main driver of future earnings. Loan portfolios are generally the biggest chunk of a bank's assets, and so analysis will focus on loan quality and the conservatism of loan loss provisioning.

- *Management* – The evaluation of management is one of the most subjective elements of bank analysis. It includes a look at the organizational structure of the bank, its strategic orientation, the track record of the management team, and the coherence of these elements. The risk management of the bank is becoming an increasingly key component of such an analysis, since a large part of bank revenue is compensation for calculated risk-taking. The quality of corporate governance by the board of directors is also an important consideration of the overall management of the bank.

- *Earnings* – The profitability level of a bank is essential to the long-term performance of the bank and its ability to increase or maintain its capital, which will impact the risk protection of its creditors. The level of volatility and the diversity of earnings are important, and the earnings are also the result of the management to control costs to bring more revenue to the bottom line.

- *Liquidity* – Liquidity, or liability management, is a measure of the ability of the bank to finance itself under stress, especially important given that access to funding is often based on perception of the creditworthiness of the bank, which is especially important for banks without a large depositor base.

FROM THE FINANCIAL STRENGTH RATING TO THE ISSUER CREDIT RATING   The credit ratings applied to a bank, referred to as counterparty, senior unsecured or issuer ratings, and those applied to specific obligations, are decided by determining the likelihood of external support (either sovereign state support or that of the bank owner) if needed. This is then combined with the bank financial strength rating to determine the relative likelihood of default of the bank, which is translated into an issuer rating. As discussed, due to the support often received by banks the likelihood of default is much lower than the likelihood of bank failure. As for any other debt rating, the ratings are subject to local and foreign currency ceilings, as appropriate. As with any other instrument rating, the credit rating applied to the individual debt obligations of a bank incorporate both the likelihood of default, and the expected recovery in the event of default.

SCALE   The scale used by the major CRAs for bank financial strength is a scale that varies from A to E, as shown by the scale used by Moody's provided in Exhibit 6.13.

Insurance Companies

DEFINITION   Insurer Financial Strength (IFS) ratings provide an assessment of the financial strength of an insurance organization and are assigned to insurance companies' policyholders obligations. The IFS ratings thus refer to the ability of an insurance company to punctually pay its obligations to policyholders. It explicitly does not consider debt obligations. For those insurance companies with debt obligations, a standard debt credit rating is issued. IFS ratings use the same scale as for debt credit ratings albeit with different descriptors attached to each rating. Thus, IFS ratings do not have their own rating symbols, as opposed

Exhibit 6.13 Moody's Bank Financial Strength Ratings

A	Banks rated A possess *superior intrinsic financial strength*. Typically, they will be institutions with highly valuable and defensible business franchises, strong financial fundamentals, and a very predictable and stable operating environment.
B	Banks rated B possess *strong intrinsic financial strength*. Typically, they will be institutions with valuable and defensible business franchises, good financial fundamentals, and a predictable and stable operating environment.
C	Banks rated C possess *adequate intrinsic financial strength*. Typically, they will be institutions with more limited but still valuable business franchises. These banks will display either acceptable financial fundamentals within a predictable and stable operating environment, or good financial fundamentals within a less predictable and stable operating environment.
D	Banks rated D display *modest intrinsic financial strength,* potentially requiring some outside support at times. Such institutions may be limited by one or more of the following factors: a weak business franchise; financial fundamentals that are deficient in one or more respects; or an unpredictable and unstable operating environment.
E	Banks rated E display *very modest intrinsic financial strength,* with a higher likelihood of periodic outside support or an eventual need for outside assistance. Such institutions may be limited by one or more of the following factors: a weak and limited business franchise; financial fundamentals that are materially deficient in one or more respects; or a highly unpredictable or unstable operating environment.
	Where appropriate, a '+' modifier will be appended to ratings below the 'A' category and a '−' modifier will be appended to ratings above the 'E' category to distinguish those banks that fall in intermediate categories

Note: Standard & Poor's and Fitch also scale from A to E with intermediary graduations, as well. Standard & Poor's also uses '+' or '−' to denote graduations, whereas Fitch graduates its ratings with A/B, B/C, C/D, and D/E and calls the rating an Individual Rating. Furthermore, Fitch uses an additional rating of 'F' to denote a bank that has defaulted or, in Fitch's opinion, would have done so if it had not received external support.
Source: Moody's Investors Service, 2007, Bank Financial Strength Ratings, *Global Rating Methodology*: February, 1–40, page 36.

to the case for Bank Financial Strength ratings. Depending on the CRA, IFS ratings are either used as the base rating from which notching of debt securities occurs (Moody's), or on the contrary IFS ratings are notched with respect to the issuer credit rating (Fitch), or the IFS rating and the issuer credit rating are determined by separate processes (S&P). An IFS rating is determined by taking into account the regulatory policyholder protection regime after an analysis of the business. Thus, in jurisdictions with a strong regulatory framework for insurance companies and priority recognition of policyholder interests, the IFS will be above the debt credit rating. However, in lenient jurisdictions with no recognition of policyholder priority, IFS ratings can be lower than debt credit ratings, at least at some CRAs.

Insurer Financial Strength ratings are thus different from Bank Financial Strength Ratings. The IFS rating provides an opinion of timely payment, but of policyholders rather than debt holders; on the other hand, Bank Financial Strength Ratings determine the likelihood that a bank will require assistance to avoid default, or, expressed differently, that it will fail. Insurance companies, including large ones, have been allowed by governments to fail without intervention.

The analysis of the business, upon which both the financial strength and debt credit-worthiness are based, is essentially the same as for banks. This is not surprising since they are both financial intermediaries. We find the same process of looking at the business profile (market position and brand, product focus and diversification), financial profile (essentially the CAMEL model) and other factors such as the regulatory, accounting, and country environment. However, as already mentioned, for insurance companies there is no consideration of government support since none is generally forthcoming.

SCALE   The IFS rating scale is the same as the standard rating scale used for debt credit ratings, going from AAA/Aaa down to C. When the rating notches down from BBB−/Baa3 to BB+/Ba1, it leaves 'secure' and enters 'vulnerable' territory. This means that the capacity to meet policyholder and contract obligations has become 'uncertain,' and the impact of any adverse business and economic factors is expected to be 'significant.' Exhibit 6.14 provides the IFS rating scale used by Fitch.

6.3.3   Structured Finance Instruments Ratings

Structured finance instruments are essentially asset-backed securities (in the original sense of pass-through securitization, refer to Section 3.3.2) divided into different tranches or classes. Each class behaves as a bond, in the sense that it will pay interests periodically and principal will be redeemed at maturity. This characteristic allows for the evaluation of the creditworthiness of these tranches using ratings on the same scale as traditional bonds. By doing so, investors make investment decisions in a familiar framework and regulators watch over markets within the established criteria system.

However, as further explained in the following paragraphs, CDO or ABS notes and traditional bonds are not all that homogeneous in how they yield payment and what the possible scenarios of payments are. More specifically, the probability distributions of losses underlying each type of instrument have different properties. Although the significance of ratings is still the same, in the sense that it is a benchmark measure of default, ratings on these two categories do not refer to the same underlying distribution of losses and hence should be interpreted accordingly.

In the case of CDOs and other structured finance instruments, the credit risk embedded arises from two underlying factors. One is the default risk linked to the collateral pool: the default of some assets in this pool would lead to losses on the aggregate principal amount of this pool and hence to potential shortfalls in the cash flows generated from the pool to pay investors duly. The other type of risk is not directly linked to defaults but arises from the transaction's structure. Such risk would affect the possibility that investors can collect sufficient and timely payments as scheduled. For this purpose, the rating analysis of each transaction is two-fold.[40]

In one part, analytical models are set to assess pool credit risk. The tools used for analyzing CDO pools may differ according to the nature of the collateral assets and across rating agencies. In the second part of the process is structural analysis. This stage deals with

---

[40] Fender, I. and Kiff, J., 2004, CDO Rating Methodology: Some thoughts on model risk and its implications, *BIS Working Papers*, No. 163, Nov. 2004, page 2.

Exhibit 6.14   Long-term Insurer Financial Strength Rating Scale: Fitch's Description

Major rating category	Fitch's description
	Secure
AAA	*Exceptionally Strong.* 'AAA' IFS ratings denote the lowest expectation of ceased or interrupted payments. They are assigned only in the case of exceptionally strong capacity to meet policyholder and contract obligations on a timely basis. This capacity is highly unlikely to be adversely affected by foreseeable events.
AA	*Very Strong.* 'AA' IFS ratings denote a very low expectation of ceased or interrupted payments. They indicate very strong capacity to meet policyholder and contract obligations on a timely basis. This capacity is not significantly vulnerable to foreseeable events.
A	*Strong.* 'A' IFS ratings denote a low expectation of ceased or interrupted payments. They indicate strong capacity to meet policyholder and contract obligations on a timely basis. This capacity may, nonetheless, be more vulnerable to changes in circumstances or in economic conditions than is the case for higher ratings.
BBB	*Good.* 'BBB' IFS ratings indicate that there is currently a low expectation of ceased or interrupted payments. The capacity to meet policyholder and contract obligations on a timely basis is considered adequate, but adverse changes in circumstances and economic conditions are more likely to impact this capacity. This is the lowest 'secure' rating category.
	Vulnerable
BB	*Moderately weak.* 'BB' IFS ratings indicate that there is a possibility that ceased or interrupted payments could occur, particularly as the result of adverse economic or market changes over time. However, business or financial alternatives may be available to allow for policyholder and contract obligations to be met in a timely manner. Obligations in this and lower categories are considered 'vulnerable'.
B	*Weak.* 'B' IFS ratings indicate two possible conditions. If obligations are still being met on a timely basis, there is significant risk that ceased or interrupted payments could occur in the future, but a limited margin of safety remains. Capacity for continued timely payments is contingent upon a sustained, favorable business and economic environment, and favorable market conditions. Alternatively, a 'B' IFS rating is assigned to obligations that have experienced ceased or interrupted payments, but with the potential for extremely high recoveries.
CCC	*Very Weak.* 'CCC' IFS ratings indicate two possible conditions. If obligations are still being met on a timely basis, there is a real possibility that ceased or interrupted payments could occur in the future. Capacity for continued timely payments is solely reliant upon a sustained, favorable business and economic environment, and favorable market conditions. Alternatively, a 'CCC' IFS rating is assigned to obligations that have experienced ceased or interrupted payments, and with the potential for average to superior recoveries.

(*continued overleaf*)

Exhibit 6.14   *(continued)*

Major rating category	Fitch's description
CC	'CC' IFS ratings indicate two possible conditions. If obligations are still being met on a timely basis, it is probable that ceased or interrupted payments could occur in the future. Alternatively, a 'CC' IFS rating is assigned to obligations that have experienced ceased or interrupted payments, with the potential for average to below-average recoveries.
C	'C' IFS ratings indicate two possible conditions. If obligations are still being met on a timely basis, ceased or interrupted payments are imminent. Alternatively, a 'C' IFS rating is assigned to obligations that have experienced ceased or interrupted payments, with the potential for below-average to poor recoveries.

Notes: '+' or '−' may be appended to a rating to indicate the relative position of a credit within the rating category. Such suffixes are not added to ratings in the 'AAA' category or to ratings below the 'CCC' category.
Source: Fitch Ratings, 2007, Fitch Ratings Definitions: Insurer financial strength ratings, Resource Library, March 26, 1–5.

contractual specifics as laid out in the CDO's documentation, or indenture. Detailed cash flow modeling, for cash-based instruments, as well as legal considerations and evaluation of any third parties involved in the deal will be implemented. Finally, all of the information is aggregated and mapped into a single, alphanumeric tranche rating benchmarked to the historical performance of other bond types.

Collateral Pool Credit Modeling

This stage is focused on assessing the default possibility embedded in the collateral pool and the level of losses in each default scenario. Generally speaking, there are mainly two approaches to model this risk. One is based on the binomial assumption of default, and the other carries out Monte Carlo simulations, often based on a structural or Merton-type model.

To explain the idea underlying the first approach, we take Moody's Binomial Expansion Technique (BET) as an epitome. In the BET, the actual portfolio is first mapped into a hypothetical portfolio that contains a number of homogeneous uncorrelated assets with the same size of holding, probability of default (PD) and recovery rate (RR). The number of assets in the hypothetical portfolio is equal to the Diversity Score (DS) of the actual pool to reflect the extent to which the actual pool is diversified across industry sectors and obligors.

Mathematically, for a collateral pool of n assets across m industry sectors and N obligors, the diversity score is calculated as follows:[41]

$$\mathrm{DS} = \sum_{k=1}^{m} G \left\{ \sum_{i=1}^{n_k} \min\{1, F_i/\overline{F}\} \right\}, \quad \text{where} \quad \overline{F} = \frac{1}{N} \sum_{i=1}^{n} F_i$$

---

[41] Fender, I. and Kiff, J., 2004, CDO Rating Methodology: Some thoughts on model risk and its implications, BIS Working Papers, No 163, Nov. 2004, page 4.

The size of the ith holding is denoted F_i, n_k is the number of assets in the kth sector and $G(x)$ is a concave function that maps the diversity among obligors in a sector into a score at the sector level. As we can see $\min\{1, F_i/\overline{F}\}$ penalizes large shares of a given asset in the portfolio. The concavity of G rewards having assets from different rather than from the same sectors and finally the diversity score is more favorable to a portfolio with assets from distinct obligors rather than from the same obligor.[42]

Consider the behavior of the hypothetical pool, built to reflect that of the actual pool, in order to derive a simplified but practical credit model.[43] Given the homogeneity of the hypothetical assets, the hypothetical pool can have DS + 1 default scenarios (i.e., with default occurring on 0 asset, 1 asset ... DS assets). The DS transformation allows to disregard any correlation between hypothetical assets. We can define the expected loss (EL) of the CDO portfolio as:[44]

$$EL = \sum_{j=1}^{DS} P_j L_j, \quad \text{where} \quad P_j = C_{DS}^j (PD)^j (1 - (PD))^{DS-j}$$

L_j denotes the percentage loss in the jth scenario. C_n^j is the combinatorial operator. Note that the formula of P_j translates the assumption of independence (all assets in the hypothetical pool are independent of one another) of the simple BET model.

When the pool is made up of two or more uncorrelated groups of assets having markedly different average properties, a modified version of BET can be used, the so-called 'multiple BET' (MBET).[45] Finally, a more recent method, called 'correlated binomial method' (CBM), is used for cash flow CDOs backed by pools, especially in the RMBS sector of highly correlated assets with low DS. This newer approach allows for explicit assumptions about correlation among collateral assets to be incorporated into the pool credit risk model and tend to generate default distribution with fatter-right-tail (higher probabilities of multiple defaults) than under the BET.[46,47]

---

[42] For illustration, see Fender, I. and Kiff, J. CDO Rating Methodology: Some thoughts on model risk and its implications, BIS working papers No 163, Nov. 2004, tables 1 and 2.

[43] Rating agencies usually select the parameters of the hypothetical portfolio to match higher order moments of the actual portfolio distribution, e.g. mean, variance, skewness or kurtosis of the actual loss distribution. By doing so, the shape of the hypothetical loss distribution is considered better fit into that of the actual one. See Gluck and Remeza 'Moody's Approach to Rating Multi-sector CDOs,' Moody's Investors Service Structured Finance Special Report, Sept. 2000.

[44] Fender, I. and Kiff, J., 2004, CDO Rating Methodology: Some thoughts on model risk and its implications, BIS Working Papers, No 163, Nov. 2004, page 6.

[45] See Cifuentes and Wilcox, 1998. 'The Double Binomial Method and Its Application to a Special Case of CBO structures,' Moody's Investors Service Structured Finance Special Report, March.

[46] See Witt, 'Moody's correlated binomial default distribution', Moody's Investors Service Structured Finance Special Report, Aug. 2004 for the detailed method.

[47] By contrast, Moody's alternative diversity score (ADS) implicitly incorporate the intra- and inter-sector default correlation assumption when mapping the actual pool into the hypothetical one. Usually the higher the correlation, the lower the score is than under the DS method. See Gluck and Remeza 'Moody's Approach to Rating Multi-sector CDOs', Moody's Investors Service Structured Finance Special Report, Sept. 2000.

The general binomial method is summarized as in Exhibit 5.

Example 6.5 The binomial method

Step: 1. Map the actual collateral pool into a hypothetical one
      2. Specify the probability of each level of loss of the hypothetical pool
      3. For each level of loss, calculate the loss of the CDO note
      4. Average the product of results from steps 2 and 3

DS *Diversity Score*	ADS *Alternative Diversity Score*	CBM *Correlated Binomial Method*
Remove effects of industry sector concentration and obligor concentration in step 1. Assets in hypothetical pools are uncorrelated. Probabilities in step 2 are modeled binomially.	Remove effects of intra- and inter-industry correlation in step 1, in addition to those removed in DS (thus a smaller number of assets than in DS). Assets in hypothetical pools are uncorrelated. Probabilities in step 2 are modeled binomially.	Assets in hypothetical pools are assumed correlated. Probabilities in step 2 are modeled through copula and in a recursive way. Multiple default probabilities are modeled higher than in DS and ADS.

Alternatively, Monte Carlo methodologies are often based on the simulation of default events within a simplified structural credit risk model. The basic intuition is that a default occurs when the value of an obligor's assets falls below that of its liabilities (same principle as in Section 6.2.2, Figure 6.2 provides a good illustration). The loss on an asset is determined by the portfolio's exposure to that asset times its recovery rate. The portfolio's total loss is then computed as the sum of the losses on each of the assets. Simulating portfolio losses a large number of times yields an estimated portfolio loss distribution. This portfolio loss distribution contains all the information required to determine the performance of each CDO tranche. The key modeling difficulties are that:

- the asset values are correlated (hence asset defaults also);
- these asset correlations need to be determined (estimated using regression analysis within a factor model or using empirical default observations, using equity return correlations as proxies) and taken into account;
- the individual asset probabilities of default and/or times to default are inputs (estimated from the agencies' extensive historical records of defaults and transitions).

All agencies make their own modeling choices and use their own extensive proprietary data to best capture these key inputs. A general simulation procedure to compute the estimated portfolio total loss distribution at a given date t, for a portfolio of N correlated assets, can be described as follows. This description is intended to provide you with a general sense of the simulation rating model of CDOs, not more. Of course, each rating agency has a specific rating model that varies across the different types of transactions[48]

- For instance, to simulate correlated asset default times:

  - Simulate a vector of N standard normal correlated random variables, or *latent variables*, y_i for each asset, with a given correlation matrix *(include the greek capital letter sigma of the line below)*.
  - Compute $\Phi(y_i) = u_i$, where Φ is the normal probability distribution function and u_i is a uniformly distributed random variable belonging to [0,1] but correlated across i, since the y_i are correlated.[49] Given the correlation structure, for each simulation run, the generated u_i will tend to be clustered in a particular way.
  - From the given u_i, calculate the simulated default time through the relation $\tau_i = S^{-1}(u_i)$, where S is the survival function, described by the credit curves. Credit curves, one for each broad rating class, are estimated using estimated probabilities of transitions between different ratings – *transition matrices*. These transition matrices are estimated using agencies' extensive proprietary historical data.

- If $\tau_i < T$, the default time is less than the CDO maturity T, then a default occurs on this asset and a realization of recovery is determined. Recovery is either fixed exogenously or is drawn from the appropriate distribution. The total loss on the portfolio up to time t is then calculated as the sum of all the individual, but correlated, asset losses:

$$L(t) = \sum_{i=1}^{n} 1_{(\tau_i < t)} E_i (1 - RR_i),$$

where $1_{(\tau_i < t)}$ is the indicator function equal to 1 if $\tau_i < t$ and equal to 0 otherwise, E_i is the exposure at default and RR_i is the recovery rate of the ith asset.[50]
- After repeating the simulation runs a sufficient number of times an estimated distribution for the total loss on the portfolio can be built, as for instance in Figure 6.3. For most portfolio, 500,000 simulation trials provide sufficient accuracy of the estimation.
- The portfolio loss distribution, *p(L)*, is then used to determine the subordination level of each CDO tranche, given the desired rating.

Note that, just as in all other rating segments Moody's approach differs from Fitch and S&P as it bases the rating of a given tranche on its expected loss (EL) while S&P and Fitch base their rating on the probability of default (PD). Assume that a subordinate note takes

---

[48] The description here is based on S&P's Evaluator model, as reviewed in de Servigny, A., and Jobst N., 2007, The Collateral Debt Obligation Methodologies Developed by Standard and Poor's, Chap. 10, *Handbook of Structured Finance*, McGraw-Hill, pages 397–463.
[49] This is the where the Gaussian copula assumption interferes.
[50] The loss on a given tranche k can then be expressed as:

$$L_k = \min\{\max\{L_r - \text{attachment point of } k, 0\}, \text{thickness of } k\}$$

The attachment point of k is the total value of the entire tranches junior to k, it is the value beyond which losses on the portfolio impact tranche k. The thickness of tranche k is its loss absorption capacity.

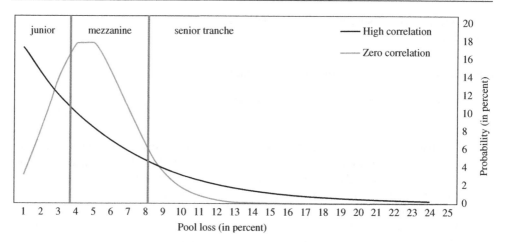

Figure 6.3 Total loss distribution

losses from 15% to 40%. Hence, in the Moody's approach, the EL, as a percentage of the tranche's value, is given by:

$$\text{EL} = \int_{15\%}^{40\%} \frac{(L - 15\%)}{40\% - 15\%} p(L) \, \mathrm{d}L + \int_{40\%}^{100\%} p(L) \, \mathrm{d}L.$$

This EL is then benchmarked to the expected loss on corporate bonds to determine the rating on this note. In this example, the S&P and Fitch default probability approach would be given by $\text{PD} = \int_{15\%}^{100\%} p(L) \, \mathrm{d}L$. In other words, the probability that this note defaults is equal to the probability that the total loss on the pool is greater than 15%. The PD is then benchmarked to the default probability of corporate bonds to give the initial rating level.

Structural analysis

The credit model will give a numerical estimation of the losses that may hit the portfolio. However, since CDOs are deal-specific instruments, other non-default risks due to the structure of the indenture need to be carefully studied.

One of these risks is market risk. The market risk affects the credit risk in CDOs directly in two ways. Often CDO deals have preset triggers to secure the payments to senior tranches. These triggers are, for instance, embedded in the over-collateralization and interest coverage of the senior tranches. Once these triggers are hit, the CDO manager needs to sell some of the portfolio assets to maintain the triggers above level or duly meet the payment requirements. Moreover, in managed deals, the manager needs to purchase new assets with the proceeds of those in the pool that have matured. Hence the market value of underlying assets is assessed upon sale or purchase and the quality of the CDO is thus not only affected by the market value of the underlying assets through the triggers but also in the general course of the portfolio management.

The second type of non-default risk affecting a CDO is the third party risk. As we know, many participants are involved in a CDO deal and their performance and creditworthiness can affect the quality of the CDO. As mentioned in the paragraph above, the ability of the manager to maintain the pool is an essential concern. Asset manager quality is often a key performance driver in the CDO market. In the ABS market the servicer's duly collecting of proceeds of the pools and distributing them correctly is essential. In some jurisdictions it may be difficult to replace a servicer, so that extra liquidity support would be necessary to account for a potentail servicer switch. Additionally, the size of the credit enhancement and liquidity facility also play an appreciable role in affecting the quality of the tranches in the CDO, especially that of the senior tranche, hence the importance of the quality of the monoline insurers. The quality of the third parties involved is sometimes also explicitly rated.

Last but not the least is the legal risk. Structured finance transactions are complex, deal specific legal transactions. The value of the structured finance instruments relies essentially on the bankruptcy remoteness of the SPV from the originator, on the tranching and priority payments (or losses) between the different classes of note holders. The rating agencies either review in-house or outsource to external lawyers the assessment of the soundness of the legal structure, based on the legal opinions of specialized law firms, requested by the originator or arranger. Rating agencies sometimes ask the arranger to provide distinct opinions from more lawyers as a prerequisite to rate a deal. Since CDOs are usually sophisticated and deal-specific, they could pose important legal issues with negotiations among relevant parties. Moreover, CDO investors often have various profiles and are subject to different jurisdictions. Reconciling this diversity in legal and regulatory aspects is also important.

Conclusion and model risk

As structured finance instruments are based on pools of assets and with properties predefined in the indenture, they are naturally suited to quantitative rating models. In some sense, the legal documentation provides the basis for the rating model's algorithm. Compared to corporate bonds or sovereigns, there is much less leeway, or degrees of freedom, in a structured finance transaction for any individual party to willingly affect the rating of the instruments, in either way, except for the manager in a managed transaction. As any mathematical model, quantitative rating models are descriptions or approximations of real-world phenomena and as such are subject to limitations. The risk that, on average, over a large sample, the rating model does not capture the actual credit risk is what is called 'model risk.' Model risk can be divided into two major categories.

PARAMETER ERROR   First is the model risk due to the choice of rating model input parameters. The concern is whether these parameter inputs are the proper ones and generate the best results possible, given the choice of the model. The default probability, the recovery rate and correlation used for each asset in the underlying pool are biased at a given point in time, since they are actually time-variant but assumed constant in many pool default models. Parameters are often calculated from historical data. Historical data can be a reasonable predictor for the future if the economic and financial environments are stable and if there is a sufficiently long, or representative, time-series. If these parameters are obtained from models on each underlying asset, then in effect the pool model depends partly on the accuracy of these sub-models. Errors in the results of a model can be magnified if the inputs to the model are from other sub-models and already contain errors.

STRUCTURAL ERROR   Aside from the parameter errors, what is more essential is the appropriateness of the model itself: whether it accurately reflects the nature and the dynamics of the underlying pool. For instance, in Merton's structural model, it is open to discussion whether an obligor's total asset values can be assumed to follow a lognormal distribution.[51] Additionally, to integrate the complexity of structured finance, the difference between the maturity date of the underlying and that of the notes needs to be considered, as well as the prepayment rate on the underlying assets that affects default probability and expected losses, etc. A common solution is to first model the pool default risk in a general way, and then to add the risks arising from the aforementioned concerns in a linear way to deliver a final risk assessment. However, under some circumstances, this cannot be done linearly and could significantly impair the predictability of the model. All the above should resort to more advanced mathematical and computational development in the future.

Last but not the least, the values that need to be modeled and used as principal criteria for credit rating evokes another concern, the foremost of which nowadays is the choice between default probability (used by S&P, Fitch) and expected losses (used by Moody's). Obviously they contain different types of information of which investors need to be wary, in order not to favor rating shopping by issuers[52].

6.4   TECHNICAL APPENDIX

Equivalent benchmark redemption yield (EBRY) is a major step in calculating Spread Over Benchmark Curve. EBRY displays the estimated yield of a benchmark that has exactly the same maturity and currency of a bond (for example, a corporate bond) for which the spread is calculated.

EBRY can be used to chart the equivalent benchmark yield together with the yield of the bond being analyzed. This shows, for example, if a credit spread narrowing was accompanied by a general decrease in the government benchmark yield.

Linear interpolation is used to estimate the yield of the equivalent government benchmark with the same maturity as the analyzed bond. For bonds with a maturity longer than the longest government benchmark, the equivalent benchmark yield is always the yield of the longest government benchmark available in the market (no extrapolation). The same holds for bonds with maturities shorter than the shortest benchmark.

In this case the equivalent benchmark bond is the shortest available benchmark in this market. The formula to calculate the linear interpolated benchmark yield (EBRY) is:

$$\text{Yield} = Y_1 \left(\frac{l_3 - l_1}{l_2 - l_1} \right) * (Y_2 - Y_1) \tag{6.11}$$

where Y_1 = yield of the benchmark with the lower maturity
$\quad\quad Y_2$ = yield of the benchmark with the higher maturity
$\quad\quad l_1$ = exact maturity in years of the lower benchmark
$\quad\quad l_2$ = exact maturity in years of the higher benchmark
$\quad\quad l_3$ = maturity of the bond being analyzed.

---

[51] Alternatively, a jump-diffusion process incorporating sudden changes in value may be more accurate to model the dynamics of an obligor's total assets.
[52] See Fender, I., and Kiff, J., 2004, CDO Rating Methodology: Some thoughts on model risk and its implications, BIS Working Papers No. 163, November 2004, pages 10, 11, 12.

Credit spread is the difference in yield between different securities due to different credit quality. In this case it is the difference in yield between the FT 1993–2006 6.25% Bond and the Equivalent Benchmark Bond.

6.4.1 Step 1: Computing the Implied Market Value of Assets and Asset Volatility

The asset value and asset volatility of the firm are estimated from the market value and volatility of equity and the book value of liabilities using BS–Merton's model. Note the necessary inputs.

(a) *Book Value of Liabilities* – The assumption here is that all the book value of liabilities would be payable in one year. Due to debt covenants, a default on a short-term liability could possibly trigger all the debt to be payable immediately. This would also affect the unlisted liabilities as these may also become payable immediately due to covenants in credit agreements, etc. This assumption is very important since taking only a portion of the liabilities would also change the estimate for the asset volatility and underestimate the actual asset value implied by the model.

(b) *Market Value of Equity* – This is the daily equity price multiplied by the number of outstanding shares.

(c) *Annual Equity Volatility* – The equity volatility has been computed using the daily returns on FT stock price. A 3-month historical daily return has been taken to compute the daily volatility of the current month end, e.g. Oct–Nov–Dec daily returns to compute the volatility for December and so on. Since the events were developing quite rapidly for FT in that period, we find it optimal to base the volatility calculations on a 3-month period. The daily volatility number has then been scaled by $\sqrt{250}$ (assuming 250 working days in a year) to obtain the annual volatility of the stock.

(d) *Risk-Free Interest Rate* – The Equivalent Benchmark Redemption Yield, with reference to the FT Long Term Bond, has been used as the risk free rate.

(e) *Computing the Asset Volatility and Value* – We exploit the option nature of equity to derive the market value and volatility of the firm's underlying assets implied by the equity's market value. In particular, we solve backwards from the option price and option price volatility for the implied asset value and asset volatility.

6.4.2 Step 2: Computing the Distance to Default

(a) *Default Point* (C) (*Moody's Definition*) – The simplified BS model assumed a single liability (or a series of liabilities with the same maturity). In practice, however, firms have several debt liabilities – France Telecom has a series of listed and unlisted debt instruments on its books. The question is how to define the default point in order to account for this variety. Moody's definition, which we will refer to as default point (C), is:

Book value of short-term liabilities + 0.5 × Book value of long-term liabilities

(b) *Expected Return on the Firm's Assets* (μ) – We are using an approximation of WACC (Weighted Average Cost of Capital) as a proxy for the expected return on the firm's assets.

- FT equity Beta is computed using the historical data for FT and MSCI returns.

  - The equity and MSCI volatility have been computed using the daily returns on FT stock price and the daily returns on MSCI. A 3-month historical daily return has been taken to compute the daily volatility of the current month end, e.g. Oct–Nov–Dec daily returns to compute volatility for December, and so on.
  - The covariance between FT and MSCI at each interval has been computed.
  - Beta by definition is:

    Covariance of FT and MSCI/Variance of MSCI

    This expression would give us the raw Beta which is translated to the adjusted beta by the formula $0.67 \times$ Raw Beta $+ 0.33$. This is the levered Beta for FT equity and thus is unlevered using the existing D/E (Book value of liabilities/Market value of equity) ratio of FT.

- To compute the target D/E ratio a list of comparables has been used, viz. British Telecom, Cable & Wireless, Deutsche Telekom, KPN, Portugal Telecom, Telefonica, Telecom Italia, Belgacom, Swisscom, Hellenic, Telenor, and Teliasonera.

  - The historical annualized average of each comparable company's D/E (Book value of debt/Market value of equity) is computed with adjustment for outliers. A pooled rolling average of this ratio is computed from 1996 to 2004 and has been used as the Target D/E ratio for relevering Beta for FT.

- The Equivalent Benchmark Redemption Yield, with reference to the FT Long Term Bond, has been used as the risk-free rate.
- A corporate tax rate of 33% has been assumed.
- A market risk premium of 4.1% has been assumed.
- Bond Beta is computed as the ratio of:

  (Spread between long-term FT bond and equivalent benchmark bond)/(Market risk premium).
  Using the above data we can compute a good approximation for the WACC.

(c) *Distance to Default*–Use Equation (6.6) to calculate the distance to default for the given default point.

6.4.3   Step 3: Calculating the Default Probability Corresponding to the Distance to Default

EDF (Expected Default Frequency)
Use Equation (6.5) to calculate the theoretical EDF for the given default point and distance to default, based *on the assumption of normality of asset return distribution*. In practice, Moody's KMV uses its extensive database to devise the actual probability of default based on small ranges of distance to default.

7

Credit Rating Performance

> Since credit ratings are probabilistic opinions about future creditworthiness, the performance of an individual credit rating opinion will not be judged on the basis of the individual outcome, but on whether the individual credit rating was formed pursuant to Moody's established processes. Where possible, the performance of credit ratings collectively will be evaluated on the basis of how they perform on a statistical basis ex-post (e.g. default studies, accuracy ratios and stability measures).[1]

This chapter deals with the relevance, performance, and stabilizer role of ratings. These are three quite different questions. To be relevant to issuers, the ratings and ratings changes have to create value for those who pay for the ratings. To be useful to investors, ratings need to perform well in predicting actual defaults and in avoiding the false prediction of defaults that never occur. This is what investors are interested in. And those responsible for the day-to-day management of the stability of the financial system have obviously a big stake in the aptitude of CRAs to handle creditworthiness assessments during periods of financial crisis. How diligent and objective did the CRAs act during periods of crisis?

7.1 RELEVANCE: RATINGS AND VALUE

Issuers want ratings to be relevant to them, i.e. increase their value above what it would have been in the absence of a rating. They largely support the cost of the CRA industry, about $6 bn in 2006 for the big three. The benefits to issuers must at least exceed that cost for the CRA industry to make economic sense. These benefits represent the savings to the issuers' businesses, from being rated in the several ways that we discussed in Section 3.2. If these savings do exist, they increase the free cash flows of the issuers and their valuations. A low creditworthy firm will only be willing to reveal its type by a poor rating if being rated per se has sufficient positive influence on the value of its expected free cash flows and of its growth options. For instance, access to funding, even if expensive, that the rating brings about will allow the firm to implement more positive NPV projects and thus create more value than it would have been able to create in the absence of that access. In all cases, rational firms will only incur the cost of the CRA industry if their values are higher than they otherwise would have been. Value impact will thus form the relevance test. And if issuers came to the conclusion that ratings have become irrelevant, they would stop supporting the CRA industry, however accurate ratings were as a benchmark likelihood and expected losses from defaults.

That increase in value could very well be hard to observe, particularly in the short run. Depending on the mix of net savings attributable to the rating action, the value impact could be on enterprise, debt or equity value – or a mixture of these. The observable impact could even be negative and yet be value accretive. Think about a scenario whereby the downgrade triggers management to finally take long postponed but badly needed corrective action to

---

[1] Moody's Investors Service, 2005, *Code of Professional Conduct*, June, SP1399, 1–16, section III,1,A,1.1, page 5.

preserve and improve enterprise value. Absent CRA monitoring and feedback, management might have taken the needed action only after a prolonged period of value destruction. The downgrade now preventing this, but at the same time revealing the bad shape of the company, may very well have a negative price impact and yet be value accretive! Briefly put, a rating action may be a key metric on the management radar screen that not only reveals danger but also triggers corrective action.

Ahold to Cut 700 Jobs to Regain Credit Rating

Royal Ahold, the owner of the Giant and Stop & Shop supermarket chains in the United States, plans to eliminate about 700 jobs at its US Foodservice unit as it cuts costs to try to regain an investment-grade credit rating. The company will take a charge of $50 million to $60 million in the fourth quarter to reflect the cost of the overhaul.[2]

A downgrade could be opposite news to different investors in the firm, and for quite different reasons. A debt downgrade could be good news for shareholders pursuant to a voluntary increase in leverage. But it could be bad news if the leverage increase is endogenous, for example when enterprise value drops – as happened in the previously discussed case of France Telecom. It could also be bad news for all investors if a downgrade reveals that the issuers' free cash flow generating power is less than what was expected. An issuer starting to pledge assets to creditors, thereby signaling to investors that the company's situation is bad, could be relatively good news for the beneficiary creditors, but bad news for other creditors and possibly for shareholders.

Ford to Back $18 Billion in New Loans with Assets[3]

Ford Motor, struggling to overcome record losses in 1996 and in need of cash to pay for its restructuring plans, was for the first time going to use assets as collateral on loans. The new debt includes $8 billion in a secured credit line to replace an unsecured $6.3 billion loan and a new $7 billion secured term loan.

For collateral, Ford is using US plants, other US automotive assets and 'all or a portion' of profitable units including Ford Motor Credit and Volvo. According to Glenn Reynolds, CEO of the research firm CreditSights in NY, Ford had 'still very low default risk, but bondholders' asset protection has been significantly eaten into.' Upon the announcement, Moody's lowered Ford's unsecured debt rating to Caa1.

Debt analysts Shelly Lombard at Gimme Credit Publications noted that Ford came to 'realize they're in worse shape than they thought and it's going to take a long time to fix this ... This subordinates [existing] bonds, but the alternative – running out of cash and filing bankruptcy – is worse.' Ford's shares fell 36 cents to close at $8.16.

This pledging of assets may nevertheless be beneficial for enterprise value because it may secure the firm continued access to badly needed liquidity in very hard times, thereby

---

[2] Bloomberg, 2005, Ahold to cut 700 jobs to regain credit rating, *International Herald Tribune*, December 31, page 13.
[3] This title and the following example are taken from Koenig, B., 2006, Ford to back $18 billion in new loans with assets, *Bloomberg News*, as reported in the *International Herald Tribune*, November 28, 503 words.

buying time and therefore increasing its chances to survive as a going concern rather than as a bundle of assets to be sold in liquidation procedures.

In all cases, a correct rating stance reduces an information asymmetry. The stance could be initiation, confirmation, inaction, or rating change. Whatever the direction of the stance, as long as it is correct, it improves the overall economic prospects of the obligor compared to what it would have been without being rated.

Take the example of the inaction of the CRAs in not downgrading France Telecom's ratings to below investment grade in the summer of 2002. This reduced the information asymmetry between the capital markets and France Telecom about the favorable prospects for the company to get out of its financial distress without defaulting. The sequence of downgrades that preceded it forced management to refocus on the company's debt service and free cash flow generating power before it was too late, rather than on building a European telecom empire. The incumbent management did not succeed rapidly enough, probably due to its own legacy and conduct of business culture. Each company strategy and focus typically needs its own leadership profile. The pressures of the downgrades and the conditional maintenance of investment grade were instrumental in creating the circumstances in which the France Telecom reference shareholder, the French State, and its Board of Directors managed a change of guard at the helm of the company without undue costly operational disruption – even if its short-term revealing influence increases the credit spreads of the issuers and reduces the stock price. Summing up, the structural relevance of credit ratings for credit spreads is a highly complex matter indeed, going beyond straightforward statistical correlation or causality tests.

The relevance of a rating is typically measured by studying security prices. One way is to relate the structure of ratings to the structure of credit spreads (Table 7.1 and Figure 7.1).

We call this structural relevance to which we devote Section 7.1.1. There, we examine the association between ratings, the initial promised yield, and the observed structure of credit

Table 7.1 Corporate bond yield spreads over Treasuries for main rating categories USA (1990–2006)

Year	Bond spreads in basis points							
	A	AA	AAA	BAA	B	BA	CA	CAA
1990	114	89	69	170	673	247		1276
1991	104	79	45	165	637	313		1571
1992	76	56	25	113	402	152		835
1993	61	30	21	113	365	250		715
1994	67	41	29	117	341	199		654
1995	82	56	53	130	351	221		868
1996	78	57	37	130	312	202		795
1997	66	61	38	92	357	235		676
1998	84	62	40	110	327	171		544
1999	107	92	55	145	410	253	1536	1215
2000	185	164	127	226	640	429	870	1150
2001	200	152	96	262	343	460	6010	1740
2002	155	108	68	220	150	367	4421	1652
2003	138	86	71	227	561	450	3225	1325
2004	98	57	60	159	286	221	1190	739
2005	89	61	60	164	258	245	1317	580
2006	113	80	65	147	339	293	1558	522

Source: Lehman Brothers

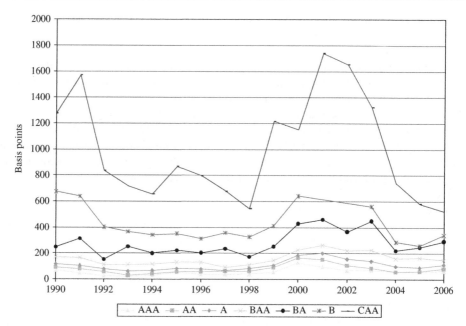

Figure 7.1 Corporate bond yield spreads over Treasuries for main rating categories USA (1990–2006)
Note: The spreads for the 'B' rating in 2001 and 2002 not being as reliable, we chose to intrapolate the data for the 'B' rating between 2000 and 2003.
Source: Datastream (Lehman Brothers).

spreads. The other way is to relate changes in ratings to changes in credit spreads or in the prices of rated and related securities. We call this impact relevance, to which we devote Section 7.1.2. There we examine the extent to which the rating changes are proactive or reactive *vis-à-vis* market information. If spreads and prices reflect ratings and rating changes, and not just the other way around, the market pays attention to ratings. They are relevant to issuer shareholders. But the market may pay attention without an observable price impact upon the announcement of a rating or rating change. For one thing, the announcement may have been fully anticipated. Or the enterprise value increase may be so favorable to bondholders that it leaves shareholders indifferent. Whatever the imperfection of spreads and price impacts as measures of relevance, one can make reasonable inference from these if properly constructed.

Summing up the question, do ratings add information to market prices, or not? Do ratings and rating changes reflect information from the market or does the market reflect information from the ratings and changes in them? This is the difficult question that we address now.

7.1.1 Structural Relevance: Rating and Credit Spreads

Two 'mega' facts about the structural relevance of ratings for credit spreads stand out. Relying on vast theoretical, econometric, and casual evidence and experience from market professionals, one can safely assert the following.

One, ratings do add information to the process whereby the market determines credit spreads. Ratings are news relative to existing publicly available information. They influence the shape of the credit risk structure of credit spreads. Ratings are not perfectly correlated with publicly observable and quantifiable information about financial conditions, industry characteristics, and management. In other words, beyond incorporating in replicable ways information in financial accounting statistics, ratings bring to the market something new about an obligors' creditworthiness.

Two, ratings have no monopoly in shaping the structure of credit spreads. Alternative credit information processors compete with CRAs in shaping spreads.[4] The influence of non-rating measures of creditworthiness on credit spreads is sometimes indiscernible from the influence of just the ratings. Taken together, non-rating measures and ratings provide the best overall fit for the credit risk structure of credit spreads, corroborating not only the relevance of the ratings but also the competitiveness of the credit information production business, beyond the arena of just the CRAs. In fact, institutional investors, banks, and specialized credit hedge funds perform their own intensive in-house credit risk analysis to prepare their price-revealing buying, holding, or selling decisions. They use CRA rating analysis as just one among many other inputs.

As we will disentangle now, credit spreads express the complex interaction between issuer credit fundamentals, instrument characteristics, and market conditions such as risk aversion and liquidity. Fundamental credit ratings are found to intermediate this interaction process in a statistically significant way. But this intermediation is not always economically determinant for the spread.

Chicken or Egg: the Degree in which Ratings Determine the Rating–Spread Structure

Do ratings affect the spread or just reflect it? What do ratings per se add in fashioning credit spreads, if anything?[5] CRAs claim that their rating actions add non-replicable accuracy and efficiency to default benchmarking. If that is true, the market will recognize that and rating actions should fashion spreads, not just be coincident with them, unless one could replicate rating actions without intervention of the raters. But this turns out not to be the case exactly – only approximately.[6]

Initially, economists found no conclusive evidence that ratings actually reveal relevant information for setting the spreads.[7] It was rather thought that CRAs and capital markets were merely in agreement at the time of a new issue as to what a B rated bond looked like as opposed to an AAA one. The agencies would add economic value, not in being relevant for setting spreads, but only in positioning the new issue on a fairly well understood credit risk spectrum and in gauging its equilibrium spread. To market bonds, this helps to determine

---

[4] As previously discussed, there are also several non-rating factors in credit spreads.

[5] We purposely use the term fashioning instead of determining. Fundamental credit ratings cannot and should not be able to determine the spreads because ratings measure the extent of default risk and its consequences whereas spreads reflect in addition to that the market taste for risk. See also again Section 2.3.2, dealing with misinterpreting credit ratings in which we already explained that ratings grade default risk, they don't price it.

[6] For foundations results on this question, see Kaplan, R.S., and Urwitz, G., 1979, Statistical models of bond ratings: a methodological inquiry, *Journal of Business*, Vol. 52, No. 2, 231–261.

[7] See Joehnk, M., and Reilly F., 1976, The association between market based risk measures for bonds and bond ratings, *Journal of Finance*, December, Vol. 31, Issue 5, 1387–1403; Weinstein, M., 1981, The systematic risk of corporate bonds, *Journal of Financial and Quantitative Analysis*, September, Vol. 16, No. 3, 257–278; and Ogden, J.P., 1987, Determinants of relative interest rate sensitivity of corporate bonds, *Financial Management*, Spring, Vol. 16, Issue 1, 22–30.

the pitch that the underwriter will make to investors, the allocation that investors wish to make to an issue, and ultimately the price and yield spread that clears the new issue market for rated bonds.[8]

But it was then discovered that market yields are 'significantly correlated with both the ratings and a set of readily available financial accounting statistics.'[9] By itself, a correlation tells nothing about causality, as both yields and ratings could very well be caused by a same common factor. But further exploring these correlations on independent cross-sectional samples of fairly liquid industrial bonds rated by both Moody's and S&P's finds interesting results. More specifically, the explanatory power of ratings by themselves is about the same as the one of observable ratios of creditworthiness by themselves – such as interest coverage, leverage, coverage volatility and size. Interestingly, combining ratings and ratios increases the power to explain the cross-section variation in yields. This means that ratios and ratings are not just linear combinations of each other. It would be wrong to say: seen one, seen the other ... On the contrary, these three results taken jointly mean that ratios and ratings exercise their own influences on yields and mutually reinforce each other in this. Bearing in mind thus how ratings and ratios interact in explaining spreads, it would be hard to reject the proposition that ratings do exercise an intermediating influence on yields and that they are therefore relevant.

In addition, ratings show in fact a slight edge in relevance over ratios to account for the spreads of below investment grade bonds. This is important. It suggests that ratings are particularly relevant when they are most needed. Thus, inasmuch information as asymmetry is more pervasive in the below investment grade universe, the value added of ratings increases with information asymmetries, as found elsewhere.

These results hold as much for issues that were rated or reviewed recently as they do for those that have had no rating action for five years or more. The market does not really depreciate ratings. It views a new or recently reviewed rating as similarly meaningful to set credit spreads as an old rating that has not been reviewed and changed recently. Respectively, it means that ratios affect yields on both new and old issues.

When testing credit ratings against sentiment to account for spreads, ratings tend to win also. New issue credit spreads do reflect objective considerations such as the credit rating. In fact, credit ratings account for the largest proportion of variations in spreads. They also have by far the highest correlation than any other variable.[10] These findings are robust with respect to variations in the seniority of the debt, term of the debt, call features, first time or seasoned issuer, underwriter reputation, state of the IPO market, or mutual fund flows. Under all these scenarios, the systematic relevance of ratings to account for spreads is confirmed.

When ratings develop while firm fundamentals remain the same, they affect spread structure! Isn't that another fascinating finding to resolve the chicken or egg enigma? Let's thank S&P and Moody's for offering in 1974 and 1982, respectively, one experiment where such

---

[8] For a classic on this, see Wakeman, L.M., 1984, The real function of bond rating agencies, in Jensen, M. and Smith, C. (eds), *The Modern Theory of Corporate Finance*, McGraw-Hill, New York, 391–396.

[9] Ederington, L.H., Roberts, B.E., and Yawitz, J.B., 1987, The informational content of bond ratings, *Journal of Financial Research*, Fall, Vol. X, No. 3, 211–226, page 211.

[10] See for instance: Fridson, M.S., and Garman, M.C., 1998, Determinants of spreads on new high-yield bonds, *Financial Analysts Journal*, March/April, Vol. 54, No. 2, 28–39. It is also noted that, while this may seem unremarkable, there is evidence that for the French bond market, a direct relationship between yield and the ratings of the largest French bond rating agency is either weak or non-existent. See Artus, P., Garrigues, J., and Sassenou, M., 1993, Interest rate costs and issuer ratings: The case of French CP and bonds, *Journal of International Securities Markets*, Autumn, Vol. 7, 211–218.

a case occurred. They announced the refinement of their rating scale adding 12 fine rating modifiers ($+/-$ or $1-2-3$, respectively) to their traditional main categories. Close inspection of the effects of the Moody's move found that its rating refinement had an independent impact on bond prices.[11] This was particularly so for the '3' modifier that increased the spreads. For another experiment we have to be grateful to Fitch credit ratings.[12] As a third rating, these have a significant incremental impact on credit spreads, which suggests that these ratings convey supplementary information that S&P and Moody's either overlooked or misinterpreted and that the market values that information.[13] What is remarkable in both cases is that it is virtually impossible to reasonably argue that causality flew from the spreads to the ratings or from a common cause to both spreads and ratings.

An extra revealing way to establish the relevance of credit ratings to bond yield spreads is to examine the bid–ask spreads on corporate bonds. Doing so, one finds that bid–ask spreads in the European corporate bond market vary with credit ratings.

> Market microstructure models of dealer markets imply that spreads should increase with the inventory bearing costs of the dealers. Inventory costs increase with the risk that the value of the security will vary a lot. In the case of bonds, this risk increases with the duration of the bond (which can be proxied by its maturity) and its credit risk (which can be proxied by its rating). Consistently with these implications of the theory, we find that bid–ask spreads in the European corporate bond market increase with maturity and decrease with credit quality.[14]

To sum up and conclude, ratings do independently fashion spreads, but they have no monopoly in doing so.

Two Chickens: Split Ratings and the Structural Relevance of Ratings for Spreads

Most issues have at least two ratings and they tend to be observationally split. This is at least the rule rather than the exception. It holds for new issue ratings and for ongoing issuer ratings. As we saw earlier for 65 993 US Domestic Public Offerings during the period 1976–2006, of the 7615 joint corporate bond ratings of Moody's and S&P, 47.2% were split on a 20 notch scale; of the 740 of Fitch and S&P, 51.1% were split; of the 737 of Fitch and Moody's, 48.4% were split.[15] For ongoing issuer ratings, a globally representative sample of about 15 000 issuer ratings that generate 51 342 matched pairs from the 11 larger CRAs rating internationally showed a similar result. The average consensus across the full

---

[11] Liu, P., Seyyed, F.J., and Smith, S.D., 1999, The independent impact of credit rating changes: the case of Moody's refinement on yield premiums, *Journal of Business Finance and Accounting*, April/May, Vol. 26(3) and (4), 337–363, page 340.

[12] Fitch stand here for both Fitch Investors Service and Duff&Phelps because the data on which the reported results are based pre-date the 1997–2000 mergers.

[13] Jewell, J., and Livingston, M., 2000, The impact of a third credit rating on the pricing of bonds, *The Journal of Fixed Income*, December, Vol. 10, 69–85, pages 69 and 83.

[14] Biais, B., Declerck, F., Dow, J., Portes, R., von Thadden, E-L., 2006, European corporate bond markets: transparency, liquidity, efficiency, Centre for Economic Policy Research, May, page 55. See also Ho, T., and Stoll, H., 1983, The dynamics of dealer markets under competition, *Journal of Finance*, September, Biais, B., 1993, Price formation and equilibrium liquidity in fragmented and centralized markets, *Journal of Finance*, Vol. 48, pages 157–185, or Biais, B., Glosten, L., and Spatt, C., 2005, Market microstructure: A survey of microfoundations, empirical results and policy implications, *Journal of Financial Markets*, Vol. 8, pp 217–264.

[15] The fraction of splits is generally even more pronounced for CD and Notes ratings, particularly between Fitch and S&P who disagree 65.9% of the time on 6919 jointly rated CDs and 62.9% of the time on 11 600 jointly rated Notes.

20-point scale was a mere 26.8%; across investment grades it was 34.4%; across speculative grades it was 16.0%.[16] What can we observe of split ratings in credit spreads? What can we learn from this about the structural relevance of ratings for spreads?

State of the art findings about split ratings in credit spreads show that spreads reflect the split. Initially, it was proposed that 'the market considers the quality of a split-rated bond to reflect the lower of the two ratings.'[17] This finding followed the analysis of a carefully selected sample of 282 investment grade and liquid corporate bonds with split ratings by Moody's and S&P in 1984. It concluded 'that risk-averse investors who face two different and imperfect sources of information about investment quality would give more credence to the lower ratings. But the analysis did not control for bond and bond market conditions. More recently, it was proposed that 'the spread on split-rated bonds is 16 to 21 bps less than that on bonds on the adjacent lower rating.'[18] These findings followed the analysis of a sample of 1512 Moody's and S&P rated municipal bonds sold in Texas between 1976 and 1983. In fact, a completely independent approach from the former one that controls for bond features and market conditions found equivalently that any one of Moody's or S&P ratings, or the average of these, produced an unbiased estimate of the actually observed reoffering spread on the full sample of 4399 US corporate bonds issued between 1983 and 1993. In addition, that analysis established that the average rating was the most efficient estimator of that spread. This finding about efficiency held also for each sub-sample of one through four notch differentials and on the investment versus non-investment grade sub-samples.[19] Yet another analysis found also that the yield on the split rated bond lies between the typical yields for the higher rating and the lower rating. Thus, the initial market pricing reflects some average of the split assigned ratings.[20]

The combined information of two ratings, split or not, brings information to the market, underscoring the structural relevance of ratings for spreads. For the case of split ratings, we just called attention to the reduction in prediction error brought about by equally weighting the two different ratings to forecast the spread of the split-rated bond. For the case of identical multiple ratings, the previously discussed analysis of municipal bonds found that these reduce investors' required yield by 2.5 bps.[21] Both types of findings allow us to share the view 'that two bond ratings are better than one.'[22] This is, of course, consistent with the fact that, observationally, split ratings occur due to systematic differences across CRAs, as seen earlier in the book. Refining the split rating analysis one step further, does the market interpret split ratings differentially for above and below investment grade bonds? In turns out that 'pricing in the investment grade sector is more conservative – placing more weight

---

[16] Barton, A., 2006, Split credit ratings and the prediction of bank ratings in the Basel II environment, Thesis submitted for the degree of Doctor of Philosophy, University of Southampton, Faculty of Law, Arts and Social Sciences, School of Management, 1–205, pages 121–122.

[17] Liu, P., and Moore, W.T., 1987, The impact of split bond ratings on risk premia, *The Financial Review*, February, Vol. 22, 71–85, page 83.

[18] Hsueh, L., and Kidwell, D., 1988, Bond ratings: are two better than one?, Spring, *Financial Management*, 46–53, page 52.

[19] Cantor, R., Packer, F., and Cole, K., 1997, Split ratings and the pricing of credit risk, *The Journal of Fixed Income*, December, 1–82.

[20] Jewell, J., and Livingston, M., 1998, Split ratings, bond yields, and underwriter spreads, *The Journal of Financial Research*, Summer, Vol. XXI, No. 2, 185–204.

[21] Hsueh, L., and Kidwell, D., 1988, Bond ratings: are two better than one?, Spring, *Financial Management*, 46–53, page 52.

[22] Hsueh, L., and Kidwell, D., 1988, Bond ratings: are two better than one?, Spring, *Financial Management*, 46–53, page 52.

on the lower rating than on the higher rating – than pricing in the full sample.'[23] In the sample below investment grade, the average rating is again relatively superior as a predictor than either a non-combined rating or one that puts more weight on the low rating than on the high one. To sum up and conclude, the findings on the extent and degree in which split ratings affect spreads document, in their own way, the structural relevance of credit ratings for credit spreads.

The Credit Spread Puzzle and the Actual Structure of the Relation between Ratings and Spreads

Having seen that ratings fashion spreads by bringing information to the market, what is the information really about and how much of the spreads does it determine? Is it information about the likely ups and downs of the spreads? Are ratings relevant to benchmark the volatility of bond returns? Once the process of market spread setting to which ratings contribute is over – say, the spread is in equilibrium – what is its structure and how much of that spread can we then attribute to ratings? Is it more or less dependent on the rating category? So, let's move from the process question of the previous section to the end result question now. To focus on this, one might even imagine, if one wishes to do so, that market participants outside of CRAs can fully replicate CRA ratings and that the market fully anticipates ratings. For our question at hand now, these points are ... fully irrelevant. From here on, we take the ratings and spreads for what they are. We simply ask: what is the end-game of the structure of the relation between them? Of course, the answer to that is as important in gauging the relevance of ratings to issuers as was our former process question.

CRAs pay most of their attention at figuring out the fundamentals of the issuer and the structure of its financing. Their work focuses on anticipating the issuer fundamentals that will drive it into default and, on analyzing the characterisitics of the debt instruments, to gauge the losses on some of the instruments in the event of a default. How much of these issuer fundamentals and instrument characteristics drive the structure of credit spreads?

The fundamental that shows up prominently in the spreads that are associated with each rating category is the expected loss on the rated instrument due to default. Table 7.2 tabulates the average spreads for the categories AAA to B for four maturity buckets from 1–3 to 7–10 years. For each spread, the table shows the corresponding expected loss in bps and as a percentage of the spread.[24] This finding documents a structure of the relation between ratings and spreads whereby the importance of expected loss as a component of the spread rises as credit ratings go down and, for a given rating, as maturity increases. For example, take the 3–5 years maturity bucket and compare the relation between expected loss to spread for an AAA bond category with the one of the B category. In the former, it is 0.18 bps relative to 63.86, or a mere 0.3%; whereas in the latter it is 400.52 bps relative to 691.81 bps or 57.9%. The lower the credit rating, the larger the expected loss component in the observed credit spread. Considering any rating level, the fraction of expected loss in the spread increases with maturity. Take the BBB category. From the shortest maturity bucket the fraction increases monotonically from 7% to 19% in the longest

[23] Cantor, R., Packer, F., and Cole, K., 1997, Split ratings and the pricing of credit risk, *The Journal of Fixed Income*, December, 1–82, page 78.
[24] Amato, J.D., and Remolona, E.M., 2003, The credit spread puzzle, *Quarterly Review*: Bank for International Settlements, December, 51–63, Table 1, page 52.

Table 7.2 Spreads and expected default losses (1997–2003)

Rating	Maturity											
	1–3 years		3–5 years		5–7 years		7–10 years	
	Spread	Expected loss	Spread	Expected loss	Spread	Expected loss	Spread	Expected loss
AAA	49.50	0.06	0%	63.86	0.18	0%	70.47	0.33	0%	73.95	0.61	1%
AA	58.97	1.24	2%	71.22	1.44	2%	82.36	1.86	2%	88.57	2.70	3%
A	88.82	1.12	1%	102.91	2.78	3%	110.71	4.71	4%	117.52	7.32	6%
BBB	168.99	12.48	7%	170.89	20.12	12%	185.34	27.17	15%	179.63	34.56	19%
BB	421.20	103.09	24%	364.55	126.74	35%	345.37	140.52	41%	322.32	148.05	46%
B	760.84	426.16	56%	691.81	400.52	58%	571.94	368.38	64%	512.43	329.40	64%

Source: Amato, J.D., and Remolona, E.M., 2003, The credit spread puzzle, *Quarterly Review*: Bank for International Settlements, December, 51–63, Table 1, page 52.

bucket. Interest coverage, capitalization, profitability, size, and stability are well-known co-determinants of rating levels and their corresponding expected default losses. The evidence presented in Table 7.2 suggests how determinant these financial fundamentals are in driving spreads.

But next to these fundamentals, a complex risk factor helps to explain spreads. Expected loss is surrounded by an in-built uncertainty. But also, a spread is a price. On top of intrinsic metrics such as expected loss and its standard deviation, the price also reflects something psychological, driving a wedge between the spread and 'risk-neutral' probability distributions. This is the aversion against uncertainty about expected loss. Bond investors will prefer low uncertainty surrounding expected loss over high uncertainty. After all, they are short the expected credit loss, meaning that the higher the loss outcome, the worse of they are. They must hate the volatility of the expected loss, just as someone who is short an option hates the volatility of the underlying! One can expect spreads to also reflect bond investors' distaste for risk and for uncertainty and the extent of that uncertainty. Of course, the degree of that uncertainty is once more a fundamental or measurable variable to which the CRAs could pay attention in their ratings, next to expected loss.[25]

That leads us to the so-called credit spread puzzle. One can see the puzzle in Table 7.2.

Spreads on corporate bonds tend to be many times wider than what would be implied by expected default alone ... In 1997–2003, for example, the average spread on BBB-rated corporate bonds with three to five years to maturity was about 170 bps at annual rates. Yet, during the same period, the average yearly loss from default amounted to only 20 basis points. In this case, the spread was more than eight times the expected loss from default.[26]

Isn't it puzzling that AAA bonds with virtually zero expected loss command spreads from 50 bps at the short end of the maturity spectrum to 74 bps at the long end?

The solution to the puzzle is the systematic risk premium that bond returns command. Think about an investment in a corporate bond in the same way as the investment in common stock. Bonds expose their investors to this economy wide risk in the same sense that common stocks expose shareholders to it.

There are two reasons why changes in corporate spreads might be systematic. First, if expected default loss were to move with equity prices, so while stock prices rise default risk goes down and as stock prices fall default risk goes up, it would introduce a systematic factor. Second, the compensation for risk required in capital markets changes over time. If changes in the required compensation for risk affects both corporate bond and stock markets, then this would introduce a systematic influence.[27]

---

[25] Gürkaynak, R., and Wolfers, J., 2006, Macroeconomic derivatives: an initial analysis of market-based macro forecast, uncertainty and risk, Working Paper 11929: National Bureau of Economic Research, January, 1–43, report for the macroeconomic level 'finding little evidence that risk-aversion drives a wedge between market prices and volatilities' (page 2). If this were to hold also at the micro-economic level for relative prices, that would suggest that eventually one should succeed in re-engineering observed spreads with pure risk neutral metrics that do not need any risk aversion parameters.

[26] Amato, J.D., and Remolona, E.M., 2003. The credit spread puzzle, *Quarterly Review*: Bank for International Settlements, December, 51–63, page 51.

[27] Agrawal, D., Elton, E., Gruber, M., and Mann, C., 2001, Explaining the rate spread on corporate bonds, *Journal of Finance*, February, Vol. LVI, No. 1, 247–277, page 267.

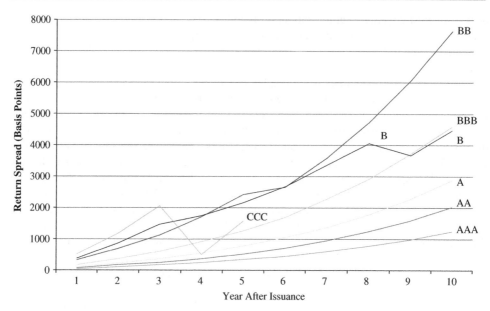

Figure 7.2 Realized return spreads on net investment in US corporate bonds over risk-free governments (1971–1987)
Source: Altman, E.I., 1989, Measuring corporate bond mortality and performance, *The Journal of Finance*, Vol XLIV, No. 4, September, 909–922, pages 919–920.

This leads to the notion of the fair risk return premium on the bond that bond investors would require for bearing non-diversifiable risk. Does the market pay that return premium as compensation?

The market rewards bond investors for bearing that systematic risk, net of realized losses from defaults and in line with the initial credit ratings of the bonds. That is established by estimates of the long-term performance of fixed-income investors over a broad spectrum of credit ratings that allow for bond mortality and loss in the event of default, as Figure 7.2 (based on Table 7.3) illustrates.

The results show that AAA-rated bonds can be expected to earn 45 bps (0.45%) more than Treasuries over one year (two semi-annual coupon payments) and 1245 bps after 10 years. BB-rated bonds earn 326 bps more than Treasuries after one year and an impressive 7637 bps after 10 years. Another way to put this is that an investment of $100 would return $76.37 more than Treasuries over 10 years.[28]

The premium that investors integrate into the rate at which they discount the expected bond cash flows has a term for market risk and a term for the exposure of the bond to that market risk. The market risk premium is the one that all assets command that are exposed to market wide risk. The exposure term is particular to a bond of a specific firm. This is called the market return sensitivity of the bond, or its beta. For instance, over the period 1990–2000, investment grade corporate debt had an estimated beta of 0.27 and high-yield

---

[28] Altman, E.I., 1989, Measuring corporate bond mortality and performance, *The Journal of Finance*, September, Vol. XLIV, No. 4, 909–922, pages 919–920.

Table 7.3 Realized return spreads in basis points on net investment in US corporate bonds over risk-free governments – compounded over time (1971–1987)

Years after issuance	Bond rating at issuance						
	AAA	AA	A	BBB	BB	B	CCC
1	45	76	104	171	326	382	519
2	100	168	223	366	684	861	1174
3	165	243	367	609	129	1460	2062
4	246	359	556	923	1710	1746	496
5	344	515	782	1250	2419	2160	1561
6	457	710	1047	1700	2648	2676	NA
7	598	949	1366	2286	3585	3365	NA
8	772	1246	1778	2911	4725	4058	NA
9	987	1591	2278	3721	6073	3673	NA
10	1245	2028	2885	4577	7637	4467	NA

Notes:
1. Return spreads are based on compound returns net of losses incurred from defaults. They reflect actual mortality rates and reinvestment rates derived from S&P Bond Guides and a number of securities firms.
2. Return spreads are based on compounding cash flows received from coupon payments, redemptions, and default recoveries.
3. Cash flows were reinvested in the same bond-rating class at prevailing interest rates at that time.
Source: Altman, E.I., 1989, Measuring corporate bond mortality and performance, *The Journal of Finance*, Vol XLIV, No. 4, September, 909–922, pages 919–920.

corporate debt beta of 0.37.[29] We can now put these two terms together to gauge the fair risk return premium on a corporate bond over that period. As the market premium is about 4.3% over that period, the premium on a typical investment grade bond is then 1.16%, and on a high-yield one it would be 1.59%.[30] All these insights combined suggest that bond spreads must reflect more than just the expected loss on the bond. This is exactly what Table 7.4, which reflects results of advanced statistical 'stock price' type of analysis of corporate bonds, documents.[31] It attributes 19.4–40.7% of the spread to that risk premium, which is a significantly larger portion than expected loss.[32] This greater importance is particularly so for the highest grade bonds where the risk premium is 3.5 to 5.5 times the expected loss. The fractional contribution of the premium increases with the expected loss, as the rating concurrently declines.[33] This risk premium is a true excess return of the bond over the default-free rate. It compensates not for the cost of the expected loss, but for the risk

---

[29] Goedhart, M., Koller, T., and Wessels, D., McKinsey & Company, 2005, *Valuation: Measuring and Managing the Value of Companies*, John Wiley & Sons, New Jersey, 1–742, page 327.
[30] Dimson, E., Marsh, P., and Staunton, M., 2002, *Triumph of the Optimists*, Princeton University Press, New Jersey, 1–339, page 310.
[31] As Agrawal, D., Elton, E., Gruber, M., and Mann, C., remind and empirically corroborate, a significant 'portion of the spread is closely related to the factors that we commonly accept as explaining risk premiums for common stocks ... Our tests support the existence of a risk premium on corporate bonds ... This occurs because a large part of the risk on corporate bonds is systematic rather than diversifiable' in 2001, Explaining the rate spread on corporate bonds, *Journal of Finance*, February, Vol. LVI, No. 1, 247–277, page 247.
[32] Making abstraction for a moment from firm exogenous forces such as income taxes on the coupon and possibly liquidity of the bond.
[33] Amato, J.D., and Remolona, E.M., 2003, The credit spread puzzle, *Quarterly Review*: Bank for International Settlements, December, 51–63, Table 2, page 54.

Table 7.4 Attributing credit spreads to expected losses and a risk premium

Authors	Spread component	Decomposing credit spreads					
		Attributed portion of spread (in percentages)					
		Rating					
		AA		A		BBB	
		Maturity					
		5	10	5	10	5	10
Elton et al. (2001)	Expected loss	3.50	8.00	11.40	17.80	20.90	34.70
	Taxes	72.60	58.00	48.00	44.10	29.00	28.40
	Risk premium	19.40	27.60	33.00	30.90	40.70	30.00
	Other	4.50	6.40	7.70	7.20	9.40	7.00

Source: Agrawal, D., Elton, E., Gruber, M., and Mann, C., 2001, Explaining the rate spread on corporate bonds, *Journal of Finance*, February, Vol. LVI, No. 1, 247–277, page 247.

of the unexpected loss![34] It is the price of unexpected credit losses.[35] If one approximates risk of unexpected loss with the volatility in put options on a firm's stock, one finds that this volatility explains about 63% of the time variation in CDS spreads.[36] The objective benchmarking of risk of unexpected loss through measures of standard deviation around the expected loss, or others, is a fascinating area of R&D at CRAs.

The premium hides in fact an extra component that we have to extract: the premium for the risk of disaster. When prices fall off the cliff, it is called a collapse or a downside jump. Imagine it graphically as a discontinuity. You are drawing a price graph, moving your pencil horizontally, or up or down, depending on the time series. But occasionally, you must lift your pencil off the paper and resume graphing at a vertical distance below the point where you lifted your pencil. Think about times of sudden panics, of self-feeding fears of collapse, of unprecedented stock market crashes of 22.6% on one day as on Monday, October 19, 1987, or of a drop of the plane due to a thin air bubble, as happened to the SSE Composite Index (Shanghai) dropping 8.8% on February 27, 2007, as Figure 7.3 shows.

Investors know that discontinuities exist, but don't know when they will occur, or how bad they will be when they occur. Crashes are always a great surprise, almost by definition. However good CRAs are in preventing surprises in defaults ... during normal times! It is an adversity to which all securities of all defaultable issuers are exposed, regardless of their credit rating. It tends to rapidly spill over from one asset class to another, from one market to another, as Figure 7.3 also illustrates. Note how within five trading days of the Shanghai stock market downside jump the average credit spread on a broad portfolio of emerging markets corporate bonds jumped up from 85 bps to 112 bps or by more than one-third and remained high until at least the end of March. So it is a broad risk than materializes very suddenly, taking almost everybody by surprise.

Investors hate being taken by such surprises. This hatred is in addition to be generally risk averse. During such extreme days, sentiment easily takes over from fundamentals and

---

[34] Ex-ante credit loss uncertainty is commonly referred to as unexpected loss.

[35] Amato, J.D., and Remolona, E.M., 2004, The pricing of unexpected credit losses, Working Paper: Bank for International Settlements, October, 1–49.

[36] Cao, C., Yu, F., and Zong, Z., 2006, The information content of option implied volatility for credit default swap valuation, Working Paper, April 9, 1–42, Table 4, page 32.

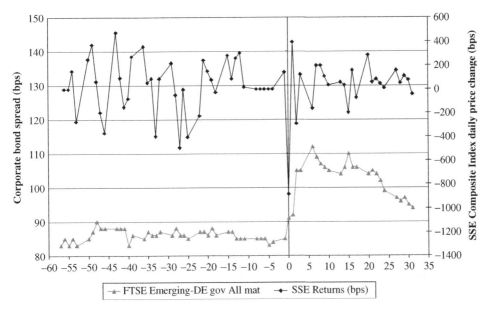

Figure 7.3 SSE Composite Index (Shanghai) price changes and spread of emerging market bonds. (Daily, January 1–March 30, 2007)

Definitions:

1. Bond spread = FTSE Euro denominated emerging market bond index, all maturities (FTSE EURO EMERGING MARKETS ALL MATS–RED. YIELD) less FTSE German government bond index, all maturities (FTSE GLOBAL GOVT. BD ALL MATS.(E)–RED. YIELD)
2. SSE Returns = (SSE(t+1) − SSE(t))/SSE(t) where SSE is the 'Shanghai SE composite–price index' from Datastream.

Source: Datastream

psychology from analysis. Risk aversion increases quite drastically and independently of credit fundamentals in these circumstances. 'Increasingly, there is statistical evidence that suggests the stock market may have a life of its own to some extent, unrelated to economic fundamentals.'[37] And as 'the informational efficiency of corporate bond prices is similar to that of the underlying stocks . . . and measures of market quality are [similar] for the bonds in our sample [to] the underlying stocks,' it is no real surprise that collapse risk transfers to the defaultable bond market.[38]

We can now assemble the full puzzle: a comprehensive financial engineering model of credit spreads documents that credit ratings embed a structure on credit spreads that reflects the economics of these spreads.[39] From what precedes, credit spreads should reflect (1) expected loss, (2) beta risk, (3) jump risk, (4) the tax differential treatment between corporate and government bond income, and (5) other factors. Do they actually do so and are

[37] Shiller, R.J., 1989, *Market Volatility*, The MIT Press, Cambridge, Massachusetts, 1–464, page 398.
[38] Hotchkiss, E.S., and Ronen T., 2002, The informational efficiency of the corporate bond market: an intraday analysis, *Review of Financial Studies*, Winter, Vol. 15, No. 5, 1325–1354, page 1325.
[39] Cremers, M., Driessen, J., and Maenhout, P., 2007, Explaining the level of credit spreads: option-implied jump risk premia in a firm value model, *Review of Financial Studies*, forthcoming, 1–48.

they structured in a meaningful and useful way according to fundamental credit ratings? The answer to both questions is by and large 'yes' (nothing is perfect). A particularly clever method has been used to reach that answer. The method replicates observed spreads for rating categories AAA to B. It does so by imposing an exhaustive spread structure on the output of a model that integrates different component drivers to produce model spreads for the different credit ratings. One driver is the time evolution of enterprise values that are correlated across firms, uncertain and subject to major shocks, which we know, for certain, can occur, but not when or with what intensity. Another driver is the arbitrage-based option valuation model. Some forms of that model engineer spreads on debt as the result of company credit fundamentals such as: business risk, as measured by the volatility of asset returns; financial leverage, as captured by the ratio of the face value of debt to the market value of the assets; the length in time of credit exposure, as captured by the maturity of the bond.[40] A third driver is the set of historical measures of input parameters needed to run and then solve the models. Table 7.5 shows the result of this major effort.[41]

Table 7.5 Comprehensive decomposition of credit spread

				Compensations in basis points for:					
Issuer rating	Model credit spreads in bps*	Income tax effect	Expected loss	Risk in Diffusion-only model	Risk in Jump-diffusion model	Unaccounted for compensation	Lehman index credit spread in bps†	10 yr cumulative default probability	Average recovery rate
AAA	82.7	35.1	3.8	11.7	47.6	−16.4	66.3	0.77%	51.31%
AA	91.6	35.1	4.8	19.4	56.5	0.3	91.9	0.99%	51.31%
A	105.7	35.0	7.6	27.1	70.7	9.7	115.4	1.55%	51.31%
BBB	152.3	34.0	21.6	68.4	118.3	18.7	171.0	4.39%	51.31%
BB	339.9	30.9	105.9	247.9	309.0	−7.3	332.6	20.63%	51.31%
B	535.9	23.6	240.5	478.7	512.3	11.9	547.8	43.91%	51.31%
AAA	100.0%	42.4%	4.5%	14.1%	57.6%	−19.8%			
AA	100.0%	38.3%	5.3%	21.2%	61.7%	0.3%			
A	100.0%	33.1%	7.2%	25.6%	66.9%	9.2%			
BBB	100.0%	22.3%	14.2%	44.9%	77.7%	12.3%			
BB	100.0%	9.1%	31.1%	72.9%	90.9%	−2.1%			
B	100.0%	4.4%	44.9%	89.3%	95.6%	2.2%			

*The model credit spread is the option-implied spread generated by the jump diffusion model. Hence the spread in the first column is the sum of the income tax effect and the risk in the jump diffusion model (column 1 = column 2 + column 5).
†The Lehman index credit spread is the empirical equivalent of the model credit spread, hence the difference, the unaccounted for compensation (column 6 = column 7 − column 1).
Source: Cremers, M., Driessen, J., and Maenhout, P., 2007, Explaining the level of credit spreads: option-implied jump risk premia in a firm value model, *Review of Financial Studies*, forthcoming, 1–48, Tables 1 and 5, page 42.

---

[40] One can think of the maturity of a bond as a binary measure of the 'temporal resolution of uncertainty (TRU)': no uncertainty about expected loss is resolved until maturity, all uncertainty is resolved at the maturity. It turns out that 'the later the uncertainty facing the firm is resolved, the larger the yields on corporate debt issued between 1987 and 1996.' See Perlich, C., and Reisz, A.S., 2006, Temporal resolution of uncertainty and corporate debt yields: an empirical investigation, *Journal of Business*, Vol. 79, No. 2, 731–770, page 731.
[41] Table 7.5, is a slight adaptation of Table 5 in Cremers, M., Driessen, J., and Maenhout, P., 2007, Explaining the level of credit spreads: option-implied jump risk premia in a firm value model, *Review of Financial Studies*, forthcoming, 1–48, page 42.

The levels and structure of the credit spreads that emerge from the model are quite revealing. One, the model spreads account for about 99% on average of the spreads for different rating categories of the historically observed and widely used Lehman index credit spreads. Two, it accounts particularly well for the spreads at the BB and B levels where the income tax effect is smallest and the expected loss factor is highest. Three, changes in the relative importance of cost factors in the spread when ratings decline make sense. As the cost of income tax is a function of the size of the coupon, and not of the spread, then, as ratings go down, its bps in the spread remain fairly constant and decline as a fraction of the spread. The cost of expected loss pattern is as it should be, and is similar to the one in Table 7.4 previously discussed, and accounting for 31% (45%) of the spread in the case of BB (B) bonds. Four, the return premium for non-diversifiable risk increases from 48 bps on AAA bonds to 512 bps on B bonds. This corresponds in order of magnitude and direction with previously discussed results. It accounts for a prominent fraction of the spread, especially for non-investment grade bonds. Five, the real novelty of the results in Table 7.5 is in the breakdown of the return premium in one for continuous or ongoing risks and one for discontinuous or jump risks. Note that the compensation for jump risk is far from trivial. For investment grade bonds, it exceeds by a factor of almost 2 the compensation for ongoing risk. It is the other way around for high-yield bonds where the allowance for expected loss is already a large component of the spread.

Summing up, bond investor revulsion against the real major uncertainty of timing and gravity of jump-downs also commands a price in the corporate bond market. It is related not so much to the estimates by credit rating agencies of expected loss, but much more to the highly uncertain unexpected loss triggered by crashes. It is the required compensation for debt exposure to sudden market-wide value breakdowns, whereby prices quickly melt down and enterprise values dip deeply unexpectedly. In fact, such 'extreme-return days play a much more significant role in shaping the market's total returns than a normal distribution suggests.'[42] Indications suggest that they are easily twice as important! And they command an extra return to compensate the corporate bond investors who take that risk.

SF VIGNETTE 7
SF Instruments Ratings and Spreads: Specificities

Critics often question the quality of structured finance ratings after observing the spread differentials with more traditional debt instruments. Spreads on rated debt instruments vary, sometimes considerably, even where the instruments have the same rating. Some attribute the differentials to investors' distrust of ratings resulting from the ineptitude of rating agencies. However, this argument is not fully well-founded but not entirely groundless either.

The spread differentials may reflect, to a certain extent, the different market perspectives of the informativeness of ratings in the corporate or structured finance segment. However, spreads should especially reflect differences in payoffs and other risks embedded in different debt instruments, as these are essential elements that investors consider (or at least should consider) when paying for a security in addition to what the current rating of a structured finance instrument strictly tells them. We highlight some components of a spread that have specific impacts and dynamics in structured finance.

---

[42] Mauboussin, M.J., 2006, *More than You Know: Finding Financial Wisdom in Unconventional Places,* Columbia University Press, New York, 1–268, page 39.

- Most generally ratings are relative assessments of probability of default or expected loss and thus depend essentially on the first moment of the distribution of possible outcomes, whereas a spread also takes into account the risk or second-order moments of the distribution of outcomes. In particular, a spread generally accounts for the uncertainty in credit loss, often called unexpected loss (standard deviation of the credit loss). By nature, a tranche's unexpected loss increases with more junior and thinner tranches.
- In case of default, subordinated tranches may have zero recovery, and if default is severe enough, investors in all but the most senior tranches may lose the entire value of their investment, even in the case of non-zero recoveries. Subordinated tranches have a wider distribution of outcomes than like-rated bond portfolios and will thus need to pay a higher spread than traditional debt instruments to compensate for the higher loss given default.
- Model risk is the risk that the tranche rating may inaccurately reflect the 'true' credit risk of the tranche because the rating model used is not the most accurate one. Model risk is expected to increase with the complexity (perceived or real) of a given instrument.
- The volatility of tranche market prices and its potentially higher correlation with market risk demands higher spreads, for a given credit risk. Note that although the prioritization rule allows senior tranches to have low default probabilities, and hence high credit ratings, the senior tranche losses occur in systematically bad economic states. However, securities that fail to deliver their payment in these economic states should also, today, have a relatively low value, because systematically bad states are the states where a dollar has the most value (marginal utility) or that investors would like to cover themselves most against.[43]
- The likely amortization profile and the uncertainty in the amortization profile of the instruments is important for those structured finance instruments that pass-through principal prepayments from the collateral pool to amortize the debt owned by investors.
- The liquidity of the instrument, i.e. how frequently it is traded and hence how easy it might be to sell in the secondary market also affects the spread of instruments. A relatively illiquid instrument will trade at a higher spread, all else equal, than a liquid instrument. Hence, subordinate tranches or bespoke instruments that have smaller volumes may trade with a liquidity premium. Related to this is how often the originator comes to market and the size of the issue. For an issuance from an originator that rarely comes to market, investors may be willing to pay only a lower price (higher spread) due to adverse selection (more opacity) concerns. Indeed, they also have fixed costs of analysis and monitoring that they'd rather spread over several related issues or over larger amounts of investment. On the other hand, the infrequent originator may provide a valuable element of diversity for investors' portfolios, and evoke a premium (in the sense of higher price).

In a more general sense, the market for structured finance works by the competing forces of demand and supply, just as other markets. Prices are set by the transitory equilibrium between buyers and sellers. All economic factors related to products that influence supply or demand can play a role in deciding the dynamic prices, credit risk is just one of them. Other characteristics embedded in the behavior of market participants can further drive prices beyond what one could consider as fundamental value or

---

[43] Refer to Coval, J., Jurek, J., and Stafford, E., 2007, Economic Catastrophe Bonds, July, HBS Finance Working Paper No. 07-102.

cost drivers of supply and demand, they would be linked to the formation of beliefs concerning future events and the specificities of behavior under uncertainty. Important among them, to name a few, are investors' risk aversion, overreaction, sentiment, etc.

In conclusion, the relation between ratings and spreads is nowadays understood as being so highly structured that it can almost be engineered. Ratings bring to the market valuable information about expected losses. The importance of this information increases as the credit quality of the issuer declines. In addition, there is scope for the CRAs to also bring valuable information about the objective volatility surrounding the expected loss because that volatility is priced in the credit spread. Were CRAs to benchmark that volatility, it could be a worthwhile strategy to separately benchmark 'smooth' ongoing volatility and 'disruptive' catastrophic volatility, because these two volatilities are priced separately in the spread. These findings support the structural relevance of credit ratings as one element in their relevance for the value of the issuer. This brings to a close our discussion of the credit fundamentals and other factors in the structure of the relation between ratings and spreads.

7.1.2   Impact Relevance: Rating Actions and Security Price Changes

It is easy to casually observe occurrences of the high impact relevance of actual or newly anticipated rating actions. Consider the following. In response to demands from market participants and the code of conduct guidelines, CRAs regularly invite market participants to comment about changes they consider in rating methods and protocols before accepting and implementing them. On November 21, 2006, Moody's requested comments on a proposal to change its rating of preferred stock and hybrid securities.[44] Hybrids are securities that contain special clauses that allow an issuer to omit scheduled payment without triggering a default. They offer the issuer financing flexibility akin to equity and tax savings like debt. Gauging the likely implications of the change, Moody's wrote: 'If implemented as proposed, the refined methodology would lead to rating downgrades for most non-cumulative preferred stock issues and for a number of hybrid securities.'

'Hybrids hit by Moody's rethink' was the headline of the *Financial Times* reporting of November 22 on Moody's request for comments, writing that: 'Bond prices of some of Europe's biggest companies were rocked yesterday by [the] announcement ... Vinci suffered the biggest price moves, as such an action would mean its bonds' ratings were cut to junk.'[45]

By revealing new information about the likelihood that Vinci's bonds could become below investment grade, Moody's request for comment reduced the demand for Vinci's bonds from those investors whose portfolio assets are subject to above investment grade rating constraints. Is this anecdotal evidence sufficiently valid to illustrate that ratings bring

---

[44] Fanger, D., Fons, J., Gates, D., and Havlicek, B., 2006, Rating preferred stock and hybrid securities: request for comment, *Rating Methodology*: Moody's Investors Service, November 21, Report 100692, 1–8, page 4, also indicates that ratings could change for roughly 300 securities.

[45] Oakley, D., 2006, Hybrids hit by Moody's rethink, *Financial Times*, November 22.

information to the markets about default prospects? Not really, because portfolio constrained holders of Vinci affected securities could very well be selling for portfolio governance reasons rather than for a rating action induced change of their own views of Vinci's default prospects. The bond price reaction could indeed have been fully due to a liquidity effect, without any change in the views that the sellers held about Vinci's default prospects.

The interplay between rating actions and security price changes is complex. Do rating changes provide additional information about default prospects that is not already factored into market prices, or do rating actions merely reflect the change in information that the capital market has already priced? In the high-yield sector in particular, news tends to alter prices rapidly. Professional investors constantly monitor issuers, issues, and markets to anticipate price-sensitive events and news about them. Do agencies lead the market, or is it the other way around?

The satellite-based telephone industry has been an interesting example of the complexity of the interplay between rating price changes. It shows how bond investor changing perceptions of default prospects and the uncertainty surrounding these, and their changing aversion against that uncertainty, can have a dramatic effect on bond prices, not waiting for rating changes. See, for example, the cases of Iridium in Figure 7.4 and of Globalstar in Figure 7.5.

Iridium – Figure 7.1 shows the yield on a defaulted bond from Iridium, the Motorola-backed provider of global mobile satellite telephone services that declared bankruptcy in August of 1999. The company was plagued from the start with faulty handsets, slow subscriber growth, and problems with the satellites. This bond, due in July 2005, went in default in January 2000. Note the sharp increase in yield during the spring of 1999 ahead of rating changes as a string of negative announcements about company prospects were made. S&P downgraded the bond to D on July 15, 1999.[46]

Globalstar – The graph in Figure 7.2. is a bond from Globalstar LP, a development stage second mover in the satellite-based telephone industry that in November 1999 completed a worldwide, low-earth orbit satellite-based telecommunications system and was expected to soon start operating it on a limited scale. Market demand remained to be demonstrated. Total cost of the 52 satellite Globalstar system was about $4.3 billion, and had been fully financed. S&P had a B rating on the bond, thinking that Globalstar could have a credible business model, and conveying that the bonds of Globalstar, while speculative, are a manageable credit risk. The rating agency has still some confidence that Globalstar will continue to honor its debt obligations as it moves forward. The stock market appeared to agree at that time. Globalstar's equity had more than doubled between the middle of December 1999 and the first week of 2000. Yet Globalstar bondholders asked a yield to maturity of approximately 23% on January 14, 2000. Bottom-line? Who got it right: the agencies and stock investors or bondholders? Let's see what happened. At the time, the stock market was at the zenith of the ICT tech bubble and optimism turned out to be short lived. Globalstar went into service on March 1, 2000, covering 25 countries by the end of the month. First quarter results (ended March 31, 2000) were disappointing, indicating that its recently launched satellite voice service has gotten off to a slower-than-expected start. The stock price tumbled. The company had experienced a number of start-up challenges and now faced near-term liquidity issues. On March 31, 2000, it had $2.1 billion of debt, $234.7 million of cash,

---

[46] Standard & Poor's, 2005, *Data from CreditPro 7.0*, June 30.

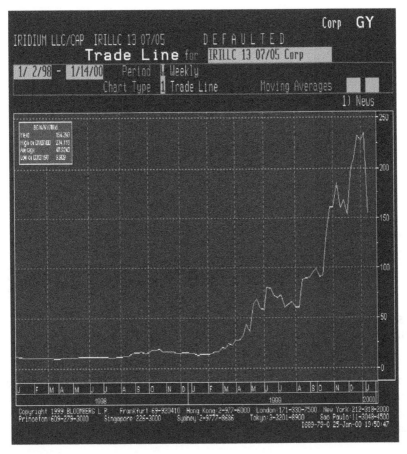

Figure 7.4 Iridium 13 percent 07/05 bond: yield to maturity (YTM) 1/2/98–1/14/00
Source: Bloomberg as of January 14, 2000.

and an undrawn $350 million bank credit facility originally set to mature in December 2000, but that could be accelerated to June 2000. In the light of these, on May 9 S&P downgraded Globalstar to B– with negative watch. During Q2, the operational ramp-up of the company's recently launched satellite voice service continued to be slow. The company's liquidity situation tightened further, the bank line was fully drawn, there was no more cash, just more debt and concerns grew regarding potential covenant violations during the first quarter of 2001. As a result, on August 22 S&P downgraded to CCC, with continuous negative watch. End of the story? On January 16, 2001, S&P lowered the rating to D, following Globalstar's announcement that it had suspended principal and interest payments on its debt obligations.[47] The bond continued trading occasionally and the last price tracked on March 23, 2001, corresponded to a yield to maturity of 135.1%.

---

[47] Standard & Poor's, 2001, Globalstar ratings lowered to 'D', removed from creditwatch, *Rating Action*, January 16.

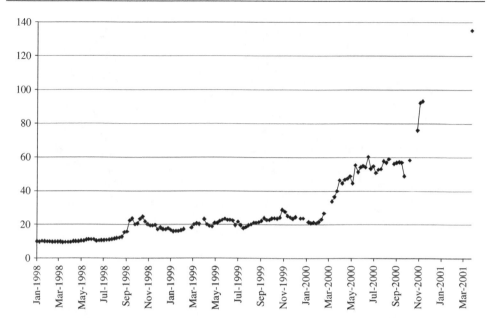

Figure 7.5   Globalstar 11.25% 06/04 bond: yield to maturity (YTM) 1/2/1998–3/2/2001
Source: Bloomberg as of June 29, 2000.

Underneath the apparent complexity, what is the structure of the relationship between changes in ratings and in issuer security prices? What regularities emerge, if any? Do casual observation, graphical inspection, empirical research, and statistical event studies reveal any robust patterns?

Stock Price Reactions to Rating Actions

Abnormal negative returns in the stock of the issuing firm precede bond rating downgrades.[48] If we consider Figures 7.6 and 7.7,[49] the following emerges.

A first regularity is that sharp price movements in an issuer share price typically precede rating actions. In both the US and Europe, the announcement, by either Fitch, Moody's or S&P, of a downgrade and also of a negative watch are both preceded by significant negative abnormal stock returns during a window of −90 days. Positive watches by S&P and Fitch are associated with positive abnormal returns, but to a lesser extent. As rating changes do not happen overnight, that should be no surprise. A rigorous reassessment process within the agency tends to precede them. The agency will typically announce when it begins an issuer's review, which could be a re-examination of an issuer general perspective, called an outlook, or the agency could focus on more short-term, specific developments, called a review. Both moves are often triggered by events or changes in circumstances that are,

---

[48] Holthausen, R., and Leftwich, R., 1986. The effect of bond rating changes on common stock prices, *Journal of Financial Economics*, Vol. 17, No. 1, pages 57–89) find that bond rating downgrades are associated with abnormal negative returns of the stock of the issuing firm.
[49] Lankova, E., Pochon, F., and Teïletche, J., 2006, Impact of agencies' decisions: comparison of French equities and international experiences, *Autorité des Marchés Financiers*, January, 1–42, page 17

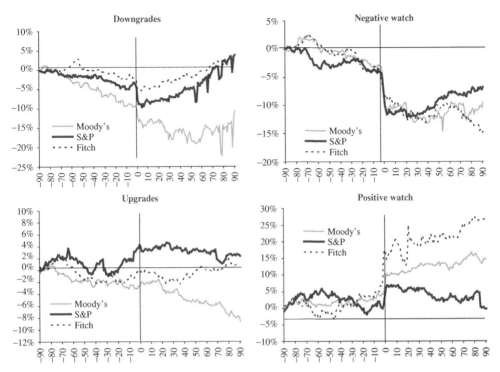

Figure 7.6 Europe: mean impact of CRA decisions on cumulative abnormal stock returns (1990–2004)

Note: The *x*-axis represents the number of days around the event, with 0 denoting the event date.

Source: Iankova, E., Pochon, F., and Teïletche, J., 2006, Impact of agencies' decisions: comparison of French equities and international experiences, *Autorité des Marchés Financiers*, January, 1–42, page 17.

to some extent, publicly known, and such circumstances explain why stock price changes often precede rating actions.[50]

The first regularity suggests that rating actions focus on material occurrences in the life of an issuer – developments that affect or could affect its enterprise value and the credit risk of the claims on it. Rating actions follow upon events that have significant value and risk implications in the life of an issuer. This is of course relevant knowledge for issuers. And to identify these occurrences CRAs use several instruments, one of which is the observation of market price signals. For example, on mm. the morning of January 12th 2004, barely a couple of weeks after Parmalat defaulted, John Doe suddenly stormed into the office of Blaise Ganguin, alerting S&P's Managing Director in Paris that the stock price of Adecco was collapsing. What was going on? Within seconds, S&P realized that Adecco had just made a statement that it was going to be late in closing its 2003 accounts and in announcing its results. Adecco's credit analyst at S&P then immediately investigated the reasons for this, S&P set meetings with Adecco's senior management, performed due diligence, a credit

---

[50] For more details, see Turner, J., 1998, A guide to market participants for monitoring Moody's credit opinions, *Special Comment*: Moody's Investors Service, July, Report 34 707, 1–8.

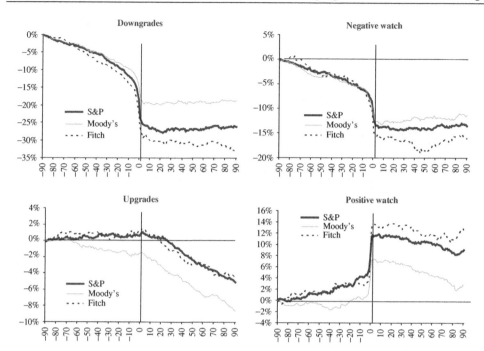

Figure 7.7   USA: mean impact of CRA decisions on cumulative abnormal stock returns (1990–2004)
Note: The *x*-axis represents the number of days around the event, with 0 denoting the event date.
Source: Iankova, E., Pochon, F., and Teïletche, J., 2006, Impact of agencies' decisions: comparison of French equities and international experiences, *Autorité des Marchés Financiers*, January, 1–42, page 18.

committee met and deliberated. Adecco was put on developing credit watch on January 12th and negative credit shortly after, on January 20th. Clearly, Adecco's announcement took S&P by surprise. But the surprise triggered an immediate investigation of the reason for the announcement, in cooperation with Adecco's senior management. This allowed S&P to reach the conclusion that little had really deteriorated in Adecco's fundamentals and its credit rating stance should be maintained.

A second regularity that Figures 7.6 and 7.7 put in evidence is that significant stock price changes still occur upon the actual announcement of the rating action. This is particularly the case for watches and for downgrades. This suggests that rating actions by themselves reveal new information to the market regarding these material events. By the time the rating action is taken, the market has not yet fully reflected the implications of these material events in the security prices of the issuer. Rating actions are an input to the price formation process; they are not just a reflection of it.

Interactions between Bond Rating Agencies and Stock Analysts

Stock and bond rating agency analyst reports and actions interact with each other. The answer to the question 'who knows what when?' is that knowledge flows both ways.

While most bond downgrades are preceded by declines in actual and forecast earnings, both actual earnings and forecasts of future earnings tend to fall following downgrades. Although part of this post-downgrade forecast revision can be attributed to negative news regarding actual earnings, most appears to be a reaction to the downgrade itself. We find little change in actual earnings following upgrades. Analysts, however, tend to increase their forecasts of future earnings.[51]

Both equity analysts and rating agency bond analysts produce at least some new information for the market that is then priced in securities. Stock prices react both to changes in analysts' earnings forecasts and to bond rating downgrades. But analysts also react to public information already in the prices. The finding that downgrades (upgrades) tend to occur following periods of negative (positive) abnormal returns illustrates that.

Rating agencies rely to some extent on inside information that is not available to stock analysts, due to securities laws. Thus, if equity analysts view ratings as reflecting at least some information that is not publicly available, it might cause them to change their earnings forecasts. Equity analysts and the market respond to downgrades and not to upgrades, because companies promptly release favorable information but are less eager to release unfavorable information. Firms tend to be a lot quicker to communicate good news than bad news. Thus, upgrades tend to be more of a response to information that the market already knows. In addition, rating agencies focus on the downside risk of a company (as opposed to upside potential), which implies that a rating agency analyst is more likely to look for unfavorable information and reveal its credit consequences. Moreover, 'the market impounds downgrade information much more quickly and efficiently than analysts do since, while market returns show no post-downgrade pattern, analysts are still revising their forecasts months later. And, we find that downgrades do presage declines in actual earnings.'[52]

7.1.3 Evaluation: How Relevant are Fundamental Credit Ratings?

Credit ratings are beyond doubt significant in the financial marketplace. Section 7.1 has analyzed credit ratings and credit spreads. It has explored the structure of the relationship between credit ratings and credit spreads and the degree in which ratings determine that structure, and we concluded that fundamental ratings contribute to shaping and determining that structure. They bring information to the secondary market and not merely synthesize it. New issue ratings influence the initial pricing of risk and not merely reflect it. Credit ratings are thus relevant for a firm's cost of capital and for its capital structure. The findings of a field survey that 'the most important factors affecting debt policy are maintaining financial flexibility and having a good credit rating' confirm our conclusion.[53]

Credit Ratings and the Cost of Capital

Credit ratings improve the accuracy of a firm's cost of capital. They achieve this by fostering the alignment of a firm's debt credit spread to the expected loss and the risk from holding that debt. It is asserted that '[firms and governments] almost certainly exaggerate the influence

---

[51] Ederington, L.H., and Goh, J.C., 1998, Bond rating agencies and stock analysts: Who knows what when?, *Journal of Financial and Quantitative Analysis*, December, Vol. 33, No. 4, 569–585, page 569.

[52] Ederington, L.H., and Goh, J.C., 1998, Bond rating agencies and stock analysts: Who knows what when?, *Journal of Financial and Quantitative Analysis*, December, Vol. 33, No. 4, 569–585, page 584.

[53] Graham, J.R., and Harvey, C.R., 2001, The theory and practice of corporate finance: evidence from the field, *Journal of Financial Economics*, May, Vol. 60, Issue 2–3, 187–243, page 2.

of rating agencies, which are as much following investor opinion as leading it,'[54] but the accumulated evidence contradicts that assertion. The relations between ratings, spreads, and security prices that we documented are fairly similar in the primary market, i.e. the association between rating and credit spreads at the time of the issue of a security, and in the secondary market – in other words, the association between credit spread changes and rating changes after trading in the rated security has started.

Ratings ameliorate the cost of capital by shedding light on the expected losses associated with different debt instruments. Variations in expected losses induce variations in the credit spread, increasing the level of cash outflows that firms must commit to purchase a given amount of cash if an expected loss increases and vice versa.

Ratings also shed light on the uncertainty surrounding these expected losses, and thus they affect the risk premium on the instrument and the required return on it. If the light signals higher uncertainty, the spread is higher, and vice versa. They thus also ameliorate the cost of capital in this way.

Ratings play a role in determining issuer fees in the new issue market and in dealer spreads in the secondary market. Split ratings increase both of these and both also increase as the rating goes down. These are additional channels by which credit ratings affect the cost of capital.

Credit Ratings and Capital Structure

Credit ratings directly affect a firm's optimal capital structure decisions and its adjustments from an actual situation to it.

Credit ratings disseminate informative views about a firm's quality. They thereby assist capital markets in setting the right cost of debt of the firm. This facilitates the firm's access to capital markets and it should thus be no surprise to observe that firms that have a debt rating have, ceteris paribus, significantly more leverage.[55]

Credit ratings influence firms in how they adjust their actual financial structure to the optimal one.[56]

7.2   PREVENTING SURPRISE IN DEFAULTS: RATING ACCURACY AND STABILITY

> *If we were able to perfectly predict the future, there would only be two ratings: 'will not default' and 'will default.'* [57]

Investors want ratings to perform, i.e. to offer the desired balance between accuracy and stability. However accurate and stable a rating system is, one always comes at the cost of the other. Arguably, for the quality of the rating process, as discussed in Section 4.3, objectivity and speed as well as fairness in the dissemination of the outcome of the process

---

[54] Brealey, R.A., and Myers, S.C., 2003, *Principles of Corporate Finance*, seventh edition, McGraw-Hill, Irwin, New York, 1–1071, page 685.

[55] Faulkender, M., and Peterson, M., 2006, Does the source of capital affect capital structure?, *Review of Financial Studies*, Vol. 19, No. 1, 45–79.

[56] Kisgen, D.J., 2000. Credit ratings and capital structure, *Journal of Finance*, Vol LXI, No. 3, June, 1035–1072.

[57] Dering, J.M., Executive Vice President for Global Regulatory Affairs and Compliance–Moody's Corporation, 2005, Remarks to the American Enterprise Institute, September 27, 1–7, page 3.

are minimum quality standards of ratings to which all concerned parties would easily agree. But, markets demand more from rating agencies than process quality. They need results. Ratings are predictive statements about defaults. And agencies cannot escape the fact that market participants want these predictions to be right. Ratings and rating changes may move market prices, but how accurate and discriminatory are they?

How can we really measure the quality of a prediction?

The accuracy of ratings can only be measured in the aggregate. Raymond McDaniel, President of Moody's Investors Service, stated the nature of the quality measurement problem very well:

> As opinions about the future, it is impossible for ratings to be statements of absolute fact. Ratings serve the public good if *in the aggregate* they have predictive content and that predictive content is communicated broadly. But however desirable, it is unfortunately impossible for any single rating opinion to be adjudged 'correct' or 'incorrect' on a case-by-case basis. That is because ratings are opinions forecasting relative future probabilities, rather than descriptive statements of past occurrences.
>
> By way of an analogy, an insurance company is uncertain as to exactly which holder will in fact draw on its policy in the future; a rating agency is uncertain about exactly which issuer will default in the future. However, insurance companies over time have learned to correlate certain factors with longevity and to assign greater or lesser weight to each factor. Thus, they can accurately predict that over the next five years more 80-year-old smokers will die than 20-year-old non-smokers; and they can accurately predict that over the same time period some 80-year-olds will live and some 20-year-olds will not. However, while they can classify people into risk categories, and provide valuable insurance products and services accordingly, they cannot guarantee future outcomes on a name-by-name basis.
>
> Therefore, to evaluate the quality of any opinion about the future on the basis of its 'rightness' is to place an inordinate burden on both the fundamental nature of opinions and on our ability as human beings to know the future. If Moody's could know the future, we would only have two ratings: 'will default' or 'will pay.' In actuality, we have a rating system with 21 broad categories, further refined by watchlists and outlooks, which provide a rank ordering of relative creditworthiness based on assessments of *probabilities* of default.[58]

How good are ratings at apprehending defaults correctly and timely? Default either occurs or it does not. How good are the credit agency ratings as indexes that indicate relative likelihoods of default? This question defines, analyzes, and evaluates what you may call the 'technical' performance of credit rating agencies.

Technical performance has multiple dimensions. One is the association of rating notches with the subsequent occurrence of defaults. Is this association stable and predictable? Another is whether rating changes lead properly to changes in default prospects, i.e. sufficiently timely and accurately. Then there is the question of how well ratings discriminate. It is trivial to see that if Jonah were to apocalyptically predict that all issues are going to default, he will have been right in catching all the eventuality defaulted issues. But of course, that is not the purpose of the exercise. Ratings must discriminate. They should correctly predict actual defaults and avoid to predict erroneously the default of bonds that do

---

[58] McDaniel, R.W., President of Moody's Investors Service, 2003, Annual meeting of the International Organization of Securities Commissions (IOSCO), Panel on the regulation of rating agencies, *Special Comment*: Moody's Investors Service, October 17, Report 79839, 1–8, page 2.

Table 7.6 Accuracy and stability summary from Moody's September 2007 quarterly update

		Accuracy measures			Stability measures	
Cohort ending	Number of defaults over prior 12 months	1-year accuracy ratio	5-year accuracy ratio	Average rating prior to default	Rating action rate	Large rating action rate
Sep-07	27	93.00%	79.20%	B3/Caa1	14.50%	1.90%
Jun-07	29	92.60%	77.30%	Caa1	15.50%	2.10%
Sep-06	32	85.30%	73.70%	B3/Caa1	20.80%	2.90%
Historical Average		84.50%	71.30%	B2	21.40%	4.80%

Source: Cantor, R., and Mann, Ch., 2007, The performance of Moody's corporate bond ratings: September 2007 Quarterly Update, *Special Comment*: Moody's Investors Service, October, Report 105286, 1–18, page 2.

not actually default. Missing actual defaults is called a Type I error. Predicting defaults that do not occur is a Type II error. The power of prediction measures the ability to avoid both Type I and Type II errors. How powerful are credit ratings in this respect? How do fundamental and technical ratings compare in this respect? This section adresses these aspects of performance.

7.2.1 Metrics of Accuracy and Stability

Accuracy and stability are two inherently conflicting characteristics of ratings. On the one hand, investors require that ratings convey reasonably good information about the riskiness of a bond. On the other hand, inasmuch as ratings are part of the investment decision process, investors need a certain level of stability, so that decisions need not be reversed on, say, a daily basis, incurring significant transaction costs.

Each of the three main CRAs publish annual and quarterly reports dedicated to accuracy and stability of their ratings, as in summary Table 7.6 from Moody's.[59]

How rating accuracy and stability is quantified is discussed below, starting first with measurement of default occurrence.

Occurrence: Default Rates

Default rate is an evident measure of incidence of defaults, which can be used as a basis for measuring the accuracy of ratings. It can be calculated, by industry, geographic location and, more relevant to our discussion, by rating grade. For a given rating category, the ratio of defaulted issuers to total issuers is calculated. The intricacy here is in the definition of the universe of issuers (or issues) in the calculation sample. Typically each CRA calculates default rates (and hence accuracy ratios based on these) using the universe of issuers it covers. Hence the influence of CRA market shares on the sample size and composition. In that sense measures of accuracy displayed by CRAs, even if similarly defined (which is not the case), may not be exactly comparable.

---

[59] Cantor, R. and Mann, Ch., 2007, The performance of Moody's corporate bond ratings: September 2007 Quarterly Update, *Special Comment*: Moody's Investors Service, October, Report 105286, 1–18, page 2.

Table 7.7 Annual global issuer-weighted default rates by whole letter rating (1970–2006)[a]

Rating	1970	1971	1972	1973	1974	1975	1976	1977	1978	1979	1980	1981	1982	1983	1984	1985	1986	1987
Aaa	0.00	0.00	0.00	0.00	0.00	0.00	0.00	0.00	0.00	0.00	0.00	0.00	0.00	0.00	0.00	0.00	0.00	0.00
Aa	0.00	0.00	0.00	0.00	0.00	0.00	0.00	0.00	0.00	0.00	0.00	0.00	0.00	0.00	0.00	0.00	0.00	0.00
A	0.00	0.00	0.00	0.00	0.00	0.00	0.00	0.00	0.00	0.00	0.00	0.00	0.25	0.00	0.00	0.00	0.00	0.00
Baa	0.54	0.00	0.00	0.46	0.00	0.00	0.00	0.29	0.00	0.00	0.00	0.00	0.32	0.00	0.37	0.00	1.36	0.00
Ba	4.25	0.87	0.00	0.00	0.00	1.03	1.00	0.52	1.08	0.49	0.00	0.00	2.74	0.91	0.83	1.40	2.04	2.72
B	19.72	0.00	7.41	3.92	10.35	6.15	0.00	3.39	5.56	0.00	4.94	4.60	2.41	6.31	6.72	8.22	11.73	6.23
Caa–C	53.33	14.29	40.00	44.44	0.00	0.00	0.00	50.00	0.00	0.00	33.33	0.00	25.00	40.00	100.00	0.00	23.53	20.00
Investment Grade	0.27	0.00	0.00	0.23	0.00	0.00	0.00	0.11	0.00	0.00	0.00	0.00	0.21	0.00	0.10	0.00	0.32	0.00
Speculative Grade	8.74	1.14	1.94	1.28	1.34	1.74	0.87	1.35	1.79	0.42	1.61	0.70	3.56	3.82	3.32	3.67	5.64	4.23
All Corporates	2.64	0.29	0.46	0.45	0.28	0.36	0.18	0.35	0.35	0.09	0.34	0.16	1.03	0.96	0.92	1.01	1.90	1.50

Rating	1988	1989	1990	1991	1992	1993	1994	1995	1996	1997	1998	1999	2000	2001	2002	2003	2004	2005	2006
Aaa	0.00	0.00	0.00	0.00	0.00	0.00	0.00	0.00	0.00	0.00	0.00	0.00	0.00	0.00	0.00	0.00	0.00	0.00	0.00
Aa	0.00	0.60	0.00	0.00	0.00	0.00	0.00	0.00	0.00	0.00	0.00	0.00	0.00	0.00	0.00	0.00	0.00	0.00	0.00
A	0.00	0.00	0.00	0.00	0.00	0.00	0.00	0.00	0.00	0.00	0.00	0.00	0.00	0.16	0.16	0.00	0.00	0.00	0.00
Baa	0.00	0.60	0.00	0.27	0.00	0.00	0.00	0.00	0.00	0.00	0.12	0.10	0.38	0.19	1.28	0.00	0.00	0.17	0.00
Ba	1.25	2.98	3.34	5.35	0.30	0.55	0.24	0.69	0.00	0.19	0.78	1.15	0.87	1.53	1.49	0.91	0.36	0.00	0.17
B	6.36	8.95	16.20	14.56	9.11	6.22	3.87	4.78	1.44	2.13	4.26	6.13	5.69	9.43	5.20	2.46	0.82	0.98	1.04
Caa–C	28.57	25.00	58.82	36.84	26.67	28.57	5.13	12.39	14.18	14.87	15.24	20.44	20.15	34.26	29.42	21.28	12.84	7.90	7.19
Investment Grade	0.00	0.29	0.00	0.06	0.00	0.00	0.00	0.00	0.00	0.00	0.04	0.04	0.13	0.13	0.51	0.00	0.00	0.06	0.00
Speculative Grade	3.60	5.80	10.08	10.40	4.84	3.67	1.94	3.33	1.67	2.06	3.52	5.83	6.27	10.59	8.25	5.13	2.41	1.80	1.57
All Corporates	1.36	2.34	3.59	3.22	1.30	0.98	0.56	1.02	0.51	0.65	1.25	2.20	2.49	3.91	3.05	1.70	0.82	0.65	0.54

[a] Includes issuers rated as of January 1 of each cohort year

Source: Cantor, R., Hamilton, D.T., Kim, F., and Ou, S., 2007, Corporate Default and Recovery Rates, 1920–2006, *Special Comment:* Moody's Investors Service, June, Report 102071, 1–48, page 20.

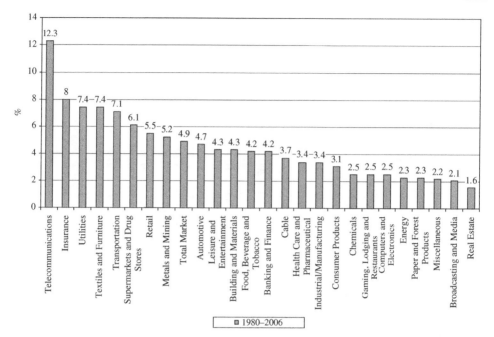

Figure 7.8   Fitch US high-yield default index: industry default rates (1980–2006)
Source: Mancuso, P., Rosenthal, E., and Verde, M., 2007, The shrinking default rate and the credit cycle – New twists, New risks, *Credit Market Research*: Fitch Ratings, February 20, page 3.

Average Annual Default Ratios per Rating Grade

For a given rating grade, take the ratio of defaulted issuers during a period to total issuers at the beginning of the period. This is a first simple indicator of the association between ratings and defaults. This ratio doesn't tell the likelihood of default of an issuer, because an issuer that didn't default this year could default next year, or during the next two years, or between now and its maturity, maybe in 10 years, and so on. But you observe the number of issuer defaults during a year, classify these according to their rating at the time of default, and divide the number of defaults of a given rating by the number of issuers of that rating at the beginning of the year. It tells you the fraction of issuers of a given rate, at the beginning of the year, that defaulted during the year. Doing this year after year produces a time series of annual default rates per broad rating category, as in Table 7.7.

One observes the inverse association for a given year between default ratios and rating. In virtually every single year, that ratio increases as the rating goes down. The average of these annual ratios over the 35-year period for all corporates across all ratings was 1.23%. For Aaa, it was zero, meaning that, of all the Aaa issuer ratings outstanding at the beginning of the year, no issuer defaulted during the year. At Baa, this average stood at 0.18%, going up to 1.15% for Ba, 5.98% for B, and 23.83% for Caa–C.

But the extent of that simple association varies considerably from year to year. For example, in 1986 1.36% of Baa ratings defaulted, even though in 22 of the 35 years none did. In fact, the coefficient of variation (standard deviation relative to the mean) for these ratios is pretty large, around one for most of them.

Figure 7.8 shows high-yield default rates over the period from 1980 to 2006 by industry in the US. Telecoms are the clear champions, which is probably not surprising given that the period includes the Internet bubble from its beginning to the end.

Types of credit instruments present an interesting way of default rate categorization. Cantor and Emery (2005) compared the default rates on loans and bonds in the US and Europe.[60] The US part of the study is based on 134 non-bankrupt defaulters – US non-financial corporations. A similar analysis was repeated on a small sample of 29 European companies. US data revealed that default rates on loans were about 20% lower than bond default rates. The explanation of the difference is that companies sometimes default on their bonds but avoid bankruptcy (23% of the sample), and hence avoid loan default. European data yielded similar results as it comes to differences in loan and bond default rates. There are, however, important differences apparently due to differences in the US and European bankruptcy legislation and corporate culture as 49% of European defaulters avoided bankruptcy. Another notable difference between European and US corporate cultures is the relatively high 'reliance on bank loans as a source of capital' in Europe.

With regard to measurement of default incidence, a better measure of association needs to integrate the 'aging effect' of defaults. At whatever grade, issues default less when they are young (first years after issue) than when they are aged. Due to the relatively large increase in new speculative grade issuance during the three years preceding the 1990–1991 recession, the default rates of 10.1% and 10.4% observed during the recession are in fact downward biased due to this 'aging effect' of defaults. Marginal default rates in the first three years after issuance start out quite low. So the actual default experience on high-yield issues of the mid-1980s was significantly worse. This led to important drops in high-yield issuance until the 'junk' sector took off again in 1993. And it suggests looking beyond average default ratios to get a good measure of the true association between ratings and defaults of the rated objects.

Remoteness: Cumulative Cohort Default Rates

Cohorts are usually defined as static pools of rated companies (e.g. in a rating category) at the beginning of a given period. Then marginal default rates are calculated for subsequent periods (e.g. months, years) as the 'ratio of the number of companies that default during a given time period' to the 'number of survived companies in the beginning of that period.' In other words, the marginal default rate shows the probability that a company belonging to a cohort will default during a time period after the cohort formation data, given that it has so far survived up to the beginning of that time period. In order to account for an investment time horizon, cumulative default rates are calculated over corresponding periods of time in a similar manner, showing the probability that a company will default at some point between the cohort date and the end of the investment time horizon.[61]

---

[60] Cantor, R., and Emery, K.M., 2005, Relative default rates on corporate loans and bonds, *Journal of Banking and Finance*, 29, 1575–1584.

[61] Mathematically, the marginal default rate in time interval t, $d(t)$, for a cohort of issuers formed on date y holding rating z is defined as the number of defaults $x(t)$ from the cohort that occur in the time interval t divided by the effective size of the cohort, $n(t)$, at the start of time t : $d_y^z(t) = x_y^z(t)/n_y^z(t)$.

Source: Cantor, R., and Hamilton, D., 2006, Measuring corporate default rates, *Special Comment*: Moody's Investors Service, November 2006, Report 100779, 1–16.

Cohort analysis commingles all issues of a rating grade issued during a given calendar year. By thus controlling for aging, one can then follow the default experience over time of a cohort.

But for identical grades and at the same age, cohorts of different years prefigure different default performances. Figure 7.9 illustrates this by graphing the realized default experience of cohorts by age 5. Consider Baa. The 1973 cohort default rate at age 5 was 1.93%. This rate was down to 0.57% for 1977 cohort, all the way up to 5.26% for the 1986 cohort, to then fall to 0% for the 1992 cohort.

This variance of default frequencies at the same age for different cohorts has serious implications. It follows that identical ratings and bond ages comprise different levels of credit risk as a function of when the bond was issued. It also raises questions about the association between credit risk and financial credit ratios. For companies that went bankrupt, credit ratios tend to have deteriorated during the period preceding bankruptcy according to a recognizable pattern, as we will see in more detail later. Therefore, as cohort default rates for a given rating increased several fold between 1970 and the late 1980s, in reciprocal manner the credit ratios of these rating categories deteriorated.[62] In other words, the relationship, at

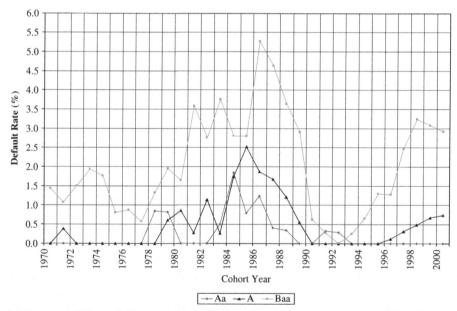

Relative scale-default rates for the same rating grade and same time horizon change over time. Higher rating grade is linked to lower default rates with exceptions in some years

Figure 7.9 Cumulative 5-year issuer weighted default rates by annual cohorts of Aa, A, and Baa corporate bonds (1970–2000)
Source: Cantor, R., Hamilton, D.T., Ou, S., and Varma, P., 2005, Default and recovery rates of corporate bond issuers, 1920–2004, *Special Comment*: Moody's Investors Service, January, Report 91233, 1–40, Exhibit 26, pages 22–32.

---

[62] Cantor, R., and Packer, F., 1994, The credit rating industry, *Quarterly Review*: Federal Reserve Bank of New York, Summer–Fall, 1–26, page 12.

a given age after issue, between a company's credit ratios and the new issue rating is far from stable. Put differently, to be able to anticipate what a key set of credit ratios for, say, a Baa company will look like, say, five years after the issue, one should be able to anticipate the relevant point in the business cycle five years hence. A probably insurmountable task.

To sum up, average annual default ratios per rating grade and cumulative cohort default rates fluctuate with the business cycle. Ratings are not only approximate in their precision about credit quality, but their associations with a given level of default frequency, and with a given set of credit ratios, are also relative to the business cycle.

Accuracy

Ratings accuracy refers to the correlation between ratings and defaults. While the idea of ratings accuracy is intuitively transparent, technically there can be multitude ways of defining it. To measure the correspondence between ratings and defaults, *default rates* are calculated by rating category.

It is useful to illustrate the accuracy of ratings through Lorenz curves combined with two extreme lines – the random line and the ideal line. The Lorenz curve was developed by Max Lorenz in 1905 to demonstrate inequalities in wealth distribution, and we are interested in inequalities of default rate distribution across rating categories. The horizontal axis represents the cumulative share of rated universe, from lowest to highest rating, and the vertical axis represents the cumulative proportion of defaults among them. Figure 7.10 represents the performance of S&P ratings based on three-year cumulative default rates for

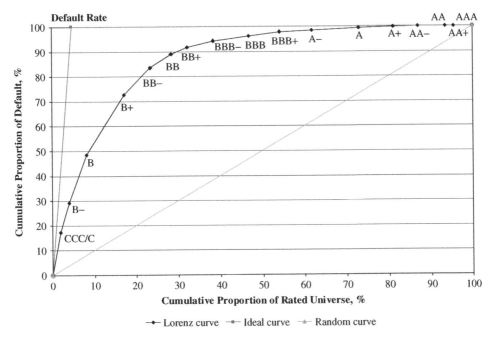

Figure 7.10   S&P Three-year relative corporate ratings performance (1981–2006)
Source: Standard & Poor's Global Fixed Income Research; Standard & Poor's CreditPro®.

the period 1981–2006. If there were no correlation between ratings and default rates (if ratings did not discriminate defaults), each rating would comprise the same default rate and hence the corresponding Lorenz curve would be the 45-degree line (the random curve). Conversely, if ratings did perfectly discriminate defaulters,[63] the Lorenz curve would be represented by the ideal curve, where the X-value of the upper leftmost point of the curve is the total proportion of defaulters: 'Default Rate' on the graph, Figure 7.10.

The accuracy ratio or Gini coefficient is a summary statistic for the Lorenz curve reflecting the overall accuracy of ratings in predicting defaults. It shows how far (or closely) the Lorenz curve is from the ideal curve. The accuracy ratio is defined as the ratio of the surface between the Lorenz curve and a random curve to the surface between the ideal curve and a random curve. In extremes, it equals 0 for the random curve and 1 for the ideal curve. The Gini coefficient implied by the data underlying Figure 7.10 equals 77%.

Unsurprisingly, ratings are more accurate over shorter term horizons, as in Figure 7.11, A comparison of Lorenz curves covering different time horizons, as in Figure 7.11, reveals that the shorter the 'forecast' period, the more accurate the ratings performance. Table 7.8 summarizes Gini coefficients corresponding to each time horizon in the graph. However, it may not always be possible to clearly differentiate Lorenz curves. The case with intersecting curves presented in Figure 7.12 shows that while one-year accuracy has been clearly better than the average over 1983–2005 for ratings of B1 and below, it is impossible to use Gini coefficients to reach to a comprehensive conclusion. It is partly due to the fact that there have been no defaults among categories from Ba1 to B1 in 2005.

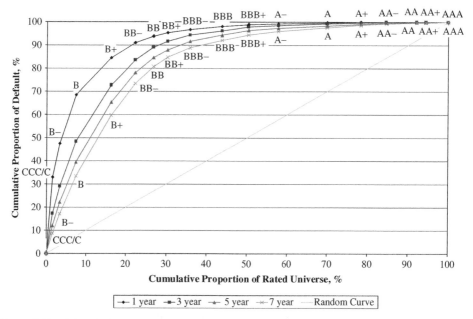

Figure 7.11   S&P relative corporate ratings performance (1981–2006)
Source: Standard & Poor's Global Fixed Income Research; Standard & Poor's CreditPro®.

---

[63] Essentially, as mentioned above, assigning perfectly two grades – will default, will not default.

Table 7.8 Gini coefficients of S&P ratings performance (1981–2006) for different time horizons

Time horizon	Gini coefficient
1 year	83%
3 year	77%
5 year	74%
7 year	71%

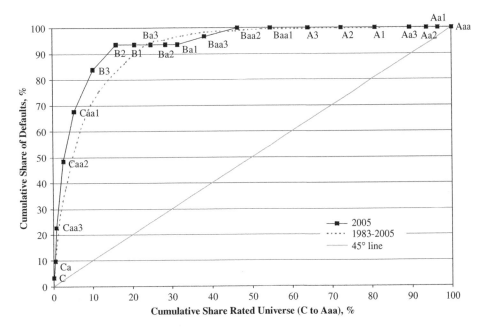

Figure 7.12 Moody's 1-year Lorenz curve
Source: Cantor, R., Hamilton, D.T., Ou, S., and Varma, P., 2006, Default and recovery rates of corporate bond issuers, 1920–2005, *Special Comment*: Moody's Investors Service, January, Report 96546, 1–52, Exhibit 9, page 11.

CRAs predict the volatility of accuracy ratios by following their continuous time-series plots. Such plots of Gini coefficients corresponding to various time horizons confirm the inverse relationship between the accuracy of ratings and time horizon.

Stability: Transition Rates and Rating Action Rates

Ratings stability refers to rating changes and their endurance. Rating transition (or migration) rates are used to examine the probability of rating evolution across rating categories over a period of time. Table 7.9 presents Standard & Poor's 1-, 3-, 5- and 7-year transition rates based on 1981–2006 data. Such tables are called credit transition (or migration) matrices.

Table 7.9 S&P global average transition rates (1981–2006) (%)

1 year	AAA	AA	A	BBB	BB	B	CCC/C	D	NR
AAA	88.34	7.84	0.47	0.09	0.09	0	0	0	3.17
AA	0.59	87.31	7.54	0.57	0.06	0.10	0.02	0.01	3.79
A	0.05	2.00	87.39	5.47	0.40	0.15	0.02	0.06	4.46
BBB	0.01	0.15	3.98	84.17	4.14	0.73	0.16	0.24	6.42
BB	0.03	0.06	0.22	5.18	75.71	7.20	0.84	1.07	9.69
B	0	0.05	0.18	0.30	5.78	72.77	4.10	4.99	11.83
CCC/C	0	0	0.26	0.39	1.10	11.15	47.49	26.29	13.34

3 years									
AAA	68.39	18.98	2.55	0.40	0.12	0.03	0.03	0.09	9.41
AA	1.41	66.46	18.06	2.38	0.41	0.25	0.02	0.10	10.92
A	0.10	4.57	67.34	12.21	1.52	0.62	0.11	0.32	13.21
BBB	0.04	0.47	9.09	60.55	8.06	2.33	0.43	1.32	17.72
BB	0.05	0.10	0.81	11.33	43.82	11.87	1.54	5.92	24.57
B	0.01	0.07	0.45	1.30	11.01	37.08	4.34	17.04	28.71
CCC/C	0	0	0.30	1.06	2.43	14.25	13.57	42.61	25.78

5 years									
AAA	53.57	23.85	5.01	1.06	0.13	0.13	0.03	0.30	15.92
AA	1.75	51.00	24.05	4.25	0.66	0.39	0.04	0.34	17.52
A	0.13	5.62	53.01	15.49	2.58	1.02	0.18	0.73	21.24
BBB	0.07	0.81	10.57	46.23	8.75	3.08	0.53	2.97	26.99
BB	0.03	0.15	1.59	12.32	27.49	10.87	1.63	11.42	34.49
B	0.03	0.07	0.58	2.07	10.06	20.41	2.90	25.73	38.14
CCC/C	0	0	0.29	1.18	2.95	9.64	3.93	51.13	30.88

7 years									
AAA	42.95	26.16	7.30	1.96	0.22	0.07	0.07	0.55	20.71
AA	1.88	40.41	26.67	5.61	0.89	0.33	0.02	0.59	23.60
A	0.14	5.92	43.76	16.47	3.19	1.16	0.18	1.29	27.89
BBB	0.11	1.13	11.25	37.29	8.08	2.90	0.43	4.19	34.62
BB	0	0.16	2.02	12.61	18.21	8.76	1.03	15.36	41.86
B	0.01	0.05	0.82	2.65	8.24	12.19	1.85	29.69	44.50
CCC/C	0	0	0.41	1.63	3.25	5.96	2.17	50.54	36.04

Source: Standard & Poor's Global Fixed Income Research and Standard & Poor's CreditPro®.

Transition tables can be read as follows. Diagonal elements are a direct measure of stability – they show the probability that the rating will stay unchanged and can be described as stability rates for a corresponding time period. One minus the value of a diagonal element is called the rating action rate and shows the fraction of issuers who underwent rating changes over the period. Numbers below the diagonal show the probability of upgrades and those above the diagonal are probabilities of downgrade.

The data shows that the higher the rating category, the more stable it is. The probability that a triple A rating will change (i.e. will be downgraded) within a year is less than 12%. It becomes, however, more likely over longer periods of time. The probability of a downgrade for a triple A exceeds 57% over a 7-year period.

The column 'D' shows in effect the probability of default for each category in the left column, over the corresponding time horizon. The trend once again confirms the logical consistency of ratings mentioned above – the lower the rating, the higher the probability of default.

Rating actions can be further subdivided into groups by the magnitude of change expressed in notches. Large rating actions (e.g. upgrades/downgrades by more than one main category) are rates to estimate the frequency of significant rating actions.

Another measure of stability, as well as a measure of the 'willingness' or 'reluctance' of CRAs to review a rating, is the rating reversal rate. It is based on the relative number of issuers who underwent rating actions in both directions within a given period of time.

The Predictive Content of Ratings in the High-Yield Market

The vast majority of bond defaults occur in the high-yield sector of the bond market. Returning to Table 7.7, what strikes is the spikes in default rates. During 1990 and 1991 it was the result of the heavy new issuance of high-yield debt in the mid-1980s followed by the 1990 recession. The spikes of 2001 and 2002 resulted from the bursting of the stock market bubble.

Table 7.10 presents default rates and losses over the period from 1978 to the second quarter of 2007 in the US high-yield sector. The year 2007 stands out with the size of the market – the total value of high-yield bonds outstanding at the end of the second quarter is almost equal to the record value in 2005. It is even more impressive given the default rate, which is one of the lowest over the period (the third lowest!), and the lowest ever default loss.[64] Note the very high (almost perfect) correlation (0.98) between default rates and default losses.

Fallen angels are bonds originally issued at investment grade but whose rating has been downgraded to speculative grade.[65] The universe of high-yield bonds can thus be subdivided into fallen angels and others, sometimes called 'original issue high-yield bonds.' The original high-yield issuance saw a steady expansion starting in the late 1970s. By the mid-1980s sufficient data had accumulated to allow for empirical research into the category, considering in particular default rate comparisons with fallen angels. One of the earliest studies[66] found that, on average, original issue high-yield bonds had a significantly higher default rate than fallen angels. Subsequent studies showed that fallen angels had a higher probability of rising back to investment grade than defaulting, as opposed to the original issue high-yield bonds which had a higher default rate compared to the probability of being upgraded to investment grade. One explanation to this phenomenon is that managers of formerly investment grade issuers have a stronger motivation to retrieve the lost status. However, looking into the temporal dynamics of defaults and rating migrations gives a better insight. Fallen angels are more likely to default than similarly rated original speculative grade bonds during the first two years following the downgrade. This difference disappears, however, in subsequent years.[67]

A more recent study covered a full high-yield cycle from the low default rates of 1997 to the other trough in early 2006. This period comprises the peak of 2002 exceeding 10%.

---

[64] Needs to be seen how annual numbers for 2007 will be affected by the unfolding sub-prime crisis.

[65] Issuers whose ratings move up from original speculative to investment grade are referred to as rising stars.

[66] Fridson, M., and Wahl, F., 1986, Fallen angels versus original issue high yield bonds, *High Performance*: The Magazine of High Yield Bonds, Morgan Stanley & Co., Inc., October, 2–8.

[67] Cantor, R., Hamilton, D., Mann, Ch., and Varma, P., 2003, What happens to fallen angels? A statistical review 1982–2003, Moody's Investors Service: *Special Comment*, July, Report: 78912, 1–10.

Table 7.10 Default rates and losses in the US high-yield sector (1978-2007Q2)

Year	Par value outstanding ($mns)	Par value of default ($mns)	Default rate (%)[a]	Weighted price after default ($)	Weighted coupon (%)	Default loss (%)[b]
2007Q2	1053 900	2 689	0.26	84.0	9.46	0.05
2006	993 600	7 559	0.76	65.3	9.33[a]	0.30
2005	1073 000	36 209	3.38	61.1	8.61	1.46
2004	933 100	11 657	1.25	57.7	10.30	0.59
2003	825 000	38 451	4.66	45.5	9.55	2.76
2002	757 000	96 858	12.79	25.3	9.37	10.15
2001	649 000	63 609	9.80	25.5	9.18	7.76
2000	597 200	30 295	5.07	26.4	8.54	3.95
1999	567 400	23 532	4.15	27.9	10.55	3.21
1998	465 500	7 464	1.60	35.9	9.46	1.10
1997	335 400	4 200	1.25	54.2	11.87	0.65
1996	271 000	3 336	1.23	51.9	8.92	1.10
1995	240 000	4 551	1.90	40.6	11.83	1.24
1994	235 000	3 418	1.45	39.4	10.25	0.96
1993	206 907	2 287	1.11	56.6	12.98	0.56
1992	163 000	5 545	3.40	50.1	12.32	1.91
1991	183 600	18 862	10.27	36.0	11.59	7.16
1990	181 000	18 354	10.14	23.4	12.94	8.42
1989	189 258	8 110	4.29	38.3	13.40	2.93
1988	148 187	3 944	2.66	43.6	11.91	1.66
1987	129 557	7 486	5.78	75.9	12.07	1.74
1986	90 243	3 156	3.50	34.5	10.61	2.48
1985	58 088	992	1.71	45.9	13.69	1.04
1984	40 939	344	0.84	48.6	12.23	0.48
1983	27 492	301	1.09	55.7	10.11	0.54
1982	18 109	577	3.19	38.6	9.61	2.11
1981	17 115	27	0.16	12.0	15.75	0.15
1980	14 935	224	1.50	21.1	8.43	1.25
1979	10 356	20	0.19	31.0	10.63	0.14
1978	8 946	119	1.33	60.0	8.38	0.59
Arithmetic average 1978–2006			3.46	44.41	10.84	2.34
Weighted average 1978–2006			4.26			2.94

Note: [a] Excludes defaulted issues. [b] Default loss rate adjusted for fallen angels is 9.3% in 2002, 1.82% in 2003, 0.59% in 2004, 1.56% in 2005, 0.322% in 2006, and 0.054% in 2007Q2.
Source: Altman, E., and Karlin, B.J., 2007, Defaults and returns on high-yield bonds and distressed debt: first half 2007, *Review, Special Report*, NYU Salomon Center, 1–25, page 11.

According to the study, fallen angels significantly outperform original issue high-yield bonds on the basis of annualized (9.85% vs 5.26%) and quarterly returns.[68]

To examine the change of default probabilities in time, consider Moody's mapping of Expected Default Frequency (EDF) values to implied ratings. For a given major rating category in a given month, Moody's calculates the median EDF corresponding to that category in the previous month. Then EDFs are mapped to fine grades using a geometric

---

[68] Fridson, M., and Sterling, K., 2006, Fallen angels: a separate and superior asset class, *Journal of Fixed Income*, Winter 2006, 22–29.

means approach to ensure the convexity of the EDF – rating relationship. Table 7.11 and Figure 7.13 show average results of such mapping for the period 1994–2005.

These show that the median EDF value for each credit category varies substantially over time. For example, the median EDF for A2 can vary from 0.275% in 2000 to 0.040% in 2005. Also, the range of EDFs covered in even the finer rating buckets can be fairly wide – for example, at the beginning of 2003, all firms with EDF values between 0.22% and 0.24% had the same credit category, A2. Similarly, all firms with EDF values between 0.98% and 1.20% fall in the Ba2 category. Therefore, knowledge of the EDF-implied credit categories does not give an exact picture of the default risk level, which is also a function of the current business cycle. Moreover, there can be significant variation in default risk levels within the same equity-implied rating category.

Measuring Relative Credit Risks

The measurement of meaningful default rates and losses for a given rating over a certain period of time is not as simple as it may sound and the number of possible alternative sampling and calculation methods is staggering when one considers all the subtleties.[69] The major approach in this regard, developed by Altman (1989),[70] measures the expected mortality of bonds in a manner similar to that used by actuaries in assessing human mortality. It considers the surviving population of bonds for various time periods in the future on the basis of their rating at issuance. Given the initial rating, it answers the following two questions:

1. What is the marginal probability of default (mortality) and loss from default during a given year after having survived an elapsed time from issuance of one year, two years, or N years?
2. What is the cumulative annual mortality rate and loss for various elapsed times from issuance?

Table 7.12, which tabulates these marginal and cumulative default (or mortality) rates[71] shows mortality rates for all S&P rated corporate bonds, according to rating category at issuance and over elapsed times from 1 to 10 years. It covers the period 1971–2006. The relationship between a high rating and a low probability of default (AAA has a cumulative 10-year mortality rate of 0.09%) and conversely a low rating and a high probability of default (CCC has one of 59.39%) is thus highly robust and holds across the whole spectrum of ratings, sample years, and time from issuance. Table 7.13 reports corresponding mortality losses and reinforces the previous results. Lower rated bonds are more likely to default as the rating declines with time from issuance in each rating category. The relationship is smooth, with progressively lower ratings corresponding to progressively higher default rates and losses.

---

[69] For the various methods and their results, see Altman E.I., Caouette, J., and Narayanan, P., 1998, *Managing Credit Risk: The Next Great Financial Challenge*, John Wiley & Sons, Inc., New York, 1–452, pages 194–201.

[70] Altman, E.I., 1989. Measuring corporate bond mortality and performance, *Journal of Finance*, Vol. 44, No. 4, September, 909–922.

[71] See Altman, E.I., and Cooke, D., 1999. Defaults and returns on high yield bonds: analysis through 1998 and default outlook for 1999–2001, Working Paper series S-99-10: New York University Salomon Center, 1–26.

Table 7.11 Moody's KMV median EDF and Moody's rating grades (1994–2005)
Average of monthly EDF observations per year

	1994	1995	1996	1997	1998	1999	2000	2001	2002	2003	2004	2005
Aaa	0.021	0.020	0.020	0.020	0.020	0.020	0.023	0.028	0.035	0.022	0.020	0.020
Aa1	0.030	0.026	0.026	0.026	0.026	0.028	0.052	0.064	0.058	0.033	0.026	0.026
Aa2	0.035	0.030	0.030	0.030	0.030	0.033	0.080	0.096	0.074	0.042	0.030	0.030
Aa3	0.051	0.041	0.037	0.034	0.039	0.051	0.121	0.134	0.103	0.063	0.038	0.033
A1	0.072	0.057	0.047	0.039	0.050	0.077	0.182	0.188	0.144	0.095	0.049	0.036
A2	0.104	0.079	0.058	0.045	0.065	0.116	0.275	0.263	0.202	0.145	0.064	0.040
A3	0.132	0.101	0.078	0.060	0.092	0.176	0.366	0.336	0.253	0.181	0.080	0.048
Baa1	0.167	0.130	0.104	0.081	0.131	0.267	0.487	0.429	0.316	0.225	0.101	0.058
Baa2	0.212	0.167	0.140	0.110	0.185	0.405	0.650	0.549	0.395	0.281	0.128	0.070
Baa3	0.311	0.254	0.217	0.177	0.304	0.600	0.842	0.717	0.524	0.376	0.160	0.089
Ba1	0.457	0.385	0.338	0.286	0.499	0.894	1.091	0.936	0.694	0.503	0.201	0.113
Ba2	0.669	0.585	0.525	0.461	0.819	1.338	1.415	1.223	0.920	0.673	0.253	0.144
Ba3	0.975	0.872	0.772	0.712	1.216	1.887	2.048	1.844	1.323	1.002	0.392	0.225
B1	1.420	1.301	1.137	1.099	1.805	2.664	2.978	2.784	1.903	1.491	0.608	0.351
B2	2.070	1.941	1.678	1.696	2.681	3.763	4.354	4.213	2.741	2.221	0.942	0.550
B3	4.173	4.000	3.626	3.652	4.866	6.210	6.831	6.684	5.011	4.311	2.466	1.720
Caa1	8.419	8.244	7.846	7.874	9.006	10.266	10.757	10.641	9.205	8.494	6.468	5.399
Caa2	17.000	17.000	17.000	17.000	17.000	17.000	17.000	17.000	17.000	17.000	17.000	17.000
Caa3	17.946	17.946	17.946	17.946	17.946	17.946	17.946	17.946	17.946	17.946	17.946	17.946
Ca	20.000	20.000	20.000	20.000	20.000	20.000	20.000	20.000	20.000	20.000	20.000	20.000
C	20.000	20.000	20.000	20.000	20.000	20.000	20.000	20.000	20.000	20.000	20.000	20.000

Note: 1994, average from March to December; 2005, average from January to November
Source: Moody's.

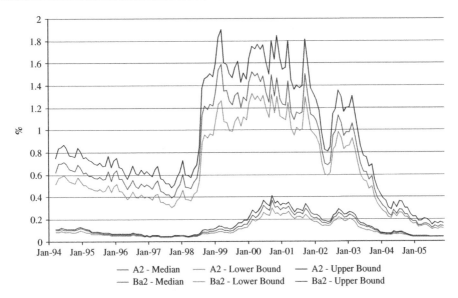

Figure 7.13 Variation of Moody's KMV median EDF and bounds for ratings A2 and Ba2 (1994–2005) [Fig. 2.7]
Source: Cantor, R., Fons, J., Mann, C., Munves, D., and Viswanathan, J., 2005, *An Explanation of Market Implied Ratings*, Moody's Investors Service, November, SP1325, 1–19, Figure 1, page 12.

SF VIGNETTE 8
Stability of Structured Finance Ratings Compared to Corporate Finance Ratings

Based on historical observations from 1984 to 2007, structured finance ratings have been globally more stable than corporate finance ratings, particularly in the AAA/Aaa notch. They are more stable in the sense that they are less likely to change rating in a given period of time than corporate ratings. This can be seen, for instance, in Table 7.15,[72] on the diagonal of the Moody's rating transition matrices.

Experience has shown however, that once a rating change does occur, the average magnitude of the rating movement is almost twice the average number of notches changed for corporate rating downgrades and upgrades. Structured instruments are highly susceptible to asset correlation changes which are affected usually by macroeconomic factors, while corporate finance instruments are affected more often by issuer specific factors. Corporations can take many decisions that can positively impact a rating or change the direction of rating paths. Whereas, in structured finance, SPVs have almost no discretionary power, or degrees of freedom, that affect the course of ratings, only eventually asset managers in dynamically managed deals. Other actions would be triggered by contractual clauses. The statistics of rating movements are generalized, as shown in Table 7.15.

The rating stability of each notch, indicated by the diagonal values in the transition matrices, declines roughly in line with the notches for both structured finance and

---

[72] Moody's Investors Service, 2008. Structured finance rating transitions 1983–2007, *Special Comment*, February, 1-74.

Table 7.12 Mortality rates by original rating, in percentage – all rated corporate bonds (1971–2006)

		Years after Issuance									
		1 (%)	2 (%)	3 (%)	4 (%)	5 (%)	6 (%)	7 (%)	8 (%)	9 (%)	10 (%)
AAA	Marginal	0.00	0.00	0.00	0.00	0.05	0.03	0.01	0.00	0.00	0.00
	Cumulative	0.00	0.00	0.00	0.00	0.05	0.08	0.09	0.09	0.09	0.09
AA	Marginal	0.00	0.00	0.30	0.14	0.02	0.02	0.00	0.00	0.05	0.01
	Cumulative	0.00	0.00	0.30	0.44	0.46	0.48	0.48	0.48	0.53	0.54
A	Marginal	0.01	0.08	0.02	0.06	0.06	0.09	0.05	0.20	0.09	0.05
	Cumulative	0.01	0.09	0.11	0.17	0.23	0.32	0.37	0.57	0.66	0.71
BBB	Marginal	0.33	3.13	1.34	1.24	0.74	0.31	0.25	0.19	0.14	0.40
	Cumulative	0.33	3.45	4.74	5.92	6.62	7.10	7.33	7.51	7.63	8.00
BB	Marginal	1.15	2.42	4.32	2.26	2.53	1.27	1.61	1.11	1.71	3.47
	Cumulative	1.15	3.54	7.72	9.88	12.10	13.20	14.60	15.56	17.00	19.88
B	Marginal	2.84	6.78	7.35	8.49	6.01	4.32	3.95	2.40	1.96	0.83
	Cumulative	2.84	9.43	16.08	23.21	27.82	30.94	35.67	35.26	36.53	37.06
CCC	Marginal	8.12	15.42	18.75	11.76	4.14	9.33	5.79	5.70	0.85	4.70
	Cumulative	8.12	22.30	36.86	44.30	46.60	51.57	54.38	56.98	57.34	59.36

Source: Altman, E.I., and Ramayanam, S., 2007, Default and returns in the high-yield bond market: 2006 in *Review and Outlook*, Special Report: NYU Salomon Center, and Leonard N. Stern School of Business, January, 1–35, page 23. (Rated by S&P at issuance based on 1955 issues, *Source*: Standard & Poor's (New York) and Altman's Compilation.)

Table 7.13 Mortality losses by original rating, in percentage – all rated corporate bonds (1971–2006)

| | | \multicolumn{10}{c}{Years after Issuance} | | | | | | | | | |
		1 (%)	2 (%)	3 (%)	4 (%)	5 (%)	6 (%)	7 (%)	8 (%)	9 (%)	10 (%)
AAA	Marginal	0.00	0.00	0.00	0.00	0.01	0.01	0.01	0.00	0.00	0.00
	Cumulative	0.00	0.00	0.00	0.00	0.01	0.02	0.03	0.03	0.03	0.03
AA	Marginal	0.00	0.00	0.05	0.04	0.01	0.01	0.00	0.00	0.02	0.00
	Cumulative	0.00	0.00	0.05	0.09	0.10	0.11	0.11	0.11	0.13	0.14
A	Marginal	0.00	0.03	0.01	0.04	0.03	0.04	0.02	0.03	0.06	0.00
	Cumulative	0.00	0.03	0.04	0.08	0.11	0.15	0.17	0.20	0.26	0.26
BBB	Marginal	0.23	2.19	1.06	0.45	0.44	0.21	0.10	0.11	0.07	0.23
	Cumulative	0.23	2.41	3.45	3.88	4.31	4.54	4.63	4.74	4.80	5.02
BB	Marginal	0.67	1.41	2.50	1.27	1.47	0.65	0.90	0.48	0.85	1.25
	Cumulative	0.67	2.07	4.52	5.73	7.12	7.72	8.55	8.99	9.76	10.89
B	Marginal	1.83	4.74	4.92	5.49	3.90	2.37	2.56	1.34	1.03	0.61
	Cumulative	1.83	6.48	11.08	15.97	18.37	19.24	21.31	22.36	23.16	23.63
CCC	Marginal	5.44	11.10	13.50	8.46	2.90	7.00	4.34	4.41	0.51	3.01
	Cumulative	5.44	15.94	27.38	33.44	35.37	39.89	42.50	45.04	45.32	46.96

Source: Altman, E.I. and Ramayanam, S., 2007. Default and returns in the high-yield bond market: 2006 in *Review and Outlook*, Special Report: NYU Salomon Center, and Leonard N. Stern School of Business, January, 1–35, page 23. (Rated by S&P at issuance based on 1777 issues. *Source:* Standard & Poor's (New York) and E. Altman's Compilation.)

Table 7.14 Global structured finance and corporate finance 12–months rating transition matrices: 1984–2007 average and 2007.

Structured finance: 1984–2007 average

From	To	Aaa	Aa	A	Baa	Ba	B	Caa and below
Aaa		98.64%	0.24%	0.07%	0.02%	0.01%	0.01%	0.01%
Aa		6.17%	91.56%	1.50%	0.44%	0.11%	0.09%	0.13%
A		1.30%	3.73%	91.61%	2.26%	0.62%	0.24%	0.23%
Baa		0.44%	0.58%	2.86%	90.68%	2.72%	1.44%	1.29%
Ba		0.16%	0.09%	0.56%	2.96%	88.34%	3.33%	4.56%
B		0.06%	0.05%	0.09%	0.41%	2.29%	87.22%	9.88%
Caa etc.		0.03%			0.09%	0.11%	0.62%	99.15%

Corporate finance: 1984–2007 average

From	To	Aaa	Aa	A	Baa	Ba	B	Caa and below
Aaa		92.80%	6.92%	0.26%		0.02%	0.00%	
Aa		1.27%	91.43%	6.96%	0.27%	0.05%	0.02%	0.01%
A		0.07%	2.96%	90.97%	5.28%	0.56%	0.11%	0.04%
Baa		0.05%	0.21%	5.38%	88.32%	4.54%	1.00%	0.51%
Ba		0.01%	0.06%	0.44%	6.48%	81.50%	9.52%	1.99%
B		0.01%	0.05%	0.19%	0.41%	6.13%	81.66%	11.54%
Caa, etc.			0.03%	0.04%	0.20%	0.69%	11.19%	87.85%

Structured finance in 2007

From	To	Aaa	Aa	A	Baa	Ba	B	Caa and below
Aaa		99.58%	0.20%	0.07%	0.06%	0.05%	0.02%	0.02%
Aa		3.65%	93.66%	0.99%	0.60%	0.44%	0.21%	0.45%
A		0.69%	3.19%	82.45%	6.92%	3.69%	1.50%	1.56%
Baa		0.36%	0.22%	1.96%	76.10%	6.87%	7.28%	7.20%
Ba		0.25%	0.09%	0.16%	1.61%	76.01%	5.91%	15.98%
B		0.14%		0.07%	0.21%	1.57%	91.66%	6.36%
Caa, etc.				0.17%	0.17%	0.17%	0.51%	98.99%

Corporate finance in 2007

From	To	Aaa	Aa	A	Baa	Ba	B	Caa and below
Aaa		95.88%	4.12%					
Aa		4.52%	91.16%	4.12%	0.10%		0.10%	
A			9.93%	87.27%	2.62%	0.06%		0.12%
Baa			1.19%	7.36%	88.55%	3.63%	0.28%	
Ba				0.19%	8.38%	88.62%	7.05%	0.76%
B		0.10%			0.20%	6.30%	83.84%	9.55%
Caa, etc.							15.98%	84.02%

Issuance in all product categories and regions is included. For structured finance instruments, the four major categories, ABS, CDO, CMBS and RMBS plus all others are included.
Source: Moody's Investors Service, 2008., Structured finance rating transitions 1983-2007, *Special Comment,* February, 1–74, page.

Table 7.15 Global SF and CF 1-year rating transition statistics

	Global structured finance		Global corporate finance	
	2007	1984–2007	2007	1984–2007
Downgrade rate	7.40%	2.34%	8.72%	13.56%
Upgrade rate	2.21%	2.47%	18.67%	9.86%
Downgrade rate (notch weighted)	3.35	0.95	0.47	1.38
Upgrade rate (notch weighted)	42.63%	9.40%	13.12%	24.27%
Rating drift (notch weighted)	5.03%	5.88%	26.45%	14.78%
Rating volatility (notch weighted)	8.47	1.60	0.50	1.64
Stability rate	−37.59%	−3.52%	13.33%	−9.49%
Withdrawal rate	47.66%	15.28%	39.57%	39.05%
Notches per downgrade per year	90.39%	95.19%	72.61%	76.59%
Notches per upgrade per year	5.76	4.01	1.50	1.79

Issuance in all product categories and regions is included.

Downgrade (Upgrade) Rate: A security is considered to have been downgraded (upgraded) if its rating at the end of a pre-specified time period is lower (higher) than at the beginning of the time period on the basis of ratings with numeric modifiers (also known as refined ratings or modified ratings). The downgrade rate is the number of securities downgraded (or upgraded) divided by the total number of outstanding securities at the beginning of the time period. Note that in measuring downgrade rates and upgrade rates, only ratings at the beginning and the end of the time period are considered. However, if a rating was withdrawn by the end of the time period, then the rating prior to withdrawal is used as the end rating. Note that a security will only be counted if it was outstanding as of the cohort formation date.

Weighted Downgrade (Upgrade) Rate is computed as the number of securities downgraded (upgraded), weighted by the number of total notches changed per downgrade (upgrade) per year, divided by the total number of outstanding securities at the beginning of the 12-month period. For example, a security downgraded from Baa1 to B1 over 12 months is counted as three downgrades in the calculation of a weighted downgrade rate, but counted as only one downgrade in the calculation of the unweighted downgrade rate.

Rating Drift is defined as the weighted upgrade rate minus the weighted downgrade rate.

Rating Volatility is defined as the weighted upgrade rate plus the weighted downgrade rate.

Rating Stability Rate is a measure of the proportion of ratings that were unchanged over a pre-specified time period. It is calculated as one minus the sum of the downgrade rate and upgrade rate.

Source: Moody's Investors Service, 2008. Structured finance rating transitions 1983-2007, *Special Comment,* February, 1-74, Exhibit 10E, page 10.

corporate finance. However, a careful induction shows that the likelihood of transitioning from higher rating categories to the lowest is different in the cohorts of investment level and below-investment level for structured finance and corporate finance, as shown in Figure 7.14 and Figure 7.15. In the investment grade category, structured instruments are more prone to default (considered as rated below Caa or below) than corporate debt instruments; and vice versa in the below-investment grade category. The understanding of rating dynamics in structured finance still requires further research. Many instruments are still very new and have not lived through an entire business cycle. However, it is clear that typical rating paths or histories of a given instrument in structured finance is likely to be very different from the typical rating path in corporate finance. Average transition statistics may conceal some of the most relevant information concerning rating dynamics in structured finance. Although the same rating scale for both corporate and structured finance instruments refers to the same ordinal default probability, the scale cannot be calibrated to refer also to the same

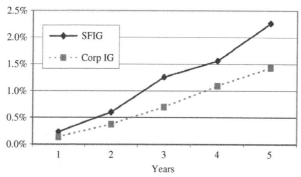

Rating categories 1983–2002 (broad rating category based, adjusted for withdrawn ratings; for corporate ratings, defaults are merged into the Caa or below category)

Figure 7.14 Cumulative frequencies of transition into the lowest rating category (Caa or below) from investment grade (IG)
Source: Moody's Investors Service, 2003. Structured finance rating transitions 1983-2002, comparison with corporate ratings and across sectors, *Special Comment,* January, 1–32, page 7.

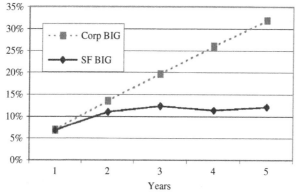

Rating categories 1983–2002 (broad rating category based, adjusted for withdrawn ratings; for corporate ratings, defaults are merged into the Caa or below category)

Figure 7.15 Cumulative frequencies of transition into the lowest rating category (Caa or below) from below investment grade (BIG)
Source: Moody's Investors Service, 2003. Structured finance rating transitions 1983–2002, comparison with corporate ratings and across sectors, *Special Comment,* January, 1–32, page 8.

transition probabilities. Because the likely rating paths are so different for ratings from both segments, we believe it could be worthwhile to signal this more clearly to investors, for instance, by including a modifier on the rating scale for structured finance instruments.

7.2.2 Analysis of the Prevention of Surprise in Defaults

The rating distribution of defaulted issues at various points prior to default for the peroid 1971 to 2002 can be seen in Table 7.16

The Quality of Ratings as a Warning Signal

Consider now bonds that actually defaulted. Did the ratings provide a coherent and consistent warning that default was about to happen? Figure 7.16 sheds light on this question by showing the rating distribution of defaulted issues at various points prior to default for the period 1983 to 2006.

This illustrates that the rating agencies reflect to investors the deterioration in credit quality of a security. Five years prior to default the median rating of defaulting companies is speculative grade. The downward slope of the average and median ratings show that these future defaulters were already experiencing downward rating pressure five years in advance of default. At 48 months before default, the median rating has fallen to B1 and falls further to B2 17 months prior to default. At the time of default, the median and average credit rating is Caa2. It is interesting to note that as the default date approaches, the pace of rating downgrade accelerates.

Moreover, as Löffler and Posch (2007) demonstrate on the example of Moody's data, ratings help to predict individual financial ratios over a horizon of up to five years.[73] The

Table 7.16 Rating distribution of defaulted issues at various points prior to default (1971–2002)

	Original rating		1 year prior		6 months prior	
	Number	Percentage	Number	Percentage	Number	Percentage
AAA	5	0.0%	0	0.0%	0	0.0%
AA	27	1.7%	0	0.0%	0	0.0%
A	115	7.1%	12	0.9%	14	1.1%
BBB	228	14.1%	127	9.6%	120	9.9%
Total Investment Grade	375	22.9%	139	10.5%	134	11.0%
BB	174	10.8%	190	14.4%	184	15.1%
B	882	54.5%	630	47.7%	566	46.5%
CCC	176	10.9%	320	24.2%	278	22.8%
CC	10	0.6%	31	2.3%	45	3.7%
C	1	0.1%	8	0.6%	7	0.6%
D	0	0.0%	4	0.3%	4	0.3%
Total Non-Investment Grade	1243	77.1%	1183	89.5%	1084	89.0%
Total	1618	100%	1322	100%	1218	100%

Note: Based on Standard & Poor's Bond Ratings.
Source: Altman, E.I., and Bana, G., 2003, Defaults and returns on high-yield bonds: The year 2002 in review and the market outlook, New York University Salomon Center, Stern School of Business Report, February, 1–64, Exhibit 7, page 48.

---

[73] Löffler, G., and Posch, P.N., 2007, How do rating agencies score in predicting firm performance?, July, SFB 649 Discussion Paper 2007-043, Humboldt Universität Berlin, 1–25.

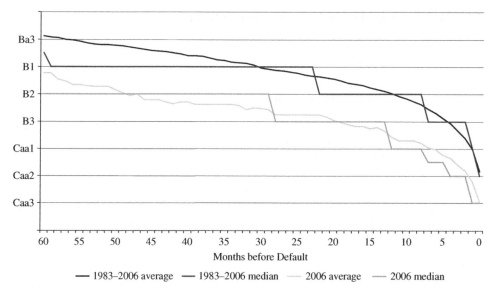

Figure 7.16 Rating distribution of defaulted issues at various points prior to default (1983–2006)
Source: Cantor, R., Hamilton, D.T., Kim, F., and Ou, S., 2007, Corporate default and recovery rates, 1920–2006, *Special Comment*: Moody's Investors Service, February 27, Report 102071, 1–48, page 6.

contribution of ratings appears to be economically significant and robust for different specifications. On the other hand, serial correlation of rating actions has been well documented. Assessment of conditional transition rates reveals a 'rating momentum.' While an upgrade is equally likely to be followed by another upgrade or a downgrade, a downgrade is nine times more likely to be followed by a downgrade than by an upgrade within a one-year horizon. Nevertheless, when transition rates are conditioned on outlooks and rating reviews as well, the serial correlation all but disappears, that is, the CRAs signal their rating action intentions through reviews and outlooks.[74]

Güttler and Wahrenburg compare the reaction of Moody's and S&P to the increasing risk of default and claim that Moody's is somewhat faster in following the actual risk of default.[75] It is interesting to see how the two firms react to each other's actions: a downgrade (upgrade) by one is usually followed by a similar action of 'greater magnitude in the short term.' More generally, a reaction by the second agency is much more likely after a downgrade rather than an upgrade by the first agency.

The Cycle Neutrality of Ratings

Many studies have been conducted to examine whether ratings are actually cycle neutral as they supposedly intend to be. An observation of upgrades and downgrades over time

---

[74] Hamilton, D.T., and Cantor, R., 2004, Rating transition and default rates conditioned on outlooks, *Journal of Fixed Income*, September, 54–70.
[75] Güttler, A. and Wahrenburg, M., 2007, The adjustment of credit ratings in advance of defaults, *Journal of Banking and Finance*, Vol. 31, 751–767.

shows that upgrades tend to fall in relation to downgrades during recessions. For example, upgrades were only 34% as a fraction of total transitions in 2001, and 19% in 2002, in comparison to 48% in 2000. During the 1990–1991 recession, this fraction fell to 24% in 1990 and 21% in 1991 compared to 32% in 1989.[76]

Another study examines the universe of US firms rated by S&P between 1981 and 2001. The study finds that a complete set of firms and ratings provides very little evidence that credit ratings are influenced by the business cycle. However, a study of a subset of observations where a rating had either just been issued or changed showed that credit ratings exhibit excess sensitivity to the business cycle. In particular, conditional on the financial and business characteristics of the firm, newly announced credit ratings were found to be related to the macroeconomy in a procyclical manner. That is, ratings were found to be conditionally better during a boom and conditionally worse during a downturn.[77]

In order to investigate the influence of cycles on ratings, Bangia et al. built a Merton-type model of asset values which they linked to a factor representing the state of the economy, contraction or expansion.[78] They documented the path-dependence of transition matrices with the state of the economy and found that ratings are less stable in a recession, in the sense that rating changes, downgrades in particular, are more likely than in an expansion, and that the volatility of transition probabilities was significantly lower in a period of recession compared to unconditional transition probabilities.

In order to reproduce the CRA rating methodologies, Löffler built a cyclical model allowing for permanent and transitory shocks.[79] The model was used to test 'through-the-cycle' and the 'point-in-time' or 'current-condition' rating approaches. The analysis revealed that, while rating stability is higher when using the through-the-cycle approach, ratings are far from being perfectly correlated with actual default risk and there is evidence of serial correlation of ratings over time. Löffler goes on to suggest, however, that some lack of 'predictability ... can stem from errors in assessing the degree of cyclicality.'

The lack of cycle neutrality of ratings could have a debilitating consequence on financial markets during bad times, given the widespread use of ratings in investment norms of institutional investors and the regulatory capital of banks. If CRA downgrades increase during recessions, when firms are already in a relatively weaker financial state, more and more debt securities can go below the minimum rating grade required by institutional investors, leading to large-scale sell-offs, rise in yields, and crashing bond prices. This could further result in reduced capacity for companies to raise fresh funds, and the reduction in regulatory capital of banks during downturns, when financial stability is most needed by market participants. However, ratings need to be sufficiently cycle neutral to bring stability, but also sufficiently timely to bring enough accuracy to maintain investors' confidence who need to continue trusting that the agencies' ratings are indicative of the true degrees of fundamental creditworthiness.

---

[76] Cantor, R., Hamilton, D.T., Ou, S., and Varma, P., 2005, Default and recovery rates of corporate bond issuers, 1920–2004, *Special Comment*: Moody's Investors Service, January, Report 91233, 1–40, Exhibit 29: Annual aggregate rating migration rates, 1983–2004, page 35.

[77] Amato, J.D., and Furfine, C.H., 2004. Are credit ratings procyclical?, *Journal of Banking and Finance*, Vol. 28, 2641–2677.

[78] Bangia, A., Diebold, F.X., Kronimus, A., Schagen, Ch., and Schuermann, T., 2002, Ratings migration and the business cycle, with application to credit portfolio stress testing, *Journal of Banking and Finance*, Vol. 26, 445–474.

[79] Löffler, G., 2004, An anatomy of rating through the cycle, *Journal of Banking and Finance*, Vol. 28, 695–720.

7.2.3 Summary, Evaluation and Conclusion

In evaluating the performance of rating agencies, the question becomes which of the two approaches – ratings on an ordinal scale or expected default frequencies on a cardinal scale – does the best job in default discrimination?[80] It has been shown that market-based measures may be better predictors of short-term default risk than agency ratings. Löffler finds that the relative power of the two measures in predicting defaults depends on the investor's investment horizon and risk appetite. His results, based on Moody's ratings and Moody's KMV EDF data from 1983 to 2002, including both US and non-US issuers, and a sample of over 290,000 issuer-months, support the agencies' claim that their policy of reducing rating volatility, that builds on through-the-cycle approach and the avoidance of frequent rating reversals is beneficial to bond investors. 'The results also suggest that widely used statistical measures of rating quality may be insufficient to judge the economic value of rating information in specific contexts.'

As explained in Chapter 3, fundamental ratings serve three complementary functions, they measure credit risk in a consistent (comparable across geographic and product segments) and contractible way. These should be kept in mind when using and evaluating ratings.

7.3 EFFICIENCY ENHANCEMENT: STABILIZATION IN TIMES OF CRISIS?

System risk managers want ratings to be stabilizers. They want ratings to keep issuers on a leash when these become irrationally exuberant. They also want ratings to reassure markets when markets become irrationally depressed. In the parlance of traditional central bank interest rate policy, they want ratings to 'lean against the wind.' Inasmuch as it is the job of central banks to properly manage money supply growth, one could say that it is the job of credit rating agencies to properly manage market participants awareness of credit quality.

So, last but not least, what value do credit ratings add in times of crisis? Think about the 1997–1998 Asian macro financial crisis, the 2000–2003 Western micro equity crisis, and the 2007-2008 subprime mortgage related crisis. The CRAs were severely criticized for having failed to properly anticipate many of the massive defaults listed in Exhibit 2.1 and for generally paying scant attention to properly monitor the issues they rate. What are the merits and remedies of these criticisms? We will address those issues in the third section of this chapter.

7.3.1 The Asian Macroeconomic Financial Crisis

The Procyclical Role of Rating Agencies: Evidence from the East Asian Crisis

We demonstrate that credit rating agencies aggravated the East Asian crisis. In fact, having failed to predict the emergence of the crisis, rating agencies became excessively conservative. They downgraded East Asian crisis countries more than the worsening in these countries' economic fundamentals would justify. This unduly exacerbated, for

---

[80] Löffler, G., 2004. Ratings versus market-based measures of default risk in portfolio governance, *Journal of Banking and Finance*, Vol. 28, No. 11, November, 2715–2746.

these countries, the cost of borrowing abroad and caused the supply of international capital to them to evaporate. In turn, lower than deserved ratings contributed – at least for some time – to amplify the East Asian crisis.[81]

The above accusation is a very grave one. The more so that one of the accusers was at that time Senior Vice President and Chief Economist of the World Bank.[82] The above blame of the CRAs was rendered almost in the heat of the crisis. What are, in retrospect and in the light of new evidence, the merits of the prosecution? But first, what entailed this crisis?

Between 1993 and 1997, international investors poured more than US$500 billion into Asian economies. When times were good, investors seemed oblivious to the lack of transparency and regulatory shortcomings in most of the regional markets. When the crisis hit in the middle of 1997 there was a stampede for the exits in which many investors got badly burned. The Asian financial crisis is a tailor-made illustration of the importance and the difficulty of making the international financial system work effectively. *The Economist* put it this way:

> Imagine yourself taking a business-school exam in international financial management. The test is a case study. It concerns Opacia, an emerging economy that is in a bit of a mess. Corporate financial statements mean little as firms routinely lend to each other off balance sheet. You have no idea how big the country's foreign liabilities are, though you know that its banks and companies like to borrow dollars short-term, usually to finance long-term local investment projects. There is no effective bankruptcy law, and corruption is rife. Question: Is this a safe place to invest money?[83]

The answer is clearly 'no,' but this did not stop a flow of money from 'sophisticated' international investors to an area of the world that looks like the fictional country of Opacia. The conventional wisdom purports that the rating agencies provided little if any warning to investors about the risks of investing in Asia. Is this borne out by the facts?

In the aftermath of the Asian financial crisis observers began to look around for somebody to blame. Among the leading suspects were the Western CRAs whose sovereign ratings of selected Asian countries Exhibit 7.1 reports and some of which Figure 7.17 describes.

This exhibit starts with what the Fitch, Moody's and S&P sovereign ratings were before the onset of the crisis that began with the devaluation of the Thai baht on July 2, 1997 for China (NR/A3/BBB+), Hong Kong (A+/A3/A+) Indonesia (BBB−/Baa3/BBB), Korea (AA−/A1/AA−), Taiwan (NR,Aa3,AA+), and Thailand (NR/A3/A). It then follows the ratings through to the first ratings recovery after the crisis to illustrate the degree of anticipation or the pace of reaction of the CRAs.

Consider Indonesia. Fitch had initiated coverage on June 4 at the BBB− level, one month before the crisis. It was not until three months after crisis, on October 10, that the first downgrade occurred, S&P downgrading Indonesia to BB−. It then took five gradual downgrades over the space of seven months for S&P to rate Indonesia CCC+ and 10

---

[81] Ferri, G., Liu, L.G., and Stiglitz, J.E., 1999, The procyclical role of rating agencies: evidence from the East Asian Crisis, *Economic Notes* by Banca Monte dei Paschi di Siena SpA, Vol. 28, No. 3, 335–355, page 335.

[82] Stiglitz, J.E. from 1997–2000, after having been Chairman, Council of Economic Advisers to the US President, 1995–1997.

[83] *The Economist*, 1999, A stitch in time, *Global Finance Survey*, January 30, Vol. 350, Issue 8104, 8–12, page 8.

Exhibit 7.1   Selected Asian sovereign ratings (long-term foreign currency) from December 1993 through the first upgrade after the crisis.

Date	Fitch	Moody's Rating	S&P Rating
China			
December 31, 1993		A3	BBB
May 14, 1997			BBB+
Devaluation of the Thai baht: July 2, 1997			
December 11, 1997	A−		
December 22, 1998	A−		
July 20, 1999			BBB
February 18, 2004			BBB+
Hong Kong			
December 31, 1993		A3	A
August 10, 1994	AA−		
August 9, 1995	A+		
May 14, 1997			A+
Devaluation of the Thai baht: July 2, 1997			
August 31, 1998			A
February 8, 2001			A+
June 25, 2001	AA−		
Indonesia			
December 31, 1993			BBB−
March 14, 1994		Baa3	
April 18, 1995			BBB
June 4, 1997	BBB−		
Devaluation of the Thai baht: July 2, 1997			
October 10, 1997			BBB−
December 21, 1997		Ba1	
December 22, 1997	BB+		
December 31, 1997			BB+
January 8, 1998	BB−		
January 9, 1998		B2	BB
January 21, 1998	B+		
January 27, 1998			B
March 11, 1998			B−
March 16, 1998	B−		
March 20, 1998		B3	
May 15, 1998			CCC+
March 30, 1999			SD (Selective Default)
March 31, 1999			CCC+
April 17, 2000			SD (Selective Default)
October 2, 2000			B−
May 21, 2001			CCC+
November 2, 2001			CCC
April 23, 2002			SD (Selective Default)
August 1, 2002	B		
September 5, 2002			CCC+
May 12, 2003			B−
September, 2003		B2	
October 8, 2003			B

(*continued overleaf*)

Exhibit 7.1 (*continued*)

Date	Fitch	Moody's Rating	S&P Rating
Korea			
December 31, 1993		A1	A+
May 3, 1995			AA−
June 27, 1996	AA−		
Devaluation of the Thai baht: July 2, 1997			
October 24, 1997			A+
November 18, 1997	A+		
November 25, 1997			A−
November 26, 1997	A		
November 27, 1997		A3	
December 10, 1997		Baa2	
December 11, 1997	BBB−		BBB−
December 21, 1997		Ba1	
December 22, 1997			B+
December 23, 1997	B−		
February 3, 1998	BB+		
February 18, 1998			BB+
January 25, 1999			BBB−
February 12, 1999		Baa3	
December 16, 1999		Baa2	
Taiwan			
December 31, 1993			AA+
March 24, 1994		Aa3	
Devaluation of the Thai baht: July 2, 1997			
July 26, 2001			AA
November 19, 2001	A+		
December 17, 2002			AA−
Thailand			
December 31, 1993		A2	A−
December 29, 1994			A
April 8, 1997		A3	
Devaluation of the Thai baht: July 2, 1997			
September 3, 1997			A−
October 1, 1997		Baa1	
October 24, 1997			BBB
November 27, 1997		Baa3	
December 21, 1997		Ba1	
January 8, 1998			BBB−
May 14, 1998	BB+		
June 24, 1999	BBB−		
June 22, 2000		Baa3	
October 8, 2003			BBB

Source: Fitch Ratings, 2006, *Complete Sovereign Rating History*, August 25; Cavanaugh, M., and Daly, K., 2006, Sovereign ratings history since 1975, *Research*: Standard & Poor's, September 11, 1–19, pages 3–19; Moody's Investors Service, 2005, *Ratings History on Each Country*, December 14.

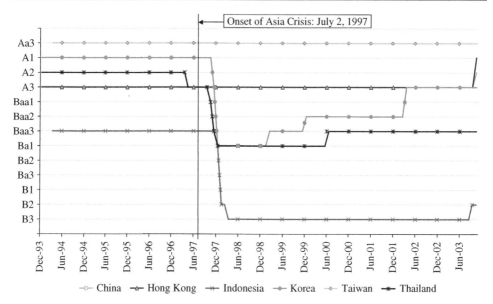

Figure 7.17   Selected Asian sovereign Moody's LT foreign currency ratings (Dec. 1993–Oct. 2003)

Source: Moody's Investors Service, 2005, *Ratings History on China, Hong Kong, Indonesia, Korea, Taiwan, and Thailand*, December 14.

additional months before selective default occurred in March 1999. It is interesting to note that Moody's and Fitch made generally fewer moves during the crisis, but maybe more drastic ones early on. Moody's, for instance, downgraded 4 notches in one step in January 1998. The pace at which the CRAs recognized recovery varied significantly, Fitch upgrading to B on August 1, 2002, S&P upgrading out of selective default to CCC+ one month later, and Moody's waiting another year before upgrading to B2.

The CRAs also moved significantly on Korea and Thailand, again with a slow start but falling to below investment grade by the year-end (with the exception of S&P for Thailand) but recovering in rating sooner than Indonesia.

In contrast the agencies had not made any big moves in 'Greater China' (mainland China, Taiwan, or Hong Kong) by the time that Indonesia, Korea, and Thailand had reached their rating depths in the winter of 1997/spring of 1998. Greater China retained investment grade all the time, Hong Kong and Taiwan maintaining A levels, and China remaining stable at the BBB level. The CRAs made the right call for Greater China on the long-term foreign currency ratings.[84]

Critics refer to data as presented in Exhibit 7.1 and Figure 7.17 to claim that instead of acting as an early warning system, the agencies belatedly reacted to events that they had not foreseen in the first place. According to *The Economist*, the agencies were at least guilty of badly misreading Asian politics and of failing to spell out the questionable assumptions that sometimes underpin their ratings.[85] It was also often a question of too little, too late.

---

[84] Maybe not for Hong Kong where they were forced to react after the fact on the domestic currency front.

[85] The *Economist*, 1997. Risks beyond measure, December 13, Vol. 345, Issue 8047, 70–71, page 70.

Yamaichi Securities (the fourth largest securities firm in Japan) was downgraded by Moody's and S&P just before it went bankrupt in November 1997, long after the international capital markets had been closed to the firm.

According to rating expert Edward Altman, the CRAs suffer from 'downward rigidity.' When they determine that a bond issuer's creditworthiness has improved and upgrade the bonds, the next rating change is equally likely to be up or down. A downgrade, however, is far more likely to be followed by another downgrade than by an upgrade. This indicates, says Altman, that the agencies tend to dole out the bad news in small packets rather than savaging the issuer (who is the source of their profits), by knocking down the issuer by more than one rating.[86]

There is some evidence that this was a problem in Asia during 1997 and 1998. The agencies did not move very quickly to warn investors of impending problems. However, it is also the case that when they did, they were highly criticized for doing so. Indeed, it is easy to forget how difficult it was in pre-crisis Asia to criticize Asian governments or companies. When Moody's lowered Thailand's short-term foreign currency debt rating in 1996, local and international bankers roundly criticized the move.[87]

There may be more to the criticism as the rating agencies tend to be very conservative and are generally unwilling to take a stand that is significantly different from that of their competitors. A herd mentality exists which may not be unlike that found in the mutual fund industry, where most fund managers end up owning the same stocks as everyone else. After all, if you are wrong about downgrading Malaysian debt you could cause serious damage to your reputation.

It also may not be fair to accuse the agencies of a reluctance to criticize their customers given the fact that they have on many occasions incurred the wrath of governments and companies by downgrading issuers at critical junctures. Moody's downgraded the long-term foreign currency debt of Thailand on April 8, 1997. This was a wake-up call to an impending crisis just before it actually began. It enraged the Thai government.[88]

Perhaps a more serious charge against the rating agencies is the fact that by centralizing staff in New York and London (with only a small number of analysts in the regional offices), they may miss developments on the ground. While the agencies argue that putting the majority of staff in one place means there will be less variability between ratings (and that people can fly into a region to get the local flavor), there is probably little doubt that credit ratings in Asia were being assigned by people who greatly underestimated the political risks.

Another criticism from market participants concerns whether the agencies had sufficient staff to stay on top of a rapidly evolving market. One banker commented, 'When you called up the rating agency and asked to have a rating done for an issuer, you'd be told to wait for one and a half months. These guys are so busy, and fair enough, they're chasing revenues

---

[86] *The Economist*, 1997. Risks beyond measure, December 13, Vol. 345, Issue 8047, 70–71, page 70.

[87] Doug Coulter lived in Asia between 1994 and 1997 and saw first hand those very same foreign investment bankers continue to hunt down financing mandates and peddle Asian stocks and bonds to Western investors even as Asian economies began to show clear signs of problems during the early months of 1997.

[88] For the trustees and managers of conservative US and European based funds that were investing a portion of their clients money in emerging markets during the boom years in Asia, 1997 was a sobering experience. Thailand provides a good example of why they were so angry with the rating agencies. In May of 1997 Thailand issued a 10-year 7.75% bond that the agencies rated A/A3. The more conservative funds that bought and held the paper did so under investment criteria that permitted A−/A3 paper or above but nothing lower. This meant that when the sovereign rating was revised closer to high yield levels, the funds were forced to sell the bonds. The spread moved from 89 bps over treasuries as of May 30 to a peak of 530 bps on October 28.

like all of us. But you have to ask, if they're that busy who've they got watching the existing ratings?'[89]

Asia (and the rest of the emerging markets) are clearly a tougher environment in which to work. One of Hong Kong's biggest fund managers is quoted as saying that 'the relative success of rating agencies only reflects the underlying system. In the US, there is full disclosure and transparency and this appears to make them more accurate. Here in Asia they're dealing with a much less transparent underlying market.'[90]

The response of the agencies to the criticism was varied. According to Paul Coughlin, the head of S&P's office in Hong Kong, 'people have got a bit carried away ... they've generalized from a few ratings that they deem a failure and concluded that all the other thousands are useless too. But if you look across the thousands of ratings we've issued does it give you a good indication of risk? Happily it does.'[91]

It is true that the rating agencies are very good at assessing risk and assigning that risk a rating. However, since the rating agencies have only been rating companies in emerging markets for a relatively short period of time, there is not yet a sufficient time frame to allow for relevant statistical analysis of rating agency performance in emerging markets. The question that skeptics have is whether a BBB company in Thailand is the same as a BBB in the US. The problem is compounded with regard to unsolicited ratings where the rating agencies are relying on public information that may not be of a high standard.

An additional problem in Asia was the fact that very few Asian companies and banks were actually rated and, more often than not, the rated companies were the better ones. This means that the rating agencies were less likely to spot the problems. For example, only 8 of Indonesia's 230 banks were rated prior to the Asian crisis. This has as much to do with the resources devoted to emerging markets as anything else.

There is also the question of whether what the agencies are saying privately and what they say publicly are the same. It is a similar criticism that might be leveled at investment banks that offer a better level of service to their richest clients.

At the end of the day, the environment in which the rating agencies operate is as important as anything else. The President of S&P notes that

> in the absence of a strong and outspoken media serving as a vehicle for communicating different opinions, there cannot be open markets because financial information providers are nothing more than extensions of the media at large. Institutional investors, securities analysts and rating services should become involved in establishing disclosure standards and markets all over the world need to appreciate the value of a true credit culture. This is a culture where risk is measured and priced according to objective standards and not on questionable relationships and implicit assurances.[92]

Ratings are not just used as a guide to the risk of default. They are also used to determine whether bonds are reasonably priced. In the end, the rating agencies may be no more or less accurate than their compatriots who make their living as equity analysts, strategists, economists, and political risk consultants.

---

[89] Irvine, S., 1998, Caught with their pants down?, *Euromoney*, January, 51–53.

[90] Irvine, S., 1998, Caught with their pants down?, *Euromoney*, January, 51–53.

[91] Irvine, S., 1998, Caught with their pants down?', *Euromoney*, January, 51–53.

[92] O'Neill, L.C., President and Chief Rating Officer–Standard & Poor's, 1999, Building the new global framework for risk analysis, Remarks to Professional bankers association at World Bank headquarters in Washington, D.C., March 26, 1–5.

7.3.2   The Western Microeconomic Equity Crisis

Rating Stability

Rating agencies use the number of rating actions, and the number of large rating actions (in excess of 2 notches within one year) as an indicator of the stability of ratings, which is an important criterion for CRA ratings

Generally speaking, 2001–2002 were watershed years for corporate rating analysis at major CRAs.[93] As Moody's pointed out, the September 2001 terrorist attacks in the United States, global economic contraction, and the highly visible financial setbacks – including some notable bankruptcies – suffered by a number of well-known US, European, and Japanese companies, sharpened the focus of capital market participants on issues of credit quality. This brought considerable attention to the CRAs downgrades of high-visibility issuers. In addition to a higher incidence of downgrades relative to upgrades in 2001, there was also a marked increase in serial downgrades of the same issuer. Moody's reported that 'roughly 20% of rating changes in 2001 represented repeat actions for the same issuer, as compared to 6% in 2000.'

But historically, CRAs had 'sought to maintain a system characterized by stable ratings, with a time horizon that extended several years and an intention to rate through the cycle.' As Standard & Poor's puts it 'The ideal is to rate "through the cycle." There is no point in assigning high ratings to a company enjoying peak prosperity if that performance level is expected to be only temporary. Similarly, there is no need to lower ratings to reflect poor performance as long as one can reliably anticipate that better times are just around the corner.'[94]

The unusually high incidence of serial rating actions in 2001 represented, in a sense, a challenge to the traditional system in which there could be an embedded 'stasis' (as Moody's puts it), or rating intertia, that favors gradual, slow adjustments leading to short-term serial correlation, rather than more fully revealing multi-notch rating changes. If there would indeed be short-term serial correlation in rating changes, this could suggest that true information about changes in quality is slow to surface in the ratings. This would then reduce the information quality of a rating at a particular point in time.[95] It could seriously call into question traditional rating analysis and the consequential rating action.

In fact, it seems that traditionally some very particular inertia prevailed indeed, independent from the notion of 'through the cycle' rating. Results of credit analysis would trigger consequential rating migration (change in notch) only when the results were 'material,' and the adjustment to the new target rating would only be partial. In other words, CRAs pursued a conservative migration policy, as evidenced in the way rating agencies achieve rating stability.[96] According to Altman and Rijken, S&P triggered a rating migration only when

---

[93] See Mahoney, C., 2002, The bond rating process in a changing environment, *Special Comment*: Moody's Investors Service, January, Report 73741, 1–4; Laserson, F., and Mahoney, C., 2002, The bond rating process: a progress report, *Rating Policy*: Moody's Investors Service, February, Report 74079, 1–4.; Cantor, R., Fons, J.S., and Mahoney, C., 2002, Understanding Moody's corporate bond ratings and rating process, *Special Comment*: Moody's Investors Service, May, Report 74982, 1–16.

[94] Standard & Poor's, 2005, *Corporate Ratings Criteria*, 1–119, page 34.

[95] Financial economists would say that changes in a price series reflect all available information about the price generating process up to the point of the latest price change if these changes are uncorrelated, or unpredictable in any sense, one from the other. They would describe such an information processor as a 'weakly efficient' one.

[96] See Altman, E.I. and Rijken, H.A., 2003, How rating agencies achieve rating stability, December, 1–48. Their findings rely on a time series of 1772 obligors with a duration of 1–21 years, the 1981–1999 sample estimation

the post-analysis credit quality would exceed a threshold level of at least 1.25 notch steps compared to the typical credit quality in a particular rating class. And if triggered, ratings are only partly adjusted, by 75%, to a target rating level, which is set about 0.3–0.6 notch steps below the actual through-the-cycle credit quality level. Target rating adjustments are split and executed on different times. Presumably, Altman argues, S&P followed a wait and see policy.

It should be no surprise that the consequences of the CRAs principle of through the cycle rating and their policy of conservative migrations, i.e. a marked degree of rating stability, contrasted heavily with the 2001–2002 context of greater volatility in credit markets and more rapid deterioration in the financial condition and liquidity prospects for obligors. As credit spreads and their volatility increase, investors become more sensitive to the 'point-in-time' perception on the creditworthiness of a company, and less to its 'through the cycle' one. So investors became more keen to have an instant outlook on the probability of default of a company, within a short- to medium-term horizon. Traditional fundamental ratings tend to rank order fairly consistently, increasing default frequencies according to declining rating grades. Yet they do not solve the kind of problem of number ordering the expected default frequency of a company, let's say, within a year or within five years, using all available market information, such as a company's stock market price and its corresponding volatility like market-implied ratings do. Their popularity has considerably increased since the 2001–2002 shocks to the creditworthiness of many companies.

7.3.3 The Subprime Mortgage Related Crisis

In this crisis, the credit rating agencies' loss of credibility with respect to investors was a key factor in destabilizing the financial markets. This loss of credibility was due partly to CRA negligence and mistakes and partly to investors' misunderstanding of the nature, the amount and the location of the risks. The most evident trigger to this loss of credibility occurred during the second week of July 2007 when S&P downgraded $7.3 billion of securities issued in 2005 and 2006 and a few weeks later, Moody's downgraded 691 securities of the 2006 vintage, originally worth $19.4 billion. In 78 cases the bonds originally had Aaa ratings, this immediately raised questions about the veracity of the rating methodologies employed by the different rating agencies. In October and November, further downgrades in the residential-mortgage-backed securities (RMBS) segment and structured investment vehicles (SIV) occurred, with par values of $22 billion and $33 billion respectively, thereby accelerating this loss of confidence.[97]

The rating agencies started warning about the state of the residential housing market before the beginning of 2006, as Exhibit 7.2, for Moody's illustrates. Some rating modifications, essentially increases in credit enhancements, had been made to take into account the worsening of underwriting standards and the slowing down of house price appreciations.[98] However, these were generally adjustments within the same rating models and frameworks. As Ashcraft and Schuermann point out: 'One must be fair to note that the downturn in

---

period and the 2000–2001 out of sample testing period. It contains 11 890 firm-year observations with a known S&P rating and 1828 firm-year observations with a non-rated S&P status.

[97] Crouhy, M., and Turnbull, S., 2008. The subprime credit crisis of 07, mimeo, March 5th, 1–42.

[98] The level of credit enhancement, say for the AAA tranche, would be the minimum percentage of portfolio loss required before the portfolio loss hits the AAA tranche, say 20%. If macroeconomic conditions worsen, this level could be increased to, say 25%, in order to protect the AAA tranche from potential losses on the portfolio.

Exhibit 7.2 Sample of Moody's publications discussing the deterioration of the subprime mortgage sector before 2007

	2005	
2004 Review & 2005 Outlook: Home Equity ABS	January 18, 2005	-*"Because these loans are generally underwritten based on lower initial monthly payments, **many subprime borrowers may not be able to withstand the payment shock once their loans reset into their fully indexed/amortizing schedule. The resulting higher default probability, which may be exacerbated with slowing home price appreciation**, could have a very negative effect on home equity performance in the future."* (Page 3) -*"**The increase in reduced documentation in the subprime sector is particularly worrisome** because for borrowers with weaker credit profiles the need for establishing repayment capability with stronger asset and income documentation becomes even more important."* (page 6) -*"Moody's increases credit enhancement on such loans to account for the lower borrower equity and the higher borrower leverage"* (page 6)
The Importance of Representations and Warranties in RMBS Transactions	Jan 14, 2005	-*"Moody's believes that representations and warranties **against the inclusion of certain loans in securitized transactions provide a small but important protection** against losses."* (Page 1) -*"**For those securitizers that don't meet standards**, Moody's would seek additional credit enhancement, or financial backing from another company, or acceptable third-party verification of compliance with the standard R&Ws."* (Page 2)
An Update to Moody's Analysis of Payment Shock Risk in Sub-Prime Hybrid ARM Products	May 16, 2005	-*"Moody's adjusts the loss coverage levels up or down by up to 15% for mortgage loans that utilize product features resulting in higher or lower levels of payment increase relative to the benchmark loan."* (Page 1)
Moody's Increases Overcollateralization Floor In Subprime Mortgage Transactions	Jul 12, 2005	-*"To increase the level of protection for investors in Moody's-rated residential mortgage-backed securities (RMBS), Moody's Investors Service has revised its overcollateralization floor for subprime mortgage transactions that include a mix of asset types, such as manufactured housing loans."* (Page 1)

(continued overleaf)

Exhibit 7.2   *(continued)*

2006		
2005 Review & 2006 Outlook: Home Equity ABS	January 24, 2006	- *"Full documentation levels fell by almost 10 percent on average per transaction from the beginning of 2004 to the end of 2005. Therefore,* **in 2005 not only did we see a proliferation of riskier "affordability" products, but also a gradual weakening of underwriting standards."** (Page 5) - *"Moody's loss expectations on the interest-only mortgages are about 15%-25% higher than that of fully amortizing mortgages."* (Page 6) - *"In Moody's view, credit risk for this product is approximately 5% higher than the standard 30 year fully amortizing product, all other credit parameters being equal."* (Page 6) - *"Moody's considers hybrid ARM loans to be riskier than equivalent fixed- rate loans primarily because of the risk of payment shock associated with adjustable-rate products."* (Page 6)
The Blurring Lines between Traditional Alternative-A and Traditional Subprime US Residential Mortgage Markets	Oct 31, 2006	*"In today's economic environment which includes declining US residential mortgage loan origination volume, originators are exploring various ways to stay competitive.* **We are seeing originators who historically specialized in either prime or subprime moving into each other's markets to maintain or increase their origination volume."** (Page 1)
Moody's Approach to Coding Subprime Residential Mortgage Documentation Programs: Updated Methodology	Nov 28, 2006	- *"The subprime residential mortgage-backed securities (RMBS) market is experiencing a decrease in the percentage of loans with full income documentation ("full income doc")."* (Page 1) - *"Less than full documentation, or in other words,* **reduced documentation ("reduced doc") programs can add to the credit risk of a loan as the borrower's financial capabilities are not fully revealed and may result in a loan that may be beyond the borrower's means."** (Page 1)

Source: Kanef, M., Asset Backed Finance Rating Group Managing Director - Moody's Investors Service, 2007, The role and impact of credit rating agencies on the subprime credit markets, Testimony before the United States Senate Committee on Banking, Housing and Urban Affairs September 26, 1–34, Annex 2, page 32. Emphasis added by authors.

housing did not surprise the rating agencies, who had been warning investors about the possibility and the impact on performance for quite some time. However, it did not appear that the agencies appropriately measured the sensitivity of losses to economic activity or anticipated the severity of the downturn.'[99]

The key credit rating agency related causes of the crisis are the lack of perspective and communication (or transparency and disclosure). These in turn are caused by a lack of competition in the rating industry, lack of accountability for transparency and diligence in the securitization process, and both are due to inadequate regulation. The regulation is inadequate in the sense that the rating industry is naturally concentrated, and that the public good nature of ratings and their crucial importance for financial market stability demand subtle monitoring. A rating agency's performance in the short term does not sufficiently affect its bottom line. For instance, rating agencies should have an incentive not to rate instruments for which there is not enough reliable information. Rating agencies have been overly protected by the NRSRO recognition system and by the extensive references to ratings in rules and regulations, as explained in Chapter 9.

Lack of perspective and depth in analysis

Structured finance ratings are still very recent. Most performance data and transition matrices of structured finance ratings, especially CDOs, dates from the last 10 years and the segment has grown tremendously both in volume and diversity of instruments. Structured finance ratings are still not that well understood and most market participants still tend to react to them (for instance in investment guidelines) as if they were corporate finance ratings. However, structured finance instruments represent claims on cash flows from a portfolio of underlying assets rather than on cash flows specific to one firm. Hence, especially in asset-backed securities (ABS) of large pools of homogenous assets where idiosyncratic risk is diversified away like residential-mortgage-backed securities (RMBS), highly rated tranches are especially vulnerable to systematic risk. Relatively small individual asset losses, but that are correlated across the pool of assets, are likely to affect even the highest rated tranches. Correlated losses occur through dependence on common risk factors, such as economic conditions but also, important in this context, the model risk by the agencies (for instance due to lack of information and diligence), and originator, arranger and servicer effects.[100]

Moreover, ratings in structured finance rely heavily on quantitative models, whereas corporate finance ratings rely on analyst judgment. It is natural that quantitative models are used for structured finance rating models, but some of the essential elements that analysts watch for in corporate credit analysis, such as moral hazard and adverse selection, should also be monitored more closely in structured finance. Rating agencies should ask themselves: what are the fundamental incentives of a given party in a structured finance transaction? Ashcraft and Schuermann identify several key market frictions in the securitization process.[101] The frictions that created a discrepancy between the credit true quality of

---

[99] Ashcraft, A., and Schuermann, T., 2008. Understanding the securitization of subprime mortgage credit, *FRBNY Staff Reports,* No. 318, March, 1–76, page 46.

[100] Hence the importance of integrating third party risks and reliability of information directly inside the simulation rating models (in the estimation of the portfolio loss), rather than ex-post.

[101] Ashcraft, A., and Schuermann, T., 2008. Understanding the securitization of subprime mortgage credit, *FRBNY Staff Report,* No. 318, March, 1–76.

the underlying assets and the credit quality accounted for by the rating agencies are: frictions between the mortgagor and the originator that lead to predatory lending, information advantage of the originator over the arranger and of the arranger over the CRAs regarding mortgage quality. Duffie, Eckner, Horel, and Saita clearly describe how including these frictions in the rating models could have improved the estimated portfolio loss:

> 'For example, sub-prime mortgage debt portfolios recently suffered losses in excess of the high confidence levels that were estimated by rating agencies. [...] An example of an important factor that was not included in most mortgage-portfolio default-loss models is the degree to which borrowers and mortgage brokers provided proper documentation of borrowers' credit qualities. With hindsight, more teams responsible for designing, rating, intermediating, and investing in sub-prime CDOs might have done better by allowing for the possibility that the difference between actual and documented credit qualities would turn out to be much higher than expected, or much lower than expected, in a manner that is correlated across the pool of borrowers. Incorporating this additional source of uncertainty would have resulted in higher prices for CDO "first-loss" equity tranches (a convexity effect). Senior CDOs would have been designed with more conservative over-collateralization, or alternatively have had lower ratings and lower prices (a concavity effect), on top of any related effects of risk premia. Perhaps more modelers should have thought to look for, might have found, and might have included in their models proxies for this moral-hazard effect. It seems optimistic to believe that they would have done so, for despite the clear incentives, many apparently did not.'[102]

The issue that this raises is why these factors where not included in the models, when it seems that rating agencies disclosed some of the underlying moral hazard and adverse selection problems. The rate of growth of the structured finance segment, the increasing complexity of the products, together with the conflict of interest that rating agencies are generally paid by arrangers or deals sponsors (directly or indirectly) for their opinions created a lack of resources and perspective to improve the rating models. The latter conflict of interest has created commercial pressure on the rating agencies as a small number of arrangers or deal sponsors represent a large amount of revenue and repeated business, at least compared to the corporate finance segment. Moreover, the pricing bias that Duffie et al. describe on the equity tranches and the senior tranches that resulted from the underestimatation of correlated losses is in favor of the originators or the banks with the selling mandates to investors (often also arrangers). Indeed, the originator often retained the equity tranche (which was worth more than it was priced) and sold the more senior tranches, at higher prices than they were worth... This certainly creates an incentive for originators and arrangers to further innovate and originate complex products.

Transparency and disclosure

Investors had an incentive to reach for yields by purchasing structured debt issues with high ratings, arrangers to maintain it this way and rating agencies to remain independent but respond to arrangers' requests with increasingly complex products. Arrangers or banks with the placing mandate had an incentive to continue selling structured finance instruments that were highly rated.

---

[102] Duffie, D., Eckner, A., Horel, G., and Saita, L., 2008. Frailty correlated default, Stanford Graduate School of Business, January, 1–56, page 3, forthcoming *Journal of Finance*.

Most investors did not realize all the risks involved in the structured finance instruments and tended to focus on the investment grade rating, as authorized by their investment guidelines, even though ratings are just benchmarks for default risk and do not consider market risk or liquidity risk. Many of the agencies' programs used for rating structured instruments were made available on their website; however, the underlying rating model, the economics behind it, its assumptions and dynamics remained nevertheless a black box. It is part of the agencies' responsibility that investors remain well informed and understand the variables that drive the output of the rating model and its robustness to varying assumptions and economic conditions.

7.3.4 Criticisms: the Ratings in Crisis?

Rating Through the Cycle

One of the biggest criticisms of the rating agencies is the fact that the agencies are reluctant to make rating changes based on cyclical considerations even though the number of defaults rises during recessions. Even if there is short-term variability in default rates of a given rating band, long-term default probabilities should be stable across the business cycle if ratings are going to be considered good long-term indicators of credit risk.

Most commercial and investment banks employ large numbers of fixed income analysts that perform a credit function similar to that performed by the agencies. If a bank has a proprietary bond trading operation, an independent credit team is needed. Many banks use rating agency research as an effective starting point for their own analysis. One of their criticisms of the rating agencies is the rather slow and bureaucratic pace at which they move. However, the rating agencies were never meant to be offering real-time information to investors.

SLUGGISHNESS   A related criticism is that rating agencies often lag behind events. Chris Legge, head of European industrial ratings at S&P, defends the agencies by pointing out that they are taking a medium-term view – over three to five years – of a company's prospects. For example, S&P kept KPN, the Dutch telecommunications group, on investment grade throughout 2000–2001 when the financial markets regarded its debt as, in effect, junk. KPN sorted out its finances and has since been upgraded.

Undoubtedly, there is a difficulty in timing: if an agency moves too soon on a downgrade, it risks being accused of triggering a company's problems. Too late and it is blamed for missing the boat. Ratings agencies argue that the key to their success has always been independent assessment and point out that 'no company has ever said it is the right time to have a downgrade.'[103] This argument is more difficult to hold in the case of structured finance. The arguments given for the belatedness in reaction to the subprime crisis is that the differences within asset classes, vintages and servicers only emerged later and over time. It is the agencies' policies to act judiciously and not to 'fire and then aim.' The sluggishness is related to the through-the-cycle policy. If it had the point-in-time rating horizon, rating agencies could adjust their ratings and track market prices.

---

[103] Legge, Chris, head of European industrial ratings at S&P, quoted in Batchelor, C., 2003, Companies and regulators go on offensive in the global ratings game, *Financial Times*, July 5.

CONSERVATISM   Another criticism is that the rating agencies tend to be conservative, and will rarely award investment grade ratings to a new, fast-growing company. According to Simon Adamson, head of financial institutions credit research at Deutsche Bank, 'the agencies have no interest to go out on a limb ... they are primarily concerned about the default rate and the timeliness of repayment so they need to be cautious.'[104]

INFREQUENT MONITORING   A further criticism of the rating agencies is that they do not offer frequent monitoring of each issuer. While the agencies will look at a company once or twice a year, a credit analyst at a financial intermediary will monitor daily developments at each company he covers much as a fund manager or an equity analyst would. Of course, one way for these investors to make money is to second-guess the ratings agencies and thus find market opportunities. It may be that there is less risk than the agencies think and that this will become apparent over time, leading to a rise in the price of the bonds and a profit for the investor who owns them. Stronger incentive could be provided for improved monitoring by having the rating fee paid out more evenly through time.

DUE DILIGENCE   Rating agencies base their analysis on all the information known to them and deemed relevant. They are explicit about the fact that they do not perform due diligence on the issuer, originator or assets and cannot require information that an issuer or deal sponsor is not willing to furnish. However, rating agencies should recall that they are free to refuse to rate. Moreover, they should be more explicit about what type of information they base their ratings on, and especially they should be able to assess how reliable their information is according to economic conditions. For instance, when asset prices increase very fast, such as during the housing bubble or internet stock bubble, the potential returns to accounting fraud increase a lot, whereas the cost of punishment remains the same.

BAND WIDTH   For banks that trade debt, the rating bands of the agencies do not provide information that is precise enough for the million dollar bets that are being taken on a daily basis. Each rating band (e.g. a BBB rated corporate) will include companies with diverse credit fundamentals whose debt trades at a variety of spreads. An extreme example of this occurred at the end of February 1999 when a B rated bond of Geberit was trading at a spread of 307 basis points at the same time as a B rated bond of Central European Media was at 1167 basis points over.[105]

Evaluation and Conclusions

In a recent book, R. Posner 'posits that Americans have a "cultural peculiarity" that holds that "human will can conquer all adversities." Thus "every non success is deemed culpable failure".'[106] CRAs are often blamed for the ills of bond investors or bond issuers. Investors complain that CRAs were late in alerting them to take shelter in anticipation of waves of

---

[104] Bream, R., 1999, Telling the wheat from the chaff, *Credit research: Euromoney*, April, Issue 360, 128–134, page 43.
[105] Bream, R., 1999, Telling the wheat from the chaff, *Credit research: Euromoney*, April, Issue 360, 128–134, page 43.
[106] Posner, R., 2006, *Preventing Surprise Attacks: Intelligence Reform in the Wake of 9/11*, Rowman & Littlefield Publishers, Inc., July, quoted in Greenway, H.D.S., 2006, Maybe no one is to blame, *International Herald Tribune*, October 11, page 5.

bond defaults that were on their way. Issuers complain that CRAs were making bad weather with their ill-advised downgrades, rather than just being the weathermen. What should be concluded from the previous analysis and how should these complaints be evaluated? Are these simply an American 'cultural peculiarity' obfuscating the self-serving lobbying of issuers to rein in the independence of the CRAs, or of investors to continuously raise the performance standards of a service for which they don't pay, or of start-up CRA contenders to discredit incumbents? Or did the CRAs actually fail in crisis?

We find that, if they were not to exist, it would be hard to engineer economically sustainable engines that perform as well as the CRAs. They occasionaly stutter or even miss a turn, but overall, they run quite well. We believe that no regulator would like to be bestowed with their job, or be able to do as good a job as the CRAs – however imperfect they are.

Part C
The Credit Rating Business

In two chapters, 'The Credit Rating Business' analyzes the credit rating industry and the regulatory oversight of credit rating agencies.

Chapter 8 analyzes the rating industry: where it comes from, what its main characteristics are, how the main players compete, and what results it produces for issuers, investors, and shareholders. It is an industry in which reputation and network effects prevail, maintaining high barriers to entry and concentration. Ratings from the same CRA offer a common standard for interpreting credit risk, and the more that standard is used, the more will we be willing to learn it. CRAs compete for the market rather than in the market, because switching from one standard to another is costly. Ratings are opinions about a possible future default. Their quality is thus only revealed over time. For investors to pay attention and for issuers to pay, they must trust the lifetime accuracy of a rating. You can only assess that using large samples, not by staring at a unique event such as the timeliness of predicting a singular default. Users thus need experience with a lot of ratings of a CRA to figure out how accurate they are. Clearly, all of that benefits incumbents who occupied the field early and acquired an installed base giving them a head start over new entrants. A small number of CRAs with the highest reputation for quality and independence will always dominate. This should not be a concern provided regulations do not protect incumbents artificially.

Chapter 9 reviews the regulatory uses of ratings and the regulation of the credit rating agencies that produce them. Regulations form an important part of how credit ratings are used in decisions about purchasing or selling and the holding or disposing of particular securities. The use of ratings in prudential, market access, and investor protection regulations is prevalent around the world, leading to several approaches to regulating the industry. Industry regulation covers industry structure and conduct of business issues. Regulatory interest in the industry has been ongoing since 2003 in the wake of the Enron scandal with a vivid renewed interest since the subprime crisis. Worldwide, the International Organization of Securities Commissions adopted a self-regulatory approach using the principle 'comply with the consensual code of conduct or explain why you don't.' The EU immediately followed suit, in March 2005. The US has eventually decided not to align itself with IOSCO and the EU, as a minority in the Congress proposed. With the Credit Rating Agency Reform Act of 2006, it decided to lower the traditional discretionary regulatory barrier to entry in the industry but also went for rather strong, imposed regulations with intrusive oversight rights granted to the SEC.

8
The Credit Rating Industry

This chapter analyzes the credit rating business, its origins, current structure, special characteristics that affect competition, and how well the industry performs. This is important because, as Chapter 3 showed, CRAs play a public interest role. Do the public interest externalities of credit ratings create a structural misalignment with the CRAs' business conduct from the perspective of maximizing shareholder value?

With overall around 160 CRAs and three global players – Fitch, Moody's and S&P – this is a small industry. The roughly 4500 professionals it employs on an industry basis tend to rank at the right end of the IQ scale and are unusually well trained and analytically skilled (be it in law, science, economics, accounting, or finance) 'knowledge workers.' Strong cognitively, they 'want a rating to be right' rather than to 'sell' it, and to have it adhering to global company standards rather than adapting these to local cultures. Traditionally a US-based industry, its rapid internationalization creates typical managerial and organizational challenges, such as, for instance, how to harness the best diverse talent of the world to ever improve activities while maintaining and strengthening one global company standard for ratings quality.

The nature of demand and supply in the credit ratings industry unavoidably leads to high degrees of industry concentration. This industry concentration supports the independence of CRAs *vis-à-vis* their issuer clients but could lead CRAs to extract economic rents from issuers. This concentration grants CRAs the power with regard to their paying issuers that they need to ensure sufficient independence. This independence is a prerequisite to guaranteeing objectivity in often extremely touchy credit rating opinions.

8.1 THE RISE OF THE CREDIT RATING AGENCIES

8.1.1 Origins

In the 19th century, the functions that are now supplied by credit rating agencies were provided by three types of institutions: the specialized business and financial press, credit reporting agencies, and investment bankers.

The specialized business press reported about business conditions for companies and industry sectors. The first was the *American Railroad Journal*, which appeared in 1832. Henry Varnum Poor became its editor in 1849, and later went on to publish *Poor's Manual of the Railroads of the United States*. In 1916, the Poor Company entered the bond rating business, and merged with Standard Statistics to form S&P in 1941.

Credit **reporting** (not rating) agencies evaluated the ability of merchants to pay their financial obligations. The first mercantile credit agency was founded in New York in 1841. Robert Dun acquired the agency and subsequently published the first creditworthiness guide in 1859. John Bradstreet founded a similar agency in 1849 and published his first credit guide in 1857. In 1933, the two businesses were consolidated into Dun & Bradstreet (D&B), and in 1962, D&B acquired Moody's Investor Services, bringing credit rating and reporting under one roof before splitting up again in 2000.

The investment banks placed the issues they had underwritten, and their reputation capital was the third proxy for credit rating agencies. By putting their reputation at stake every time they underwrote a security, the investment banks helped the securities market and brought together users and suppliers of capital.

The first CRA was established by John Moody in 1909 and combined the three functions in a single business, laying the foundation of the CRA industry and its reputation capital. There have been four major growth phases in the CRA industry, as summarized in Exhibit 8.1.

The first phase lasted from 1909 to 1943. The First World War and the prosperous 1920s led to a large number of private and public issues. The 1930s saw the first regulatory uses of credit ratings, and the expansion of bond markets lasted till the end of the Second World War. The second phase, 1944–1969, i.e. the era after the Second World War, was one of

Exhibit 8.1   History of growth of CRA industry

Pre-CRA

1832	1849	1841	1849
The American Railroad Journal	*Poor's Manual of the Railroads of the United States*	The first mercantile credit agency (acquired by Robert Dun in 1859)	John Bradstreet agency

CRA

Phase 1 (1909–1943): Establishment of the CRA industry

1909	1916	1930	1933	1941
John Moody's agency	Entry of the Poor company into the rating business. John Knowles Fitch founds Fitch Ratings	First regulatory uses of credit ratings	Consolidation of Dun & Bradstreet (D&B)	Merger of the Poor company with Standard Statistics

Phase 2 (1944–1969): Period of economic stability and low demand for ratings

1962
D&B acquires Moody's Investor Services

Phase 3 (1970–2001): Period of major economic shocks; development of demand for CRA services

1970	1975	1995	2000
Penn Central defaults on its commercial paper. Issuer-pays model is introduced as a result.	SEC established the list of nationally recognized statistical rating organizations (NRSRO)	Fitch Ratings becomes part of Fimalac SA.	Fitch Ratings acquires Duff & Phelps Credit Rating Co.

Phase 4 (2002–present): Rapid development of financial innovations. Expansion of CRAs outside the US.

financial and economic stability. As a result, bond ratings were not as relevant during this period, and leading agencies apparently employed only a few analysts each, with revenues coming from the sale of research reports to investors.

The third phase was characterized by major real shocks from 1970 through 2001. During this time, the global financial system became market-based, moving from fixed to flexible exchange rates, from quantitative credit controls to price-based money supply management, and from price control to market pricing. The regulation of financial institutions shifted from business to functional competition among all market participants, and business funding switched from institutions to markets.[1] Chapter 3 described how this initiated a phase of rapid expansion in the need for credit ratings, with Figure 3.6 showing an increase in the number of global rated corporate issuers from about 1000 in 1970 to nearly 6000 by 2006. There were also three waves of increases in the relative importance of speculative grade issuer ratings, as Figure 8.1 illustrates. The three expansions of the early 1970s, late 1980s and 1990s all saw a spurt in speculative grade issuers.

Although this receded somewhat afterwards, it nevertheless highlights a structural trend toward a greater number of default-prone issuers seeking funding through security issues.

The fourth phase of CRA industry development, from 2002 to the present, is characterized by significant changes in the industry itself, along with continued expansion. Changes are driven by a spate of unexpected corporate bankruptcies, the tremendous growth of the structured finance market, and the rapid adoption of the Internet as a powerful force for

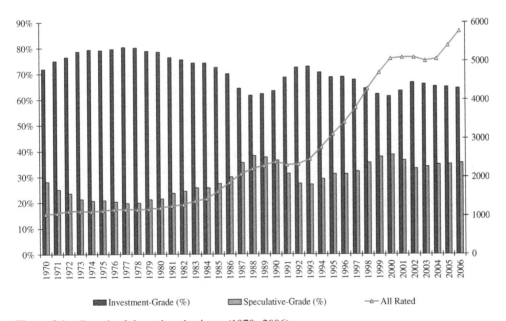

Figure 8.1 Growth of the ratings business (1970–2006).
Source: Moody's Investors Service, 2007, *Corporate Default and Recovery Rates, 1920–2006*, Exhibit 33.

[1] See Bodie, Z., Crane, D.B., Froot, K.A., Mason, S.P., Merton, R.C., Perold, A.F., Sirri, E.R., and Tufano, P., 1995. *The Global Financial System: A Functional Perspective*, Harvard Business School Press, Boston, Massachusetts, 1–291 for one of the first cogent analyses of these dynamics.

infomediaries, including CRAs. At the same time, capital market instruments have become increasingly complex and pervasive. As the range of issuers, securities, and investors have expanded, ratings have become increasingly more relevant to the savings investment process through the capital markets. The faster expansion of ratings outside rather than inside the US creates demanding management challenges for traditionally US-based business.

8.1.2 Macroeconomic Forces Shaping the Current Industry

Six main macroeconomic factors shaped the current CRA industry. They are: financial disintermediation, institutionalization of investments, accelerated rate of industry change, complex financial innovations, the globalization of international capital markets, and the growth in regulatory uses of ratings.

Financial Disintermediation

Financial disintermediation is the substitution of bank-based funding, i.e. loans, by market-based funding, i.e. securities (as discussed in Chapter 3). This de-linking of the original relationship between the provider of the funds and its user created a new need for due diligence, and has been a central force in the increasing demand for bond ratings by market participants.

When commercial banks lend to corporates, their own credit committees scrutinize the companies, their management, and their balance sheets, and bank relationship officers keep in close contact with corporate clients. In the more transactional, anonymous, and dispersed capital markets, with a broader investor base and trading in already issued securities, commercial bank analysts have no incentive to do the credit analysis for new bond issues. Fixed income analysts from investment banks could have replaced the commercial bank credit analysts, but did not, because the underwriting and trading revenue that investment banks generate compensates them for taking short-term market risks and for their commercial effort, not for taking long-term credit risks. Investment banks purchase bonds from the issuers, pay the amount of the issue, and re-sell the issue, hopefully instantaneously and with a profit margin, to their buy-side customers or their sub-underwriters. Investment banks intend to be exposed to the issuers and the prices the issues command in the market for an extremely short time. The focus of the fixed income analysts at the investment bank is thus very much on market pricing, not on long-term creditworthiness.

Nor did the corporate finance departments of investment banks replace the commercial bank. Their function is to conduct credit analysis and to form credit rating opinions, as rating advisory is an integral part of the services that the investment bank offers its clients. But rating advisory is aimed at assisting the client in deciding its capital and debt structure and how best to access the capital markets. Thus the compensation structure is geared toward originating and executing major transactions, not toward developing and maintaining a credit rating business.

Assisting a client's choice of capital structure and access to the capital markets is also quite different from rating its debt. The former requires a deep grasp of the client's long-term creditworthiness and is very much prescriptive, while the latter requires the right positioning of the debt on the default risk spectrum and is descriptive, as we saw in Section 2.3.2. Capital structure assessment looks predominantly – if not exclusively – at the shareholders' perspective, whereas a credit rating looks at the downside from the creditors' perspective.

There was thus a gap in the market for credit analysis. The commercial and investment banks had no business reasons to incur the costs of credit analysis for bonds. The CRAs filled the gap, incurred the costs and passed them on to the issuers. Since issuers were already used to incurring costs on credits granted and funded by commercial banks – either explicitly as commissions or provision income related to the loan, or implicitly as part of the commercial margin in the rate of interest charged on the loan – this did not mark a major change in the cost of obtaining funding.

Financial disintermediation has considerably increased the demand for credit ratings in Europe. As Figure 3.26 shows, this process has been well underway in the US since the early 1990s, but still in its infancy in Europe. The rating agencies expect to see further growth in their European business and regard Euroland as a key battleground in the coming years. In fact, disintermediation in Europe has been cited as a leading demand factor by all three leading CRAs. To quote S&P,

> The Financial Services segment expects that the European Monetary Union will continue to facilitate disintermediation with borrowers obtaining increasingly more financing through the public debt markets rather than banks. This trend and the anticipated economic recovery should lead to continued growth in 2005.[2]

Industry observers point out that rating analysis may be called for outside the US in particular. In Europe, and in emerging markets, reliable data and relevant information about issuers is generally less available: as one analyst notes,

> at a rating agency, you have access to confidential information. This is a competitive advantage of the agency, particularly in Europe, since knowledge is power. In the US, by contrast, information is so freely available that the competitive advantage of ratings agencies over the market is not as great as it is in Europe.[3]

There is also a belief that credit research will become increasingly important in Europe as its high-yield market develops. As one professional puts it: 'With companies often raising high-yield finance in preference to an equity IPO, credit analysts are often the first to get to know some companies.'

To sum up, commercial banks let the CRAs expand. Their withdrawal from long-term lending to corporations stimulated the need for credit ratings, creating an opportunity that CRAs seized in the US and are now seizing in Europe.

Disintermediation and securitization go hand in hand.

Institutionalization of Investments

The institutionalization of investments created new uses for credit ratings and opportunities for CRAs. Section 3.1.1 described extensively the institutionalization movement: where it came from, how it happened, and how extensive and widespread it is nowadays. With increasing amounts of the total investment in the capital markets being made indirectly,

---

[2] The McGraw-Hill Company, 2005. Annual Report, 2004, February 25, 1–70, page 38.
[3] See fixed income analyst at Merrill Lynch, Pinto, M., 1998. Can the agencies play catch-up?, *Euroweek* special reports – The Euro Supplement, June 1, 84.

institutional investors have emerged as the single most important class of investors for most issuers, and an important contributor to the rise of CRAs.

Fixed income institutional investors link portfolio allocations to rating standards. They therefore use ratings in their bond purchase decisions, and to ensure subscription, issuers must get their issues rated by an appropriate CRA.

Fixed income institutional investors also link portfolio performance to bond indices, which have been created using the various rating classes. As trading instruments, these indices reduce the costs of portfolio adjustments, and as benchmarks for portfolio performance, they facilitate performance evaluation. Bond indices use rating classes as defined by various rating agencies, and the inclusion, or not, of the ratings of a particular agency has wide-ranging reputation effects. Merrill Lynch announced in October 2004, and Lehman Brothers in January 2005, that they would start using Fitch ratings, in addition to those from Moody's and S&P, when calculating the index quality assigned to individual securities.[4] Understandably, Fimalac, Fitch's parent company, mentioned this event in its annual report and its marketing manager celebrated it.[5]

Accelerating Rate of Industry Change

The accelerating rate of industry change broadens the need for credit ratings, because there are ever more issuers with uncertain prospects. This doesn't mean that issuers become worse, or that overall stock market volatility increases. As a matter of fact, there is no discernible statistically significant trend in market volatility for the period 1926 through 1997.[6] For the more recent 1986 through 2007 period, the CBOE stock market volatility index shown in Figure 8.1 stood at 20.3% on average, with a standard deviation of 4.1% on average.

But when the prospects of ever more issuers become uncertain, it implies that it becomes harder to determine if any particular issuer is a good or a bad one. It gets more difficult to discriminate. This creates an interest in seeing companies that were never rated in the past now being rated, because it becomes tougher for a good company to convince investors that it is not a lemon. The accelerating rate of industry change also deepens the need for credit ratings, because the pace of innovation means that the enterprise value of traditionally rated companies shifts gradually from the value of its assets in place to the value of its growth options. Business risk and management opportunity for risk shifting both increase, and may both contribute to the rise in a company's idiosyncratic volatility, i.e. the volatility due to what happens in the company, rather than in the business cycle. A recent rise in this phenomenon was documented initially by Campbell et al. (2001), who found that 'over the period from 1962 to 1997 there has been a noticeable increase in firm-level volatility relative to market volatility. Accordingly, correlations among individual stocks and the explanatory power of the market model for a typical stock have declined, whereas the number of stocks needed to achieve a given level of diversification has increased.'[7]

---

[4] Galdi, P., 2004. Upcoming changes in global bond index rules, Merrill Lynch, October 13, 1–8, page 2; Lehman Brothers, 2005. Lehman Brothers to include Fitch ratings in global family of indices, January 24, 1–3, page 1.
[5] Fimalac SA, 2006. Annual Report, 2005, 1–211, page 9.
[6] Campbell, J.Y., Lettau, M., Malkiel, B.G., and Xu, Y., 2001. Have individual stocks become more volatile? An empirical exploration of idiosyncratic risk, *Journal of Finance*, February, Vol. 56, No. 1, 1–43, page 9.
[7] Campbell, J.Y., Lettau, M., Malkiel, BG., and Xu, Y., 2001. Have individual stocks become more volatile? An empirical exploration of idiosyncratic risk, *Journal of Finance*, February, Vol. 56, No. 1, 1–43, page 1.

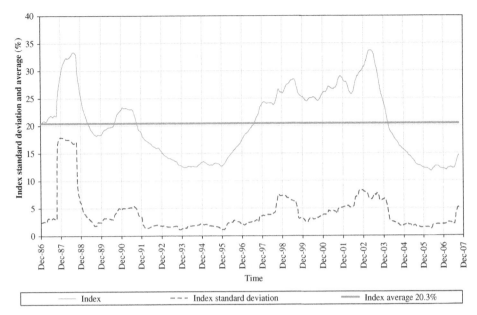

Figure 8.2 US stock market volatility (1986–2007).
Source: Chicago Board Options Exchange.

Industry change thus creates growth opportunities for CRAs. Each time it becomes harder
to apprehend an issuer's future; and it becomes more efficient for investors to broaden their
spectrum of diversification. This creates an opportunity for CRAs to deepen their ratings
and broaden their rated universe. Investors' interest in ratings for resolving information
asymmetry goes up with the number of information asymmetries to be resolved. The more
uncertain an issuer's performance, the higher the value of a rating in resolving the corresponding information asymmetry. And, of course, each time the rated universe expands,
it doesn't readily contract to its original size. Newly rated public debt issuers invest significantly in their initial rating, and have a stake in maintaining it. Similarly, CRAs become
more sophisticated in their rating actions with each wave, and have no desire to revert
to cruder methods. For the fixed income investor, increased risk shows up most tangibly
in waves of expanding default rates. This is exactly what has happened since the early
1970s, as discussed in Section 2.1. Often waves of change bring about economic crises
that are test periods for ratings. In addition to the crises already described (e.g. the Asian
financial meltdown in 1997, Russian defaults in 1998, the Enron and Parmalat scandals
in the 2000s, and the subprime meltdown in 2007), there have also been a large number
of defaults in the commercial paper market and of long-term bond issues, particularly by
unrated companies. According to Moody's, corporate bond default rates in Europe reached
a record 20.1% peak in 2002, but receded dramatically in 2003, finishing the year at 6.9%.
Moody's volume-weighted default rate also declined from as high as 57.1% in 2002 to 6.7%
in 2003. Nine Moody's-rated European corporate issuers defaulted in 2003 on $3.5 billion,
compared with 28 Moody's-rated issuers that defaulted on over $42 billion in 2002. How-
ever, given the history of economic volatility, periods of relative economic stability do not
imply reduced relevance for CRAs. As opinions of future risk, credit ratings assume even
greater significance in periods of frequent economic highs and lows.

Complex Financial Innovations

Financial innovation has been another source of opportunities for CRAs. The introduction of new products and the development of technology that makes the trade of such products possible, drive disintermediation and capital market expansion. All the more so as financial products become more complex and innovative, and, as we saw above, disintermediation and capital market expansion by themselves stimulate the need for credit ratings.

The proliferation of structured finance instruments as investment products exemplifies how innovation leads to rating needs. New issuance of securitized assets has shown an increasing trend across the globe, e.g. the expansion in SPVs for securitized asset pools as discussed in Section 3.3. Figure 8.3 and Figure 8.4 show that while the US continues to lead in terms of new issuance against these pools, Europe has shown higher growth rates in recent years. The SPVs issue different tranches of securities with decreasing credit rights on the pool and declining ratings, going down from AAA to B+ or below. Rating these tranches is one of the more legally and mathematically complex tasks for a CRA. It should therefore be no surprise that this has been the fastest growing segment of the ratings business in recent years, particularly in Europe, where securitization issuance has been growing fastest in recent years.

Globalization of International Capital Markets

International bond financing has overtaken international bank lending, and provides a further opportunity for CRAs. Figure 3.2 and Figure 3.3 documented the time path of these movements. What happened? After disintermediation within national markets, commercial banks began to withdraw from international lending, and, following the 1998 international financial crisis, international bank lending decreased substantially, especially toward developing countries, as demonstrated in Figure 3.29b. From 1999 through 2004, bank debtors

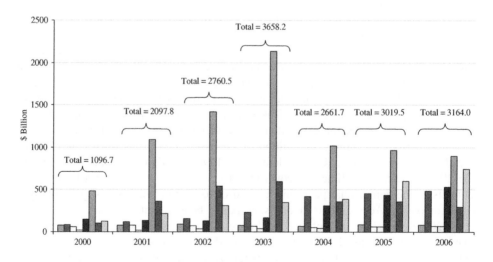

Figure 8.3 US securitization issuance (2000–2006).
Sources: Bond Market Association, *Research Quarterly*, Feb. 2001, Feb. 2002, Feb. 2003, Feb. 2004, Feb. 2005 and Feb. 2006.

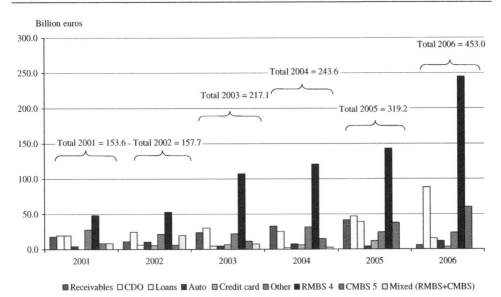

Figure 8.4 European securitization issuance (2001–2006).

reimbursed net $27.1 billion, more than half the inflow that occurred in 1998. In the meantime, bond financing expanded by $159.1 billion, and credit analysts at the CRAs took over from the credit analysts for international lending at commercial banks.

Investors' desire for international diversification in their portfolio of investments created yet another opportunity for CRAs.[8] Flexible exchange rates reduced the correlation of securities returns across currencies. Concurrently, cross-currency portfolio investments became more important due to improved understanding and acceptance of the return/risk benefits of international portfolio diversification.[9] This was a boon for existing CRAs because cross-border investors tend to have little detailed knowledge about the countries, and companies, whose bonds they are being offered, making credits rating an ever more important source of qualified credit information.

International diversification also fed innovation and trading, both of which are good for credit ratings. Bond investment portfolios became more efficiently diversified geographically and across sectors than bank loan portfolios. Credit risk in commercial bank loan portfolios was less diversified than in corporate bond portfolios because the scope of commercial bank lending was significantly narrower than the investment scope for capital market investors. This has two consequences, which are both favorable for credit ratings: (1) it allowed markets to pay higher prices for risky bonds than banks for loans, stimulating the growth of the markets at the expense of bank lending; (2) it induced commercial banks to securitize their loan books and to use credit derivatives and credit swaps markets, to better diversify their credit risk. This second consequence further explains why commercial banks are so much more interested in the credit derivatives and credit swap markets than the managers of highly diversified corporate bond portfolios.

---

[8] This interest of course supported the demand to take up the offering in the global bond markets. This was needed for a market to exist, it is not sufficient that there is a supply.

[9] See Solnik, B.H., 1988. *International Investments*, Addison-Wesley Publishing Company, 1–387 for the first seminal explanation of these.

The demand for global ratings was born, and CRAs expanded their rating activities globally to respond to this need. As a result, they ended up occupying center stage in the world theater of capital markets.

Growth in Regulatory Uses of Credit Ratings

The regulatory uses of ratings (discussed extensively in Section 9.1) not only created a captive demand for credit ratings per se by market participants, but also designated particular CRAs as beneficiaries. The growing use of rating references for regulatory purposes in the US has meant that demand for the fog-piercing services from these beneficiaries was not solely market-based.[10] Globally, recently adopted regulatory capital requirements for financial institutions (see Section 9.1.1) will substantially expand those regulatory demands. 'Accordingly, though the logic of why financial markets might want credit rating firms' assistance in fog piercing remains impeccable, the actual practice of regulation has meant that the current presence of the major incumbents is no automatic assurance that they continue to meet the market test.'[11]

The regulatory endorsement of ratings from particular CRAs was a sign of their success, not the maker of it. The widespread regulatory use of ratings shifted the demand for ratings upward. It did not create it. The CRAs had already developed successfully in response to market forces without a regulatory license to start their business and to make it successful.[12] In a sense, the regulators jumped on the bandwagon of the CRAs' success. They were almost free-loading on the CRAs' efforts to benchmark default prospects by adopting the CRAs' output, rather than producing it themselves.

The paradox is that now the regulators have started regulating the CRAs, as we shall discuss in Chapter 9. In brief, the rationale for these regulations is dual. One, there is the importance of credit ratings for the securities markets and credit risk assessment. The regulators thus want to ensure that ratings are high quality. Two, regulatory uses of credit ratings reduce competition in the credit rating industry. The regulatory thus want to enhance fair competition.

8.1.3   The Current Structure of the Industry

There are currently about 150 local and international CRAs around the world, up from approximately 130 in 2000.[13] The major US agencies have all established operations and joint ventures abroad to meet the globalization of capital markets, and the increasing importance of credit ratings in markets outside the US. Exhibit 8.2 lists all the independent credit rating agencies across the world with their location. The most striking feature of the industry

---

[10] Fog piercing refers to the role of CRAs in 'helping lenders pierce the fog of asymmetric information that surrounds lending relationships,' see White, L.J., 2001, *The Credit Rating Industry*, an industrial organization analysis, prepared for the conference on rating agencies in the global financial system, New York University, June, 1–38, page 4.

[11] White, L.J., 2001. *The Credit Rating Industry*: an industrial organization analysis, prepared for the conference on rating agencies in the global financial system, New York University, June, 1–38, page 5.

[12] Contra, see Partnoy, F., 1999. The Siskel and Ebert of financial markets?: Two thumbs down for the credit rating agencies, *Washington University Law Quarterly*, Vol. 77, No. 3, 619–715, who espouses the 'regulatory license view' of credit ratings.

[13] See Estrella, A., 2000. Credit ratings and complementary sources of credit quality information, Basel Committee on Banking Supervision, Working Papers No. 3: Bank for International Settlements, Basel, August, 1–186.

Exhibit 8.2   Rating agencies around the world (2006)

	Main office	Affiliate	Branch	Countries	Offices					
					North America	Europe	Asia Pacific	Latin America	Middle East	Total
Moody's	1	9	20	25	6	7	9	4	4	**30**
S&P	1	6	22	23	7	7	9	4	2	**29**
Fitch	2	17	27	37	8	8	15	12	3	**46**
A.M. Best	1				1					**1**
Egan-Jones	1				1					**1**
Dominion Bond Rating Service	1				1					**1**
Weiss Ratings	1				1					**1**
GovernanceMetrics International, Inc.	1				1					**1**
Lace Financial	1				1					**1**
European Rating Agency	1	1	1	3		3				**3**
Bulgarian Credit Rating Agency	1					1				**1**
First Turkish Credit Rating Agency	1					1				**1**
CofaceRating	1					1				**1**
R@S Rating Services AG	1					1				**1**
URA UNTERNEHMENS RATINGAGENTUR AG	1					1				**1**
EuroRatings AG	1					1				**1**
Global Rating	1					1				**1**
Companhia Portuguesa de Rating	1					1				**1**
Rus-Rating	1					1				**1**
Expert RA Rating Agency	1					1				**1**
IC Rating – Rating Information center	1					1				**1**
Swiss Public Financial Rating SA:										
ComRating	1					1				**1**
CoreRatings	1					1				**1**
Credit-Rating	1					1				**1**
JCR VIS Credit Rating	1	2		3			2		1	**3**
Credit Rating Agency of Bangladesh (CRAB)	1						1			**1**
Vishal Group Limited	1						1			**1**
Rapid Rating Pty Ltd.	1						1			**1**
Sino-Hawk Credit Rating Co., Ltd	1						1			**1**
China Lianhe Credit Rating Co., Ltd	1						1			**1**
Great Wall Credit Rating Co.	1						1			**1**
Shanghai Far East Credit Rating Co., Ltd	1						1			**1**
Credit Analysis & Research Ltd (CARE)	1						1			**1**

(*continued overleaf*)

Exhibit 8.2 (*continued*)

	Main office	Affiliate	Branch	Countries	Offices					
					North America	Europe	Asia Pacific	Latin America	Middle East	Total
Rating and Investment Information, Inc.	1						1			1
Mikuni & Co., Ltd	1						1			1
Japan Credit Rating	1						1			1
Kazkommerts Securities	1						1			1
Rating Agency Malaysia (RAM)	1						1			1
Malaysian Rating Corporation (MARC)	1						1			1
Philippine Rating Services Corporation (PhilRatings)	1						1			1
DP Credit Rating	1						1			1
TRIS Rating	1						1			1
National Information and Credit Evaluation (NICE)	1						1			1
Seoul Credit Rating & Information	1						1			1
Ecuability SA	1							1		1
SR Rating	1							1		1
Austin Rating Clasificadora de Risco	1							1		1
Equilibrium Clasificadora de Riesgo	1							1		1
Class & Asociados SA Clasificadora de Riesgo	1							1		1
Pacific Credit Rating	1							1		1
Capital Intelligence	1								1	1
Credit Rating & Collection (CRC)	1								1	1
Agusto & Co.	1								1	1
Global Credit Rating Co.	1								1	1
	56	35	70	91	27	39	55	26	14	161

Source: International Rating Group (IRG).

today is that over 80% of all rated issues outstanding are in the hands of just two CRAs, namely Moody's and S&P. Fitch, with a market share of 14%, is a distant third.[14] In this section, we first characterize the three global players and then look at the competitive fringe.

The Dominant Firms

Today, the industry can best be described as an oligopoly of three dominant global credit rating agencies, with a competitive fringe of specialized agencies. By 2000, each of the three leading agencies serving the needs of international bond investors provided significant coverage of most categories of issuers around the world, as Table 8.1 documents.

---

[14] Many issues are rated by more than one agency, generally by two agencies and sometimes three.

Table 8.1 Issuer rating coverage (%) by major credit rating agencies (January 2000)

	Bank			Industrials and Corporates			Sovereigns		
	Fitch	Moody's	S&P	Fitch	Moody's	S&P	Fitch	Moody's	S&P
United States	22	88	42	7	80	67	100	100	100
Europe, Middle East, Africa	36	69	39	18	70	71	58*	100*	71*
Asia	13	91	22	1	90	30	44*	100*	94*
Latin America	22	85	26	5	51	76	22*	100*	74*
Total	27	80	37	8	78	66	49*	100*	76*

	Sub-sovereigns			Insurance			Structured finance		
	Fitch	Moody's	S&P	Fitch	Moody's	S&P	Fitch	Moody's	S&P
United States	NA	NA	NA	0*	24*	100*	44	55	73
Europe, Middle East, Africa	42*	88*	100*	2*	19*	100*	12	62	64
Asia	0*	100*	0*	0*	40*	100*	8	46	75
Latin America	20*	100*	70*	0*	0*	100*	5	43	59
Total	NA	NA	NA	0.38*	23*	100*	35	55	71

*Due to lack of data, the highest number of rated issuers by one of 3 credit rating agencies (Fitch, Moody's, and S&P) is assumed to be the total rated issuers, then the coverage is calculated based on this total number.

Notes:

1. 'NA' indicates figures were not available.
2. Due to the difficulty in obtaining consistent statistics relating to the total number of entities eligible to seek a rating across member countries of the Basel Committee, 'coverage' is calculated as being the proportion of institutions rated by an agency relative to the total rated population (defined as being the set of entities rated by at least one of the four rating agencies above); under these conditions, 'coverage' is not an absolute indicator of the 'reach' of a rating agency.
3. For insurance firms, ratings are CPA (Claims Paying Ability), a measure of a company's ability to pay out their insurance claims rather than the likelihood of them defaulting on the repayment of issued debt.

Source: Estrella, A., 2000, Credit ratings and complementary sources of credit quality information, Basel Committee on Banking Supervision, Working Papers No. 3: Bank for International Settlements, Basel, August, 1–186, pages 33, 34.

CRAs are differentiated along several dimensions: the extent and type of coverage (geography and industry of issuer, instruments), methodology (statistical modeling or fundamental credit analysis), pricing model (issuer fee or subscription), type of scale (ordinal with actual probability of default/PD-estimation or cardinal with estimates of relative default probabilities), and size.

The three dominant players – S&P, Moody's, and Fitch – follow a similar pattern: they are large, have a global focus, and provide cross-industry, issuer and instrument specific ratings. They take an analytical approach with committee reporting, use ordinal scales, and have an issuer-pays business model. This blanket coverage has led to a combined revenue growth for the three leaders of 17% per year from 1998 to 2005, as Figure 8.5 shows, Fitch having the most impressive growth at 24%. Moody's Investors Service is the oldest and, along with S&P, is dominant among the major CRAs.[15] In recent years, Fitch has built up significant market share through a series of acquisitions as well as through organic growth.

By and large, the three agencies are comparable in the most important dimensions. In terms of performance, investors generally perceive all three agencies as equivalent even though, when it comes to choosing a rating agency, some biases and differences remain, in particular in favor of the more established incumbents.[16] In the older markets, such as the US corporate debt markets, most issuers automatically get ratings from two or three

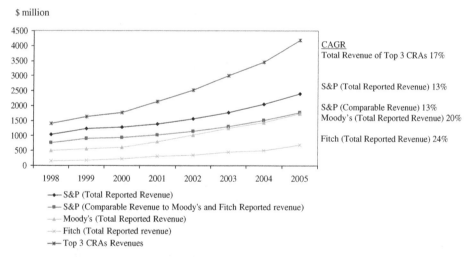

Figure 8.5   Revenue comparison of three major CRAs (1998–2005).
Notes:

1. Given that only the consolidated revenue is disclosed for S&P, comparable revenue of S&P for 2005 has been estimated from Moody's September 2006 presentation and extrapolated to previous years in the same ratio (approx. 74% of total)
2. Total Revenue for top 3 CRAs has been obtained by adding the reported revenues of Moody's and Fitch and the comparable revenues for S&P
3. CAGR is the Compound Annual Growth Rate of the $ million value

Sources: Annual Reports; Moody's Investors Service, 2006, Investor Presentation, September.

---

[15] Reinebach, A., 1998. Inroads overseas help US rating agencies to level the playing field, *The Investment Dealers' Digest*, August 3, Vol. 64, Issue 31, page 11.
[16] This fact emerged from interviews with rating advisory businesses.

agencies. The third rating is often requested when the first two ratings are split. Given that issuers can choose to keep an initial rating confidential, issuers in rated markets with only one rating are perceived more negatively by investors, by default, it is often assumed that other ratings would have been lower.

Differences between the three agencies remain, so that they are not quite viewed as perfect substitutes for each other. These differences mainly result from how their businesses developed over time. Table 8.2 summarizes the main mergers and acquisitions in the rating industry and shows movements toward concentration in the industry and, in particular, the arrival of Fitch as a major challenger to the dominant duopoly. Governance structure, methodological emphasis, rating-related services, and cultures are still different and provide valuable diversity. Moreover, as capital markets are in constant mutation, they also vary in their expertise and coverage, and this is likely to remain so, as agencies need to constantly adapt themselves to fast-changing financial and regulatory environments.

STANDARD & POOR'S   This section refers to S&P's Credit Market Services, which is responsible for its credit rating activity. Credit Market Services is part of the Financial Services division of S&P's parent company McGraw-Hill, which provides financial services related to equities, including the development and management of benchmark equity indices known throughout the world, and independent equity and mutual fund research. S&P also provides valuation advisory services, credit analysis, and exposure management products, investor education, and data services through its subsidiary Capital IQ.

As described earlier, S&P traces its roots to 1860, when Henry Varnum Poor published his *History of Railroads and Canals of the United States*. He was one of the first in the financial information industry to emphasize 'the investor's right to know.' Poor's Publishing Company issued its first ratings guide in 1916. Standard Statistics Company published its first ratings publication in 1922, and the two merged to form S&P in 1941. In the tradition of synergies between publishing companies and providers of financial information, The McGraw-Hill Companies, a publicly traded company headquartered in New York, acquired S&P in 1966. In 2004, S&P Financial Services contributed 39% of The McGraw-Hill Group's overall revenue and 65% of the operating profit.

From S&P's birth in 1941 to the early 1970s, business was relatively stable. But as market-based funding became more commonplace in the late 1960s and early 1970s, demand for ratings started to grow rapidly. The early 1970s also saw the first of three growth spurts in the number of speculative or junk bonds offered, which added to the increased need for ratings. In 1974, S&P refined its ratings by adding '+' (plus) and '−' (minus) to each generic category from 'AA' to 'B' to indicate whether a bond is ranked at the high end or the low end of a rating category. It thus moved from a 10-point to a 22-point scale.[17] Concurrently, S&P took the major step of deciding to charge issuers for their ratings, as investor subscriptions could no longer meet the costs the company incurred, not only in terms of demand, but also in terms of the ever-more sophisticated analysis required. Perhaps not coincidentally, 1974 saw the start of more than 25 years of annual dividend raises for the parent company McGraw-Hill.[18]

The birth of the structured finance market was marked in 1975, when S&P began rating mortgage-backed securities, the first of the new complex securities products. In the same

---

[17] The modifiers were in fact later introduced for the CCC category.
[18] Lazo, S.A., 1996. Just call it McGraw-High – profits, shares, dividends up; stock to split, *Barron's*, February, 786 words.

Table 8.2 M&A of global agencies and NRSRO designation (pre- Credit Rating Agency Reform Act of 2006 NRSRO designation)

Credit rating agency	Ratings first issued in	Year of initial NRSRO designation	Corporate actions
Moody's Investors Service (Moody's)	1909	1975	1962: Acquired by The Dun & Bradstreet Corporation (D&B) 2000: Spun off by D&B into a division of a new company, Moody's Corporation 2002: Moody's Corporation acquired KMV
Standard & Poor's (S&P)	1916	1975	1941: Poor's Publishing Co merges with Standard Statistics Company, Inc. to form S&P 1966: Acquired as a division by The McGraw-Hill Companies, Inc. 2000: Acquires Canadian Bond Rating Service 2002: Acquires Default Filter
Fitch Ratings (Fitch)	1924 (Fitch Publishing Company)	1975	1997: Fitch Investors Service L.P. (New York based) merges with Fimalac S.A. (Fimalac)-owned IBCA Ltd (London based), renamed Fitch IBCA 2000: Acquires Duff & Phelps Credit Rating Co. (Duff & Phelps or DCR) to create Fitch-IBCA Duff & Phelps on June 1. 2000 end: Acquires Thomson Bankwatch, renamed Fitch Ratings 2002: Acquires NetRisk and Credit Ratings System 2004: Acquires Algorithmics, creates Fitch Group consisting of Fitch Ratings and Algorithmics 2006: Divests 20% minority stake to Hearst
Duff & Phelps	1982	1982	1991: Acquires McCarthy Crisanti & Maffei, Inc. 2000: Acquired by Fitch IBCA
McCarthy Crisanti & Maffei, Inc.	1975	1983	1985: Acquired by Xerox Corporation 1991: Acquired by Duff & Phelps
IBCA Limited and its subsidiary, IBCA, Inc.	1978	1990	1991: Acquired by Fimalac 1997: Merges with Fitch Ratings
Thomson BankWatch, Inc.	1974	1991	1989: Sold by Keefe, Bruyette and Woods to Thomson 2000: Acquired by Fitch
Dominion Bond Rating Service	1976	2003	
A.M. Best Company, Inc.	1906	2005	1905: Purchased Insurers Reporting Company 1947: Purchased Flitcraft Inc

Sources: Cantor, R. and Packer, F., 1994. The credit rating industry, *Quarterly Review*: Federal Reserve Bank of New York, Summer–Fall, 1–26, page 2; Sylla, R., 2001. An historical primer on the business of credit ratings, NY University Salomon Center, Conference on rating agencies and the global financial system, June 1, 1–29, pages 8, 9; US Securities and Exchange Commission, 2005, Proposed rule – definition of Nationally Recognized Statistical Rating Organizations, April 19, 1–74, page 9; *The New York Times*, 1997. Merger to create large credit rating agency, October 17; Company websites Moody's Investors Service website: http://www.moodys.com, About Moody's, Moody's history; Moody's Corporation, 2001. *Annual Report 2000*, March 15, 1–50, page 4; Moody's Corporation, 2003. *Annual Report 2002*, March 15, 1–58; Fimalac SA, 2006. Annual Report 2005, 1–211.

year, the SEC introduced Nationally Recognized Statistical Rating Organization (NRSRO) status as a regulatory aid, and in 1976, S&P was one of the first ratings agencies to receive this designation, along with Moody's and Fitch.[19] Regulatory uses for ratings added to market demand, and in the same year, S&P restructured along product lines and issued the first structured finance rating. In the late 1970s, S&P introduced their seminar series, aimed at explaining ratings and ratings criteria to investors, and published the first book on rating criteria.

Ratings up to this time were limited to the US market, but the globalization of capital markets, which began in the 1980s, saw a period of rapid growth and expansion for S&P. The entry of institutions, such as municipalities, into the global equities markets saw S&P start to rate Municipal Notes in 1982, and soon new financial products were coming thick and fast. S&P started rating Money Market Mutual Funds and Bond Funds in 1984, and in 1986 introduced ratings for asset-backed securities. By 1990, non-US insurance ratings were growing, and S&P responded by acquiring Insurance Solvency International, to add this service to the company's portfolio of offerings. Ratings for derivative products companies were introduced in 1992. The addition of new products meant that S&P continued to report growth in 1994 and 1995, even though the number of new issues in the US bond market fell over those two years. Barron's reported that record 1995 profits for McGraw-Hill included 'growth at Standard & Poor's Ratings, despite a decline in the number of new issues in the US bond market for the second consecutive year.'[20]

The growth in the ratings universe was not just in terms of new products, but also in terms of new markets. The company opened its first foreign office in London in 1984, and its second in Japan, in 1985. Expansion into continental Europe followed, with S&P's first acquisition, a 50% stake in French credit rating company Agence France d'Evaluation Financière (ADEF) being announced in 1990. The *Financial Times* reported that 'S&P said it aimed to integrate the French agency into its own operations over the next two years, but that ADEF's ratings would continue to be used in the French domestic market.'[21] This first step seems to have given S&P an early-mover advantage over Moody's in France and Europe, and the acquisition was completed when S&P bought ADEF outright in 1996. Leo O'Neill, president and head of the rating department at S&P, was reported as saying that taking control of ADEF had two purposes: firstly, to complete the integration of French activities into S&P's international network and, secondly, to develop Paris operations into a regional center covering France, Belgium, Italy, and Luxembourg.[22]

Other overseas ventures included the acquisition of Australian Ratings in 1996, and a merger with Canadian Bond Ratings Service (CBRS), a major Canadian bond rating agency, in 2000.[23] The Canadian merger, like the purchase of ADEF in France, was designed to help S&P to grow in a new market and to expand CBRS's reach overseas. The integration of rating cultures was somewhat of a challenge, because out of 504 matched pairs of ratings,

---

[19] We will refer to this NRSRO status as the 'old NRSRO' or 'initial NRSRO' status, in opposition to the recent more clarified and transparent criteria to become NRSRO since the Credit Rating Agency Reform Act of 2006.

[20] Lazo, S.A., 1996. Just call it McGraw-High – profits, shares, dividend up; stock to split, *Barron's*, February, 786 words.

[21] *Financial Times*, 1990. Standard and Poor's acquires 50% stake in debt rating agency, January 26, 121 words.

[22] *Les Echos*, 1996. Standard & Poor's acquires remainder of S&P-ADEF, January 18, 191 words.

[23] CBRS: Canadian Bond Rating Service was created in 1972 and at the time of the acquisition had a portfolio of about 470 Canadian issuers. (To B or not to B)

65.1% were in disagreement – among the highest on the North American scene.[24] But it was commercially worth the effort, CBRS president Brian Neysmith commenting that:

> one of the major rationales for the merger was the fact that now, between combining their operations here and our operations, we now have a critical mass to completely to serve every single facet in the Canadian market and serve any Canadian borrower and any investor who's interested in Canadian debt almost any place in the world.[25]

The combined agency was the largest in Canada, but Neysmith did not expect competition to fall, pointing out that 'There's still Moody's, us and DBRS and of course we expect Fitch...to make a decent attack on the Canadian market ... four very good competitors.'[26] S&P also strengthened its position in Asia-Pacific by becoming a major shareholder of Indian rating agency CRISIL in 2005, cementing a relationship that had begun in 1996. Twenty years after the London office opened, S&P operates in 21 countries and markets around the world, from Stockholm to Moscow and from Mexico City to Sydney.

It seems that this combined strategy of new products and new countries has been effective as, in 2002, Jennifer Ablan of Barron's reported that 'much of S&P's recent growth has been driven by the company's international expansion and the acquisition and development of supplementary risk-analysis products.'[27] She went on to point out that securitization financings had 'mushroomed in popularity in the US and Europe in recent years.' Clearly S&P had positioned itself well – that same year, the McGraw-Hill's Financial Services unit, which includes S&P, was referred to as 'the straw that stirs the drink' in The McGraw-Hill group.[28] Indeed, the continuing success of S&P has prompted suggestions that McGraw-Hill might follow the example of Dun & Bradstreet, which spun off Moody's in 2000. In 2006, the Moody's stock was 'valued at $18 billion, roughly the same amount as McGraw-Hill.'[29]

S&P is widely accepted by investors in both the US and European markets. It rated 94% of the rated dollar volume of the US debt market in 2005 and 85% of the rated dollar volume of the European debt market, including all structured finance categories and corporates for both US and Europe, and also municipals for the US debt market. The US market is usually considered as a 'rated market' for industry insiders, as issuers almost always get two ratings if not three. S&P has a policy of systematically rating issuers in the US debt market, whether solicited or not. This is not yet the case in Europe, and S&P still tends to be the preferred agency for European corporate issuers seeking only one rating. The growth of S&P from 1998 through 2005 can be seen in Figure 8.6.

Overseas activity today produces 31.3% of total revenues. The US contributes roughly 60% of the business, with Europe at about 20–25% and the balance from the rest of the world (see Figure 8.7).

S&P is the largest agency in terms of number of analysts, has 1422 credit analysts including credit analyst supervisors, and is relatively close to Moody's in the number of

[24] Barton, A., 2006. Split credit ratings and the prediction of bank ratings in the Basel II environment, Thesis submitted for the degree of Doctor of Philosophy, University of Southampton, Faculty of Law, Arts and Social Sciences, School of Management, 1–205, page 115.

[25] Musero, F., 2000. S&P Acquires CBRS, Private Placement Letter, November 6, 680 words.

[26] Musero, F., 2000. S&P Acquires CBRS, Private Placement Letter, November 6, 680 words.

[27] Ablan, J., 2002. A triple-A for effort: thanks to its fast-growing financial services business, McGraw-Hill merits a re-rating, Barron's, July 22, 2119 words.

[28] Ablan, J., 2002. A triple-A for effort: thanks to its fast-growing financial services business, McGraw-Hill merits a re-rating, Barron's, July 22, 2119 words.

[29] Bary, A., 2006. Free S&P, Barron's, January 30, 1562 words.

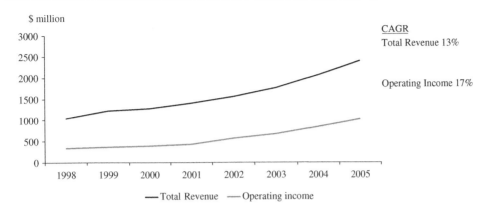

Figure 8.6 S&P Growth.
Notes: Total Reported Figures for the Financial Services Segment of McGraw-Hill Companies, i.e. includes ratings, ratings-related and non-ratings-related products and services; CAGR is the Compound Annual Growth Rate of the $ million value.
Source: The McGraw-Hill Companies, Annual Reports, 1998 through 2005.

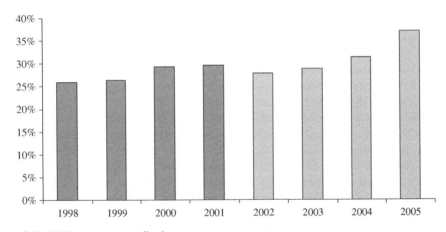

Figure 8.7 S&P overseas contribution to revenue.
Notes: 1998–2001, percentages are of Credit Market Services (or equivalent) Revenue (includes ratings and related revenues e.g. from research and risk management tools and services); 2002–2005, percentages are of total Financial Services Revenue (includes in addition to the above, non ratings related revenue, e.g. from portfolio services).
Source: The McGraw-Hill Companies, Annual Reports, 1998 through 2005.

issues it covers, according to the 2008 NRSRO certification filing. Unfortunately, the product split for S&P is not readily available, as The McGraw-Hill Companies consolidated annual report only gives total figures for entire divisions. Overall, S&P seems to have the broadest and most balanced coverage of the major CRAs, with a strong number of issuers outstanding in all segments (Exhibit 8.3). S&P is perceived as being slightly more 'quantitative' in communication and rating guidance than its major competitors. For instance, in 2005, S&P Ratings Services published more than 500 000 ratings.

Exhibit 8.3 Size comparison of leading CRAs, 2007

Rating agency	Global/regional	No. of analysts (incl. analyst supervisors)	Ratings o/s
Moody's	Global	>1321 credit analysts	113 000 Corporations and FI >154 000 Municipal and Sovereigns >108 000 SF issues
S&P	Global	>1422 credit analysts	77 900 Corporations and FI 976 000 Municipal and Sovereigns 187 600 SF issues
Fitch	Global	>1165 credit analysts	83 436 Corporations and FI 765 699 Municipal and Sovereigns 70 731 SF issues

Sources: Fitch Ratings website: http://www.fitchratings.com; Moody's Investors Service website: http://www.moodys.com; Standard & Poor's website: http://www.standardandpoors.com, NRSRO filings, item 6 and exhibit 8.

MOODY'S   In 1996, in a Public Broadcasting Service (PBS) interview, Pulitzer Prize winning journalist Thomas Friedman said:

> There are two superpowers in the world today in my opinion. There's the United States and there's Moody's Bond Rating Service. The United States can destroy you by dropping bombs, and Moody's can destroy you by downgrading your bonds. And believe me, it's not clear sometimes who's more powerful.[30]

Moody's describes itself today as 'an essential component of the global capital markets. It provides credit ratings, research, tools and analysis that help to protect the integrity of credit.'[31] John Moody (1868–1958) laid the foundations in 1900 for what is now Moody's Investors Service, when he published *Moody's Manual of Industrial and Corporation Securities*. In 1909, Moody published the first bond ratings as part of *Moody's Analyses of Railroad Securities*. It was here that the Aaa through C symbols were used to rank securities in terms of credit risk for the first time on a 9-point scale.[32] Moody's was incorporated in 1914, when it began expanding ratings coverage to bonds issued by US cities and other municipalities as well as utility and industrial bonds. By 1924, Moody's ratings covered nearly 100% of the US bond market. During the Great Depression, overall bond default rates soared, but most of those rated highly by Moody's continued to meet scheduled payments.

Dun & Bradstreet purchased Moody's Investors Service in 1962. Ten years later, Moody's began to assign short-term ratings after Penn Central defaulted on its commercial paper, and also began to rate bank deposits. Moody's changed its business model to issuer pays around the same time as S&P and in 1976 became one of the first agencies to be given the initial NRSRO status, along with S&P and Fitch. While enjoying the benefits of NRSRO status,

---

[30] Public Broadcasting Service, 1996. Free Market Sociey, Transcript of interview between David Gergen and Thomas L. Friedman, February 13.

[31] Moody's Investors Service website: http://www.moodys.com, Shareholder relations.

[32] Perhaps not surprisingly, there was great opposition among the rated companies and on Wall Street as well. According to Moody's, John Moody later noted that 'a storm of opposition was raised … not to mention ridicule from some quarters … but the ratings took hold with dealers and investment houses … Long before 1914 the Railroad Manual was a recognized authority and Moody's ratings had become an important factor in the bond trading and bond selling field.'

Moody's called on the SEC to 'allow more rather than fewer entities to be registered as NRSROs' because 'increased competition could increase the number of valuable opinions available to the financial markets.'[33]

Moody's Corporation was spun off from Dun & Bradstreet in 2000, a move that was intended to 'unlock significant value for the shareholders of the Dun & Bradstreet Corporation,' according to a statement by Clifford L. Alexander Jr, former Chairman and CEO of Dun & Bradstreet, who became Chairman of Moody's following the separation.[34] Under the Moody's Corporation umbrella, Moody's Investors Service provided ratings, and Moody's Risk Management Services (MRMS) aimed to help financial institutions in their loan decisions.

In 2002, Moody's Corporation acquired KMV, a company providing quantitative credit risk management tools, for $210 million. The acquisition was part of a planned phase of investment spending aimed at helping the company to develop new products and enter new markets. KMV was combined with MRMS and christened Moody's KMV. John Rutherford Jr, President and CEO of Moody's Corporation, said of the acquisition, 'We expect to develop Moody's KMV into an important new business alongside our core Moody's Investors Service (MIS) business.'[35] The independent research provider, Economy.com, was acquired in 2005 and renamed Moody's Economy.com, but despite adding this 'second string' of research products and software to their offering, approximately 80% of Moody's revenues still derives from ratings.[36]

As capital markets globalized in the early 1980s, both Moody's and S&P recognized the need for a local presence in overseas markets if they were to truly understand regional circumstances and maintain the quality of their ratings. But while S&P opened their first foreign office in London, Moody's chose to start in Tokyo, in 1985. Moody's did not open an office in Europe until the London office opened in 1987, followed by a Paris office a year later, which meant that S&P had a head start in Europe.

Moody's initially compensated for a relatively weaker presence in Europe than S&P and Fitch by issuing more unsolicited ratings. However, in 2000 the company responded to concerns over unsolicited ratings expressed by leading participants in the European market. In a speech to the Association of French Treasurers (AFTE), Moody's Investors Service President Raymond McDaniel described how the company had changed the conditions under which such ratings would be issued in 2000, 'effectively ending the practice in Europe.'[37] But Europe remained a strategic target for growth. In the 2000 Annual Report, the company stated that '[e]ach year since 1997, Moody's has assigned first-time ratings to about 100 European corporations,' estimating that 'there are still 1500 unrated European institutions with revenues of over 1 billion euros.'[38]

---

[33] Regulatory Comment. Letter from Dering, J.M., Executive Vice President–Global Regulatory Affairs & Compliance, Moody's Investors Service, 2007. Proposed rules regarding oversight of credit rating agencies registered as Nationally Recognized Statistical Rating Organizations, to Nancy M. Morris, Secretary, Securities and Exchange Commission, March 12.

[34] Moody's Corporation, 2001. Annual Report 2000, March 2001, 1–50.

[35] Moody's Corporation, 2002. Moody's Corporation completes acquisition of KMV; purchase of pioneer in quantitative credit tools complements Moody's core credit ratings business, Press release, April 15.

[36] Moody's Corporation, 2006. Annual Report 2005, 1–94.

[37] McDaniel, R., 2003. The role and function of rating agencies: evolving perceptions and the implications for regulatory oversight. Report based on a speech presented to the Association of French Treasurers (AFTE) on 5 February 2003 in Paris, France by Raymond McDaniel, President–Moody's Investors Service, Special Comment, February, 1–8.

[38] Moody's Corporation, 2001. Annual Report 2000, March 15, 1–50.

Moody's has also cited the drive toward monetary union in Europe as a boost to ratings growth, because it opened the door to far greater borrowing and investment between member countries of the European Union. The company pointed out that scope for growth in Europe was underscored by the fact that while only 25% of credit financing in the US was supplied by banks, in the Netherlands, Switzerland, and the UK this figure was 50%, rising to over 70% in Germany, France, and Italy.[39] The move into Europe continues, more recently with the 2006 acquisition of CRA Rating Agencies in the Czech Republic, which is now the headquarters for Moody's Central Europe.

Further internationalization occurred in the 1990s, when securitization expanded outside the US, and by 2001 Moody's could list offices in 16 countries, including the newly opened Beijing office, and joint ventures in a further six.[40] Between 1996 and 2000, Moody's international revenues grew from $63 million to $173 million. By 2005, international revenues contributed 37% of the $1732 million total, or $640.8 million, and compound annual growth rates in Europe (32%) and the rest of the world (26%) outstripped that of the US at 20%.[41]

When corporate borrowing started to move away from banks and into the debt markets in the 1970s and early 1980s, Moody's ratings business grew rapidly and its rating products were adapted. On April 26, 1982, it refined its rating system for the first time by adding numerical modifiers to each rating category, moving from a 9-point scale to a 21-point scale, as S&P had done in 1974. The modifiers 1, 2 and 3 indicated whether the debt issues ranked at the high end, the mid-range (the generic category under the old system), or the low end of the generic category, respectively. The 1980s also saw the beginnings of a boom in sovereign ratings and Moody's was just one step ahead of S&P because in the 1970s, while S&P was only rating the US and Canada, Moody's was also rating Australia.[42]

The rush of new financial products to meet demand for borrowing opened up new revenue streams for Moody's. In the first annual report published by the new Moody's Corporation in 2000, President and CEO John Rutherfurd Jr pointed out that 'investment financed by debt drives Moody's revenues' because 'debt sold in public capital markets usually require ratings.'[43] But the same report also noted the success of two relatively new product offerings, ratings for Collateralized Debt Obligations (CDOs) and for syndicated bank loans. Other recent additions for Moody's include assigning ratings to issuers of securities, insurance company obligations, bank deposits and other bank debt, managed funds and derivatives.[44]

Analysts tend to agree with Moody's view of new products being important contributors to the company's growth. Morgan Stanley analysts believe 'that interest rates and new debt issuance trends are not the sole drivers of growth at [Moody's].'[45] Structured finance in 2005, 'fueled by US residential mortgage-backed and home equity loans' 'accounted for the bulk of [Moody's] revenue upside.'[46] In 2003, a JPMorgan report pointed out that

---

[39] Moody's Corporation, 2002. Annual Report 2001, March 15, 1–47.
[40] Moody's Corporation, 2002. Annual Report 2001, March 15, 1–47.
[41] Moody's Corporation, 2006. Annual Report 2005, 1–94.
[42] Klein, A., 2004. Smoothing the way for debt markets, *Washington Post*, November 23.
[43] Moody's Corporation, 2001. Annual Report 2000, March 15, 1–50.
[44] Moody's Investors Service website: http://www.moodys.com, Investor Relations, Corporate Profile.
[45] Apgar, P.E., Arthur, D., and Monaco, L., 2005. Moody's, Equity Research report: Morgan Stanley, April 27, 1–16.
[46] Apgar, P.E., Arthur, D., and Monaco, L., 2005. Moody's, Equity Research report: Morgan Stanley, April 27, 1–16.

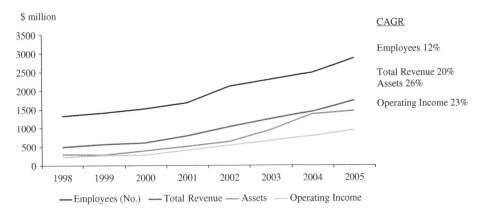

Figure 8.8 Moody's growth.
Notes: Total reported figures of the company, i.e. includes Ratings, Research and Risk Management Products (i.e. KMV); CAGR is the Compound Annual Growth Rate of the $ million value.
Source: Moody's Corporation, Annual Reports, 1998 through 2005.

'structured finance . . . has accounted for the lion's share of Moody's growth since 1996.'[47] Moody's growth from 1998 through 2005 can be seen in Figure 8.8.

Today, Moody's Corporation is a publicly traded company, listed on the New York Stock Exchange since September 30, 2000, when it was spun off from Dun & Bradstreet. Moody's Corporation is now the parent company of Moody's Investors Services, Moody's KMV, and Moody's Economy.com. Major shareholders include Warren Buffett's Berkshire Hathaway, which owns 16.1% of Moody's Corporation shares, and Davis Selected Advisers, which owns 6.3%.[48]

Moody's provides services in fixed income securities markets, including credit ratings and investor-oriented credit research (including in-depth research on major issuers, industry studies, special comments, and credit opinion handbooks) provided through Moody's Investor Services. Moody's KMV develops and distributes quantitative credit assessment products and services for banks and investors in credit-sensitive assets, credit training services, and credit process software.

US revenues contribute roughly 60%, of the business, with Europe at about 20–25%, and the balance from the rest of the world. Research and Moody's KMV have shown the highest growth rates among the various products recently, followed by structured finance (see Figure 8.9).

Moody's today operates in over 26 countries outside the US, employs over 100 credit analysts in Europe, and 60 more in Asia. The total number of analysts is over 1000. The firm's ratings and analysis products track more than US$30 trillion of debt issued in domestic and international markets, and in 2006 covered approximately 12 000 corporations and financial institutions, more than 29 000 public finance issuers, over 96 000 structured finance transactions, and 100 sovereign issuers[49] (see Figure 8.10).

---

[47] Crockett, B., Lowe, J., and Searby, F., 2003. Moody's attractive business, but growth hiatus in 2004, North American Equity Research: JPMorgan, October 14, 1–44.
[48] Crockett, B., Lowe, J., and Searby, F., 2003. Moody's attractive business, but growth hiatus in 2004, North American Equity Research: JPMorgan, October 14, 1–44.
[49] Reuters website: http://stocks.us.reuters.com/stocks/fullDescription.asp?symbol=MCO, full description on Moody's.

$ million

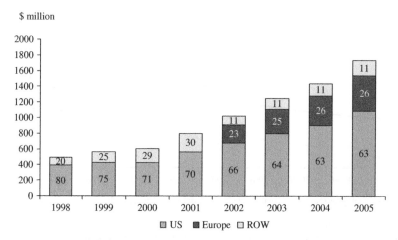

Figure 8.9   Moody's geographical contribution to total revenue.
Notes: Histogram heights represent Total Reported Revenue in $ millions (i.e. Sum of Ratings, Research and Risk Management Products Revenue); Revenue from Europe is included in ROW prior to 2002 due to lack of availability of separate data; Figures in histograms are percentage contribution of the Geographical Segment Revenue to Total Revenue and add to 100; CAGR is the Compound Annual Growth Rate of the $ million value.
Source: Moody's Corporation, Annual Reports, 1998 through 2005.

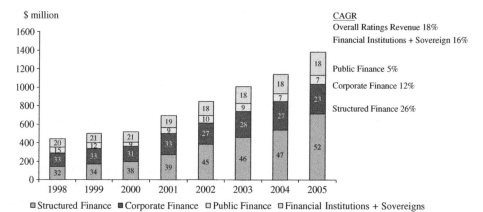

Figure 8.10   Moody's segment-wise contribution to ratings revenue.
Notes: Histogram heights represent Ratings Revenue in $ millions (Total Reported Revenue less Research and Risk Management Products Revenue); Figures in histograms are percentage contribution of the Product Segment Revenue to Ratings Revenue and add to 100; CAGR is the Compound Annual Growth Rate of the $ million value.
Source: Moody's Corporation, Annual Reports, 1998 through 2005.

FITCH   The Fitch story is slightly different from that of Moody's or S&P. While the bigger firms have grown their ratings groups largely organically, making tactical acquisitions to expand their geographical range, today's Fitch Group is the result of a complex series of mergers and acquisitions that brought not only geographical reach but also additional products and ratings expertise. A series of 'marriages made in heaven' enabled the driving force behind the modern Fitch Group, French entrepreneur Marc Ladreit de Lacharrière, to capitalize on the original Fitch's position as the third ratings agency with the initial NRSRO status and develop a company that can rightfully be said to compete with the two giants.

Like S&P and Moody's, Fitch Group began life in the early 20th century. John Knowles Fitch founded The Fitch Publishing Company in New York on December 24, 1913, planning to publish financial statistics. The first *Fitch Bond Book* and *Fitch Stock and Bond Manual* soon appeared and, in 1924, the company published its first securities ratings book using the AAA to D scale.

The arrival of NRSRO status in 1975 saw Fitch's importance in the rating world recognized alongside S&P and Moody's, but recapitalization and the introduction of a new management team in 1989 suggest that for the business itself not everything was rosy. After 1989, however, things started to take off. Fitch enjoyed the boom brought about by financial disintermediation and the introduction of structured finance just as much as Moody's and S&P.

In 1997, IBCA Limited announced that 'it was in talks to buy Fitch Investors Service.'[50] IBCA was owned by French company Fimalac SA, of which the controlling shareholder was Marc Ladreit de Lacharrière. Founded in 1978, IBCA was based in London and originally specialized in credit ratings for banking and financial institutions, and government agencies. The eventual deal in October 1997, whereby Fimalac acquired Fitch for $175 million and then merged it with IBCA, created the third largest ratings company after S&P and Moody's. The *Financial Times* said of the deal that IBCA was 'just about the only serious challenger to the might of the US credit ratings agencies led by Moody's and Standard & Poor's, merging with Fitch pushes it into the big league.'[51]

With the merger, IBCA gained the presence in America that it lacked and Fitch gained international reach and coverage of sovereigns, corporates, and financial institutions. Fitch IBCA maintained dual headquarters in New York and London, and by 1999 had 400 analysts in 21 offices around the world, covering over 1400 issuers (1000 financial institutions and 400 corporates). The Fitch website describes the deal as a 'merger [that] represented the first step in Fitch Ratings' plan to meet investors' need for an alternative, global, full service rating.'

The next step shortly emerged. In April of 2000, Fitch IBCA announced that it had acquired Duff & Phelps Credit Rating Co., a company founded in 1974 and headquartered in Chicago, for $528 million.[52] Duff & Phelps Credit Ratings Co was a relative newcomer to the ratings scene. The company's connections to public utilities ratings went back to 1932, but it had only begun providing bond ratings for a wider range of companies in 1982. Duff & Phelps had seen rapid growth in the 1990s, and by 1999 had over 300 analysts in 30 offices, rating over 100 000 issues across more than 50 countries. The acquisition was a natural fit inasmuch as 701 matched pairs of ratings of the same bond, issued the year preceding the merger, the consensus between them was 65%, the highest in the industry.[53] The acquisition increased Fitch IBCA's global reach, bringing in offices and affiliates in Latin America and Asia, as well as the US and the UK. Fimalac President and CEO de

---

[50] *The Economist*, 1997. The would-be king of credit ratings, August 16, 765 words.

[51] *Financial Times*, 1997. Credit due, October 20, 217 words.

[52] PR Newswire, 2000. Fitch IBCA and Duff & Phelps Credit Rating Co. announce merger agreement, March 7, 800 words.

[53] Security Data Corporation, 2007. US Domestic Public Offerings Data Base, Non-convertible, non-short-term debt. All issuers and issue types.

Lacharrière said of the deal, 'For many years now Fimalac has been interested in developing a European owned alternative to the major US agencies. Through the development of Fitch IBCA, and with the acquisition of Duff & Phelps, we now have achieved our goal.'

But things didn't stop there. Fitch IBCA announced its next acquisition later in 2000, when it bought Toronto-based ratings company Thomson Financial BankWatch from the Canadian media giant, The Thomson Corporation. BankWatch specialized in interbank credit ratings, and had 1100 employees operating across 75 countries. The fit between the two was also a natural one inasmuch as out of 620 matched pairs of ratings, the agreement was also high at 61.5%. Fitch commented that the deal 'will strengthen our international banking coverage.'[54]

The choice to grow through acquisitions as well as organically helped Fitch to leapfrog more quickly into a competitive position *vis-à-vis* Moody's and S&P than organic growth alone might have done. These two acquisitions broadened and strengthened Fitch's ratings offerings as well as dramatically increasing the company's presence around the world. At the same time, the company also broadened its portfolio outside the core ratings business, firstly by acquiring specialist financial training firm CCR in 2002, and, secondly, by acquiring the enterprise risk management company Algorithmics in 2004 to boost Fitch's own risk practice. Both additional offerings gave Fitch access to a wider base of companies, people, and information in the financial world.

While Fitch used acquisitions to provide quantum leaps in growth, the company also launched a number of new ratings products and ensured that its offerings evolved with the markets. Issuer Reporting Standards were launched in 2003, a European Property Market Metric appeared in 2004, and Issuer Default and Recovery Ratings were launched in 2005. Recovery Ratings are scaled from RR1/outstanding to RR6/poor, and in 2006, they were incorporated into ratings for Collateralized Loan Obligations (CLOs). This reflected the increasing complexity of the different loans underlying CLOs, and aimed to give investors a deeper understanding of potential credit losses associated with those underlying loans.

In 2006, Fitch took the bold step of setting up a new specialist rating agency, Derivative Fitch. This signaled the importance of the credit derivatives sector, with the Fitch press release announcing the launch of Derivative Fitch pointing out that,

> With the credit derivatives market now approaching $33 trillion in notional value outstanding, the market has become a dynamic element of the global financial economy, as many participants utilize credit derivatives to manage their risk profiles.[55]

While the Fitch Group was growing, parent company Fimalac was also changing. Fitch Ratings contributed 36% of Fimalac's revenue and 68% of the operating profit in 2004. Acknowledging this, Fimalac decided to refocus its business strategy entirely on the financial services sector. With the sale of tools company Facom in 2005, Fimalac divested itself of the last of its various unrelated businesses and became the parent company of a pure-play financial services.

Nowhere was this quality more evident than in the fact that, between October 2004 and February 2005, Merrill Lynch, Lehman Brothers, and CalPERS all announced that they would be including Fitch Ratings alongside those of Moody's and S&P in their indices

---

[54] *Business Publisher*, 2000. Thomson sells BankWatch Ratings Service; acquires Argentinian publisher, October 17, 207 words.

[55] *Businesswire*, 2006. Fitch Ratings launches new rating agency, *Derivative Fitch*, October 18, 1050 words.

and investment guidelines. Merrill Lynch planned to take an average of the three ratings, Lehman Brothers to use the middle rating of the three, and CalPERS specified in their Statement of Investment Policy that investments 'must have a minimum credit rating of a single A from at least two of the three nationally recognized credit rating agencies (Moody's Investor Service, Standard & Poor's, and Fitch Ratings).'[56] While all three changes would require some adjustments to current recommendations, Merrill Lynch pointed out that,

> It is worth noting that of the 2300 bonds [out of 18 818 in total] whose rating will change under the new methodology, Moody's and S&P ratings match only 5% of the time, whereas Fitch matches either Moody's or S&P 65% of the time.'[57]

Today's Fitch Group (see Exhibit 8.4) comprises Fitch Ratings, Fitch Training, and Algorithmics. The Group is a majority-owned subsidiary of Fimalac SA, which is listed on Euronext. Fimalac owns 80% of the Fitch Group, the remaining 20% was sold to the Hearst Group in 2006.[58]

Including ratings, research, and risk management revenues, the US contributes roughly 60% of the business, with Europe at about 20–25%, and the balance from the rest of the world (Figure 8.11). Growth rates have been higher in Europe and the rest of the world than in the US.

Exhibit 8.4   Fitch Group's historical diagram.

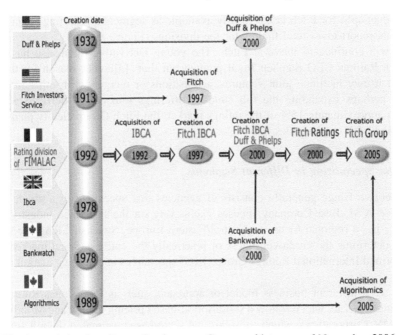

Source: Fimalac website: http://www.fimalac.com, Company history as of November 2006.

---

[56] California Public Employees' Retirement System, 2005. CalPERS Statement of Investment Policy for Credit Enhancement Program, February 14, 1–11.

[57] Merrill Lynch, 2004. Upcoming changes in Global Index Rules, Bond Indices, October, 1–8, page 3.

[58] Fimalac SA, 2006. Annual Report 2005, 1–211.

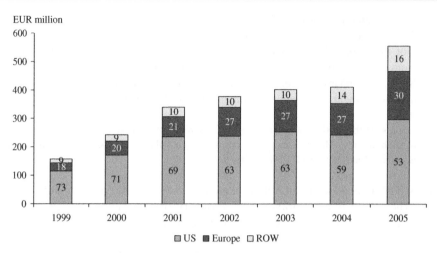

Figure 8.11 Fitch geographical contribution to total revenue.
Notes: Histogram heights represent Total Reported Revenue in EUR millions (i.e. Sum of Ratings, Research and Risk Management Products Revenue); Figures in histograms are percentage contribution of the Geographical Segment Revenue to Total Revenue and add to 100; CAGR is the Compound Annual Growth Rate of the EUR million value.
Source: Fimalac SA, Annual Reports, 1999 through 2005.

The product split for Fitch is not readily available as segmental reporting in the consolidated annual report gives total figures for the divisions (Figure 8.12).

Things will continue to move at Fitch. The young Derivative Fitch also has plans to grow. Fitch Ratings CEO Stephen Joynt pointed out that '[a]nother reason for this initiative is that it may facilitate joint ventures, acquisitions or mergers with other information providers, perhaps expanding the full suite of offerings into equity derivatives.'[59] Currently with approximately 15% of the ratings market, the Fitch Group clearly plans to keep Moody's and S&P on their toes.

The Fringe: Specializing in Different Segments

The competitive fringe generally consists of agencies that specialize in a given segment. For instance A.M. Best Company focuses exclusively on the insurance industry, Capital Intelligence has a regional focus, on Central/Eastern Europe, Swedish CRAs use statistical models to determine the creditworthiness of practically the entire national market, and the recently formed International Ratings Group (IRG) specializes in emerging market corporate debt.

Some have a different business model or approach, such as Egan-Jones Rating Co. or Rapid Ratings Pty Ltd, which follow a subscription-based pricing model, and Moody's KMV (earlier KMV Corporation), which uses cardinal-scale-based estimated default frequencies (EDF) PD.[60]

---

[59] Scholtes, S., 2006. Fitch unveils new agency, *Financial Times*, October 18.
[60] Estrella, A., 2000. Credit ratings and complementary sources of credit quality information, Basel Committee on Banking Supervision, Working Papers No. 3: Bank for International Settlements, Basel, August, 1–186, pages 14–27.

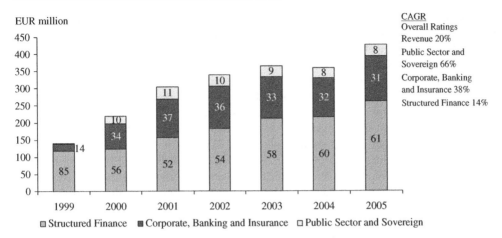

Figure 8.12 Fitch segment-wise contribution to ratings revenue.
Notes: Histogram heights represent Ratings Revenue in EUR millions (Total Reported Revenue less Research and Risk Management Products Revenue); Figures in histograms are percentage contribution of the Product Segment Revenue to Ratings Revenue and add to 100; CAGR is the Compound Annual Growth Rate of the EUR million value.
Sources: Fimalac SA, Annual Reports, 1999 through 2005; Fimalac SA, 2006, *Investor Presentation*, March 16, 1–74.

In addition to the three leading CRAs, Dominion Bond Ratings Service (DBRS) and A.M. Best Company also had the initial NRSRO status. Founded in 1976 and headquartered in Canada, DBRS is a privately held, full-service credit agency. It has 30 analysts and rates around 500 corporations world wide, as well as Canadian government securities. DBRS provides ratings on commercial paper, bonds, preferred shares and asset-backed securities and is currently expanding into global sovereign issues and European financial ones

EGAN-JONES   Egan-Jones is a small but vocal ratings agency based in the Philadelphia area of Pennsylvania. Privately owned, the company has a subscriber-based business model and receives no fees from issuers of the entities it rates. It is reported not to 'meet with companies or use inside information in its credit analyses,' because, according to cofounder Sean Egan, 'We think [insider access] is an accident waiting to happen.'[61]

The company differentiates itself loud and clear from its much larger issuer-pays business model competitors. This is not only because of the seemingly unassailable position that the old NRSRO status had conferred on Fitch, Moody's, S&P, DBRS and A.M. Best, but also because Egan-Jones sees the biggest share of the market go to two companies that it believes are old-fashioned, slow, and beset by conflicts of interest.

Egan-Jones first applied for NRSRO status in 1998, and finally achieved it late December 2007, thanks to the new criteria for NRSRO of the Credit Rating Agency Reform Act of 2006, for which Egan-Jones actively lobbied, and successfully so. This is a turning point for Egan-Jones, that plans to expand into more diverse products and increase its number of analysts.

---

[61] Reason, T., 2003. Good to rate, *CFO Magazine*, September 1, 2003.

In testimony to the Senate Committee on Banking, Housing, and Urban Affairs, Egan stated that 'the ratings industry is suffering from a state that is hard to characterize as anything other than dysfunctional.'[62] Egan has repeatedly underscored the lack of competition under the old NRSRO system, calling it a 'partner monopoly,' and loses no opportunity to point out that his company was quicker to downgrade ratings for troubled corporates such as WorldCom, Enron, and the Ford Motor Company than the NRSRO agencies.[63] 'Egan-Jones makes a practice of alerting investors to corporate credit problems well before they are acknowledged by management,'[64] – a quotation among several along similar lines provided by Egan-Jones in their submissions to the SEC and on their website. As of March 2008, the annual certification forms of the NRSRO status indicate that Egan-Jones have 62 ratings outstanding on financial institutions, brokers and dealers, 46 on insurance companies and 803 corporate ratings outstanding. Moreover, exhibit 8 indicates they have 12 credit analysts and 3 credit analyst supervisors.

DBRS   The Dominion Bond Rating Service, better known as DBRS, was founded in 1976 in Toronto, Canada, by Walter Shroeder. The company prides itself in remaining privately owned, with no affiliation to any financial institution, and Shroeder is still the company's President. DBRS uses traditional ratings scales, for instance, commercial paper and short-term debt is rated from R-1 (high) via R-5 to D, while bond and long-term debt from the more familiar AAA through D. The company originally covered corporates and financial institutions.

DBRS considers itself different from other agencies in several respects. Operationally, DBRS rates through economic cycles to prevent rating adjustments due to external conditions, provides detailed rationales for ratings, and separates long-term and short-term debt ratings. Strategically, the company positions itself as offering a fresh, more up-to-date methodology, with greater transparency in its methodologies than other agencies, and lower fees than Moody's, S&P, or Fitch. DBRS has also attracted staff from rival agencies to help to drive growth.

DBRS was granted the old NRSRO status in February 2003, after almost three years of negotiation with the Securities and Exchange Commission (SEC). This made DBRS only the fourth agency with NRSRO status, joining the 'big three.' DBRS acknowledged that recognition from the SEC would help it to expand in the US, and put them 'on a level playing field' with their competitors.[65]

DBRS' next challenge to the big three was to launch in Europe. DBRS Europe was established in 2006, with headquarters in London and affiliates in Frankfurt and Paris, staffed with several recruits from Moody's. The *Financial Times* reported that 'DBRS is believed to be planning a sales pitch founded on giving clients the same quality of research as the big agencies but for lower fees,' noting that '[i]n recent years, clients of the Big Three ... have seen the fees they pay for their ratings soar.'[66]

---

[62] Egan, S., 2005. Testimony to Senate Committee on Banking, Housing, and Urban Affairs: The Role of Credit Rating Agencies in the Capital Markets, February 8, 1–12.

[63] Egan, S.J., 2002. Statement of Egan Jones on Credit Rating Agencies, letter submitted to the SEC, November 10, 2002.

[64] Egan, S.J., 2002. Statement of Egan Jones on Credit Rating Agencies, letter submitted to the SEC, November 10, 2002.

[65] Wiggins, J., 2003. US gets fourth ratings agency, *Financial Times*, February 25, 2003.

[66] Jenkins, P., 2006. DBRS to challenge big agencies, *Financial Times*, January 10, 2006.

Just two months after its geographical expansion, DBRS announced a product expansion – it was to start issuing sovereign ratings, focusing initially 'on countries whose major industries are those in which DBRS has a strong track record of analytical expertise.'[67] The leader of DBRS' Sovereign team, David Roberts, commented that 'globalization has transformed the financial markets. Yet the traditional ways of evaluating a sovereign's rating and its impact on a corporate's credit in the country haven't always kept up with the changing fundamentals of sovereign credit risks.'[68]

Another boost to competition among ratings agencies came in June 2006, when DBRS announced that it would establish a European structured finance group to rate complex debt instruments. Apea Koranteng, tasked by DBRS to set up the structured finance group, commented that the announcement reflected 'the importance of the region to global capital markets and the high demand for credit ratings as capital markets activity increases.'[69] Unfortunately, early January 2008, DBRS closed its European offices, as it was forced to downsize as the issuance of structured finance instruments dropped dramatically because of the subprime meltdown.

According to the June 2008 annual certification forms to the NRSRO status, DBRS had 78 credit analysts and 22 supervisors. It had 855 ratings outstanding of financial institutions, 35 of insurance companies, 590 of corporates, 840 of asset backed securities and 45 of municipals and sovereigns. In 2005, the company reported more than 4500 subscribers and over 64 000 hits accessing rating information per month on the DBRS website.[70] In April 2007, the company announced that it had been recognized by 11 European Union countries 'as an eligible External Credit Assessment Institution.' This allows DBRS ratings to be used for the type of risk analysis required by the Basel II framework, ticking yet another competitive box in its efforts to challenge the big three.

A.M. BEST COMPANY   A.M. Best differs from the other agencies discussed here in that, until recently, it was totally specialized on the insurance industry. The company was founded in 1899 by Alfred Magilton Best. Having had various jobs in the insurance industry since the age of 15, Best decided by the age of 21 that the industry needed 'some place where any one interested – whether insured, agent or broker – could obtain a reliable report upon the financial condition and operating methods of insurance companies.'[71] The company grew by gradually covering the different insurance segments, originally publishing *Best's Insurance Reports*, and then introducing ratings, starting with Property/Casualty in 1906. Major insurance events such as the Baltimore Conflagration in 1904 and the San Francisco earthquake in 1907 were major drivers of growth.

While financial disintermediation and the growth of capital markets around the world led other agencies to expand out of the US, for A.M. Best it was the globalization of the insurance market that took it overseas. Although the company had been reporting on European insurers since it was founded, the first non-US *Best's Insurance Reports* were published in 1985. A.M. Best Europe Limited was launched in 1997, and that same year,

---

[67] DBRS, 2006. DBRS Launches Sovereign Ratings Operations, Company press release, DBRS, March 22, 2006.

[68] DBRS, 2006. DBRS Launches Sovereign Ratings Operations, Company press release, DBRS, March 22, 2006.

[69] Davies, P.J., 2006. DBRS moves into structured finance, *Financial Times*, June 5, 2006.

[70] Keogh, M, 2005. DBRS's Response to the CEBS consultation paper on the recognition of external credit assessment institutions, letter to the Committee of European Banking Supervisors (CEBS), September 27, 2005.

[71] Best, A., 1949. A junior clerk at fifteen, *Best's Review magazine*.

the company issued the first ever rating of Lloyd's. A year later, the company purchased UK company Financial Intelligence & Research Ltd (FI&R), which specialized in the UK insurance market.[72] The company's second overseas office was established in Hong Kong on December 6, 1999. In the same year, A.M. Best set up operations in Canada through the acquisition of Toronto-based Trac Insurance Services. However, the Canadian office was closed in 2003, as the company 'consolidated all Canadian operations . . . into its corporate headquarters.'[73]

Despite the company's specialization and position in the insurance industry, NRSRO recognition was considered important for growth. In 2002, chief rating officer at A.M. Best, Larry Mayewski, commented that NRSRO status was 'the Good Housekeeping seal of approval,' and that A.M. Best was ' "strongly considering" applying.'[74] Later that year, Mayewski pointed out that 'there are still companies that would like to see us with the NRSRO designation before they'll do business with us.'[75] A.M. Best announced that it had achieved NRSRO status on March 3, 2005, and President and Chairman Arthur Snyder said 'we . . . look forward to expanding and enhancing our services to the market-place.'[76]

The changing relationship between the insurance and banking industries led A.M. Best to announce in October 2006 that it was introducing ratings for US banks and bank holding companies. The company again took the specialist route, choosing segments that 'traditionally have not received comprehensive rating coverage,' and stating that it would be rating 'US banks with asset sizes ranging from approximately $100 million . . . to $40 billion, with a specific focus on the mid-sized and small banks.'[77]

Today, the company calls itself the 'largest and longest-established company devoted to issuing in-depth reports and financial strength ratings about insurance organizations.'[78] The company's database is claimed to be 'the most comprehensive source of insurance company financial and operating figures available.'[79] According to the June 2008 annual certification forms to the NRSRO status, AM Best had 85 credit analysts and 46 supervisors. It had 3 ratings outstanding of financial institutions, 6129 of insurance companies, 2696 of corporate issuers, and 54 of asset backed securities. A.M. Best issues *Financial Strength, Issuer Credit* and *Debt Ratings*. Company ratings and insurer profiles are provided free of charge on the company's website. The company covers 23 countries from its Europe offices, including Bahrain and Egypt in the Middle East, Pakistan, and South Africa. The Hong Kong office covers 13 countries across the Asia-Pacific region, from India to Malaysia and from Japan to New Zealand.

INTERNATIONAL RATINGS GROUP The International Ratings Group (IRG) was launched in February 2006 and brings a new business model to the ratings industry, by not only specializing on one area of the ratings spectrum but also by sharing best practice and

[72] A.M. Best, 2007. website, www.Europe.ambest.com/aboutambest.html

[73] Insurance Canada, 2003, A.M. Best consolidates Canadian Operations, www.insurance-canada.ca, January 10, 2003.

[74] Wiggins, J., 2002. Lesser-known ratings groups seek high status, *Financial Times*, May 20, 2002.

[75] Wiggins, J., 2002. A chance to step into the light, *Financial Times*, December 9, 2002.

[76] A.M. Best, 2005. A.M. Best Granted NRSRO Status by the US Securities and Exchange Commission, Company press release, March 3, 2005.

[77] A.M. Best, 2006. A.M. Best introduces interactive rating services on US Banks and Bank Holding Companies', press release, October 2, 2006.

[78] A.M. Best, 2007. website, www.ambest.com/about/

[79] A.M. Best, 2007. website, www.ambest.com/about/history.html

resources to achieve economies of scale. IRG comprises a network of established ratings companies, Global Credit Rating Co. (GCR) in South Africa, Pacific Credit Rating Co. (PCR), which has offices in six Latin American countries with plans to open offices in five more, and JCR-VIS Credit Rating Co. Ltd (JCR-VIS) in Pakistan. The companies operate under the umbrella brand of IRG. The group specializes in emerging markets, which GCR Chairman Dave King pointed out are 'fundamentally different to the developed markets in the US and Western Europe.'[80]

8.2   INDUSTRY SPECIFICS AND HOW THEY AFFECT COMPETITION

In this section we analyze the factors affecting the competitive structure of the industry.

8.2.1   Agencies Compete for the Market rather than in the Market

Credit Ratings are Experience Goods

A credit rating is a benchmark probability of default, at a given point in time, conditional on the information possessed by the rater. So before buying a rating, or even at the time the rating is issued, market participants cannot really assess the quality of the prediction. They can just assess the general reasoning behind the rating action and the methodology used. Unlike sweaters, you cannot test how good a rating fits before paying for it. You can only look in the mirror when the issue has come to maturity. Therefore, by definition it is a good, whose quality is only revealed over time. We can only have a more precise idea of the accuracy ex-post once we have the information of whether it defaulted or not. Even then, this measure of quality is very rough. Statistically, the quality of a rating, say a Moody's Baa1, can only be measured using large enough samples of different issues rated Baa1 by Moody's over time, and by comparing the benchmark probabilities of default associated with Baa1 with the realized frequencies of default over time. One could also compare benchmark probabilities of default with realized frequencies of default across firms. But generally, users of ratings will have to form beliefs concerning the quality of a rating. These beliefs are constantly updated as new ratings are produced and default-like events occur. The formation and update of these beliefs constitute an agency's reputation capital. And vice-versa: the reputation of a firm forms the beliefs that are held by the users of ratings.

As producers of experience goods, reputation is the crucial competitive advantage that an agency needs to build. The value of a rating to the market will depend on the reputation of the agency producing it. How investors perceive the quality (accuracy of estimate) of a rating determines the benefit of that rating to the issuer, in terms of improving its cost of debt, i.e. it needs an unbiased rating that reflects its credit risk efficiently.

Certainly incumbent firms with a strong reputation will have an advantage compared to relatively unknown agencies or entrants. Moreover, the greater volume of ratings and the longer track-record will give incumbents an early-mover advantage.[81] However, reputation

---

[80] IRG, 2006. 'Regional Rating Agencies Announce Formation of International Ratings Group,' IRG press release, February 22, 2006.
[81] McDaniel, R.W., President of Moody's Investors Service, 2005. Examining the role of credit rating agencies in the capital markets, Testimony before the US Senate Committee on Banking, Housing, and Urban Affairs, February 8, 1–14, page 11.

is a capital that can depreciate. It would be very interesting to study the impact on market shares after a given agency 'fails to predict' default-related events. This would give an idea of how strong the market discipline is on CRAs.

Switching Costs Limit the Number of CRAs in a Market

Investors will form and update their beliefs concerning the reputation of an agency and its ratings in different segments. Also, investors need to translate a rating on an ordinal scale into the type of risks they are willing to take. In some sense, ratings from a given CRA provide investors with a common language or standard to interpret credit risk. Switching from one language to another is costly. As we described in Chapter 3, investors will desire consistency and comparability in credit opinions. So for a given agency's reputation, the more widely its ratings are used and accepted by market participants, the greater the utility of its ratings to investors, and therefore issuers. Bond portfolio managers look for complete coverage of investment opportunities. Portfolio sponsors want to be in good company when setting portfolio constraints. Hence the network externality characteristic associated with ratings. S&P, Moody's, and Fitch have become *de facto* dominant standards in the credit rating markets. However, dominant firm reversals in industries with network effects exist, and there are several mitigating factors in this industry that increase the chances of a given market tipping in favor of a new entrant. We will see in a later section the strategies that can be used to unseat a dominant player.

Issuers will value the ratings of companies that investors value. The agency that is most trusted at removing information asymmetry should normally improve its spread most. However, besides switching costs for investors, there are also direct switching costs for issuers. Issuers build a trust relationship with just one or two CRAs. Fundamental credit analysis involves valuable CEO and executive management time as well as the exchange of sensitive information. There is a sunk cost involved in starting a rating process with a new agency. Moreover, the marginal benefit to an issuer from having an extra rating on a given issue decreases substantially with the number of ratings. Indeed, once information asymmetry is lifted through a rating, the remaining asymmetry is very small; however, CRAs still incur the same marginal cost (and charge the same fee) for producing a rating, even when that issue has already been rated by a competitor.

Because of the switching costs for both investors and issuers, it is unlikely that the market for credit ratings can sustain a large number of agencies in each segment. However, as we have seen, the industry is segmented along several dimensions, giving some room for specialized firms.

Other Barriers to Entry and Early-Mover Advantages

As we have seen above, some intrinsic characteristics result in barriers to entry in the credit rating industry. But there are others, some exogenous, such as the ones created by regulations, and some endogenous. Endogenous barriers to entry are those that incumbents build in order to protect themselves and maintain their dominance.

REGULATIONS   Credit ratings are used in several regulations and, since recognition systems exist to determine which CRAs' ratings are eligible in applying regulations, this use of ratings influences competition in the industry. As an example, we discuss below the US recognition system, as it was in effect until mid-2007. Although the NRSRO status is now granted in a more transparent way, without any tacit market share criteria, the status is still in many regulations and has greatly affected the competitive dynamics and structure of the industry.

Since 1975, the US Securities and Exchange Commission (SEC) relied on ratings from market-recognized, credible rating agencies to distinguish between grades of creditworthiness in various regulations under federal securities laws. The SEC granted or refused 'Nationally Recognized Statistical Rating Organization,' or NRSRO, status, and recognized it through the no-action letter process.[82]

NRSRO status and the exclusive recognition of NRSRO ratings for particular purposes have restricted competition in the industry. Entrance to several lines of rating agency activity are clearly influenced by the SEC's control over NRSRO status, and, under most ratings-dependent regulations in the US the only ratings that matter are those issued by an NRSRO.

Fitch, Moody's, and S&P received the initial NRSRO status in 1975. Since then, several rating agencies have entered the sector and achieved the requisite level of market recognition to be designated NRSRO. However, each of these NRSROs was subsequently acquired by or merged into another NRSRO, with the result that, until February 2003, there were only three NRSROs. In February 2003, Dominion Bond Ratings Service was awarded NRSRO designation, bringing the total number of NRSROs up to four. In March 2005, a fifth rating agency, A.M. Best Company, Inc., was designated under the old NRSRO status.

The principal test which the SEC applies to grant NRSRO status, is that the agency be 'nationally recognized by the predominant users of ratings in the United States as an issuer of credible and reliable ratings.'[83] This means in effect that the capital markets – arguably the toughest and most competitive market anywhere – must 'already place substantial weight on the judgment of the rating agency,' and leads to something akin to a 'chicken and egg' problem for agencies wishing to obtain NRSRO status, which they view as necessary or, at a minimum, very important for becoming a substantial presence in the industry.[84] This clearly favors incumbents and acts as a substantial barrier to entry for new rating agencies.[85] The SEC has acknowledged this, but is grappling with how exactly to open up the market since users of credit ratings and others point out that there must be substantive threshold standards for achieving NRSRO status for that term to have meaning.[86]

Are the extraordinary shareholder results for Moody's until late 2006 due to the NRSRO factor? Some, certainly; but generally, NRSRO status is just a partial explanation for CRA industry concentration. The industry was concentrated before NRSRO was introduced in

[82] US Securities and Exchange Commission, 2003. Report on the role and function of credit rating agencies in the operation of the securities market, January, 1–45, page 5.
[83] US Securities and Exchange Commission, 1994. Nationally Recognized Statistical Rating Organizations, August 31, File No. S7-23-94, 1–12.
[84] Cantor, R. and Packer, F., 1994. The credit rating industry, Quarterly Review: Federal Reserve Bank of New York, Summer-Fall, 1–26, page 8.
[85] Basel Committee on Banking Supervision, 1999. A new capital adequacy framework: a consultative paper, Bank for International Settlements, Basel, June, 1–62, proposes as criteria for recognition as an eligible external credit assessment institution: objectivity, independence, transparency, credibility, international access and resources and the possession of a track record, pages 29–35.
[86] Nazareth, A.L., Director, Division of Market Regulation – U.S. Securities and Exchange Commission, 2003. Rating the rating agencies: the state of transparency and competition, Testimony before the House Subcommittee on Capital Markets, Insurance, and Government Sponsored Enterprises, Committee on Financial Services, April 2, 1–8.

1975. Concentration exists today in the EU, where NRSRO does not apply. Concentration is largely due to the reputation and networking first mover's advantages that benefits incumbents. The NRSRO status, as it had been defined until September 2006, has reinforced this tendency; it has not created it, as is sometimes claimed.[87]

LEARNING CURVE   Another advantage that incumbents have over entrants is that they have more experience in producing credit ratings and hence have learned how to do so more efficiently. The credit rating's black box becomes a very efficient machine once the process has been viewed, corrected, and reviewed over time. This is the learning curve advantage, whereby firms' average costs decrease as they accumulate experience and knowledge in a given market. According to this, all else being equal, incumbents should have lower average costs. Of course, if the knowledge of the efficient process is embedded in a handful of analysts and directors, these could always be hired away by a new entrant in the industry, so this advantage will only be sustainable as long as incumbent CRAs are able to retain their analysts.

INSTALLED BASE AND THE CASE FOR UNSOLICITED RATINGS   DBRS – New rating agencies will have difficulty getting started without doing unsolicited ratings or at least doing benchmark reports. These ratings are not done by new CRAs to put pressure on entities to obtain solicited ratings, but to start up operations or to gain exposure to new markets. Today, DBRS has a general policy to stay out of unsolicited ratings if at all possible, but DBRS started by doing over 100 unsolicited ratings. Despite present opinions with respect to our involvement in unsolicited ratings, DBRS would never have been created, had it not been able to do unsolicited ratings at the start.[88]

Agencies benefit by establishing themselves as a standard and by building a reputation that is continuously evaluated by investors through an up-to-date, dense track record. They should therefore actively seek to increase this track record, as it can positively enhance their reputation, help them to develop expertise in a segment, and preempt other firms by locking in investors and issuers who are unwilling to switch agency. This should encourage agencies to race for an installed base of clients, especially in growing segments. One way of doing this is by providing unsolicited ratings.[89] Unsolicited ratings are a sunk cost. They can be viewed as the industry equivalent of advertising or distributing free software, and are necessary for entrants to be able to credibly challenge incumbents. This is what we mean by agencies competing for the market rather than in the market. They tend to focus on capturing a whole market by going for volume and establishing a strong reputation, rather than competing fiercely for each individual issue and taking the risk of compromising their reputation or providing individual fee discounts.

Exhaustive reliable evidence for unsolicited ratings is difficult to find. We know that they have been used extensively in the aggregate and they have been used by all issuer-pays rating agencies, including the three global ones. Until the 1970s, all ratings were

---

[87] The standard reference for the regulatory license view of credit ratings is Partnoy, F., 1999. The Siskel and Ebert of financial markets?: Two thumbs down for the credit rating agencies, *Washington University Law Quarterly*, Vol. 77, No. 3, 619–715.

[88] Schroeder, W.J., CFA, President – Dominion Bond Rating Service, 2001. DBRS Response to the January 2001 Basel Committee on banking supervision draft, May 28, 1–5.

[89] Unsolicited ratings are also discussed in section 4.2.1. on the rating action. Agencies also refer to unsolicited ratings as public information ratings, because it is often the case. However, it happens that some unsolicited ratings contain private information and some public information ratings are actually solicited.

unsolicited, because all ratings were delivered under the investor-pays model, and this also corresponds to the publisher status protected by the right of free press in the US.

The practice of unsolicited ratings does not seem to have had as much bad press in the US as in Europe. For instance S&P almost systematically rates all US debt without bad publicity. All major agencies have used unsolicited ratings to penetrate the European market, with varying amounts of negative publicity. Fitch has probably issued the most unsolicited ratings, thanks to which investors now consider it as an acceptable alternative to the S&P–Moody's duopoly. Unsolicited ratings have had especially bad press during the reform of CRA regulations and in the light of potential conflicts of interest in the aftermath of the auditors' roles in the major corporate bankruptcies. However, in this industry, unsolicited ratings should really be considered as a necessary tool for entering competitors to have a chance at entering the market at all.

8.2.2 The Business Model and Profit Drivers

As we saw in Chapter 3, direct demand for ratings comes from both investors and issuers, and both are willing to pay for them. CRAs are formally independent from both parties. In the following, we discuss CRAs' business models and the drivers of price, mark-up, volume, and cost.

The Business Model

There are two pricing models prevalent among rating agencies today. One is the subscription-based model, where users such as institutional investors and broker-dealers are charged for ratings. The other, followed by the old NRSROs, is the issuer-pays pricing model. Here, although traditionally the primary commitment of the agencies is to the investment community, they are primarily paid by the issuers whose securities they rate.

Prior to 1970, all agencies provided ratings free of charge to issuers and sold their publications to investors for a fee. The subscribers-pay model however, turned out to be unsustainable. While it guaranteed the agencies independence from the issuer being rated, it did not provide sufficient revenues to support their operations, since the publications could easily be copied. During the US recession of 1970, the dynamics of the industry changed. The railroad company Penn Central defaulted on US$82 million of commercial paper obligations. The commercial paper market had grown quickly in the 1960s, with little regard for credit quality. If a borrower was well known, he could easily tap the short-term commercial paper market. When Penn defaulted, the creditworthiness of many sound companies was questioned and investors stopped rolling over their short-term paper. This prompted a liquidity crisis and more defaults. Issuers became willing to pay for a rating in order to demonstrate to the market that they were a sound credit. With the demand for ratings rising, the rating agencies found themselves able to charge a fee for their services. This practice grew to the point where, by 1987, nearly 80% of S&P's revenues came from issuer fees.[90] The balance came from selling research and ratings information to large institutional investors, corporations, and libraries.

The justification for charging issuers is two-fold. Firstly, issuers receive substantial value through the publication of independent ratings that gives them access to public debt markets

---

[90] Ederington, L.H., Roberts, B.E., and Yawitz, J.B., 1987, The informational content of bond ratings, *Journal of Financial Research*, Fall, Vol. 10, No. 3, 211–226, page 12.

and improve the cost of capital. Secondly, rating agencies need these revenues to be able to sustain the costs of their activity.

While both issuers and investors rely on ratings, issuers have a higher willingness-to-pay than investors. This is due to two attributes of ratings for investors: non-excludability of rating information and redundance of any specific rating. Firstly, it is impossible to exclude any investor from the knowledge of a credit rating once it has become available to some investors. An investor cannot 'consume' a rating, knowledge is a non-depletable good in the sense that a rating will still exist once an investor has bought the information, but even more than that, the investor will not be able to exclude any other investor from this information, as most of it will be transferred through the pricing of the rated issue in question. A 'bulk' ratings subscription service that covers the universe that the subscriber specifies could be highly valuable for investors. Unfortunately, such a service is impractical because of the expectation that a rating action on any specific instrument will become simultaneously available to all investors through public dissemination. Because ratings are publicly disseminated, investors do not need to purchase ratings, as they are freely available.

Secondly, the same rating that may be 'required' for an issuer is rather 'redundant' for the investor. There is a substantial difference between issuers and investors in their need for a rating on any single debt instrument. The rating of a particular bond promotes its broad marketability and is therefore valuable for the issuer. But investors can select from a wide range of alternative bonds and are, therefore, more interested in the general existence and application of ratings than in any individual rating. If, for example, a rating is not assigned to a particular bond, in most cases an investor's motivation to request and pay for a rating on that bond is low, even if it were the only investor to have this information. There are many other rated bonds or investment opportunities that the investor can choose from. For issuers it is more interesting to pay for the rating themselves and have access to a much broader investor base than not pay for the rating and have only a couple of investors invest in the issue and split the total amount of the corresponding fee schedule; which they would not even be willing to do because of the automatic dissemination of the rating information.

Summing up, a rating is a public good in the economic sense that it is non-depletable once it is produced and made available, and that it is difficult to exclude anyone from its consumption. Combining the public availability of ratings with the relative indifference of investors toward any single rating, it follows that investors can benefit from ratings by consuming them without a compelling need to support the cost-base that produces them. Ratings become a free good. An issuer does not have the same tolerance as an investor for missing a rating on its bond. It does not have the same range of choices in accessing capital that an investor has in deploying capital. In order for an issuer to make its bonds marketable, it will probably choose to have that bond rated.

So where does the subscription-based model apply? Credit rating agencies that use market implied ratings rather than fundamental credit analysis, based mostly on public information, use investor subscriptions as unique source of income. The reason for this is that the cost of producing a market implied rating is much lower than that of a fundamental credit rating. Because the market segment for fundamental credit ratings is the dominating one, we focus on this business model and profit drivers. In Section 6.2.3 we discuss the complementarity between market-implied ratings and traditional credit ratings.

Fee Schedule Drivers

In the issuer-pays pricing model, the fees that are charged by the agencies vary according to the size and type of security being analyzed. A typical up-front fee on a new long-term corporate bond issue ranges between 4 and 5 bps of the principal amount. Thus a typical fee for a US$200 million 10-year bond issue would be somewhere in the range of US$80 000 to $100 000. Frequent issuers (companies issuing rated securities more than five or six times per year) often receive negotiated rates based on the total value of issuance.[91] In addition, more complex securities generally carry higher fees since the rating agency must spend considerably more time and due diligence rating a complex structured finance transaction, as opposed to a plain vanilla bond issue from a regular issuer.

An assessment of the fee schedules of the three main CRAs shows that the fee for a long-term bond rating typically consists of an up-front initial fee, that is generally a fixed percentage of the amount of the debt issue (with stated maximum and minimum fees), and an annual surveillance fee. Commercial paper and medium-term notes have separate fee schedules. Fees are mostly similar across the three major agencies, with Fitch being somewhat lower. Table 8.3 shows Moody's fee schedule for 2000 and 2007, suggesting the following observations.

Firstly, rating fees that depend on the value of the debt issue imply that the total fees paid increase with the volume of debt. It is unlikely that CRAs have costs that increase commensurately with the size of the issue even though more of their reputation capital is at stake and their legal exposure increases. It seems more likely that issuers' willingness to pay for a rating increases with the size of the issue. We identified some of the main benefits from getting a rating in Section 3.1.1, as lowering the cost of debt, increasing the liquidity in the trading of the issue, and getting access to a much broader investor base. These three benefits certainly increase with the size of the issue probably at least in a linear way. Hence, this fee schedule is also consistent with second-degree price discrimination, according to which a firm (here the CRA) will extract more rents from the buyer of its service (here the issuer) as its willingness to pay increases. This is typical of industries with a certain degree of market power.

Table 8.3 Moody's fee schedule for long term debt for corporates in Europe (2000 and 2007).

Moody's (€)	2007	2000
Bond rating	Initial fee 43 500[a] 4.5 bp on initial 500 mn Additional 3 bp for issues over 500 mn Min of 43 500 Max of 372 000 Surveillance 25 300	Initial fee 23 750[a] 3.25 bp on initial 473 mn Additional 2 bp for issues over 500 mn Min of 23 750 Max of 189 000 nil

Sources: Moody's Investors Service, 2000, Moody's Rating Fee Guide – Corporates, January, 1–3; Moody's Investors Service, 2007, Fee Guide for Per Issue Fees, January, 1–2.
[a](The initial fee is for a first issue with Moody's only.)

[91] S&P has a frequent issuer program whereby issuers who come to market more than five or six times per year may pay a flat yearly fee for unlimited ratings advisory service. No further information regarding such programs or tariff levels is available since the rating agencies consider such information to be proprietary.

A second observation is the significant increase in fees over the years 2001–2007, a period during which the practices of CRAs were called into question. A survey conducted in 2004 by the Association of Finance Professionals found that 52% of financial professionals indicated that the cost of credit ratings had increased by at least 11% over the previous three years, including 19% of respondents indicating that costs had increased by at least 25% over that time period.[92,93] These observations point toward the low bargaining power of buyers. The three major CRAs are predominant. Their ratings are almost universally required by issuers for access to institutional investors.

However, these observations have to be mitigated by two other facts. At the end, the credit rating cost is small relative to the total issuing cost, and relative to total company costs they are minuscule. It is, however, a source of irritation for treasurers because CRA invoices are important in their operating budget, and CRAs charge increasingly for every service rendered and are stiff in sticking to their fee schedules. Interviews with the Association of Corporate Treasurers revealed that there is in effect really little scope for bargaining and negotiation. Treasurers dealing with agencies are dependent on the rating, and at the same time feel that the pricing is not necessarily proportional to the agencies' costs. Issuers would, a priori, feel more comfortable with a fee based on the agency's time, more like typical lawyer or consultant services. We further discuss why the current type of fee structure may be efficient in the section on the price–cost margin.

Another important fact to keep in mind is that the agencies have been under a lot of scrutiny and pressure over the last seven years after the major bankruptcies in the US and Europe, as regulatory reform was under way. In addition to the publication of strict codes of conduct, agencies have internally developed major initiatives like transparency initiatives to increase the transparency of the rating process, of methodologies, of revealing potential conflicts; quality initiatives, and especially quality of governance initiatives and forensic accounting initiatives. Even if the initiatives have not been sufficient to guard markets earlier against the subprime crisis agencies' costs have increased over the last five to seven. This is an efficient reason to increase fees as it is directly linked with an expected increase of quality of ratings.

Other Sources of CRA Revenue

Today, CRAs provide a host of services apart from credit ratings. These include risk solutions to help corporations and financial institutions to manage their credit exposures, research and indices on mutual, insurance and pension funds, data services on corporations, securities, indices and funds.

As noted in the overall revenue charts in Section 8.1.3, while ratings continue to form the bulk of rating agency revenues (80% for Moody's and 90% for Fitch), those other products, including research and analytical products, are growing faster than the rating products. This product diversification is thus reducing the dependence of rating agency revenues on debt issuance trends. Overseas operations have similarly reduced dependence

---

[92] The Association for Financial Professionals (AFP) represents more than 14 000 finance and treasury professionals representing more than 5000 organizations.

[93] Kaitz, J.A., President and Chief Executive Officer – the Association of Finance Professionals, 2005, Testimony before the Committee on Banking, Housing, and Urban Affairs, United State Senate, February 8, 1–24, page 3.

on domestic debt issuance. Morgan Stanley equity research analysts comment on Moody's for Q1 of 2005,

> First quarter results speak to the diversity of Moody's revenue basis and our belief that interest rates and new debt issuance trends are not the sole drivers of growth at Moody's. For example, the Corporate Finance revenue was up 9.5%. despite a 20%+ drop in corporate issuance in the US Revenue from overseas, bank loan ratings, and enhanced analytical products more than offset softness in ratings revenue for US corporates.

The Price–Cost Margin

We do not have a direct measure of the price–cost margin. Measures of prices can be observed through the fee schedules but true marginal costs are difficult to determine. We do know that most of the marginal costs per rating (additional costs incurred for each additional rating) are driven by analyst labor time. Moody's 2004 accounts show that operating, general, and administrative expenses represented 94.9% of expenses, of which compensation amounted to about 71%. As financial products become more sophisticated and more specific, the labor market for analysts also becomes tighter, and CRAs compete with investment banks for high-quality analysts who are not only more and more specialized and quantitative, but are also required to have a solid background in business and economics. Competencies have become much more specific with the segmentization of the industry, and the profile of an expert in sovereign ratings will be very different from that of an expert in structured finance. Overall, analyst compensation is relatively high even though there is a discount in the base salaries compared to similar competencies in an investment bank; but the major difference lies in the bonuses. Credit analysts are totally disconnected with the commercial aspect of issues. They have no incentives related to the commercial aspect of a rating in stark contrast to investment banks' high-powered incentive schemes. A major credit analyst that changes agency does not bring with him issuers and issues he has been following. Credit analysts' bonuses are driven by individual performance of the ratings and overall firm performance. Certainly, analysts leave CRAs and move to investment banks when they recruit aggressively and the bonuses are high. Generally, credit analysts seem to enjoy working in rating agencies rather than banking because they value the less commercial, more collegial and academic corporate culture. Given that fees do not seem to vary with market conditions (other than the deeper trend of fee increases) and that credit analysts' salaries increase when the issuing volume is high, CRA margins may be slightly countercyclical.

We have previously seen that the bargaining power of issuers is low with respect to CRAs. This is not surprising because issuers have very few close substitutes to getting a rating in many markets. In the most mature markets, where two ratings per issue is the norm, issuers do not seriously consider issuing without a credit rating; this would be a negative signal to the market with respect to the quality of the issue and hence would be too costly. Distant substitutes would be a bank loan, or raising equity or convertible debt, but these options are very limited, generally less flexible, and more expensive. CRAs thus still have some leeway in terms of pricing before issuers move away from them.

Fees do not vary much with characteristics of issuers, issues, and market timing (i.e. volume and utilization rates of rating analysts). They rather vary in a simple, predictable and observable way. For most goods, it is the pricing mechanism that allows supply to meet demand in an efficient way. Generally prices vary with the essential characteristics of the goods that affect its production costs and the buyer's willingness to pay for these characteristics. Hence one expects prices to vary with these characteristics. Here the pricing mechanism is a simple posted pricing rule, which does not mean that the price–cost margin does not vary across issues, on the contrary. Two issues of the same type of bond, with the same issuing volume, issued with the same rating can have very different costs in terms of analyst time spent on the issue, depending for instance on the issuer's industry. The main advantage of this relatively simple pricing rule is that it decreases transaction costs as it reduces the scope for negotiation and the role of prices as an adjustment variable. Certainly one could see that transaction costs are decreased this way. But another point that came out from several interviews with market participants, other than the agencies themselves, is that it adds distance in the relationship between the issuer and the agency from the commercial aspect. The risk expressed is that allowing for price negotiation would be like opening a 'can of worms' or conflicts of interest. The simple pricing rule can be viewed as a commitment mechanism not to enter into lengthy negotiation and adjusting the rating agency's service as a function of the negotiation. We believe that the lack of a simple public pricing rule in the structured finance market has contributed to the loosening of standards and conduct inside the rating agencies.

Volume

INDUSTRY VOLUME DRIVERS   Since the amount of rating fees generated is linked to the size of a bond issue, debt issuance trends significantly affect the ratings revenues of the CRAs. Revenues are thus affected by the factors that affect issuance volumes. We examine below the three main trends that affect debt issuance, and thus ratings revenues.

A low interest rate scenario favors new issuance, as borrowers make use of the opportunity to borrow at low costs. For instance, rising interest rates in the US in the second half of 2004 led to a decline of 27% in issuance of asset-backed securities, while the same grew in Europe by 10.2% due to the accommodative interest rate policy. For corporate borrowers, the spreads over treasury yields also affect new bond issuance. Higher spreads increase borrowing costs, and provide higher return to investors, with the same amount of investments leading to a dual negative impact on bond issuance. Spreads are affected by a combination of credit quality and economic conditions.

Good economic conditions encourage expansionary business activities and the consequent use of debt to finance it. In addition, economic growth increases investor confidence, which reduces risk premia and thus corporate spreads, encouraging new bond issuance, which in turn increases the demand for ratings. On the other hand, economic downturn and volatility increases investor demand for assurances on credit quality, which in turn results in a need for credit ratings.

Credit quality is typically measured by default rates, downgrade ratios (ratio of down-grades to total rating actions), and outlooks in watchlists. Credit quality deterioration negatively affects investors' appetite for risk and vice versa. Moreover, as noted above, a slowdown in deterioration of credit quality reduces corporate spreads, which in turn raises new bond issuance and therefore the demand for ratings.

AGENCY SPECIFIC VOLUME DRIVERS   The most important predictor of agency-specific vol-ume drivers, in segments other than structured finance, is a CRA's installed base in that segment. It results directly from the reputation that the agency has built, and comprises sophisticated and unsophisticated investors' beliefs concerning the quality of the CRA's ratings. Installed base, or the number past issues and issues outstanding rated, depends on a dense performance track record, and this track record can be affected by unsolicited ratings. This may explain how Fitch was able to build up demand for its ratings, as it produces unsolicited ratings that are highly researched, probably thanks to a low number of issuers followed per analyst. Market shares in structured finance seem to depend less on installed base. We believe that there are two main reasons for this. One is the fact that each structured finance transaction is akin an initial rating because each SPV is created specifically for a transaction. There is no large switching cost for an issuer of a structured finance transaction as there could be for a corporation that switches rating agency. The second one is that issuers in structured finance are known for a practice known as ratings shopping. Ratings shopping is prevalent in structured finance because the issuer expects to capture the return from shopping, whereas for corporate debt investors understand the differences in approach of the agencies sufficiently to reflect them in the spreads. It is as if investors understood the methodology so well that, disregarding which rating agency is selected, the issuer ends-up with the same spread. Whereas in structured finance 'If the market does not wholly understand the differences between the two approaches, [], CDO issuers may be able to lower funding costs by strategic selection of which agency to employ for which type of tranche.'[94]

Average Costs and Fixed Costs

Other than the unsolicited ratings and installed base, the fixed costs associated with setting up as a CRA are relatively low, and are essentially composed of establishing offices and creating an initial network of contacts, which requires management time and overhead.

Given the increasing specialization of the industry and products, there are fixed costs associated with entering a segment that requires investing in specific tools and training. Some segments, such as general corporate issues, are likely to be less specialized than structured finance transactions and sovereign ratings.

There are some economies of scope, whereby the average costs of credit analysis in two related products are certainly lower than the sum of the average costs that two separate agencies would incur to analyze credit risk in these products separately. An illustration of this is that Fitch systematically has a credit analyst participate in rating reviews outside their domain of expertise. It is not clear how these economies of scope are likely to vary, given the increasing specialization of the industry. Increasingly, CRAs are organized in separate divisions according to product specificities and analysts are encouraged to develop a domain of expertise.

Economies of scale certainly exist if you consider the average costs of analyzing issues from the same issuer. Once you have rated an issuer and one or two issues, the cost of producing a rating on a third issue will certainly be smaller, which explains why rating agencies are keen on locking their issuers into a long-term relationship.

---

[94] *The citation refers to the expected loss versus the probability of default approach, but the principle can be extended to other methodological differences and mis-understandings by the market.* Pereytatkin, V., Perraudin, W., 2003, Expected loss and probability of default approaches to rating collateralised debt obligations and the scope for 'ratings shopping', Credit Ratings, methodologies, rationale and default risk, ed. M.K. Ong, Risk Books, 495–506, page 496.

8.2.3   Some Dynamic Aspects of Competition among CRAs: A Small Number of Players can be Consistent with Intense Rivalry

Reputation, installed base, and network effects feed into a greater demand for ratings and reinforce an *incumbent's first-mover advantages.* So clearly, establishing a brand name is one of the critical factors in building a successful CRA. Both S&P and Moody's have been able to leverage their reputation capital, acquired in the US capital markets, to build market share in Europe, Asia, and Latin America in recent years.

There are high barriers to entry in the industry but lower mobility barriers within the industry and across segments. Incumbents can leverage their reputation and expertise advantage into complementary goods and segments. But to some extent so can specialized firms on the fringe. How difficult it is for specialized fringe firms to enter neighboring segments remains to be investigated. The case of DBRS and how it entered the European financial institutions market, provides an interesting example.

DBRS already has an impressive rating coverage on North American financial institutions – both in the United States and in Canada. Now, in addition to North America, we are focusing our skills on rating European banking entities and keeping investors apprised of pertinent market activities here.

Based on our global expansion, early this summer DBRS started to publish its first ratings and research on various European financial institutions. We rate their deposits and the full panoply of securities: medium-term notes, commercial paper, various categories of subordinated debt and hybrids, as well as, going forward, covered bonds. These are [given in Example 8.1]:[95]

Example 8.1

Germany	Hypo Real Estate Group; WestLB
Ireland	Anglo Irish Bank; International Securities Trading Corporation
Netherlands	ABN AMRO Bank
Norway	DnB NOR
Spain	Banco Popular; Caixa Catalunya; Caja Madrid
Switzerland	Credit Suisse
United Kingdom	Barclays Plc

In an industry where installed base is such a crucial driver of agency-specific demand for ratings, the existence of market segments with high growth rates is of crucial importance for competition. Rapidly developing macroeconomic factors and trends such as globalization and structuring are a real opportunity for the fringe. Investment in unsolicited ratings should show a high return if it increases an agency's installed base beyond a certain tipping point, so the harshest battles for an installed base would be expected in new and strongly growing segments. This is what has been observed in the structured finance area, with the anticompetitive complaints concerning the practice of 'notching' and a loosening of diligence and procedures in a fight amongst the rating agencies to become the dominant agency or standard in all and each of the segments in the rapidly expanding structured finance area.

---

[95] Dominion Bond Rating Service, 2006, DBRS *New European Banking Weekly*, October 5, Issue 1. DBRS was forced to close its offices in Europe early 2008, as a result of the subprime crisis, but the rating of European financial institutions still remains.

Other successful growth and entry strategies would be mergers and acquisitions to reach critical size and enter new markets. The advantage for users of ratings here is that investor and issuer switching costs are internalized in the new CRA. When two rating agencies merge, they have to merge their rating scales and procedures. In other words, it is the merged agency, and not the investors, that translate both rating scales and methodologies in a common one. And obviously, mergers help entrant firms, in that they reduce the number of competitors. This strategy has made the success of Fitch whether in the US or overseas.

Another strategy is to include products, like Moody's KMV, within the same agency. These are complements not substitutes, and enhance an agency's overall reputation and visibility among investors who use KMV products. Not least, continuously innovating and remaining at the cutting edge of credit analysis research is essential to be able to compete, it can also become an advantage if an agency creates a valuable, unique innovation.

The distorting effect of NRSRO status is expected to be reduced since the Credit Rating Agency Reform Act of 2006 came into force in 2007. It is discussed extensively in Chapter 9.

It is true that S&P and Moody's have historically dominated the credit rating industry. However, there is no doubt that the rating agency business is slowly becoming more competitive. The advent of Fitch as a global rating agency and true alternative to S&P and Moody's is the compelling illustration of this. This can be seen by the fact that CRAs are moving into one another's turf and launching new products in an effort to increase revenues. For example, the agencies have followed each other in introducing rating advisory services, which allow issuers and financial advisers to get 'a more definitive response' to inquiries on the ratings impact of big corporate events or recovery ratings.

8.3 INDUSTRY PERFORMANCE

8.3.1 Performance for CRA Shareholders

The value that CRAs add to their shareholders is a critical component of their business model and profit drivers. In corporate finance, we teach that it is hard to generate sustainable, valuable free cash flows that translate into shareholder' value without competitive products and services that satisfied clients are willing to purchase at a good price. Growth in revenues and in shareholder value could thus be key indicators of CRAs' business model and value-added.

Aggregated credit rating revenues of Fitch, Moody's, and S&P grew at a compounded annual growth rate of 17% during 1998–2005, reaching $4.9 billion.

What about free cash flow generation, profitability, and shareholder value creation? Since September 20, 2000, Moody's has been listed on the NYSE. It is the only pure credit rating company the stock market 'plays.' The results of Fitch's and S&P's credit rating business are confounded with those of other lines of business for parent companies Fimalac and McGraw-Hill, respectively, and thus harder to observe. So we are obliged to focus on Moody's.

For the period 2000–2004, Moody's reported average ROA of over 45% per year and average growth in EPS of around 25% per year. Figure 8.13 shows that, through 2005, the company repurchased stock worth about $1.5 billion and reached a stock market capitalization of around $18 billion, more than quadrupling its $4 billion IPO value. Until late 2007, Moody's was a real free cash-flow generating engine, and financial analysts describe it as one of the best performing stocks in the business services/publishing sector.

It is unclear to what extent Moody's performance is typical of a CRA. Figure 8.14 shows the stock price evolution of Fimalac, McGraw-Hill, and Moody's, and some indices from October 2000 through October 2007.

Is Moody's credit rating business really outperforming Fitch (a business line of Fimalac) and S&P (a business line of McGraw-Hill)? Hearst's acquisition of a 20% minority stake in Fitch Group from Fimalac SA shows that it is performing at a very comparable level. The agreement was signed in March 2006, and the deal value for 20% was based on a Fitch Group enterprise value of US$ 4.4 billion, which was itself derived by applying a Moody's multiple of 17-fold to the Fitch Ratings EBITDA.

Figure 8.13 and Figure 8.14 confirm that CRAs have been able to capture their share of the value created through the tremendous global growth of the credit market and structured finance transactions. CRAs have kept up for a while with the growing markets, increased their fees and probably kept their costs under control, but unfortunately it seems like they have not been able to invest sufficiently in their analysts, in innovating, and maintaining timely and high-quality service to issuers and investors in the structured finance segment. They have been struggling to adapt their rating and management processes to the extremely rapid rate of innovation.

8.3.2 Performance of Ratings as a Public Good

Serving Issuers or Investors?

It is often argued that CRAs have a clear conflict of interest because they serve two masters: the investors and the issuers. Investors want the ratings to be objective and useful for making inferences about default probability and loss in the event of default. Issuers want the ratings

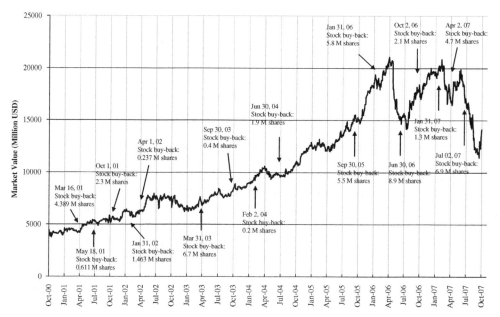

Figure 8.13 Moody's market capitalization and share buy-backs (2000–2007).
Source: Thomson Datastream.

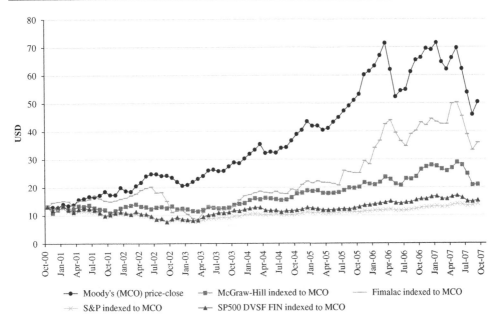

Figure 8.14 Stock price evolution of Fimalac, McGraw-Hill, and Moody's and some indices (2000–2007).
Source: Thomson Datastream.

to be favorable in order to decrease their cost of capital and increase their access to capital markets. Since the issuers supply the rating agencies with most of their revenue in fees, a conflict seems to exist. It is even possible that public listings of ratings businesses (first Moody's and then Fitch) may increase the conflict of interest by shifting the emphasis to commercial gains, rather than the provision of a 'public good.' Despite this apparent conflict, however, the payment arrangements have not eroded the credibility of the agencies in the traditional segments and many argue before the subprime mortgage crisis:

> While the current payment structure may appear to encourage agencies to assign higher ratings to satisfy issuers, the agencies have an overriding incentive to maintain a reputation for high-quality, accurate ratings...Over the years, the discipline provided by reputation considerations appears to have been effective, with no major scandals in the ratings industry of which we are aware.[96]

The 2002 SEC hearings agreed:

> In general, hearing participants did not believe that reliance by rating agencies on issuer fees leads to significant conflicts of interest or otherwise calls into question the overall objectivity of credit ratings. While the issuer-fee model naturally creates the potential for conflict of interest and ratings inflation, most were of the view that this conflict is manageable and, for the most part, has been effectively addressed by the credit rating agencies. The rating agencies take the position that their reputation for issuing objective and credible ratings is of paramount

---

[96] Cantor, R., and Packer, F., 1994, The credit rating industry, *Quarterly Review*: Federal Reserve Bank of New York, Summer-Fall, 1–26, page 4.

importance, and that they would be loathe to jeopardize that reputation to mollify a particular issuer.[97] Furthermore, the rating agencies have implemented a number of policies and procedures designed to assure the independence and objectivity of the ratings process, such as requiring ratings decisions to be made by a ratings committee, imposing investment restrictions, and adhering to fixed fee schedules. In addition, they assert that rating analyst compensation is merit-based (e.g. based on the demonstrated accuracy of their ratings), and is not dependent on the level of fees paid by issuers the analyst rates. While most hearing participants agreed that, for the most part, the rating agencies had effectively managed this potential conflict, they stressed the importance of credit rating agencies implementing stringent firewalls, independent compensation, and other related procedures.[98]

So, while the agencies are 'paid for their services, they generally behave more like academic research centers than like businesses. Analysts, for example, never discuss the cost of a rating in their discussions with clients. They are engaged in pure analysis, and do not even have to concern themselves with a budget.'[99] Although this may seem surprising in the more recent context of the subprime crisis, this reputation for independence from conflicts of interests is pervasive in the non-structured finance related segments. It has been shown empirically, on a dataset of about 2000 bond credit rating migrations from S&P and Moody's from 1997 to 2002, that rating changes do not appear to be importantly influenced by rating agency conflicts of interest, but, rather, suggest that rating agencies are motivated primarily by reputation-related incentives.'[100] A more recent academic study, mostly executed prior to the subprime crisis, based on interviews and surevys, of key market participants mostly in the U.K. including both issuers and investors finds that all interviewees were confident in the independence of the CRAs they dealt with. The main objective of the study is to identify the characteristics that market participants, such as financial managers, investors and other interested parties, value in a CRA. The study finds relative agreement amongst the participants and the ranking of essential characteristics is as follows: 'reputation, trust, and values, followed by characteristics of transparency, timeliness, expertise, investor orientation; methodology, co-operation; independence; issuer orientation; internal process; and responsiveness.'[101] Interestingly, this study relates to the auditing literature as an approach to a model of rating quality. There is one key difference that we highlight which is the possibility to quantitatively measure the performance of ratings at maturity, as discussed in the previous chapter. Indeed, this is the ultimate measurable feedback of ratings' quality that will enhance the reputation building incentives of agencies. Given these performance statistics, investors and issuers can objectively evaluate the rating agencies, even if it is with a lag.

It seems as though reputation mechanisms have kept moral hazard temptation at bay in the traditional rating segments. We review the specific issues of conflicts of interest in the structured finance segment and the shortcomings of the rating agencies in that area in

---

[97] Fees from any single issuer typically comprise a very small percentage – less than 1% – of a rating agency's total revenue.

[98] US Securities and Exchange Commission, 2003, Report on the role and function of credit rating agencies in the operation of the securities market, January, 1–45, page 23.

[99] Caouette, J.B., Altman, E.I., and Narayanan, P., 1998, *Managing Credit Risk: The Next Great Financial Challenge*, John Wiley & Sons, Inc., New York, 1–452, page 70.

[100] Covitz, D., Harrison, P., 2003. Testing conflicts of interest at bond rating agencies with market anticipation: evidence that reputation incentives dominate, working paper, Federal Reserve Board, December, 1–37, page 2.

[101] Duff, A., Einig, S., 2007. Credit Rating Agencies: Meeting the Needs of the Market?, The Institute of Chartered Accountants of Scotland. On page 55 a consultant is quoted in this study as: 'I've seen clients kicking and screaming, but they [the CRA] stuck to their opinion. I think they're independent.'

section 7.3 on the subprime crisis. However, there have been allegations of anticompetitive practices in the industry.[102] These practices include: agencies that provide an unsolicited rating of a company along with a bill for the service; forcing rated companies to purchase other services, known as tying; and lowering the ratings on asset-backed securities unless a substantial portion of the assets making up those securities are also rated by the agency, known as notching.

Unsolicited Ratings

CRAs have been charged with misusing unsolicited ratings to extract revenue from the rated issuer. By its nature, an unsolicited rating relies on poorer information than a solicited one. Remember from Section 4.1 how important it is for the analyst to know and understand the issuer in depth in order to be able to make a fair assessment of its creditworthiness. For businesses with high information asymmetries due to the complexity, proprietary nature, or sheer confidentiality of their business, it would be impossible to form a fair opinion without at least some access to confidential information. For example, banks would say that it is impossible to conduct a fair unsolicited rating on them because the rater needs to know what is in the loan book, and the loan book is private and confidential. An architect, designer, manufacturer of advanced aircraft or any R&D intensive company would argue similarly. Suppose a CRA published an unsolicited rating on such a company. Wouldn't this put pressure on 'good' companies to go for a solicited and paid rating that in all likelihood would be more favorable because it would be based on more relevant, accurate information? This is what the charge of 'extracting revenue' refers to.

However, CRAs dismiss the charge as unfounded. They argue that unsolicited ratings are issued in response to meaningful interest in the investor community for cases where there is adequate public disclosure. For example, on November 20, 2006, Fitch assigned Pernod Ricard S.A., the second largest spirits company, a BBB minus senior unsecured and Issuer Default Rating (IDR). The press release stated that this rating has 'been initiated by Fitch as a service to Investors. The issuer did not participate in the rating process other than through the medium of its public disclosure.'[103] Presumably, there are few information asymmetries in a Ricard pastis, a Havana Club rum or a Chivas whisky. Moreover, there is public disclosure of unsolicited ratings as such. So this may very well have been a Fitch Initiated Rating to help Fitch enter the French corporate market, and provide valuable competition.

Rating agencies are often reluctant to issue ratings on an unsolicited basis, partly because they would, to some extent, be based on information that did not come from the actual issuer. Since the presumption is that the company being rated knows its business better than anyone else, this would tend to undermine the value of any unsolicited rating. The rating agency foots the bill for unsolicited issues. However given the fact that substantially less due diligence is required (the issuer is not likely to open its doors to the rating agency in the case of an unsolicited rating) the costs to the agency of completing an unsolicited rating tend to be lower.

The CRAs have slightly different policies with regard to assigning ratings not requested by the issuer. Both S&P and Moody's rate all SEC-registered, US corporate securities,

---

[102] Include citations from Partnoy, F., 1999, The Siskel and Ebert of financial markets?: Two thumbs down for the credit rating agencies, *Washington University Law Quarterly*, Vol. 77, No. 3, 619–715.
[103] Fitch Ratings, 2006, Fitch rates Pernod Ricard IDR 'BBB'; stable outlook, Press release, November 20, 1–2.

regardless of whether the rating was requested and paid for by the issuer.[104] They publicly release all of their ratings.

When Moody's does undertake an unsolicited rating, it informs the issuer and gives company management the opportunity to participate in (and pay for) the ratings process. Moody's often rates non-registered structured securities and foreign bonds on an unsolicited basis as well. Unsolicited ratings are often assigned to large, liquid foreign issues that are expected to be heavily traded. Moody's will indicate in a press release when a newly rated issuer chooses not to participate in the ratings process.

In 1996, S&P ended a long-standing policy of only assigning ratings to registered securities or upon request.[105] It began assigning unsolicited ratings using its standard rating scale with a 'pi' notation (for 'public information') to indicate that the rating was unsolicited. Most observers feel that S&P changed its policy in order to better compete with Moody's.

Similarly, Fitch did not publish unsolicited ratings before 2001. In 2001, the Fitch Initiated Ratings (FIR) program was introduced, which targeted high-profile market participants or issuers with discrepancy in market opinions not traditionally rated by Fitch. Ratings published under this program are identified as such in the original publication concerning the rating. Fitch states that it will only publish an FIR if it concludes that there is sufficient information available to allow an educated opinion, and, in all cases, such ratings are uncompensated and Fitch does not assess or seek fees for the analysis. There is no difference in the analytical process or criteria for FIRs, although the level of management involvement varies. Procedures relative to the publication of the ratings are also the same and Fitch contacts the issuer prior to publishing a new rating or subsequent rating action to the marketplace.

Those in favor of unsolicited ratings argue that they provide a check against ratings shopping. This is the practice of hiring only those agencies that are expected to provide a favorable rating. Furthermore, a company may be willing to take the chance (however small) that a third rating agency will assign a slightly higher rating, particularly if the firm thinks they have been undervalued by S&P and Moody's.[106] The incremental cost of a third credit rating is small compared to the potential savings that an investment grade rating could make for a company rated below investment grade by Moody's or S&P.

An unsolicited rating may end up being lower than what a solicited one would have been: firstly, because unsolicited ratings are likely to be based on incomplete information since contact with the issuer is limited, and secondly, the agency will be more cautious, having had less access to information. In other words, unsolicited ratings may be downward biased. Findings from a pooled time-series cross-sectional data analysis from S&P covering 265 firms in 15 countries during the period of 1998–2000 document this bias, as Table 8.4 shows.[107] The mean rankings in the tables indicate that unsolicited ratings, on average,

---

[104] 'As a matter of policy, in the U.S., we assign and publish ratings for all public corporate debt issues over $100 million–with or without a request from the issuer. Public transactions are defined as those registered with the SEC, those with future registration rights, and other 144A deals that have broad distribution,' Standard and Poor's, 2005, *Corporate Ratings Criteria*, 1–119, page 15.

[105] Standard & Poor's, 1996. Behind the ratings: substantially broader ratings coverage for banks, *Research*, November 27, 1–2, page 1.

[106] Reinebach, A., 1998b, Study shows third rating shrinks spreads, *The Investment Dealers' Digest*, Vol. 64, page 8.

[107] Poon, W.P.H., 2003, Are unsolicited credit ratings biased downward?, *Journal of Banking and Finance*, April, Vol. 27, Issue 4, 593–614. The null hypothesis that solicited and unsolicited ratings have identical mean rankings is rejected at the 1% level for all three panels in Table 8.4.

Table 8.4 Downward bias of unsolicited ratings (2001).
A study of 595 issuer long-term ratings across 15 countries by S&P between 1998 and 2000.

Sub-sample	No. of observations	Mean rank
Overall sample: Solicited rating	272	349
Unsolicited rating	323	255
Excluding Japanese issuers: Solicited rating	193	163
Unsolicited rating	107	128
Japanese issuers: Solicited rating	79	225
Unsolicited rating	216	120

Mean ranks for 32 pairs of Japanese issuers with similar financial profiles

Sub-sample	No. of observations	Mean rank
Solicited rating	32	41.2
Unsolicited rating	32	23.8

To control difference in sovereign risk, 32 pairs of matching issuers with similar financial profile are selected only from the Japanese sub-sample (representing about half of the overall sample) for this Mann–Whitney U test. A Japanese issuer from the solicited group is paired with another Japanese issuer from the unsolicited group by matching ICOV, ROA, DTC, and SDTD. Each pair of issuers has a similar financial profile. Specifically, the absolute differences in these ratios between the two groups fall within the following ranges: ICOV 1-time, ROA 1%, DTC 0.1, and SDTD ±0.1.

Note: The ratings are coded on a six-point ordinal scale where AA or above = 6, A = 5, BBB = 4, BB = 3, B = 2, and CCC or below = 1.
Source: Poon, W.P.H., 2003, Are unsolicited credit ratings biased downward?, *Journal of Banking and Finance*, April, Vol. 27, Issue 4, 593–614, pages 606–607.

are lower than solicited ratings for the overall sample and all sub-samples. This downward bias could be because those issuers who choose not to obtain rating services from S&P have weaker financial profiles. In order to remove this self-selection bias, the same study is conducted on a sub-sample of Japanese firms paired according to similar financial profiles, with the conclusion that even after controlling for differences in sovereign risk and key financial characteristics, the mean ranking of unsolicited ratings is still lower than that for solicited ratings.

It is thus possible that a CRA takes the opportunity to subtly reward the firms that pay with a higher rating. A possible example where CRAs may have abused the practice of issuing unsolicited ratings is the story of the German insurance company, Hannover Re, published in the *Washington Post*.[108]

> Moody's exerted subtle pressure on the company to pay for the ratings that it was issuing on the company on an unsolicited basis. Since the company was already a client of two other rating companies, it refused to solicit Moody's services. Moody's began evaluating Hannover anyway, giving it weaker marks over successive years and publishing the results while seeking

---

[108] Klein, A., 2004, Credit raters' power leads to some abuses, some borrowers say, *The Washington Post*, November 24, page A01.

Hannover's business. Still, the insurer refused to pay. Then in 2003, even as other credit raters continued to give Hannover a clean bill of health, Moody's cut Hannover's debt to junk status. Shareholders worldwide, alarmed by the downgrade, dumped the insurer's stock, lowering its market value by about $175 million within hours.

Sean Egan, MD, Egan-Jones Ratings Co., quoted this article at the Senate Hearings held on credit rating agencies in February 2005. Raymond McDaniel, President of Moody's Investors Service, defended Moody's by emphasizing that the downgrade in fact happened after payment was received from Hannover Re.[109]

However, as Caouette et al. (1998) point out, if investors were to lose confidence in an agency's ratings, issuers would no longer believe they could lower their funding costs by obtaining ratings from that agency. Every time a rating is assigned, the agency's name, integrity, and credibility are on the line and subject to inspection by the whole invest-ment community.[110] This view is supported by the reputation hypothesis mentioned earlier, suggesting that the key success factor in building a successful CRA is the development of a strong reputation in the international financial community. For a CRA to preserve its reputation while also assigning unsolicited ratings, it is of paramount importance to announce clearly if and when a rating is unsolicited, both at initiation and follow-ups.

Notching

In the course of the Congress Hearings on Rating Agencies, allegations were made that the largest rating agencies had abused their dominant position by engaging in a practice known as notching. Notching occurs when a CRA refuses to provide an overall rating for a structured finance instrument, or gives an unfavorable rating, unless a substantial portion of the assets in the underlying pool are also rated by that CRA.[111] This is a complaint that has been publicly stated by Fitch for several years. 'Through their discriminatory practice known as "notching," Moody's and S&P successfully alter competition in the commercial and residential mortgage-backed securities markets (RMBS) by leveraging their monopoly position in other markets.'[112] For example, if a CDO based exclusively on a pool of RMBS is only rated by S&P or Moody's if they also rate at least 80% of the RMBS', any originator of RMBS will initially pick the agency that leads the market in the RMBS segment. Hence, stifling competition. A practice such as notching can certainly affect the market dynamics in favor of the dominant firms, thereby reducing competition in the RMBS rating segment, which seemed to already lack market discipline.

The arguments in favor of notching compare the case of a rating agency X relying on the ratings of agency Y for the pool of assets on which its CDO is based, to a lawyer relying

---

[109] United States Senate Committee on Banking, Housing, and Urban Affairs, 2005, Examining the role of credit rating agencies in the capital markets: Open session hearing, February 8.

[110] Caouette, J.B., Altman E.I., and Narayanan, P., 1998, *Managing Credit Risk: The Next Great Financial Chal-lenge*, John Wiley & Sons, Inc., New York, 1–452, page 70.

[111] US Securities and Exchange Commission, 2003, Report on the role and function of credit rating agencies in the operation of the securities market, January, 1–45, page 24.

[112] Stroker, N., Group Managing Director–Fitch Ratings, 2005, Legislative Solutions for the Credit Rating Agency Duopoly Relief Act of 2005, Statement to the House Subcommittee on Capital Markets, Insurance and Government Sponsored Enterprises, June 29, 1–24, page 4. For instance, according to comments submitted Fitch, Moody's refuses to rate a given structured finance transaction if the less than 80% of the underlying pool of assets is rated by Moody's also.

on someone else's opinion in order to form its own opinion. The question of independence and diversity of rating opinions is clearly at stake. But still, the above argument does not seem as convincing in defense of notching as it has become clearer recently that the rating agencies did not mind relying on third parties' due diligence when these are not competitors. The question of notching is complicated and merits further investigation in order to find the most efficient arrangement.

8.3.3 Performance for Issuers

The important CRA performance metrics from the issuer's perspective would be the fee, the decrease in terms of cost of credit compared to best available alternatives, accuracy and stability of the ratings, and quality of the service.

We have mentioned that issuers only have distant substitutes for ratings, which directly implies that the CRAs probably provide issuers with a competitive cost of credit. The immense growth volume of rated issues in the last 15 years talks for itself. Another implication of the lack of substitutes is the low bargaining power of issuers with respect to the fees.

The fact that the industry is so concentrated and that CRAs compete for the market rather than in the market, implies that issuers may suffer from a lack of choice among agencies and that agencies may not be as competitive in terms of service. Issuers get locked into a relationship with an agency once the agency has produced its initial rating. Agencies do not have a strong incentive to maintain a high quality of service in terms of availability of analysts, response time, and flexibility, which is consistent with our discussions with issuers and treasury associations.

Finally, issuers have a strong preference for credit ratings that are not only accurate but also stable: 'They want ratings to reflect enduring changes in credit risk because rating changes have real consequences – due primarily to ratings-based portfolio governance rules and rating triggers – that are costly to reverse.'[113] Here, credit-focused CRAs differentiate themselves clearly from CRAs that provide market-implied ratings and carefully gauge the trade-off between increasing accuracy of short-term ratings while reducing rating stability. In this sense, rating outlooks and watches are useful in providing more information on credit quality without affecting stability too much.

8.3.4 Performance for Investors

The main performance criteria for investors are accuracy and timeliness. Accuracy is discussed in Chapter 7. Timeliness is certainly an important dimension that, in the aggregate, could affect investors' portfolio performance substantially. Timeliness may especially be an issue when the financial markets are bullish and when CRAs are understaffed, especially if the issuing volume at the time is high.

Often investors subscribe to ratings information services provided by CRAs, and hence expect a certain level of service such as a large range of information and in-depth reports, seminars and opportunities for discussion or explanations on given ratings.

---

[113] Cantor, R., and Mann, C., 2006, Analyzing the tradeoff between ratings accuracy and stability, *Special Comment*: Moody's Investors Service, September, Report 99100, 1–8.

8.4 CONCLUSION

Changes in regulatory recognition systems and a growing consensus that competition can improve the functioning of the rating industry could increase competition from new and existing firms. The high industry growth rates (see Figure 8.14) also encourage new entrants.

The growth of a number of competing agencies has provided a much greater level of competition to Moody's and Standard & Poor's in recent years.[114] Many argue that Moody's and Standard & Poor's together represent one of the most powerful groups in the international financial markets and share concern over the power and influence of these two agencies. It is seen that a greater level of competition to the two agencies would be a healthy development in the marketplace.

There is no doubt that Moody's and S&P have built strong brand names and are seen as the pace-setters in the industry. However, it also seems that, due to fast-growing capital markets in the US, Europe, and the emerging countries, there is room for growth among all of the industry players. Indeed, the vast majority of corporations are still unrated.

Competitors of Moody's and S&P point to evidence that competition in the ratings business is good for clients. A 1998 study shows that a third corporate debt rating can affect bond spreads.[115] The study examined the behavior of more than 235 bonds rated by Fitch, Moody's, and S&P between 1991 and 1995. It found that for corporate bonds similarly rated by Moody's and S&P, the presence of a higher Fitch rating resulted in a lower spread. For bonds rated Baa2/BBB for example, a Fitch rating saved the issuer 23 basis points.[116] The lower the rating, the more a third rating generally helped. For B2/B rated securities, issuers saved 86 basis points. The yield differential was significant as well when Moody's and S&P gave a split rating and Fitch was being utilized to serve as a tie-breaker. Where S&P offered an A rating and Moody's a Baa2 or vice versa, an A rating from Fitch resulted in a 98 basis point advantage for the issuer.[117] The findings thus provide quantitative support to an argument that S&P and Moody's competitors have been making for years: third ratings are noticed by the capital markets and can often help issuers to achieve a lower total cost of capital.

---

[114] Reinebach, A., 1998b, Study shows third rating shrinks spreads, *The Investment Dealers' Digest*, Vol. 64, page 8.
[115] Reinebach, A., 1998b, Study shows third rating shrinks spreads, *The Investment Dealers' Digest*, Vol. 64, page 8.
[116] How significant might that be to a CFO? Consider a corporation issuing a US$250 million bond. A 23 basis point savings would amount to approximately US$600 000 per year. Perhaps almost enough to pay the CFO's annual pre-bonus salary.
[117] This would save our CFO approximately US$2,500,000 per year, significantly more than he would have to pay Fitch and his investment bankers to obtain the rating.

9
Regulatory Oversight of the Credit Rating Industry

It is clear that today's CRA industry presents plenty of public interest externalities. The quality, volume, cost and price of its output have repercussions for the efficiency of resource allocation in the economy. This is due to the success of CRAs in becoming a pillar of the informational infrastructure of world capital markets, and the extent to which regulators use credit ratings. Few industries driven by shareholder value have no public interest externalities, and in the financial sector, all sub-sectors (insurance companies, stock exchanges, equity analysis, auditors, etc.) are implicated. The solution adopted for these sectors has been to impose regulatory constraints on behavior aimed at maximizing private value in order to reconcile this with the public interest. And so it is with the CRA industry.

This chapter reviews the regulatory uses of credit ratings and the regulation of the credit rating agencies that produce them. While related, the former is not necessary for the latter and the latter doesn't fully follow from the former. Even if ratings were not used for regulatory purposes, the sheer commercial market success of the credit rating agencies' product has created its own public interest externalities. This alone would have eventually resulted in a call for some sort of regulatory oversight – however relevant, useful, or wasteful this may be. But that same commercial success made regulators decide to use ratings for their own prudential regulatory purposes. Paradoxically, this adoption was later used to justify regulatory oversight of CRAs to ensure that they did a good job.

Economic crises and government attempts to deal with these led to the use of ratings in regulation. It started with the change in the US Comptroller of the Currency's (OCC) valuation of bonds in national bank portfolios after the onset of the second banking crisis in March 1931.[1]

> Banks had to dump their assets on the market, which inevitably forced a decline in the market value of those assets and hence of the remaining assets they held. The impairment in the market value of assets held by banks, particularly in their bond portfolios, was the most important source of impairment of capital leading to bank suspensions, rather than the default of specific loans or of specific bond issues.[2]

For bonds in which there was an active market and continuous price quotations, bank examiners impaired the capital of banks to the full extent of the drop in market value

---

[1] Friedman, M., and Schwartz, A.J., 1963. *A Monetary History of the United States 1867–1960*, Princeton University Press, Princeton, New Jersey, 1–860, give an extremely lucid account of the process on page 312: 'In their search for liquidity [during the onset of the first banking crisis, October 1930], banks and others were inclined first to dispose of their lower-grade bonds ... hence ... their prices fell. The decline in bond prices itself contributed ... to the subsequent banking crises. It made banks more fearful of holding bonds and so fostered declines in prices. By reducing the market value of the bond portfolios of banks, declines in bond prices in turn reduced the margin of capital as evaluated by bank examiners, and in this way contributed to subsequent bank failures.'

[2] Friedman, M., and Schwartz, A.J., 1963. *A Monetary History of the United States 1867–1960*, Princeton University Press, Princeton, New Jersey, 1–860, page 355.

below face value, regardless of credit quality. To alleviate the pressure on banks capital as measured by banking examiners, the Comptroller changed the valuation regulations and 'ruled that national banks would be required to charge off no depreciation [to market value] on bonds of the four highest ratings.'[3] Thus, publicly traded bonds rated BBB or higher by at least one credit rating agency could now be carried at book value. Otherwise, the bonds would have to be written down and 25% of the resulting book losses would be charged against capital. This was the first regulatory use of credit ratings.

The more recent spate of ratings reverses in the Asian financial crisis, the corporate scandals in the US and Europe and the latest subprime crisis repeatedly prompted calls to regulate the industry, or strengthen the existing regulation. In Europe, the scandals led the EU executive to begin analyzing the issue of credit rating agencies in April 2002.[4] In the US, it led to the July 2002 'Sarbanes–Oxley Act,' which ordered a study of the credit ratings industry.[5] Regulation in the aftermath of these studies occurred first in Europe, with the adoption of EU regulatory policy as defined in the December 2005 'Communication from the Commission on Credit Rating Agencies.'[6] Nine months later, the US adopted the 'Credit Ratings Reform Act of 2006' and in June 2007 the SEC adopted the final rule that provides it with the authority to implement oversight rules with respect to registered rating agencies.[7] The scandals had highlighted that credit rating agencies had to be competent, diligent, transparent, independent, and trustworthy for the stability and proper functioning of capital markets. They brought to the foreground issues such as inadequate due diligence, apparent conflicts between the commercial and deontological interests of CRAs, inadequate explanation of ratings, and unfair commercial practices.[8] Each one of these could prevent CRAs from producing reliable, timely, and fair ratings. The subprime crisis, starting very shortly after in the summer of 2007, raised again these issues applied more specifically to the structured finance market and has started a new round of regulatory proposals.[9]

9.1 THE REGULATORY USES OF RATINGS

Credit ratings are used in decisions about purchasing, selling, holding or disposing of particular securities. In 1936, the Office of the Comptroller and the US Federal Reserve went further than the Comptroller's 1931 ruling on valuation, now 'prohibiting banks from holding bonds not rated BBB or above by at least two agencies. The new rules had far-reaching

---

[3] Friedman, M., and Schwartz, A.J., 1963. *A Monetary History of the United States 1867–1960*, Princeton University Press, Princeton, New Jersey, 1–860, page 319, n. 22.

[4] At the Oviedo Informal ECOFIN Council.

[5] United States Congress, 2002. Sarbanes–Oxley Act of 2002, January 23, 1–66, Title VII, Section 702.

[6] Commission of the European Communities, 2005. Communication from the Commission on Credit Rating Agencies, December 23, 2005/11990, 1–9.

[7] US Securities and Exchange Commission, 2007. Oversight of Credit Rating Agencies Registered as Nationally Recognized Statistical Rating Organizations, Securities Exchange Act of 1934, Release No. 55857, June, 72 FR 33564, 1–284.

[8] US Securities and Exchange Commission, 2003. Concept release: rating agencies and the use of credit ratings under the federal security laws, June, page 2, and Technical Committee of International Organization of Securities Commissions, 2003. Report on the activities of credit rating agencies, September, OICV-IOSCO PD 153, 1–20, page 15.

[9] US Securities and Exchange Commission, 2008. Proposed rules for Nationally Recognized Statistical Rating Organizations, June 11, 1–168 and the Technical Committee of International Organisation of Securities Commissions, 2008, Code of Conduct Fundamentals for Credit Rating Agencies, revised May, OICV-IOSCO PD 271, 1–14.

consequences, because 891 of the 1975 bonds listed on the New York Stock Exchange were rated below BBB in 1936.'[10] These regulations remain in force today.

The use of ratings in regulations is most widespread in, but not limited to, the US. In June 2005, US Congress hearings reported that at least 8 Federal statutes, 47 Federal rules, and 100 State laws made reference to them.[11] These regulations affect not only banks, but also broker-dealers, insurers, pension funds, and mutual funds. They restrict or prohibit the purchase of securities with 'low' ratings (usually below BBB), impose variable equity capital requirements depending on the rating of the holdings, and ease the issuance conditions or disclosure requirements for securities carrying a 'satisfactory' rating.[12] One can summarize the key purposes of these uses under three broad categories: prudence, from which follows, for instance the setting of minimum capital adequacy requirements for banks and broker dealers; investor protection, for instance, minimum rating requirements for investments by pension funds; and the integrity of security markets, for instance the regulation of market access as a function of the rating of the security. Exhibit 9.1 tabulates the various uses of these ratings in the US, which we will discuss in some detail later in this section.

As of July 1st 2008, the SEC has proposed a rule in three sections that would substantially reduce the regulatory reliance on credit ratings of NRSROs. This is an unprecedented move towards decreasing the use of NRSRO ratings and an open door to omitting any reference to them at all and hence eliminating any undue reliance on NRSRO ratings specifically by market participants.[13]

The regulatory use of ratings is less widespread and codified in Europe. This is particularly true at the level of the European Union. Several European States use credit ratings standards for similar purposes to the US and with comparable techniques. Supervisors of insurance companies use ratings to calculate technical reserves, to determine eligible counterparties or in the context of the stress testing that insurance companies are obliged to apply.[14] However, ratings-based regulation is much less common overall in Europe than in the US.[15] As an example, Exhibit 9.2 shows the main uses of ratings in regulation in France, demonstrating that, while ratings are indeed used in some regulations, the number of uses does not come anywhere close to what it is in the US.

At the EU level, the one regulation using credit ratings extensively is the 2006 Capital Requirements Directive (CRD), discussed in detail below. Upon the advice of the Committee

---

[10] Cantor, R., and Packer, F., 1994. The credit rating industry, *Quarterly Review*: Federal Reserve Bank of New York, Summer–Fall, 1–26, page 6.

[11] 'The NRSRO concept, after all, has become embedded in many areas of the law. The term is used in about 8 federal statutes, 47 federal rules, and more than 100 state laws.' Kanjorski, P.E., Ranking democratic member, 2005, Opening statement at the hearing entitled 'Legislative solutions for the credit rating industry' before the House Subcommittee on Capital Markets, Insurance and Government Sponsored Enterprises, June 29, 1–6.

[12] Gonzalez, F., Hass, F., Johannes, R., Persson, M., Toledo, L., Violi, R., Wieland, M., and Zins, C., 2004. Market dynamics associated with credit ratings, Occasional Paper No. 16: European Central Bank, June, 1–40, page 9.

[13] US Securities and Exchange Commission, 2008. Proposed rule – References to ratings of Nationally Recognized Statistical Rating Organizations, July 1st, release 34-58070, 1–75. US Securities and Exchange Commission, 2008, Proposed rule – Security ratings, July 1st, release 33-8940, 1–77. US Securities and Exchange Commission, 2008, Proposed rule – References to ratings of Nationally Recognized Statistical Rating Organizations, July 1st, release IC-28327, 1–70.

[14] The Committee of European Securities Regulators (CESR), 2004. CESR's technical advice to the European Commission on possible measures concerning credit rating agencies, Consultation Paper, November, Reference CESR/04-612b, 1–86, page 15.

[15] Gonzalez, F., Hass, F., Johannes, R., Persson, M., Toledo, L., Violi, R., Wieland, M., and Zins, C., 2004. Market dynamics associated with credit ratings, Occasional Paper No. 16: European Central Bank, June, 1–40, page 9.

Exhibit 9.1   Selected uses of ratings in regulation in the US (1931–2000)

Year adopted	Ratings dependent regulation	Minimum rating	How many ratings?	Regulator/Regulation	Use
1931	Required banks to mark-to-market lower rated bonds	BBB	2	OCC and Federal Reserve Examination Rules	Prudence
1936	Prohibited Banks from purchasing 'speculative securities'	BBB	Unspecified	OCC, FDIC and Federal Reserve joint statements	Prudence
1951	Imposed higher capital requirement on insurers' lower rated bonds	Various	NA	NAIC mandatory reserve requirement	Capital Adequacy Requirement
1975	Imposed higher capital haircuts on broker dealers' below investment grade bonds	BBB	2	SEC amendment to rule 15c3-1, the uniform net capital rule	Capital Adequacy Requirement
1982	Eased disclosure requirements for investment grade bonds	BBB	1	SEC adoption of integrated disclosure system	Easier Market Access
1984	Eased issuance of non agency mortgage-backed securities	AA	1	Congressional promulgation of the secondary Mortgage Market Enhancement Act of 1984	Easier Market Access
1987	Permitted margin lending against MBS and (later) foreign bonds	AA	1	Federal Reserve regulation T	Prudence
1989	Allowed pension funds to invest in high rated ABS	A	1	Department of Labor relaxation of ERISA restriction	Investor Protection
1989	Prohibited S&Ls from investing in below investment grade bonds	BBB	1	Congressional promulgation of the Financial Institutions Recovery and Reform Act of 1989	Investor Protection
1991	Required money market mutual funds to limit holdings of low rated paper	A1*	1	SEC amendment to rule 2a-7 under the Investment Company Act of 1940	Investor Protection
1992	Exempted issues of certain ABS from registration as a mutual fund	BBB	1	SEC adoption of Rule 3a-7 under the Investment Company Act of 1940	Easier Market Access
1994	Imposes varying capital charges on banks and S&Ls of different tranches of ABS	AAA and BBB	1	Federal Reserve, OCC, FDIC, OTS Proposed Rule on Recourse and Direct Substitutes	Capital Adequacy Requirement

Exhibit 9.1 *(continued)*

Year adopted	Ratings dependent regulation	Minimum rating	How many ratings?	Regulator/Regulation	Use
1998[a]	Department of Transportation can only extend credit assistance to projects with an investment grade rating	BBB	1	Transport Infrastructure Finance and Innovation Act 1998	Prudence
1999[a]	Restricts the ability of national banks to establish financial subsidiaries	A	1	Gramm-Leach-Biley Act of 1999	Prudence
2000[b]	Loan by non profit corporation eligible for guarantee under the Act provided that such corporation has one or more issues of outstanding long-term debt that is rated within the highest 3 rating categories of an NRSRO (District of Columbia – Appropriations Legislation)	A	1	Public Law 106-553	Prudence

[a]Estrella, A., 2000, Credit ratings and complementary sources of credit quality information, Basel Committee on Banking Supervision, Working Papers No. 3: Bank for International Settlements, Basel, August, 1–186, page 54.
[b]United States Congress, 2000, Public law 106-553: Federal funding, fiscal year 2001, December 21, 1–151, page 130; US Securities and Exchange Commission, 2005, Proposed rule – definition of Nationally Recognized Statistical Rating Organizations, April 19, 1–74, pages 6–9.
Source: (1931–1994): Cantor, R. and Packer, F., 1994, The credit rating industry, *Quarterly Review*, Federal Reserve Bank of New York, Summer–Fall, 1–26, page 6.

of European Securities Regulators (CESR), the European Commission (the EU executive) has been reluctant to extend the regulatory use of ratings to other applications.[16] It holds that

> the use of ratings in European legislation should not simply be encouraged in a general way without a case-by-case analysis of the different proposals. In any event, it would be necessary to identify all the alternatives capable of achieving the regulatory objectives sought by the use of ratings in the legislation. A detailed study of the strengths and weaknesses of each alternative, including the use of ratings, should be prepared prior to any conclusion.[17]

---

[16] European Commission, 2004. Call to CESR for technical advice on possible measures concerning credit rating agencies, July 27, 1–10, Item 3.5.
[17] The Committee of European Securities Regulators (CESR), 2005. The use of ratings in private contracts, Technical advice to the European Commission on possible measures concerning credit rating agencies, March, CESR/05-139b, 1–93, page 40.

Exhibit 9.2 Selected uses of ratings in regulation in France

Year adopted	Ratings dependent regulation	Minimum rating	How many ratings?	Regulator/regulation	Use
1988	Any Securitized debt fund making a public offering requires a rating	NA	NA	Article L 214-44 of the Monetary and Financial Code	Prudence
1991	Allowed money market funds to hold up to 25% of their assets in the form of securities issued by a single credit institution if the institution was rated			Decree	Prudence
1988	Issuers of money market securities must disclose the rating assigned to their issuance program before each issue			Decree 2004-865 of 24 Aug. 2004, amending decree 92-137 of Feb. 1992	Prudence
1988	Required a rating for admission to trading on a regulated market or for the issue of financial instruments including a component of debt securities. In November 2003, this requirement was extended to issuers whose shares were already listed if they wanted to make a public offering of debt securities (except for debt securities that are or could be convertible).			Reg. 88-04, Reg. 98-04 and the Commission decision of 9 Nov. 1990	Investor protection

Source: Autorité des Marchés Financiers, 2005, *2004 AMF Report on Rating Agencies*, January, 1–76, pages 37, 38.

The use of credit ratings in regulations is nevertheless prevalent around the world. For example, in Canadian securities regulation, at least 10 National Instruments or National Policies as well as various provincial securities rules and regulatory instruments use the concept of approved credit ratings. In addition, references to ratings obtained from rating agencies (although not necessarily references to specific rating agencies) appear in at least 8 Federal statutes or regulations promulgated under Federal legislation, and at least 37 Canadian provincial statutes (or regulations) in addition to securities laws.[18] With examples drawn from a number of countries where ratings-based regulations are in existence, we now turn to the three broad categories of uses of credit ratings: prudence, market access, and investor protection.

---

[18] Nicholls, C.C., 2005. *Public and Private Uses of Credit Ratings*, Policy Series: Capital Markets Institute (Canada), August, 1–47, page 15.

9.1.1 Prudence

Prudential regulations aim at ensuring the stability of financial institutions in order to maintain market confidence. The early US regulations of 1931 and 1936 are prudential. The norms usually relate to capital and other risk management standards and are intended to mitigate the possibility that firms will be unable to meet their liabilities and commitments to consumers and counterparties.[19] Examples of prudential guidelines relating to better risk management include bank exposure limits for different borrowers according to industry, sector, individual or group (i.e. common management control),[20] frameworks for lending to risky sectors such as venture capital (which may contain stipulations with respect to the maximum tenor, documentation, classification of the asset in the bank's books, etc.), barring end uses for which certain types of loans may be granted, rules on valuations of investment portfolios of financial institutions (which further translates into capital adequacy), etc. Exhibit 9.1 shows the uses of credit ratings in the US in prudential regulations.

The most incisive prudential regulation consists of minimum regulatory capital requirements imposed on financial firms. In these, regulators use credit ratings to induce financial intermediaries to finance their credit portfolios with a proportion of equity that corresponds to the credit risks of the portfolio.[21] In 1975, the US SEC used ratings in such regulation for the first time, in its net capital rule for broker-dealers. The net capital rule requires broker-dealers, when computing net capital, to deduct certain percentages of the market value of their proprietary securities positions from their net worth, depending on the ratings of these securities.[22] In Europe, ratings are used in the financial regulation of banks, primarily to determine the capital requirement to back earning assets. The Financial Services Authority (FSA) in the UK, for example, allows debt securities of any issuer to qualify for reduced risk weightings if they are rated investment grade by at least one among Fitch, Moody's, or S&P.[23]

In the global arena, this works through the Basel Committee on Banking Supervision (the Committee). For credit risk, the 1988 Basel Capital Accord (Basel I) had used regulatory fiat to decide the credit risk class of an asset.[24] But this mechanism biased the amount of capital to be held against risk classes at the extreme end of the risk spectrum: too much capital for low credit risk; insufficient for high risk. Overall, banks hold larger fractions of low-risk than high-risk assets. As a result, Basel I increased the capital intensity of bank lending and made high-quality borrowing from banks uncompetitive relative to issuing securities to investors not subject to these capital requirements.

In 1993, the Committee started distinguishing between bank assets held for 'lending' purposes, and those for 'trading' purposes. It then proposed market risk charges to debt

---

[19] The gist of this definition has been taken from The Financial Services Authority, 2001. *Interim Prudential Sourcebook for Investment Businesses*, June, Chapter 1, page 1.

[20] For example, Indian Term Lending institutions are subject to 'individual and group borrower exposure limits' by the Indian Central Bank, the Reserve Bank of India (Reserve Bank of India, 2005, Master circular – exposure norms for financial institutions, August 13, 1–23, page 1), as well as limits on some industry sectors such as stock markets, venture capital, etc.

[21] See Caouette, J.B., Altman, E.I., and Narayanan, P., 1998. *Managing Credit Risk: the Next Great Financial Challenge*, John Wiley & Sons, Inc., New York, 1–452, Table 6.1, page 66 for the uses of ratings by US regulators.

[22] US Securities and Exchange Commission, 2003. Report on the role and function of credit rating agencies in the operation of the securities market, January, 1–45, page 6.

[23] The Financial Services Authority, 2001. *Interim Prudential Sourcebook: Banks*, June, page 173–175.

[24] In January 2001, this was superseded by the Second Consultative Paper titled 'The New Basel Capital Accord', which was in turn superseded by the Third Consultative Paper (published in April 2003).

securities held in trading books to replace credit risk weights. These charges were going to use for the first time credit ratings among other criteria to determine the level of the charge.[25]

In the aftermath of the 1997–1998 turbulences in the world financial system, and with the objectives of ensuring that credit risk in lending was priced properly and improving the use of capital in the banking sector, this Committee extended more economic based credit risk weightings to the banks' 'lending' book. It issued a 'New Capital Adequacy Framework' proposal in June 1999. This proposal interprets the credit risk of an asset as its probability of default combined with the expected loss in the event of default. To determine the asset basis on which required capital is computed, the asset weights used for different assets are made a function of these assets' credit risk. And the credit risk, also called credit quality, of the asset itself can be gauged by two approaches. Under the standardized approach, credit quality may be determined by reference to the external credit assessments (ECAs, i.e. credit ratings) of the External Credit Assessment Institutions (ECAIs, i.e. CRAs). Under the alternative, internal ratings-based (IRB) approach, the prudential authority can permit a bank to use its own credit ratings if properly based on verified EDF and LGD estimates by the bank. This proposal led to the 2004 New Basel Capital Accord (Basel II).[26] Exhibit 9.3 shows the asset weights, transposing the six credit quality steps used in the accord to the rating scales in Exhibit 2.4. Basel II tightens up the relationship between ordinal ratings and cardinal default probabilities. It links ratings more closely to the amount of equity that banks need in order to fund an asset and therefore to the cost of credit.[27] For the members of the EU, this is encapsulated in the CRD.[28,29] This Directive provides for the use of 'external credit assessments' (ECAs) in the determination of credit risk weights (and consequential capital requirements) applied to a bank or investment firm's exposures, in application of Basel II.[30]

9.1.2 Market Access

Regulators also use credit ratings as an eligibility criterion for issuers tapping the capital markets. They often use the rating to differentiate the compliance/due diligence/information requirements that the issuer must fulfill in order to be granted access to the market. The use of credit ratings to control market access is widespread globally, as the following examples illustrate.

The US SEC adopted several such regulations under the Securities Act of 1933. Offerings of certain non-convertible debts, preferred securities, and asset-backed securities that

---

[25] Basel Committee on Banking Supervision, 1993. The supervisory treatment of market risks: consultative proposal, Bank for International Settlements, Basel, April, 1–61, pages 15–19.

[26] The new accord calls this 'the standardized approach to credit risk,' see Basel Committee on Banking Supervision, 2006. *International Convergence of Capital Measurement and Capital Standards: A Revised Framework*, Bank for International Settlements, Basel, June, 1–347, page 19.

[27] See Basel Committee on Banking Supervision, 1999. A new capital adequacy framework: a consultative paper, Bank for International Settlements, Basel, June, 1–62, and Fleming, S., 1999, *Disarming Bank Credit Risk*, Institutional Investor – International Edition, August, Vol. 24, Issue 8, 28–35, pages 29–34.

[28] European Parliament and Council, 2006. Directive 2006/48/EC of June 14, 2006 relating to the taking up and pursuit of the business of credit institutions (recast), *Official Journal of the European Union*, June 30, 1–200, page L177, Title V, Chapter 2: Technical instruments of prudential supervision.

[29] Basel Committee on Banking Supervision, 2006. *International Convergence of Capital Measurement and Capital Standards: A Revised Framework*, Bank for International Settlements, Basel, June, 1–347.

[30] Commission of the European Communities, 2005. Communication from the commission on credit rating agencies, December 23, 2005/11990, 1–9, page 4 (as produced in the *Official Journal of the European Union*, 2006/C59/02, March 11, 2006, 1–5).

Exhibit 9.3 The New Basel Capital Accord – Standardized Approach for risk weighting banking book exposures (June 2004)

Rating ranks		Corporates	Sovereigns	Banks			Securitization exposure
				Option 1	Option 2		
Alphanumeric	Numeric				Long term	Short term	Long term
(1)	(2)	(3)	(4)	(5)	(6)	(7)	(8)
AAA	1	20%	0%	20%	20%	20%	20%
AA+	2	20%	0%	20%	20%	20%	20%
AA	3	20%	0%	20%	20%	20%	20%
AA−	4	20%	0%	20%	20%	20%	20%
A+	5	50%	20%	50%	50%	20%	50%
A	6	50%	20%	50%	50%	20%	50%
A−	7	50%	20%	50%	50%	20%	50%
BBB+	8	100%	50%	100%	50%	20%	100%
BBB	9	100%	50%	100%	50%	20%	100%
BBB−	10	100%	50%	100%	50%	20%	100%
BB+	11	100%	100%	100%	100%	50%	350%
BB	12	100%	100%	100%	100%	50%	350%
BB−	13	100%	100%	100%	100%	50%	350%
B+	14	150%	100%	100%	100%	50%	Deduction
B	15	150%	100%	100%	100%	50%	Deduction
B−	16	150%	100%	100%	100%	50%	Deduction
CCC+	17	150%	150%	150%	150%	150%	Deduction
CCC	18	150%	150%	150%	150%	150%	Deduction
CCC−	19	150%	150%	150%	150%	150%	Deduction
CC	20	150%	150%	150%	150%	150%	Deduction
C	21	150%	150%	150%	150%	150%	Deduction
Unrated		100%	100%	100%	50%	20%	Deduction

Rating ranks	Securitization exposure
	Short term
	(9)
A-1/P-1	20%
A-2/P-2	50%
A-3/P-3	100%
All other ratings or unrated	Deduction

Notations follow the methodology used by one institution, S&P. The use of S&P's credit ratings is an example only.

Source: Basel Committee on Banking Supervision, 2004, *International Convergence of Capital Measurement and Capital Standards: a Revised Framework*, Bank for International Settlements, Basel, June, 1–251, pages 15–19, 120.

are rated investment grade by at least one NRSRO, can be registered on Form S-3 – the Commission's 'short-form' registration statement – without the issuer satisfying a minimum public float test.[31] Similarly, the SEC's adoption of Rule 3a-7 under the Investment Company Act of 1940 (in 1992), exempted issues of certain ABS from registration as a mutual

---

[31] US Securities and Exchange Commission, 2005. Proposed rule – definition of Nationally Recognized Statistical Rating Organizations, April 19, 1–74, page 7.

fund. One of the criteria for such an exemption was that the security be '... rated, at the time of initial sale, in one of the four highest categories assigned long-term debt or in an equivalent short-term category (within either of which there may be sub-categories or gradations indicating relative standing) by at least one nationally recognized statistical rating organization ... '[32]

Another example from the US defined the term 'mortgage related security.'[33] This required, among other things, that such securities be rated in one of the two highest rating categories by at least one NRSRO.[34]

Similarly, the French Autorité des Marché Financiers (AMF) requires that any securitized debt fund making a public offering be rated. Issuers of money market securities must disclose the rating assigned to their issuance program before each issue.[35] The stock market regulator requires issuers to disclose a rating from a specialized agency for issues of securities, other than money market securities, that are aimed at the general public. Back in 1988, the Commission des Opérations de Bourse (which was then the stock market regulator) could require a rating for an issue's admission to trading on a regulated market or for the issue of financial instruments, including a component of debt securities. In November 2003, this requirement was extended to issuers whose shares were already listed if they wanted to make a public offering of debt securities (except for debt securities that are or could be convertible).[36]

Canada, under national Securities Laws, also refers to credit ratings when granting market access. For example, dealers in guaranteed or short-term debt do not need to be registered if the debt has an approved credit rating.[37]

In India, a company must obtain a credit rating from any one of the CRAs recognized by the Reserve Bank of India (RBI) to be eligible to issue Commercial Paper.[38] The minimum credit rating needs to be P-2 from CRISIL or an equivalent rating from other agencies.[39] The Central Bank of India, for instance, in its guidelines on 'Securitization of Standard Assets,'[40] stipulates that

> the securities issued by the SPV (Special Purpose Vehicle) shall compulsorily be rated by a rating agency registered with SEBI[41] and such rating at any time shall not be more than 6 months old. The credit rating should be publicly available. For the purpose of rating and subsequent updating, the SPV should supply the necessary information to the rating agency in a timely manner. Commonality and conflict of interest, if any, between the SPV and the rating agency should also be disclosed.

---

[32] United States Congress, Investment Company Act of 1940. Rule 3a-7 – Issuers of Asset-Backed Securities.

[33] See Section 3(a)(41) of the Securities Exchange Act of 1934 introduced as part of the Secondary Mortgage Market Enhancement Act of 1984 revised through September 30, 2004, 1–259.

[34] US Securities and Exchange Commission, 2005. Proposed rule – definition of Nationally Recognized Statistical Rating Organizations, April 19, 1–74, page 8.

[35] Autorité des Marchés Financiers (AMF), 2005. *2004 AMF Report on Rating Agencies*, January, 1–76, page 37.

[36] Autorité des Marchés Financiers (AMF), 2005. *2004 AMF Report on Rating Agencies*, January, 1–76, page 38.

[37] Nicholls, C.C., 2005. *Public and Private Uses of Credit Ratings*, Policy series: Capital Markets Institute (Canada), August, 1–47, page 38.

[38] The RBI currently recognizes four CRAs for this purpose, and in general as well – Credit Rating Information Services of India Ltd (CRISIL) which has an affiliation with S&P, the Investment Information and Credit Rating Agency of India Ltd (ICRA) which has an affiliation with Moody's, the Credit Analysis and Research Ltd (CARE) and FITCH Ratings India Pvt. Ltd (*Source*: Reserve Bank of India). Interestingly, credit rating agencies in India are regulated under The Securities and Exchange Board of India Act, 1992. Under this Act, CRAs need to register with SEBI, and the Act confers powers on SEBI to regulate CRAs.

[39] The second highest grade in CRISIL's P-1 to P-5 Short Term Instruments Rating Scale.

[40] Reserve Bank of India, 2006. *Guidelines on Securitization of Standard Assets*, February 2, 1–23.

[41] The Securities and Exchange Board of India, which is the regulatory authority for the Indian securities market.

9.1.3 Investor Protection

While the goal of every financial regulation can ultimately be traced to investor protection, certain regulations serve this end more directly. Examples of these can be found in many countries, and in particular those regulations that govern the activities of collective investment vehicles that serve the interests of a large number of investors.

Examples of such regulations in the US can be found in Exhibit 9.1. Rule 2a-7 of the US Investment Company Act of 1940 limits money market funds to investing only in high-quality short-term instruments, and NRSRO ratings can be used as benchmarks for establishing minimum quality investment standards. Under Rule 2a-7, a money market fund is limited to investing in securities rated by an NRSRO in the two highest ratings categories for short-term debt (or un-rated securities of similar quality), and there are limitations on the amount of securities the fund can hold that are not rated in the highest rating category (or are not un-rated securities of similar quality).[42] Pension fund investments in ABS were allowed only in 1989, and only in those securities with an investment grade rating. In the same year, Congressional promulgation of the Financial Institutions Recovery and Reform Act of 1989 prohibited Savings and Loans from investing in bonds below investment grade.

In India, the RBI imposes several minimum rating standards to protect investors. For example, it requires that a NBFC (Non-Banking Financial Company) must have a minimum investment grade credit rating from an approved CRA[43] for it to accept public deposits.

In France, money market fund portfolios have been subject to credit rating restrictions since 1991. For example, they can only hold up to 25% of their assets in the form of securities issued by a single credit institution if the institution in question is rated.

Similarly, in Canada, there are several such regulations. Under the Canada Marine Act (a Federal regulation), a port authority may invest in debt that is rated by at least two specified rating agencies, one of which must be Moody's or S&P, if either of them assigns a rating for the investment. Several other regulations at the provincial level involving investments by credit unions, school boards, power authorities, municipalities, etc., specify minimum ratings for eligible debt securities.[44] And under a Federal statute, a money market mutual fund, among other things, must have at least 95% of its assets invested in cash, cash equivalents, or debt issued by an issuer whose commercial paper has received an approved credit rating (specific credit rating organizations are listed).[45]

In summary, the regulatory use of ratings has become widespread. It covers several applications: prudence, particularly capital requirements; market access; and investor protection. It spans the globe: any economy with investable financial assets and institutionalized intermediation has ratings-based regulations, to a greater or lesser extent. This has undoubtedly sharpened the interest of market participants and the public at large in credit ratings. It has also encouraged issuers of securities to have their securities rated, probably making the demand for ratings, especially from the dominant agencies, stronger than it might otherwise have been. This undoubtedly contributed to impulses to regulate the credit rating industry.

---

[42] US Securities and Exchange Commission, 2005. Proposed rule – definition of Nationally Recognized Statistical Rating Organizations, April 19, 1–74, page 6.

[43] Same as those mentioned in footnote 38.

[44] Nicholls, C.C., 2005. *Public and Private Uses of Credit Ratings*, Policy series: Capital Markets Institute (Canada), August, 1–47, pages 28–30.

[45] Nicholls, C.C., 2005. *Public and Private Uses of Credit Ratings*, Policy series: Capital Markets Institute (Canada), August, 1–47, page 29.

9.2   THE REGULATION OF THE INDUSTRY

'The Siskel and Ebert of financial markets? two thumbs down for the credit rating agencies.' This was the title of a 1999 article that argued:

> In place of ratings-dependent regulation, I recommend a replacement: simply substitute credit spreads, the market risk measure of bonds, for credit ratings. Credit spreads are more accurate than credit ratings...'[46]

However ill-conceived the above recommendation, and unsubstantiated the assertion upon which it is based, the Siskel and Ebert call was ahead of reverses for the CRAs and laid the doctrinal foundations for US regulatory reform. The key reforms three years later came about through a multi-constituent consultation process within and between Europe, the US, and the international regulatory and industry communities, with actual legislative work getting under way in the US in 2005–2006.

This section covers the regulatory oversight of both industry structure and business conduct. Both deal with the prescriptions of proper behavior and the power of enforcement that an oversight authority should have. Industry structure regulations aim at maintaining a level playing field on which the CRAs compete for business without reducing the intensity of competition or access to the field. While trying to avoid imposing undue rigidity and costs, the regulations for conduct of business have three main purposes. One is to ensure that investors obtain the trade-offs between stability and accuracy of ratings that they desire. The other is to protect issuers from possible market power abuses by the CRAs. And last, but not least, that credit ratings strengthen the information infrastructure of capital markets rather than weaken it.

We cover industry regulation at the global, EU, and US levels. World wide, the International Organization of Securities Commissions (IOSCO) adopted a Code of Conduct as the basis of a self-regulatory approach for industry oversight. It uses the 'comply or explain' principle. This means incorporate the elements of the Code into CRA proprietary Code and where those specific provisions are not appropriate (and have not been fully incorporated), explain why. The EU followed suit. The US legislator, with the 'Credit Rating Agency Reform Act of 2006' (the 'Rating Agency Act'), went for rather strong imposed regulations with intrusive oversight rights granted to the SEC. In June 2007, the SEC released the final implementation rules of the Rating Agency Act. As the regulation of the credit rating industry is still being evaluated and in flux, and was so even before the subprime crisis, we discuss the regulatory options, we review the global initiative for voluntary self-regulation that the IOSCO undertook in 2004, and follow-ups in the EU in 2005 and the US in 2006. To conclude the chapter, we analyze and evaluate the regulatory regimes.

9.2.1   The Regulatory Options

Industry Structure Issues

Open access is clearly one option, implying no targeted interference in industry structure. The CRA industry would of course be subject to the usual anti-trust, fairness in competition

---

[46] Partnoy, F., 1999. The Siskel and Ebert of financial markets?: two thumbs down for the credit rating agencies, *Washington University Law Quarterly*, Vol. 77, No. 3, 619–715, page 624.

and general competition, and common law requirements applicable to all industry and commerce. But under an open access regime, no government or regulatory body distorts the market outcomes of natural supply and demand conditions. These conditions would not be distorted through the use of selected agencies' ratings in regulations nor through licensing mechanisms.

Alternatively, controlled access is rooted in the practice of recognition of certain agencies for the regulatory use of their ratings. For example, on the use of external ratings by central bank regulators, 'virtually all countries use credit ratings in financial regulation', and 'tend to recognize the large global rating agencies, with very few exceptions.'[47] These findings imply that controlled access may indeed be more prevalent world-wide than open access. Formal recognition of a CRA to permit the regulatory use of its credit ratings is firmly entrenched in the US. There, the SEC has exercised the authority to express a *nihil obstat* against the use of the NRSRO label by a particular CRA since 1975. Several non-US and international regulations make the use of ratings contingent on the ratings being from one of these NRSROs.

The NRSRO practice, as it was prior to the Rating Agency Act, is an artificial barrier to entry. Firms that do not have a similar 'stamp of approval' claim that it is difficult to compete with NRSROs. Representatives of the NRSROs tend to play down the effect of the regulatory use of ratings on their business. They attribute their standing to their reputation, availability of historical performance, and the fact that the market does not demand more than 2–3 ratings. They emphasize that the proliferation of rating agencies since the 1970s (e.g. Duff & Phelps, IBCA Limited and IBCA Inc., Thomson BankWatch, Inc., all began issuing ratings in the 1970s or 1980s and later became NRSROs) is proof that regulatory barriers of entry are not insurmountable.[48] In fact, Moody's has gone on record to say that they do not oppose the discontinuance of the NRSRO system. 'We do not believe that our business depends on the continuance of the NRSRO system.'[49] However, potential entrants push the need for greater competition in the industry and are of the view that the designation system has substantially hindered their rate of growth.[50] We agree in the arguments of both sides, in the sense that even without the old NRSRO recognition system the industry would be dominated by a few large agencies, but there would be more niche players enhancing competition and providing well-needed market discipline.

The US Rating Agency Act replaced one form of controlled access with another. Interestingly, the US debate prior to the reform focused on removing the artificiality of the barrier while maintaining the quality of ratings. It centered on replacing the rather opaque NRSRO 'subjective' recognition system with an 'objective' registration system. All qualifying CRAs desirous of having their ratings used in regulations can request registration. The need for registration was designed to ensure the quality of ratings. This new system does not do away with controlled access, but in fact replaces the current form of control with another.

---

[47] Estrella, A., 2000. Credit ratings and complementary sources of credit quality information, Basel Committee on Banking Supervision, Working Papers No. 3: Bank for International Settlements, Basel, August, 1–186, page 3. These findings apply to the study sample of G12 countries plus a few additional ones including Austria, Malaysia, Portugal, and Spain.

[48] US Securities and Exchange Commission, 2003. Report on the role and function of credit rating agencies in the operation of the securities market, January, 1–45, page 38.

[49] McDaniel, R.W., President – Moody's Investors Service, 2005. Examining the role of credit rating agencies in the capital markets, Testimony before the US Senate Committee on Banking, Housing, and Urban Affairs, February 8, 1–14, page 13.

[50] US Securities and Exchange Commission, 2003. Report on the role and function of credit rating agencies in the operation of the securities markets, January, 1–45, page 38.

Conduct of Business Issues

Conduct of business deals with certain inherent industry practices that could compromise the goal of producing unbiased and efficient ratings. The regulatory options deal with issues of conflict of interest, information flow, fairness of commercial practices, level of due diligence and the degree of oversight that regulatory authorities could apply to how well CRAs discharge themselves in respecting prescribed standards of conduct. These range from low to strong regulatory oversight.

Low regulatory oversight characterizes the regulatory scenario where no particular government agency exercises oversight authority in most jurisdictions.[51] Even in the US, until the Rating Agency Act, the SEC's powers over the rating agencies were limited to the ability to withhold NRSRO status. However, the SEC had neither authority nor set procedures for ongoing monitoring once the designation has been given. CRAs are thus only loosely regulated under such a regime.

Under moderate oversight, the CRAs adhere to a code of conduct. This is a set of voluntary and commonly accepted principles. CRAs implement internal rules of conduct according to the mechanism: 'comply with the code or, if not, explain.' In other words, there is no formal regulatory authority exercising oversight, but rather monitored self-regulation, whereby CRAs adhere to common standards of functioning. The advantage of such an approach is that it is flexible and therefore easier to implement. It works toward CRA integrity by encouraging transparency.

The strong oversight scenario grants formal legal authority for regulators to supervise CRAs. The authority would devolve power to the regulator to take action against CRAs for non-compliance with stated policies, to demand records, to conduct inspections and examinations.

The trade-offs with respect to each one of the three approaches involves issues such as enforceability, the costs of regulation (administration and distortion of market forces), and the detrimental impact of regulation on the quality, innovativeness, diversity, and independence of credit ratings, were widely discussed. As can be expected, incumbents favor fewer regulations and more flexibility. In comparison, non-NRSROs, while not overtly propounding regulatory control over the business operations of CRAs, highlight inherent issues with the business models of incumbent NRSROs. They were largely in favor of some sort of regulatory action in the field, especially those aimed at increasing competition. At the other end of the spectrum, some investors, who feel the most hit in incidents of perceived ratings failure, prefer tighter regulation.[52] But CRA independence in reaching a rating action is of paramount importance and where does one draw the line between the regulation of process and regulation of content? For instance, the debt of sovereign governments is rated, and concerns were raised that administrative requirements of regulatory agencies may be used to exert indirect pressure for higher ratings of government debt.[53] The differing views emerge below as we review the IOSCO Code of Conduct, the EU, and lastly the US regulatory regimes.

---

[51] Technical Committee of International Organization of Securities Commissions (IOSCO), 2003. Report on the activities of credit rating agencies, September, OICV-IOSCO PD 153, 1–20, page 6.
[52] This is the case among some US investors but was less the feeling among European investors.
[53] Katiforis, G., 2004. Report on role and methods of rating agencies, European Parliament, January 29, Session document A5-0040/2004, 1–11, recital 12, page 7.

9.2.2 Worldwide Regulatory Initiative: the 2004 IOSCO Code of Conduct

IOSCO laid out a set of guidelines for CRAs aimed at addressing key issues that were thought to affect their proper functioning. IOSCO itself is a committee comprising approximately 100 of the world's securities regulatory authorities. It laid out its principles in two steps: a 'Statement of Principles Regarding the Activities of the Credit Rating Agencies'[54] in September 2003, and a 'Code of Conduct Fundamentals for Credit Rating Agencies' in December 2004.

National regulators from several countries drafted this code jointly in broad consultation with market participants These included issuers, investors, intermediaries, and rating agencies in their respective jurisdictions. The IOSCO Technical Committee formed a Task Force, chaired by a commissioner of the US SEC, Roel C. Campos, and representatives from the securities regulating organizations of 13 countries. The Task Force prepared a questionnaire that was circulated among all the members and also to DBRS, Fitch, Moody's, and S&P. Subsequently the Task Force consulted with the Basel Committee on Banking Supervision and with senior representatives from the four CRAs mentioned.

The IOSCO Technical Committee was in charge of the effort, laying down four key principles:

1. Rating actions should reduce information asymmetry.
2. Rating actions should be independent and objective.
3. CRAs should pursue transparency and disclosure.
4. CRAs should maintain in confidence all non-public information.

In September 2003, this committee had issued a report on the activities of CRAs backing up its Statement of Principles. Principle 1 deals with the quality and integrity of the rating process; 2 with the independence and conflicts of interest of analysts; 3 with the transparency and timeliness of ratings disclosure, and 4 with the preservation of confidential information. These principles are high-level objectives that CRAs, regulators, issuers, and other market participants should strive toward in order to protect the integrity and analytical independence of the credit rating process.

In October 2004, the Committee published its Consultation Report soliciting comments from various market participants. This report offered more detailed guidance to CRAs on how the objectives of the CRA Principles could be achieved in practice. It received 45 extensive comments coming from 21 different countries, which were all published.[55]

The Code Fundamentals, adopted in December 2004, prescribe that the CRAs should each adopt, publish, and adhere to its Code of Conduct. This should contain measures that deal with:

(1) the quality and integrity of the rating process;
(2) CRA independence and avoidance of conflicts of interest;
(3) CRA responsibilities to the investing public and issuers;
(4) disclosure of its code of conduct and communication with market participants.

---

[54] Statement of the Technical Committee of IOSCO, 2003. IOSCO Statement of Principles Regarding The Activities of Credit Rating Agencies, September 25, 1–4.

[55] Technical Committee of International Organization of Securities Commissions (IOSCO), 2004. Code of conduct fundamentals for credit rating agencies, Consultation report, October, OICV-IOSCO PD 173, 1–13.

Under each of these sections, the Fundamentals enumerate specific provisions, in total 52, that we will analyze below in comparison with EU and US regulatory approaches.[56] Importantly, the Code of Conduct mentions that the Code Fundamentals should be fully supported by the CRA management and backed by strong compliance and enforcement mechanisms.

The Code Fundamentals are not designed to be rigid or formulaic. They are designed to offer CRAs a degree of flexibility in how these measures are incorporated into the individual codes of conduct of the CRAs themselves, according to each CRA's specific legal and market circumstances.[57] IOSCO has arrived at the conclusion that a flexible approach can be more easily enforced than a universal code. A degree of flexibility is considered appropriate because rating agencies vary considerably in size, rating methods, and business model and IOSCO remains neutral toward these.

Moreover, the Fundamentals are to be implemented through a 'comply or explain' mechanism. Specifically, rating agencies are to voluntarily adopt their own Code, and then periodically publish its compliance with the Fundamentals or explain why they are unable to satisfy specific provisions. Thus, IOSCO does not recommend additional regulatory mechanisms for implementation. However, in its report of September 2003, it advises any jurisdiction that is considering implementation of additional regulation for CRAs, to take into account the issues described above, as they may affect the decision of whether to regulate, the shape of such regulation, and how to frame regulations that address them. The Technical Committee envisioned to revise the Code Fundamentals should experience dictate that a revision is necessary. The Technical Committee consulted with CRAs on the implementation of the Code of Conduct and published a report subsequently.[58] As soon as April 2007, at the early signs of the subprime mortgage meltdown the Technical Committee asked for an analysis of the role of CRAs in the structured finance market. After consultation with market participants on proposed amendments to the IOSCO Code of Conduct it published the new version of the Code of Conduct Fundamentals for Credit Rating Agencies.[59]

9.2.3   The 2005 European Union Policy on Credit Rating Agencies

The EU adopted a policy of moderate oversight with two types of instruments to implement it in December 2005.[60] One is self-regulation by the CRAs, the other is EU generic, non-CRA targeted, legislation. Under self-regulation, CRAs are advised to respect the IOSCO principles in their own Codes of Conduct. The relevant EU legislation is Competition Law and three framework laws passed under the 1999 Financial Services Action Plan (FSAP).[61]

---

[56] Technical Committee of International Organization of Securities Commissions (IOSCO), 2004. Code of conduct fundamentals for credit rating agencies, December, OICV-IOSCO PD 180, 1–12, page 3.

[57] Technical Committee of International Organization of Securities Commissions (IOSCO), 2004. Code of conduct fundamentals for credit rating agencies, December, OICV-IOSCO PD 180, 1–12, page 3.

[58] Technical Committee of International Organization of Securities Commissions (IOSCO), 2007. Review of implementation of the IOSCO fundamentals of a code of conduct for credit rating agencies, February, OICV-IOSCO PD 233, 1–18.

[59] Technical Committee of International Organization of Securities Commissions (IOSCO), 2008. Code of conduct fundamentals for credit rating agencies, Revised May, OICV-IOSCO PD 271, 1–14.

[60] Commission of the European Communities, 2005. Communication from the commission on credit rating agencies, December 23, 2005/11990, 1–9 (as published in the *Official Journal of the European Union*, 2006/C59/02, March 11, 2006, 1–5).

[61] The European Commission, 1999. Financial Services: Implementing the framework for financial markets: Action plan, Communication of the Commission, May 5, COM(1999)232, 11.05.99, 1–32. The FSAP was designed to open up a single market for financial services in the EU. Begun in 1999, it comprises 42 measures designed to

They are the 2003 Market Abuse Directive (MAD) which tackles the issue of insider dealing and market manipulation; the previously discussed 2006 CRD, and the 2004 Markets in Financial Instruments Directive (MiFID) which regulates the provision of investment services and activities, and defines investment advice.[62]

But the Commission kept the option to take legislative action in any one or a combination of events: (1) if compliance with EU rules or the IOSCO code by the CRAs is unsatisfactory and damaging to EU capital markets; (2) if new circumstances arise – including serious problems of market failure; (3) if changes occur in the way CRAs are regulated in other parts of the world. In addition, the Commission would assess whether the the ECAI recognition criteria set out in the CRD could be used in the future for conduct of business regulation of CRAs, if this appears necessary.

To assess the likelihood that the Commission might exercise the option to tighten its regulatory approach to the industry, one must know how the current policy arose. It was far from a done deal at the outset, with the legislators pushing for intrusive targeted regulation and the executive, with the support of technical expert groups, resisting in favor of relying more on market-based forces and generic EU law.

In January 2004, the European Parliament placed its first milestone on the path toward shaping EU policy. Within the Parliament, the Committee on Economic and Monetary Affairs (CEMA) had started work in April 2003, on its own initiative. As a result, it identified the following agenda of concerns: (a) oligopolistic and American dominated industry; (b) spectacular recent rating performance reverses; (c) the regulatory uses of ratings, and (d) potential conflicts of interest for CRAs in the normal course of business. CEMA resolved to instruct the Executive to examine the need for targeted legislative proposals to deal with its agenda and to recommend regulating the industry along the following lines. Firstly, CRAs active in Europe should be asked to register with a European Union Ratings Authority. This would imply periodic reporting to this authority and supervision by this authority of the proper conduct of rating activity. Secondly, rules could eventually be introduced to regulate, in the interests of market stability, the use made of ratings by private agents and regulators. Thirdly, the Moody's–S&P industry duopoly had to be confronted by means of a possible break-up of the agencies along lines of specialization. The implementation of such policies, however, should not interfere with the independence of opinion of CRAs.[63] The European Parliament backed away from the policy recommendations in favor of strong, targeted regulation, but endorsed the agenda and the request to the executive to examine the need for targeted legislative proposals to deal with it.[64]

---

harmonize the member states' rules on securities, banking, insurance, mortgages, pensions and all other forms of financial transaction. By the end of 2006, almost all of these measures have been adopted.

[62] (1) Market Abuse Directive ('MAD') along with its implementing regulation and directives for prevention of market manipulation and insider trading (Directive 2003/6/EC of 28/01/03 (OJ 2003 L 96/16); Commission Directive 2003/124/EC of 22/12/03 (OJ 2003 L 339/70); Commission Directive 2003/125/EC of 22/12/03 (OJ 2003 L 339/73); Commission Directive 2004/72/EC of 29/04/04 (OJ 2003 L 162/70) and Commission Regulation (EC) No 2273/2003 of 22/12/03 (OJ 2003 L 336/33)); (2) Capital Requirements Directive ('CRD') (Re-casting Directive 2000/12/EC of the European Parliament and of the Council of 20 March 2000 relating to the taking up and pursuit of the business of credit institutions) and Council Directive 93/6/EEC of March 15, 1993 on the capital adequacy of investment firms and credit institutions and (3) Markets in Financial Instruments Directive ('MiFID') (Directive 2004/39/EC of 21/04/04 (OJ 2004 L 145/1) covering the provision of investment advice).

[63] Katiforis, G., 2004. Report on role and methods of rating agencies, European Parliament, January 29, Session document A5-0040/2004, 1–11.

[64] European Parliament, 2004. Resolution on role and methods of rating agencies, February 10, P5_TA-PROV(2004)0080, 1–4.

The next milestone was reached in March 2005. The Executive had put the Parliament's agenda on conduct of business issues for analysis and advice to the Committee of European Securities Regulators (CESR).[65,66] It found that the aim of ensuring transparency and thoroughness in ratings could be achieved by adherence to a Code of Conduct – in particular, that of the IOSCO. The various options for code enforcement that the CESR evaluated were the monitoring of market developments, third party certification, and setting up of a recognition/regulation regime. In order to assess both CRA compliance with the Code and the effectiveness of the Code in achieving its objectives, the CESR recommended that market developments be monitored. Such a wait and see approach was also expected to reveal whether there was any need for a regulatory mechanism at all. The absence of a regulatory mechanism to enforce the Code could, of course, result in lack of compliance/implementation. But this approach would help to avert the costs of setting up a formal regulatory mechanism, namely administration costs and the costs of market failure due to governmental intervention. As a further disadvantage, a regulatory mechanism could give investors the perception that ratings give an absolute quality guarantee and threaten the independence of CRAs. It could also give new entrants a badge of respectability when this is not the role of regulation. The option of a third party certifier is also not recommended, given the absence of an obvious body that could serve this role and the issues it would raise with respect to the legal powers of such a body, and its ability to understand the policies and procedures of CRAs enough to enforce them. The CESR thus came out in favor of moderate oversight through self-regulation by CRAs following IOSCO, backed up with the reliance on EU generic, non-CRA targeted, legislation.[67]

Several pieces of generic legislation contributed other milestones in shaping EU policy. The Market Abuse Directive (MAD) was adopted in 2003, and the Markets in Financial Instruments Directive (MiFID) in 2004.[68] Furthermore, the Capital Requirements Directive (CRD) was being operationalized, allowing institutions to use credit ratings to determine the risk weight of their exposures and therefore the required capital. The condition was that the proper regulatory authority had recognized the CRA whose ratings were being used, according to the recognition criteria laid down in the CRD.[69]

The last milestone was the June 2005 Committee of European Banking Supervisors (CEBS) guidelines for implementing the CRA recognition criteria.[70] They cover the procedure for application to obtain ECAI status, the criteria themselves, and the process of mapping the credit ratings to risk weights of exposures. The criteria are grouped under methods (objectivity, independence, ongoing review, transparency) and individual credit assessments (credibility and market acceptance, transparency, and disclosure). They attempt to create a

---

[65] European Commission, 2004. Call to the CESR for technical advice on possible measures concerning credit rating agencies, July 27, 1–10.

[66] The Committee of European Securities Regulators (CESR), 2005. The use of ratings in private contracts, Technical advice to the European Commission on possible measures concerning credit rating agencies, March, CESR/05-139b, 1–93.

[67] The Committee of European Securities Regulators (CESR), 2005. The use of ratings in private contracts, Technical advice to the European Commission on possible measures concerning credit rating agencies, March, CESR/05-139b, 1–93.

[68] See footnote 62.

[69] Committee of European Banking Supervisors, 2006. *Guidelines on the Recognition of External Credit Assessment Institutions*, January 20, 1–40, page 1.

[70] Committee of European Banking Supervisors, 2005. Consultation paper on the recognition of external credit assessment institutions, June 29, 1–37. For their final form, see Committee of European Banking Supervisors, 2006. Guidelines on the recognition of external credit assessment institutions, January 20, 1–40.

single-market level playing field across jurisdictions in Europe, reduce administrative costs, and bring about convergence and common understanding of recognition criteria across the various European authorities. While these guidelines deal extensively with recognition criteria for ECAIs, it is made clear that 'ECAI recognition for capital purposes does not in any way constitute a form of regulation of ECAIs or a form of licensing of rating agencies to do business in Europe. Its sole purpose is to provide a basis for capital requirement calculations in the Standardized Approach and the Securitization Ratings Based Approaches.'[71]

In the EU, the regulation of CRAs now stands firmly on four legs of EU generic, non-CRA targeted, legislation. Built between 2002 and 2005, the regulation was articulated in the December 2005 Commission communication, to which the quotes in the following summary refer.

One, EU competition law fully covers the *industry structure and competitive practices* issues that the CRA industry may encounter. The EU Executive, as the enforcement authority, came to the conclusion that 'there is [currently] no indication of any anti-competitive practices in this industry ... it does not therefore see currently the need for action.' Furthermore, the Executive does not consider the high degree of industry concentration a point of concern, since 'in this particular industry, excessive fragmentation could have adverse consequences' (i.e. CRAs may face undue pressure to issue favorable ratings in order to attract clients).

Two, possible *conflicts between a CRA's commercial interest in selling ancillary services and deontological duties in deciding a rating action* with respect to the same issuer are regulated by the MiFID. 'Issuing a credit rating will normally not result in the CRA also providing "investment advice" so that MiFID is not applicable to the rating process of credit rating agencies.' 'However, CRAs that do also provide investment services and activities on a professional basis may require authorization. In such cases, the MiFID provisions regarding conduct of business and organizational requirements will apply.' These 'may require an appropriate degree of separation of investment services from the credit rating process so that these services may not interfere with the quality and objectivity of credit ratings.'

Three, the *regulatory use of credit ratings in computing regulatory capital requirements* is regulated by the CRD. The regulatory authorities will only accept for that purpose 'the use of ratings provided by recognized CRAs.' To be recognized, the ratings 'must be objectively and independently assigned and reviewed on an ongoing basis'; 'rating procedures must be sufficiently transparent'; ratings must be 'recognized in the market as credible and reliable by their users'; they must be 'accessible at equivalent terms to all interested parties.' The recognition of this particular regulatory use of the rating should in principle not bear upon 'the broader conduct of business issues,' but could possibly 'be used in the future for conduct of business regulation.'

Four, in the field of *conflicts of interest, fair representation of investment recommendations and the access to inside information*, the provisions of the MAD constitute a comprehensive legal framework for CRAs. Accordingly, credit ratings do not constitute a recommendation but they are regarded as opinions on creditworthiness. Nevertheless CRAs are to implement 'procedures to ensure that credit ratings published by them are fairly presented'; are prohibited 'to disseminate false or misleading information, constituting market manipulation'; must disclose 'any significant interests or conflicts of interest concerning the issues or the

---

[71] Committee of European Banking Supervisors, 2006. *Guidelines on the Recognition of External Credit Assessment Institutions*, January 20, 1–40, page 1.

issuers they rate'; 'owe a duty of confidentiality' to the issuer who 'allows a CRA access to inside information,' i.e. prohibition from trading on the information or disclosing it.

Next to the application of EU generic legislation on competition and financial markets to CRAs, under self-regulation, CRAs are advised to incorporate the IOSCO principles into their own Codes of Conduct. The EU Executive is to closely monitor CRAs compliance with the IOSCO code through annual reports from the CESR, the first one to be delivered by the end of 2006.[72] Interestingly, the Executive expects from this annual report a 'thorough assessment of the level of day to day application of the IOSCO code in practice including consultation of all stakeholders.' This is more than the CESR is able and willing to deliver. It holds the view 'to rely on self-regulation as regards the implementation of the provisions of the IOSCO Code by CRAs.' In addition, 'it is not in a position to conduct such an assessment in absence of legislation and of necessary enabling supervisory authority.'[73] Instead, the CESR has engaged in a series of dialogues with prominent CRAs to review the implementation of the IOSCO Code. This exchange between the EU Executive and the CESR as a quasi-regulatory body may indicate that the Executive may in fact be thinking along lines of stronger oversight than it has so far professed. It is quite plausible that the EU Executive was affected by concurrent developments in the US, where the possibility of regulatory oversight of the credit rating industry, backed up by enabling supervisory authority for the SEC, was looming large. More recently, following the meltdown in the US subprime mortgage market, the CESR has been further monitoring the self-regulatory approach and examining the role of the rating agencies in the structured finance market.[74] The pressure for stronger direct oversight of the rating agencies is increasing.

9.2.4 The US 'Credit Rating Agency Reform Act of 2006'

After four years of preparation, the US signed 'The Credit Rating Agency Reform Act of 2006' into law on September 19. This was to improve ratings quality 'by fostering accountability, transparency, and competition in the CRA industry.'[75] The act vests vigorous oversight authority in the SEC to grant access to the registered pool of CRAs and to monitor proper business conduct of those who are in the pool. It replaces the 'opaque' prevailing NRSRO designation system with a more transparent and objective alternative registration system. It limits the authority of the SEC to those CRAs that seek recognition. The bill was introduced on the premise that it would encourage competition in the industry and that by doing so ratings quality would improve. Oversight of registered CRAs includes a duty of record keeping and reporting, and the SEC rights of inspection, examination, and enforcement. For example, under the section 'Accountability for Rating Procedures,' the bill gives the SEC the authority to take action against a CRA that contravenes the information provided during the application process, or in later reports submitted under the bill. It also gives the SEC the right of censure, denial, or suspension of registration.

---

[72] The Committee of European Securities Regulators (CESR), 2006. Report to the European Commission on the compliance of credit rating agencies with the IOSCO code, December, CESR/06-545, 1–122.

[73] The Committee of European Securities Regulators (CESR), 2006. Letter from European Commission re annual reports on credit rating agencies and The Committee of European Securities Regulators' answer, May 17, 1–3.

[74] The Committee of European Securities Regulators (CESR), 2008. Second report to the European Commission on the compliance of credit rating agencies with the IOSCO code and the role of credit rating agencies in structured finance, May, CESR/08-277, 1–68.

[75] United States Senate, 2006. Credit Rating Agency Reform Act of 2006 (S. 3850), 109th Congress, 2D Session, September 22, in effect since July 1, 2007, after the SEC released its final implementation rule.

The real impact of new legislation depends on how stable and broadly shared its origins are. These will influence the likelihood of future law reversals and the determination of how the act will be implemented. And implementation by itself is of course what counts. It is therefore of more than speculative interest to understand how and why the Reform Act came about, first through the work at the SEC, and then in Congress.

The US Securities and Exchange Commission

Complying with Sarbanes–Oxley, the SEC spent the period from 2002 through 2005 study-ing the issues facing the CRA industry and designing measures to resolve them. In November 2002, it held public hearings. In January 2003 the SEC published its 'Report on the role and function of credit rating agencies in the operation of the securities market.' And in June 2003, an initial SEC rule concept invited comments from market participants, other regulators, and the public at large. Both of these deal with greater regulatory oversight of CRAs and the need to reduce potential regulatory barriers to entry brought about by the prevailing NRSRO system in the regulatory use of ratings. Due to the SEC's lack of statu-tory oversight rights, the hearings and publications focused primarily on the existence and process of the NRSRO system.

The first result was to come out in favour of maintaining access control to the regulatory uses of CRAs credit ratings.[76] Removal of the NRSRO designation system would necessitate replacing ratings in regulations with alternative benchmarks (for example, credit spreads), or replacing the designation with an alternative recognition system.[77] As per the SEC Proposed Rule,

> Most of the 46 commenters responding to the 2003 Concept Release supported retention of the NRSRO concept. They generally represented that, among other things, eliminating the NRSRO concept would be disruptive to the capital markets, and would be costly and complicated to replace. Only four commenters supported elimination of the concept, and there was limited discussion of regulatory alternatives.[78]

The next result was to reach consensus on improving the process. 'The Commission's process of recognizing NRSROs has come under criticism for being opaque and lengthy,' as per the SEC report itself.[79] Criticism included lack of clarity on how the SEC conducts its assessment of the stated criteria, ambiguity in the minimum standards required for meeting those criteria, lack of explanation on why the status is denied, and long response times. 'For over a decade, R&I and its predecessors have engaged the SEC in an effort to receive NRSRO designation.'[80] R&I is a credit rating agency headquartered in Tokyo and well-recognized in the broader Asian market. R&I first applied to the SEC in 1990, subsequently

---

[76] US Securities and Exchange Commission, 2003. Report on the role and function of credit rating agencies in the operation of the securities market, January, 1–45, page 10.
[77] US Securities and Exchange Commission, 2003. Report on the role and function of credit rating agencies in the operation of the securities market, January, 1–45, page 39.
[78] US Securities and Exchange Commission, 2005. Proposed rule – definition of Nationally Recognized Statistical Rating Organizations, April 19, 1–74, page 17.
[79] US Securities and Exchange Commission, 2003. Report on the role and function of credit rating agencies in the operation of the securities market, January, 1–45, page 40.
[80] Harada, Y., Executive Vice President – Rating and Investment Information, Inc., 2005. Examining the role of credit rating agencies in the capital markets, Testimony before Committee on Banking, Housing, and Urban Affairs, United States Senate, February 8, 1–8, page 4.

received no formal response from the SEC, submitted fresh requests in 1998 and 2002, and has still not received a final decision. In the words of the MD of another non-NRSRO CRA,

> We applied for NRSRO designation in July 1998, approximately eight years ago. Despite our success in issuing timely, accurate ratings, we are not designated and even after multiple requests, have not been told what is needed to be designated. In 2003, an SEC official told us that the SEC hesitated to tell us what the specific criteria were since we would probably meet them and the SEC would have to designate us.[81]

A substantial change that these comments suggested was that the crucial NRSRO designation variable, 'national recognition,' should be eliminated. This criterion had drawn virtually unanimous criticism. In addition, the concept release reflected that market participants generally agreed that firms with a particular specialization (industry, product, or geography) should be eligible for NRSRO recognition, if they have demonstrated their expertise.[82]

Integrating these outcomes, the SEC released a revised rule proposal on the definition of NRSROs in 2005.[83] This proposal sought to define the term NRSRO based on fulfillment of three conditions: (1) issuance of publicly available (at no cost) credit ratings that are current assessments on specific securities; (2) general acceptance of the ratings, including for a particular geography or industry segment; and (3) use of systematic procedures and sufficient financial resources to ensure credible ratings, manage conflicts of interest, etc. Importantly, it did away with the national recognition criterion, which had been widely agreed to be the most restrictive criterion for new agencies wishing to enter the NRSRO group, and replaced it with a general acceptance criterion.

The most vociferous comment on this revised SEC proposed rule, either for or against, was from the community of CRAs aspiring to become NRSROs.[84] They argued that it reinforced the barriers to entry that the SEC was already accused of having created with the NRSRO system. The three key conditions drew criticism. The first was the criterion of public dissemination of ratings at 'no cost.' Rating agencies such as Egan-Jones Ratings Co. and Rapid Ratings Pty Ltd contended that this presumed that aspiring NRSROs follow 'issuer pays' business models. However, there are firms that follow 'subscriber pays' business models, who would not be able to apply for the NRSRO status given the no cost criterion, since charging large numbers of subscribers is at the heart of this business model.

The second area of criticism was the allusion to 'general acceptance' by the market. Although the SEC had said that NRSROs issuing ratings in a particular geographical or

---

[81] Egan, S.J., 2005, Managing Director – Egan-Jones Ratings Company, 2005. Legislative Solutions for the Credit Rating Agency Duopoly Relief Act of 2005, Testimony before the House Subcommittee on Capital Markets, Insurance and Government Sponsored Enterprises, June 29, 1–7.

[82] US Securities and Exchange Commission, 2003. Report on the role and function of credit rating agencies in the operation of the securities markets, January, 1–45, page 39 and Joynt, S.W., 2005. Examining the role of credit rating agencies in the capital markets, Testimony before the US Senate Committee on Banking, Housing, and Urban Affairs, February 8, 1–10, page 5.

[83] US Securities and Exchange Commission, 2005. Proposed rule – definition of Nationally Recognized Statistical Rating Organizations, April 19, 1–74,

[84] Egan-Jones Ratings Company, 2005. Comments on SEC proposed rule – Definition of Nationally Recognized Statistical Rating Organizations, May 26, 1–7, and Caragata, P.J., Managing Director and Chief Executive Officer – Rapid Ratings Pty. Ltd, 2005. Comments on SEC proposed rule – Nationally Recognized Statistical Rating Organizations, August 6, 1–25.

industrial segment would also be considered for NRSRO status, the feeling among several market participants was that the term was really a cosmetic change to the earlier term, national recognition. Finally, aspiring NRSROs were of the view that the proposed criteria were designed to suit the ratings approach of existing NRSROs.

> Although the SEC has indicated an openness to quantitatively oriented ratings agencies qualifying for NRSRO status, the recently proposed NRSRO definitions are biased against quantitative firms. For example, the SEC notes in its release accompanying the rulemaking, a number of benchmarks, including the experience and training of analysts, number of issues covered by each analyst, and information sources within issuers as determinative of operational integrity. These criteria, and the level of operational funding needed to support the functions, while relevant to qualitative rating organizations (Type 1: paid by issuers), have little relevance to organizations such as Rapid Ratings and other quantitative firms that determine their ratings based on software models and public information (Type 2: paid by investors and other subscribers).[85]

To oversee conduct of business, the SEC engaged the industry along IOSCO lines, because it did not have statutory authority. The SEC discussed a voluntary framework of standards with existing NRSROs that would address important issues such as potential conflicts of interest. The framework envisaged enhanced oversight of NRSROs by providing a means by which SEC staff could assess on an ongoing basis whether an NRSRO continued to meet the NRSRO definition.[86]

However, despite all its initiatives, the SEC avoided a hard stand on the issue of regulatory oversight. SEC Chairman William Donaldson passed on the responsibility to the US Congress, stating: 'The Commission believes that to conduct a rigorous program of NRSRO oversight, more explicit regulatory authority from Congress is necessary. We believe that a well-thought-out regulatory regime could provide significant benefits in such areas as record-keeping and addressing conflicts of interest in the industry.'[87] He further explained that even with respect to the voluntary framework being discussed with the NRSROs, such a framework if adopted would not give the Commission the authority that would be conferred by actual legislation, as the SEC would not have enforcement power, or the right to direct inspection. A few months later, the new Chairman, Christopher Cox, somewhat revised this stand with the statement that, 'we can issue no-action letters, and can bring enforcement actions for violation of antifraud provisions of the securities laws.'[88] He also said that efforts to establish a voluntary framework with the CRAs has been underway since 2004 and that 'We need to be prepared alternatively with our own action.' He indicated that the SEC might be 'proceeding apace' even without legislation.

---

[85] Roberts, R., 2005. The credit rating agency duopoly relief act of 2005. Testimony before the Committee on Financial Services, United States House of Representatives, Rapid Ratings Pty Ltd, November 29, 1–17, pages 8, 11.

[86] Donaldson, W.H., Chairman – US Securities and Exchange Commission, 2005. Chairman SEC, The State of the Securities Industry, Testimony before the Committee on Banking, Housing, and Urban Affairs, United States Senate, March 9, 1–13, page 6.

[87] Donaldson, W.H., Chairman – US Securities and Exchange Commission, 2005. Chairman SEC, The State of the Securities Industry, Testimony before the Committee on Banking, Housing, and Urban Affairs, United States Senate, March 9, 1–13, page 5.

[88] Cox, C., Chairman – US Securities and Exchange Commission, 2006. A review of current securities issues, Testimony before Committee on Banking, Housing, and Urban Affairs, United States Senate, April 25, 1–12.

US Congress

Congress eventually pre-empted any notable outcome from the efforts of the SEC by passing the Reform Act. The Enron Corporation had filed for bankruptcy protection on December 2, 2001 and the country moved quickly: In the United States, whenever there is a major problem in our capital markets, we shine a light on it and move quickly to clean it up.'[89] So in January 2002, the US Senate started a wide-ranging review, taking charge of the CRA agenda as a private sector watchdog of financial oversight. This led to a series of hearings on rating the CRAs in March, first in a sequence of events and reports filled with testimonies from representatives of the SEC, major CRAs, associations of corporate treasurers, intermediaries, academics, etc. that underscored the legislative process. After another set of hearings in March 2005, it was clear that the NRSRO system could not continue in its current form, nor would a cosmetic change be sufficient. It was by now widely accepted that the SEC criterion of national recognition for granting NRSRO status to a CRA to license its ratings for regulatory uses was a classic Catch 22. As Committee Chairman Shelby of the US Senate put it poignantly on March 7: 'to receive the license, a firm must be nationally recognized, but it cannot become nationally recognized without first having the license.' By mid-2005, the SEC had prepared a legislative framework ('SEC Legislative Framework') laying out some of the tenets of potential legislation for the industry.[90,91] This led to the first legislative initiative in June 2005, with the deposition in the House of the 'Credit Rating Agency Duopoly Relief Act of 2005' proposal, H.R. 2990.[92]

H.R. 2990 was a reaction to the SEC's lethargy in taking a stand on opening the industry and on overseeing CRAs. H.R. 2990 explicitly opposed the SEC designation system and Rule Proposal. '... Congress finds that ... the SEC ... has, through its designation of certain credit rating agencies as NRSRO, created an artificial barrier to entry for new participants; and ... will, in its latest proposed rule defining NRSROs, codify and strengthen this barrier.'[93] It tried to force a regime change in the way CRAs compete in the US by abolishing that barrier, instructing the SEC to grant NRSRO status to CRAs that are simply registered and have been in business for at least three consecutive years. Registration entails disclosing rating procedures and methods, statistics on ratings performance, and policies and procedures to handle conflicts of interest and non-public information. Any wannabe CRA could comply with these conditions, considerably flattening the world of credit ratings. The credible threat of new entrants would reinvigorate competition. This would encourage CRAs to increase their investment in quality, facilitate reversals of market dominance, and improve choices for issuers.

As far as overseeing CRAs goes, H.R. 2990 can be said to be a mixed bag. It reinvents the wheel by codifying the current practices of CRAs, such as disseminating rating criteria and

---

[89] Paulson, H.M., Treasury Secretary, 2006. Remarks on the competitiveness of US capital markets, economic club of New York, New York, NY, November 20, 1–12, page 1.

[90] US Securities and Exchange Commission, 2005. Staff outline of key issues for a legislative framework for the oversight and regulation of credit rating agencies (Introduced into the record by Ranking Democratic Member Paul E. Kanjorski in his Opening Statement at the Hearing entitled 'Legislative Solutions for the Credit Rating Industry' before the House Subcommittee on Capital Markets, Insurance and Government Sponsored Enterprises, on 29 June 2005), June 6, 1–3.

[91] The NRSROs opposed this framework.

[92] United States House of Representatives, 2005. H.R. 2990 introduced by Mr Fitzpatrick, referred to the House Committee on Financial Services, June 20.

[93] United States House of Representatives, 2005. H.R. 2990 introduced by Mr Fitzpatrick, referred to the House Committee on Financial Services, June 20, page 3.

performance, and establishing policies for dealing with conflicts of interest and non-public information, already well-documented on the CRAs' own websites. It includes potentially dangerous features, such as granting the SEC intrusive regulatory authority over CRAs.

H.R. 2990 found many supporters but drew strong opposition from the NRSROs on the matter of overly intrusive oversight. '... we believe that H.R. 2990, ... could unnecessarily inject the SEC into the substance of the credit ratings process and result in a dilution of the quality and diversity of ratings, thus undermining the benefits of ratings to the market.'[94] The NRSROs also contended that by increasing regulation-related costs for new entrants, it could even hamper competition: '... the Act ... as proposed impose(s) a substantial and ill-defined regulatory burden on rating agencies, which itself could create a new barrier to entry,' as Nancy Stroker, MD of Fitch, put it.[95]

NRSROs also reacted negatively to replacing the SEC designation system in its revised rule proposal with the open registration system. While supporting the objectives of greater competition and transparency, NRSROs were skeptical as to whether the bill would actually achieve these objectives. For one, it did not provide clear legislative standards by which the SEC would assess the reliability of ratings and decide whether or not to approve the registration of a rating organization. In the absence of proper legislation to deter rating agencies from competing by issuing more favorable ratings than other rating agencies, the introduction of too many new agencies could actually reduce the reliability of ratings.[96]

Further, the NRSROs declared the bill unconstitutional: 'The very notion that a bona fide publisher – whether it be *Business Week*, *The Wall Street Journal* or S&P – can be required under the threat of penalty to obtain a government license, adhere to government dictates about its policies and procedures, and/or submit to intrusive examinations before being permitted to disseminate its opinions to the public is inconsistent with core First Amendment principles.'[97,98]

After a number of changes, the House approved the bill on July 12, 2006.[99,100] The need for compulsory registration of any rating agency was removed. Another major change dealt with the NRSROs' concern about excessive interference by the SEC, through the inclusion of the Limitation Clause which stated that 'The rules and regulations applicable to NRSROs the Commission may prescribe pursuant to this Act shall be narrowly tailored to meet

---

[94] Bolger, R.M., Managing Director, Global Regulatory Affairs & Associate General Counsel–Standard & Poor's, 2005. The Credit Rating Agency Duopoly Relief Act of 2005. Testimony before the House Subcommittee on Capital Markets, Insurance and Government Sponsored Enterprises, June 29, 1–17, page 2.

[95] Stroker, N., Group Managing Director – Fitch Ratings, 2005. Legislative Solutions for the Credit Rating Agency Duopoly Relief Act of 2005, Statement to the House Subcommittee on Capital Markets, Insurance and Government Sponsored Enterprises, June 29, 1–24, page 2.

[96] Stroker, N., Group Managing Director – Fitch Ratings, 2005. Legislative Solutions for the Credit Rating Agency Duopoly Relief Act of 2005, Statement to the House Subcommittee on Capital Markets, Insurance and Government Sponsored Enterprises, June 29, 1–24, page 4.

[97] The First Amendment states in part: 'Congress shall make no law ... abridging the freedom of speech, or of the press.' What credit rating agencies do in analyzing debt and assessing the likelihood of repayment of the debt and then putting a sort of shorthand label [like triple-A] on it is very similar to what recognized journalists do in covering the market. As a result, there is a substantial body of law that has developed concluding that rating agencies are protected by the First Amendment in what they do.

[98] Bolger, R.M., Managing Director, Global Regulatory Affairs & Associate General Counsel – Standard & Poor's, 2005. The Credit Rating Agency Duopoly Relief Act of 2005, Testimony before the House Subcommittee on Capital Markets, Insurance and Government Sponsored Enterprises, June 29, 1–17, page 2.

[99] United States House of Representatives, 2006. Amendment in the nature of a substitute to H.R. 2990 offered by Mr Oxley of Ohio, June 13, 1–24. H.R. 2990 ordered reported to the House with a favorable recommendation, with an amendment, by a voice vote.

[100] Initially introduced into the House as H.R. 2990, the CRA Duopoly Relief Act of 2005 (see below).

the requirements of this Act applicable to NRSROs and shall not purport to regulate the substance of credit ratings or the procedures and methodologies by which such NRSROs determine credit ratings.' However, the clause does not seem to have allayed all fears of the incumbents. In a letter to the US House of Representatives, the President of S&P expressed the view that 'Notwithstanding the bill's statement of principle that the SEC will not have a role in assessing rating agencies' processes and procedures, in reality, H.R. 2990 would improperly involve the SEC in determining the appropriate "procedures and methodologies" to be employed by NRSROs.'[101]

Shortly thereafter, the US Senate Committee approved 'The CRA Reform Act of 2006,' different in several key respects to H.R. 2990.[102] Firstly, perhaps owing to inputs from the SEC, which were apparently missing in the case of H.R. 2990, it did away with the strongly worded clause blaming the SEC for strengthening its self-created artificial barriers to entry into the CRA industry.

Secondly, it contained the Limitation Clause which was missing from the earlier versions of H.R. 2990.

Thirdly, it addressed concerns about infringement of First Amendment rights by making it clear that under the bill, the rating agencies are not waiving their First Amendment free speech protections or any other federal rights.

Fourthly, the concern of 'quality over quantity' due to a disclosure-based registration process was addressed through the requirement that CRAs applying for registration provide certification by at least 10 Qualified Institutional Buyers, who have used the ratings of that agency for at least the immediately preceding three consecutive years.

Fifthly, the Act dealt with the issue of conflicts of interest due to economic pressures more clearly by demanding a list of the 20 largest issuers or subscribers.

Finally, the Reform Act made rule-making in certain areas of CRA procedure mandatory for the SEC, rather than optional as in the matter of conflicts of interest, or protection of non-public information. The Reform Act requires that these rules be issued in final form, and become effective not later than 270 days from the enactment of the legislation. It also links the effective date of the legislation to the issuance of these rules in final form.

The Reform Act has found favor with several market participants, including AFP, BMA and, to some extent, the CRAs themselves. The reaction of incumbents has been more muted than to H.R. 2990. While Fitch has actually endorsed the bill, representatives of S&P and Moody's have said that they support the goals of the bill, but will continue to work with the lawmakers to try to obtain further changes. 'We support the goals of the bill and believe the current version takes a constructive approach to increasing competition and transparency in the credit rating industry,' said Marjory Appel, a spokesperson at Standard & Poor's. 'We are encouraged that further improvements and clarifications will be made in order to safeguard the independence of the credit rating agency process.' 'We're supportive of these goals,' said Fran Laserson, a spokesperson for Moody's. 'We'll continue to communicate with lawmakers' because Moody's wants to assure the legislation does not result in any 'unintended market consequences,' she said. Notwithstanding this hope for further improvements and clarifications, the Reform Act proceeded to pass the full Senate on September 23, 2006, and the US House of Representatives on September 27, 2006. It was signed into law by the President on September 29, 2006.

---

[101] Corbet, K.A., President – Standard & Poor's, 2006. Letter to United States House of Representatives re H.R. 2990, July 10, 1–9.
[102] On August 2, 2006.

9.3   ANALYSIS AND EVALUATION

9.3.1   The EU and the US Approaches Compared

Recognition Criteria to Allow the Regulatory Use of a CRA's Ratings

The EU has no targeted industry entrance or exit requirements nor recognition criteria for
the regulatory use of a CRA's ratings, yet. The common corporate and competition law
principles apply. If the natural course of competition leads to industry concentration, so be
it. This may in fact be in the interest of investors because it protects CRAs from undue
commercial pressure, minimizes their switching costs and learning of various rating methodologies. The only exception to this principle is one detailed rule for the use of a CRA's
credit ratings in the computation of bank capital requirements – albeit not a minor one.

   In the US, the Rating Agency Act does away with the no-action letter procedure and
requires instead that entities that wish to be NRSROs should register with the SEC, thereby
giving the SEC a much clearer and more active role in the recognition process, which
resembles more a registration process. The application process and timelines for responses
by the SEC have been defined clearly in the Reform Act – approval to be granted within
90 days, or else proceedings, **including grounds for denial**, to be instituted within 120 days
of filing the application, with a decision mandatory at the end of this period, or within a
maximum period of another 90 days. More specifically, at the time of application, a rating
agency is required to have been in the business of issuing credit ratings for at least three
consecutive years, and to have written certifications from at least ten qualified institutional
buyers (QIBs), in each category of rated obligors. The purpose is to ensure that the quality
of registered agencies is maintained. Whether this would once again introduce a 'chicken
and egg' situation remains to be seen, though the bill has been supported in general by the
parties who stand to gain by greater competition, including investor and issuer associations.

   With respect to the European approach on recognition criteria, the most extensive work,
as noted above, has been conducted by CEBS. While these guidelines do not profess to
address the regulation of CRAs in Europe, the EC does recognize in its stated policy that it
will closely monitor developments relating to the recognition of ECAIs to see '. . . whether
the ECAI recognition criteria could be used in the future for conduct of business regulation
of credit rating agencies, if this appears to be necessary.' In this context, a comparison of
the CEBS criteria and the criteria laid out in the Rating Agency Act is worth while.

   The CEBS spells out technical criteria for general rating methods and for individual
rating actions.[103] The former must satisfy detailed conditions with respect to objectivity,
independence, ongoing review, and transparency and disclosure. The latter must pass the
tests of credibility and market acceptance, and transparency and disclosure of the rating
assessments. The guidelines give detailed directions on what factors the authorities must
consider in determining whether a criterion has been met or not. They also require ECAIs
to demonstrate that they have met the criteria and provide detailed guidelines on the issues
that ECAIs must cover for such demonstration.

   On the other hand, the Rating Agency Act basically lists a series of information requirements. These deal with policies for preventing misuse of non-public information, any
conflicts of interest, organization structure, whether it has a code of conduct, a list of
the 20 largest issuers or subscribers, and certifications from at least 10 QIBs that have used

---

[103] Committee of European Banking Supervisors, 2006. *Guidelines on the Recognition of External Credit Assessment
Institutions*, January 20, 1–40.

the CRA's rating in the last three years. This makes the Rating Agency Act criteria simpler to understand than the CEBS guidelines, but leaves the SEC with a lot of discretion on how exactly to interpret information received from CRAs, and what merit-based criteria to apply.

At the same time, parallels can be drawn between the broad goals of CEBS and the information requirements of the Rating Agency Act. For example, the objectivity goal of CEBS requires, 'In meeting this criterion, an ECAI will need to demonstrate that its methodology incorporates factors known to be relevant in determining an entity's creditworthiness. This demonstration should, to the fullest extent possible, be supported by statistical evidence that the methodology has produced accurate credit assessments in the past.' In comparison, the Rating Agency Act requires information on credit ratings performance measurement statistics over short-term, mid-term, and long-term periods (as applicable); as well as on procedures and methodologies used in determining credit ratings. Similarly, the independence criterion of the CEBS guidelines requires that ratings be free from political influence and economic pressures, and defines the conflicts of interest that can arise from these pressures. In tandem, the Rating Agency Act requires information on organization structure, any conflicts of interest relating to the issuance of credit ratings, a list of the top 20 issuers or subscribers, and whether the CRA has an internal code of conduct.

Another area of similarity is the 'credibility and market acceptance' criterion of the CEBS guidelines, which is mirrored in the Rating Agency Act requirement for certifications by at least ten QIBs. These criteria seem to present the same problem as the current national recognition criterion in the US. The Rating Agency Act requirement seems to have been added over the original version of the bill to solve the quantity over quality issue, but could lead again to the basic problem of lesser known firms being unable to get recognition and so remain unknown. The CEBS guidelines do qualify this criterion by saying that it is not a necessary criterion, and that in its absence, the competent authorities would need to do a more thorough assessment of the ECAI in question. 'Stronger market acceptance is not a prerequisite, but rather a factor which is relevant in determining the intensity of assessment of other factors.'[104] However, the criterion could well become a source of barrier for entry to lesser-known CRAs.

This problem has been highlighted by a relatively prominent CRA, DBRS, which although well known in the US, may have problems of market acceptability in Europe. For agencies that are much less well known than DBRS, the problem could be much more acute. The situation is summed up by the following quotation from the DBRS response to the CEBS guidelines.

> ...DBRS submits that the European market is quite different from the US, and that for DBRS to demonstrate strong market acceptance in member states would be somewhat more difficult.... DBRS suggests that for credit rating agencies that are relatively less well known in Europe or in a particular member state, supervisory authorities should be encouraged to undertake a greater level of assessment.... other indicators of market credibility should be permitted, e.g. ... many institutions plan to use an ECAI's credit assessment; however, DBRS requests that the term 'large number of institutions' be clearly defined. Other indications of market acceptance should also be included,... planned ECAI usage by broker-dealers, and the number and type of citations of the ECAI in well-known industry journals or newspapers (international and/or

---

[104] Committee of European Banking Supervisors, 2006. *Guidelines on the Recognition of External Credit Assessment Institutions*, January 20, 1–40, page 17.

local). Moreover, DBRS suggests that a reasonable time frame such as three to four years be permitted to establish broad market acceptance in the international European community.[105]

Disclosure Requirements

The CEBS guidelines include adherence to a code of conduct and the public disclosure of such a code. They require that the principles of the methodology ECAIs use to formulate credit assessments be made publicly available so as to allow all potential users to decide whether they are derived in a reasonable way. However, the guidelines leave the form and extent of such disclosure to the ECAIs, instead of prescribing a rigid disclosure framework.

ECAIs are also required to disclose any changes in methodology. The guidelines specify that disclosure methods could include display in the public area of the ECAIs' Internet website, or free-of-charge distribution of written publications on request. Also, ECAIs are required to ensure that individual credit assessments are accessible at equivalent terms at least to all credit institutions having a legitimate interest in these assessments. Proper differentiation is made between ECAIs that charge subscribers and those that charge issuers, with the stipulation that the complete range of an ECAI's credit assessments be potentially available to all subscribing institutions (in the case of the former) and to the public (in the case of the latter).

The Rating Agency Act and the SEC rule require that a recognized CRA makes all information filed with SEC in the application publicly available, except for: the certification from qualified institutional buyers, the list of the largest users of rating services by net revenue, the financial statements and the total and median annual compensation of credit analysts. Essentially this information is: the credit ratings performance measurement statistics, a description of the procedures and methodologies used in determining the credit ratings, policies and procedures implemented to prevent the misuse of material, nonpublic information, the organizational structure of the agency, the code of ethics, identification of conflicts of interests related to the issuance of ratings, policies and procedures to address and manage these conflicts, information regarding the number of analysts, of analyst supervisors and analyst qualifications. In the SEC rule, analyst, and analyst supervisors, experience and training, the number of ratings per category and the financial statements are taken as criteria for ascertaining if a CRA has sufficient resources to issue reliable ratings.[106]

Management of Conflicts of Interest

In Europe, legislation has been passed under the Financial Services Action Plan to address some of the issues in the functioning of CRAs. In the field of conflicts of interest, the provisions of the Market Abuse Directives constitute a comprehensive legal framework for CRAs. In order to prevent insider dealing and market manipulation, Directive 2003/125/EC addresses the disclosure of conflicts of interest. Moreover, it states that a CRA must disclose any significant interests or conflicts of interest concerning the financial instruments or the issuers to which their credit ratings relate. Additionally, it follows from the Directive 2003/6/EC that, where a CRA knew, or ought to have known, that the credit rating was false

---

[105] Keogh, M., Managing Director, Policy – Dominion Bond Rating Service, 2005. Response to CEBS consultation paper on the recognition of external credit assessment institutions, September 27, 1–8, page 6.
[106] US Securities and Exchange Commission, 2007. Final rule – oversight of credit rating agencies as Nationally Recognized Statistical Rating Organization, June 26, 1–28, for the entire section.

or misleading, the prohibition to disseminate false or misleading information, constituting market manipulation, may apply to their credit ratings. Considering these provisions, it is clear that CRAs need to implement internal procedures and policies to ensure objective, independent, and accurate credit ratings that will benefit investor confidence.[107]

In addition, conflicts of interest arising from a CRA providing ancillary services are addressed by the Markets in Financial Instruments Directive (MiFID). This directive applies to CRAs when they cross the limits of providing 'investment advice.' In such situations, they require authorization and the MiFID provisions regarding conduct of business and organizational requirements will apply to the firm and its undertaking of investment services and activities. Where, for example, a credit rating agency provides investment services (such as investment advice) to clients that fall under the MiFID, the provisions on conflicts of interest will apply to protect the interest of those who receive these services. The provisions on conflicts of interest may require an appropriate degree of separation of investment services from the credit rating process, so that ancillary services do not interfere with the quality and objectivity of credit ratings.

The Rating Agency Act also stipulates the condition of implementation of systematic procedures by the CRAs, and makes rule-making mandatory for the SEC. The final rule requires that an NRSRO informs of any potential conflict of interest relating to the issuance of credit ratings and provides as guidance a list of ten different generic conflicts of interest. The agency can choose to provide its own description of conflicts or just check whether any of the list are applicable. Then an NRSRO is required to disclose the policies and procedures it establishes, maintains, and enforces to address and manage these conflicts. Proprietary information that may diminish the effectiveness of these procedures is not required. 'The Commission shall issue final rules in accordance with subsection (n) to prohibit, or require the management and disclosure of, any conflicts of interest relating to the issuance of credit ratings by a nationally recognized statistical rating organization, including, without limitation, conflicts of interest relating to . . . .' The subsection (n) referred to in this clause requires that these rules be issued in final form, and become effective, not later than 270 days from the enactment of the legislation. It also links the effective date of the legislation to the issuance of these rules in final form.

In addition, the Rating Agency Act requires that at the time of application, rating agencies provide a list of the 20 largest issuers and subscribers that use the services of the CRA. This provision clearly addresses the conflict arising from the dependence of CRAs on a few large issuers for a large proportion of their overall revenue.

Protection of Confidential Information that CRAs Receive from Issuers

The Market Abuse Directive in Europe, apart from containing provisions on managing conflicts of interest, also has provisions that relate to CRAs' access to inside information. With respect to the legal treatment of this access, the Directive prohibits any person possessing inside information from using that information by acquiring or disposing of financial instruments to which that information relates. Inside information is defined as information of a precise nature which has not been made public, relating, directly or indirectly, to one or more issuers of financial instruments and which, if it were made public, would be likely

---

[107] Commission of the European Communities, 2005. Communication from the Commission on Credit Rating Agencies, December 23, 2005/11990, 1–9, entire section from page 4.

to have a significant effect on the price of those financial instruments or on the price of related derivative financial instruments. As a rule, an issuer must disclose inside information as soon as possible. Consequently, there will be few circumstances in which an issuer can legitimately be in possession of information that has not already been disclosed to the market. If an issuer decides to allow a CRA access to inside information, the CRA would owe a duty of confidentiality as required by Article 6(3) of Directive 2003/6/EC. Considering these provisions, it is clear that CRAs need to implement internal procedures and policies to ensure objective, independent, and accurate credit ratings that will benefit investor confidence.[108]

The Rating Agency Act makes rule-making by the SEC mandatory. As with management of conflicts of interest, the SEC's final rule it stipulates that policies and procedures should be established to maintain, enforce and prevent the misuse of material nonpublic information. These policies and procedures should include those designed to prevent: the inappropriate dissemination within and outside the rating agency of material nonpublic information obtained in connection with the rating process, a person inside the rating agency from trading on the material nonpublic information, the inappropriate dissemination of a rating action within or outside the rating agency before it is made public.

Prohibition of Certain Commercial Practices

The SEC's final rule prohibits any act or practice relating to the issuance of credit ratings by an NRSRO that the SEC determines to be unfair, coercive, or abusive, including the asking of fees for unsolicited ratings, making the issuance of credit ratings conditional on the issuer's purchase of other services or products, lowering the rating of an asset pool or refusing to rate an asset-backed security unless a portion of the constituent elements is also rated by the agency and engaging in this practice for an anticompetitive purpose (notching), linking a credit rating to the fee received from the rated party for the rating or other products and services. The paragraph concerning notching should be difficult to implement, as notching clearly has an anticompetitive effect, but it would be very difficult to show that the purpose of the notching was anticompetitive. Many arguments, some of them quite reasonable, have been given in favor of notching.

The EC and CEBS guidelines have no targeted rules on this. In the EU, generic competition law applies.

Regulatory Inspection Rights

The current regulatory regime in Europe is one of moderate oversight, with no real regulatory authority exercising supervision over CRAs. Since the SEC's final rule is effective, on June 26, 2007, the current regulatory regime in the US is one of strong oversight with the SEC exercising supervision over CRAs.

In contrast, the Rating Agency Act requires the CRAs to file any certified financial statements that the SEC may require. In addition, the bill requires annual certification by CRAs that information supplied at the time of application continues to be accurate. The SEC's final rule requires a prompt amendment if any of the information provided becomes

---

[108] Commission of the European Communities, 2005. Communication from the Commission on Credit Rating Agencies, December 23, 2005/11990, 1–9, entire section from page 4.

materially inaccurate. This does not concern the statistics, financial statements, headcounts and rating count, but it does concern all the procedures and methodologies used to determine ratings, to prevent conflicts of interest and misuse of nonpublic information, the organization structure and the code of ethics. The Rating Agency Act also allows the SEC the right of censure, denial, or suspension of registration where an NRSRO fails to furnish these certifications.[109] More specifically, the final SEC rule adds section 17g-2 to the general rules and regulations of the Securities Exchange Act of 1934 which requires NRSROs to make and retain an extensive amount of complete books and records. In particular, any record relating to each rating action whether public or private rating. Moreover, NRSROs must retain for three years internal records, including nonpublic information and work papers used to form the basis of a credit rating or the basis of a credit analysis report, any internal audit plans and reports and any external and internal communications, including electronic communications received or sent by NRSRO employees that relate to initiating, determining, maintaining or changing a credit rating. Regarding this section, the SEC reiterates that the purpose of examining these records is to review whether an NRSRO adheres to its procedures and methodologies, but not to regulate the substance of credit ratings or the procedures and methodologies, as this is indeed explicitly forbidden.

The SEC will censure, place limitations on the activities, functions, or operations of, suspend for a period not exceeding 12 months, or revoke the registration of any NRSRO if it finds that any such action is necessary for the protection of investors and in the public interest and that such NRSRO, or any person associated with it (whether prior to or subsequent to becoming so associated):

  (i) has committed certain acts, offences or crimes in contravention of the Securities Exchange Act in the last 10 years;
 (ii) fails to furnish the certifications required; or
(iii) fails to maintain adequate financial and managerial resources to consistently produce credit ratings with integrity.

The CEBS guidelines provide for ongoing review of the eligibility of recognized CRAs. This includes the ECAIs reporting any material change to competent authorities, and an in-depth analysis of each ECAI's eligibility at least every five years.

With respect to general business conduct, the CESR has set up a voluntary framework of cooperation with CRAs to review implementation of the IOSCO Code. The framework includes: (i) each CRA will send an annual letter to the CESR, which will be made public, outlining how it has complied with the IOSCO Code and indicating any deviations from the Code; (ii) the CESR and each CRA will meet annually to discuss any issues related to implementation of the IOSCO Code; and (iii) CRAs will provide an explanation to the national CESR member where any substantial incident has occurred with a particular issuer in its market. Here again, there are no explicit inspection rights by CESR over CRAs.[110]

---

[109] This is in rather stark contrast to the debate surrounding the 2005 SEC proposed rule that talked of difficulties in examining NRSROs arising from, among other things, the lack of record-keeping requirements tailored to NRSRO activities, the NRSROs' assertions that the document retention and production requirements of the Investment Advisers Act of 1940 are inapplicable to the credit rating business, and their claims that the First Amendment shields them from producing certain documents to the Commission.

[110] The Committee of European Securities Regulators (CESR), 2005. Dialogue with rating agencies to review how the IOSCO Code is being implemented, December 13, Reference 05-751, 1–7.

9.3.2 The Positions of the Main Stakeholders

The positions of the main stakeholders are dated from before the SEC released the final rule on the oversight of the credit rating agencies registered as NRSROs, in June 2007. We have decided to leave most of the section because a large part of the debate is still relevant as Europe is considering the strong oversight option, and perhaps to recall that some of the incentives of the rating agencies would have been different the past years, as the structured finance market was expanding, had the regulatory framework for rating agencies and NRSROs been different. Moreover, the Rating Agency Act has been in effect just one year, so that the impact is still difficult to evaluate.

Investors

Investors bear the brunt of wrong rating calls on corporate credit quality. Hence, it is not surprising that investors hold the most extreme view on regulation of the industry. The view of this community, represented by organizations such as the Investment Company Institute, is that the current regulatory structure governing NRSROs should be improved by: (1) improving the initial recognition process through, among other things, formal SEC action in recognizing NRSROs, rather than the current staff no-action letters; (2) strengthening the system of oversight of credit rating agencies (direct, ongoing oversight, record-keeping requirements, annual certifications by CRAs, annual public comment, frequent examinations of CRAs, as opposed to current frequency of once every five years); (3) disclosure of the resources, standards, procedures, and policies employed by the agencies in their rating process; (4) instituting a new public comment and review process regarding rating agencies' performance, standards, and methodologies; and (5) holding rating agencies legally accountable for their ratings.[111]

With regard to the SEC Proposed Rule, the ICI supports the adoption of a formal definition of 'NRSRO.' 'This would facilitate much-needed competition among credit rating agencies. At the same time, however, we believe the Commission must ensure that a regulatory oversight process is in place to protect the integrity and quality of the credit ratings process.'[112]

At the same time, the Investment Management Association, which represents the UK-based investment management industry, holds a completely different view with respect to regulatory oversight of the CRA industry.

> The IMA urges that securities regulators do not bring CRAs into their regulatory oversight or supervision. [As noted above], ratings are merely opinions and there will be a range of opinions in the wider market about any borrower or bond. That leads to healthy markets. There is a real danger of investors being misled as to the quality of a rating if there appears to be some formal regulatory 'endorsement' of the CRA. The IMA believes that market mechanisms will enforce compliance with the Code Fundamentals, although this would be more achievable if investors and not issuers paid for a credit rating.[113]

[111] Lancellotta, A.B.R., Senior Counsel – Investment Company Institute, 2003. Comment on SEC concept release regarding rating agencies and the use of credit ratings under the Federal Securities Laws, July 28.
[112] Lancellotta, A.B.R., Senior Counsel – Investment Company Institute, 2005. Comments on SEC proposed rule – definition of Nationally Recognized Statistical Rating Organization, June 9, 1–5, page 1.
[113] Rae, L., Senior Adviser – Investment Operatings, Investment Management Association, 2004. Comments on IOSCO October 2004 draft: Code of Conduct Fundamentals for Credit Rating Agencies, November 8, 1–2, page 2.

The European Banking Federation (EBF) also took a significant position on CRA policy in favor of the IOSCO Code, arguing that 'Legislation is not the appropriate route in this regard. Self-regulation through an international Code of Conduct would establish a well-functioning balance between the different interests of rating agencies, investors, and issuers.'[114]

Issuers

The *Code of Standard Practices for Participants in the Credit Rating Process* represents best the view of issuers. It was developed in 2004 by The Association of Corporate Treasurers (ACT), London, England, The Association for Financial Professionals (AFP), United States, and the Association Française Des Trésoriers D'Entreprise (AFTE), Paris, France. The AFP has expressed these views in several forums, a summary of which is given below

1. *Need for immediate action.* There is a need for action to address the issues facing the credit rating industry, as confidence in rating agencies and their ratings has diminished over the past few years.[115] 'Despite the increasing reliance on credit ratings, even after more than 10 years of examining the role and regulation of credit rating agencies, the Securities and Exchange Commission has not taken any meaningful action to address the concerns of issuers and investors.'[116]
2. *Regulatory action needed for increasing competition.* 'The SEC's NRSRO designation system is an artificial barrier to entry which has led to a concentration of market power with the recognized rating agencies and a lack of competition and innovation in the credit ratings market.'[117] Recommends that 'the SEC maintain the NRSRO designation and clearly articulate the process by which qualified credit rating agencies can attain the NRSRO designation.'[118] 'The criteria that CRAs must meet to receive regulatory approval should be based on whether the agency can consistently produce credible and reliable ratings over the long-term, not on methodology. The determination of whether ratings are credible and reliable may be based on market acceptance, quantitative analysis, or other methods developed by relevant regulators.'[119]
3. *Regulatory action needed for ongoing oversight of CRAs.* '... the Commission must ensure that, on an ongoing basis, NRSROs continue to issue credible and reliable ratings. Further, the Commission must periodically verify that NRSROs have and adhere to policies that protect non-public information and prevent conflicts of interest and unfair

---

[114] European Banking Federation (EBF), 2004. Response to CESR's call for evidence on credit rating agencies (CRAs), August 24, 1–4.

[115] Kaitz, J.A., President and Chief Executive Officer – Association for Finance Professionals, 2005. Examining the role of credit rating agencies in the capital markets, Testimony before the Committee on Banking, Housing, and Urban Affairs, United States Senate, February 8, 1–24, page 4.

[116] Kaitz, J.A., President and Chief Executive Officer – The Association for Finance Professionals, 2005. Examining the role of credit rating agencies in the capital markets, Testimony before the Committee on Banking, Housing, and Urban Affairs, United States Senate, February 8, 1–24, page 4.

[117] Kaitz, J.A., President and Chief Executive Officer – The Association for Finance Professionals, 2005. Examining the role of credit rating agencies in the capital markets, Testimony before the Committee on Banking, Housing, and Urban Affairs, United States Senate, February 8, 1–24, page 4.

[118] Kaitz, J.A., President and Chief Executive Officer – The Association for Finance Professionals, 2005. Examining the role of credit rating agencies in the capital markets, Testimony before the Committee on Banking, Housing, and Urban Affairs, United States Senate, February 8, 1–24, pages 4, 5.

[119] Association for Financial Professionals, Association Française Des Trésoriers D'Entreprise, and Association of Corporate Treasurers, 2004. Code of Standard Practices for Participants in the Credit Rating Process, April 14, 1–48, page 1.

and abusive practices.'[120] 'Regulators should periodically review each recognized CRA to ensure that it continues to meet the recognition criteria.'[121]

4. *Legislative action, if necessary, to enforce recommended regulatory action.* 'Chairman Shelby and members of the Committee, we strongly recommend that you hold the SEC accountable by demanding immediate action on the issues that have been raised here today. If the SEC does not act immediately to aggressively address each of the concerns we have outlined, we urge you act to restore investor confidence in the credit ratings process through action by this Committee.'[122]

5. *Industry Code as a complement to regulatory action.* Apart from the specific regulation recommended in 2 and 3 above, the treasury associations are of the view that 'regulation should only provide a minimal fail-safe framework for CRA regulation and that the more flexible and adaptable industry code of standard practices must play a complementary role to such regulation.'[123] Thus, the treasury associations recommend a 'minimum regulatory framework,' based on oversight of adherence to documented policies, rather than prescription of the policies themselves.

The reaction to the various reform initiatives follows from the above approach. For example, the Association of Finance Professionals has supported H.R. 2990 as it considers recent initiatives by the SEC inadequate. It believes that ongoing oversight by the SEC is important and that the legislation adequately provides for this authority. The AFP also supports the 'transparent' registration system over the 'ambiguous' NRSRO recognition system

> The Credit Rating Agency Duopoly Relief Act of 2005 would require the SEC to register credit rating agencies within 90 days of application based on the criteria recommended by AFP. By eliminating the ambiguous NRSRO designation process in favor of a more transparent registration process, the Act will foster meaningful competition in the credit ratings market. The recent SEC proposal falls short in this regard. As such, AFP supports the legislative proposal before the Committee today.[124]

More recently, the AFP has expressed its strong support to the Reform Act.

> Today's action is the next critical step following the House of Representatives passage of its version of the bill to address the lack of competition in the credit ratings market. On behalf of our membership, we commend Chairman Shelby and Senator Sarbanes for moving this important legislation forward. We urge the full Senate to take action on the bill as soon as possible.[125]

---

[120] Kaitz, J.A., President and Chief Executive Officer – The Association for Finance Professionals, 2005, Comments on SEC proposed rule – definition of Nationally Recognized Statistical Rating Organization, June 7, 1–7, page 2.
[121] Association for Financial Professionals, Association Française Des Trésoriers D'Entreprise, and Association of Corporate Treasurers, 2004. Code of Standard Practices for Participants in the Credit Rating Process, April 14, 1–48, page 1.
[122] Kaitz, J.A., President and Chief Executive Officer – The Association for Finance Professionals, 2005. Examining the role of credit rating agencies in the capital markets, Testimony before the Committee on Banking, Housing, and Urban Affairs, United States Senate, February 8, 1–24, page 6.
[123] Association for Financial Professionals, Association Française Des Trésoriers D'Entreprise, and Association of Corporate Treasurers, 2004. Code of Standard Practices for Participants in the Credit Rating Process, April 14, 1–48, page 7.
[124] Kaitz, J.A., President and Chief Executive Officer – The Association for Financial Professionals, 2005. Legislative solutions for the rating agency duopoly, Testimony before the Committee on Financial Services, Subcommittee on Capital Markets, Insurance and Government Sponsored Enterprises, United States House of Representatives, June 29, 1–12, page 3.
[125] Kaitz, J.A., President and Chief Executive Officer – The Association for Financial Professionals, 2006. AFP commends Senate Banking Committee on credit rating agency reform, August 2, 1–1.

At the same time, the AFP does not support the SEC's proposed rule. It believes that 'the SEC's heavy reliance on market acceptance, coupled with prescriptive input and methodology requirements, will erect an even more formidable barrier to entry into the credit ratings market than already exists.'[126] It is also very concerned about the lack of any proposal to conduct ongoing oversight of NRSROs, and states support for any future legislative action that will give oversight authority to the SEC. 'Unfortunately, we do not believe that the SEC proposal would foster a truly competitive market and fails to address the need for ongoing oversight of the credit ratings market.'[127]

In line with the view expressed in point 5 above, the treasury associations have broadly supported the IOSCO Code. 'The Treasury Associations do not see the need for specific regulation of CRAs except in certain very selected ways. Accordingly the Treasury Associations generally welcome the IOSCO publication of a code with its inherent flexibility.'[128]

They have also broadly supported the CESR approach (with suggestions for some amendments), but do not rule out the possibility of regulation or registration going forward, 'We believe that the IOSCO code should be allowed to bed in for a couple of years before any additional provisions by way of registration requirements or regulation are introduced.'[129]

The German industry federation (BDI) also took the significant position that 'to enforce the code, it favors a market approach which has proved its worth in practice. Should there be discrepancies between the standards of the individual agencies and the IOSCO requirements, the rating agencies must comply or explain. In addition, rating agencies are expected to provide organizational measures to ensure compliance with the code. Should the procedure not prove successful in practice, formal regulatory steps should not be excluded. First, however, experience should be gathered with the code. It would be desirable if the European Union would adhere to the IOSCO requirements for the time being. A special regulation for the EU would involve the danger of access to the global capital markets becoming more difficult for EU issuers.'[130]

Intermediaries

Given the symbiotic nature of the relationship between intermediaries, such as investment banks on the one hand and CRAs on the other, the views of the former are similar to those of the latter. The Bond Market Association (BMA), which represents securities firms and banks that underwrite, distribute, and trade debt securities in the United States and

---

[126] Kaitz, J.A., President and Chief Executive Officer – The Association for Finance Professionals, 2005. Comments on SEC proposed rule – definition of Nationally Recognized Statistical Rating Organization, June 7, 1–7, page 2.
[127] Kaitz, J.A., President and Chief Executive Officer – The Association for Financial Professionals, 2005. Legislative solutions for the rating agency duopoly, Testimony before the Committee on Financial Services, Subcommittee on Capital Markets, Insurance and Government Sponsored Enterprises, United States House of Representatives, June 29, 1–12, page 3.
[128] Association for Financial Professionals, Association Française Des Trésoriers D'Entreprise, and Association of Corporate Treasurers, 2004. Comments on IOSCO October 2004 draft: *Code of Conduct Fundamentals for Credit Rating Agencies*, November, 1–38, page 5.
[129] Association Française Des Trésoriers D'Entreprise, and Association of Corporate Treasurers, 2005. Comments on consultation paper: CESR's technical advice to the European Commission on possible measures concerning credit rating agencies, January, 1–21.
[130] Federation of German Industries, 2004. BDI position on the CESR consultation paper on a possible regulation of rating agencies, January 28, 1–8.

internationally, has expressed its view in various forums on CRAs, and a summary of their view on key points is given below.[131]

1. *Degree of Oversight* – '... do not believe that regulation of the credit rating process is necessary or desirable, since government regulation would tend to result in less diversity of opinion and would be less responsive to new product developments.'[132] However, 'We believe the Commission either has or should have the authority to determine whether a rating agency meets or continues to meet the requirements for designation as an NRSRO. We do not, however, believe that more extensive regulation of rating agencies is warranted.'[133] 'Believes that credit rating agencies should have policies and procedures to ensure the independence of the credit rating process.'[134]
2. *Competition* – Barriers to entry in the CRA industry are natural rather than the result of any anticompetitive behavior from the more established CRAs.[135]
3. *Recognition System* – 'Believes that the criteria adopted by regulators for approving NRSROs or ECAIs should be flexible enough to allow increased competition between a larger number of entities, while ensuring that designated rating agencies have the expertise to produce accurate ratings. In the US, this means eliminating the current requirement that a rating agency be widely recognized, rather than accepted in a defined sector of the market.'[136]
4. *Ratings Model* – Does not support firms that use only quantitative models. 'Association does not favor granting the NRSRO designation to firms that use solely quantitative models and do not request that an issuer's senior management participate in the rating process free of charge. There is substantial volatility in ratings based solely on quantitative models and such ratings often give false positive results regarding credit problems.'[137]

As such, the BMA supports the IOSCO Code 'We support a code of conduct based approaches to issues with CRAs and therefore commend IOSCO for its initiative to provide consistent guidance and set clear expectations for all participants in the market.'[138]

---

[131] Green, M.S., President – The Bond Market Association, 2005. Examining the role of credit rating agencies in the capital markets, Testimony before Committee on Banking, Housing, and Urban Affairs, United States Senate, February 8, 1–8, page 5.

[132] Green, M.S., President – The Bond Market Association, 2005. Examining the role of credit rating agencies in the capital markets, Testimony before Committee on Banking, Housing, and Urban Affairs, United States Senate, February 8, 1–8, page 5.

[133] Fernandez, F.A., Senior Vice President and Chief Economist, and Gross, M.E., Senior Vice President and Regulatory Counsel – The Bond Market Association, 2005. Comment on SEC proposed rule – definition of Nationally Recognized Statistical Rating Organization, June 9, 1–9, page 9.

[134] Green, M.S., President – The Bond Market Association, 2005. Examining the role of credit rating agencies in the capital markets, Testimony before Committee on Banking, Housing, and Urban Affairs, United States Senate, February 8, 1–8, page 5.

[135] The Bond Market Association, 2005. Response to CESR's technical advice to the European Commission on possible measures concerning credit rating agencies (CRAs) – Consultation paper November 2004, January 28, 1–24, page 3.

[136] Green, M.S., President – The Bond Market Association, 2005. Examining the role of credit rating agencies in the capital markets, Testimony before Committee on Banking, Housing, and Urban Affairs, United States Senate, February 8, 1–8, page 5.

[137] The Bond Market Association, 2005. Legislative solutions for the rating agency duopoly, Statement for the record before the Committee on Financial Services, Subcommittee on Capital Markets, Insurance and Government Sponsored Enterprises, United States House of Representatives, June 29, 1–11, page 9.

[138] The Bond Market Association, 2004. Public comments on IOSCO October 2004 draft: *Code of Conduct Fundamentals for Credit Rating Agencies*, November 6, 1–12.

It also supports the CESR approach of allowing market mechanisms to oversee the implementation of a CRA Code of Conduct. The BMA's response to CESR's consultation on the issue of CRAs states that, 'We strongly believe that enforcement of the IOSCO Code by the market offers the strongest, most cost-efficient and most immediate answer to current regulatory concerns.'

It follows that the BMA does not support the much more strict regulatory regime proposed by H.R. 2990. 'For several reasons [which we articulate below], however, as currently drafted, H.R. 2990 could ultimately dilute the important role credit rating agencies play in the capital markets.' The concerns noted in this document include lack of merit-based criteria, with registration simply on the basis of disclosure of specified information, the inclusion of firms using only quantitative modeling, inclusion of firms that do not provide credit ratings free of cost, and the granting of 'anti-trust jurisdiction to SEC' for prohibition of anticompetitive practices common to CRAs.

Finally, the BMA broadly supports the SEC proposed rule, and reiterates that even though BMA supports SEC oversight to ensure that recognized NRSROs continue to meet the acceptance criteria, it does not support more extensive regulation (see point 1 above).

9.3.3 Comments and Evaluation on Regulatory Options

In this section we comment and evaluate the three main regulatory options as described in Section 7.2., in light of the regulatory options followed by Europe and the US and the main stakeholders' positions.

The Low Regulatory Oversight Approach

The low regulatory oversight is characterized by no oversight authority in most jurisdictions. There are no set procedures for ongoing monitoring and no code of conduct or self-regulatory approach. If the regulatory framework stops here, the market is basically very free to provide for a natural discipline. Without any NRSRO obstacle to competitors and any regulations and guidelines based on the NRSRO status, this market discipline could potentially be effective in maintaining the reputation mechanism to manage the conflicts of interest and enhance rating quality. However credit ratings are quite special products and the industry dynamics rather unique. No matter how credible the threats of new entrants, reputation and network effects will continue to prevail in this industry, maintaining high barriers to entry and industry concentration. Of course, market dominance reversals will occur, but given the public good aspect of credit ratings in terms of stability of financial markets, it is not clear that, without any enhanced monitoring and disclosure, the dominance reversals would occur in a timely and non-disruptive manner. This is the fundamental rationale for monitoring the industry. It is costly for issuers and investors to switch rating agency, hence, it all the more crucial for the well-functioning of financial markets that they be very well informed and active in their evaluation of ratings. This requires some guardrails.

The low oversight approach was obviously incompatible with the old NRSRO status embedded in so many regulations. The old NRSRO status coupled with low or no oversight, encourages passivity from investors who outsource the safety decision regarding an investment and passivity within the rating agencies who have a very large guaranteed market share and revenue. If the CRAs' bottom line is not affected in the short or medium run by extra diligence, then it is unlikely that they will pro-actively invest in being more diligent.

The Strong Regulatory Oversight Approach

The strong oversight approach grants formal legal authority for regulators to supervise CRAs. The authority can take action against CRAs for non-compliance with stated policies, to demand records, conduct inspections and examinations. This approach may be effective in identifying ex-post shortcomings in rating processes of the agencies, and it can perhaps even prevent some shortcomings but it is extremely costly and intrusive for the CRAs. Heavy administrative scrutiny imposes fixed costs, diversion of attention and diversion of scarce resources on NRSROs. These risk discouraging new entry, replacing the previous barrier to entry with a new one. If entry into the industry is painful, it will not occur. Incumbents will not feel the same pressure to perform, once again lowering the quality of ratings.

The Rating Agency Act and the SEC make it clear that they may not regulate the substance of the credit ratings or the procedures or methods by which an NRSRO determines credit ratings, however it is a fine line between the regulation of the process and compliance to a process versus the regulation of the content. For the SEC's approach to be failproof, the following condition needs to hold. Given a CRA's set of procedures and methods for determining credit ratings and all its records related to the rating of a specific issue, compliance or non-compliance could be declared unambiguously according to the accepted procedures and methodologies. Unfortunately, that condition can only hold if rating methodologies and procedures are completely described. Procedures and methodologies would even only be completely describable if an outsider provided with the complete exhaustive methodologies and procedures, along with all the relevant private information, could do a unique mapping onto a credit rating. While one can try to describe the methodologies and procedures used to determine a rating in extensive detail, the very essence of ratings, makes it impossible to extract the algorithm of a deliberative process that maps a methodology and an issuer's information set into a unique rating. If it were possible, CRAs would not exist, or they would just be a computer program using certified information as input. Hence, there will always be a point where the regulator needs to interpret the rating agency's intent behind the actions. Moreover, given the the examination threat by the SEC, the rating agencies potentially have an incentive to establish excessively cautious or ambiguous procedures and methodologies.

Another major issue with the strong oversight approach with intrusive inspection rights, is that it 'gives a sense that the SEC is good at conducting rating process control and thus at vouching for rating quality'.[139] Market participants will have fewer incentives than they otherwise would have to incur costly monitoring expenses. They would disengage from their own indirect monitoring, provided by their competitive choices, and the quality of ratings would go down.

To summarize, we find that the strong oversight approach to regulate is not only very costly, but that it risks providing the wrong incentives to market participants and CRAs themselves. Especially there are more effective ways that can provide the right incentives. All the more that we are at a unique time when there are regulatory initiatives and discussions about finally suppressing the reference to NRSRO ratings in federal regulations, and in discouraging them in guidelines.[140] This is a necessary condition for any regulatory oversight

---

[139] This section is based on Langohr, H., Langohr, P., 2007. Comments to the SEC's proposed rule S7-04-07, SEC website, March 12, 1–21.
[140] US Securities and Exchange Commission, 2008. Proposed rule – References to ratings of Nationally Recognized Statistical Rating Organizations, July 1st, File No. S7-19-08, 1–75; US Securities and Exchange Commission, 2008.

of the rating agencies to be successful. We have gotten rid of the restricted access to NRSRO, now we have to make sure that investors and issuers actively monitor the agencies.

The Moderate Regulatory Oversight Approach

The moderate regulatory oversight approach is one where the CRAs adhere to a code of conduct, but there is no formal regulatory authority exercising oversight, but rather monitored self-regulation. The approach is flexible, easy to implement, and works towards CRA integrity by encouraging transparency.

In order to encourage CRAs to disclose their conduct, a mechanism by which users and buyers of ratings rate the degree of compliance of the rating agencies to a code of conduct could be especially useful. If market participants rate on a scale from 1 to 10, to what extent they believe a given CRA adheres to each item on the common code of conduct, and if aggregate ratings across all market participants were computed and disclosed, this would help investors evaluate the confidence they should put in a given 'rated' credit rating. For instance, if a rating agency X were to have a bad score on 'separation between credit analysts and marketers of rating transactions,' then investors may not place much confidence on ratings of agency X, and rating advisors would not recommend its issuer-client to buy a credit rating from agency X. Eventually, if a bond is only rated by agencies that have relatively low scores on the code of conduct, it is likely to exhibit a greater spread, comparable to a risk premium, than if the agencies had high conduct scores. Thanks to this revelation mechanism, rating agencies' incentives could be aligned with those of the financial market as a whole. The key is that rating agencies should have a direct positive impact on their bottom line by not rating transactions that do not have enough information. 'Not rating a given issue' could then be a credible signal to market participants that rating agency X is not free riding on its reputation.

NRSROs will not free-ride on their reputation for integrity and accuracy if the risk of substantially depreciating it is high. The main benefit of this approach is that it aligns incentives, encourages entry, and is almost costless. It requires some trust in the industry's competitive dynamics and market participants' capacity to make market discipline effective, just as one requires trust in any type of public or private monitoring activity. It is a difficult time to trust the rating agencies and the financial market, however it should also be a difficult time to trust legislative rules, as some of them regarding the rating agencies, have had dramatic indirect effects. Should regulators treat the symptoms or look for the root cause?

Proposed rule – Security ratings, July 1st, File No. S7-19-08, 1–77; US Securities and Exchange Commission, 2008. Proposed rule – References to ratings of Nationally Recognized Statistical Rating Organizations, July 1st, File No. S7-19-08, 1–70.

10

Summary and Conclusions

10.1 THE CHALLENGES FACING RATING AGENCIES TODAY

Like most businesses, CRAs continuously face challenges. We comment on just a few of them. The CRAs' legitimacy and acceptability have been questioned. Are codes of conduct the answer? Innovations in financial engineering are challenging the traditional methods of CRAs. In the face of that, what is CRAs' uniqueness as an infomediary? Is growth a curse for CRAs?

10.1.1 From Regulatory Legitimacy to Market Legitimacy

The former Nationally Recognized Statistical Rating Organization (NRSRO) status from 1975 to 2007 and the prevailing embeddedness of ratings in many investment rules and regulations, has nudged investors into using ratings in a passive way, thereby nudging rating agencies out of market discipline. The key challenge for the rating agencies is to regain their credibility, acquire market legitimacy by embracing the fundamental principles behind their codes of conduct and anticipate market needs even further. For this to happen the deep cultural change associated with moving from a protected oligopoly to a competitive one, where users of ratings evaluate the agencies, is necessary. This can only happen if the regulators level the playing field as much as possible.

Indeed, the excessive reliance on ratings created and maintained opaqueness between the ratings and investors. This opaqueness hinders CRA independence and competition and hence negatively affects the quality of ratings. If investors do not fully integrate the differences in methodologies, rating models and quality of assets across rating agencies and products, prices and spreads will not reflect this variation, thereby allowing more informed issuers to take advantage of this inefficient pricing. For instance, this opaqueness has created the opportunity for issuers of structured finance instruments to game the ratings. Regulations apply ratings of structured finance in the same way as ratings for corporates, many investment funds use the same guidelines for corporate bonds as for structured finance products, whereas these financial products react completely differently to market risks and liquidity risks. If investors focus on credit risk because it is measured in investment guidelines, and are rewarded for yield, they will generate a demand for products with high ratings and high yields. Such high yields imply that these products have more and different risks embedded in them. Hence the opportunities that arrangers were able to take advantage of by specifically creating tranches of structured finance instruments to be highly rated. Moreover, given the opaqueness they were also able to sell highly rated instruments at relatively high prices and retain undervalued equity tranches, given the real nature of the underlying risks.

Obviously some of the structured finance ratings' methodologies were flawed and assumptions on correlation and recovery wrong. But the reason this was allowed to happen is that, in the short run, rating agencies did not have sufficient incentives to get it right and invest more resources to better analyze the products and perform more robustness tests of their rating models. In a naturally very concentrated industry, were most users of ratings do not directly pay for them, the former NRSRO status that prevailed for 32 years and the embeddedness of ratings in rules and regulations protected the agencies excessively from any competitive threat. This does not prohibit rivalry amongst the agencies of being intense, as the practices of ratings' shopping and notching suggest, but the big three are still too comfortable in the industry when their quality is not closely monitored by their users. *Although in the long run CRAs have an incentive to provide the best possible quality in order to remain a recognized agency that investors systematically refer to, in the short run their profits increase much more by rating more issues than from improving their quality.* Given the context of rating shopping, improved methodology and due diligence would have scared away some arrangers or originators to a rival's more lenient rating. The rating agencies' individual reputation for due diligence, independence, disclosure and accuracy is not sufficiently at stake. As an industry their credibility has been hit collectively very hard, but individually their fundamental incentive for quality in the short run is still not sufficiently strong.

Is a voluntary code of conduct the solution? At this time, the EU still allows the CRAs to do their job without license and intrusive prescriptions about how to issue a credit rating, leaving the market open to entry and relying instead on self-reinforcing transparency about respecting the IOSCO Code about the conduct of a ratings business. This is a wise decision, subject to an important caveat.

First, to appreciate the impact of such codes of conduct, one has to distinguish between two phases: the construction and initial implementation of the code, and life afterwards. Stakeholder efforts to construct the code in a consensual way are genuinely constructive. They create a period of intense 're-awareness' in the industry. They make stakeholders take stock of what the industry's role is and develop a better understanding of the minimum degree of coordination in the conduct of the business that is required to best serve issuers and investors. In other words, they help stakeholders to reach a level of agreement about industry driving principles and standards that are easily adaptable, without colluding over pricing. In this regard, preparation work under the guidance of IOSCO has been highly expert and insightful. And emphasizing the fundamentals of the industry at the beginning of the consultation process, as summed up in Exhibit 10.1 has been extremely useful. Senior management of CRAs, fully aware of these principles, seized the opportunity offered by the code to implement or accelerate changes within their own organizations that they intended to make anyway. By facilitating internal change in this way, codes of conduct are part of the change equation toward the better.

But what about life afterwards? There is a real danger that codes and regulations could undermine the responsibilities of boards and senior management who, now that they have

Exhibit 10.1   Principles for the activities of credit rating agencies (2004)

1. Rating actions should reduce information asymmetry.
2. Rating actions should be independent and objective.
3. CRAs should pursue transparency and disclosure.
4. CRAs should keep confidential all non-public information.

Source: Technical Committee of International Organization of Securities Commissions, 2003, IOSCO Statement of principles regarding the activities of credit rating agencies, September 25, 1–4.

lists of things to do, can simply check them off without worrying about the principles involved. If something does not appear on the code list, you do not have to think about it. So there is an issue. Is life after the code really more principled and responsible, or less? It is true that the subprime crisis occurred while the CRAs had already adopted the IOSCO code. However, several mitigating factors should be considered before judging of the performance of the code of conduct. The former NRSRO status has only effectively been abolished in June 2007, as the subprime crisis was just revealing itself but after the vast volume of problematic Residential Mortgage Backed Securities (RMBS) and CDOs had been issued and rated. The US market shares of the rating agencies widely influence their market shares in Europe and the rest of the world, so that deregulating the US market is a necessary condition for the European or code of conduct approach. Moreover, market participants are still influenced by the embeddedness of ratings in many rules and regulations and tend to consider ratings as a parameter outside their choice set.

A feature of a code of conduct is that each measure can be complied with to a certain extent. Typically agencies can voluntarily adopt the code and disclose whether they comply or explain why not. But there is a whole range of degrees by which a rating agency can comply with a code. Basic compliance with the code of conduct may not create a competitive industry. For instance Exhibit 10.2 transcribes measure 1.7 of the revised IOSCO code of conduct. Compliance to this measure is very subjective, indeed, how much skilled personnel is 'sufficient personnel with sufficient skill sets to make a proper rating assessment'? What benchmark should be used to assess whether there has been compliance?

The code of conduct could provide a unique framework for the users of ratings, for instance organized as associations, to monitor and evaluate the agencies' individual performances or degree of compliance with their code of conduct. Whether this degree of compliance is perceived or real, this would incentivize rating agencies not only to be transparent, but to disclose and actively communicate its methodologies, processes, and performance in an investor friendly way (not regulator-friendly way). It may then finally be in a rating agency's short term interest to refuse to rate a certain structure or issue, and disclose that it has refused to do so, in order to build a genuine reputation for diligence and independence. Financial markets will then progressively mostly trust ratings from the diligent agencies, spreads on issues rated by these will decrease relatively, thereby increasing demand for ratings from this agency.

Exhibit 10.2   Measure 1.7 of the quality of the rating process in the revised IOSCO Code of Conduct (2008)

1.7 A CRA should ensure that it has and devotes sufficient resources to carry out high-quality credit assessments of all obligations and issuers it rates. When deciding whether to rate or continue rating an obligation or issuer, it should assess whether it is able to devote sufficient personnel with sufficient skill sets to make a proper rating assessment, and whether its personnel likely will have access to sufficient information needed in order to make such an assessment. A CRA should adopt reasonable measures so that the information it uses in assigning a rating is of sufficient quality to support a credible rating. If the rating involves a type of financial product presenting limited historical data (such as an innovative financial vehicle), the CRA should make clear, in a prominent place, the limitations of the rating.

Source: Technical Committee of International Organisation of Securities Commissions, 2008. Code of conduct fundamentals for credit rating agencies, revised May, OICV-IOSCO PD 271, 1–14, pages 4–5.

The challenge of re-earning market legitimacy is as much the rating agencies' challenge as the regulators'. The agencies' challenge is to improve organizations to set a better culture and the regulators' is to design the right mechanism that will promote this culture. Authorizing and forbidding certain actions in given contingencies and creating institutions that have enforcement powers could do some of the trick, but never can all contingencies be covered, and if incentives are not aligned there will always be a way to game the system to increase its profits.

10.1.2 Financial Innovation

The advent of continuously better economic theory, financial modelling, richer databases, usable numerical methods, powerful statistical tests, user friendly software and the faster and wider diffusion of all these through the Internet has the potential to rock the foundations of traditional qualitative ordinal credit ratings. In the face of all this, traditional ordinal credit ratings resemble a Delphic pronouncement.

Innovations in financial engineering seem to challenge the traditional role and functions of CRAs. Is this role compromised? No, innovations continuously refine, solidify, and clarify differences in opinions. As we have discussed in Chapter 3, fundamental credit ratings are unique in that they offer a consistent across products and borders, contractible, ordinal measure of default likelihood. They are unique in that they can integrate private information and are independent from market sentiment. As discussed in **Chapter 4** and as the France Telecom case showed, several mathematical financial models, fed with the proper data, extract issuer default probabilities from market prices. Agencies are now under pressure to show the same responsiveness in their credit rating actions by changing their ratings at the same speed and to the same extent as default probabilities extracted from market prices change. But this is not their function. Their function is to help coordinate investor beliefs on the long term perspectives of a company, which, in the France Telecom case, eventually allowed the company to continue funding its recovery at a not-prohibitive cost.

We reviewed how these market-implied ratings (MIRs) or cardinal default probabilities are highly sensitive to changing market conditions. The reasons are that these MIRs reflect as much appetite for risk as risk, and as much changes in liquidity for the instrument as changes in its value. In addition, the purpose of credit analysis is not to achieve superior valuation in order to make buying or selling decisions. It is rather to produce relevant insight in the lasting downside characteristics of free cash flow distributions of an issuer. Credit Default Swaps (CDS) valuations provide us with market willingness-to-pay for credit insurance, this information is closely related to credit worthiness but is not independent from market sentiment. Morgan Stanley and Goldman Sachs now use the credit insurance market's view of their own creditworthiness as a basis for their lending decisions. The direct cost of protection of their own debt is a better measure to guard themselves against the sudden loss of confidence and withdrawal of market funding, but this does not imply that 'the derivatives market has replaced rating agencies as the final word on creditworthiness.'[1] Loss of confidence and creditworthiness are two distinct concepts, even though they mutually affect each other. Prices of credit insurance are also shaped by ratings. If the use of the ratings changes and adapts itself to innovations, their essential functions remain the same. Rating agencies should stick to their guns of fundamental analysis, undisturbed by market

---

[1] Sender, H., 2008. MS and Goldman change approach to lending, *Financial Times*, August 17th.

exuberance or depression and by the perpetually moving pendulum of market liquidity. They and market participants should treat MIRs and CDS valuations for what they are: complements rather than substitutes of fundamental traditional ratings.

Although the fundamental functions of credit ratings prevail in an environment of fast paced financial innovation, the content and tools of credit risk analysis change with new products. There are now structured finance instruments based on market values, such as the Structured Investment Vehicle Lite (SIV-Lite) that change the nature of the rating analyst's work to analyzing market value, pricing and liquidity of assets. Moreover, the subprime crisis has revealed needs such as liquidity ratings, and more explicit measures of transition risk, and robustness. These are challenges for the incumbent rating agencies, but also great opportunities for new entrants or competitors from related market segments.

10.1.3   Growth and Globalization

Lastly, CRAs have been growing extremely rapidly. Could this be a curse?

Credit rating is a labor-intensive activity. There are relatively limited economies of scale in the production of ratings. As a CRA needs to produce more ratings, it needs to recruit more people and provide them with the tools to work. How does a CRA respond to the conflicting needs to expand rapidly the number of analysts they put to work on the one hand and to preserve a relatively homogeneous and consistent credit analytical culture across regions, offices, sectors, products, etc., on the other? Inevitably, the ratio of highly seasoned analysts to junior ones has to decrease, making it extremely difficult to absorb incoming talent while preserving the tried and tested fundamental credit rating culture. This presents a knotty problem for the management of a credit rating agency, for which the only solution we can offer is to invest even more in analyst training and education and learn to refuse to rate certain products and issues, for which there is not enough quality information or analyst training.

10.2   CONCLUSION

To conclude, among the many challenges CRAs face, they must assume their public role through impeccable business conduct. There is no doubt credit rating agencies are among the more powerful and less understood financial institutions on the planet. There are numerous stories that illustrate the power of the rating agencies, but the following may be one of the best to show how much of that power is often just imaginary. The anecdote goes as follows.[2]

After an eleven-year hiatus, Harvard Business School reinstated the GMAT in 1996 as a requirement for admission to the Graduate School of Business in part because the credit rating agencies demanded it. The agencies felt the GMAT was a valid indicator of student quality and gave them an additional quantitative tool with which to compare Harvard graduates with the graduates of other top US universities. HBS reinstated the test despite the fact that statistical studies carried out by the school failed to find a link between performance on the GMAT and future success, either at HBS or in the workplace following graduation. Is this acceptable?

---

[2] The source is an unidentified capital markets practitioner.

After having heard this story, of course we submitted it to the Admission department of Harvard Business School for confirmation. It turned out to be one of those fantasies that are nice to tell at parties, but have no foundation.

Despite the criticism levelled at the rating agencies in recent years, it is likely the case (like so many other maligned institutions) that if they were abolished we would have to create identical institutions to replace them. It is also true that the recurring financial crises that take place in both the developed and the developing world at the very least provide the rating agencies and investors with 'lessons learned' that will help to build stronger and more vibrant financial markets and rating agencies in the future.

As the President of S&P remarked in 1999:

> No one ever appointed any of our organizations as the capital markets' watchdogs and none of us should reasonably aspire to that role. In the final analysis, the activities of all players in modern financial markets are based on opinions – from lenders to traders to hedge funds to credit analysts to the international financial institutions. All of us play roles in helping to formulate opinions about risk. Those opinions are then translated into the constant pricing and trading of a whole range of financial assets. What is most important is for all of us to realize that efficient financial markets depend on differences in those opinions.[3]

Rating agencies are no official watchdogs but ratings are unique and more complex beasts than first appears. Given their importance, perception of what ratings really are and really measure is still too approximate. For instance, what is the process behind the rating through-the-cycle? What is the frequency and nature of the monitoring? How far does due diligence go? Ratings are meant to be exogenous, in the sense that they are outside indicators, but at the same time the embeddedness of ratings in many contracts, rules and regulations implies that ratings have direct real effects and tend to become endogenous, especially around the investment grade border.

Ratings are very visible. Indeed, we have qualified them as contractible in the sense that they are observable and verifiable, and hence are ideal candidates for performance evaluation purposes. However, very often the performance that is evaluated (for instance yield subject to risk restrictions) is much broader than just measurable by a credit rating. Credit ratings have too often been assimilated to the overall measure of financial risk of debt instruments, hence creating distortions and arbitrage opportunities. This is not a small matter. The extent to which ratings are embedded in rules and regulations and monitored by market participants makes them essential keys to efficient and stable financial markets. The macroeconomic consequences of prudential uses of credit ratings beyond the scope of their purpose may not be as desirable as the intentions that produced the regulations. Ratings are far from perfect, but the quality of ratings would increase if they were used for what they are and nothing else. They would then be evaluated and monitored according to the right criteria. Regulations should help align the interests of various stakeholders in this market.

Credit ratings will remain a fascinating business for quite some time and will hopefully get much further research. It is indeed a fine line to manage and monitor a business that at the same time rates the issuers that pays them, serves investors, is prescribed by regulators and has such a large public interest component in its impact on the efficiency and stability of financial markets.

---

[3] O'Neill, L.C., President and Chief Rating Officer - Standard & Poor's, 1999. Building the new global framework for risk analysis, Remarks to Professional bankers association at World Bank headquarters in Washington, D.C., March 26, 1–5.

References

1 CREDIT RATING AGENCY DOCUMENTS

1.1 Egan-Jones

Egan, S.J., 2002. Statement of Egan Jones on credit rating agencies, letter submitted to the SEC, November 10, 1–90.

Egan, S.J., 2005. Managing Director–Egan-Jones Ratings Company, Examining the role of credit rating agencies in the capital markets, Testimony to Senate Committee on Banking, Housing and Urban Affairs, February 8, 1–12.

Egan, S.J., 2005. Managing Director–Egan-Jones Ratings Company, Legislative solutions for the Credit Rating Agency Duopoly Relief Act of 2005, Testimony before the House Subcommittee on Capital Markets, Insurance, and Government Sponsored Enterprises, June 29, 1–7.

1.2 Fitch

Albertson, T., Duignan, K., Mah, S.K., Merrick, S., Metz, M., and Verde, M., 2002. Structured finance rating transition study, *Credit Market Research*: Fitch Ratings, May 8, 1–8.

Bettini, D., Buckley, K.M., Carter, G., Meyer, D.L., and Waterman, C., 2005. Quantitative insurer financial strength ratings methodology: European insurers, *Criteria Report*: Fitch Ratings, March 7, 1–11.

Fimalac S.A., 2006. Investor Presentation, March 16, 1–74.

Fimalac S.A., *Annual Report*, 1998 through 2005.

Fitch Ratings, 2005. International long-term credit ratings, *Fitch Ratings Definitions*, 1–2.

Fitch Ratings, 2005. Recovery ratings: Exposing the components of credit risk: *Special Report*, July 26, 1–8.

Fitch Ratings, 2005. Reference fee schedule 2005–Corporate – EMEA, 1–1.

Fitch Ratings, 2005. *Code of Conduct*, April, 1–13.

Fitch Ratings, 2006. Corporate rating methodology, *Corporate Finance Criteria Report*, June 13, 1–7.

Fitch Ratings, 2007. Fitch CDS implied ratings model, *Research Special Report*, June 13.

Fitch Ratings, 2007. Fitch equity implied rating and probability of default model, *Quantitative Financial Research Criteria Report*, June 13, 1–19.

Fitch Ratings, 2007. Insurer financial strength ratings, *Fitch Ratings Definitions*, March 26, 1–5.

Fitch Ratings, 2007. International short term ratings, *Fitch Ratings Definitions*, March 26, 1–3.

Fitch Ratings, 2007. Introduction to ratings, *Fitch Ratings Definitions*, March 26, 1–4.

Fitch Ratings, 2007. Global bank individual ratings transition and failure study – 1990-2006, *Special Report*, June 12, 1–20.

Greening, T., Kastholm, D.R., Pitman, T., and Stringer, T., 2006. Corporate rating methodology, *Criteria report:* Fitch Ratings, June 13, 1–7.

Joynt, S.W., President and Chief Executive Officer–Fitch Ratings, 2002. Comment on the role and function of rating agencies in the operation of securities markets, letter submitted to SEC, November 12, 1–8.

Joynt, S.W., 2005. President and Chief Executive Officer–Fitch Ratings, Examining the role of credit rating agencies in the capital markets, Testimony before the U.S. Senate Committee on Banking, Housing and Urban Affairs, February 8, 1–10.

Mancuso, P., Rosenthal, E. and Verde, M., 2007. The shrinking default rate and the credit cycle – new twists, new risks, *Credit Market Research*: Fitch Ratings, February 20.

May, W., Needham, C., and Verde, M., 2006. Recovery ratings reveal diverse expectations for loss in the event of default, *Credit Market Research*: Fitch Ratings, December 14, 1–11.

Stroker, N., 2005. Group Managing Director–Fitch Ratings, Legislative solutions for the Credit Rating Agency Duopoly Relief Act of 2005, Statement to the House Subcommittee on Capital Markets, Insurance and Government Sponsored Enterprises, June 29, 1–24.

1.3 Moody's

Bodard, E., Foley, M., Hilderman, M., Keller, T., Takizawa, Y., and Turner, J., 1998. Industrial company rating methodology, *Special Comment*: Moody's Investors Service, July, Report 36188, 1–16.

Bodard, E., Fisher, A., Konefal, R., and Winzer, C., 2001. France Telecom analysis, *Global Credit Research*: Moody's Investors Service, June 25, Report 68080, 1–16.

Bodard, E., Hu, C.M., Lau, C., Otsuki, E., and Stumpp, P., 2006. Rating transitions for investment-grade issuers subject to event risk: request for comment, *Rating Methodology*: Moody's Investors Service, July, Report 98024, 1–8.

Bodard, E., Gates, D., Hu, C.M., Lau, C., and Otsuki, E., 2006. Event risk and investment grade non-financial companies, *Rating Practice*: Moody's Investors Service, October, Report 97134, 1–4.

Cantor, R., Emery K., and Stumpp P., 2006. Probability of default ratings and loss given default assessments for non-financial speculative-grade corporate obligors in the United States and Canada, *Rating Methodology*: Moody's Investors Service, August, Report 98771, 1–16.

Cantor, R., Fons, J.S., and Mahoney, C., 2002. Understanding Moody's corporate bond ratings and rating process, *Special Comment*: Moody's Investors Service, May, Report 74982, 1–16.

Cantor, R., Fons, J.S, Mann, C., Munves, D., and Viswanathan, J., 2005. *An Explanation of Market Implied Ratings*, Moody's Investors Service, November, SP1325, 1–19.

Cantor, R. and Hamilton, D., 2006. Measuring corporate default rates, *Special Comment*: Moody's Investors Service, November, Report 100779, 1–16.

Cantor, R., Hamilton, D.T, Kim, F., and Ou, S., 2007. Corporate default and recovery rates, 1920–2006, *Special Comment*: Moody's Investors Service, June, Report 102 071, 1–48.

Cantor, R., Hamilton, D., Mann, Ch. and Varma, P., 2003. What happens to fallen angels? A statistical review 1982-2003, *Special Comment*: Moody's Investors Service, July, Report: 78912, 1–10.

Cantor, R., Hamilton, D.T, Ou, S., and Varma, P., 2004. Default and recovery rates of corporate bond issuers: A statistical review of Moody's ratings performance, 1920-2003, *Special Comment*: Moody's Investors Service, January, Report 80989, 1–40.

Cantor, R., Hamilton, D.T, Ou, S., and Varma, P., 2005. Default and recovery rates of European corporate issuers, 1985–2004, *Special comment*: Moody's Investors Service, February, Report 91623, 1–20.

Cantor, R., Hamilton, D.T, Ou, S., and Varma, P., 2005. Default and recovery rates of corporate bond issuers, 1920-2004, *Special Comment*: Moody's Investors Service, January, Report 91233, 1–40.

Cantor, R., Hamilton, D.T, Ou, S., and Varma, P., 2006. Default and recovery rates of corporate bond issuers, 1920-2005, *Special Comment*: Moody's Investors Service, March, Report 96546, 1–51.

Cantor, R. and Mann, C., 2006. Analyzing the tradeoff between rating accuracy and stability, *Special Comment*: Moody's Investors Services, September, Report 99100, 1–8.

Cantor, R. and Mann, C., 2007. The performance of Moody's corporate bond ratings: September quarterly update, *Special Comment*: Moody's Investors Service, October, Report 105286, 1–18.

Cifuentes, A. and Wilcox, C., 1998. The double binomial method and its application to a special case of CBO structures, *Structured Finance Special Report*: Moody's Investors Service, March, 1–6.

Coppola, M., and Stumpp, P., 2002. Moody's analysis of US corporate rating triggers heightens need for increased disclosure, *Special Comment*: Moody's Investors Service, July, Report 75412, 1–16.

Cotton, C., and Zarin, F., 1998. Rating methodology: responses to frequently asked questions concerning confidential information, *Special Comment*: Moody's Investors Services, October, Report 38862, 1–4.

Dering, J.M., 2005. Executive Vice President–Global Regulatory Affairs and Compliance–Moody's Corporation, Remarks to the American Enterprise Institute, September 27, 1–7.

Dering, J.M., 2007. Executive Vice President–Global Regulatory Affairs and Compliance, Moody's Corporation, Proposed rules regarding oversight of credit rating agencies registered as Nationally Recognized Statistical Rating Organizations, Letter to Nancy M Morris, Secretary, Securities and Exchange Commission, March 12.

Fanger, D., Fons, J., Gates, D., and Havlicek B., 2006. Rating preferred stock and hybrid securities: Request for comment, *Rating Methodology*: Moody's Investors Service, November 21, Report 100692, 1–8.

Gluck, J. and Remeza, H., 2000. Moody's approach to rating multi-sector CDOs, *Structured Finance Special Report*: Moody's Investors Service, September 20, 1–20.

Laserson, F., and Mahoney, C., 2002. The bond rating process: A progress report, *Rating Policy*: Moody's Investors Service, February, Report 74079, 1–4.

Mahoney C., 2001. The truth about bank credit risk, *Special Comment*: Moody's Investors Service, April, 1–8.

Mahoney, C., 2002. The bond rating process in a changing environment, *Special Comment*: Moody's Investors Service, January, Report: 73741, 1–4.

Marjolin, B., 2007. *Securitization*–ESSEC Presentation, Moody's Investors Service, March 16.

Marshella, T., Rowan, M., and Subhas, M., 1999. Moody's analytical framework for speculative grade ratings, *Global Credit Research*: Moody's Investors Service, May, Report 40026, 1–8.

McDaniel, R.W., 2003. President of Moody's Investors Service, Annual meeting of the International Organization of Securities Commissions (IOSCO), Panel on the regulation of rating agencies, *Special Comment*: Moody's Investors Service, October 17, Report 79839, 1–8.

McDaniel, R.W, 2003. The role and function of rating agencies: evolving perceptions and the implications for regulatory oversight, Report based on a speech presented to the Association of French Treasurers (AFTE) on 5 February 2003 in Paris, France by Raymond McDaniel, President, *Special Comment*: Moody's Investors Service, February, 1–8.

McDaniel, R.W., 2005. President of Moody's Investors Service, Examining the role of credit rating agencies in the capital markets, Testimony before the U.S. Senate Committee on Banking, Housing and Urban Affairs, February 8, 1–14.

Moody's Corporation, *Annual Report*, 1998 through 2005.

Moody's Investors Service, 1999. How to use Moody's rating, *Ratings*.

Moody's Investors Service, 2000. Moody's rating fee guide – Corporates, January, 1–3.

Moody's Investors Service, 2002. Liquidity Rating Assessment on France Telecom 2002.

Moody's Investors Service, 2003. Structured finance rating transitions 1983-2002, comparison with corporate ratings and across sectors, *Special Comment*, January, 1–32.

Moody's Investors Service, 2004. Global cigarette and smokeless tobacco industry, *Rating Methodology*, December, 1–28.

Moody's Investors Service, 2004. Guide to Moody's ratings, rating process, and rating practices, June, Report 87615, 1–48.

Moody's Investors Service, 2005. *Annual Default and Recovery Study: 1920-2004*, June 29.

Moody's Investors Service, 2005. *Code of Professional Conduct*, June, SP1399, 1–16.

Moody's Investors Service, 2005. Fee guide for per issue fees, January, 1–2.

Moody's Investors Service, 2005. Global telecommunications industry, *Rating Methodology*, February, 1–24.

Mody's Investors Service, 2005. *Ratings History on China, Hong Kong, Indonesia, Korea, Taiwan, and Thailand*, December 14.

Moody's Investors Service, 2006. *Annual Default and Recovery Study: 1920-2005*, 1–42.

Moody's Investors Service, 2006. *Investor Presentation*, September.

Moody's Investors Service, 2006. Default and recovery rates of corporate bond issuers, 1920-2005, *Special Comment*, March, 1–52.

Moody's Investors Service, 2007. Bank financial strength ratings, *Global Rating Methodology*, February, 1–40

Moody's Investors Service, 2007. *Moody's Rating Symbols and Definitions*, March, 1–52.
Moody's Investors Service, 2007. Structured finance rating transitions 1983-2006, *Special Comment*, January, 1–76.
Moody's Investors Service, 2007. Global telecommunications industry: *Rating Methodology*, December, 1–36.
Moody's Investors Service, 2007. Global tobacco industry: *Rating Methodology*: November, 1–33.
Moody's Investors Service, 2008. Structured finance rating transitions 1983-2007, *Special Comment*, February, 1-74.
Rutherfurd Jr, J., 2005. Senior Adviser – Moody's Corporation, Rating agencies and auditors, IOSCO Technical Committee meeting, Panel 5: Securities regulation and financial stability – learning the lessons of recent corporate failures, Frankfurt, Germany, October 6, 1–18.
Truglia, V., Cailleteau, P., 2006. A guide to Moody's sovereign ratings, *Special Comment*: Moody's Investors Service, August, 1–10.
Turner, J., 1998. A guide to market participants for monitoring Moody's credit opinions, *Special Comment:* Moody's Investors Service, July, Report 34707, 1–8.
Witt, G. 2004. Moody's correlated binomial default distribution, *Structured Finance Special Report*: Moody's Investors Service, August 10, 1–20.

1.4 Moody's KMV

Arora, N., Bohn, J.R., and Zhu, F., 2005. Reduced form vs. structural models of credit risk: a case study of three models, Moody's KMV, February 17, 1–39.
Crosbie, P. and Bohn, J., 2003. Modeling default risk, *Modeling Methodology*: Moody's KMV, December 18, 1–31.
Dwyer, D. and Qu, S., 2007. *EDF™ 8.0 Model enhancements*, Moody's KMV, January, 1–36.
Korablev, I. and Dwyer, D., 2007. Power and level validation of Moody's KMV EDF credit measures in North-America, Europe and Asia, *Modeling Methodology:* Moody's KMV, September 10, 1–56.
Vasicek, O.A., 1984. Credit valuation, *White Paper*: KMV Corporation, March 22, 1–16.

1.5 Rating and Investment Information

Harada Y., 2005. Executive Vice President–Rating and Investment Information, Inc., Examining the role of credit rating agencies in the capital markets, Testimony before Committee on Banking, Housing and Urban Affairs, United States Senate, February 8, 1–8.

1.6 Rapid Ratings

Caragata, P.J., 2005. Managing Director and Chief Executive Officer–Rapid Ratings Pty. Ltd., Comments on SEC proposed rule–Nationally Recognised Statistical Rating Organisations, August 6, 1–25.
Roberts, R., 2005. The Credit Rating Agency Duopoly Relief Act of 2005, Testimony before the Committee on Financial Services, United States House of Representatives, Rapid Ratings Pty. Ltd., November 29, 1–17.

1.7 Standard and Poor's

Beers, D.T., 2006. Credit FAQ: The future of sovereign credit ratings, *Research*: Standard & Poor's, September 5, 1–8.
Beers, D.T., and Cavanaugh, M., 2005. Sovereign credit ratings: A primer, *Criteria*: Standard & Poor's, September 27, 1–17.
Beers, T., and Cavanaugh, M., 2006. Sovereign credit ratings: A primer, *Criteria:* Standard & Poor's, October, 1–17

Bolger, R.M., 2005. Managing Director, Global Regulatory Affairs and Associate General Counsel–Standard & Poor's, The Credit Rating Agency Duopoly Relief Act of 2005, Testimony before the House Subcommittee on Capital Markets, Insurance and Government Sponsored Enterprises, June 29, 1–17.

Cavanaugh, M., and Daly, K., 2006. Sovereign ratings history since 1975, *Research*: Standard & Poor's, September 11, 1–19.

Corbet, K.A., 2005. President–Standard & Poor's, Examining the role of credit rating agencies in the capital markets, Testimony before the Committee on Banking, Housing and Urban Affairs, United States Senate, February 8, 1–12.

Corbet, K.A., 2005. President–Standard & Poor's, Comments on SEC proposed rule–Definition of Nationally Recognised Statistical Rating Organisation, June 9, 1–17.

Corbet, K.A., 2006. President–Standard & Poor's, Letter to United States House of Representatives re H.R. 2990, July 10, 1–9.

Ganguin, B., Jones, R., and Six, J.M., 2006. It's all a game of snakes and ladders for the top 50 European corporate entities, *Industry Report Card*: Standard & Poor's, November 2, 1–22.

Ganguin, B., and De Toytot, A., 2006. Private equity activity and uncertainty threaten the outlook for European credit quality in 2007, *Research*: Standard & Poor's, December 13, 1–7.

Griep, C.M., 2002. Higher ratings linked to stronger recoveries, *Research*: Standard & Poor's, March 11, 1–6.

Marshall, S., Carvalho, L., Jones, R., 2006. Global reinsurance companies bounce back from a catastrophe riddled 2005, *Industry Report Card*: Standard & Poor's, April 5, 1–18.

O'Neill, L.C., 1999. President and Chief Rating Officer–Standard & Poor's, Building the new global framework for risk analysis, Remarks to Professional bankers association at World Bank headquarters in Washington, D.C., March 26, 1–5.

Samson, S.B., 2002. S&P releases survey on rating triggers, contingent calls on liquidity, *Research*: Standard & Poor's, May 15, 1–2.

Samson, S.B., Sprinzen, S., Dubois-Pelerin, E., 2006. Standard & Poor's role in the financial markets; ratings definitions; the rating process, *Corporate Ratings Criteria*: Standard & Poor's, March 9, 1–13.

de Servigny, A., Jobst, N. 2007. The collateral debt obligation methodologies developed by Standard and Poor's, Chapter 10, *Handbook of Structured Finance*, Standard & Poor's, McGraw-Hill, 397–463.

Standard & Poor's, 1996. Behind the ratings: substantially broader ratings coverage for banks, *Research*: Standard & Poor's, November 27, 1–2.

Standard & Poor's, 1998. *Corporate Credit Ratings: a Guide*.

Standard & Poor's, 2001. Evaluating the Issuer, *Corporate Ratings Criteria*, September 7, 1–123.

Standard & Poor's, 2002. *Global cash flow and synthetic CDO criteria*, March 21, 1–167.

Standard & Poor's, 2004. *Rating Definitions and Terminology*, March 18, 1–12.

Standard & Poor's, 2005. Fee schedule for European corporates, utilities, and financial institutions, January 1, 1–4.

Standard & Poor's, 2005. *Corporate Ratings Criteria*, 1–119.

Standard & Poor's, 2005. *Standard & Poor's Ratings Services Code of Conduct*, October, 1–16.

Standard & Poor's, 2006. Global reinsurance companies bounce back from a catastrophe riddled 2005, *Industry Report Card*, April 5, 3–12.

Standard & Poor's, 2006. The future of sovereign ratings, *Research*, September 5.

Standard & Poor's, 2006. *Corporate Ratings Criteria*, 1–128.

Standard & Poor's, 2007. Recovery analytics update: Enhanced recovery scale and issue ratings framework, *Commentary Report*, May 30, 1–4

The McGraw Hill Companies, *Annual Report*, 1998 through 2006.

Tillman, V.A., 2003. Executive Vice President–S&P Credit Market Services, Standard & Poor's, Comments on the hearing on rating the rating agencies–The state of transparency and competition, submitted to the Committee on Financial Services, the Subcommittee on Capital Markets, Insurance and Government Sponsored Enterprises, United States House of Representatives, April 2, 1–12.

Vazza, D., Aurora, D., Schneck, R., 2005. Annual global corporate default study–corporate defaults poised to rise in 2005, *Research*: Standard & Poor's, January 31, 1–60.

2   INTEREST GROUP DOCUMENTS

2.1   Association of Finance Professionals

Association for Financial Professionals, Association Française des Trésoriers d'Entreprise, and Association of Corporate Treasurers, 2004. *Code of Standard Practices for Participants in the Credit Rating Process*, April 14, 1–48.

Association for Financial Professionals, Association Francaise des Trésoriers d'Entreprise, and Association of Corporate Treasurers, 2004. Comments on IOSCO October 2004 draft: Code of conduct fundamentals for credit rating agencies, November, 1–38.

Association Francaise Des Trésoriers D'Entreprise, and Association of Corporate Treasurers, 2005. Comments on consultation paper: CESR's technical advice to the European Commission on possible measures concerning credit rating agencies, January, 1–21.

Kaitz, J.A., 2005. President and Chief Executive Officer–Association for Financial Professionals, Examining the role of credit rating agencies in the capital markets, Testimony before the Committee on Banking, Housing and Urban Affairs, United States Senate, February 8, 1–24.

Kaitz, J.A., 2005. President and Chief Executive Officer–Association for Financial Professionals, Comments on SEC proposed rule–Definition of Nationally Recognised Statistical Rating Organisation, June 7, 1–7.

Kaitz, J.A., 2005. President and Chief Executive Officer–Association for Financial Professionals, Legislative solutions for the rating agency duopoly, Testimony before the Committee on Financial Services, Subcommittee on Capital Markets, Insurance and Government Sponsored Enterprises, United States House of Representatives, June 29, 1–12.

Kaitz, J.A., 2006. President and Chief Executive Officer–Association for Financial Professionals, AFP commends Senate Banking Committee on credit rating agency reform, August 2, 1–1.

2.2   Bank for International Settlements

Amato, J.D., and Remolona, E.M., 2003. The credit spread puzzle, *BIS Quarterly Review*, December, 51–63.

Amato, J.D., and Remolona, E.M., 2005. The pricing of unexpected credit losses, *BIS Working Papers*, No.190, November, 1–49.

Bank for International Settlements, International banking and financial market developments, *BIS Quarterly Review*, November 1997, November 1998, November 1999, August 2000, December 2003, June 2006.

Bank for International Settlements, The international debt securities market, *BIS Quarterly Review*, September 2001, March 2005, June 2005.

Basel Committee on Banking Supervision, 1993. The supervisory treatment of market risks, *Consultative Proposal*, Bank for International Settlements, Basel, April, 1–59.

Basel Committee on Banking Supervision, 1999. A new capital adequacy framework, *Consultative Paper*, Bank for International Settlements, Basel, June, 1–62.

Basel Committee on Banking Supervision, 2004. International convergence of capital measurement and capital standards: a revised framework, Bank for International Settlements, Basel, June, 1–251.

Basel Committee on Banking Supervision, 2006. International convergence of capital measurement and capital standards: a revised framework, Bank for International Settlements, Basel, June, 1–347.

Committee on the Global Financial System, 2005. The role of ratings in structured finance: Issues and implications, Bank for International Settlements, January, 1–63.

Estrella, A., 2000. Credit ratings and complementary sources of credit quality information, *Basel Committee on Banking Supervision Working Paper,* No.3, Bank for International Settlements, Basel, August, 1–186.

Fender, I. and Kiff, J., 2004. CDO rating methodology: Some thoughts on model risk and its implications, *BIS Working Papers*, No. 163, November, 1–23.

Micu, M., Remolona, E. and Wooldridge, P., 2006. The price impact of rating announcements: which announcements matter?, *BIS Working Papers,* No. 207, June, 1–31.

2.3 The Bond Market Association

Fernandez, F.A., 2005. Senior Vice President and Chief Economist, and Gross, M.E., Senior Vice President and Regulatory Consel–The Bond Market Association, Comment on SEC proposed rule–Definition of Nationally Recognised Statistical Rating Organisation, June 9, 1–9.

Green, M.S., 2005. President–The Bond Market Association, Examining the role of credit rating agencies in the capital markets, Testimony before the Committee on Banking, Housing and Urban Affairs, United States Senate, February 8, 1–8.

The Bond Market Association, *Research Quarterly*, February 2001, February 2002, February 2003, February 2004, February 2005, February 2006.

The Bond Market Association, 2004. Public comment on IOSCO October 2004 draft: Code of conduct fundamentals for credit rating agencies, November 6, 1–12.

The Bond Market Association, 2005. Response to CESR's technical advice to the European Commission on possible measures concerning credit rating agencies (CRAs)–Consultation Paper November 2004, January 28, 1–24.

The Bond Market Association, 2005. Legislative solutions for the rating agency duopoly, Statement for the Record before the Committee on Financial Services, Subcommittee on Capital Markets, Insurance and Government Sponsored Enterprises, United States House of Representatives, June 29, 1–11.

2.4 The Committee of European Securities Regulators (CESR)

The Committee of European Securities Regulators (CESR), 2004. CESR's technical advice to the European Commission on possible measures concerning credit rating agencies, *Consultation Paper*, November, Reference CESR/04-612b, 1–86.

The Committee of European Securities Regulators (CESR), 2005. The use of ratings in private contracts, Technical advice to the European Commission on possible measures concerning credit rating agencies, March, CESR/05-139b, 1–93.

The Committee of European Securities Regulators (CESR), 2005. Dialogue with rating agencies to review how the IOSCO code is being implemented, December 13, Reference 05-751, 1–7.

The Committee of European Securities Regulators (CESR), 2006. Letter from European Commission re annual reports on credit rating agencies and The Committee of European Securities Regulators' answer, May 17, 1–3.

The Committee of European Securities Regulators (CESR), 2006. Update on CESR's dialogue with credit rating agencies to review how the IOSCO code of conduct is being implemented – Annexes, July 6, Reference 06-220 Annexes, 1–135.

2.5 Committee of European Banking Supervisors

Committee of European Banking Supervisors, 2005. Consultation paper on the recognition of external credit assessment institutions, June 29, 1–37.

Committee of European Banking Supervisors, 2006. *Guidelines on the Recognition of External Credit Assessment Institutions*, January 20, 1–40.

2.6 European Central Bank

European Central Bank, 2000. *Monthly Bulletin*, January, 1–120.

European Central Bank, 2004. *The Monetary Policy of the ECB*, 1–128.

European Central Bank, 2006. Euro area statistics: section 3.2–Main liabilities of non-financial sectors, June.

Gonzalez, F., Hass, F., Johannes, R., Persson, M., Toledo, L., Violi, R., Wieland, M., and Zins, C., 2004. Market dynamics associated with credit ratings, *Occasional Paper* no. 16: European Central Bank, June, 1–40.

2.7 European Commission

Commission Directive 2003/124/EC of 22/12/03 (OJ 2003 L 339/70).
Commission Directive 2003/125/EC of 22/12/03 (OJ 2003 L 339/73).
Commission Directive 2004/72/EC of 29/04/04 (OJ 2003 L 162/70).
Commission of the European Communities, 2004. Proposal, Re-casting Directive 2000/12/EC of the European Parliament and of the Council of 20 March 2000, 1–174.
Commission of the European Communities, 2005. Communication from the Commission on credit rating agencies, December 23, 2005/11990, 1-9 (as published in the Official Journal of the European Union, 2006/C59/02, March 11, 2006, 1-5).
Commission Regulation (EC) No 2273/2003 of 22/12/03 (OJ 2003 L 336/33).
Council Directive 93/6/EEC of 15 March 1993.
Directive 2003/6/EC of 28/01/03 (OJ 2003 L 96/16).
Directive 2004/39/EC of 21/04/04 (OJ 2004 L 145/1) ('MiFID').
European Commission, 1999. Financial Services: Implementing the framework for financial markets: Action plan, *Communication of the Commission*, May 5, COM(1999)232, 11.05.99, 1–32.
European Commission, 2004. Call to CESR for technical advice on possible measures concerning credit rating agencies, July 27, 1–10.

2.8 European parliament

European Parliament and Council, 2006. Directive 2006/48/EC of June 14, 2006 relating to the taking up and pursuit of the business of credit institutions (recast), *Official Journal of the European Union*, June 30, 1–200.
European Parliament, 2004. Resolution on role and methods of rating agencies, February 10, P5_TA-PROV(2004)0080, 1–4.
Katiforis, G., 2004. Report on role and methods of rating agencies, European Parliament, January 29, Session document A5-0040/2004, 1–11.

2.9 European Securitisation Forum

European Securitisation Forum, *ESF Securitisation Data Report*, Spring 2002, Winter 2003, Winter 2004, Winter 2005, Winter 2006.

2.10 Federal Reserve System

Board of Governors of the Federal Reserve System, 2005. Flow of funds accounts of the United States historical data: 1965-1994, December 8.
Board of Governors of the Federal Reserve System, 2006. Flow of funds accounts of the United States historical data: 1995-2005, September 19, 1–109.
Board of Governors of the Federal Reserve System, 2006. Flow of funds accounts of the United States, Federal Reserve statistical release, September 19, 1–124.

2.11 Banks and Financial Advisory Companies.

Apgar, P.E., Arthur, D., and Monaco, L., 2005. Moody's, *Equity Research Report*: Morgan Stanley, April 27, 1–16.
Crockett, B., Lowe, J., and Searby, F., 2003. Moody's attractive business, but growth hiatus in 2004. *North American Equity Research*: JPMorgan, October 14, 1–44.
Fitzgerald I., 2005. *Uncertainty in the European Loan Market*, Lloyd's TSB, June 13, 1–3.
Fridson, M. and Wahl, F., 1986. Fallen Angels versus original issue high yield bonds, High Performance: *The Magazine of High Yield Bonds*, Morgan Stanley & Co., Inc., October, 2–8.
Galdi, P., 2004. Upcoming changes in global bond index rules, Merrill Lynch, October 13, 1–8.

Lehman Brothers, 2005. Lehman Brothers to include Fitch ratings in global family of indices, January 24, 1–3.

Merrill Lynch, 2004. Merrill Lynch announces changes in global bond index rules, October 14, 1–2.

Merrill Lynch, 2005. EMU Corporate Index, November 30.

Morgan Stanley Credit Advisory Group, 2006. Pros and cons of obtaining credit ratings, Overview of the credit rating process – *Morgan Stanley's Integrated Rating Advisory Approach*, December 12, 1–3.

UBS Global Equity Research, 2007. First Read: Fimalac, *UBS Investment Research*, January 26, 1–5.

2.12   Financial Press

Ablan, J., 2002. A triple-A for effort: thanks to its fast-growing financial services business, McGraw-Hill merits a re-rating, *Barron's*, July 22, 2119 words.

Areddy, J.T., 2006. Chinese firms disclose more–Transparency shows ties to government as scandals unfold, *Wall Street Journal Europe*, November 13.

Associated Press Newswires, 2005. Standard & Poor's lowers Italy's credit outlook from stable to negative, August 8.

Bary, A., 2006. Free S&P, *Barron's*, January 30, 1562 words.

Batchelor, C., 2003. Companies and regulators go on offensive in the global ratings game, *Financial Times*, July 5.

BBC News, 2001. Kensington wins top credit rating, March 5.

BBC News, 2002. France Telecom in 9bn-euro bailout, December 4.

BBC News, 2005. GM and Ford downgraded to junk, May 5.

BBC News, 2005. Philippines' credit woes escalate, July 13.

Beales, R, 2006. DBRS to launch country ratings, Financial Times, 22 March.

Benoit, B., and Bream, R., 2003. S&P downgrades ThyssenKrupp, *Financial Times*, February 22.

Best, A, 1949. A junior clerk at fifteen, *Best's Review magazine*.

Blitz, R., and Larsen, P.T., 2006. PartyGaming bank loan talks, *Financial Times*, October 4.

Bloomberg News, 2005. Ahold to cut 700 jobs to regain credit rating, *International Herald Tribune*, December 31.

Bloomberg News, 2006. Doubt on lender's debt Citigroup sees advance in global equity market, October 17, as reported in *International Herald Tribune*.

Bloomberg News, 2007. Some take refuge in poison puts, *International Herald Tribune*, April 4.

Bream, R., 1999. Telling the wheat from the chaff, Credit research, *Euromoney*, April, Issue 360, 128–134.

Business Publisher, 2000. Thomson sells BankWatch Ratings Service; Acquires Argentinian publisher, October 17.

Business Wire, 2006. Fitch Ratings launches new rating agency, Derivative Fitch, October 18, 1050 words.

Cass, D., 2000. Moody's launches risk model, *Risk*, June, Vol. 13, No. 6, 14–15.

Covel, S., and Hawkins Jr., L, 2005. High fuel prices, Delphi woes pressure GM's credit ratings, *Wall Street Journal Europe*, September 29.

Credit, 2006. Upgrading the rating process, October, 1–6.

Davies, P J, 2006. DBRS moves into structured finance, *Financial Times*, June 5.

Delaney, K.J., 2002. France Inc. is fuming at top rating agencies–anger over downgrades is sign of new accountability; Search for a scapegoat, *Wall Street Journal Europe*, November 20.

Di Leo, L., and Perry, J., 2006. Italy credit downgrade may undermine euro zone, *Wall Street Journal*, October 20.

Duin, S., 2006. Warning: PGE hasn't redlined this column, *Oragonian*, December 14.

Duyn, A.V., 2001. Telecoms operators look set for long stay in debt markets: Equity markets' cooling sentiment means companies must turn to debt financing to fund 3G networks, *Financial Times*, March 16.

Economist, 1997. Risks beyond measure, December 13, 70–71.

Economist, 1997. The would-be king of credit ratings, August 16, 765 words.

Economist, 1999. A stitch in time, Global Finance Survey, January 30, 8–12.

Fay, S., Girard, L., 2001. France Télécom boucle une émission obligatoire record, *Le Monde*, March 9.

Financial Times, 1990. Standard and Poor's acquires 50% stake in debt rating agency, January 26, 121 words.

Financial Times, 1997. Credit due, October 20, 217 words.

Fleming, S., 1999. Disarming bank credit risk, Institutional Investor-International Edition, Vol. 24, No. 8, August, 28–34.

Fridson, M., and Wahl, F., 1986. Fallen angels versus original issue high yield bonds, *High Performance*: The Magazine of High Yield Bonds, Morgan Stanley & Co., Inc., October, 2–8.

Giddy, I., 2001. France Telecom confirms ABS, Article compiled by Giddy, I. of New York University, February 27.

Insurance Canada, 2003. A.M. Best consolidates Canadian Operations, www.insurance-canada.ca, January.

Irvine, S., 1998. Caught with their pants down?, *Euromoney*, January.

Jaquiss, N., 2006. The producer – How PGE manipulated the record to try to raise our electricity rates, *Willamette Week Online*, December 6.

Jaquiss, N., 2006. An Oregon senator wants regulators to look at PGE-Standard & Poor's dealings, *Willamette Week*, December 13.

Jenkins, P, 2006. DBRS to challenge big agencies, *Financial Times*, January 10.

Winter, J., head of European investment banking at Barclays Capital, as quoted in Oakley, D., 2007. Ford bond a matter of timing, *Financial Times*, February 14.

Johnston, D.C., 2006. Objectivity of a rating questioned, *New York Times*, December 12.

Klein, A., 2004. Credit raters' power leads to some abuses, some borrowers say, *Washington Post*, November 24.

Klein, A., 2004. Smoothing the way for debt markets, *Washington Post*, November 23.

Koenig, B., 2006. Ford to back $18 billion in new loans with assets, Bloomberg News, *International Herald Tribune*, November 28, 503 words.

Lazo, S.A., 1996. Just Call It McGraw-High – profits, shares, dividends up; stock to split, *Barron's*, February, 786 words.

Les Echos, 1996. Standard & Poor's acquires remainder of S&P-ADEF, January 18, 191 words.

Monnelly, M., 2002. Bon voyage, *Breakingviews*, May 24.

Monnelly, M., 2002. Bon's chance, *Breakingviews*, May 28.

Musero, F., 2000. S&P Acquires CBRS, *Private Placement Letter*, November 6, 680 words.

New York Times, 1997. Merger to create large credit rating agency, October 17.

Oakley, D., 2007. Ford bond a matter of timing, February 14, *Financial Times*, page 41.

Oakley, D., 2006. Hybrids hit by Moody's rethink, *Financial Times*, November 22.

Partnoy, F., 2006. Take away the credit rating agencies' licences, *Financial Times*, March 13.

Pinto, M., 1998. Can the agencies play catch-up?, Special reports: The Euro-Supplement, *Euroweek*, June 1.

Greenway H.D.S., 2006. Maybe no one is to blame, *International Herald Tribune*, October 10.

PR Newswire, 2000. Fitch IBCA and Duff & Phelps Credit Rating Co. announce merger agreement, March 7, 800 words.

Raynes, P., 2002. Piece of Schmid, *Breakingviews*, May 30.

Reinebach, A., 1998. Inroads overseas help US rating agencies to level the playing field, *The Investment Dealers Digest*, August 3, Vol. 64, Issue 31, 11–11.

Reinebach, A., 1998. Study shows third rating shrinks spreads, *The Investment Dealers Digest*, Vol. 64.

Salas, C., and Hassler, D., 2007. CDOs may bring subprime-like bust for LBOs and Junk Debt, *Bloomberg.com*, March 13.

Schepp, D., 2002. Family cedes control at Adelphia, *BBC News*, May 23.

Scholtes, S., 2006. Hedge funds to use high-tech filter to harvest market gossip, *Financial Times*, September 21, 1–1.

Scholtes, S., 2006. Fitch unveils new agency, *Financial Times*, October 18.

Sender, H., 2008. MS and Goldman change approach to lending, *Financial Times*, August 17.

Tett, G., 2006. London borough wins elite credit rating, *Financial Times*, May 29.

Wall Street Journal, 2001. France Telecom expects revenue to grow at double-digit pace, March 23.

Wall Street Journal, 2001. France Telecom may be near big push in Eurobond market, August 3.

Wall Street Journal, 2001. France Telecom group may raise stake in Telekomunikacja Polska., August 22.

Wall Street Journal, 2001. France Telecom says its debt won't derail some expansion, September 7.

Wall Street Journal, 2001. France Telecom bonds pressured by downgrade, September 26.

Wiggins, J, 2002. Lesser-known ratings groups seek high status, *Financial Times*, May 20 .

Wiggins, J, 2002. A chance to step into the light, *Financial Times*, December 9.

Wiggins, J, 2003. US gets fourth ratings agency, *Financial Times*, February 25.

2.13   France Telecom

BBC News, 2002. France Telecom in 9bn-euro bailout, December 4.

France Telecom, 2001. Note d'Operation, February 12, 1–170.

France Telecom, 2001. Note d'Operation, May 28.

France Telecom, 2001. Financial analyst presentation – Half-year results, September 6.

France Telecom, 2002. Financial analyst presentation – Annual results 2001, March 21.

France Telecom, 2002. France Telecom posts its best-ever operating income in 2001 but net income is negative after non-recurring provisions, *Press Release*, March 21.

France Telecom, 2002. Thierry takes helm at France Telecom, Statement of Thierry Breton as new head of France Telecom, *Press Release*, October 3.

France Telecom, *Annual Report*, 1996 through 2005.

France Telecom, Form 20-F for the fiscal year ended: December 31, 1996, 1997, 1998, 1999, 2000, 2001, 2002, 2003, 2004.

Ministère de l'Economie, des Finances et de l'Industrie, 2002. Soutien de l'Etat au plan d'action approuvé par le conseil d'administration de France Télécom, *Communiqué*, December 4.

Moody's Investors Service, 2001. France Telecom analysis, *Global Credit Research*, June.

Moody's Investors Service, 2005. France Telecom rating history, *Ratings Interactive*, March 14.

2.14   International monetary fund

International Monetary Fund, 2005. Globalisation and External Imbalances, *Staff Survey*, April, 109–156.

2.15   International Organisation of Securities Commissions (IOSCO)

Technical Committee of International Organisation of Securities Commissions, 2003. IOSCO Statement of principles regarding the activities of credit rating agencies, OICV-IOSCO, September 25, 1–4.

Technical Committee of International Organisation of Securities Commissions, 2003. Report on the activities of credit rating agencies, September, OICV-IOSCO PD 153, 1–20.

Technical Committee of International Organization of Securities Commissions, 2004. Code of conduct fundamentals for credit rating agencies, *Consultation Report,* October, OICV-IOSCO PD 173, 1–13.

Technical Committee of International Organization of Securities Commissions, 2004. Code of conduct fundamentals for credit rating agencies, December, OICV-IOSCO PD 180, 1–12.

Technical Committee of International Organisation of Securities Commissions, 2008. Code of conduct fundamentals for credit rating agencies, revised May, OICV-IOSCO PD 271, 1–14.

2.16   Miscellaneous

ABB Ltd, 2006. Form 20-F for fiscal year ended December 31, 2005.

ABB Ltd, 2003. Form 20-F for fiscal year ended December 31, 2002, filed with United States Securities and Exchange Commission, June 30, File No: 001-16429, 1–224.

Alcatel, *Annual Report*, 2002.

Association of Corporate Treasurers, 2006. *The Treasurer's Handbook 2006*.

Autorité des Marchés Financiers (AMF), 2005. *2004 AMF Report on Rating Agencies*, January, 1–76.

BDO International, Deloitte, Ernst & Young, Grant Thornton International, KPMG International, and PricewaterhouseCoopers International Limited, 2006. Global capital markets and the global economy: a vision from the CEOs of the International Audit Networks, November, 1–24.

Biais, B., Declerck, F., Dow, J., Portes, R., and von Thadden, E.L., 2006. European corporate bond markets: transparency, liquidity, efficiency, Report commissionned by Association of British Insurers, City of London, European high-yield association, European Primary Dealers' Association, International Capital Market Association, Investment Management Association and London Investment Banking Association from *Centre for Economic Policy Research*, May, 1–81.

California Public Employees' Retirement System, 2005. CalPERS Statement of Investment Policy for Credit Enhancement Program, February 14, 1–11.

Diabré, Z., 2002. Associate Administrator–United Nations Development Programme, Partnership with the private sector for financing Africa's growth through NEPAD, Statement on April 15 in Dakar, Senegal, 1–5.

Embassy of Ukraine to the United States of America, 1998. President Kuchma Receives Co-Chairperson Of Ukrainian-German Interbank Group, *Press Release*, September 29.

Entergy Corporation, 2005. Entergy Corporation's New Orleans subsidiary files Chapter 11 petition, *Press Release*, September 23.

European Banking Federation, 2004. Response to CESR's call for evidence on credit rating agencies, August 24, 1–4.

Federation of German Industries, 2004. BDI position on the CESR consultation paper on a possible regulation of rating agencies, January 28, 1–8.

Financial Services Authority, 2001. Interim Prudential Sourcebook: *Banks*, June.

Financial Services Authority, 2001. Interim Prudential Sourcebook: *Investment Businesses*, June, Chapter 1.

Jankova, E., Pochon, F., and Teïletche, J., 2006. Impact of agencies' decisions: comparison of French equities and international experiences, Autorités des Marchés Financiers, January, 1–42.

Kanjorski, P.E., 2005. Ranking democratic member, Opening Statement at the Hearing entitled 'Legislative solutions for the credit rating agencies' before the House Subcommittee on Capital Markets, Insurance and Government Sponsored Enterprises, June 29, 1–6.

Keogh, M., 2005. Managing Director, Policy – Dominion Bond Rating Service, Response to CEBS consultation paper on the recognition of external credit assessment institutions, September 27, 1–8.

Lancellotta, A.B.R., Senior Counsel–Investment Company Institute, 2003. Comment on SEC concept release regarding rating agencies and the use of credit ratings under the Federal Securities Laws, July 28.

Lancellotta, A.B.R., 2005. Senior Counsel–Investment Company Institute, Comments on SEC proposed rule–Definition of Nationally Recognised Statistical Rating Organisation, June 9, 1–5.

Langohr, H., Langohr, P., 2007. Comments to the SEC's proposed rule S7-04-07, SEC website, March 12, 1–21.

Ministère de l'Economie, des Finances et de l'Industrie, 2002. Situation financière de France Télécom, *Communiqué*, September 12.

Ministère de l'Economie, des Finances et de l'Industrie, 2002. France Télécom, *Communiqué*, October 2.

Ministère de l'Economie, des Finances et de l'Industrie, 2002. Soutien de l'Etat au plan d'action approuvé par le conseil d'administration de France Télécom, *Communiqué*, December 4.

Nicholls, C.C., 2005. Public and private uses of credit ratings, *Policy Series*: Capital Markets Institute (Canada), August, 1–47.

Paulson, H.M., Treasury Secretary, 2006. Remarks on the competitivness of U.S. capital markets economic club of New York, New York, NY, November 20, 1–12.

Public Broadcasting Service, 1996. Paraphrased from Friedman, T., The News Hour with Jim Lehrer: Interview with Thomas L. Friedman, February 13.

Public Broadcasting Service, 1996. Free Market Sociey, Transcript of interview between David Gergen and Thomas L. Friedman, February 13.

Rae, L., Senior Advisor – Investment Operatings, Investment Management Association, 2004. Comments on IOSCO October 2004 draft: Code of conduct fundamentals for credit rating agencies, November 8, 1–2.

Reserve Bank of India, 2005. Master circular–exposure norms for financial institutions, August 13, 1–23.

Reserve Bank of India, 2006. Guidelines on securitisation of standard assets, February 2, 1–23.

Russell Reynolds Associates, 2005. International survey of institutional investors: a world of risk, Business Evolves, *Leadership Endures Series* Ndeg 8, 1–21.

Schroeder, W.J., 2001. CFA, President – Dominion Bond Rating Service, DBRS response to the January 2001 Basel Committee on Banking Supervision draft, May 28, 1–5.

Stevens, P.S., 2005. President–Investment Company Institute, The Credit Rating Agency Duopoly Relief Act, Testimony before the Committee on Financial Services, United States House of Representatives, November 29, 1–14.

Stevens, P.S., 2006. President–Investment Company Institute, Letter to Chairman Honorable Richard Shelby and Ranking Minority Member, Honorable Paul Sarbanes, Senate Committee on Banking, Housing and Urban Affairs, July 31, 1–2.

Working Group of Investment Institutions ('Gang of 26'), 2003. Improving market standards in the Sterling and Euro fixed income credit markets, *Proposals Paper*, October, 1–8.

2.17   Securities and Exchange Commission (SEC)

Cox, C., 2006. Chairman–U.S. Securities and Exchange Commission, A review of current securities issues, Testimony before Committee on Banking, Housing and Urban Affairs, United States Senate, April 25, 1–12.

Donaldson, W.H., 2005. Chairman–U.S. Securities and Exchange Commission, The state of the securities industry, Testimony before the Committee on Banking Housing and Urban Affairs, United States Senate, March 9, 1–13.

Lancellotta, A.B.R., 2002. Senior Counsel–Investment Company Institute, SEC hearing on issues relating to credit rating agencies, November 21.

Macdonald, M.S., 2002. Vice President, Finance and Treasurer–Ford Motor Company, Transcript of SEC hearings on the current role and function of the credit rating agencies in the operation of the securities markets, November 15.

Nazareth, A.L., 2003. Director, Division of Market Regulation–U.S. Securities and Exchange Commission, Rating the rating agencies: The state of transparency and competition, Testimony before the House Subcommittee on Capital Markets, Insurance, and Government Sponsored Enterprises, Committee on Financial Services, April 2, 1–8.

The Securities Exchange Act of 1934 introduced as part of the Secondary Mortgage Market Enhancement Act of 1984 revised through September 30, 2004, 1–259.

U.S. Securities and Exchange Commission, 1994. Nationally Recognized Statistical Rating Organizations, August 31, File No. S7-23-94, 1–12.

U.S. Securities and Exchange Commission, 2003. Rating agencies and the use of credit ratings under the federal security laws, *Concept Release*, June.

U.S. Securities and Exchange Commission, 2003. Report on the role and function of credit rating agencies in the operation of the securities market, January, 1–45.

U.S. Securities and Exchange Commission, 2005. Definition of Nationally Recognised Statistical Rating Organisations, *Proposed Rule*, April 19, 1–74.

U.S. Securities and Exchange Commission, 2005. Staff outline of key issues for a legislative framework for the oversight and regulation of credit rating agencies (Introduced into the record by Ranking Democratic Member Paul E. Kanjorski in his Opening Statement at the Hearing entitled Legislative Solutions for the Credit Rating Industry before the House Subcommittee on Capital Markets, Insurance and Government Sponsored Enterprises), June, 1–3.

U.S. Securities and Exchange Commission, 2007. Oversight of credit rating agencies as Nationally Recognized Statistical Rating Organizations, *Proposed Rule*, February 2, File No. S7-04-07, 1–196.

U.S. Securities and Exchange Commission, 2008. References to ratings of Nationally Recognized Statistical Rating Organizations, *Proposed Rule,* July 1st, File No. S7-19-08, 1–75.

U.S. Securities and Exchange Commission, 2008. Security ratings, *Proposed Rule,* July 1st, File No. S7-19-08, 1–77.

U.S. Securities and Exchange Commission, 2008. References to ratings of Nationally Recognized Statistical Rating Organizations, *Proposed Rule*, July 1st, File No. S7-19-08, 1–70.

U.S. Securities and Exchange Commission, 2008. Proposed rules for Nationally Recognized Statistical Rating Organizations, June 11, File No. S7-13-08, 1–168.

2.18   US Congress

House Committee on Financial Services, 2006. President signs credit rating agency reform act of 2006. S.3850, into law, *Press Release*, September 29.

United States Congress, Investment Company Act of 1940, Rule 3a-7–Issuers of Asset-Backed Securities.

United States Congress, 2000. Public law 106-553: Federal funding, fiscal year 2001, December 21, 1–151.

United States Congress, 2002. Sarbanes-Oxley Act of 2002, January 23, 1–66.

United States Congress, 2006. Credit Rating Agency Reform Act of 2006 (S. 3850), 109th Congress, 2D Session, September 27.

United States House of Representatives, 2005. H.R. 2990 introduced by Mr Fitzpatrick of Pennsylvania, referred to the House Committee on Financial Services, June 20.

United States House of Representatives, 2006. Amendment in the nature of a substitute to H.R. 2990 offered by Mr. Oxley of Ohio, June 13, 1–24.

United States House of Representatives, 2006. H.R. 2990, Short Title: Credit Rating Duopoly Relief Act of 2006 (Version H.R. 2990 RFS–Referred to Senate Committee after being received from House of Representatives), July 13, 1–26.

United States Senate, 2006. Credit Rating Agency Reform Act of 2006 (S. 3850), 109th Congress, 2D Session, September 22.

United States Senate Committee on Banking, Housing, and Urban Affairs, 2005. Examining the role of credit rating agencies in the capital markets: Open Session Hearing, February 8.

2.19   The World Bank

The World Bank, 1994. World debt table: external finance for developing countries 1994-1995, *A World Bank book*, December, 1–30.

The World Bank, *Global Development Finance*, 2000, 2001, 2004, 2005, and 2006.

3   ACADEMIC RESEARCH

3.1   Articles

Agrawal, D., Elton, E.J., Gruber, M.J., and Mann, C., 2001. Explaining the rate spread on corporate bonds, *Journal of Finance*, Vol. 26, No. 1, February, 247–277.

Aguiar, J.M., and Altman, E.I., 2005. Defaults and returns in the high yield bond market: the year 2004 in review and market outlook, *NYU Salomon Center and Leonard N. Stern School of Business Special Report*, January, 1–49.

Akerlof, G.A., 1970. The market for 'lemons': quality uncertainty and the market mechanism, *Quarterly Journal of Economics*, Vol. 84, No. 3, August, 488–500.

Altman, E.I., 1968. Financial ratios, discriminant analysis and the prediction of corporate bankruptcy, *Journal of Finance*, Vol. 23, No. 4, September, 589–609.

Altman, E.I., 1989. Measuring corporate bond mortality and performance, *Journal of Finance*, Vol. 44, No. 4, September, 909–922.

Altman, E.I., 2006. Default recovery rates and LGD in credit risk modelling and practice: an updated review of the literature and empirical evidence, *mimeo,* November, 1–36.

Altman, E.I., and Bana, G., 2003. Defaults and returns on high-yield bonds: The year 2002 in review and the market outlook, NYU Salomon Center, Stern School of Business Report, February, 1–64.

Altman, E.I., Brady, B., Resti, A., and Sironi, A., 2005. The link between default and recovery rates: Theory, empirical evidence, and implications, *Journal of Business*, Vol. 78, No. 6, November, 2203–2227.

Altman, E.I., and Cooke, D., 1999. Defaults and returns on high yield bonds: analysis through 1998 and default outlook for 1999-2001, *NYU Salomon Center Working Papers*, No. S-CDM-99-01, January, 1–26.

Altman, E., and Karlin, B.J., 2007. Defaults and returns on high-yield bonds and distressed debt: first half 2007, *Review, Special Report*, NYU Salomon Center, 1–25.

Altman, E.I., and Ramayanam, S., 2007. Default and returns in the high-yield bond market: 2006, *Review and Outlook, Special Report*: NYU Salomon Center, and Leonard N. Stern School of Business, January, 1–35.

Altman, E.I., and Rijken, H.A., 2004. How rating agencies achieve rating stability, *Journal of Banking and Finance*, Vol. 28, No. 11, November, 2679–2714.

Amato, J.D., and Furfine, C.H., 2004. Are credit ratings procyclical?, *Journal of Banking and Finance*, Vol. 28, No. 11, November, 2641–2677.

Arrow, K., 1964. The role of securities in the optimal allocation of risk-bearing, *Review of Economic Studies*, Vol. 31, No. 2, April, 91–96.

Artus, P., Garrigues, J., and Sassenou, M., 1993. Interest rate costs and issuer ratings: The case of French CP and bonds, *Journal of International Securities Markets*, Vol. 7, Autumn, 211–218.

Ashcraft, A., and Schuermann, T., 2008. Understanding the securitization of subprime mortgage credit, *FRBNY Staff Reports,* No. 318, March, 1–76.

Baker, H.K., and Mansi, S.A., 2002. Assessing credit rating agencies by bond issuers and institutional investors, *Journal of Business Finance and Accounting*, Vol. 29, No. 9/10, November/December, 1367–1398.

Bangia, A., Diebold, F.X., Kronimus, A., Schagen, Ch., and Schuermann, T., 2002. Ratings migration and the business cycle, with application to credit portfolio stress testing, *Journal of Banking andnance*, Vol. 26, No. 2/3, March, 445–474.

Barton, A., 2006. *Split credit ratings and the prediction of bank ratings in the Basel II environment*, Thesis submitted for the degree of Doctor of Philosophy, University of Southampton, Faculty of Law, Arts and Social Sciences, School of Management, 1–205.

Beattie, V., and Searle, S., 1992. Bond ratings and inter-rate agreement, *Journal of International Securities Markets*, Vol. 6, Summer, 167–172.

Bharath, S.T., and Shumway, T., 2008. Forecasting default with the Merton distance to default model, *Review of Financial Studies*, Vol. 21, No. 3, May, 1339–1369.

Biais, B., 1993. Price formation and equilibrium liquidity in fragmented and centralized markets, *Journal of Finance*, Vol. 48, No. 1, March, 157–185.

Biais, B., Glosten, L., and Spatt, C., 2005. Market microstructure: A survey of microfoundations, empirical results, and policy implications, *Journal of Financial Markets,* Vol. 8, No. 2, May, 217–264.

Black, F., and Scholes, M., 1973. The pricing of options and corporate liabilities, *Journal of Political Economy*, Vol. 81, No. 3, May/June, 637–654.

Blume, M.E., and Keim, D.B., 1987. Lower grade bonds: Their risks and returns, *Financial Analysts Journal*, Vol. 43, No. 4, July/August, 26–33.

Boot, A., and Thakor, A., 1993. Security design, *Journal of Finance*, Vol. 48, No. 4, September, 1349–1378.

Brander, J., and Lewis, T., 1986. Oligopoly and financial structure: the limited liability effect, *American Economic Review*, Vol. 76, No. 5, December, 956–970.

Brennan, M., and Schwartz, E., 1988. The case for convertibles, *Journal of Applied Corporate Finance*, Vol. 1, No. 2, Summer, 55–64.

Brunner, K., 1987. The perception of man and the conception of society: two approaches to understanding society, *Economic Inquiry*, Vol. 25, No. 3, July, 367–388.

Campbell, J.Y., Lettau, M., Malkiel B.G., and Xu, Y., 2001. Have individual stocks become more volatile? An empirical exploration of idiosyncratic risk, *Journal of Finance*, Vol. 56, No.1, February, 1–43.

Cantor, R., 2004. An introduction to recent research on credit ratings, *Journal of Banking and Finance*, Vol. 28, No. 11, November, 2565–2573.

Cantor, R., and Emery, K.M., 2005. Relative default rates on corporate loans and bonds, *Journal of Banking and Finance*, Vol. 29, No. 6, June, 1575–1584.

Cantor, R., Gwilym, O.A., and Thomas, S., 2007. The use of credit ratings in investment management in the U.S. and Europe, *Journal of Fixed Income*, Vol. 17, No. 2, Fall, 13–26.

Cantor, R., and Packer, F., 1994. The credit rating industry, *Quarterly Review*, Federal Reserve Bank of New York, Vol. 19, No. 2, Summer/Fall, 1–26

Cantor, R., and Packer F., 1996. Determinants and impact of sovereign credit ratings, *Economic Policy Review*, Vol. 2, No. 3, October, 37–53.

Cantor, R., and Packer, F., 1997. Differences of opinion and selection bias in the credit rating industry, *Journal of Banking and Finance*, Vol. 21, No. 10, October, 1395–1417.

Cantor, R., Packer, F., and Cole, K., 1997. Split ratings and the pricing of credit risk, *Journal of Fixed Income*, Vol. 7, No. 3, December, 72–82.

Cao, C., Yu, F., and Zhong, Z., 2006. The information content of option-implied volatility for credit default swap valuation, *FDIC Center for Financial Research Working Papers*, No. 2007-08, April, 1–43.

Coase, R.H., 1937. The nature of the firm, *Economica, New Series*, Vol. 4, No. 16, November, 386–405.

Corrigan, B., and Dawes, R.M., 1974. Linear models in decision making, *Psychological Bulletin*, Vol. 81, No. 2, February, 95–106.

Coval, J., Jurek, J., and Stafford, E., 2007. Economic catastrophe bonds, *HBS Finance Working Papers*, No. 07-102, July, 1–44.

Covitz, D., and Harrison, P., 2003. Testing conflicts of interest at bond rating agencies with market anticipation: evidence that reputation incentives dominate, *Federal Reserve Board Finance and Economics Discussion Series*,No. 2003-68, December, 1–37.

Cremers, M., Driessen, J., and Maenhout, P., 2005. Explaining the level of credit spreads: Option-implied jump risk premia in a firm value model, *BIS Working Papers*, No. 191, July, 1-48, forthcoming in *Review of Financial Studies*.

Crouhy, M., and Turnbull, S., 2008. The subprime credit crisis of 07, mimeo, March 5th, 1–42.

DeMarzo, P.M., 2005. The pooling and tranching of securities: A model of informed intermediation, *Review of Financial Studies*, Vol. 18, No. 1, Spring, 1–35.

DeMarzo, P.M., and Duffie, D., 1999. A liquidity-based model of security design. *Econometrica*, Vol. 67, No. 1, January, 65–99.

Duffie, D., Eckner, A., Horel, G., and Saita, L., 2008. Frailty correlated default, Stanford Graduate School of Business, January, 1-56, forthcoming *Journal of Finance*.

Diamond, D.W., 1984. Financial Intermediation and Delegated Monitoring, *Review of Economic Studies*, Vol. 51, No. 166, July, 393–414.

Driessen, J., 2005. Is default event risk priced in corporate bonds? *Review of Financial Studies*, Vol. 18, No. 1, Spring, 165–195.

Ederington, L.H., 1986. Why split ratings occur, *Financial Management*, Vol. 15, No. 1, Spring, 37–47.

Ederington, L.H., and Goh, J.C., 1998. Bond rating agencies and stock analysts: Who knows what when?, *Journal of Financial and Quantitative Analysis*, Vol. 33, No. 4, December, 569–585.

Ederington, L.H., Roberts, B.E., and Yawitz, J.B., 1987. The informational content of bond ratings, *Journal of Financial Research*, Vol. 10, No. 3, Fall, 211–226.

Faulkender, M., and Peterson, M.A., 2006. Does the source of capital affect capital structure? *Review of Financial Studies*, Vol. 19, No. 1, Spring, 45–79.

Ferri, G., Liu, L.-G., and Stiglitz, J.E., 1999. The procyclical role of rating agencies: Evidence from the East Asian crisis, *Economic Notes*, Vol. 28, No. 3, November, 335–355.

Fridson, M.S., and Garman, M.C., 1998. Determinants of spreads on new high-yield bonds, *Financial Analysts Journal*, Vol. 54, No. 2, March/April, 28–39.

Fridson, M., and Sterling, K., 2006. Fallen Angels: A separate and superior asset class, *Journal of Fixed Income*, Vol. 16, No. 3, Winter, 22–29.

Fulop, A., 2006. Feedback effects of rating downgrades, September, *ESSEC Working Papers*, No. DR0616, October, 1–40.

Gilson, S.C., 1989. Management turnover and financial distress, *Journal of Financial Economics*, Vol. 25, No. 2, December, 241–262.

Gorton, G., and Souleles, N.S., 2006. Special purpose vehicles and securitization, in M. Carey and R.M. Stulz (eds), *The Risks of Financial Institutions*, University of Chicago Press, Chicago and London, 549–597.

Graham, J.R., and Harvey, C.R., 2001. The theory and practice of corporate finance: evidence from the field, *Journal of Financial Economics*, Vol. 60, No. 2/3, May, 187–243.

Grossman, S.J., and Hart, O.D., 1986. The costs and benefits of ownership: A theory of vertical and lateral integration, *Journal of Political Economy*, Vol. 94, No. 4, August, 691–719.

Gürkaynak, R., and Wolfers, J., 2006. Macroeconomic derivatives: an initial analysis of market-based macro forecast, uncertainty and risk, *National Bureau of Economic Research Working Papers*, No. 11929, January, 1–43.

Güttler, A. and Wahrenburg, M., 2007. The adjustment of credit ratings in advance of defaults, *Journal of Banking and Finance*, Vol. 31, No. 3, March, 751–767.

Halov, N., and Heider F., 2006. Capital structure, risk and asymmetric information, *mimeo*, April, 1–58.

Hamilton, D.T., and Cantor, R., 2004. Rating transition and default rates conditioned on outlooks, *Journal of Fixed Income*, Vol. 14, No. 2, September, 54–70.

Ho, T.S.Y., and Stoll, H.R., 1983. The dynamics of dealer markets under competition, *Journal of Finance*, Vol. 38, No. 4, September, 1053–1074.

Holthausen, R.W., and Leftwich, R.W., 1986. The effect of bond rating changes on common stock prices, *Journal of Financial Economics*, Vol. 17, No. 1, September, 57–89.

Hotchkiss, E.S., and Ronen, T., 2002. The informational efficiency of the corporate bond market: an intraday analysis, *Review of Financial Studies*, Vol. 15, No. 5, Winter, 1325–1354.

Hsueh, L., and Kidwell, D., 1988. Bond ratings: are two better than one? *Financial Management*, Vol. 17, No. 1, Spring, 46–53.

Jarrow, R.A., and Protter, P., 2004. Structural versus reduced form models: a new information based perspective, *Journal of Investment Management*, Vol. 2, No. 2, May, 1–10.

Jensen, M.C., 1986. Agency costs of free cash flow, corporate finance, and takeovers, *American Economic Review*, Vol. 76, No. 2, May, 323–329.

Jensen, M.C., and Meckling, W.H., 1976. Theory of the firm: managerial behavior, agency costs and ownership structure, *Journal of Financial Economics*, Vol. 3, No. 4, October, 305–360.

Jewell, J., and Livingston, M., 1998. Split ratings, bond yields, and underwriter spreads, *Journal of Financial Research*, Vol. 21, No. 2, Summer, 185–204.

Jewell, J., and Livingston, M., 2000. The impact of a third credit rating on the pricing of bonds, *Journal of Fixed Income*, Vol. 10, No. 3, December, 69–85.

Joehnk, M.D., and Reilly, F.K., 1976. The association between market based risk measures for bonds and bond ratings, *Journal of Finance*, Vol. 31, No. 5, December, 1387–1403.

Kaplan, R.S., and Urwitz, G., 1979. Statistical models of bond ratings: A methodological inquiry, *Journal of Business*, Vol. 52, No. 2, April, 231–261.

Kealhofer, S., 2003. Quantifying credit risk I: Default prediction, *Financial Analysts Journal*, Vol. 59, No. 1, January/February, 30–44.

Kisgen, D.J., 2006. Credit ratings and capital structure, *Journal of Finance*, Vol. 61, No. 3, June, 1035–1072.

Leland, H.E., and Pyle, D.H., 1977. Informational asymmetries, financial structure and financial intermediation, *Journal of Finance*, Vol. 32, No. 2, May, 371–387.

Liu, P., and Moore, W.T., 1987. The impact of split bond ratings on risk premia, *Financial Review*, Vol. 22, No. 1, February, 71–85.

Liu, P., Seyyed, F.J., and Smith, S.D., 1999. The independent impact of credit rating changes: the case of Moody's refinement on yield premiums, *Journal of Business Finance and Accounting*, Vol. 26, No. 3/4, April, 337–363.

Livingston, M., Naranjo, A., and Zhou, L., 2007. Split bond ratings and rating migration, *Journal of Banking and Finance*, Vol. 32, No. 8, August, 1613–1624.

Löffler, G., 2004. An anatomy of rating through the cycle, *Journal of Banking and Finance*, Vol. 28, No. 3, March, 695–770.

Löffler, G., 2004. Ratings versus market-based measures of default risk in portfolio governance, *Journal of Banking and Finance*, Vol. 28, No. 11, November, 2715–2746.

Löffler, G., 2007. The complementary nature of ratings and market-based measures of default risk, *Journal of Fixed Income*, Vol. 17, No. 1, Summer, 38–47.

Löffler, G., and Posch, P.N., 2007. How do rating agencies score in predicting firm performance, *SFB 649 Discussion Paper Series*, No. 2007-043, Humboldt Universität Berlin, July, 1–25.

Maskin, E., and Tirole, J., 1999. Unforeseen contingencies and incomplete contracts, *Review of Economic Studies*, Vol. 66, No. 226, January, 83–114.

Melnik A., and Nissim, D., 2004. Issue costs in the Eurobond market: The effects of market integration, *Journal of Banking and Finance*, Vol. 30, No. 1, January, 157–177.

Merton, R., 1974. On the pricing of corporate debt: The risk structure of interest rates, *Journal of Finance*, Vol. 29, No. 2, May, 449–470.

Merton, R.C., 1990. The financial system and economic performance, *Journal of Financial Services Research*, Vol. 4, No. 4, December, 263–300.

Mitchell, J., 2005. Financial intermediation theory and the sources of value in structured finance markets, *National Bank of Belgium Documents Series*, No. 71, July, 1–15.

Mora, N., 2006. Sovereign credit ratings: Guilty beyond reasonable doubt?, *Journal of Banking and Finance*, Vol. 30, No. 7, July, 2041–2062.

Morgan, D., 2002. Rating banks: Risk and uncertainty in an opaque industry, *American Economic Review*, Vol. 92, No. 4, September, 874–888.

Ogden, J.P., 1987. Determinants of relative interest rate sensitivity of corporate bonds, *Financial Management*, Vol. 16, No. 1, Spring, 22–30.

Parrino, R., 1997. Spinoffs and wealth transfers: The Marriott Case, *Journal of Financial Economics*, Vol. 43, No. 2, February, 241–274.

Partnoy, F., 1999. The Siskel and Ebert of financial markets?: Two thumbs down for the credit rating agencies, *Washington University Law Quarterly*, Vol. 77, No. 3, 619–712.

Perlich, C., and Reisz, A.S., 2006. Temporal resolution of uncertainty and corporate debt yields: an empirical investigation, *Journal of Business*, Vol. 79, No. 2, March, 731–770.

Perraudin, W., 2007. Securitization in Basel II, in A. de Servigny and N. Jobst (eds), *Handbook of Structured Finance*, McGraw-Hill, New-York, 675–696.

Perraudin, W., and Taylor, A.P., 2004. On the consistency of rating and bond market yields, *Journal of Banking and Finance*, Vol. 28, No. 11, November, 2769–2788.

Poon, W.P.H., 2003. Are unsolicited credit ratings biased downward?, *Journal of Banking and Finance*, Vol. 27, No. 4, April, 593–614.

Renault, O., 2007. Cash and synthetic CDOs, in A. de Servigny and N. Jobst (eds), *Handbook of Structured Finance*, McGraw-Hill, New-York, 373–396.

Seyhun, H.N., 1986. Insiders' profits, costs of trading, and market efficiency, *Journal of Financial Economics*, June, Vol. 16, No. 2, June, 189–212.

Smith, C., and Warner, J., 1979. On financial contracting: an analysis of bond covenants, *Journal of Financial Economics*, Vol. 7, No.2, June, 117–161.

Stiglitz, J.E., and Weiss, A., 1981. Credit rationing in markets with imperfect information, *American Economic Review*, Vol. 71, No. 3, June, 390–410.

Sylla, R., 2001. An historical primer on the business of credit ratings, World Bank Conference: *The Role of Credit Rating Reporting Systems in the International Economy*, March, 1–29.

Tompson, G.R., and Vaz., P., 1990. Dual bond ratings: a test of the certification function of rating agencies, *Financial Review*, Vol. 25, No. 3, August, 457–471.

Wakeman, L.M., 1984. The real function of bond rating agencies, in M. Jensen and C. Smith (eds), *The Modern Theory of Corporate Finance*, McGraw-Hill, New York, 391–396.

Weinstein, M., 1977. The effect of a rating change announcement on bond price, *Journal of Financial Economics*, Vol. 5, No. 3, December, 329–350.

Weinstein, M., 1981. The systematic risk of corporate bonds, *Journal of Financial and Quantitative Analysis*, Vol. 16, No. 3, September, 257–278.

White, L.J., 2002. The credit rating industry: An industrial organization analysis, in R.M. Levich, G. Majnoni and C.M. Reinhart (eds), *Ratings, Rating Agencies and the Global Financial System*, Kluwer, Boston, 41–63.

Wruck, K.H., 1990. Financial distress: reorganization and organization efficiency, *Journal of Financial Economics*, Vol. 27, No. 2, October, 419–444.

3.2 Books and Book articles

Altman, E.I., Avery, R., Eisenbeis, R., and Sinkey J., 1981. *Application of Classification Techniques in Business, Banking and Finance*, JAI Press, Conn., 1–418.

Bester, H., and M. Hellwig, M., 1987. Moral hazard and credit rationing: an overview of the issues, in Bamberg, G., and Spremann, K., 1987, *Agency Theory, Information, and Incentives*, Heidelberg, Springer, 1–533.

Bodie, Z., Crane, D.B., Froot, K.A., Mason, S.P., Merton, R.C., Perold, A.F., Sirri, E.R., and Tufano, P., 1995. *The Global Financial System: a Functional Perspective*, Harvard Business School Press, Boston, Massachusetts, 1–291.

Brealey, R.A., and Myers, S.C., 2003. *Principles of Corporate Finance*, seventh edition, McGraw-Hill, Irwin, New York, 1–1071.

Brouw, R., 1968. *De Techniek van de Kredietonderhandeling*, Standaard Wetenschappelijke Uitgeverij Antwerpen Universitaire Pers Rotterdam, Antwerpen, 1–376.

Caouette, J.B., Altman, E.I., and Narayanan, P., 1998. *Managing Credit Risk: The Next Great Financial Challenge,* John Wiley & Sons, Inc., New York, 1–452.

Carey, M., and Stulz, R.M., ed., *The Risks of Financial Institutions*, University of Chicago Press, Chicago and London

Chernow, R., 1990. *The House of Morgan: An American Banking Dynasty and the Rise of Modern Finance*, Touchstone, New York, 1–812.

Crouhy, M., Galai, D., and Mark, R., 2000. *Risk Management,* McGraw-Hill, New York, 1–717.

Duff, A., Einig, S., 2007. *Credit Rating Agencies: Meeting the Needs of the Market?*, The Institute of Chartered Accountants of Scotland, Edinburgh, 1–126.

Dimson, E., Marsh, P., and Staunton, M., 2002. *Triumph of the Optimists*, Princeton University Press, New Jersey, 1–339.

Friedman, M., and Schwartz, A.J., 1963. *A Monetary History of the United States 1867-1960*, Princeton University Press, Princeton and Oxford, New Jersey, 1–860.

Ganguin, B. and Bilardello, J., 2005. *Fundamentals of Corporate Credit Analysis*, Standard & Poor's, McGraw-Hill, 1–438.

Gerst, C., D. Groven, 2004. *To B or not to B: Le Pouvoir des Agences de Notation en Question*, Village Mondial, 1–220.

Goedhart, M., Koller, T., and Wessels, D., McKinsey & Company, 2005. *Valuation: Measuring and Managing the Value of Companies*, John Wiley & Sons, New Jersey, 1–742.

Hickman, W.B., 1958. *Corporate Bond Quality and Investors Experience*, Princeton University Press, New Jersey, 1–536.

Jorion, P, 2001. *Value at Risk*, second edition, McGraw-Hill, New York, 1–544.

Mauboussin, M.J., 2006. *More than You Know: Finding Financial Wisdom in Unconventional Places*, Columbia University Press, New York, 1–268.

Mehrling, P., 2005. *Fischer Black and the Revolutionary Idea of Finance*, John Wiley & Sons, Inc., Hoboken, New Jersey, 1–374.

Millner, H., 1999. *Pearls of Wisdom*, Clarion, England, 1–287.

de Servigny, A., Jobst, N. 2007. *The Handbook of Structured Finance*, Standard & Poor's, McGraw-Hill, 1–784.

Shapiro, C., and Varian, H.R., 1999. *Information Rules: A Strategic Guide to the Network Economy*, Harvard Business School Press, Boston, Massachusetts, 1–352.

Shiller, R.J., 1989. *Market Volatility*, MIT Press, Cambridge, Massachusetts, 1–464.

Shiller, R.J., 2003. *The New Financial Order: Risk in the 21st Century*, Princeton University Press, Princeton and Oxford, 1–366.

Sinclair, T.J., 2005. *The New Masters of Capital*, Cornell University Press, Ithaca and London, 1–186.

Solnik, B.H., 1988. *International Investments*, Addison-Wesley Publishing Company, 1–387.

Theys, T., Young, P., 1999. *Capital Market Revolution: The Future of Markets in an Online World*, Financial times & Prentice Hall, Great Britain, 1–212.

Tirole, J., 2006. *The Theory of Corporate Finance,* Princeton University Press, Princeton and Oxford, 1–644.

Webster's New World Dictionary of the American Language, 1970, Second college edition, The World Publishing Company, New York and Cleveland, 1–1692.

Williamson, O.E., 1975. *Markets and Hierarchies: Analysis of Antitrust Implications*, Free Press, New York, 1–286.

Index

A status, 75
A1 status, 208–211
A3 status, 211–219
AA status, 76
Aa1 status, 198–202
Aa2 status, 200–202
Aaa status, 75–76, 198
ABS *see* asset-backed securities, 6
accelerating rates of chance, 380–381
acceptability challenges, 473–476
accountability, 85–86
accuracy, 124–126, 188, 332–356
accuracy ratio, 340
acquisitions
    Fitch, 398–402
    France Telecom, 203
ACT (Association of Corporate Treasurers), 462
Adecco, 329
Adelphia Communications, 77, 172
adverse selection, 93, 111–126
adviser-intermediary preparations, 165–168
AFP (Association for Financial Professionals),
    462
African credibility crisis, 135–136
AFTE (Association Française Des Trésoriers
    D'Entreprise), 462
after-sales service, 174–175
agencies, origins, 2, 375–378
agency bond ratings initiation, 2
agency-specific volume drivers, 416–417
aging effects of defaults, 337
Ahold, 308
airline unsecured debt, 77
Alapage.com, 205
alternative diversity scores, 300
Altman's Z-scores, 250, 252, 284
Altman, Edward, 361
A.M. Best Company, 390, 402, 405–406, 409
Ambition 2005 restructuring plan, 242, 244
America West's unsecured debt, 77

American Stock Exchange (AMEX), 152
AMF (Autorité des Marché Financiers), 438
amortization profiles, 324
arbitrage opportunities, 102–103
Asia
    corporate ratings, 149–150
    financial crisis, 16, 356–362, 430
    sovereign ratings, 135
asset-backed floating-rate notes, 95
asset-backed securities (ABS), 6, 103, 141–149,
    296
assets
    bank financial strength ratings, 293
    default probability extraction, 276–284
    divestiture, 245–247
    France Telecom, 247, 252
    implied market values, 305
    manager contracts, 104–106
    pledging, 308–309
    pools, 35, 92–94, 130–133, 141–149
    swap spreads, 65
Association for Financial Professionals (AFP),
    462
Association Française Des Trésoriers
    D'Entreprise (AFTE), 462
Association of Corporate Treasurers (ACT), 462
asymmetric information, 116–124
see also information asymmetry
Atlas-Global One, 203, 205
auditors, 86
Australia, 134, 391
average costs, 417
average credit spreads, 68

B status, 3–6
Baa1 status, 219–221
Baa3 status, 222–229
balance sheets, 132, 230–232
band widths, 370
Bank for International Settlements (BIS), 15

bankruptcy
  bank financial strength ratings, 292–293
  corporate default definitions, 30–31
  introduction, 13–16
  rating process quality, 189
  Special Purpose Vehicles, 32–35
  value of the firm in default, 261
banks
  banking crisis regulations, 429–430
  demand for ratings, 108
  failure, 292–293
  financial strength ratings, 291–296
  funding substitution, 378–379
  loan transactions, 108–109
  rating initiation, 167–168
BankWatch, 400
Barings, 292
barriers to entry, 407–411, 418
Basel Capital Accord, 132, 435
Basel Committee on Banking Supervision, 15,
  435
Basel II, 132, 436
BBB status, 76
Belgacom, 216
below-investment status, 76–77
benchmark measures, 78
  default probability, 79
  default prospect benchmarking, 1–8
  Equivalent Benchmark Redemption Yield, 281
Best, Alfred Magilton, 405
BET (Binomial Expansion Technique), 298
beta risk, 321
bid-ask spreads, 313
Binomial Expansion Technique (BET), 298
BIS (Bank for International Settlements), 15
BITCO, 206, 207
Black and Scholes, 274–276, 279–280
Black–Scholes–Merton model, 281
BMA see Bond Market Association, 15
boards of directors, 110
Bon, Michel, 198–199, 210, 221–224, 230,
  247–248, 253–254
Bond Market Association (BMA), 15, 464
bonds
  capital market globalization, 382–384
  credit spreads, 64–74, 313–325
  default prospect benchmarking, 8
  fixed income institutional investors, 380
  France Telecom, 244
  impact relevance, 325–331
  market access, 104
  market credit spreads, 64–74
  maturity, 70–71
  product segment markets, 138–141
  rating actions, 325–331
  rating relevance, 313–315

  return volatility, 315
borrowers demand for ratings, 91–99
borrowing costs, 64
bottoming out, France Telecom, 238
Bradstreet, John, 375
Brady bonds, 135
Breton, Thierry, 238, 242, 246, 254
British Telecom, 212, 213
Bulgaria, 76
business analysis, 1–8
business conduct regulations, 442
business continuity, 28–29
business models
  France Telecom, 198
business risk analysis, 258–259
business risk scores, 266, 268, 271

Cable and Wireless Communications (CWC),
  202
California Public Employees Retirement Scheme
  (CalPERS), 105, 106, 400
Canada, 392, 434, 438, 439
Canadian Bond Ratings Service (CBRS), 391
capital
  bank financial strength ratings, 293
  costs, 85, 305, 331
  demand, 92–94
  requirements, 132, 431, 446
  structure, 332
  supply, 102–103
capital markets
  corporations, 129
  emerging markets, 149, 150, 157
  Europe, 156
  France Telecom, 200
  globalization, 382–384
  sovereign ratings, 135
Capital Requirements Directive (CRD), 431, 446
cardinal rating scales, 72–74, 274–276
Casema, 203, 245
cash collateralized debt obligations, 147–149
cash flows, 3, 67, 141–149, 244–245
CBM (correlated binomial method), 300
CBRS (Canadian Bond Ratings Service), 391
CDO see Collateralized Debt Obligations
CDS (credit default swaps), 147
CEBS see Committee of European Banking
  Supervisors
CEMA (Committee on Economic and Monetary
  Affairs), 445
certifications, 119
CESR see Committee of European Securities
  Regulators, 23
change acceleration rates, 380–381
change of control covenants, 106, 120–121
Chapter 11, 28–30

chicken or egg problem, 311–313
China, 360
CI-Telecom, 203
client issuer after-sales service, 174–175
CLO (Collateralized Loan Obligations), 103, 400
CMO (collateralized mortgage obligations), 143
Code of Standard Practices, 191–193, 462
Codes of Conduct
    acceptability challenges, 469–472
    industry regulations, 440
    legitimacy challenges, 469–472
cohort default rate remoteness, 337–339
collateral
    clauses, 107–108
    demand for ratings, 109–110
    pool credit modeling, 298–302
Collateralized Debt Obligations (CDO)
    demand for ratings, 102
    Moody's structure, 396
    structured finance instruments, 142, 296, 303
Collateralized Loan Obligations (CLO), 103, 400
collateralized mortgage obligations (CMO), 143
Commercial Paper, 50, 436–438
Commission on Credit Rating Agencies, 430
Committee of European Banking Supervisors
    (CEBS), 446, 455, 459–460
Committee of European Securities Regulators
    (CESR), 23
    credit rating definitions, 23–88
    demand for ratings, 106
    industry regulations, 461
    introduction, 15
    regulatory uses of ratings, 431
Committee on Economic and Monetary Affairs
    (CEMA), 445
common standards, 89–91
communicating ratings, 172–173
Communication from the Commission on Credit
    Rating Agencies, 430
company-specific default drivers, 39
company-specific risk, 259
comparison means, 90, 97
competition
    credit rating industry, 407–419
    demand for ratings, 96–97
    dynamic aspects, 418–419
Competition Law, 444, 447
complex debt ratings, 405
complex financial innovations, 383
conduct of business, 442
see also Codes of Conduct
confidentiality, 183–185, 193, 458–459
conflicts of interest
    rating process quality, 187–188
Congress, 452–454
conservatism, 370

conservative migration policy, 363
consolidation, France Telecom, 231–232, 234,
    245–247
contestability, 85–86
contractor's demand for ratings, 104–110
corporate Aa1 status, 198
corporate bonds, 65, 66
    credit spread definitions, 65, 67
    default prospect benchmarking, 8
    Europe, 150, 150, 154–157
    fundamental ordinal scale, 54–55
    product segment markets, 138–149
    spread dispersion, 69
    United States, 149, 150–153
corporate credit, 144, 257–273
corporate debt instruments, 260–265
corporate defaults, 24–40
    Damova, 27–28
    definitions, 27–35
    drivers, 35–39
    internationally traded debts, 25–27
    recovery rates, 39–40
    sovereign ratings, 287, 291
    Telecom Argentina, 28
corporate finance ratings stability, 350, 347–352
corporate funding, 152, 154
corporate issuers, 128–130
corporate ratings
    Asia, 149–150
    demand, 91
    Europe, 150, 150, 154–157
    industry segment markets, 128–130
    market implied ratings, 274–276
    ordinal ratings, 257–273
    United States, 149–153
corporate scandals, 430
correctly interpreting vs. misinterpreting ratings,
    78–84
correlated binomial method (CBM), 300
costs
    capital, 331
    fixed income investors, 99–102
    price-cost margins, 415–416
    switching, 408
Coughlin, Paul, 362
country ceilings, 135, 149, 291
country risk, 258, 270–271
coverage ratios, 222–224
CRD (Capital Requirements Directive), 431, 446
credibility, 456
credit default swaps (CDS), 147
credit derivatives markets, 145
credit exposure, 83
Credit Market Services, 389–394
credit protection, 218
credit quality, 416

credit rating analysis
  equivalent benchmark redemption yield, 304
  financial strength ratings, 291–296, 297
  France Telecom, 197–256
  fundamental corporate credit ratings, 257–273
  fundamental ordinal ratings, 257–273
  market implied ratings, 274–276
  ordinal ratings, 257–273
  performance, 307–371
  sovereign ratings, 286–291
  special sector ratings, 286
  structured finance instrument ratings, 296–304
credit rating business
  accelerating rates of chance, 380–381
  bank-based funding substitution, 378–379
  capital market globalization, 382–384
  change acceleration rates, 380–381
  competitive structure, 407–419
  complex financial innovations, 383
  current structure, 384–407
  disintermediation, 378–379
  financial innovations, 383
  globalization, 382–384
  history, 375–378
  industry performance, 419–428
  innovations, 383
  institutionalization of investments, 379–380
  international capital market globalization,
       382–384
  investment institutionalization, 379–380
  macroeconomic shaping factors, 378–384
  origins, 375–378
  performance, 419–428
  shaping factors, 378–384
  structure, 384–419
credit rating determination, 266–272
credit rating foundations, 23–88
  raison d'être, 89–160
  accountability, 85–86
  auditors, 86
  contestability, 85–86
  corporate defaults, 24–40
  credit rating segments, 126–157
  credit risk, 80, 82–84
  debt, 81–82
  definitions, 23–24
  demand for ratings, 89–110
  economic function, 89–160
  equity, 84
  functions, 89–110
  geographical segment markets, 149–157
  industry segment markets, 126–138
  information asymmetry, 111–126
  initiating rating processes, 161–170
  insurance, 86
  maintaining ratings, 170–193

measures of credit risk, 80, 82–84
  need for ratings, 89–110
  obligor location, 149–157
  obtaining credit ratings, 98
  opinion, 85–86
  original economic function, 89–160
  price issues, 82–84
  product segment markets, 138–149
  rating scales, 40–74
  rating segments, 126–157
  scales, 40–74
  segments, 126–157
  sovereign debt, 82
  special issues, 85–86
credit rating industry, 375–428
  competitive structure, 407–419
  current structure, 384–407
  history, 375–378
  market competition, 407–411
  origins, 375–378
  performance, 419–428
  regulation, 429–430, 440–468
  structure, 384–419
credit rating markets
  industry segments, 126–138
  rated issuer types, 126–149
  scale and scope, 126–157
  segments, 126–157
credit rating notching, 262–263
credit rating performance, 307–371
  accuracy, 332–356
  efficiency enhancement, 356–371
  impact relevance, 310, 325–331
  relevance, 307–332
  stability, 332–356
  structural relevance, 310–325
  surprise in default prevention, 332–356
  value of ratings, 307–332
Credit Rating Reform Act of
  credit rating definitions, 23–88
Credit Rating Reform Act of 2006, 430
  rating initiation, 168
credit rationing, 112, 124, 125
credit reporting, 90, 375
credit risk
  corporate debt instruments, 260–265
  credit rating foundations, 81–84
  fundamental ordinal ratings, 257–273
  institutional investors, 99–104, 105
  metrics, 345–347
  ordinal ratings, 257–273
  rating functions, 89–91
credit scores, 266–272
credit spreads, 70–71
  bond maturity, 70–71
  creditworthiness, 56, 74

definitions, 65–67
equivalent benchmark redemption yield, 304
expected returns, 67
maturity buckets, 70–71
patterns, 68–70
rating relevance, 310–325
rating scales, 64–74
returns, 67–68
SFI specificities, 323–325
structural relevance, 310–325
transitory market conditions, 71–72
credit valuation, 73
Credit Watch, 3, 7, 176
creditworthiness, 56, 74
   credit spreads, 56, 67
   entrepreneurs, 114–116
   France Telecom, 256
   market implied ratings, 284–286
crisis, 14
   Asian financial crisis, 16, 356–362, 430
   regulation changes, 429–430
   stability, 356–371
   subprime crisis, 369–371
   Western microeconomic equity crisis, 363–364
Crown Castel Int'l Corporation, 204
cumulative cohort default rates, 337–339
cumulative default rates, 337–339, 345, 348, 349
Cumulative Value Rights (CVR), 210
currency
   sovereign ratings, 136–138, 287
current structure of rating business, 384–407
cushion ratios, 250
CVR (Cumulative Value Rights), 210
CWC (Cable and Wireless Communications), 202
cycle neutrality, 80, 354–355

D ratings, 27–28
D&B (Dun & Bradstreet), 375, 394
Damova, 27–28
DBRS see Dominion Bond Rating Service
DCR see Duff & Phelps Credit Rating Co., 54
de-linking, 92–94, 141
debt
   adverse selection, 113–121
   capital, 128, 200
   consolidation, 218
   information asymmetry, 113–124
   maturity extensions, 246
   moral hazard problem, 121–124
   obligations, 134
   priority ranking, 262
debtor-in-possession packages, 28–29
default

see also corporate defaults, 25, 27
bank financial strength ratings, 292–293
equivalent benchmark redemption yield, 306
frequencies, 102
losses, 343–347
occurrence, 334
points, 229–238, 252, 252
probability
   bank financial strength ratings, 293
   benchmark measures, 78
   collateral pool credit modeling, 298
   determination on market prices, 276–284
   equivalent benchmark redemption yield, 306
   Expected Default Frequency, 73, 276, 277, 280–284
   France Telecom, 251, 281–284
   market-implied scales, 73–74
   recovery ratings, 263–264
   sovereign ratings, 287, 291
prospect benchmarking, 1–8
rates
   cohort analysis, 337–339
   long-term scales, 48–50
   macroeconomic activity, 36
   metrics, 343–347
   remoteness, 337–339
   short-term ratings, 53
ratios, 336–337
recovery rates, 39–40
risk, 80
   benchmark measures, 78
   de-linking, 141
   indices, 48–50
   market implied ratings, 274–276
   sovereign ratings, 134
surprise in default prevention, 332–356
value of firm in default, 261
demand for ratings
   borrowers, 91–99
   contractors, 104–110
   credit rating foundations, 89–110
   fixed income investors, 99–104
   institutional investors, 99–104, 105
   issuers, 91–99
   prescribers, 104–110
   private contractors, 106–109
   rating triggers, 106–109
   stakeholders, 104–110
   structured finance instruments, 92–94, 102–103
Derivative Fitch, 400, 402
Deutsche Post World Net (DPWN), 64, 162–163
Deutsche Telekom (DT), 200–201, 206, 213
developing country sovereign ratings, 289
diffusion, 192, 322

Digita, 207
diligence, 189–191
Directives, 197, 445, 457–459
disaster risks, 320–321
disclosure
    rating actions, 170–171
    rating process quality, 191–193
    rating triggers, 108
discontinuities, 320–321
disintermediation, 152, 155–157, 378–379
dispersion, 68–70, 136–138
distance to default, 277–278, 305–306
distress, 262
distribution patterns, 68–70
diversification, 383
diversity scores, 298
divestiture, 245–247
documentation see rating actions
Doe, John, 329
Domestic Public Offerings, 54
Dominion Bond Rating Service (DBRS)
    NRSRO status, 390, 409
    structure, 404–405
Donaldson, William, 451
DPWN see Deutsche Post World Net, 64
Drexel Burnham Lambert, 144
drivers of corporate defaults, 35–39
DT see Deutsche Telekom
Duff & Phelps Credit Rating Co. (DCR), 54,
    390, 399
Dun & Bradstreet (D&B), 375, 394
Dun, Robert, 375
Duopoly Relief Act 2005, 451, 452, 463
dynamic aspects of competition, 418–419

early mover advantages, 407–411
earnings, 294
East Asian crisis, 356–362
EBF (European Banking Federation), 462
EBITDA, 109, 222–224, 227, 233, 243, 420
EBRY see Equivalent Benchmark Redemption
    Yield
ECA (external credit assessments), 436
ECAI see External Credit Assessment
    Institutions
ECMS, France Telecom, 204, 207
economic analysis, information asymmetry,
    111–126
Economic and Monetary Union (EME), 156
economic conditions, industry competition, 416
economic function, 89–160
economic research, 19
economic sector default drivers, 36–39
EDF see Expected Default Frequency, 79
efficiency
    Asian macro financial crisis, 356–362

enhancement, 356–371
industry performance, 427
subprime crisis, 369–371
Western microeconomic equity crisis,
    363–364
Egan, Sean, 426
Egan-Jones Ratings Co. (EJRC), 189, 403–404,
    426
El Salvador, 204
electronic quotation, 153
eligibility criterion regulations, 436–438
ElTele Ost, 204
EME (Economic and Monetary Union), 156
emerging markets, 149, 150, 157
EMTN (Euro Medium Term Notes), 200
Energis, 77
Enron, 14, 189, 190, 452
Entergy Corporation, 28–29
entrepreneurs, 113–124
entry barriers, 407–411, 418
Equant, 210–211, 234, 236
equity, 84
    credit rating foundations, 83
    default probability extraction, 276–284
    demand for ratings, 108
    equivalent benchmark redemption yield, 304
    France Telecom, 200–201, 231–232, 234,
        247, 249
    special purpose vehicles, 130–133
    Western microeconomic equity crisis,
        363–364
Equivalent Benchmark Redemption Yield
    (EBRY), 281–304
errors, 187, 303
estimated default frequency see Expected
    Default Frequency, 73
Euro investment corporate bonds, 68–70
euro issuance, 138–141
Euro Medium Term Notes (EMTN), 200
Eurobonds, 96, 163
Europe
    capital markets, 156
    corporate bonds/ratings, 152–157
    monetary union, 396
European Banking Federation (EBF), 462
European Commission, 23, 433, 444
European Parliament, 445
European Property Market Metric, 400
European Union (EU)
    capital markets, 156
    Directives, 197, 445, 457–459
    industry regulations, 440, 444–468
    legitimacy challenges, 472
    prudence, 435–436
    regulatory uses of ratings, 431, 435–436
    telecommunications industry, 197

evaluating France Telecom, 247–256
Expected Default Frequency (EDF), 73
  default probability, 73, 276, 277, 280–284
  equivalent benchmark redemption yield, 306
  Moody's KMV, 73, 346, 347
expected losses, 67, 299, 315–325
expected returns, 67–68, 305
experience goods, 407–408
External Credit Assessment Institutions (ECAI),
  436, 446, 455
external credit assessments (ECA), 436
EU *see* European Union

facility tours, 165
fair representation, 447
fair risk return premiums, 318–321
fallen angels, 343
FCF (free cash flow), 3, 244–245
Fedders Corporation, 76–77
Federal Home Loan Mortgage Corporation
  (Freddie Mac), 143
Federal Reserve Website, 54
fees, 184, 413–414
Fimalac, 400, 419–420
financial business strength ratings, 291–296
financial disintermediation, 152, 155–157,
  378–379
financial distress, 31
financial engineering, 472
financial innovations, 383
financial institution's demand for ratings, 91
Financial Intelligence & Research Ltd (FL&R),
  406
financial market credit spreads, 43, 64–74
financial ratios, 269, 272
financial risk analysis, 259–260
financial risk scores, 266, 268, 268–269, 271
financial sector corporate issuers, 130
Financial Services Action Plan (FSAP), 444,
  457–458
Financial Services Authority (FSA), 435
financial strength ratings, 291–296
  banks, 291–296
  insurance companies, 291–292, 294–296
fine ratings, 47, 55–56, 149
FIPS (fixed income pricing systems), 153
First Amendment, 182–183, 454
Fitch
  acquisitions, 398–402
  Asian financial crisis, 357
  BankWatch, 400
  conflicts of interest, 187–188
  credit rating definitions, 24
  credit spread structural relevance, 313–315
  current structure, 398–402
  dominance, 386–389

Duff & Phelps Credit Rating Co., 399
  fundamental ordinal scale, 55–63
  industry competitive structure, 409
  industry performance, 419–420
  insurer financial strength ratings, 294, 297
  NRSRO status, 390, 399, 409
  split ratings, 55–63
  Thomson Financial BankWatch, 400
Fitch Investor Services, 399
Fitch Publishing Company, 399
Fitch Ratings, 376, 420
Fitch Training and Algorithms, 401
fixed costs, 422
fixed income investors, 99–104, 380
fixed income pricing systems (FIPS), 153
FL&R (Financial Intelligence & Research Ltd),
  406
floating-rate notes, 95
follow-up ratings, 174–179
Ford Motor Company, 172, 308
foreign currency sovereign ratings, 136–138,
  287
forensic experience, 189
Fortune 500, 91
foundations in credit ratings *see* credit rating
  foundations, 23–88
Framework Directive, 197
France
  government, 242–244, 253–254
  regulatory uses of ratings, 431, 432, 439
France Telecom, 198–229
  1995–2002, 198–229
  2002–2004, 229–247
  A1 status, 208–211
  A3 status, 211–219
  Aa1 status, 198–202
  Aa2 status, 200–202
  Aaa status, 198
  acquisition history, 202–203
  analysis, 247–256
  asset divestiture, 245–247
  Atlas-Global One, 203, 205
  Baa1 status, 219–221
  Baa3 status, 222–229
  Bon, Michel, 198–199, 221–224, 230,
    247–248, 253–254
  bond markets, 244
  bottoming out, 238
  Breton, Thierry, 238, 242, 246, 254
  business model, 198–199
  Cable and Wireless Communications, 202,
    214
  consolidation, 231–232, 234, 245–247
  corporate Aa1 status, 198
  coverage ratios, 222–224
  credit rating analysis, 197–256

France Telecom (*continued*)
  credit rating determination, 266–272
  credit risk measures, 80
  default points, 229–238
  default probability, 250, 280–284
  Deutsche Telekom, 199–201, 206, 213, 214
  divestiture, 245–247
  EBITDA, 222–224, 227, 233, 243
  EDF extraction, 281–284
  Equant, 210–211
  equity, 200–201, 231–232, 234, 248
  evaluation, 247–256
  financial engineering challenges, 472
  free cash flow, 244–245
  French government, 242–244, 253–254
  fundamental ratings, 248–253
  Global One, 199, 203, 205, 208, 210–211,
    238
  historical market values, 249, 249
  information asymmetry, 309
  Internet, 199
  IPO, 200, 210–219
  issuers ratings value, 254–256
  liquidity, 218, 229–230, 244
  market-implied ratings, 248–253
  Minitel, 199
  Mobilecom, 205, 208, 223, 225, 235
  near speculative grade, 198–229
  NTL, 202, 205, 237
  Orange, 202–229, 234
  performance indicators, 214
  Prime-3 rating, 226–229
  public Aa1 status, 200–202
  rating evolution, 198–229
  rating triggers, 107
  recovery, 229–247
  repurchase authority, 218–219
  restructuring plan, 242–244
  rights offering, 245
  risk shifting, 248–253
  sovereign ratings, 198–229, 250
  Sprint, 199, 203, 204, 208, 212
  state support, 242–243, 253–254
  syndicated loans, 222–224, 244
  Telecom Italia, 201, 213, 215
  Telefonica, 201, 213, 215
  Thomson Multimedia, 238
  TPSA, 206, 211, 224
  United Kingdom, 201–202, 208–209
  value added, 254–256
  Vodafone, 201, 208–209, 218–219
  Wanadoo, 199, 222, 244
  Wind, 205, 206, 235, 245
fraud, 87–88
Freddie Mac (Federal Home Loan Mortgage
  Corporation), 143

free cash flow (FCF), 3, 244–245
French government, 242–244, 253–254
FSA (Financial Services Authority), 435
FSAP *see* Financial Services Action Plan
functions, credit rating foundations, 89–110
fundamental ordinal scale, 43–64
  corporate credit ratings, 257–273
  credit spread structural relevance, 311
  Fitch, 44, 47, 49–50, 55–63
  France Telecom, 248–253
  inter-rate agreements, 54–64
  long-term scales, 44–52
  Moody's, 44, 47, 49, 55–63, 73
  multiple ratings, 54–64
  relevance, 311, 331–332
  short-term ratings, 44, 50–54
  split ratings, 54–64
  Standard & Poor's, 44, 47, 55–63

Genentech Inc., 75
General Motors (GM) Corp., 3–6, 76, 96
geographical segment markets, 149–157
Germany, 64
  Deutsche Post World Net, 64, 162–163
  Deutsche Telekom, 200–201, 206, 213, 214
  industry federation, 464
Gini coefficient, 340
Ginnie May (National Mortgage Association),
  143
Global Credit Rating, 407
global level industry regulations, 440
Global One, 199, 203, 205, 208, 210–211, 238
globalization, 382–384, 405, 473
Globalstar, 326–327
GM *see* General Motors, 3–6, 76
governance constraints/guidelines, 104–106
governments
  demand for ratings, 91
  France, 242–244, 253–254
  sovereign ratings, 133–138, 149, 286–291
  United States, 143
Greater China, 360
gross issuance, 138–141
growth
  challenges, 473
  regulatory uses of ratings, 384
  structured finance instruments, 145–147

harmonization, 197
health care costs, 3
Hellenic, 216
high-yield bonds, 66, 72, 343–345
history
  credit rating industry, 375–378
  sovereign ratings, 134

see also origins, credit rating business
home equity loans, 150
Home Loan Mortgage Corporation, 143
Hong Kong, 358, 362
House of Representatives, 451, 454, 463
House of the Credit Rating Agency Duopoly
    Relief Act 2005, 451, 463
Hurricane Katrina, 28–29
hybrid securities, 325

IBCA Limited, 390, 399, 400
ICI (Investment Company Institute), 461
identification issues, 103
IMF *see* International Monetary Fund, 15
impact relevance, 310, 325–331
impairment, 35
implied market values *see* market-implied
    ratings
income statements, 230–232
income tax, 322
incorporated asset pools, 91
incumbent credit rating agencies, 466
independence, 188
India, 436–438
Indice Multimedia, 207
Indonesia, 358, 360
industry, 36–39
    corporate default drivers, 35–39
    performance, 419–428
    regulations, 429–430, 440–468
        business conduct, 442
        conflicts of interest, 447, 454, 457–458
        Credit Rating Reform Act 2006, 440, 441,
            454
        European Union, 440, 444–468
        intermediary stakeholders, 464–466
        investor stakeholders, 461–462
        IOSCO, 440, 443–444, 448, 464–466
        issuer stakeholders, 462–464
        NRSRO, 436, 440–442, 449, 459
        recognition criteria, 455–457
        regulatory options, 440–442
        SEC, 436, 448–451, 455–457, 459, 464,
            465
        stakeholders, 461–466
        United States, 440, 448–468
        World-wide, 440, 443–444
    segment markets, 126–138
        bond issuance, 139
        corporate issuers, 128–130
        sovereigns, 133–138
        special purpose vehicles, 127, 130–133
    structure issues, 440–441
    see also credit rating industry
information asymmetry, 111–126
    raison d'être of ratings, 89

adverse selection, 113–121, 126
    debt claim issuers, 113–124
    entrepreneurs, 113–124
    information exchanges, 9–13
    moral hazard, 111–113, 121–125
    rating relevance, 309
information exchanges, 9–13
initial public offerings (IPO), 124–126,
    166–167, 200, 211–219
initial ratings, 162–163
initiating rating processes, 161–170
innovation, 383, 472
insolvency, 261, 263
institutional investors, 99–104, 105
institutionalization of investments, 104–106,
    379–380
instrument characteristics, 311
instrument ratings
    determination, 272–273
    MDM Bank, 94–95
    product segment markets, 138–149
    scales, 43
insurance, 86, 291–292, 294–296
inter-rate agreements, 54–64
interest group documents, 18
interest rates, 416
intermediary stakeholders, 464–466
internal ratings, 436
international bonds, 138–141
international capital market globalization,
    382–384
International Group of Treasury Associations, 15
International Monetary Fund (IMF), 15,
    135–136
International Organization of Securities
    Commissions (IOSCO), 23
    credit rating definitions, 23
    industry regulations, 440, 443–444, 464–466
    introduction, 15
International Ratings Group (IRG), 402, 406
international securities investments, 99–102
internationally traded debts, 25–27
Internet, 173–174, 199
interpretation of credit ratings, 74–75
interviews, 164–165
intuition, 111–113
investment banks, 110
Investment Company Institute (ICI), 461
investment grade ratings, 75–76
investment holding risks, 99–104
investment institutionalization, 104–106,
    379–380
investors
    demand for ratings, 99–104, 106
    demand for structured finance instruments,
        102–103

investors (*continued*)
   experience, 8
   industry performance, 420–423, 427
   information asymmetry, 113–124
   product segment markets, 149
   protection, 439
   rating performance, 420–423
   stakeholders, 461–462
   structured finance instruments, 102–103, 144
IOSCO *see* International Organization of
   Securities Commissions, 23
IPO *see* initial public offerings
IRG (International Ratings Group), 402, 406
Iridium, 326
Islamic finance rating criteria, 401
Issuer Default Ratings, 400
issuer ratings
   credit spread structural relevance, 311
   financial strength ratings, 294
   France Telecom, 254–256
   industry segment markets, 126–138
   MDM Bank, 94–95
   notching, recovery prospects, 262
   preparation, 163–165
   product segment markets, 138–149
   quality distributions, 46
   rating process quality, 189
   rating scales, 43
Issuer Reporting Standards, 400
issuer stakeholders, 462–464
issuer-pays pricing business models, 411–412
issuers
   demand for ratings, 91–99
   industry performance, 420–423, 427
   information asymmetry, 113–124
   rating performance, 420–423

Japan, 361
JCR-VIS Credit Rating Co. Ltd, Pakistan, 407
Joynt, Stephen W., 187–188
jump risk, 321, 322
junk bonds, 76–77, 389

Kealhofer, S., 276
KMV ratings, 73
Korablev–Dwyer, 284
Korea, 359, 360
KPN, 212, 213, 215, 218
Kulczyk Holding, 209, 237

la République Française, 230–238
Lafarge Group, 110
Latin America, 134
learning curves, 410
Leeson, Nick, 292
legal liability, 182–183

legal risk, 303
legislation, 444–468
legitimacy, 469–472
Lehman Brothers, 400
Lehman index, 322
lending profitability, 154–157
liability, 182–183, 231–232, 234, 305
liberalization, 198
Limitation Clause, 454
liquidity
   bank financial strength ratings, 294
   credit spread structural relevance, 311, 325
   France Telecom, 218, 229–230, 244
   General Motors Corp., 4–5
   rating triggers, 107
local currency sovereign ratings, 287
long-term
   fundamental ordinal scale, 51, 52
long-term fundamental ordinal scale, 44–50
long-term scales, 47, 44–52
Lorenz curves, 339–341
loss given default, 263
Lynch, Merrill, 400

macroeconomic activity, 36
macroeconomic shaping factors, 378–384
MAD *see* Market Abuse Directive
maintenance, rating process, 170–193
Malaysia, 361
manager contracts, 104–106
Mannesmann AG, 209
Manual of the Railroads of the United States,
   375, 376, 389
marginal default rates, 345, 348, 349
Market Abuse Directive (MAD), 446, 458–459
market acceptance, 456
market access, 104, 436–438
market competition, 407–411
market completeness, 103
market credit spreads, 43, 64–74, 311
market frictions, 111–112
market gearing, 248
market participants, 89–91
market prices/pricing, 40, 67, 276–284
market risk, 83, 302, 318–320, 324
market yields, 305, 312
market-implied ratings (MIR)
   corporate ratings, 274–276
   credit rate analysis, 274–276
   default probabilities, 72–74
   equivalent benchmark redemption yield, 305
   financial engineering challenges, 472
   France Telecom, 248–253
   information asymmetry, 9
   rating scales, 43, 72–74
   uses, 285

Markets in Financial Instruments directive
    (MiFID), 446, 458
Marks & Spencer, 120–121
Marriott Corporation, 112
maturity buckets, 70–71
Mauritius Telecom, 206
MBET (multiple Binomial Expansion
    Technique), 299
MBS *see* mortgage-backed securities
McCarthy Crisanti & Maffei, Inc., 390
McDaniel, Raymond, 333
McGraw Hill Companies *see* Standard & Poor,
    3–6
MDM Bank, 94–95
mean recovery rates, 40, 41
mean square prediction, 314–315
measures of credit risk, 80, 82–84
meetings, rating preparation, 164–165
mergers *see* acquisitions
Merrill Lynch, 200
Merton-type models, 298
metrics
    accuracy, 334–352
    credit risk, 345–347
    default losses, 343–347
    default occurrence, 334
    default rates, 343–347
    European Property Market Metric, 400
    stability, 334, 334, 343–347
microeconomic equity crisis, 363–364
MiFID *see* Markets in Financial Instruments
    directive
migration, 178–181, 363
Minitel, 199
MIR *see* market-implied ratings
misinterpreting vs. correctly interpreting ratings,
    78–84
Mobilecom, 205, 208, 223, 225, 235
model risk, 303–304
monetary union, 15, 135–136, 156, 396
Monte Carlo simulations, 298
Moody's
    Asian financial crisis, 357, 361
    Binomial Expansion Technique, 298
    corporate defaults, 25, 27
    credit rating definitions, 24
    credit spread structural relevance, 313–315
    current structure, 394–397
    Deutsche Post World Net, 162
    dominance, 386–389
    fee schedules, 413–414
    France Telecom, 83, 199, 202, 208–211,
        219–221, 224–229, 239–240, 244, 249
    fundamental ordinal scale, 47, 51, 55–63, 73
    industry performance, 419–420, 423–426
    insurer financial strength ratings, 294, 295

internationalization, 396
NRSRO status, 390, 394, 409
origins, 375–378
Philippines, sovereign ratings, 287
rating follow-ups, 175–176
rating preparation, 162, 165
rating process quality, 189
rating triggers, 108–109
sovereign ratings, 136
split ratings, 55–63
Western microeconomic equity crisis,
    363–364
Moody's Corporation, 396
Moody's Economy.com, 397
Moody's Investor Services, 333, 394, 396,
    397
Moody's KMV
    current structure, 401
    default probability extraction, 276
    EDF values, 73, 344, 346
    France Telecom, 248, 252
    ordinal rating scale, 73
Moody's Risk Management Services (MRMS),
    395
Moody, John, 2, 68, 394
moral hazard
    adverse selection problem in debt,
        119–121
    asymmetric information, 122–124
    bank financial strength ratings, 293
    credit rationing, 124, 125
    economics of ratings, 111–113, 125
    information asymmetry, 11, 111–113,
        121–124, 126
Morgan Stanley, 162–163
mortality rates, 345, 348, 349
mortgage-backed securities (MBS), 103, 143,
    146
mortgages
    collateralized mortgage obligations,
        143
    Federal Home Loan Mortgage Corporation,
        143
    Home Loan Mortgage Corporation, 143
    structured finance instruments, 143
MRMS (Moody's Risk Management Services),
    395
multiple Binomial Expansion Technique
    (MBET), 299
multiple ratings, 54–64

name recognition, 96–97
National Mortgage Association (Ginnie May),
    143
National Transcommunications Limited (NTL),
    202, 205, 237

Nationally Recognized Statistical Rating
    Organization (NRSRO)
  A.M. Best Company, 402, 405–406
  barriers to entry, 408–411
  Dominion Bond Rating Service, 403
  Egan-Jones Rating Co., 403–404
  industry competition, 418
  industry regulations, 440–442
  industry structure, 390, 397, 399
near speculative grade, 198–229
need for credit ratings, 89–110
NEPAD (New Partnership for Africa's
    Development), 135–136
neutrality of ratings, 80, 354–355
New Capital Adequacy Frameworks, 436
New Century Financial Corporation, 31
New Orleans, 28–29
New Partnership for Africa's Development
    (NEPAD), 135–136
New York Stock Exchange (NYSE), 152
Neysmith, Brian, 392
no-action letter processes, 409
non-convertible debts, 54
non-payment, 27
non-public information, 183–185, 192
Norinchukin Finance (Cayman) Ltd, 75
Nortel, 204, 234
notching
  credit ratings, 262–263, 263
  instrument rating determination, 272–273
  issuer credit rating, 262
  sovereign ratings, 291
Noyer, Christian, 109–110
NPV, 114–116, 121–123, 307
NRSRO see Nationally Recognized Statistical
    Rating Organization
NTL see National Transcommunications Limited
NYSE (New York Stock Exchange), 152

objectivity in rating process quality, 189
obligations, 138, 149–157
obligor location, 149–157
observable ratings, 90
observed bond market credit spreads, 64–74
obtaining ratings, 98, 161–193
OCC see Office of the Comptroller of the
    Currency
Oda, 204
Office of the Comptroller of the Currency
    (OCC), 429–430
one-step-at-a-time credit protection, 218
opinion, 85–86
Optimus, 203
option pricing theory, 274–276
Orange, 202, 205–209, 211–219, 221,
    225–229, 234

ordinal ratings see fundamental ordinal scale,
    43–64
original economic function, 89–160
origins, credit rating business, 375–378
see also history
OTC (over-the-counter) market, 152
outlooks, 176
over-the-counter (OTC) market, 152
overall credit rating, 266–272

Pacific Credit Rating Co. (PCR), 407
parameter errors, 303
Parmalat, 14, 87, 189, 190
patterns of credit spreads, 68–70
PCR (Pacific Credit Rating Co.), 407
Peer Analysis tool, 405
Penn Central, 50, 376, 411
pension plans, 236
performance
  credit rating industry, 419–428
  default prospect benchmarking, 7
  recovery ratings, 265, 264–265
  shareholders, 419–420
Pernod Ricard S.A., 423
Philippines, 287
pledging assets, 308
poison puts, 106, 120–121
pooling, 35
  asset pools, 33, 92–94, 130–133, 141–149
  credit modeling, 298–302
  demand for ratings, 92–94
  equilibrium, 118–121
Poor, Henry Varnum, 1–2, 375, 389
Portland General Electrical Co., 170
Portugal Telecom, 215
prediction, rating stability, 343–345
preferred stock securities, 325
prescriber's demand for ratings, 104–110
press releases, 172
prestige factors, 96–97
pricing, 82–84
  credit rating foundations, 82–84
  grids, 108
  market prices/pricing, 40, 67, 276–284
  price-cost margins, 415–416
  rating follow-ups, 185
  security prices, 309, 325–331
  sovereign ratings, 136
  stock prices, 328–330
Prime-3 rating, 226–229
prioritization rule, 324
priority ranking, 262
private contractor's demand for ratings,
    106–109
probability of default see default/dots
product segment markets, 138–149

bonds, 138–141
  obligations, 138
profit drivers, 411–417
prohibiting practices, 459
prudence, 435–436
PTK Centertel, 206
public Aa1 status, 200–202
public corporate governance reform, 135–136
public good, 420–427
put options, 251

qualified institutional buyers (QIB), 455
quality, 46–47
  issuer credit ratings, 46
  preventing surprise in defaults, 353–354
  rating process, 187–193
  warning signals, 353–354

R&I agency, 449
raison d'être, 89–160
Rapid Ratings, 402
rated issuer types, 126–149
rating actions
  communication, 172–173
  disclosure, 170–171
  France Telecom, 251
  impact relevance, 325–331
  initiation and maintenance, 170–174
  Internet, 173–174
  introduction, 18
  rating reports, 171
  rating stability, 341–343
  stock prices, 328–330
  Western microeconomic equity crisis,
    363–364
rating adviser-intermediary, 165–168
rating agency supplier, 168–170
rating basis disclosure, 191–193
rating committees, 169–170, 287
rating constraints, 104–106
rating dispersions, 136–138
rating distributions, corporate issuers, 128–129
rating evolution, 198–229
rating follow-ups
  agreement letters, 179
  communication, 172–173
  confidentiality, 183–185
  fees, 184
  France Telecom, 248
  liability, 182–183
  migration, 178–181
  pricing, 185
  rating maintenance, 174–179
  rating transitions, 180–181
  surveillance, 175–176
rating guidelines, 104–106

rating initiation, 169–170
rating maintenance, 170–193
  follow-up ratings, 174–179
rating preparation, 161–170
  adviser-intermediary, 165–168
  issuer clients, 163–165
  rating agency supplier, 168–170
rating process
  initiation, 161–170
  maintenance, 170–193
  quality, 187–193
rating procurement, 161–193
rating reports, 171
rating scales, 64–74
  bond market credit spreads, 64–74
  cardinal rating scales, 72–74, 274–276
  credit spreads, 64–74
  financial market credit spreads, 43, 64–74
  foundations, 40–74
  fundamental ordinal scale, 43–64, 257–273,
    311, 331–332
  insurer financial strength ratings, 295
  market credit spreads, 43, 64–74
  market-implied credit ratings, 43, 72–74
  observed bond market credit spreads, 64–74
  rating interpretation, 74–75
  recovery ratings, 264, 265
rating stability, 363–364
rating through the cycle, 369
rating transitions, 180
rating triggers, 106–109
RatingsDirect, 173–174
RBI (Reserve Bank of India), 436–439
recession periods, 128–130
recognition criteria, 455–457
recovery ratings
  collateral pool credit modeling, 298
  corporate default, 39–40, 41
  credit spread structural relevance, 322
  default, 39–40
  definition, 264
  Fitch, 400
  fundamental ordinal ratings, 262–265
  notching, 262
  performance, 264–265
  scales, 264
recovery scale, 272
recovery, France Telecom, 229–247
regulated investor's demand for ratings, 97
Regulation Fair Disclosure, 192
regulations
  agencies, 429–430, 440–468
  barriers to entry, 408–411
  credit rating industry, 429–430, 440–468
  eligibility criterion, 436–438
  entry barriers, 408–411

regulations (*continued*)
  France Telecom, 198
  introduction, 13–16
  investor protection, 439
  market access, 436–438
  prudence, 435–436
  ratings use, 384, 429–430
  sovereign governments, 149
relevance of ratings, 307–332
REMM (resourceful, evaluative, maximizing
    men), 31
remoteness, 337–339
Remu Catalana, 205
repurchase authority, 218–219
research, 19, 168–169
Reserve Bank of India (RBI), 436–439
Residential Capital Corp, 7–8
resourceful, evaluative, maximizing men
    (REMM), 31
restructuring plans, 242–244
returns, credit spreads, 64, 67–68
revenue
  Fitch, 401
  industry competitive structure, 413–417
reviews, 175, 176
rights offering, 245
risk aversion, 54, 311, 321
risk in diffusion model, 322
risk management, 132
risk of disaster, 320–321
risk premiums, 67, 318–321
risk shifting, 112, 248–253
risk solutions, 414
Royal Borough of Kensington and Chelsea,
    London, 97
Russian finance, 135
Russian MDM Bank, 94–95

S&P *see* Standard & Poor, 3–6
Sarbanes-Oxley Act 2002, 430, 449
satellite-based telephone industry, 326–328
scale of credit rating markets, 126–157
scales *see* rating scales, 64–74
Schmid, Gerhard, 208, 225
scope of credit rating markets, 126–157
scores
  collateral pool credit modeling, 298
  credit rating determination, 266–272
  instrument rating determination, 272–273
  Z-scores, 250, 252, 284
SEC *see* Securities and Exchange Commission
second ratings, 98
Second World War, 376
sector ratings, 286
Securities and Exchange Commission (SEC)
  agency origins, 385

barriers to entry, 408–411
credit rating definitions, 23
Credit Rating Reform Act 2006, 455–457
industry performance, 421–422
industry regulations, 448–451, 455–457
securities markets *see* information asymmetry
securitization structures, 34
securitized asset pools, 130–133
Security Data Corporation, 54
security prices, 309, 325–331
segmented markets, 102–103, 126–157
self-regulation, 444
Sema Group Plc, 203
Senior Unsecured instrument ratings, 94–95
separating equilibrium, 112, 114–116
serial rating actions, 363
SFI *see* structured finance instruments
shaping factors, 378–384
shareholders, 231–232, 397, 419–420
shirking, 112
short-term ratings, 44, 50–54
  fundamental ordinal scale, 44, 50–54
  General Motors Corp., 4–6
Shroeder, Walter, 404
sluggishness, 369
soft factor limits, 270–271
Sonatel, 203, 204
sovereign debt, 82
sovereign ratings
  Asian financial crisis, 357
  bond issuance, 139
  Bulgaria, 76
  credit rating analysis, 287
  determinants, 287
  Dominion Bond Rating Service, 409
  France Telecom, 198–229, 249, 251
  industry segment markets, 133–138
  recovery ratings, 264
  regulatory frameworks, 149
  Standard & Poor, 136, 287, 289
Soviet Union, 135
Special Purpose Vehicles (SPV)
Special Purpose Entities (SPE) *see* Special
    Purpose Vehicles
  asset pools, 130–133
  bankruptcy-remote structures, 32–35
  cash flow streams, 141–149
  industry segment markets, 127, 130–133
  securitized asset pools, 130–133
  Taganka Car Loan Finance Plc, 95
speculative bonds, 389
speculative grade firms, 129
speculative status, 76–77
split ratings, 54–64, 313–315
spread, 68–70
  dispersion, 68–70

over benchmark curves, 304
see also credit spreads
Sprint, 199, 203, 204, 208
SPV *see* Special Purpose Vehicles
stability
  corporate finance ratings, 347–352
  credit rating performance, 332–356
  crisis episodes, 356–371
  metrics, 334–352
  rating predictive content, 343–345
  structured finance ratings, 350, 347–352
  Western microeconomic equity crisis,
    363–364
stakeholders, 104–110, 461–466, 470
Standard & Poor (S&P), 3–6
  acceptability challenges, 469–472
  Asian financial crisis, 357, 361
  corporate default definitions, 27–28
  credit rating definitions, 24
  credit risk analysis, 260
  credit spread structural relevance, 313–315
  current structure, 389–394
  Damova, 27–28
  debt, 81–82
  dominance, 386–394
  foreign offices, 391
  France Telecom, 239–240
  fundamental ordinal scale, 47, 55–63
  industry performance, 419–420, 424
  insurer financial strength ratings, 294
  Internet, 173–174
  legitimacy challenges, 469–472
  NRSRO status, 390, 409
  origins, 375
  Portland General Electrical Co., 170
  rating follow-ups, 175–176
  rating interpretation, 74–75
  rating preparation, 167
  rating process quality, 187, 192
  rating triggers, 108
  sovereign ratings, 136, 287, 291
  split ratings, 55–63
  Ukraine's bond conversion, 29–30
state support, 242–243, 253–254
step-up clauses, 221
stock overhangs, 218–219
stock prices, 328–330
story bonds, 71
strategic move access, 97
strength ratings, 291–296
structural analysis, 302–303
structural errors, 303–304
structural relevance, 310–325
structure
  credit rating business, 384–419
  industry regulations, 440–441

structured finance instruments (SFI)
  asset-backed securities, 141–149, 296
  capital demand, 92–94
  collateral pool credit modeling, 298–302
  credit rating analysis, 296–304
  credit spread structural relevance, 323–325
  demand for ratings, 92–94, 102–103
  growth, 145–147
  investor demand, 102–103
  pool credit modeling, 298–302
  product segment markets, 141–149
  rating process specificities, 185
  stability, 347–352
  structural analysis, 302–303
structured finance market origins, 389
subprime crisis, 369–371
subscription-based business models, 411, 412
sunk costs, 410
super poison puts, 106
supporting materials, 18–19
surprise in default prevention, 332–356
surveillance, 175–176
Swiss-Swedish electrical engineering group
    crisis, 108–109
Swisscom, 216
switching costs, 408
symmetric information, 113–122
syndicated loans, 222–224, 244, 396
synthetic collateralized debt obligations, 145,
    147–149
systematic risks, 317

Taganka Car Loan Finance Plc, 95
Taiwan, 359
Tanzi, Calizo, 87
tax differential treatment, 321
Technical Committee, 443–444
technical default, 27
Telecom Argentina, 28
Telecom Italia, 201, 213, 215
telecoms industry
  impact relevance, 326–328
  market gearing, 248
  see also France Telecom
Telefonica, 201, 213, 215
Telekomunikacja Polska SA (TPSA), 206, 209,
    220, 235
Telenor, 217
Teliasonera, 217
terrorist attacks, 363
Tetra Pak, 87
Thailand, 359, 360, 361, 362
The American Railroad Journal, 1–2
third party assessments, 141
third party risk, 302
Thomson Bond Watch, Inc., 390

Thomson Financial BankWatch, 400
Thomson Microelectronics, 203
Thomson Multimedia, 238–239
through the cycle ratings, 364
timeliness, 189–191
tobacco industry, 269
Total Operational Performance (TOP), 242
Toyota Motor Corporation, 96
TPSA *see* Telekomunikacja Polska SA
tranching, 92–94, 141–143, 149, 324
transition matrices, 301
transition rates, 342, 341–343
transitory market conditions, 71–72
transparency, 191–193
Treasury Association, 464
treasury bonds, 65–68
Type I/Type II errors, 187

UK *see* United Kingdom
Ukraine's bond conversion, 29–30
UMTS (Universal Mobile Telecommunications
    System), 197
UNDP (United Nations Development
    Programme), 136
United Auto Workers, 3
United Kingdom (UK), 201–202, 208–209, 435
United Nations Development Programme
    (UNDP), 136
United States (US)
    Congress, 452–454
    corporate bonds, 150–153
    corporate ratings, 149–153
    Federal Home Loan Mortgage Corporation,
        143
    House of Representatives, 451, 454, 463
    industry regulations, 440, 448–468
    investor protection regulations, 439
    National Mortgage Association, 143
    over-the-counter market, 152
    regulatory uses of ratings, 432, 430–434, 439
Universal Mobile Telecommunications System
    (UMTS), 197
unrespected financial commitments, 77–86
unsolicited ratings, 410–411, 420–427
untranched pass-through securities, 143
US *see* United States

V-K (Vasicek–Kealhofer) model, 276, 281
value of firm in default, 261
value-added
    adverse selection frictions, 111–112
    France Telecom, 254–256
    investors demand, 102–103
    SPV bankruptcy-remote structures, 35
Vasicek, Oldrich, 73, 274, 285
Vasicek–Kealhofer (V–K) model, 276, 281
verifiable ratings, 90
Vinci bonds, 325–326
Vodafone, 201, 208–209, 218–219
volatility
    default probability extraction, 279
    equivalent benchmark redemption yield, 305
    France Telecom, 247, 249, 256
    ratings relevance, 315
Volker measures, 45
volume drivers, 416–417

WACC (weighted average cost of capital), 305
Wanadoo, 199, 209, 244
warning signals, rating quality, 353–354
watches
    BankWatch, 400
    Credit Watch, 3, 7, 176
    sovereign ratings, 291
    watchlists, 176
weighted average cost of capital (WACC), 305
Western microeconomic equity crisis,
    363–364
Wind, 205, 206, 235, 245
World Bank, 97, 135–136, 357
World-wide industry regulations, 440,
    443–444
WorldCom, 14, 189, 190

Yamaichi Securities, 361
yields, 65–67
    credit spread definitions, 65–67
    Equivalent Benchmark Redemption Yield,
        281, 304
    market yields, 305, 312
    yield to maturity, 82–84

Z-scores, 250, 252, 284

Printed and bound by CPI Group (UK) Ltd, Croydon, CR0 4YY

16/04/2025

14658507-0004